ITALIAN
ENGLISH
ILLUSTRATED DICTIONARY

FREE AUDIO APP

Author

Thomas Booth worked for 10 years as an English teacher in Poland, Romania, and Russia. He now lives in England, where he works as an editor and English-language materials writer. He has contributed to a number of books in the *English for Everyone* series.

ITALIAN
ENGLISH
ILLUSTRATED DICTIONARY

PRODUCED BY
Author / Editor Thomas Booth
Senior Art Editor Sunita Gahir
Art Editors Ali Jayne Scrivens, Samantha Richiardi
Illustrators Edward Byrne, Gus Scott
Project Manager Sunita Gahir / bigmetalfish design

DK UK
Senior Editors Amelia Petersen, Christine Stroyan
Senior Designers Clare Shedden, Vicky Read
Managing Art Editor Anna Hall
Managing Editor Carine Tracanelli
Jacket Editors Stephanie Cheng Hui Tan, Juhi Sheth
Jacket Development Manager Sophia MTT
Production Editors Gillian Reid, Robert Dunn, Jacqueline Street
Production Controller Sian Cheung
Publisher Andrew Macintyre
Art Director Karen Self
Publishing Director Jonathan Metcalf

Translation Andiamo! Language Services Ltd

DK INDIA
Desk Editors Joicy John, Tanya Lohan
DTP Designers Anurag Trivedi, Satish Gaur,
Jaypal Chauhan, Bimlesh Tiwary, Rakesh Kumar
DTP Coordinator Pushpak Tyagi
Jacket Designer Vidushi Chaudhry
Senior Jackets Coordinator Priyanka Sharma Saddi
Managing Editor Saloni Talwar
Creative Head Malavika Talukder

First published in Great Britain in 2023 by
Dorling Kindersley Limited
DK, One Embassy Gardens, 8 Viaduct Gardens,
London, SW11 7BW

The authorized representative in the EEA is
Dorling Kindersley Verlag GmbH. Arnulfstr. 124,
80636 Munich, Germany

Copyright © 2023 Dorling Kindersley Limited
A Penguin Random House Company
10 9 8 7 6 5 4 3 2 1
001–334032–Jun/2023

A CIP catalogue record for this book is available from the British Library
ISBN: 978-0-2416-0150-1

Printed and bound in China

All images © Dorling Kindersley Limited
For further information see: www.dkimages.com

For the curious
www.dk.com

MIX
Paper | Supporting
responsible forestry
FSC™ C018179

This book was made with Forest
Stewardship Council™ certified
paper - one small step in DK's
commitment to a sustainable future.
For more information go to
www.dk.com/our-green-pledge

Contents

IL TEMPO LIBERO LEISURE

L'AMBIENTE ENVIRONMENT

IL MONDO NATURALE NATURAL WORLD

IL RIFERIMENTO REFERENCE

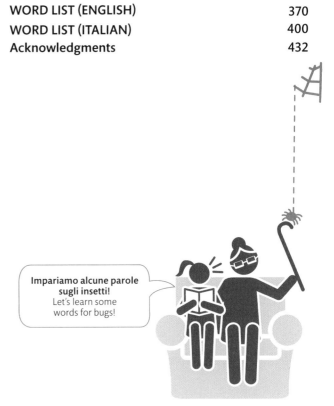

Impariamo alcune parole sugli insetti!
Let's learn some words for bugs!

Ho letto più di 10.000 parole!
I have read more than 10,000 words!

How to use this book

This *Italian English Illustrated Dictionary* will help you to understand and remember more than 10,000 of the most useful words and phrases in Italian. Each of the 180 units in the dictionary covers a practical or everyday topic (such as health, food, or the natural world), and words are shown in a visual context to fix them in your memory along with their English equivalent. Using the audio app that accompanies the dictionary will help you learn and remember the new vocabulary.

Unit number The book is divided into units. The unit number helps you to find the unit easily when searching through the contents page.

Illustrated scenes Many units include illustrated scenes that make vocabulary easy to understand and remember.

English words The English translation is provided for each word.

Module numbers Most units are broken down into modules. Every module is identified with a unique number, so you can locate the audio on the app.

Illustrations All the entries in the dictionary are illustrated, helping you to understand and memorize new vocabulary.

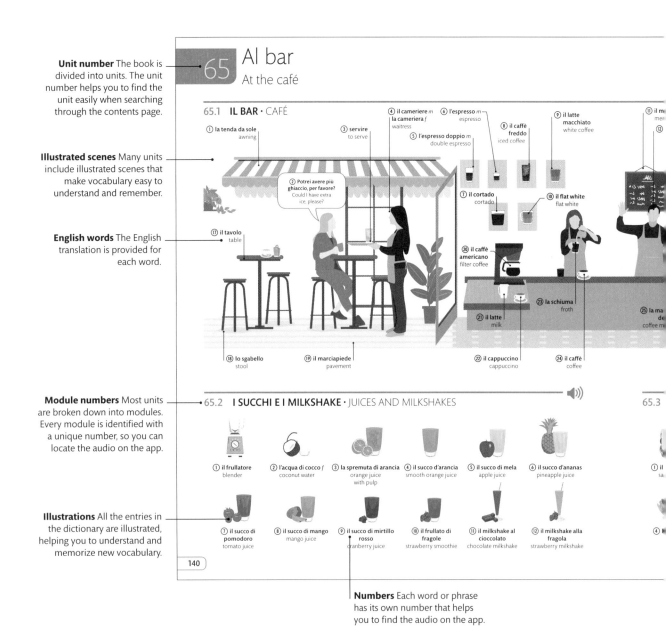

65 Al bar
At the café

65.1 IL BAR · CAFÉ

① la tenda da sole — awning
② Potrei avere più ghiaccio, per favore? — Could I have extra ice, please?
③ servire — to serve
④ il cameriere *m* la cameriera *f* — waitress
⑤ l'espresso doppio *m* — double espresso
⑥ l'espresso *m* — espresso
⑦ il cortado — cortado
⑧ il caffè freddo — iced coffee
⑨ il latte macchiato — white coffee
⑩ il flat white — flat white
⑪ il m... — mer...
⑫
⑰ il tavolo — table
⑱ lo sgabello — stool
⑲ il marciapiede — pavement
⑳ il caffè americano — filter coffee
㉑ il latte — milk
㉒ il cappuccino — cappuccino
㉓ la schiuma — froth
㉔ il caffè — coffee
㉕ la ma... de... coffee m...

65.2 I SUCCHI E I MILKSHAKE · JUICES AND MILKSHAKES
65.3

① il frullatore — blender
② l'acqua di cocco *f* — coconut water
③ la spremuta di arancia — orange juice with pulp
④ il succo d'arancia — smooth orange juice
⑤ il succo di mela — apple juice
⑥ il succo d'ananas — pineapple juice
① il sa...

⑦ il succo di pomodoro — tomato juice
⑧ il succo di mango — mango juice
⑨ il succo di mirtillo rosso — cranberry juice
⑩ il frullato di fragole — strawberry smoothie
⑪ il milkshake al cioccolato — chocolate milkshake
⑫ il milkshake alla fragola — strawberry milkshake

140

Numbers Each word or phrase has its own number that helps you to find the audio on the app.

Gender and articles

All nouns in the dictionary are preceded by the definite article ("the"). In Italian, nouns are masculine or feminine. The definite articles used for singular masculine nouns are "il" or "lo" and for feminine nouns "la". Plurals are indicated with "i" or "gli" for masculine, "le" for feminine. When nouns start with a vowel so that the articles "lo" and, "la" lose their vowel –"l'"–, the gender is indicated with *m* or *f*.

il cotone
cotton

i fusilli
fusilli

la medicina
medicine

lo zio
uncle

gli elastici
rubber bands

le monete
coins

l'ospedale *m*
hospital

Word lists

The Italian and English word lists at the back of the book contain every entry from the dictionary. All the vocabulary is listed in alphabetical order, and each entry is followed by the unit number or numbers in which it is found, enabling you to look up any word in either Italian or English. The Italian words are listed without their articles, so that you can search for words alphabetically. The English word list also provides information about the part of speech (for example noun, verb, or adjective) of each word.

Audio app

The *Italian English Illustrated Dictionary* is supported by a free audio app containing every Italian word and phrase in the book. Listen to the audio and repeat the words and phrases out loud, until you are confident you understand and can pronounce what has been said. The app can be found by searching for "DK Illustrated Dictionary" in the App Store or Google Play.

See also Each unit has a "see also" box that directs you to other units with useful or related vocabulary.

See also
27 La cucina e le stoviglie · Kitchen and tableware **52** Bere e mangiare Drinking and eating **66** Al bar (continua) · At the café continued **70** Il fast food · Fast food **72** Il pranzo e la cena · Lunch and dinner

Speech bubbles Useful expressions and examples of real-life Italian appear in speech bubbles throughout the book.

01 Le parti del corpo
Parts of the body

IL CORPO UMANO · THE HUMAN BODY

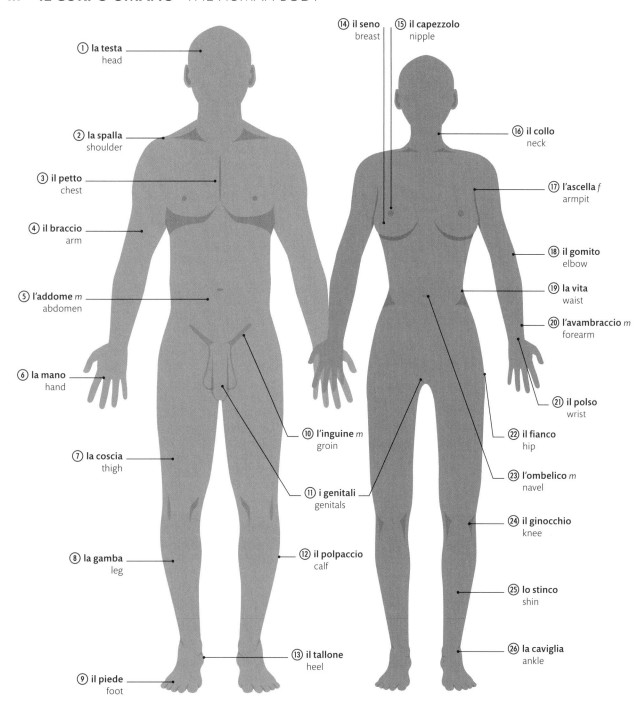

① la testa — head
② la spalla — shoulder
③ il petto — chest
④ il braccio — arm
⑤ l'addome *m* — abdomen
⑥ la mano — hand
⑦ la coscia — thigh
⑧ la gamba — leg
⑨ il piede — foot
⑩ l'inguine *m* — groin
⑪ i genitali — genitals
⑫ il polpaccio — calf
⑬ il tallone — heel
⑭ il seno — breast
⑮ il capezzolo — nipple
⑯ il collo — neck
⑰ l'ascella *f* — armpit
⑱ il gomito — elbow
⑲ la vita — waist
⑳ l'avambraccio *m* — forearm
㉑ il polso — wrist
㉒ il fianco — hip
㉓ l'ombelico *m* — navel
㉔ il ginocchio — knee
㉕ lo stinco — shin
㉖ la caviglia — ankle

See also
02 Le mani e i piedi · Hands and feet **03** I muscoli e lo scheletro · Muscles and skeleton
04 Gli organi interni · Internal organs **19** Le malattie e le lesioni · Illness and injury
20 Andare dal medico · Visiting the doctor **22** Il dentista e l'ottico · The dentist and optician

1.2 IL VISO · FACE

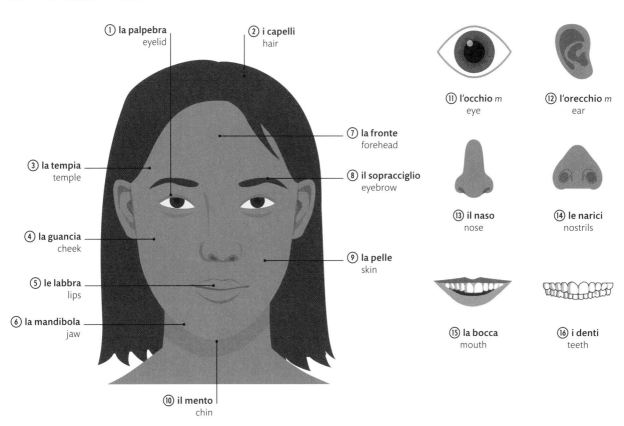

① la palpebra
eyelid

② i capelli
hair

③ la tempia
temple

④ la guancia
cheek

⑤ le labbra
lips

⑥ la mandibola
jaw

⑦ la fronte
forehead

⑧ il sopracciglio
eyebrow

⑨ la pelle
skin

⑩ il mento
chin

⑪ l'occhio *m*
eye

⑫ l'orecchio *m*
ear

⑬ il naso
nose

⑭ le narici
nostrils

⑮ la bocca
mouth

⑯ i denti
teeth

1.3 GLI OCCHI · EYES

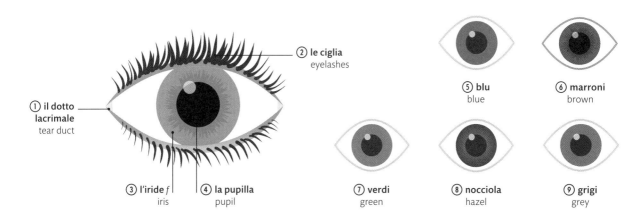

① il dotto
lacrimale
tear duct

② le ciglia
eyelashes

③ l'iride *f*
iris

④ la pupilla
pupil

⑤ blu
blue

⑥ marroni
brown

⑦ verdi
green

⑧ nocciola
hazel

⑨ grigi
grey

2.1 LE MANI · HANDS

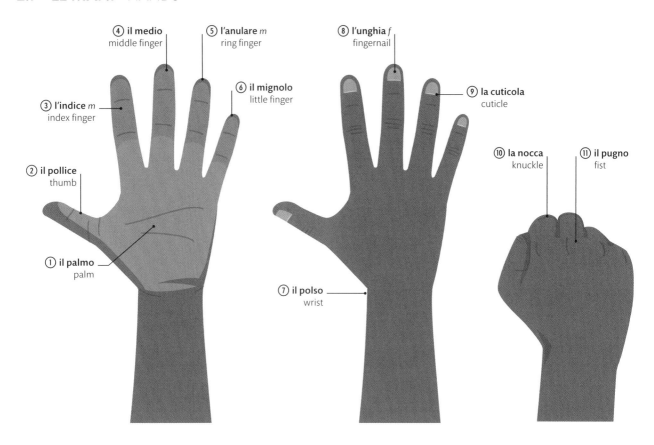

④ **il medio**
middle finger

⑤ **l'anulare** *m*
ring finger

⑧ **l'unghia** *f*
fingernail

③ **l'indice** *m*
index finger

⑥ **il mignolo**
little finger

⑨ **la cuticola**
cuticle

② **il pollice**
thumb

⑩ **la nocca**
knuckle

⑪ **il pugno**
fist

① **il palmo**
palm

⑦ **il polso**
wrist

2.2 I VERBI DEL CORPO · BODY VERBS

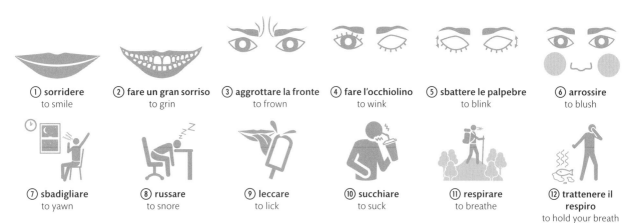

① **sorridere**
to smile

② **fare un gran sorriso**
to grin

③ **aggrottare la fronte**
to frown

④ **fare l'occhiolino**
to wink

⑤ **sbattere le palpebre**
to blink

⑥ **arrossire**
to blush

⑦ **sbadigliare**
to yawn

⑧ **russare**
to snore

⑨ **leccare**
to lick

⑩ **succhiare**
to suck

⑪ **respirare**
to breathe

⑫ **trattenere il respiro**
to hold your breath

See also
01 Le parti del corpo • Parts of the body **03** I muscoli e lo scheletro
Muscles and skeleton **19** Le malattie e le lesioni • Illness and injury
20 Andare dal medico • Visiting the doctor **21** L'ospedale • The hospital

2.3 **I PIEDI** · FEET

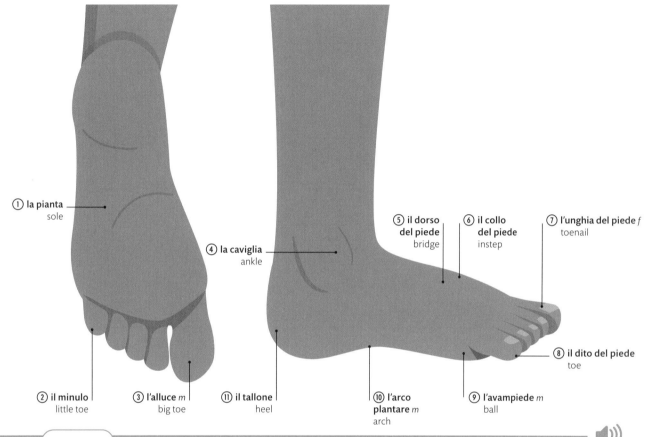

① **la pianta**
sole

④ **la caviglia**
ankle

⑤ **il dorso del piede**
bridge

⑥ **il collo del piede**
instep

⑦ **l'unghia del piede** *f*
toenail

⑧ **il dito del piede**
toe

② **il minulo**
little toe

③ **l'alluce** *m*
big toe

⑪ **il tallone**
heel

⑩ **l'arco plantare** *m*
arch

⑨ **l'avampiede** *m*
ball

Ha ha!

⑬ **ridere**
to laugh

⑭ **piangere**
to cry

⑮ **sospirare**
to sigh

⑯ **salutare con la mano**
to wave

⑰ **fare spallucce**
to shrug

⑱ **inchinarsi**
to bow

⑲ **applaudire**
to clap

⑳ **sudare**
to sweat /
to perspire

㉑ **tremare**
to shiver

㉒ **starnutire**
to sneeze

㉓ **scuotere la testa**
to shake
your head

㉔ **annuire**
to nod

15

I muscoli e lo scheletro
Muscles and skeleton

3.1 I MUSCOLI
MUSCLES

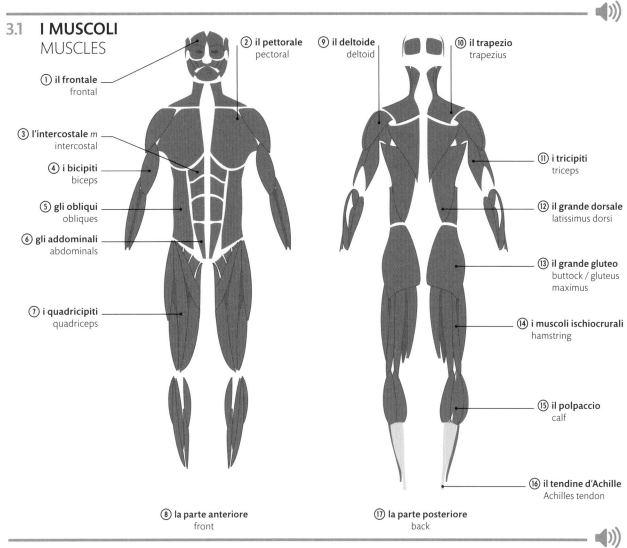

① il frontale
frontal

② il pettorale
pectoral

③ l'intercostale *m*
intercostal

④ i bicipiti
biceps

⑤ gli obliqui
obliques

⑥ gli addominali
abdominals

⑦ i quadricipiti
quadriceps

⑨ il deltoide
deltoid

⑩ il trapezio
trapezius

⑪ i tricipiti
triceps

⑫ il grande dorsale
latissimus dorsi

⑬ il grande gluteo
buttock / gluteus maximus

⑭ i muscoli ischiocrurali
hamstring

⑮ il polpaccio
calf

⑯ il tendine d'Achille
Achilles tendon

⑧ la parte anteriore
front

⑰ la parte posteriore
back

3.2 I DENTI · TEETH

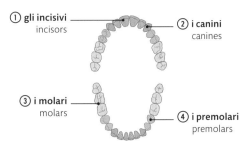

① gli incisivi
incisors

② i canini
canines

③ i molari
molars

④ i premolari
premolars

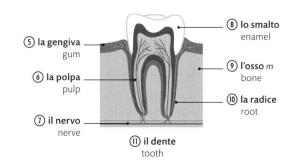

⑤ la gengiva
gum

⑥ la polpa
pulp

⑦ il nervo
nerve

⑧ lo smalto
enamel

⑨ l'osso *m*
bone

⑩ la radice
root

⑪ il dente
tooth

See also
01 Le parti del corpo • Parts of the body **02** Le mani e i piedi • Hands and feet
04 Gli organi interni • Internal organs **19** Le malattie e le lesioni • Illness and
injury **20** Andare dal medico • Visiting the doctor **21** L'ospedale • The hospital

3.3 LO SCHELETRO · SKELETON

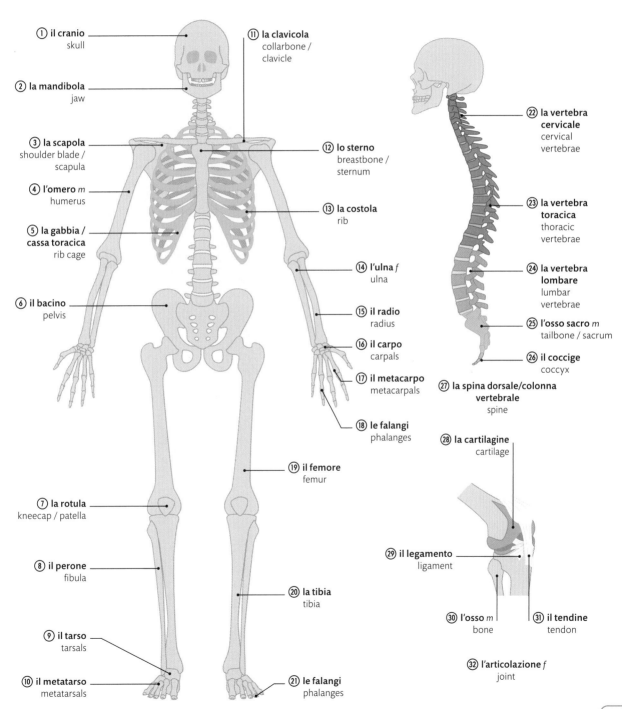

① il cranio
skull

② la mandibola
jaw

③ la scapola
shoulder blade /
scapula

④ l'omero *m*
humerus

⑤ la gabbia /
cassa toracica
rib cage

⑥ il bacino
pelvis

⑦ la rotula
kneecap / patella

⑧ il perone
fibula

⑨ il tarso
tarsals

⑩ il metatarso
metatarsals

⑪ la clavicola
collarbone /
clavicle

⑫ lo sterno
breastbone /
sternum

⑬ la costola
rib

⑭ l'ulna *f*
ulna

⑮ il radio
radius

⑯ il carpo
carpals

⑰ il metacarpo
metacarpals

⑱ le falangi
phalanges

⑲ il femore
femur

⑳ la tibia
tibia

㉑ le falangi
phalanges

㉒ la vertebra
cervicale
cervical
vertebrae

㉓ la vertebra
toracica
thoracic
vertebrae

㉔ la vertebra
lombare
lumbar
vertebrae

㉕ l'osso sacro *m*
tailbone / sacrum

㉖ il coccige
coccyx

㉗ la spina dorsale/colonna
vertebrale
spine

㉘ la cartilagine
cartilage

㉙ il legamento
ligament

㉚ l'osso *m*
bone

㉛ il tendine
tendon

㉜ l'articolazione *f*
joint

04 Gli organi interni
Internal organs

4.1 GLI ORGANI INTERNI · INTERNAL ORGANS

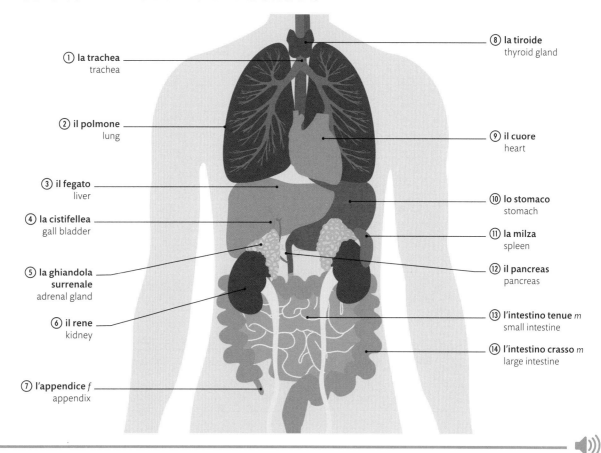

① **la trachea**
trachea

② **il polmone**
lung

③ **il fegato**
liver

④ **la cistifellea**
gall bladder

⑤ **la ghiandola
surrenale**
adrenal gland

⑥ **il rene**
kidney

⑦ **l'appendice** *f*
appendix

⑧ **la tiroide**
thyroid gland

⑨ **il cuore**
heart

⑩ **lo stomaco**
stomach

⑪ **la milza**
spleen

⑫ **il pancreas**
pancreas

⑬ **l'intestino tenue** *m*
small intestine

⑭ **l'intestino crasso** *m*
large intestine

4.2 I SISTEMI E GLI APPARATI · BODY SYSTEMS

① **l'apparato respiratorio** *m*
respiratory

② **l'apparato digerente** *m*
digestive

③ **il sistema nervoso**
nervous

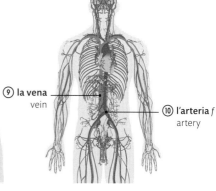

⑨ **la vena**
vein

⑩ **l'arteria** *f*
artery

④ **l'apparato
urinario** *m*
urinary

⑤ **il sistema
endocrino**
endocrine

⑥ **il sistema
linfatico**
lymphatic

⑦ **l'apparato
riproduttivo** *m*
reproductive

⑧ **l'apparato
cardiocircolatorio** *m*
cardiovascular

See also
01 Le parti del corpo • Parts of the body **03** I muscoli e lo scheletro
Muscles and skeleton **19** Le malattie e le lesioni • Illness and injury
20 Andare dal medico • Visiting the doctor **21** L'ospedale • The hospital

4.3 **LA TESTA** · HEAD

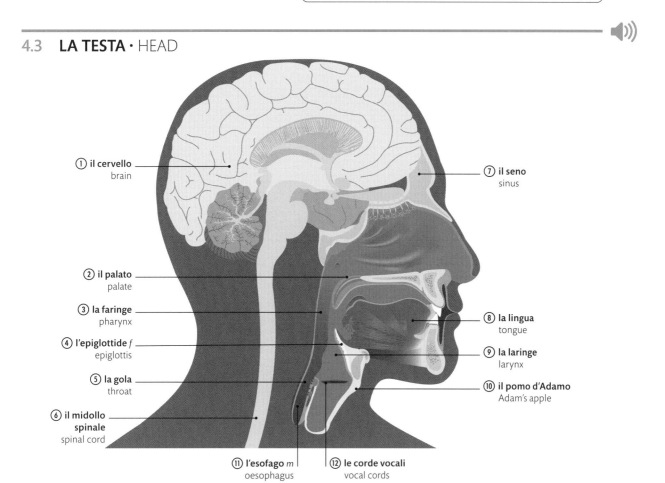

① **il cervello**
brain

⑦ **il seno**
sinus

② **il palato**
palate

③ **la faringe**
pharynx

④ **l'epiglottide** *f*
epiglottis

⑧ **la lingua**
tongue

⑨ **la laringe**
larynx

⑤ **la gola**
throat

⑩ **il pomo d'Adamo**
Adam's apple

⑥ **il midollo spinale**
spinal cord

⑪ **l'esofago** *m*
oesophagus

⑫ **le corde vocali**
vocal cords

4.4 **GLI ORGANI RIPRODUTTIVI** · REPRODUCTIVE ORGANS

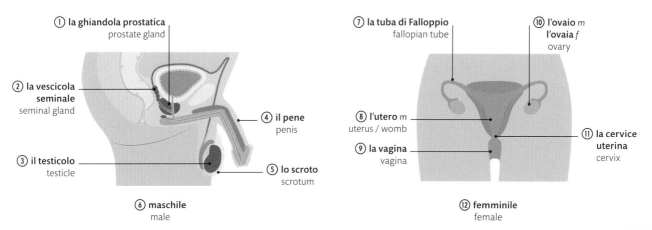

① **la ghiandola prostatica**
prostate gland

② **la vescicola seminale**
seminal gland

③ **il testicolo**
testicle

④ **il pene**
penis

⑤ **lo scroto**
scrotum

⑥ **maschile**
male

⑦ **la tuba di Falloppio**
fallopian tube

⑩ **l'ovaio** *m*
l'ovaia *f*
ovary

⑧ **l'utero** *m*
uterus / womb

⑨ **la vagina**
vagina

⑪ **la cervice uterina**
cervix

⑫ **femminile**
female

La famiglia
Family

5.1 LA FAMIGLIA DI CARLO · CARLO'S FAMILY

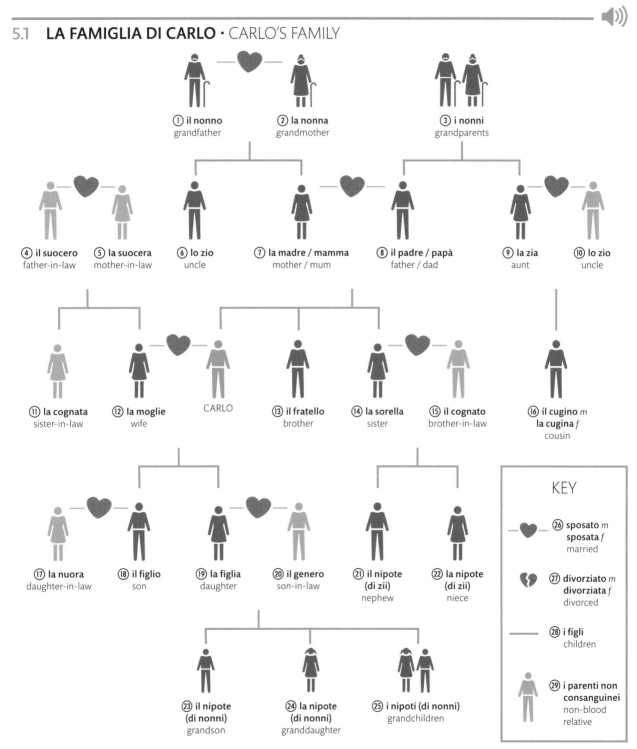

① **il nonno**
grandfather

② **la nonna**
grandmother

③ **i nonni**
grandparents

④ **il suocero**
father-in-law

⑤ **la suocera**
mother-in-law

⑥ **lo zio**
uncle

⑦ **la madre / mamma**
mother / mum

⑧ **il padre / papà**
father / dad

⑨ **la zia**
aunt

⑩ **lo zio**
uncle

⑪ **la cognata**
sister-in-law

⑫ **la moglie**
wife

CARLO

⑬ **il fratello**
brother

⑭ **la sorella**
sister

⑮ **il cognato**
brother-in-law

⑯ **il cugino** *m*
la cugina *f*
cousin

⑰ **la nuora**
daughter-in-law

⑱ **il figlio**
son

⑲ **la figlia**
daughter

⑳ **il genero**
son-in-law

㉑ **il nipote (di zii)**
nephew

㉒ **la nipote (di zii)**
niece

㉓ **il nipote (di nonni)**
grandson

㉔ **la nipote (di nonni)**
granddaughter

㉕ **i nipoti (di nonni)**
grandchildren

KEY

㉖ **sposato** *m*
sposata *f*
married

㉗ **divorziato** *m*
divorziata *f*
divorced

㉘ **i figli**
children

㉙ **i parenti non consanguinei**
non-blood relative

See also
07 Life events · Gli eventi della vita **08** Pregnancy
and childhood · La gravidanza e l'infanzia

5.2 LA FAMIGLIA DI SARA
SARA'S FAMILY

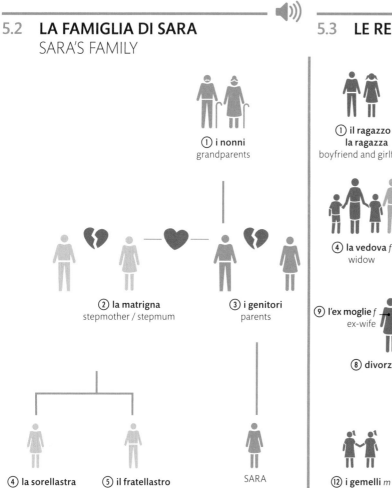

① **i nonni**
grandparents

② **la matrigna**
stepmother / stepmum

③ **i genitori**
parents

④ **la sorellastra**
stepsister

⑤ **il fratellastro**
stepbrother

SARA

5.3 LE RELAZIONI · RELATIONSHIPS

① **il ragazzo e
la ragazza**
boyfriend and girlfriend

② **il partner** *m*
la partner *f*
partner

③ **il genitore single**
single parent

④ **la vedova** *f*
widow

⑤ **sposato** *m*
sposata *f*
married

⑥ **il marito**
husband

⑦ **la moglie**
wife

⑨ **l'ex moglie** *f*
ex-wife

⑩ **l'ex marito** *m*
ex-husband

⑧ **divorziato** *m* / **divorziata** *f*
divorced

⑪ **i fratelli**
siblings

⑫ **i gemelli** *m*
le gemelle *f*
twins

⑬ **i tre gemelli**
triplets

⑭ **il figlio unico** *m*
la figlia unica *f*
only child

5.4 CRESCERE · GROWING UP

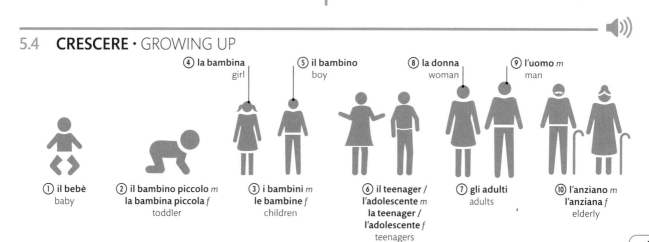

① **il bebè**
baby

② **il bambino piccolo** *m*
la bambina piccola *f*
toddler

③ **i bambini** *m*
le bambine *f*
children

④ **la bambina**
girl

⑤ **il bambino**
boy

⑥ **il teenager /
l'adolescente** *m*
**la teenager /
l'adolescente** *f*
teenagers

⑦ **gli adulti**
adults

⑧ **la donna**
woman

⑨ **l'uomo** *m*
man

⑩ **l'anziano** *m*
l'anziana *f*
elderly

6.1 I SENTIMENTI E GLI STATI D'ANIMO · FEELINGS AND MOODS

① **contento** *m*
contenta *f*
pleased

② **allegro** *m*
allegra *f*
cheerful

③ **felice**
happy

④ **felicissimo** *m*
felicissima *f*
delighted

⑤ **al settimo cielo**
ecstatic

⑥ **divertito** *m*
divertita *f*
amused

⑦ **grato** *m* / **grata** *f*
grateful

⑧ **fortunato** *m*
fortunata *f*
lucky

⑨ **interessato** *m*
interessata *f*
interested

⑩ **curioso** *m*
curiosa *f*
curious

⑪ **affascinato** *m*
affascinata *f*
intrigued

⑫ **sbalordito** *m*
sbalordita *f*
amazed

⑬ **sorpreso** *m*
sorpresa *f*
surprised

⑭ **orgoglioso** *m*
orgogliosa *f*
proud

⑮ **entusiasta**
excited

⑯ **elettrizzato** *m*
elettrizzata *f*
thrilled

⑰ **calmo** *m*
calma *f*
calm

⑱ **rilassato** *m*
rilassata *f*
relaxed

⑳ Grazie. Il pranzo era molto buono.
Thank you. I really enjoyed the meal.

⑲ **riconoscente**
appreciative

㉑ **sicuro** *m*
sicura *f*
confident

㉒ **fiducioso** *m*
fiduciosa *f*
hopeful

㉓ **comprensivo** *m*
comprensiva *f*
sympathetic

㉔ **infastidito** *m*
infastidita *f*
annoyed

㉕ **geloso** *m*
gelosa *f*
jealous

㉖ **imbarazzato** *m*
imbarazzata *f*
embarrassed

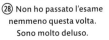

(28) **Non ho passato l'esame nemmeno questa volta. Sono molto deluso.**
I failed the exam again. I'm very disappointed.

(27) **deluso** *m* **delusa** *f*
disappointed

(29) **preoccupato** *m* **preoccupata** *f*
worried

(30) **ansioso** *m* **ansiosa** *f*
anxious

(31) **nervoso** *m* **nervosa** *f*
nervous

(32) **impaurito** *m* **impaurita** *f*
frightened

(33) **spaventato** *m* **spaventata** *f*
scared

(34) **terrorizzato** *m* **terrorizzata** *f*
terrified

(35) **triste**
sad

(36) **scontento** *m* **scontenta** *f*
unhappy

(37) **addolorato** *m* **addolorata** *f*
tearful

(38) **infelice**
miserable

(39) **depresso** *m* **depressa** *f*
depressed

(40) **solo** *m* / **sola** *f*
lonely

(41) **irritato** *m* **irritata** *f*
irritated

(42) **frustrato** *m* **frustrata** *f*
frustrated

(43) **arrabbiato** *m* **arrabbiata** *f*
angry

(44) **furioso** *m* **furiosa** *f*
furious

(45) **disgustato** *m* **disgustata** *f*
disgusted

(46) **poco entusiasta**
unenthusiastic

(47) **stanco** *m* **stanca** *f*
tired

(48) **esausto** *m* **esausta** *f*
exhausted

(49) **confuso** *m* **confusa** *f*
confused

(50) **annoiato** *m* **annoiata** *f*
bored

(51) **distratto** *m* **distratta** *f*
distracted

(52) **serio** *m* **seria** *f*
serious

(53) **indifferente**
indifferent

(54) **stressato** *m* **stressata** *f*
stressed

(55) **colpevole**
guilty

(56) **per nulla colpito** *m* **per nulla colpita** *f*
unimpressed

(57) **turbato** *m* **turbata** *f*
upset

(58) **scioccato** *m* **scioccata** *f*
shocked

07 Gli eventi della vita
Life events

I RAPPORTI · RELATIONSHIPS

① il vicino *m*
la vicina *f*
neighbour

② l'amico *m*
l'amica *f*
friend

③ il conoscente *m* /
la conoscente *f*
acquaintance

④ il collega *m*
la collega *f*
colleague

⑤ l'amico di penna *m*
l'amica di penna *f*
pen pal

⑥ la coppia
couple

⑦ il migliore amico *m*
la migliore amica *f*
best friend

⑧ il partner *m*
la partner *f*
partner

⑨ Vuoi sposarmi?
Will you marry me?

⑩ la fidanzata
fiancée

⑪ il fidanzato
fiancé

⑫ la coppia di fidanzati
engaged couple

⑬ la sposa
bride

⑭ lo sposo
groom

⑮ la coppia sposata
married couple

7.2 GLI EVENTI DELLA VITA · LIFE EVENTS

① nascere
to be born

② il certificato di nascita
birth certificate

③ andare alla scuola materna
to go to nursery

④ iniziare la scuola
to start school

⑤ fare amicizia
to make friends

⑥ vincere un premio
to win a prize

⑦ laurearsi
to graduate

⑧ emigrare
to emigrate

⑨ trovare un lavoro
to get a job

⑩ innamorarsi
to fall in love

⑪ sposarsi
to get married

See also
05 La famiglia · Family **08** La gravidanza e l'infanzia · Pregnancy and childhood **19** Le malattie e le lesioni · Illness and injury **73** A scuola · At school **80** All'università · At college **92** Fare domanda per un lavoro · Applying for a job **131** Il viaggio e l'alloggio · Travel and accommodation

7.3 LE FESTE E LE CELEBRAZIONI · FESTIVALS AND CELEBRATIONS

① **il compleanno**
birthday

② **il regalo**
present

③ **il biglietto di buon compleanno**
birthday card

④ **il Natale**
Christmas

⑤ **il Capodanno**
New Year

⑥ **il carnevale**
carnival

⑦ **il Ringraziamento**
Thanksgiving

⑧ **la Pasqua**
Easter

⑨ **Halloween** *m*
Halloween

⑩ **il Kwanzaa**
Kwanzaa

⑪ **la Pasqua ebraica**
Passover

⑫ **il Diwali**
Diwali

⑬ **il giorno dei morti**
Day of the Dead

⑭ **la Eid al-Fitr**
Eid al-Fitr

⑮ **l'Holi** *f*
Holi

⑯ **Hanukkah** *f*
Hanukkah

⑰ **Baisakhi / Vaisakhi** *m*
Baisakhi / Vaisakhi

⑫ **il matrimonio**
wedding

⑬ **la luna di miele**
honeymoon

⑭ **l'anniversario** *m*
anniversary

⑮ **avere un bambino**
to have a baby

⑯ **il battesimo**
christening / baptism
⑰ **l'acqua santa** *f*
holy water

⑱ **il bar mitzvah / bat mitzvah** *m*
bar mitzvah / bat mitzvah

⑲ **andare in pellegrinaggio alla Mecca**
to go on Hajj

⑳ **andare in pensione**
to retire

㉑ **divorziare**
divorce

㉒ **fare testamento**
to make a will

㉓ **morire**
to die

㉔ **il funerale**
funeral

8.1 LA GRAVIDANZA E IL PARTO · PREGNANCY AND CHILDBIRTH

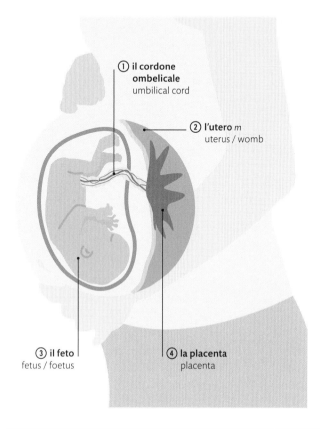

① il cordone ombelicale
umbilical cord

② l'utero m
uterus / womb

③ il feto
fetus / foetus

④ la placenta
placenta

⑧ l'embrione m
embryo

⑤ il test di gravidanza
pregnancy test

⑥ incinta
pregnant

⑦ l'ecografia f
ultrasound

⑨ la data prevista per il parto
due date

⑩ l'ostetrica f
midwife

⑪ il ginecologo m
la ginecologa f
obstetrician

⑫ la nascita
birth

⑬ il neonato m
la neonata f
newborn baby

⑭ la vaccinazione
vaccination

⑮ l'incubatrice f
incubator

8.2 I GIOCHI E I GIOCATTOLI · TOYS AND GAMES

① la bambola
doll

② la casa delle bambole
doll's house

③ il peluche
soft toy

④ il gioco da tavolo
board game

⑤ i mattoncini
building blocks / building bricks

⑥ la palla
ball

⑦ la trottola
spinning top

⑧ lo yo-yo
yo-yo

⑨ la corda per saltare
skipping rope

⑩ il trampolino
trampoline

⑪ il puzzle
jigsaw puzzle

⑫ il trenino elettrico
train set

See also
05 La famiglia · Family **13** Gli indumenti · Clothes **20** Andare dal medico · Visiting the doctor
21 L'ospedale · The hospital **30** La camera da letto · Bedroom

8.3 L'INFANZIA · CHILDHOOD

① **il passeggino**
buggy

② **la carrozzina**
pram

③ **il seggiolone**
high chair

④ **il ciuccio**
dummy

⑤ **il sonaglio**
rattle

⑥ **il baby monitor**
baby monitor

⑦ **il cancelletto di sicurezza**
stair gate

⑧ **la culla di vimini**
Moses basket

⑨ **la vaschetta per il bagnetto**
baby bath

⑩ **il vasino**
potty

⑪ **la salvietta umidificata**
wet wipe

⑫ **il bambino piccolo** *m*
la bambina piccola *f*
toddler

⑬ **la crema per irritazioni da pannolino**
nappy rash cream

⑭ **il pannolino**
nappy

⑮ **la borsa per pannolini**
changing bag

⑯ **il box**
playpen

⑱ **la tettarella**
teat

⑰ **il biberon**
bottle

⑲ **il latte in polvere**
baby formula

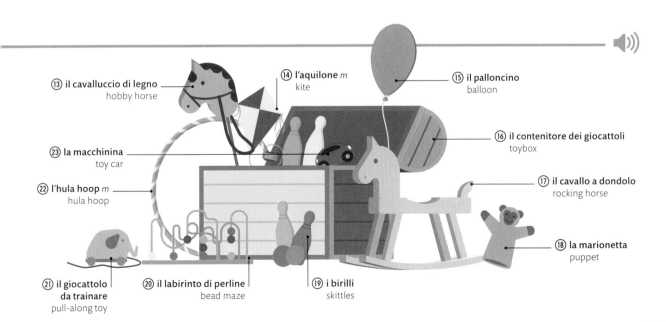

⑬ **il cavalluccio di legno**
hobby horse

⑭ **l'aquilone** *m*
kite

⑮ **il palloncino**
balloon

⑯ **il contenitore dei giocattoli**
toybox

⑰ **il cavallo a dondolo**
rocking horse

⑱ **la marionetta**
puppet

㉓ **la macchinina**
toy car

㉒ **l'hula hoop** *m*
hula hoop

㉑ **il giocattolo da trainare**
pull-along toy

⑳ **il labirinto di perline**
bead maze

⑲ **i birilli**
skittles

09 Le attività quotidiane
Daily routines

LA MATTINA E IL POMERIGGIO · MORNING AND AFTERNOON

① **suona la sveglia**
alarm goes off

② **svegliarsi**
to wake up

③ **alzarsi**
to get up

④ **fare la doccia**
to take (or have)
a shower

⑤ **fare il bagno**
to take (or have)
a bath

⑥ **truccarsi**
to put on makeup

⑦ **radersi**
to shave

⑧ **lavarsi i capelli**
to wash your hair

⑨ **asciugarsi i capelli**
to dry your hair

⑩ **stirare una camicia**
to iron a shirt

⑪ **vestirsi**
to get dressed

⑫ **lavarsi i denti**
to brush your teeth

⑬ **lavarsi il viso**
to wash your face

⑭ **pettinarsi**
to brush your hair

⑮ **fare il letto**
to make the bed

⑯ **fare colazione**
to have (or eat)
breakfast

⑰ **preparare il pranzo al sacco**
to pack your lunch

⑱ **uscire di casa**
to leave the house

⑲ **andare al lavoro**
to go to work

⑳ **andare a scuola**
to go to school

㉑ **guidare**
to drive

㉒ **prendere l'autobus**
to catch the bus

㉓ **prendere il treno**
to catch the train

㉔ **leggere un giornale**
to read a newspaper

㉕ **arrivare**
to arrive

㉖ **arrivare in anticipo**
to arrive early

㉗ **arrivare in orario**
to arrive on time

㉜ Mi dispiace di essere di nuovo in ritardo.
I'm sorry I'm late again.

㉘ **pranzare**
to have (or eat)
lunch

㉙ **controllare le e-mail**
to check your emails

㉚ **fare una pausa**
to have a break

㉛ **arrivare in ritardo / essere in ritardo**
to arrive late / to be late

See also
11 Le abilità e le azioni • Abilities and actions **29** Cucinare • Cooking **81** Al lavoro • At work
82 In ufficio • In the office **171** Feelings and moods • I sentimenti e gli stati d'animo
178 I verbi comuni • Common phrasal verbs

9.2 LA SERA · EVENING

① **finire di lavorare**
to finish work

④ **Casa dolce casa!**
There's no place
like home!

② **uscire dal lavoro**
to leave work

③ **fare gli straordinari**
to work overtime

⑤ **arrivare a casa**
to arrive home

⑥ **preparare la cena**
to cook dinner

⑦ **cenare**
to have (or eat) dinner

⑧ **sparecchiare**
to clear the table

⑨ **lavare i piatti**
to wash up

⑩ **ascoltare la radio**
to listen to the radio

⑪ **guardare la TV**
to watch TV

⑫ **bere tè o caffè**
to drink tea or coffee

⑬ **portare fuori la spazzatura**
to take out the rubbish

⑭ **mettere a letto i bambini**
to put the children to bed

⑮ **andare a letto**
to go to bed

⑯ **impostare la sveglia**
to set the alarm

⑰ **addormentarsi**
to go to sleep

9.3 LE ALTRE ATTIVITÀ
OTHER ACTIVITIES

① **fare i compiti**
to do homework

② **portare a spasso il cane**
to walk the dog

③ **dare da mangiare al cane / al gatto**
to feed the dog / cat

④ **fare la spesa**
to buy groceries

⑤ **uscire con gli amici**
to go out with friends

⑥ **andare al bar**
to go to a café

⑦ **chiamare un'amico m / un'amica f / chiamare i familiari**
to call a friend / to call your family

⑧ **tagliare l'erba**
to mow the lawn

⑨ **fare esercizio fisico**
to exercise

⑩ **giocare con i bambini**
to play with your kids

⑪ **pagare le bollette**
to pay the bills

⑫ **fare un riposino**
to take a nap

⑬ **lavare l'auto**
to clean the car

⑭ **suonare uno strumento musicale**
to play a musical instrument

⑮ **chiacchierare con gli amici**
to chat with friends

⑯ **chattare online**
to chat online

⑰ **innaffiare le piante**
to water the plants

⑱ **spedire un pacco**
to send a package / parcel

10 I tratti della personalità
Personality traits

10.1 DESCRIVERE LE PERSONALITÀ · DESCRIBING PERSONALITIES

① **amichevole**
friendly

② **scortese**
unfriendly

③ **loquace**
talkative

④ **entusiasta**
enthusiastic

⑤ **serio** *m*
seria *f*
serious

⑥ **assertivo** *m*
assertiva *f*
assertive

⑦ **critico** *m*
critica *f*
critical

⑧ **premuroso** *m*
premurosa *f*
caring

⑨ **sensibile**
sensitive

⑩ **insensibile**
insensitive

⑪ **ragionevole**
reasonable

⑫ **irragionevole**
unreasonable

⑬ **gentile**
kind

⑭ **sgarbato** *m*
sgarbata *f*
unkind

⑮ **riservato** *m*
riservata *f*
secretive

⑯ **maturo** *m*
matura *f*
mature

⑰ **immaturo** *m*
immatura *f*
immature

⑱ **cauto** *m* / **cauta** *f*
cautious

⑲ **generoso** *m*
generosa *f*
generous

⑳ **coraggioso** *m*
coraggiosa *f*
brave

㉑ **divertente**
funny

㉒ **meschino** *m*
meschina *f*
mean

㉓ **paziente**
patient

㉔ **impaziente**
impatient

㉕ **pigro** *m* / **pigra** *f*
lazy

㉖ **ottimista**
optimistic

㉗ **estroverso** *m*
estroversa *f*
outgoing

㉘ **appassionato** *m*
appassionata *f*
passionate

㉙ **educato** *m* / **educata** *f*
polite

㉚ **maleducato** *m*
maleducata *f*
rude

㉛ **timido** *m*
timida *f*
shy

㉜ **intelligente**
intelligent

㉝ **nervoso** *m*
nervosa *f*
nervous

㉞ **sicuro** *m* / **sicura** *f*
confident

㉟ **sciocco** *m*
sciocca *f*
silly

㊱ **egoista**
selfish

See also
05 La famiglia • Family **06** I sentimenti e gli stati d'animo • Feelings and moods **11** Le abilità e le azioni • Abilities and actions **93** Le competenze sul luogo di lavoro • Workplace skills

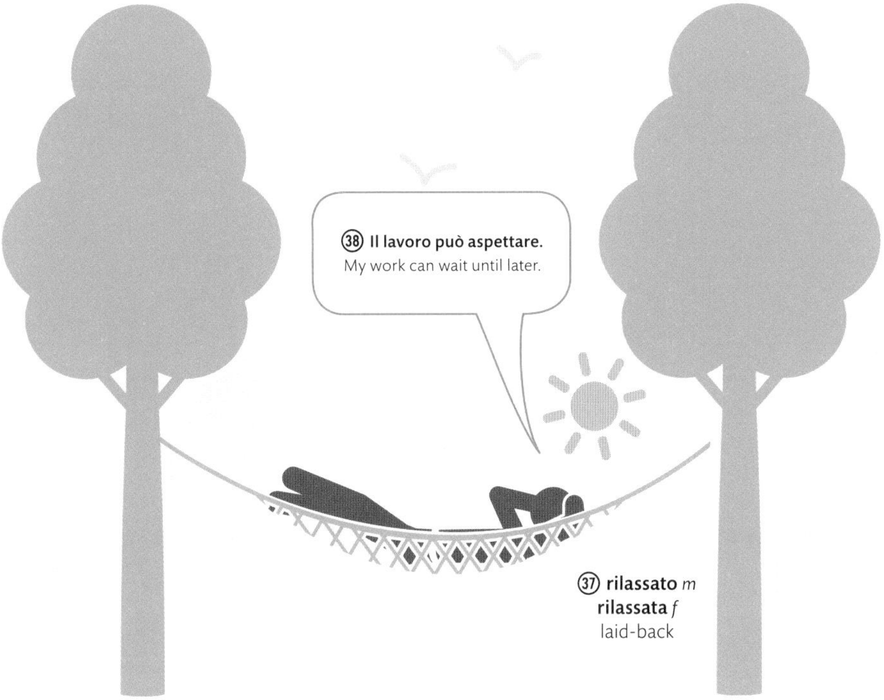

㊳ **Il lavoro può aspettare.**
My work can wait until later.

㊲ **rilassato** *m*
rilassata *f*
laid-back

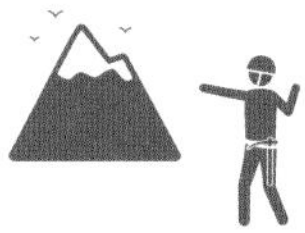

㊴ **ambizioso** *m*
ambiziosa *f*
ambitious

㊵ **spontaneo** *m*
spontanea *f*
spontaneous

㊶ **romantico** *m*
romantica *f*
romantic

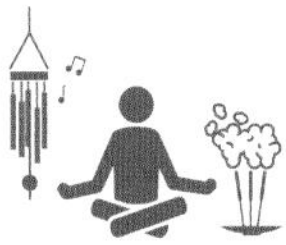

㊷ **calmo** *m* / **calma** *f*
calm

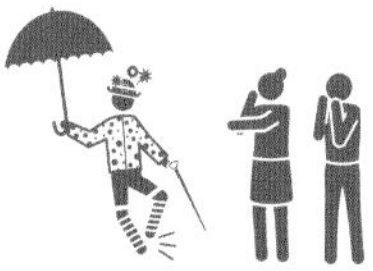

㊸ **eccentrico** *m*
eccentrica *f*
eccentric

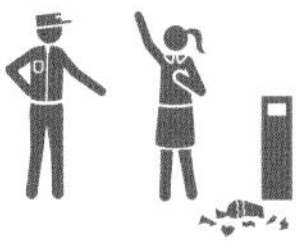

㊹ **onesto** *m* / **onesta** *f*
honest

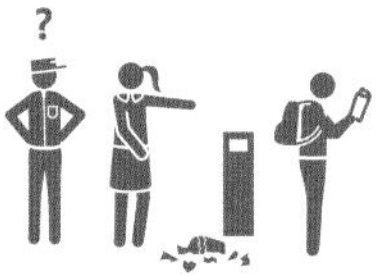

㊺ **disonesto** *m*
disonesta *f*
dishonest

㊻ **di conforto**
supportive

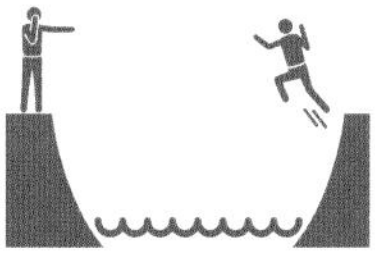

㊼ **impulsivo** *m*
impulsiva *f*
impulsive

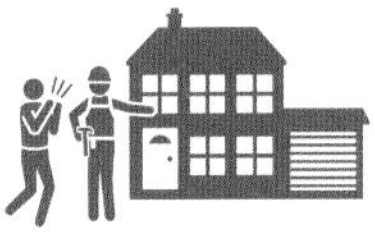

㊽ **affidabile**
reliable

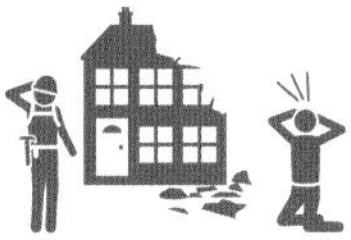

㊾ **inaffidabile**
unreliable

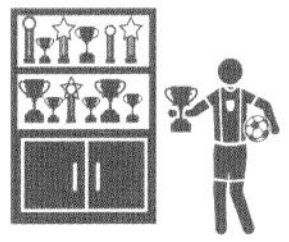

㊿ **talentuoso** *m*
talentuosa *f*
talented

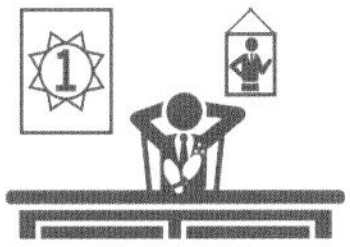

(51) **arrogante**
arrogant

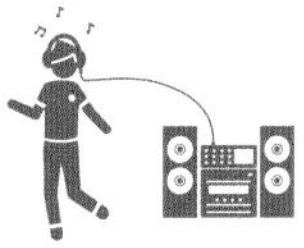

(52) **attento** *m*
attenta *f*
considerate

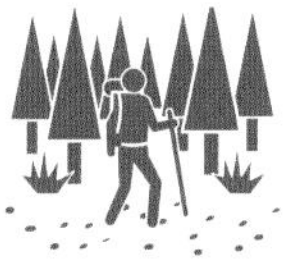

(53) **avventuroso** *m*
avventurosa *f*
adventurous

(54) **disponibile**
approachable

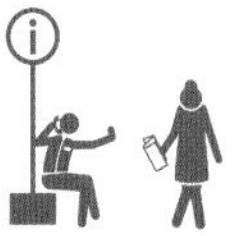

(55) **inavvicinabile**
unapproachable

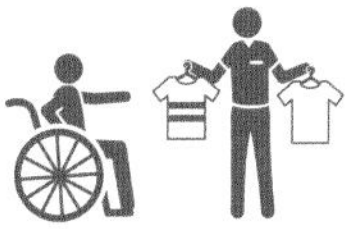

(56) **deciso** *m* / **decisa** *f*
decisive

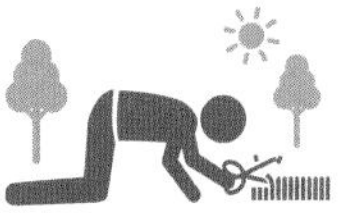

(57) **meticoloso** *m*
meticolosa *f*
meticulous

(58) **goffo** *m*
goffa *f*
clumsy

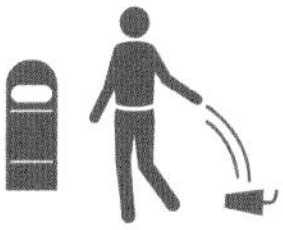

(59) **irriguardoso** *m*
irriguardosa *f*
thoughtless

11 Le abilità e le azioni
Abilities and actions

11.1 DESCRIVERE LE ABILITÀ E LE AZIONI
DESCRIBING ABILITIES AND ACTIONS

⑩ Amo ballare.
I love to dance.

⑪ Anch'io!
Me too!

① **vedere**
to see

② **assaggiare**
to taste

③ **annusare**
to smell

④ **andare carponi**
to crawl

⑤ **colpire**
to hit

⑥ **giocare**
to play

⑦ **calciare**
to kick

⑧ **lanciare**
to throw

⑨ **ballare**
to dance

⑫ **afferrare**
to catch

⑬ **correre**
to run

⑭ **saltellare**
to hop

⑮ **saltare**
to jump

⑯ **muoversi furtivamente**
to creep

⑰ **scuotere**
to shake

⑱ **lavorare**
to work

⑲ **soffiare**
to blow

⑳ **fare (un pupazzo di neve)**
to make (a snowman)

㉑ **compitare**
to spell

㉒ **fare (i compiti)**
to do (homework)

㉓ **copiare**
to copy

㉔ **costruire**
to build

㉕ **scavare**
to dig

㉖ **riparare**
to repair

㉗ **aggiustare**
to fix

㉘ **sedersi**
to sit down

㉙ **alzarsi**
to stand up

㉚ **capire**
to understand

㉛ **cadere**
to fall

㉜ **sollevare**
to lift

㉝ **aggiungere**
to add

㉞ **sottrarre**
to subtract

㉟ **contare**
to count

See also
09 Le attività quotidiane • Daily routines **93** Le competenze sul luogo di lavoro • Workplace skills **178** I verbi comuni • Common phrasal verbs

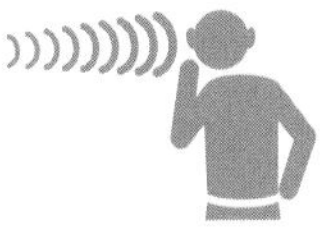

㊱ **ascoltare**
to listen

㊲ **parlare**
to talk

㊳ **parlare**
to speak

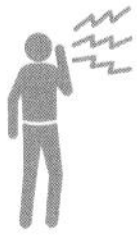

㊴ **gridare**
to shout

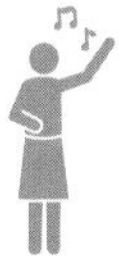

㊵ **cantare**
to sing

㊶ **recitare**
to act

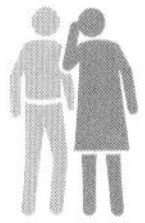

㊷ **sussurrare**
to whisper

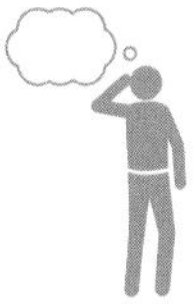

㊸ **pensare**
to think

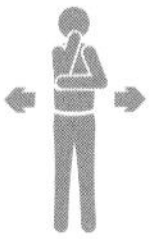

㊹ **decidere**
to decide

㊺ **ricordare**
to remember

㊻ **dimenticare**
to forget

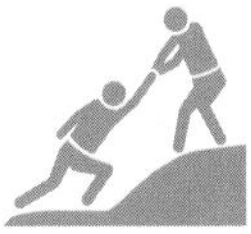

㊼ **aiutare**
to help

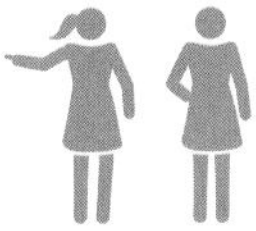

㊽ **indicare**
to point

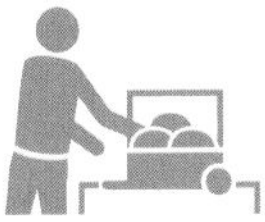

㊾ **impacchettare**
to pack

㊿ **spacchettare**
to unpack

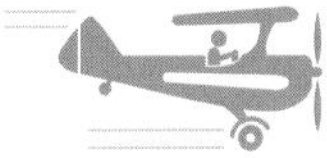

(51) **volare**
to fly

(52) **andare in**
to ride

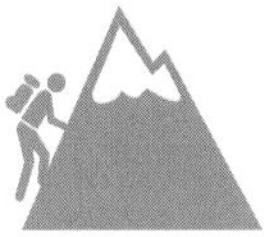

(53) **scalare**
to climb

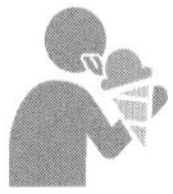

(54) **leccare**
to lick

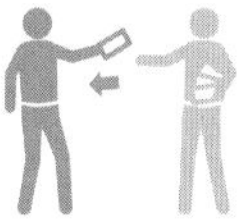

(55) **prendere**
to take

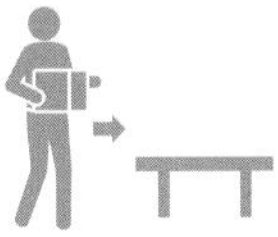

(56) **portare**
to bring

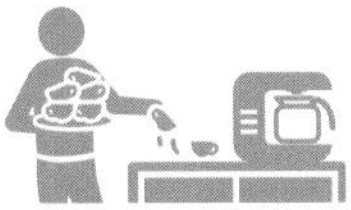

(57) **ritirare**
to pick up / to collect

(58) **entrare**
to enter

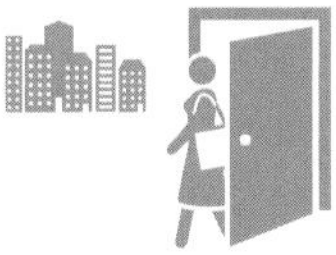

(59) **uscire**
to exit

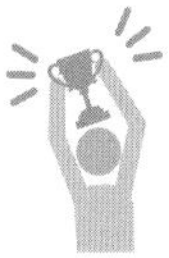

(60) **vincere**
to win

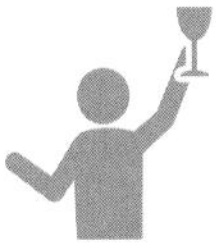

(61) **sollevare**
to raise

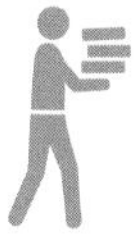

(62) **portare**
to carry

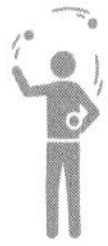

(63) **fare il giocoliere**
to juggle

(64) **tenere**
to hold

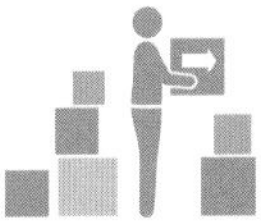

(65) **spostare**
to move

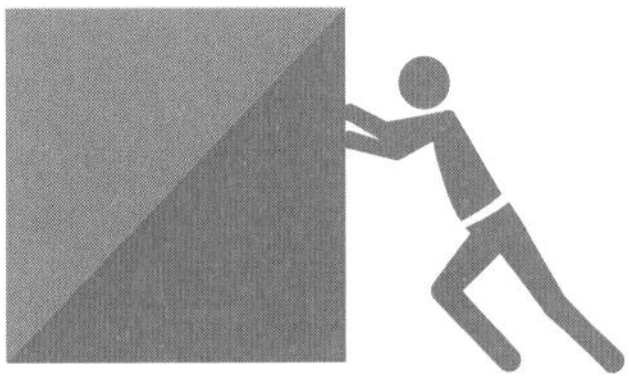

(66) **spingere**
to push

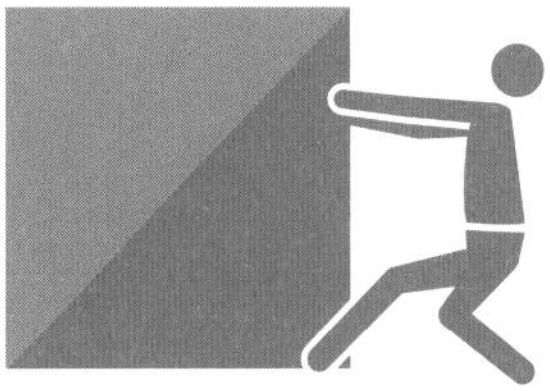

(67) **tirare**
to pull

12 L'aspetto e i capelli
Appearance and hair

12.1 L'ASPETTO GENERALE
GENERAL APPEARANCE

① **di media altezza**
medium height

② **alto** m **alta** f
tall

③ **basso** m **bassa** f
short

④ **bella**
beautiful

⑤ **bello**
handsome

⑥ **giovane**
young

⑦ **di mezza età**
middle-aged

⑧ **anziano** m **anziana** f
old

⑨ **i pori**
pores

⑩ **le lentiggini**
freckles

⑪ **le rughe**
wrinkles

⑫ **le fossette**
dimples

⑬ **il neo**
mole

12.2 I CAPELLI · HAIR

① **acconciare i capelli**
to style your hair

② **lavarsi i capelli**
to wash your hair

③ **farsi tagliare i capelli**
to have (or get) your hair cut

④ **legare i capelli**
to tie your hair back

⑤ **farsi crescere i capelli**
to grow your hair

⑥ **radersi**
to shave

⑦ **i capelli lunghi**
long hair

⑧ **i capelli corti**
short hair

⑨ **i capelli lunghi fino alle spalle**
shoulder-length hair

⑩ **la riga laterale**
side parting

⑪ **la riga centrale**
centre parting

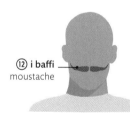 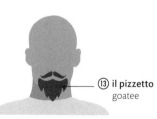

⑫ **i baffi**
moustache

⑬ **il pizzetto**
goatee

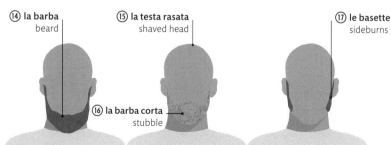

⑭ **la barba**
beard

⑮ **la testa rasata**
shaved head

⑰ **le basette**
sideburns

⑯ **la barba corta**
stubble

⑱ **i peli del viso**
facial hair

See also
13-15 Gli indumenti • Clothes **16** Gli accessori
Accessories **17** Le scarpe • Shoes **18** La bellezza • Beauty

㉑ **i capelli a spazzola**
crew cut

⑳ **calvo** *m* / **calva** *f*
bald

㉑ **i capelli lisci**
straight hair

㉒ **i capelli mossi**
wavy hair

㉓ **i capelli ricci**
curly hair

㉔ **i capelli crespi**
frizzy hair

㉕ **la coda di cavallo**
ponytail

㉖ **la treccia**
plait

㉗ **i codini**
pigtails

㉘ **il caschetto**
bob

㉙ **il taglio corto**
crop

㉚ **la parrucca**
wig

㉛ **la treccia alla francese**
French plait

㉜ **lo chignon**
bun

㉝ **le mèches**
highlights

㉞ **la pettinatura afro**
Afro

㉟ **le treccine**
braids

㊱ **le treccine aderenti alla testa**
cornrows

㊲ **i capelli normali**
normal hair

㊳ **i capelli grassi**
greasy hair

㊴ **i capelli secchi**
dry hair

㊵ **la forfora**
dandruff

㊶ **il gel per capelli**
hair gel

㊷ **lo spray per capelli**
hair spray

㊸ **i capelli neri**
black hair

㊹ **i capelli castani**
brown hair

㊺ **i capelli biondi**
blond / blonde hair

㊻ **i capelli rossi**
red hair

㊼ **i capelli ramati**
auburn hair

㊽ **i capelli grigi**
grey hair

㊾ **la piastra per capelli**
hair straightener

㊿ **il ferro arricciacapelli**
hair curler

51 **la spazzola**
hairbrush

52 **il pettine**
comb

53 **le forbici per capelli**
hair scissors

54 **il phon**
hair dryer

13 Gli indumenti
Clothes

13.1 DESCRIVERE GLI INDUMENTI · DESCRIBING CLOTHES

① la pelle / il cuoio
leather

② il cotone
cotton

③ di lana
woollen

④ la seta
silk

⑤ sintetico *m*
sintetica *f*
synthetic

⑥ il denim / jeans
denim

⑦ tinta unita
plain

⑧ a righe
striped

⑨ a quadri /
a scacchi
checkered

⑩ a pois
polka dot

⑪ con motivo
cachemire
paisley

⑫ con motivo
scozzese
plaid

⑬ largo *m* / larga *f*
loose / baggy

⑭ aderente
fitted

⑮ stretto *m*
stretta *f*
tight

⑯ stropicciato *m*
stropicciata *f*
crumpled

⑰ corto *m* / corta *f*
cropped

⑱ vintage
vintage

13.2 GLI ABITI DA LAVORO E LE UNIFORMI · WORK CLOTHES AND UNIFORMS

① il cappello
da cuoco
chef's hat

② la giacca
da cuoco
chef's coat

③ la divisa da cuoco
chef's uniform

④ il grembiule
apron

⑤ il camice da
laboratorio
lab coat

⑥ l'uniforme da
pompiere *f*
firefighter's uniform

⑦ la tuta
da lavoro
coveralls

See also
12 L'aspetto e i capelli • Appearance and hair **14–15** Gli indumenti (continua) • Clothes continued **16** Gli accessori • Accessories **17** Le scarpe • Shoes

13.3 GLI INDUMENTI DEI BAMBINI · KIDS' AND BABIES' CLOTHES

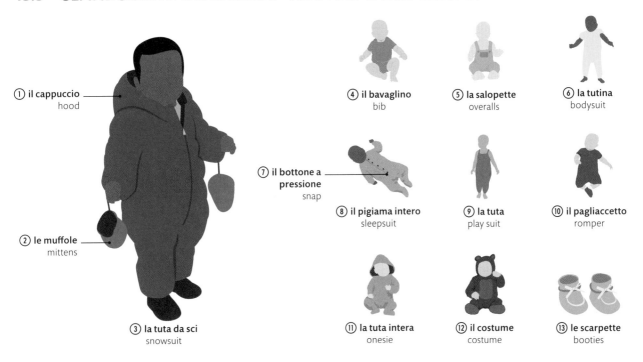

① **il cappuccio**
hood

② **le muffole**
mittens

③ **la tuta da sci**
snowsuit

④ **il bavaglino**
bib

⑤ **la salopette**
overalls

⑥ **la tutina**
bodysuit

⑦ **il bottone a pressione**
snap

⑧ **il pigiama intero**
sleepsuit

⑨ **la tuta**
play suit

⑩ **il pagliaccetto**
romper

⑪ **la tuta intera**
onesie

⑫ **il costume**
costume

⑬ **le scarpette**
booties

⑭ **la camicia della divisa scolastica**
school shirt

⑮ **la cravatta della divisa scolastica**
school tie

⑪ **la giacca ad alta visibilità**
high-visibility jacket

⑧ **l'uniforme militare** *f*
military uniform

⑨ **la divisa chirurgica**
scrubs

⑩ **i pantaloni cargo da lavoro**
cargo pants

⑫ **la pettorina da lavoro**
tabard

⑬ **la divisa scolastica**
school uniform

Gli indumenti (continua)
Clothes continued

14.1 L'ABBIGLIAMENTO INFORMALE · CASUAL CLOTHES

① Preferisco questo abbigliamento informale ai miei abiti da lavoro formali.
I prefer this casual outfit to my formal work clothes.

⑦ Dopo il lavoro, mi piace indossare un paio di jeans e una T-shirt.
After work, I like to change into jeans and a T-shirt.

② la camicetta / blusa
blouse

③ il maglione
sweater / jumper

④ la gonna
skirt

⑤ la piega
pleat

⑥ l'orlo *m*
hem

⑧ la T-shirt
T-shirt

⑨ le righe
stripes

⑩ i jeans
jeans

⑪ la felpa
sweatshirt

⑫ gli shorts
shorts

⑬ i bermuda
bermuda shorts

⑭ il cardigan
cardigan

⑮ la canotta
tank top

⑯ il vestito
dress

⑰ i leggings
leggings

⑱ la camicia a maniche corte
short-sleeved shirt

⑲ la polo
polo shirt

⑳ il cappello da sole
sun hat

㉑ la maglia con scollo a V
V-neck

㉒ la maglia girocollo
round neck

See also
12 L'aspetto e i capelli • Appearance and hair **15** Gli indumenti (continua) • Clothes continued **16** Gli accessori • Accessories **17** Le scarpe • Shoes

14.2 GLI INDUMENTI DA NOTTE
NIGHTWEAR

① **la sottoveste**
camisole

② **le pantofole**
slippers

③ **la mascherina per gli occhi**
eye mask

④ **il pigiama**
pyjamas

⑤ **la camicia da notte**
nightgown / nightie

⑥ **la vestaglia**
dressing gown

14.3 LA BIANCHERIA INTIMA · UNDERWEAR

① **le mutandine**
knickers

② **le mutande**
pants

③ **i boxer**
boxer shorts

④ **i calzini**
socks

⑤ **il reggiseno**
bra

⑥ **la sottoveste**
slip dress

⑦ **la canottiera**
vest

⑧ **i collant**
tights

⑨ **le calze**
stockings

⑩ **il corsetto**
basque

⑪ **la giarrettiera**
garter

⑫ **il reggicalze**
suspenders

14.4 I VERBI PER L'ABBIGLIAMENTO · VERBS FOR CLOTHES

① **indossare**
to wear

② **andare bene**
to fit

③ **mettere**
to put on

④ **togliere**
to take off

⑤ **allacciare**
to fasten

⑥ **slacciare**
to unfasten

⑦ **stare bene a (qualcuno)**
to suit (someone)

⑧ **cambiarsi**
to change / to get changed

⑨ **appendere**
to hang up

⑩ **piegare**
to fold

⑪ **fare il risvolto**
to turn up

⑫ **provare qualcosa**
to try something on

15.1 L'ABBIGLIAMENTO FORMALE · FORMAL WEAR

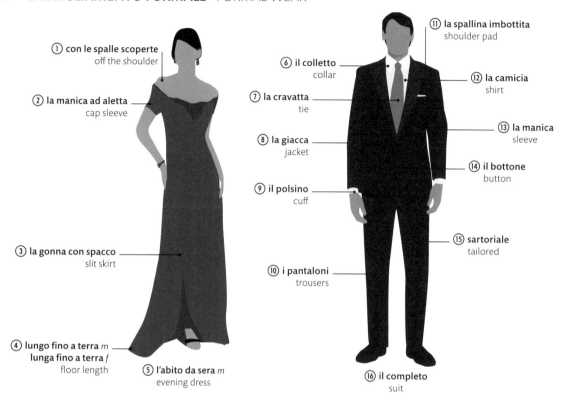

① con le spalle scoperte
off the shoulder

② la manica ad aletta
cap sleeve

③ la gonna con spacco
slit skirt

④ lungo fino a terra *m*
lunga fino a terra *f*
floor length

⑤ l'abito da sera *m*
evening dress

⑥ il colletto
collar

⑦ la cravatta
tie

⑧ la giacca
jacket

⑨ il polsino
cuff

⑩ i pantaloni
trousers

⑪ la spallina imbottita
shoulder pad

⑫ la camicia
shirt

⑬ la manica
sleeve

⑭ il bottone
button

⑮ sartoriale
tailored

⑯ il completo
suit

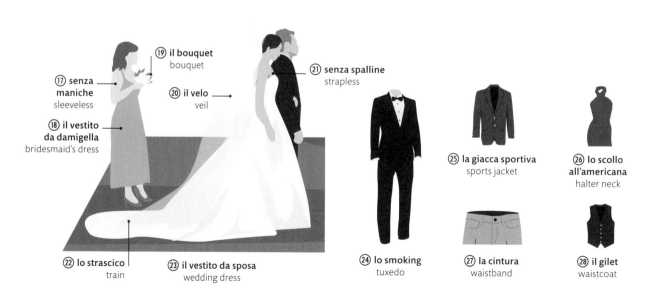

⑰ senza maniche
sleeveless

⑱ il vestito da damigella
bridesmaid's dress

⑲ il bouquet
bouquet

⑳ il velo
veil

㉑ senza spalline
strapless

㉒ lo strascico
train

㉓ il vestito da sposa
wedding dress

㉔ lo smoking
tuxedo

㉕ la giacca sportiva
sports jacket

㉖ lo scollo all'americana
halter neck

㉗ la cintura
waistband

㉘ il gilet
waistcoat

See also
12 L'aspetto e i capelli • Appearance and hair **16** Gli accessori • Accessories
17 Le scarpe • Shoes

15.2 I CAPPOTTI · COATS

① l'impermeabile *m*
raincoat

② il cappuccio
hood
③ la giacca a vento
anorak

④ il montgomery
duffle coat

⑤ il poncho
poncho

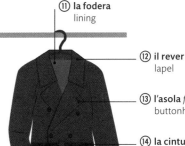

⑪ la fodera
lining
⑫ il rever
lapel
⑬ l'asola *f*
buttonhole
⑭ la cintura
belt
⑮ la tasca
pocket

⑥ la giacca di jeans
denim jacket

⑦ il giubbotto
imbottito
quilted jacket

⑧ il bomber
bomber jacket

⑨ la mantella
cloak

⑩ il trench
trench coat

15.3 L'ABBIGLIAMENTO SPORTIVO
SPORTSWEAR

① la tuta da
ginnastica
tracksuit

② il reggiseno
sportivo
sports bra

③ i pantaloni
della tuta
sweatpants

④ il body
leotard

⑥ il boccaglio
e la maschera
snorkel
and mask
⑨ gli occhialini
goggles
⑦ le pinne
fins /
flippers

⑤ la maglia
da calcio
football shirt

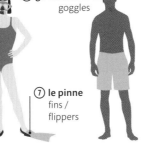
⑧ il costume
da bagno
swimsuit
⑩ il costume
da bagno
swimming trunks

15.4 GLI ABITI TRADIZIONALI
TRADITIONAL CLOTHES

① l'agbada *m*
agbada

② l'abito da
flamenco *m*
flamenco dress

③ i lederhosen
lederhosen

④ il kimono
kimono

⑤ il thawb
thawb

⑥ il sari
sari

⑦ il kilt
kilt

⑧ il sarong
sarong

⑨ la camicetta
folkloristica
folk blouse

16.1 GLI ACCESSORI DI MODA · FASHION ACCESSORIES

① **i guanti**
gloves

② **il manico**
handle

③ **l'ombrello** *m*
umbrella

④ **il fazzoletto**
handkerchief

⑤ **la fibbia**
buckle

⑥ **la cintura**
belt

⑦ **la sciarpa**
scarf

⑧ **la cravatta**
tie

⑨ **il fermacravatta**
tie-pin

⑩ **il papillon**
bow tie

⑪ **la spilla**
badge

⑫ **il cerchietto**
Alice band

16.2 I GIOIELLI · JEWELLERY

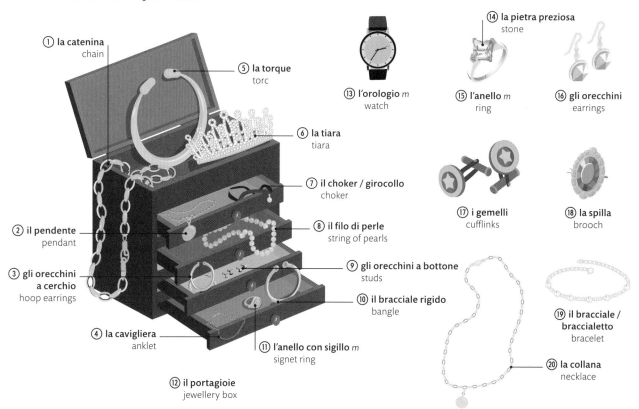

① **la catenina**
chain

② **il pendente**
pendant

③ **gli orecchini a cerchio**
hoop earrings

④ **la cavigliera**
anklet

⑤ **la torque**
torc

⑥ **la tiara**
tiara

⑦ **il choker / girocollo**
choker

⑧ **il filo di perle**
string of pearls

⑨ **gli orecchini a bottone**
studs

⑩ **il bracciale rigido**
bangle

⑪ **l'anello con sigillo** *m*
signet ring

⑫ **il portagioie**
jewellery box

⑬ **l'orologio** *m*
watch

⑭ **la pietra preziosa**
stone

⑮ **l'anello** *m*
ring

⑯ **gli orecchini**
earrings

⑰ **i gemelli**
cufflinks

⑱ **la spilla**
brooch

⑲ **il bracciale / braccialetto**
bracelet

⑳ **la collana**
necklace

See also
12 L'aspetto e i capelli · Appearance and hair **13-15** Gli indumenti · Clothes
17 Le scarpe · Shoes

16.3 I COPRICAPI · HEADWEAR

① **il basco**
flat cap

② **il cappello da baseball**
baseball cap

③ **il berretto con pon pon**
bobble hat

④ **l'hijab** *m*
hijab

⑤ **la kippah**
yarmulke

⑥ **il turbante**
turban

⑦ **il berretto**
beret

⑧ **il fedora**
fedora

⑨ **il berretto alla Sherlock Holmes**
deerstalker

⑩ **il fez**
fez

⑪ **il cappello da cowboy**
cowboy hat

⑫ **il sombrero**
sombrero

⑬ **il cappello da sole**
sun hat

⑭ **la coppola**
newsboy cap

⑮ **il panama**
panama

⑯ **la paglietta**
boater

⑰ **il berrettino**
beanie

⑱ **la cloche**
cloche

16.4 LE BORSE · BAGS

① **la valigetta**
briefcase

② **lo zaino**
backpack / rucksack

③ **il portafoglio**
purse

⑦ **il manico**
handle

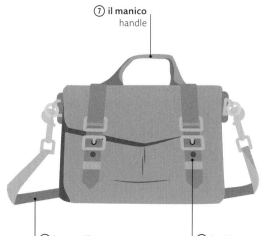

⑧ **la tracolla**
shoulder strap

⑨ **la chiusura**
fastening

⑩ **la borsa a tracolla**
shoulder bag

④ **il borsone**
holdall

⑤ **la borsa**
handbag

⑥ **la valigia**
suitcase

17 Le scarpe
Shoes

17.1 LE SCARPE E GLI ACCESSORI · SHOES AND ACCESSORIES

① **le scarpe col tacco**
high-heeled shoes

② **le scarpe basse**
flats

③ **le infradito**
flip-flops

④ **le espadrillas**
espadrilles

⑤ **le scarpe con tacco a rocchetto**
kitten heels

⑥ **le scarpe con tacco a spillo**
stilettos

⑦ **i sandali**
sandals

⑧ **i sandali in gomma**
jelly sandals

⑨ **i sandali alla schiava**
gladiator sandals

⑩ **i sandali con zeppa**
wedge sandals

⑪ **le scarpe con cinturino a T**
T-strap heels

⑫ **le scarpe con plateau**
platforms

⑬ **le scarpe con tacco e cinturino alla caviglia**
ankle strap heels

⑭ **le scarpe spuntate**
peep toes

⑮ **le scarpe con tacco aperte sul tallone**
slingback heels

⑯ **le ballerine**
ballet flats

⑰ **le mule**
mules

⑱ **le scarpe Mary Jane**
Mary Janes

17.2 GLI STIVALI · BOOTS

① **gli stivali da lavoro**
work boots

② **gli stivaletti Chelsea**
Chelsea boots

③ **gli scarponcini da trekking**
hiking boots

④ **gli stivaletti**
ankle boots

⑥ **la zip**
zip

⑤ **lo stivale alto**
thigh-high boot

⑦ **gli stivaletti chukka**
chukka boots / desert boots

⑧ **il laccio**
lace

⑩ **l'occhiello** *m*
eyelet

⑨ **la suola**
sole

⑪ **il tacco**
heel

⑫ **gli stivaletti stringati**
lace-up boots

⑬ **gli stivali al ginocchio**
knee-high boots

⑭ **gli stivali di gomma**
wellington boots

⑮ **gli stivali da cowboy**
cowboy boots

See also
12 L'aspetto e i capelli · Appearance and hair **13-15** Gli indumenti · Clothes
16 Gli accessori · Accessories **40** Gli attrezzi da giardinaggio · Garden tools

⑲ **le scarpe Oxford**
Oxfords

⑳ **le scarpe Derby**
Derby shoes

㉑ **le scarpe senza lacci**
slip-ons

㉒ **i mocassini**
moccasins

㉓ **la forma per stivali**
boot shapers

㉔ **la forma per scarpe**
shoe trees

㉕ **gli zoccoli**
clogs

㉖ **le scarpe con fibbia**
buckled shoes

㉗ **le ciabatte slider**
slides

㉘ **le pantofole**
slippers

㉙ **i lacci delle scarpe**
shoelaces

㉚ **le solette**
insoles

㉛ **i loafer**
loafers

㉜ **le scarpe da barca**
boat shoes

㉝ **le scarpe per bambini**
kids' shoes

㉞ **le scarpe brogue**
brogues

㉟ **il lucido da scarpe**
shoe polish

㊱ **la spazzola da scarpe**
shoe brush

17.3 **LE SCARPE SPORTIVE** · SPORTS SHOES

① **le scarpe da corsa con tacchetti**
running spikes

② **le scarpe da baseball**
baseball cleats

③ **le scarpe da corsa**
running shoes

④ **le scarpe da ginnastica alte**
high-tops

⑤ **le scarpe da golf**
golf shoes

⑦ **la linguetta**
tongue

⑥ **la scarpa da ginnastica**
trainer

⑧ **la scarpa da ciclismo**
cycling shoe

⑨ **lo scarpone da sci**
ski boot

⑩ **le scarpe da scoglio**
water shoes

⑪ **gli stivali da equitazione**
riding boots

⑫ **gli stivali Tabi**
tabi boots

⑬ **le scarpe da calcio**
football boots

18 La bellezza
Beauty

18.1 IL TRUCCO · MAKEUP

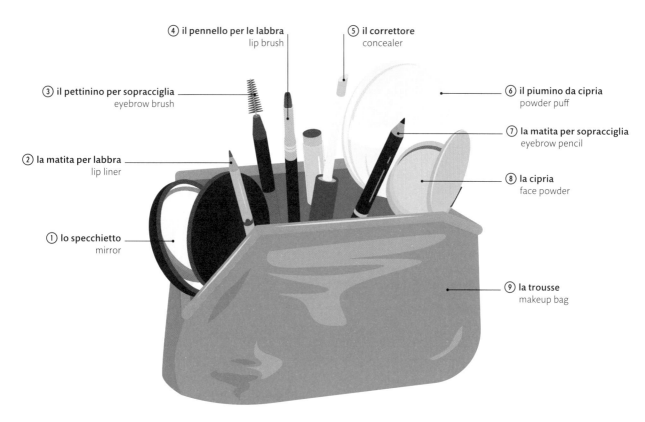

④ il pennello per le labbra
lip brush

⑤ il correttore
concealer

③ il pettinino per sopracciglia
eyebrow brush

⑥ il piumino da cipria
powder puff

⑦ la matita per sopracciglia
eyebrow pencil

② la matita per labbra
lip liner

⑧ la cipria
face powder

① lo specchietto
mirror

⑨ la trousse
makeup bag

⑩ il fard
blusher

⑪ l'eyeliner m
eyeliner

⑫ l'ombretto m
eyeshadow

⑬ il fondotinta
foundation

⑭ il mascara
mascara

⑮ il rossetto
lipstick

18.2 IL TIPO DI PELLE · SKIN TYPE

① normale
normal

② secca
dry

③ grassa
oily

④ sensibile
sensitive

⑤ mista
combination

See also
12 L'aspetto e i capelli • Appearance and hair **13-15** Gli indumenti • Clothes
16 Gli accessori • Accessories **17** Le scarpe • Shoes **31** Il bagno • Bathroom

18.3 LA MANICURE · MANICURE

① **le forbicine per le unghie** nail scissors
② **il tagliaunghie** nail clippers
③ **lo smalto per le unghie** nail polish / nail varnish
④ **il solvente per unghie** nail polish remover
⑤ **la limetta per unghie** nail file
⑥ **la crema per le mani** hand cream

18.4 GLI ARTICOLI DA TOELETTA E I TRATTAMENTI DI BELLEZZA
TOILETRIES AND BEAUTY TREATMENTS

① **la crema idratante** moisturizer
② **il tonico** toner
③ **il detergente per il viso** face wash
④ **il detergente** cleanser
⑤ **il profumo** perfume
⑥ **il dopobarba** aftershave

⑦ **il burrocacao** lip balm
⑧ **il bagnoschiuma** bubble bath
⑨ **i batuffoli di cotone** cotton balls
⑩ **la tinta per capelli** hair dye
⑪ **le pinzette** tweezers
⑫ **la ceretta** wax

⑬ **la pedicure** pedicure
⑭ **l'autoabbronzante** *m* self-tanning lotion
⑮ **il guanto per autoabbronzante** tanning mitt

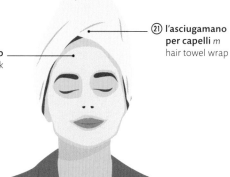

㉑ **l'asciugamano per capelli** *m* hair towel wrap
⑳ **la maschera per il viso** face mask

⑰ **i tubi UV** UV tubes

⑯ **il lettino abbronzante** sun bed
⑱ **gli occhiali protettivi per abbronzatura** tanning goggles
⑲ **facciale** facial

Le malattie e le lesioni
Illness and injury

19.1 LE MALATTIE · ILLNESS

① l'influenza f
flu

② il raffreddore
cold

③ la tosse
cough

④ il naso che cola
runny nose

⑤ il virus
virus

⑥ la febbre
fever

⑦ i brividi
chill

⑧ il mal di gola
sore throat

⑨ la tonsillite
tonsillitis

⑩ il mal di testa
headache

⑪ l'emicrania f
migraine

⑫ le vertigini
dizzy

⑬ l'intossicazione alimentare f
food poisoning

⑭ l'avvelenamento m
poisoning

⑮ l'eruzione cutanea f
rash

⑯ la varicella
chickenpox

⑰ il morbillo
measles

⑱ la parotite
mumps

⑲ l'eczema m
eczema

⑳ l'asma f
asthma

㉑ l'allergia f
allergy

㉒ la febbre da fieno
hay fever

㉓ l'infezione f
infection

㉔ il diabete
diabetes

㉕ lo stress
stress

㉖ l'epistassi f
nosebleed

㉗ la nausea
nausea

㉘ l'appendicite f
appendicitis

㉙ l'ipertensione f
high blood pressure

㉚ i sintomi
symptoms

㉛ il crampo
cramp

㉜ il mal di schiena
backache

㉝ il dolore
pain

㉞ il mal di stomaco
stomach ache

㉟ l'insonnia f
insomnia

㊱ la diarrea
diarrhoea

See also
01 Le parti del corpo · Parts of the body **03** I muscoli e lo scheletro · Muscles and skeleton **04** Gli organi interni · Internal organs **20** Andare dal medico · Visiting the doctor **21** L'ospedale · The hospital

19.2 LE LESIONI · INJURY

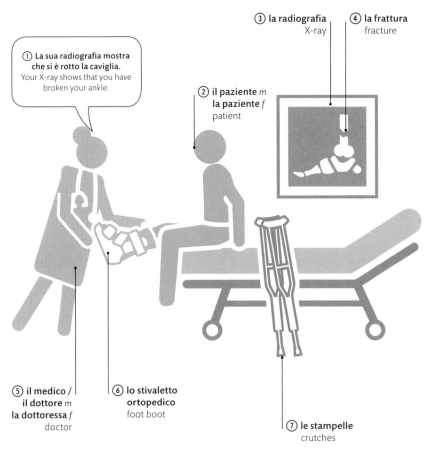

① La sua radiografia mostra che si è rotto la caviglia.
Your X-ray shows that you have broken your ankle.

③ **la radiografia**
X-ray

④ **la frattura**
fracture

② **il paziente** *m*
la paziente *f*
patient

⑤ **il medico /**
il dottore *m*
la dottoressa *f*
doctor

⑥ **lo stivaletto**
ortopedico
foot boot

⑦ **le stampelle**
crutches

⑧ **la slogatura**
sprain

⑨ **l'osso rotto** *m*
broken bone

⑩ **il reggibraccio**
sling

⑪ **il colpo di frusta**
whiplash

⑫ **il collare**
neck brace

⑬ **il taglio**
cut

⑭ **la sbucciatura**
graze

⑮ **l'ematoma** *m*
bruise

⑯ **la scheggia**
splinter

⑰ **la scottatura**
sunburn

⑱ **la bruciatura**
burn

⑲ **il morso**
bite

⑳ **la puntura**
sting

㉑ **l'incidente** *m*
accident

㉒ **la ferita**
wound

㉓ **l'emorragia** *f*
haemorrhage

㉔ **la vescica**
blister

㉕ **la commozione**
cerebrale
concussion

㉖ **la ferita**
alla testa
head injury

㉗ **la scossa**
elettrica
electric shock

20.1 LE CURE · TREATMENT

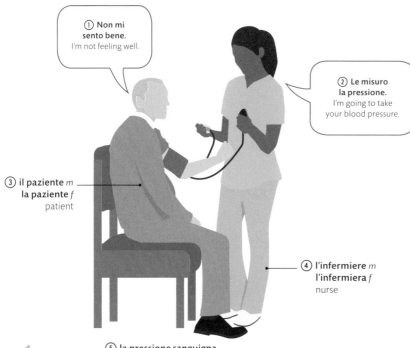

① Non mi sento bene.
I'm not feeling well.

② Le misuro la pressione.
I'm going to take your blood pressure.

③ il paziente *m*
la paziente *f*
patient

④ l'infermiere *m*
l'infermiera *f*
nurse

⑤ la pressione sanguigna
blood pressure

⑥ il medico /
il dottore *m*
la dottoressa *f*
doctor

⑦ lo studio medico
doctor's surgery

⑧ la sala d'attesa
waiting room

⑨ l'appuntamento *m*
appointment

⑩ la visita medica
medical examination

⑪ la vaccinazione
inoculation / vaccination

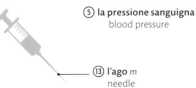

⑫ la siringa
syringe

⑬ l'ago *m*
needle

⑭ l'esame del sangue *m*
blood test

⑮ i risultati dell'esame
test results

⑯ la ricetta
prescription

⑰ il farmaco
medicine / medication

⑱ le pastiglie /
le compresse
pills / tablets

⑲ la bilancia
scales

⑳ lo stetoscopio
stethoscope

㉑ l'inalatore *m*
inhaler

㉒ lo spray nasale
nasal spray

㉓ la mascherina
face mask

㉔ il reggibraccio
sling

㉕ la fasciatura
dressing

㉖ la garza
gauze

㉗ il nastro medico
tape

㉘ il termometro
thermometer

㉙ il termometro auricolare
ear thermometer

See also
01 Le parti del corpo • Parts of the body **02** Le mani e i piedi • Hands and feet
03 I muscoli e lo scheletro • Muscles and skeleton **04** Gli organi interni • Internal organs
19 Le malattie e le lesioni • Illness and injury **21** L'ospedale • The hospital

20.2 IL KIT DI PRONTO SOCCORSO · FIRST-AID KIT

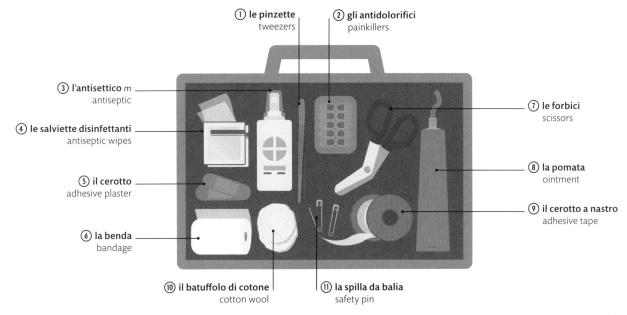

① **le pinzette**
tweezers

② **gli antidolorifici**
painkillers

③ **l'antisettico** *m*
antiseptic

④ **le salviette disinfettanti**
antiseptic wipes

⑤ **il cerotto**
adhesive plaster

⑥ **la benda**
bandage

⑦ **le forbici**
scissors

⑧ **la pomata**
ointment

⑨ **il cerotto a nastro**
adhesive tape

⑩ **il batuffolo di cotone**
cotton wool

⑪ **la spilla da balia**
safety pin

20.3 I VERBI PER DESCRIVERE LE MALATTIE · VERBS TO DESCRIBE ILLNESS

① **vomitare**
to vomit

② **starnutire**
to sneeze

③ **tossire**
to cough

④ **fare male**
to hurt / to ache

⑤ **sanguinare**
to bleed

⑥ **svenire**
to faint

⑦ **stendersi**
to lie down

⑧ **riposare**
to rest

⑨ **dimagrire**
to lose weight

⑩ **ingrassare**
to gain weight

⑪ **bere acqua**
to drink water

⑰ **le compressioni toraciche**
chest compressions

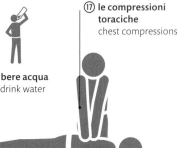

⑫ **fare esercizio fisico**
to exercise

⑬ **guarire**
to heal

⑭ **riprendersi**
to recover

⑮ **sentirsi meglio**
to feel better

⑯ **rianimare**
to resuscitate

21.1 IN OSPEDALE · AT THE HOSPITAL

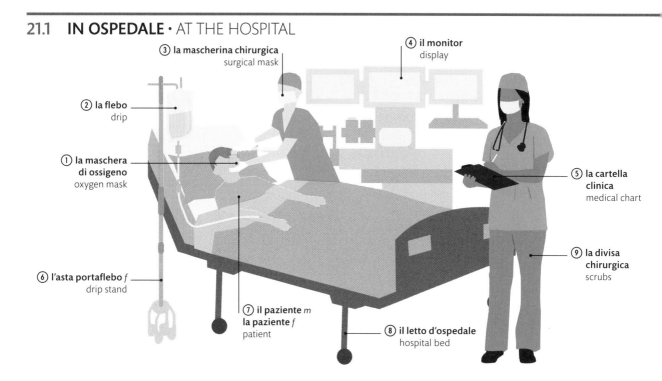

③ **la mascherina chirurgica** surgical mask

④ **il monitor** display

② **la flebo** drip

① **la maschera di ossigeno** oxygen mask

⑤ **la cartella clinica** medical chart

⑨ **la divisa chirurgica** scrubs

⑥ **l'asta portaflebo** *f* drip stand

⑦ **il paziente** *m* **la paziente** *f* patient

⑧ **il letto d'ospedale** hospital bed

⑩ **l'ospedale** *m* hospital

⑪ **l'ambulanza** *f* ambulance

⑫ **il paramedico** paramedic

⑬ **la barella** stretcher

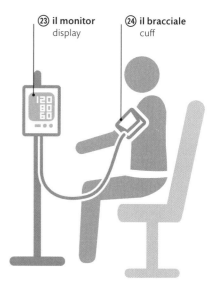

㉓ **il monitor** display

㉔ **il bracciale** cuff

⑭ **il chirurgo** *m* **la chirurga** *f* surgeon

⑮ **il medico / il dottore** *m* **la dottoressa** *f* doctor

⑯ **l'infermiere** *m* **l'infermiera** *f* nurse

⑰ **il portantino** porter

⑱ **la sedia a rotelle** wheelchair

⑲ **l'ecografia** *f* scan

⑳ **la radiografia** X-ray

㉑ **l'esame del sangue** *m* blood test

㉒ **il misuratore di pressione** blood pressure monitor

See also
01 Le parti del corpo · Parts of the body 03 I muscoli e lo scheletro · Muscles and skeleton
04 Gli organi interni · Internal organs 19 Le malattie e le lesioni · Illness and injury
20 Andare dal medico · Visiting the doctor

21.2 I REPARTI · DEPARTMENTS

㉕ il bisturi
scalpel

㉖ i punti
stitches

㉗ la chirurgia plastica
plastic surgery

㉘ la terapia
treatment

㉙ l'operazione f
operation

㉚ il tavolo operatorio
operating table

㉛ la sala operatoria
theatre

㉜ il pronto soccorso
A&E

㉝ il reparto di terapia intensiva
intensive care unit

㉞ la sala risveglio
recovery room

㉟ la stanza privata
private room

㊱ il reparto
ward

㊲ il reparto pediatrico
children's ward

㊳ il reparto maternità
maternity ward

㊴ ricoverare
to admit

㊵ dimettere
to discharge

㊶ il paziente ambulatoriale
outpatient

① l'otorinolaringoiatria f
ENT (ear, nose, and throat)

② la cardiologia
cardiology

③ l'ortopedia f
orthopaedics

④ la neurologia
neurology

⑤ la radiologia
radiology

⑥ la patologia
pathology

⑦ la pediatria
paediatrics

⑧ la dermatologia
dermatology

⑨ la ginecologia
gynaecology

⑩ la chirurgia
surgery

⑪ la fisioterapia
physiotherapy

⑫ l'urologia f
urology

⑬ la maternità
maternity

⑭ la psichiatria
psychiatry

⑮ l'oculistica f
ophthalmology

⑯ l'endocrinologia f
endocrinology

⑰ l'oncologia f
oncology

⑱ la gastroenterologia
gastroenterology

22.1 LO STUDIO DENTISTICO · DENTAL SURGERY

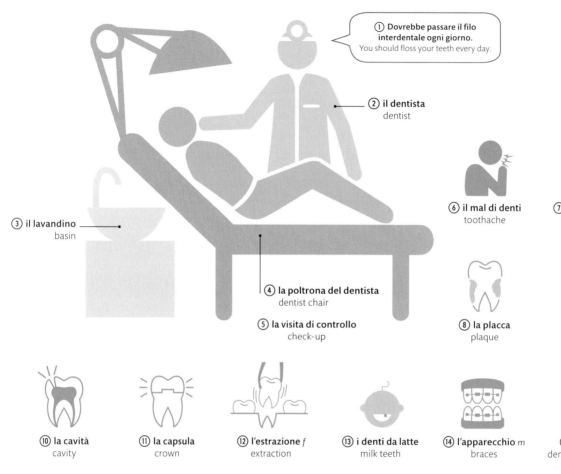

① Dovrebbe passare il filo interdentale ogni giorno.
You should floss your teeth every day.

② **il dentista**
dentist

③ **il lavandino**
basin

④ **la poltrona del dentista**
dentist chair

⑤ **la visita di controllo**
check-up

⑥ **il mal di denti**
toothache

⑦ **l'otturazione** *f*
filling

⑧ **la placca**
plaque

⑨ **la carie**
decay

⑩ **la cavità**
cavity

⑪ **la capsula**
crown

⑫ **l'estrazione** *f*
extraction

⑬ **i denti da latte**
milk teeth

⑭ **l'apparecchio** *m*
braces

⑮ **la dentiera**
dentures / false teeth

⑯ **la radiografia dentale**
dental X-ray

⑰ **l'anamnesi dentale** *f*
dental history

⑱ **il trapano**
drill

⑲ **lo specchietto**
dental mirror

⑳ **la sonda**
probe

㉑ **lo scovolino interdentale**
interdental brush

㉒ **lo sbiancante**
whitening

㉓ **l'igienista dentale** *m / f*
dental hygienist

㉔ **il filo interdentale**
dental floss

㉕ **passare il filo interdentale**
to floss

㉖ **spazzolare**
to brush

㉗ **sciacquare**
to rinse

See also
01 Le parti del corpo • Parts of the body **03** I muscoli e lo scheletro • Muscles and skeleton
20 Andare dal medico • Visiting the doctor **21** L'ospedale • The hospital **31** Il bagno • Bathroom

22.2 L'OTTICO · OPTICIAN

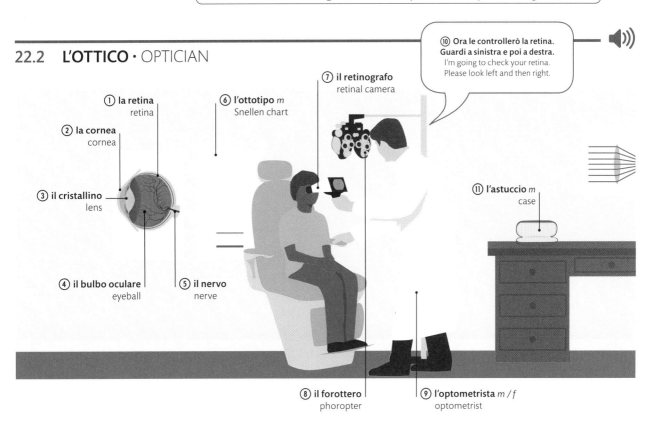

① **la retina**
retina

② **la cornea**
cornea

③ **il cristallino**
lens

④ **il bulbo oculare**
eyeball

⑤ **il nervo**
nerve

⑥ **l'ottotipo** *m*
Snellen chart

⑦ **il retinografo**
retinal camera

⑧ **il forottero**
phoropter

⑨ **l'optometrista** *m / f*
optometrist

⑩ **Ora le controllerò la retina.
Guardi a sinistra e poi a destra.**
I'm going to check your retina.
Please look left and then right.

⑪ **l'astuccio** *m*
case

⑫ **la vista**
vision

⑬ **presbite**
long-sighted

⑭ **miope**
short-sighted

⑮ **la lacrima**
tear

⑯ **la cataratta**
cataract

⑰ **l'astigmatismo** *m*
astigmatism

⑱ **gli occhiali
da lettura**
reading glasses

⑲ **gli occhiali bifocali**
bifocal

⑳ **il monocolo**
monocle

㉑ **il binocolo**
opera glasses

㉒ **gli occhiali**
glasses

㉓ **la lente**
lens

㉔ **gli occhiali
da sole**
sunglasses

㉕ **il panno per la
pulizia delle lenti**
lens cleaning cloth

㉖ **le lenti
a contatto**
contact lenses

㉗ **la soluzione per
lenti a contatto**
contact lens solution

㉘ **il portalenti**
lens case

㉙ **il collirio**
eye drops

23 La dieta e l'alimentazione
Diet and nutrition

23.1 LO STILE DI VITA SANO · HEALTHY LIVING

① le proteine
protein

② i carboidrati
carbohydrates

③ le fibre
fibre

④ i latticini
dairy

⑤ i legumi
pulses

⑥ lo zucchero
sugar

⑦ il sale
salt

⑧ i grassi saturi
saturated fat

⑨ i grassi insaturi
unsaturated fat

⑩ le calorie
calories / energy

⑪ le vitamine
vitamins

⑫ i minerali
minerals

⑬ il calcio
calcium

⑭ il ferro
iron

⑮ il colesterolo
cholesterol

⑯ la depurazione
detox

⑰ la dieta
equilibrata
balanced diet

⑱ la dieta
ipocalorica
calorie-controlled diet

⑲ il negozio di
cibi biologici
health food shop

⑳ la sezione di
alimenti biologici
organic food section

㉑ i prodotti agricoli locali
local produce

㉒ Mi piace acquistare
frutta e verdura
biologiche.
I like to buy organic fruit
and vegetables.

㉓ il mercato agricolo
farmers' market

See also
03 I muscoli e lo scheletro • Muscles and skeleton **19** Le malattie e le lesioni • Illness and injury
24 Il corpo sano, la mente sana • Healthy body, healthy mind **29** Cucinare • Cooking
48 Il supermercato • The supermarket **52-72** Gli alimenti • Food

23.2 LE ALLERGIE ALIMENTARI
FOOD ALLERGIES

㉔ **gli alimenti lavorati**
processed food

㉕ **i supercibi**
superfoods

㉖ **biologico** *m*
biologica *f*
organic

① **l'allergia alla frutta a guscio** *f*
nut allergy

② **l'allergia alle arachidi** *f*
peanut allergy

③ **l'allergia ai frutti di mare** *f*
seafood allergy

㉗ **l'integratore** *m*
supplement

㉘ **gli additivi**
additives

㉙ **senza latticini**
dairy-free

④ **l'intolleranza al lattosio** *f*
lactose intolerant

⑤ **l'intolleranza al glutine** *f*
gluten intolerant

⑥ **l'intolleranza ai latticini** *f*
dairy allergy

㉚ **vegetariano** *m*
vegetariana *f*
vegetarian

㉛ **vegano** *m*
vegana *f*
vegan

㉜ **pescetariano** *m*
pescetariana *f*
pescatarian

⑦ **l'allergia al grano** *f*
wheat allergy

⑧ **l'allergia alle uova** *f*
egg allergy

⑨ **l'allergia al sesamo** *f*
sesame allergy

㉝ **senza glutine**
gluten-free

㉞ **perdere peso / dimagrire**
to lose weight

㉟ **i cibi pronti**
convenience food

⑩ **l'allergia alla soia** *f*
soya allergy

⑪ **l'allergia al sedano** *f*
celery allergy

⑫ **l'allergia ai solfiti** *f*
sulphite allergy

㊱ **ipercalorico** *m*
ipercalorica *f*
high-calorie

㊲ **ipocalorico** *m*
ipocalorica *f*
low-calorie

㊳ **ridurre**
to cut down on

⑭ **l'allergia alla senape** *f*
mustard allergy

㊴ **rinunciare a**
to give up

㊵ **mettersi a dieta**
to go on a diet

㊶ **mangiare troppo**
to overeat

⑬ **allergico** *m* / **allergica** *f*
allergic

⑮ **intollerante**
intolerant

Il corpo sano, la mente sana
Healthy body, healthy mind

24.1 **LO YOGA** · YOGA

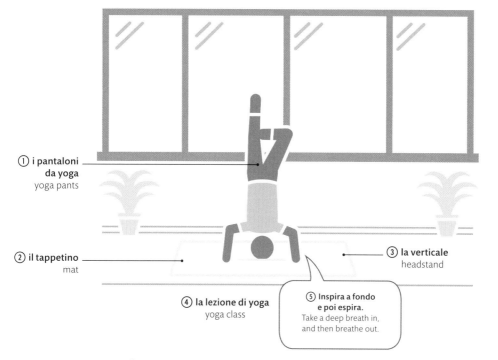

① **i pantaloni da yoga**
yoga pants

② **il tappetino**
mat

③ **la verticale**
headstand

④ **la lezione di yoga**
yoga class

⑤ **Inspira a fondo e poi espira.**
Take a deep breath in, and then breathe out.

⑥ **la posizione del bambino**
child's pose

⑦ **la posizione del cobra**
cobra pose

⑧ **la posizione del guerriero**
warrior pose

⑨ **la torsione da seduti**
seated twist

⑩ **la posizione del triangolo**
triangle pose

⑪ **il piegamento in avanti da seduti**
seated forward fold

⑫ **la posizione del cadavere**
corpse pose

⑬ **la posizione del corvo**
crow pose

⑭ **la posizione della sedia**
chair pose

⑮ **la posizione della montagna**
mountain pose

⑯ **la posizione del ponte**
bridge pose

⑰ **la posizione della panca**
plank pose

⑱ **la posizione dell'arco**
bow pose

⑲ **la posizione del piccione**
pigeon pose

⑳ **la posizione dell'albero**
tree pose

㉑ **il cane a testa in giù**
downward dog

㉒ **la posizione dell'angolo legato**
bound ankle pose

㉓ **la posizione del cammello**
camel pose

㉔ **la posizione della ruota**
wheel pose

㉕ **la posizione della mezza luna**
half moon pose

㉖ **la posizione del delfino**
dolphin pose

See also
03 I muscoli e lo scheletro · Muscles and skeleton **04** Gli organi interni · Internal organs **19** Le malattie e le lesioni · Illness and injury **20** Andare dal medico · Visiting the doctor **21** L'ospedale · The hospital **23** La dieta e l'alimentazione · Diet and nutrition **29** Cucinare · Cooking

24.2 I TRATTAMENTI E LE TERAPIE · TREATMENTS AND THERAPY

① **il massaggio**
massage

② **lo shiatsu**
shiatsu

③ **la chiropratica**
chiropractic

④ **l'osteopatia** f
osteopathy

⑤ **la riflessologia**
reflexology

⑥ **la meditazione**
meditation

⑦ **il reiki**
reiki

⑧ **l'agopuntura** f
acupuncture

⑨ **l'ayurveda** f
ayurveda

⑩ **l'ipnoterapia** f
hypnotherapy

⑪ **l'idroterapia** f
hydrotherapy

⑫ **l'aromaterapia** f
aromatherapy

⑬ **l'erbalismo** m
herbalism

⑭ **gli oli essenziali**
essential oils

⑮ **l'omeopatia** f
homeopathy

⑯ **l'agopressione** f
acupressure

⑰ **la cristalloterapia**
crystal healing

⑱ **la naturopatia**
naturopathy

⑲ **il feng shui**
feng shui

⑳ **la poesiaterapia**
poetry therapy

㉑ **l'arteterapia** f
art therapy

㉒ **la pet therapy**
pet therapy

㉓ **la naturoterapia**
nature therapy

㉔ **la musicoterapia**
music therapy

㉕ **il rilassamento**
relaxation

㉖ **la mindfulness**
mindfulness

㉗ **l'assistente socio-psicologico** m / **l'assistente sociopsicologica** f
counsellor

㉘ **la psicoterapia**
psychotherapy

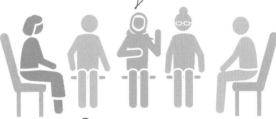
㉚ **Oggi parleremo dello stress sul lavoro.**
Today, we're talking about stress at work.

㉙ **la terapia di gruppo**
group therapy

25.1 LE CASE · HOUSES

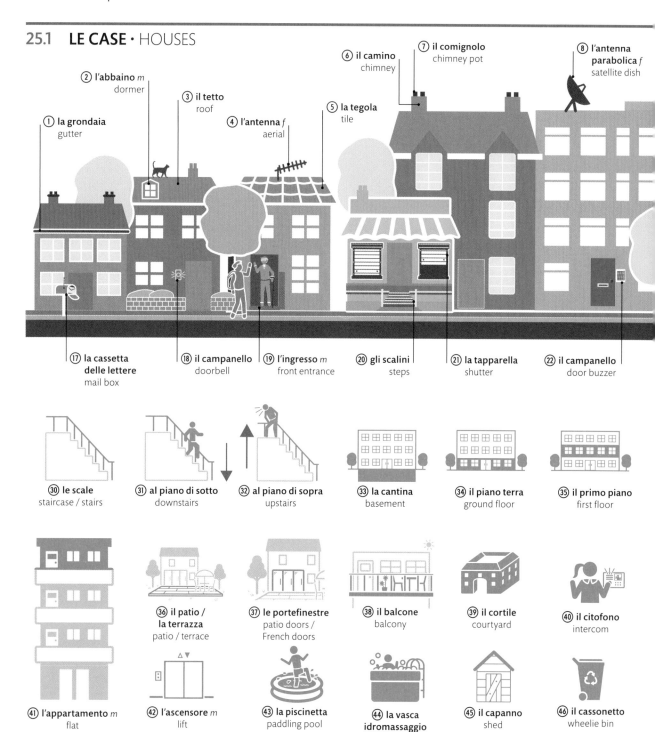

⑥ il camino
chimney

⑦ il comignolo
chimney pot

⑧ l'antenna
parabolica *f*
satellite dish

② l'abbaino *m*
dormer

③ il tetto
roof

⑤ la tegola
tile

④ l'antenna *f*
aerial

① la grondaia
gutter

⑰ la cassetta
delle lettere
mail box

⑱ il campanello
doorbell

⑲ l'ingresso *m*
front entrance

⑳ gli scalini
steps

㉑ la tapparella
shutter

㉒ il campanello
door buzzer

㉚ le scale
staircase / stairs

㉛ al piano di sotto
downstairs

㉜ al piano di sopra
upstairs

㉝ la cantina
basement

㉞ il piano terra
ground floor

㉟ il primo piano
first floor

㊱ il patio /
la terrazza
patio / terrace

㊲ le portefinestre
patio doors /
French doors

㊳ il balcone
balcony

㊴ il cortile
courtyard

㊵ il citofono
intercom

㊶ l'appartamento *m*
flat

㊷ l'ascensore *m*
lift

㊸ la piscinetta
paddling pool

㊹ la vasca
idromassaggio
jacuzzi

㊺ il capanno
shed

㊻ il cassonetto
wheelie bin

See also
32 La casa · House and home **34** Le faccende domestiche · Household chores **37** La decorazione
Decorating **42-43** In città · In town **44** Gli edifici e l'architettura · Buildings and architecture

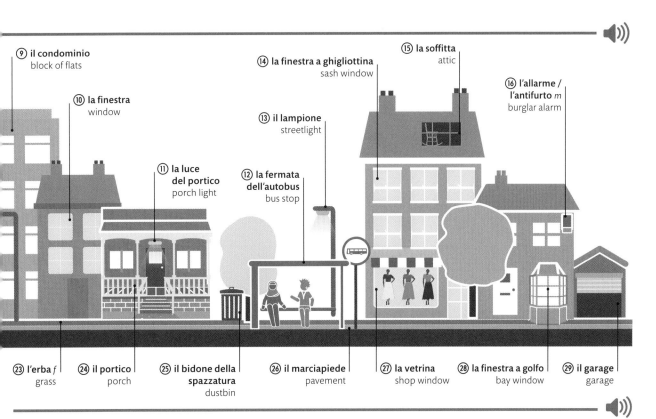

⑨ **il condominio**
block of flats

⑩ **la finestra**
window

⑪ **la luce del portico**
porch light

⑫ **la fermata dell'autobus**
bus stop

⑬ **il lampione**
streetlight

⑭ **la finestra a ghigliottina**
sash window

⑮ **la soffitta**
attic

⑯ **l'allarme / l'antifurto** *m*
burglar alarm

㉓ **l'erba** *f*
grass

㉔ **il portico**
porch

㉕ **il bidone della spazzatura**
dustbin

㉖ **il marciapiede**
pavement

㉗ **la vetrina**
shop window

㉘ **la finestra a golfo**
bay window

㉙ **il garage**
garage

25.2 L'ATRIO · HALLWAY

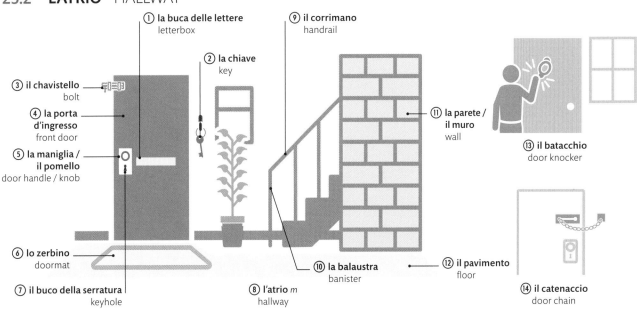

① **la buca delle lettere**
letterbox

② **la chiave**
key

③ **il chavistello**
bolt

④ **la porta d'ingresso**
front door

⑤ **la maniglia / il pomello**
door handle / knob

⑥ **lo zerbino**
doormat

⑦ **il buco della serratura**
keyhole

⑧ **l'atrio** *m*
hallway

⑨ **il corrimano**
handrail

⑩ **la balaustra**
banister

⑪ **la parete / il muro**
wall

⑫ **il pavimento**
floor

⑬ **il batacchio**
door knocker

⑭ **il catenaccio**
door chain

61

26.1 IL SALOTTO · LIVING ROOM

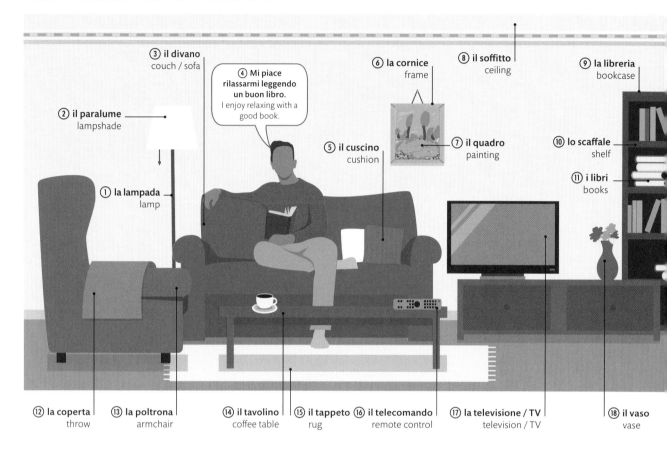

③ **il divano**
couch / sofa

④ **Mi piace rilassarmi leggendo un buon libro.**
I enjoy relaxing with a good book.

⑥ **la cornice**
frame

⑧ **il soffitto**
ceiling

⑨ **la libreria**
bookcase

② **il paralume**
lampshade

⑤ **il cuscino**
cushion

⑦ **il quadro**
painting

⑩ **lo scaffale**
shelf

① **la lampada**
lamp

⑪ **i libri**
books

⑫ **la coperta**
throw

⑬ **la poltrona**
armchair

⑭ **il tavolino**
coffee table

⑮ **il tappeto**
rug

⑯ **il telecomando**
remote control

⑰ **la televisione / TV**
television / TV

⑱ **il vaso**
vase

⑲ **il caminetto**
fireplace

⑳ **la mensola del caminetto**
mantlepiece

㉑ **le veneziane**
Venetian blinds

㉒ **le tende avvolgibili**
roller blind

㉓ **le tende**
curtains

㉔ **le tende di tulle**
net curtain

㉕ **il divano letto**
sofa bed

㉖ **la sedia a dondolo**
rocking chair

㉗ **lo sgabello**
foot stool

㉘ **l'applique** f
wall light

㉙ **lo studio**
study

See also
25 Un luogo in cui vivere • A place to live **27** La cucina e le stoviglie • Kitchen and tableware
34 Le faccende domestiche • Household chores **71** La colazione • Breakfast **72** Il pranzo e la
cena • Lunch and dinner **136** L'home entertainment • Home entertainment

26.2 LA SALA DA PRANZO · DINING ROOM

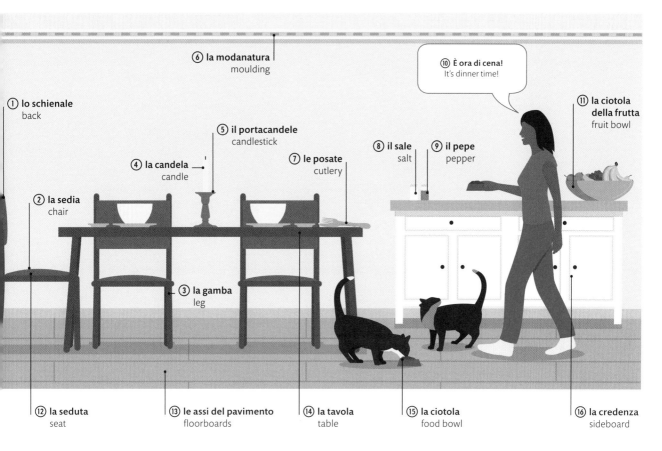

① lo schienale
back

② la sedia
chair

③ la gamba
leg

④ la candela
candle

⑤ il portacandele
candlestick

⑥ la modanatura
moulding

⑦ le posate
cutlery

⑧ il sale
salt

⑨ il pepe
pepper

⑩ È ora di cena!
It's dinner time!

⑪ la ciotola
della frutta
fruit bowl

⑫ la seduta
seat

⑬ le assi del pavimento
floorboards

⑭ la tavola
table

⑮ la ciotola
food bowl

⑯ la credenza
sideboard

⑰ **preparare la tavola**
to set the table

⑱ **la tovaglia**
tablecloth

⑲ **la tovaglietta
all'americana**
place mat

⑳ **la colazione**
breakfast

㉑ **il pranzo**
lunch

㉒ **la cena**
dinner

㉓ **l'ospite** *m / f*
host / hostess

㉔ **affamato** *m*
affamata *f*
hungry

㉕ **pieno** *m* / **piena** *f*
full

㉖ **la porzione**
portion

㉘ **l'ospite** *m / f*
guest

㉗ **la cena**
dinner party

27 La cucina e le stoviglie
Kitchen and tableware

27.1 GLI ELETTRODOMESTICI DA CUCINA
KITCHEN APPLIANCES

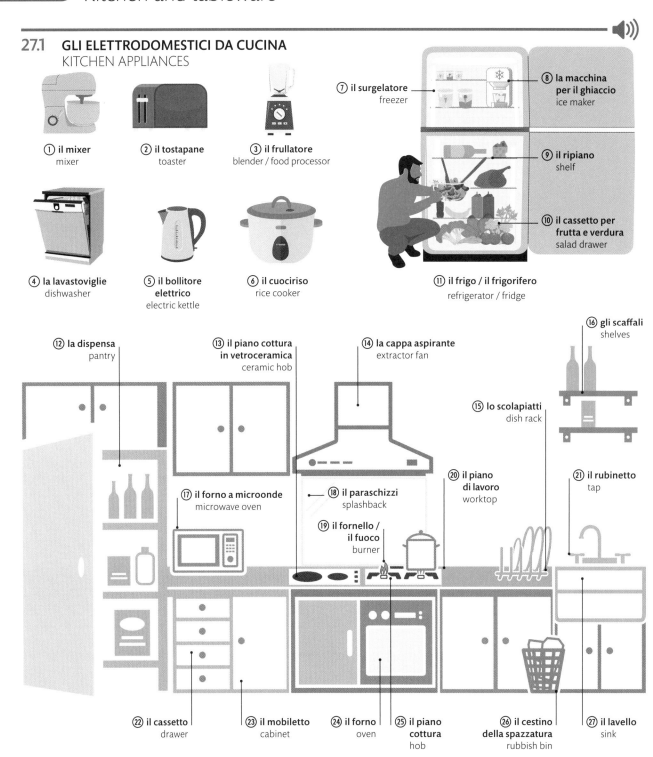

① **il mixer**
mixer

② **il tostapane**
toaster

③ **il frullatore**
blender / food processor

④ **la lavastoviglie**
dishwasher

⑤ **il bollitore elettrico**
electric kettle

⑥ **il cuociriso**
rice cooker

⑦ il surgelatore
freezer

⑧ **la macchina per il ghiaccio**
ice maker

⑨ **il ripiano**
shelf

⑩ **il cassetto per frutta e verdura**
salad drawer

⑪ **il frigo / il frigorifero**
refrigerator / fridge

⑫ **la dispensa**
pantry

⑬ **il piano cottura in vetroceramica**
ceramic hob

⑭ **la cappa aspirante**
extractor fan

⑮ **lo scolapiatti**
dish rack

⑯ **gli scaffali**
shelves

⑰ **il forno a microonde**
microwave oven

⑱ **il paraschizzi**
splashback

⑲ **il fornello / il fuoco**
burner

⑳ **il piano di lavoro**
worktop

㉑ **il rubinetto**
tap

㉒ **il cassetto**
drawer

㉓ **il mobiletto**
cabinet

㉔ **il forno**
oven

㉕ **il piano cottura**
hob

㉖ **il cestino della spazzatura**
rubbish bin

㉗ **il lavello**
sink

See also
28 Gli utensili da cucina • Kitchenware **29** Cucinare • Cooking
59 Le erbe e le spezie • Herbs and spices **60** Nella dispensa • In the pantry
71 La colazione • Breakfast **72** Il pranzo e la cena • Lunch and dinner

27.2 LE STOVIGLIE · TABLEWARE

① **la forchetta**
fork

⑦ **le posate**
cutlery

⑬ **le stoviglie**
crockery

⑲ **il posto a tavola**
place setting

㉕ **il portauovo**
egg cup

㉛ **i calici**
stemware

② **il coltello**
knife

⑧ **il coltello
da burro**
butter knife

⑭ **la tazzina da caffè**
coffee cup

⑳ **il tovagliolo**
napkin

⑯ **il set da sushi**
sushi set

㉜ **i bicchieri**
glasses / glassware

③ **il cucchiaio**
tablespoon

⑨ **le bacchette**
chopsticks

⑮ **la tazza da tè**
teacup

㉑ **il portatovagliolo**
napkin ring

㉗ **la caraffa graduata**
measuring jug

㉝ **il barattolo**
jar

④ **il cucchiaino**
teaspoon

⑩ **il mestolo**
ladle

⑯ **la tazza**
mug

㉒ **la ciotola**
bowl

㉘ **il tumbler**
tumbler

㉞ **il bicchiere**
beaker

⑤ **il cucchiaio da minestra**
soup spoon

⑪ **il piatto piano**
dinner plate

⑰ **la caffettiera**
espresso maker

㉓ **il piatto fondo /
la scodella**
soup bowl

㉙ **il bicchiere
da vino**
wineglass

㉟ **il bicchiere
da sakè**
sake cup

⑥ **il cucchiaio
da portata**
serving spoon

⑫ **il piattino**
side plate

⑱ **la teiera**
teapot

㉔ **la ciotola
del riso**
rice bowl

㉚ **il bicchiere
da birra**
pint glass

㊱ **il sottobicchiere**
coaster

28.1 GLI UTENSILI DA CUCINA · KITCHEN EQUIPMENT

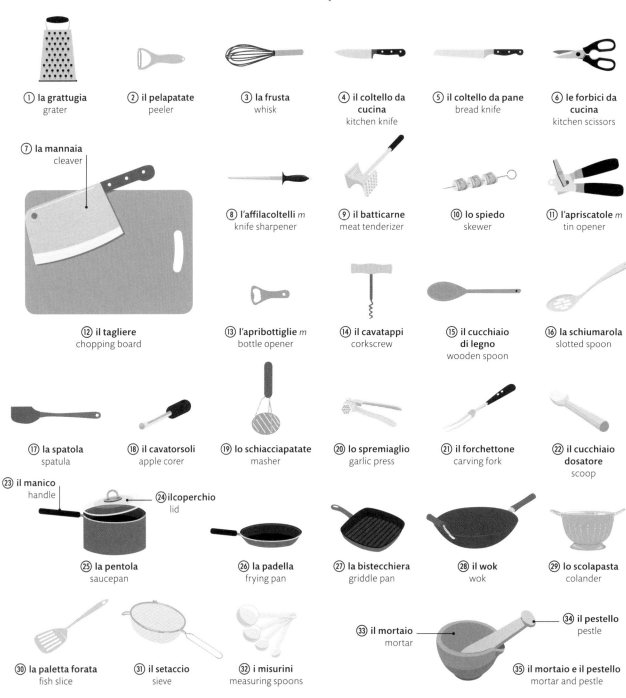

① **la grattugia**
grater

② **il pelapatate**
peeler

③ **la frusta**
whisk

④ **il coltello da cucina**
kitchen knife

⑤ **il coltello da pane**
bread knife

⑥ **le forbici da cucina**
kitchen scissors

⑦ **la mannaia**
cleaver

⑧ **l'affilacoltelli** *m*
knife sharpener

⑨ **il batticarne**
meat tenderizer

⑩ **lo spiedo**
skewer

⑪ **l'apriscatole** *m*
tin opener

⑫ **il tagliere**
chopping board

⑬ **l'apribottiglie** *m*
bottle opener

⑭ **il cavatappi**
corkscrew

⑮ **il cucchiaio di legno**
wooden spoon

⑯ **la schiumarola**
slotted spoon

⑰ **la spatola**
spatula

⑱ **il cavatorsoli**
apple corer

⑲ **lo schiacciapatate**
masher

⑳ **lo spremiaglio**
garlic press

㉑ **il forchettone**
carving fork

㉒ **il cucchiaio dosatore**
scoop

㉓ **il manico**
handle

㉔ **ilcoperchio**
lid

㉕ **la pentola**
saucepan

㉖ **la padella**
frying pan

㉗ **la bistecchiera**
griddle pan

㉘ **il wok**
wok

㉙ **lo scolapasta**
colander

㉚ **la paletta forata**
fish slice

㉛ **il setaccio**
sieve

㉜ **i misurini**
measuring spoons

㉝ **il mortaio**
mortar

㉞ **il pestello**
pestle

㉟ **il mortaio e il pestello**
mortar and pestle

See also
27 La cucina e le stoviglie • Kitchen and tableware **29** Cucinare • Cooking
59 Le erbe e le spezie • Herbs and spices **60** Nella dispensa • In the pantry
71 La colazione • Breakfast **72** Il pranzo e la cena • Lunch and dinner

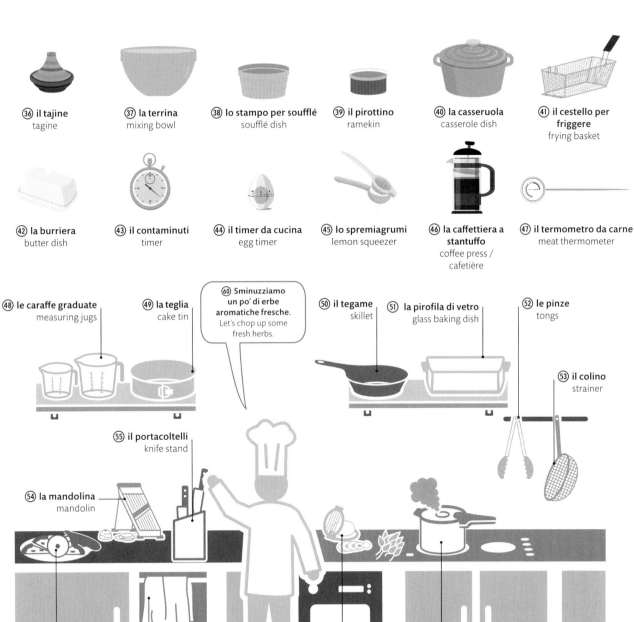

㊱ **il tajine**
tagine

㊲ **la terrina**
mixing bowl

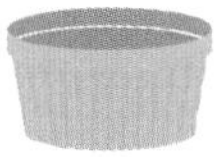

㊳ **lo stampo per soufflé**
soufflé dish

㊴ **il pirottino**
ramekin

㊵ **la casseruola**
casserole dish

㊶ **il cestello per friggere**
frying basket

㊷ **la burriera**
butter dish

㊸ **il contaminuti**
timer

㊹ **il timer da cucina**
egg timer

㊺ **lo spremiagrumi**
lemon squeezer

㊻ **la caffettiera a stantuffo**
coffee press / cafetière

㊼ **il termometro da carne**
meat thermometer

㊽ **le caraffe graduate**
measuring jugs
㊾ **la teglia**
cake tin
(60) **Sminuzziamo un po' di erbe aromatiche fresche.**
Let's chop up some fresh herbs.
㊿ **il tegame**
skillet
(51) **la pirofila di vetro**
glass baking dish
(52) **le pinze**
tongs
(53) **il colino**
strainer
(55) **il portacoltelli**
knife stand
(54) **la mandolina**
mandolin
(56) **la rotella tagliapizza**
pizza cutter
(57) **il canovaccio**
tea towel
(58) **il tagliauova**
egg slicer
(59) **la pentola a pressione**
pressure cooker

29 Cucinare
Cooking

29.1 I VERBI DELLA CUCINA · COOKING VERBS

① **cospargere** to sprinkle

② **cuocere in forno** to bake

③ **guarnire** to garnish

④ **ungere** to grease

⑤ **stendere** to roll

⑥ **assaggiare** to taste

⑬ **Lo guarnirò con un po' di erbe fresche.** I'll garnish this with some fresh herbs.

⑭ **tagliare a pezzetti** to chop

⑫ **saltare in padella** to stir-fry

⑳ **grigliare** to grill

㉑ **arrostire** to roast

㉒ **friggere** to fry

㉓ **far bollire / fare in camicia (le uova)** to poach

㉔ **cuocere a fuoco lento** to simmer

㉕ **bollire** to boil

㉖ **congelare** to freeze

㉗ **aggiungere** to add

㉘ **mescolare** to mix

㉙ **mescolare** to stir

㉚ **sbattere con la frusta** to whisk

㉛ **schiacciare** to mash

㉜ **tagliare a fette** to slice

㉝ **un pizzico** a pinch

㉞ **un goccio** a dash

㉟ **una manciata** a handful

㊱ **macinare** to mince

㊲ **sbucciare** to peel

㊳ **tagliare** to cut

㊴ **grattugiare** to grate

㊵ **versare** to pour

See also
27 La cucina e le stoviglie • Kitchen and tableware **28** Gli utensili da cucina • Kitchenware
59 Le erbe e le spezie • Herbs and spices **60** Nella dispensa • In the pantry **62-63** La panetteria
The bakery **71** La colazione • Breakfast **72** Il pranzo e la cena • Lunch and dinner

⑦ **cuocere al vapore**
to steam

⑧ **Potresti tagliare una carota a dadini? Grazie!**
Can you dice a carrot for me, please?

⑨ **sbattere le uova**
to beat eggs

⑩ **Ho bruciato le cipolle. Sono rovinate!**
I've burned the onions. They are ruined!

⑪ **cuocere in microonde**
to microwave

⑮ **sciogliere il burro**
to melt butter

⑯ **affettare**
to carve

⑰ **tagliare a dadini**
to dice

⑱ **bruciare**
to burn

⑲ **saltare**
to sauté

29.2 CUOCERE IN FORNO · BAKING

① **il grembiule**
apron

② **il guanto da forno**
oven glove

③ **la teglia**
cake tin

④ **la teglia da flan**
flan tin

⑤ **il tegame da forno**
pie dish

⑥ **il pennello per dolci**
pastry brush

⑦ **il mattarello**
rolling pin

⑧ **la placca da forno**
baking tray

⑨ **la teglia da muffin**
muffin tray

⑩ **la gratella**
cooling rack

⑪ **la glassa**
icing

⑫ **la sac-a-poche**
piping bag

⑬ **la bilancia**
scales

⑭ **la caraffa graduata**
measuring jug

⑮ **decorare**
to decorate

30 La camera da letto
Bedroom

30.1 LA CAMERA DA LETTO · BEDROOM

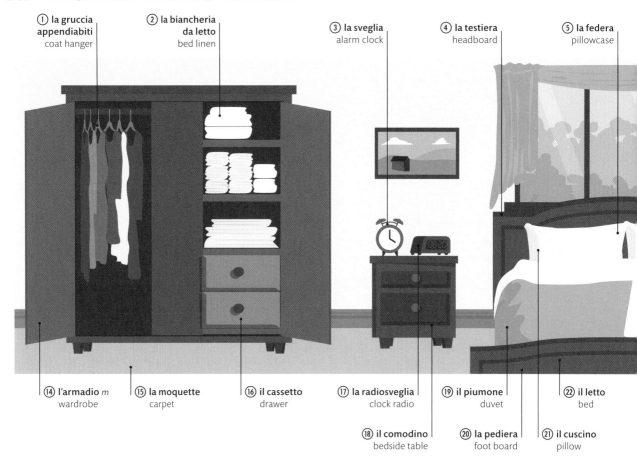

① **la gruccia appendiabiti** coat hanger

② **la biancheria da letto** bed linen

③ **la sveglia** alarm clock

④ **la testiera** headboard

⑤ **la federa** pillowcase

⑭ **l'armadio** *m* wardrobe

⑮ **la moquette** carpet

⑯ **il cassetto** drawer

⑰ **la radiosveglia** clock radio

⑲ **il piumone** duvet

㉒ **il letto** bed

⑱ **il comodino** bedside table

⑳ **la pediera** foot board

㉑ **il cuscino** pillow

㉗ **il letto singolo** single bed

㉘ **il letto matrimoniale** double bed

㉙ **la rete** bedspring

㉚ **l'ottomana** *f* Ottoman

㉛ **la cassapanca** linen chest

㉜ **il copriletto** throw

㉝ **la trapunta** quilt

㉞ **la coperta** blanket

㉟ **la coperta elettrica** electric blanket

㊱ **l'armadio a muro** *m* built-in wardrobe

㊲ **la borsa dell'acqua calda** hot-water bottle

See also
08 La gravidanza e l'infanzia • Pregnancy and childhood **13-15** Gli indumenti
Clothes **25** Un luogo in cui vivere • A place to live **32** La casa • House and home

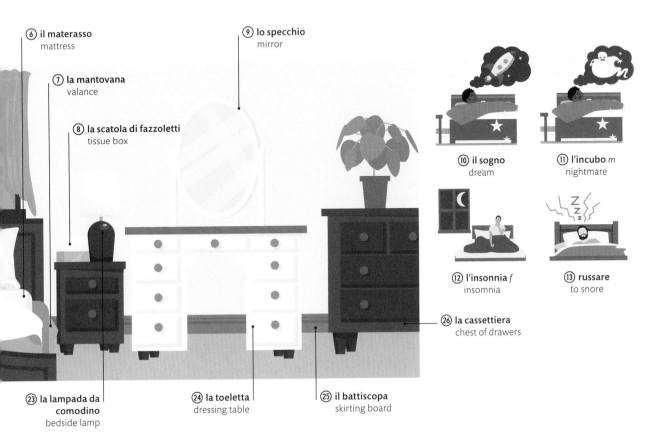

⑥ **il materasso**
mattress

⑨ **lo specchio**
mirror

⑦ **la mantovana**
valance

⑧ **la scatola di fazzoletti**
tissue box

⑩ **il sogno**
dream

⑪ **l'incubo** *m*
nightmare

⑫ **l'insonnia** *f*
insomnia

⑬ **russare**
to snore

㉖ **la cassettiera**
chest of drawers

㉓ **la lampada da comodino**
bedside lamp

㉔ **la toeletta**
dressing table

㉕ **il battiscopa**
skirting board

30.2   LA STANZA DEL BEBÈ · NURSERY

① **il baby monitor**
baby monitor

② **il lettino**
cot

③ **le sbarre**
bars

④ **il lenzuolo**
sheet

⑤ **la culla di vimini**
Moses basket

⑥ **la luce notturna**
night light

⑦ **la giostrina**
mobile

⑧ **il materassino del fasciatoio**
changing mat

⑨ **il fasciatoio**
changing table

⑩ **l'orsacchiotto** *m*
teddy bear

⑪ **il pavimento**
floor

31.1 IN BAGNO · IN THE BATHROOM

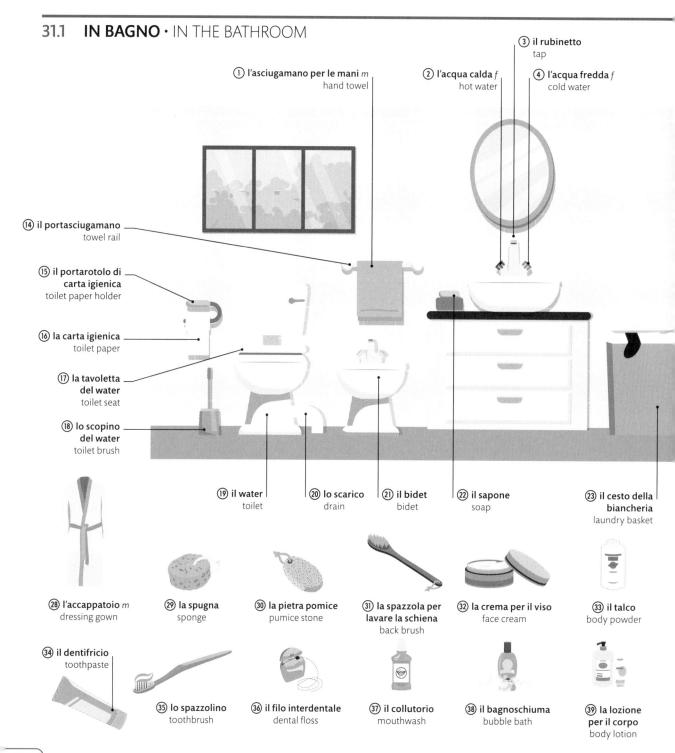

③ il rubinetto
tap

① l'asciugamano per le mani *m*
hand towel

② l'acqua calda *f*
hot water

④ l'acqua fredda *f*
cold water

⑭ il portasciugamano
towel rail

⑮ il portarotolo di
carta igienica
toilet paper holder

⑯ la carta igienica
toilet paper

⑰ la tavoletta
del water
toilet seat

⑱ lo scopino
del water
toilet brush

⑲ il water
toilet

⑳ lo scarico
drain

㉑ il bidet
bidet

㉒ il sapone
soap

㉓ il cesto della
biancheria
laundry basket

㉘ l'accappatoio *m*
dressing gown

㉙ la spugna
sponge

㉚ la pietra pomice
pumice stone

㉛ la spazzola per
lavare la schiena
back brush

㉜ la crema per il viso
face cream

㉝ il talco
body powder

㉞ il dentifricio
toothpaste

㉟ lo spazzolino
toothbrush

㊱ il filo interdentale
dental floss

㊲ il collutorio
mouthwash

㊳ il bagnoschiuma
bubble bath

㊴ la lozione
per il corpo
body lotion

See also
18 La bellezza • Beauty **25** Un luogo in cui vivere • A place to live **32** La casa House and home **33** Gli impianti elettrico e idraulico • Electrics and plumbing

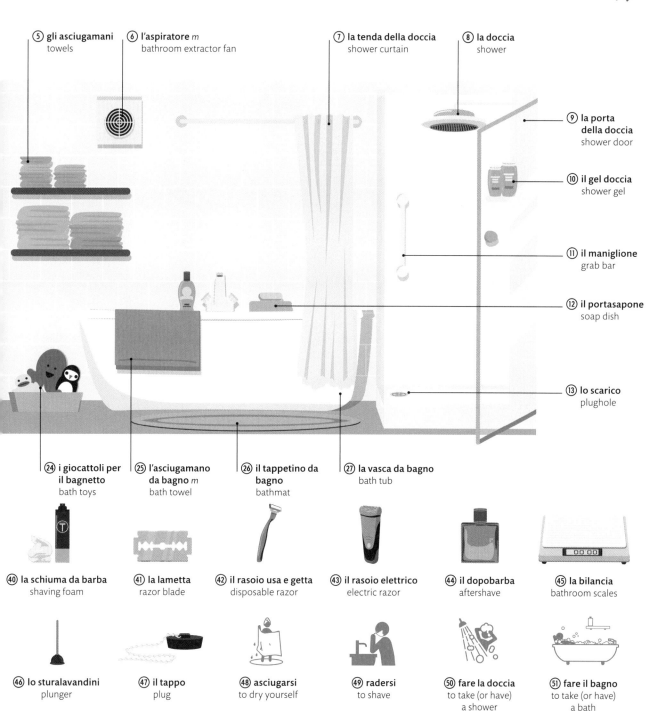

⑤ **gli asciugamani**
towels

⑥ **l'aspiratore** *m*
bathroom extractor fan

⑦ **la tenda della doccia**
shower curtain

⑧ **la doccia**
shower

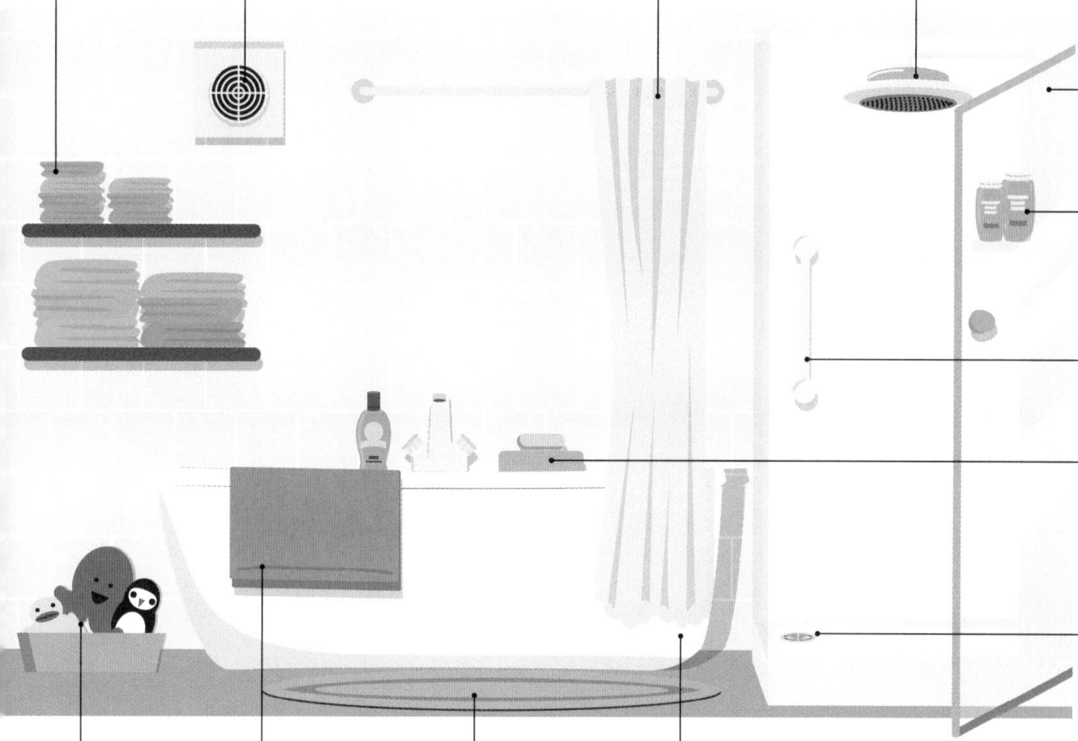

⑨ **la porta della doccia**
shower door

⑩ **il gel doccia**
shower gel

⑪ **il maniglione**
grab bar

⑫ **il portasapone**
soap dish

⑬ **lo scarico**
plughole

㉔ **i giocattoli per il bagnetto**
bath toys

㉕ **l'asciugamano da bagno** *m*
bath towel

㉖ **il tappetino da bagno**
bathmat

㉗ **la vasca da bagno**
bath tub

㊵ **la schiuma da barba**
shaving foam

㊶ **la lametta**
razor blade

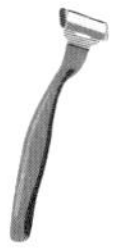

㊷ **il rasoio usa e getta**
disposable razor

㊸ **il rasoio elettrico**
electric razor

㊹ **il dopobarba**
aftershave

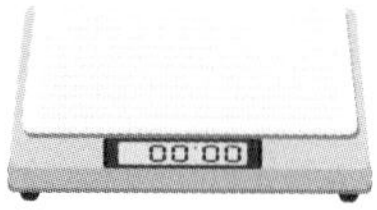

㊺ **la bilancia**
bathroom scales

㊻ **lo sturalavandini**
plunger

㊼ **il tappo**
plug

㊽ **asciugarsi**
to dry yourself

㊾ **radersi**
to shave

㊿ **fare la doccia**
to take (or have) a shower

(51) **fare il bagno**
to take (or have) a bath

32 La casa
House and home

32.1 I TIPI DI CASE · TYPES OF HOUSE

① **la casa indipendente**
detached house

② **la casa bifamiliare**
semi-detached

③ **la casa a schiera**
terraced house

④ **la casa di città**
town house

⑤ **il cottage**
cottage

⑥ **la villa**
villa

⑦ **il bungalow**
bungalow

⑧ **la villa**
mansion

⑨ **la roulotte**
caravan

⑩ **la baita**
cabin

⑪ **la casa sull'albero**
tree house

⑫ **lo chalet**
chalet

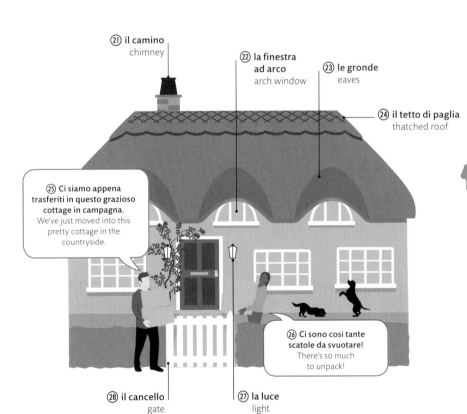

㉑ **il camino**
chimney

㉒ **la finestra ad arco**
arch window

㉓ **le gronde**
eaves

㉔ **il tetto di paglia**
thatched roof

㉕ **Ci siamo appena trasferiti in questo grazioso cottage in campagna.**
We've just moved into this pretty cottage in the countryside.

㉖ **Ci sono così tante scatole da svuotare!**
There's so much to unpack!

㉘ **il cancello**
gate

㉗ **la luce**
light

㉙ **il cottage con il tetto di paglia**
thatched cottage

⑬ **la iurta**
yurt

⑭ **la capanna**
hut

⑮ **il wigwam**
wigwam

⑯ **l'igloo** m
igloo

⑰ **il tepee**
teepee

⑱ **la casa galleggiante**
houseboat

⑲ **la casa prefabbricata**
prefab house

⑳ **la palafitta**
stilt house

See also
25 Un luogo in cui vivere • A place to live **33** Gli impianti elettrico e idraulico • Electrics and plumbing **35** I lavori di miglioria della casa • Home improvements **37** La decorazione Decorating **42-43** In città • In town **44** Gli edifici e l'architettura • Buildings and architecture

32.2 L'ACQUISTO E L'AFFITTO DI UNA CASA · BUYING AND RENTING A HOUSE

① **l'agente immobiliare** m / f
estate agent

② **l'immobile** m
property

③ **vedere una casa**
to view a house

④ **arredato** m **arredata** f
furnished

⑤ **non arredato** m **non arredata** f
unfurnished

⑥ **open space**
open-plan

⑦ **il parcheggio**
parking space

⑧ **il magazzino**
storage

⑨ **risparmiare**
to save up

⑩ **acquistare**
to buy

⑪ **possedere**
to own

⑫ **le scatole**
boxes

⑬ **il nastro adesivo**
tape

⑭ **le chiavi**
keys

⑮ **imballare**
to pack

⑯ **il camion dei traslochi**
removal van

⑰ **traslocare**
to move out

⑱ **trasferirsi**
to move in

⑲ **spacchettare**
to unpack

⑳ **dare in affitto**
to rent out

㉑ **prendere in affitto**
to rent

㉒ **il contratto d'affitto**
lease / tenancy agreement

㉓ **l'affittuario** m **l'affittuaria** f
tenant

㉔ **il padrone di casa** m **la padrona di casa** f
landlord

㉕ **la cauzione**
deposit

㉖ **dare il preavviso**
to give notice

㉗ **l'ipoteca** f
mortgage

㉘ **le bollette**
bills

㉙ **l'inquilino** m **l'inquilina** f
lodger

㉚ **il coinquilino** m **la coinquilina** f
housemate

㉛ **l'area residenziale** f
residential area

33.1 L'ELETTRICITÀ · ELECTRICITY

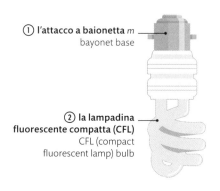

① l'attacco a baionetta m
bayonet base

② la lampadina fluorescente compatta (CFL)
CFL (compact fluorescent lamp) bulb

③ la lampadina a incandescenza
incandescent bulb

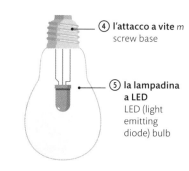

④ l'attacco a vite m
screw base

⑤ la lampadina a LED
LED (light emitting diode) bulb

⑥ le lampadine
light bulbs

⑦ la presa elettrica
socket

⑧ l'interruttore m
light switch

⑨ la corrente continua
direct current

⑩ la corrente alternata
alternating current

⑪ il generatore
generator

⑫ la stufetta a gas
gas space heater

⑬ il radiatore a olio
oil-filled radiator

⑭ la stufetta
fan space heater

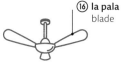

⑯ la pala
blade

⑮ il ventilatore da soffitto
ceiling fan

⑰ il ventilatore
fan

⑱ l'aria condizionata f
air conditioning

⑲ la corrente elettrica
power

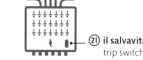

㉑ il salvavita
trip switch

⑳ il quadro elettrico
fuse box

㉒ l'ampere m
amp

㉓ sotto tensione
live

㉔ neutro
neutral

㉕ i cavi
wires

㉖ la messa a terra
earthing

㉗ il voltaggio
voltage

㉘ la spina
plug

㉙ lo spinotto
pin

㉟ Stacca la corrente prima di toccare un cavo sotto tensione.
Switch off the power before touching a live wire.

㉚ il contatore elettrico
electricity meter

㉛ il trasformatore
transformer

㉜ l'interruzione di corrente f
power cut

㉝ la rete elettrica
mains supply

㉞ il cablaggio
wiring

See also
31 Il bagno · Bathroom **35** I lavori di miglioria della casa · Home improvements
36 Gli attrezzi · Tools **37** La decorazione · Decorating **87** Le costruzioni · Construction

33.2 L'IMPIANTO IDRAULICO · PLUMBING

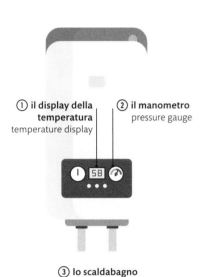

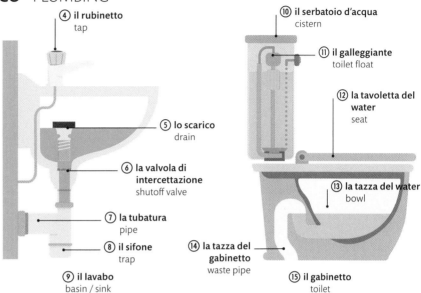

④ **il rubinetto**
tap

⑩ **il serbatoio d'acqua**
cistern

⑪ **il galleggiante**
toilet float

① **il display della temperatura**
temperature display

② **il manometro**
pressure gauge

⑫ **la tavoletta del water**
seat

⑤ **lo scarico**
drain

⑥ **la valvola di intercettazione**
shutoff valve

⑬ **la tazza del water**
bowl

⑦ **la tubatura**
pipe

⑧ **il sifone**
trap

③ **lo scaldabagno**
boiler

⑨ **il lavabo**
basin / sink

⑭ **la tazza del gabinetto**
waste pipe

⑮ **il gabinetto**
toilet

⑯ **il radiatore**
radiator

⑰ **il rubinetto**
tap

⑱ **avere una perdita**
to spring a leak

⑲ **chiamare un idraulico**
to call a plumber

⑳ **riparare**
to repair

㉑ **installare**
to install

33.3 I RIFIUTI · WASTE

② **il cestino per la raccolta differenziata**
recycling bin

③ **l'unità per la raccolta differenziata** f
sorting unit

④ **il contenitore per il compost**
food compost bin

⑤ **il sacco dell'immondizia**
bin liner

① **il cestino della spazzatura**
rubbish bin

⑥ **i rifiuti biodegradabili**
biodegradable waste

⑦ **i rifiuti pericolosi**
hazardous waste

⑧ **i rifiuti elettrici**
electrical waste

⑨ **i rifiuti edili**
construction waste

34 Le faccende domestiche
Household chores

34.1 I LAVORI DI CASA · HOUSEHOLD TASKS

① **cambiare le lenzuola**
to change the sheets

② **fare il letto**
to make the bed

③ **dare da mangiare agli animali**
to feed the pets

④ **annaffiare le piante**
to water the plants

⑤ **lavare l'auto** *f*
to wash the car

⑥ **spazzare il pavimento**
to sweep the floor

⑦ **lavare il pavimento**
to scrub the floor

⑧ **pulire il forno**
to clean the oven

⑨ **pulire le finestre**
to clean the windows

⑩ **sbrinare il frigo**
to defrost the freezer

⑪ **passare l'aspirapolvere sul tappeto** *m*
to vacuum the carpet

⑫ **spolverare**
to dust

⑬ **pulire il bagno**
to clean the bathroom

⑭ **riordinare**
to tidy

⑮ **fare la spesa**
to buy groceries

⑯ **fare il bucato**
to do the laundry

⑰ **stendere il bucato**
to hang out clothes

⑱ **stirare**
to do the ironing

⑳ **Solitamente faccio i lavori di casa alla sera.**
I usually do the housework in the evening.

⑲ **passare il mocio**
to mop the floor

㉑ **piegare i vestiti**
to fold clothes

㉒ **preparare la tavola / apparecchiare**
to set the table

㉓ **sparecchiare**
to clear the table

㉔ **riempire la lavastoviglie**
to load the dishwasher

㉕ **svuotare la lavastoviglie**
to unload the dishwasher

㉖ **pulire le superfici**
to wipe the surfaces

㉗ **lavare i piatti**
to do the dishes

㉘ **asciugare i piatti**
to dry the dishes

㉙ **portare fuori la spazzatura**
to take out the rubbish

See also
09 Le attività quotidiane • Daily routines **25** Un luogo in cui vivere • A place to live **33** Gli impianti elettrico e idraulico • Electrics and plumbing **35** I lavori di miglioria della casa • Home improvements **37** La decorazione • Decorating **39** Il giardinaggio • Practical gardening

34.2 IL BUCATO E LE PULIZIE · LAUNDRY AND CLEANING

① **la spugnetta abrasiva**
scouring pad

② **la spugna**
sponge

③ **il panno**
cloth

④ **il panno per spolverare**
duster

⑤ **il piumino per la polvere**
feather duster

⑥ **il lavavetri**
squeegee

⑦ **il secchio**
bucket

⑧ **il mocio**
mop

⑨ **lo spazzolone**
scrubbing brush

⑩ **la paletta**
dustpan

⑪ **la scopetta**
brush

⑫ **la scopa**
broom

⑬ **il cestino per la raccolta differenziata**
recycling bin

⑭ **il sacco dell'immondizia**
bin liner

⑮ **il lucidante**
polish

⑯ **il detergente per superfici**
surface cleaner

⑰ **il detergente per bagno**
toilet cleaner

⑱ **la tavoletta attiva**
toilet block

⑳ **il tubo di aspirazione**
suction hose

⑲ **l'aspirapolvere** *m*
vacuum cleaner

㉑ **i guanti di gomma**
rubber gloves

㉒ **l'aceto bianco** *m*
white vinegar

㉓ **i panni sporchi**
dirty washing

㉔ **il cesto della biancheria**
laundry basket

㉕ **la lavatrice**
washing machine

㉖ **l'asciugatrice** *f*
tumble dryer

㉗ **il ferro da stiro**
iron

㉘ **l'asse da stiro** *m*
ironing board

㉙ **la molletta**
clothes peg

㉚ **il filo stendibiancheria**
clothesline / washing line

㉛ **il detersivo per il bucato**
laundry detergent

㉜ **l'ammorbidente** *m*
fabric softener

㉝ **la lavastoviglie**
dishwasher

㉞ **le pastiglie per lavastoviglie**
dishwasher tablets

㉟ **il detersivo per piatti**
washing-up liquid

㊱ **la candeggina**
bleach

I lavori di miglioria della casa

Home improvements

35.1 GLI ATTREZZI E GLI UTENSILI PER IL BRICOLAGE · TOOLS AND DIY EQUIPMENT

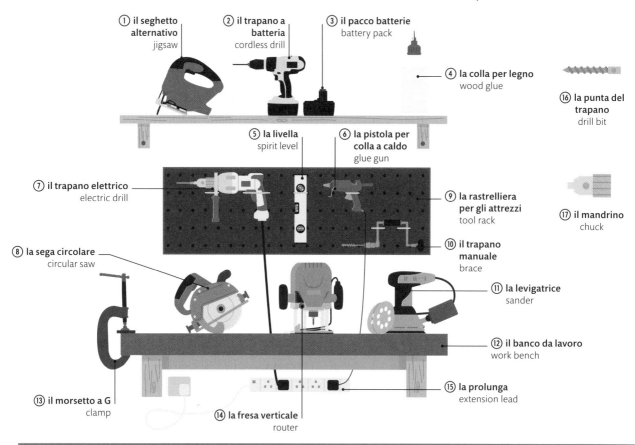

① **il seghetto alternativo**
jigsaw

② **il trapano a batteria**
cordless drill

③ **il pacco batterie**
battery pack

④ **la colla per legno**
wood glue

⑯ **la punta del trapano**
drill bit

⑤ **la livella**
spirit level

⑥ **la pistola per colla a caldo**
glue gun

⑦ **il trapano elettrico**
electric drill

⑨ **la rastrelliera per gli attrezzi**
tool rack

⑰ **il mandrino**
chuck

⑩ **il trapano manuale**
brace

⑧ **la sega circolare**
circular saw

⑪ **la levigatrice**
sander

⑫ **il banco da lavoro**
work bench

⑬ **il morsetto a G**
clamp

⑭ **la fresa verticale**
router

⑮ **la prolunga**
extension lead

35.2 I VERBI DEL BRICOLAGE · DIY VERBS

① **tagliare**
to cut

② **segare**
to saw

③ **trapanare**
to drill

④ **martellare**
to hammer

⑩ **la lega per saldatura**
solder

⑪ **la saldatrice**
soldering iron

⑤ **piallare**
to plane

⑥ **tornire**
to turn

⑦ **intagliare**
to carve

⑧ **piastrellare**
to tile

⑨ **saldare**
to solder

See also
33 Gli impianti elettrico e idraulico · Electrics and plumbing **36** Gli attrezzi Tools · **37** La decorazione · Decorating **87** Le costruzioni · Construction

35.3 I MATERIALI · MATERIALS

① il legno
wood

② il legno massiccio
hardwood

③ il legno tenero
softwood

④ la faesite
hardboard

⑤ il truciolato
chipboard

⑥ il compensato
plywood

⑦ l'MDF *m*
MDF

⑧ le piastrelle
tiles

⑨ il cemento
concrete

⑩ il metallo
metal

⑪ il fil di ferro
wire

⑫ il lastricato
flagstone

⑬ l'isolamento *m*
insulation

⑭ la sabbia
sand

⑮ la ghiaia
gravel

⑰ Sto costruendo un nuovo ampliamento.
I'm building a new extension.

⑱ il vetro
glass

⑯ i mattoni
bricks

⑲ la malta
mortar

---

⑫ posare la moquette
to fit a carpet

⑬ sturare il lavandino
to unblock the sink

⑭ rifare l'impianto elettrico della casa
to rewire the house

⑮ posare i mattoni
to lay bricks

⑯ convertire il loft
to convert the attic / loft

⑰ realizzare le tende
to make curtains

⑱ appendere gli scaffali
to put up shelves

⑲ cambiare una lampadina
to change a light bulb

⑳ sturare il water
to unblock the toilet

㉑ abbattere un muro
to knock down a wall

㉒ dipingere un muro
to paint a wall

㉓ riparare una recinzione
to fix a fence

81

36 Gli attrezzi
Tools

LA CASSETTA DEGLI ATTREZZI · TOOLBOX

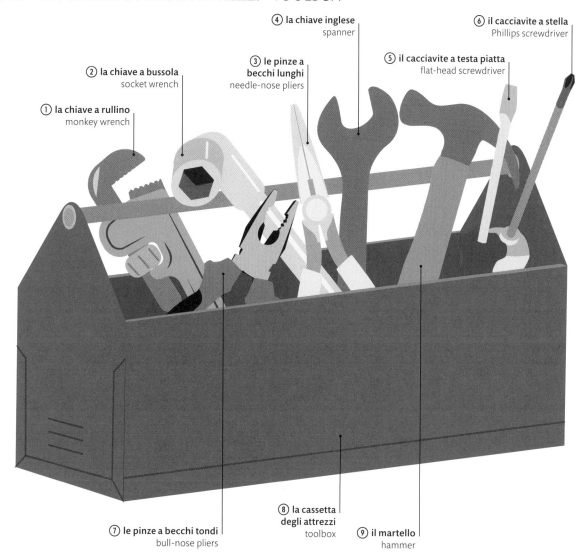

④ **la chiave inglese**
spanner

⑥ **il cacciavite a stella**
Phillips screwdriver

③ **le pinze a becchi lunghi**
needle-nose pliers

⑤ **il cacciavite a testa piatta**
flat-head screwdriver

② **la chiave a bussola**
socket wrench

① **la chiave a rullino**
monkey wrench

⑧ **la cassetta degli attrezzi**
toolbox

⑦ **le pinze a becchi tondi**
bull-nose pliers

⑨ **il martello**
hammer

36.2 **LE PUNTE DEL TRAPANO ·** DRILL BITS

① **la punta da metallo**
metal bit

② **la punta da muro**
masonry bit

③ **la punta da legno**
carpentry bit

④ **la punta piatta da legno**
flat wood bit

⑤ **la punta di sicurezza**
security bit

⑥ **l'alesatore** *m*
reamer

See also
33 Gli impianti elettrico e idraulico · Electrics and plumbing
35 I lavori di miglioria della casa · Home improvements
37 La decorazione · Decorating **87** Le costruzioni · Construction

36.3 GLI ATTREZZI · TOOLS

① la cintura porta attrezzi
tool belt

② il chiodo
nail

③ la vite
screw

④ il bullone
bolt

⑤ la guarnizione
washer

⑥ il dado
nut

⑦ le brugole
hex keys / Allen keys

⑧ il metro a nastro
tape measure

⑨ il taglierino
utility knife

⑩ il seghetto
hacksaw

⑪ la sega per tenoni
tenon saw

⑫ la sega
handsaw

⑬ la pialla
plane

⑭ il trapano manuale
hand drill

⑮ la chiave inglese
spanner

⑯ lo scalpello
chisel

⑰ la lima
file

⑱ la pietra per affilare
sharpening stone

⑳ il piolo
rung

㉑ le pinze spelafili
wire strippers

㉒ il tronchese
wire cutters

㉓ il nastro isolante
insulating tape

㉔ il tagliatubi
pipe cutter

㉕ lo sturalavandini
plunger

㉖ il mazzuolo
mallet

㉗ l'ascia *f*
axe

㉘ la lana d'acciaio
wire wool

㉙ la carta vetrata
sandpaper

㉚ gli occhiali protettivi
safety goggles

⑲ la scala
ladder

㉛ la saldatrice
soldering iron

㉜ la lega per saldatura
solder

㉝ la fiala
vial

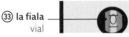
㉞ la livella
spirit level

83

37.1 LA RISTRUTTURAZIONE DELLA CASA · HOUSEHOLD RENOVATION

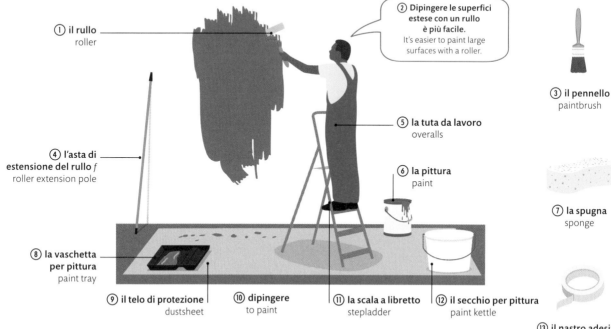

① il rullo
roller

② Dipingere le superfici estese con un rullo è più facile.
It's easier to paint large surfaces with a roller.

③ il pennello
paintbrush

⑤ la tuta da lavoro
overalls

④ l'asta di estensione del rullo *f*
roller extension pole

⑥ la pittura
paint

⑦ la spugna
sponge

⑧ la vaschetta per pittura
paint tray

⑨ il telo di protezione
dustsheet

⑩ dipingere
to paint

⑪ la scala a libretto
stepladder

⑫ il secchio per pittura
paint kettle

⑬ il nastro adesivo di carta
masking tape

⑭ il taglierino
craft knife

⑮ il filo a piombo
plumb line

⑯ la carta vetrata
sandpaper

⑰ lo stucco
filler

⑱ l'acqua ragia *f*
white spirit

⑲ lo sverniciatore
paint stripper

⑳ l'intonaco *m*
plaster

㉑ la vernice di base
primer

㉒ la mano di fondo
undercoat

㉓ l'emulsione *f*
emulsion

㉔ opaco *m* / opaca *f*
matte

㉕ lucido *m*
lucida *f*
gloss

㉖ lo stencil
stencil

㉗ il solvente
solvent

㉘ il sigillante per bagno
sealant / caulk

㉙ la malta
grout

㉚ l'impregnante *m*
wood preserver

㉛ la vernice
varnish

See also
32 La casa · House and home **33** Gli impianti elettrico e idraulico · Electrics and plumbing **34** Le faccende domestiche · Household chores **35** I lavori di miglioria della casa · Home improvements

㉜ **le forbici**
scissors

㉝ **la carta di fondo**
lining paper

㉞ **la macchina per rimuovere la carta da parati**
wallpaper stripper

㉟ **il raschietto**
scraper

㊱ **il rotolo di carta da parati**
wallpaper roll

㊲ **il bordo della carta da parati**
wallpaper border

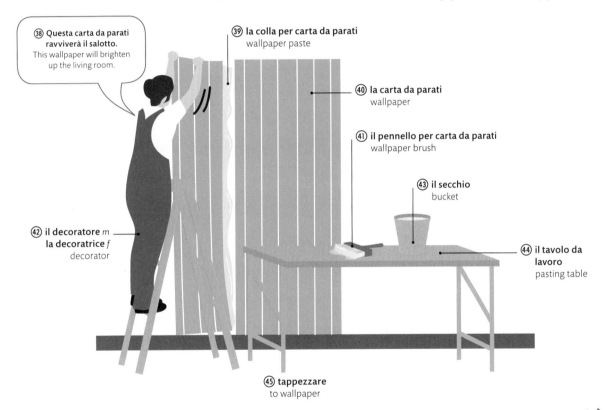

㊳ **Questa carta da parati ravviverà il salotto.**
This wallpaper will brighten up the living room.

㊴ **la colla per carta da parati**
wallpaper paste

㊵ **la carta da parati**
wallpaper

㊶ **il pennello per carta da parati**
wallpaper brush

㊸ **il secchio**
bucket

㊷ **il decoratore** *m*
la decoratrice *f*
decorator

㊹ **il tavolo da lavoro**
pasting table

㊺ **tappezzare**
to wallpaper

37.2 I VERBI DELLA DECORAZIONE · VERBS FOR DECORATING

① **staccare**
to strip

② **stuccare**
to fill

③ **scartavetrare**
to sand

④ **intonacare**
to plaster

⑤ **appendere**
to hang

⑥ **piastrellare**
to tile

38 Le piante da giardino e le piante da appartamento · Garden plants and houseplants

38.1 LE PIANTE DA GIARDINO E I FIORI · GARDEN PLANTS AND FLOWERS

① il dente di leone
dandelion

② l'enagra *f*
evening primrose

③ il cardo
thistle

④ il tulipano
tulip

⑤ il mughetto
lily of the valley

⑥ il garofano
carnation

⑧ la margherita
daisy

⑨ il ranuncolo
buttercup

⑩ il papavero
poppy

⑪ la viola del **pensiero**
pansy

⑫ il geranio
geranium

⑬ la digitale
foxglove

⑮ il lupino
lupin

⑯ la rosa
rose

⑰ il girasole
sunflower

⑱ l'orchidea *f*
orchid

⑲ la begonia
begonia

⑳ il giglio
lily

㉒ la viola
violet

㉓ il croco
crocus

㉔ la giunchiglia
daffodil

㉕ il lillà
lilac

㉖ la gardenia
gardenia

㉗ la lavanda
lavender

㉟ il caprifoglio
honeysuckle

㉙ la calendula
marigold

㉚ l'azalea *f*
azalea

㉛ il crisantemo
chrysanthemum

㉜ il rododendro
rhododendron

㉝ l'ibisco *m*
rose of Sharon / hibiscus

㊱ l'iris *f*
iris

㊲ il loto
lotus

㊳ il glicine
wisteria

㊴ la margherita **africana**
African daisy

㊵ l'ortensia *f*
hydrangea

⑦ **l'erica** *f*
heather

⑭ **la camelia**
camellia

㉑ **il ginerio**
pampas grass

㉘ **la protea**
protea

㉞ **il rosmarino**
rosemary

㊶ **l'alloro** *m*
bay tree

38.2 **LE PIANTE DA APPARTAMENTO** · HOUSEPLANTS

① **lo spatifillo**
peace lily

② **la sansevieria**
snake plant

③ **la pianta ragno**
spider plant

④ **la yucca**
yucca

⑤ **la dracena**
dragon tree

⑥ **il bonsai**
bonsai tree

⑦ **l'aracea americana** *f*
Swiss cheese plant

⑧ **le piante grasse**
succulents

⑨ **la pianta delle monete cinesi**
Chinese money plant

⑩ **il fico del caucciù**
rubber plant

⑪ **il falso papiro**
umbrella plant

⑫ **l'hypoestes phyllostachya** *f*
polka dot plant

⑬ **il pothos regina di marmo**
marble queen

⑭ **il pothos Jade**
jade pothos

38.3 **L'ANATOMIA DEL FIORE**
FLOWER ANATOMY

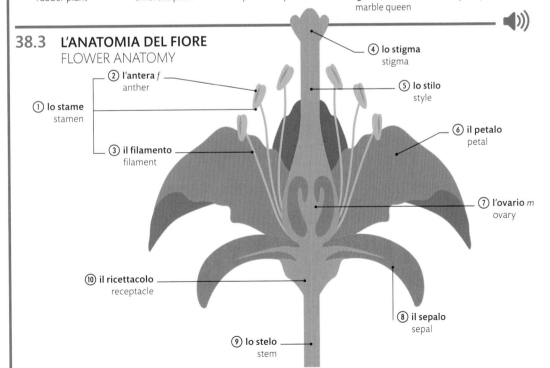

② **l'antera** *f*
anther

① **lo stame**
stamen

③ **il filamento**
filament

④ **lo stigma**
stigma

⑤ **lo stilo**
style

⑥ **il petalo**
petal

⑦ **l'ovario** *m*
ovary

⑧ **il sepalo**
sepal

⑩ **il ricettacolo**
receptacle

⑨ **lo stelo**
stem

See also
39 Il giardinaggio · Practical gardening **40** Gli attrezzi da giardinaggio · Garden tools
41 Le caratteristiche del giardino · Garden features **167-169** Le piante e gli alberi · Plants and trees

39 Il giardinaggio
Practical gardening

39.1 I VERBI DEL GIARDINAGGIO · GARDENING VERBS

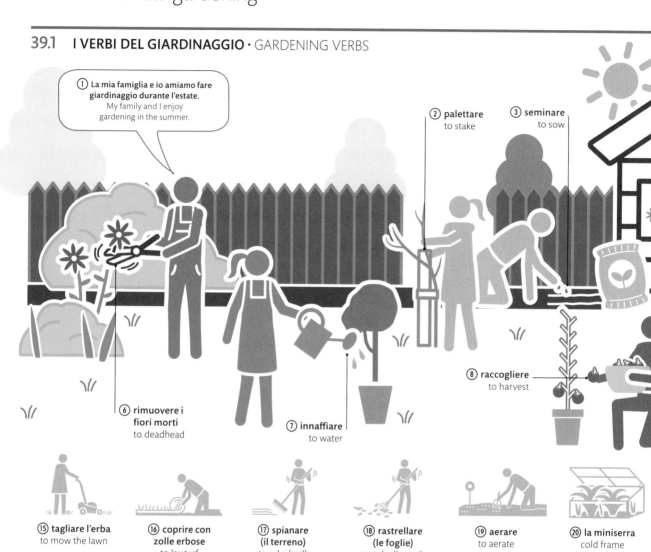

① **La mia famiglia e io amiamo fare giardinaggio durante l'estate.**
My family and I enjoy gardening in the summer.

② **palettare**
to stake

③ **seminare**
to sow

⑧ **raccogliere**
to harvest

⑥ **rimuovere i fiori morti**
to deadhead

⑦ **innaffiare**
to water

⑮ **tagliare l'erba**
to mow the lawn

⑯ **coprire con zolle erbose**
to lay turf

⑰ **spianare (il terreno)**
to rake (soil)

⑱ **rastrellare (le foglie)**
to rake (leaves)

⑲ **aerare**
to aerate

⑳ **la miniserra**
cold frame

㉔ **innestare**
to graft

㉕ **far crescere**
to propagate

㉖ **piantare**
to plant

㉗ **pacciamare**
to mulch

㉘ **togliere le erbacce**
to do the weeding

㉙ **trapiantare**
to transplant

㉞ **coltivare**
to cultivate

㉟ **potare**
to trim

㊱ **sfrondare**
to prune

㊲ **tagliare**
to chop

㊳ **setacciare**
to sieve

㊴ **progettare l'architettura paesaggistica**
to landscape

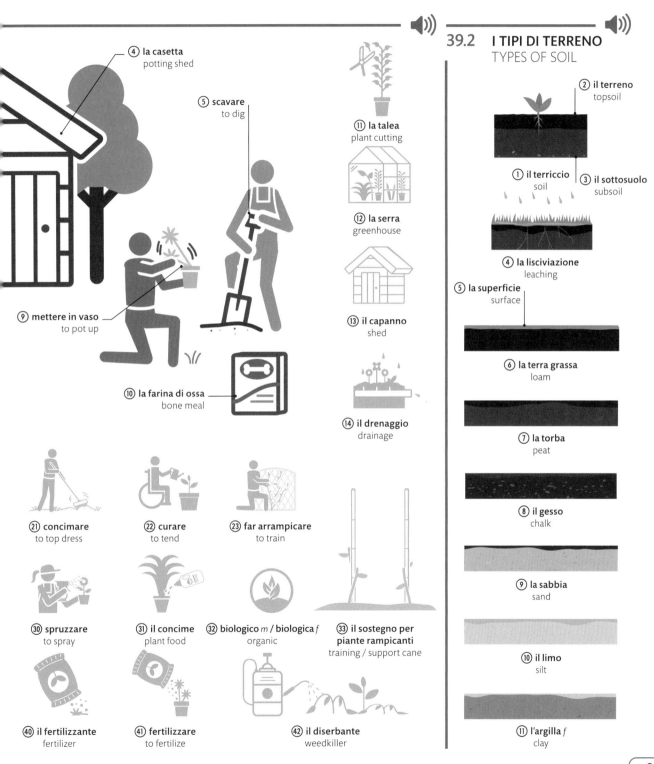

See also
38 Le piante da giardino e le piante da appartamento • Garden plants and houseplants **40** Gli attrezzi da giardinaggio • Garden tools **41** Le caratteristiche del giardino • Garden features **167-169** Le piante e gli alberi • Plants and trees

④ **la casetta**
potting shed

⑤ **scavare**
to dig

⑪ **la talea**
plant cutting

⑫ **la serra**
greenhouse

⑬ **il capanno**
shed

⑨ **mettere in vaso**
to pot up

⑩ **la farina di ossa**
bone meal

⑭ **il drenaggio**
drainage

39.2 I TIPI DI TERRENO
TYPES OF SOIL

② **il terreno**
topsoil

① **il terriccio**
soil

③ **il sottosuolo**
subsoil

④ **la lisciviazione**
leaching

⑤ **la superficie**
surface

⑥ **la terra grassa**
loam

⑦ **la torba**
peat

⑧ **il gesso**
chalk

⑨ **la sabbia**
sand

⑩ **il limo**
silt

⑪ **l'argilla** *f*
clay

㉑ **concimare**
to top dress

㉒ **curare**
to tend

㉓ **far arrampicare**
to train

㉚ **spruzzare**
to spray

㉛ **il concime**
plant food

㉜ **biologico** *m* / **biologica** *f*
organic

㉝ **il sostegno per piante rampicanti**
training / support cane

㊵ **il fertilizzante**
fertilizer

㊶ **fertilizzare**
to fertilize

㊷ **il diserbante**
weedkiller

40.1 L'ATTREZZATURA PER IL GIARDINAGGIO · GARDENING EQUIPMENT

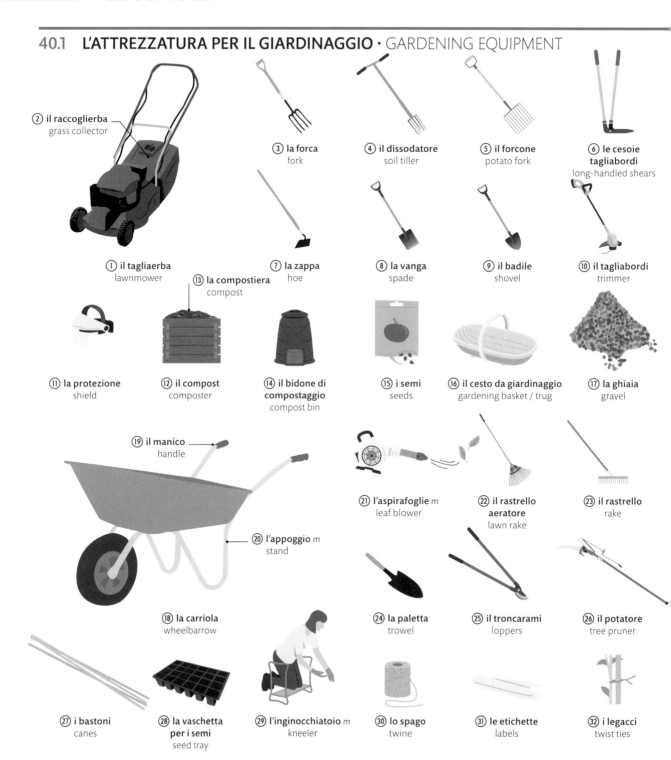

② il raccoglierba
grass collector

③ la forca
fork

④ il dissodatore
soil tiller

⑤ il forcone
potato fork

⑥ le cesoie tagliabordi
long-handled shears

① il tagliaerba
lawnmower

⑦ la zappa
hoe

⑧ la vanga
spade

⑨ il badile
shovel

⑩ il tagliabordi
trimmer

⑪ la protezione
shield

⑫ il compost
composter

⑬ la compostiera
compost

⑭ il bidone di compostaggio
compost bin

⑮ i semi
seeds

⑯ il cesto da giardinaggio
gardening basket / trug

⑰ la ghiaia
gravel

⑲ il manico
handle

⑳ l'appoggio m
stand

⑱ la carriola
wheelbarrow

㉑ l'aspirafoglie m
leaf blower

㉒ il rastrello aeratore
lawn rake

㉓ il rastrello
rake

㉔ la paletta
trowel

㉕ il troncarami
loppers

㉖ il potatore
tree pruner

㉗ i bastoni
canes

㉘ la vaschetta per i semi
seed tray

㉙ l'inginocchiatoio m
kneeler

㉚ lo spago
twine

㉛ le etichette
labels

㉜ i legacci
twist ties

See also
38 Le piante da giardino e le piante da appartamento • Garden plants and houseplants **39** Il giardinaggio • Practical gardening **41** Le caratteristiche del giardino • Garden features **167-169** Le piante e gli alberi • Plants and trees

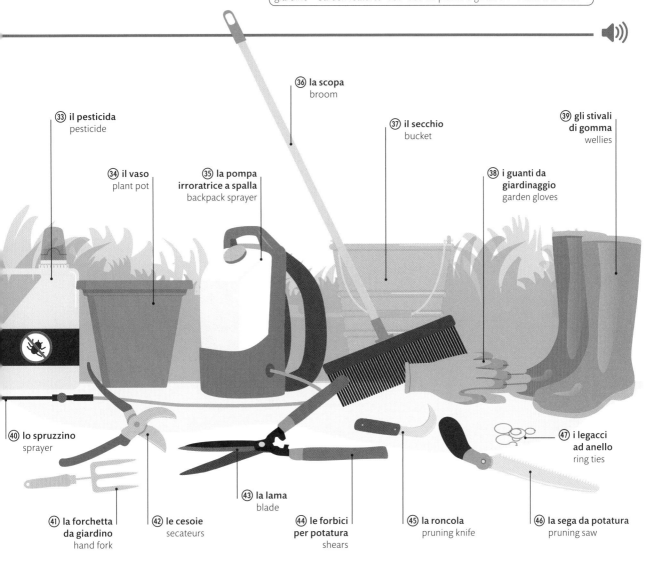

㉝ **il pesticida**
pesticide

㉞ **il vaso**
plant pot

㉟ **la pompa irroratrice a spalla**
backpack sprayer

㊱ **la scopa**
broom

㊲ **il secchio**
bucket

㊳ **i guanti da giardinaggio**
garden gloves

㊴ **gli stivali di gomma**
wellies

㊵ **lo spruzzino**
sprayer

㊶ **la forchetta da giardino**
hand fork

㊷ **le cesoie**
secateurs

㊸ **la lama**
blade

㊹ **le forbici per potatura**
shears

㊺ **la roncola**
pruning knife

㊻ **la sega da potatura**
pruning saw

㊼ **i legacci ad anello**
ring ties

40.2 **L'ANNAFFIATURA** · WATERING

① l'annaffiatoio *m*
watering can

② l'ugello **spruzzatore** *m*
spray nozzle

③ l'irrigatore **a pioggia** *m*
sprinkler

④ l'avvolgitubo *m*
hose reel

⑤ l'ugello *m*
nozzle

⑥ **la canna da giardino**
garden hose

41 Le caratteristiche del giardino
Garden features

41.1 I TIPI DI GIARDINO E GLI ORNAMENTI · GARDEN TYPES AND FEATURES

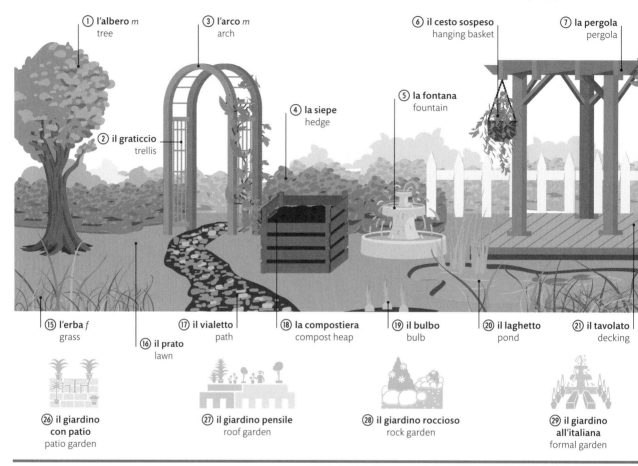

① l'albero *m*
tree

② il graticcio
trellis

③ l'arco *m*
arch

④ la siepe
hedge

⑤ la fontana
fountain

⑥ il cesto sospeso
hanging basket

⑦ la pergola
pergola

⑮ l'erba *f*
grass

⑯ il prato
lawn

⑰ il vialetto
path

⑱ la compostiera
compost heap

⑲ il bulbo
bulb

⑳ il laghetto
pond

㉑ il tavolato
decking

㉖ il giardino
con patio
patio garden

㉗ il giardino pensile
roof garden

㉘ il giardino roccioso
rock garden

㉙ il giardino
all'italiana
formal garden

41.2 I TIPI DI PIANTE · TYPES OF PLANTS

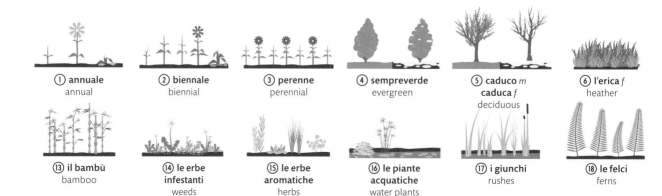

① annuale
annual

② biennale
biennial

③ perenne
perennial

④ sempreverde
evergreen

⑤ caduco *m*
caduca *f*
deciduous

⑥ l'erica *f*
heather

⑬ il bambù
bamboo

⑭ le erbe
infestanti
weeds

⑮ le erbe
aromatiche
herbs

⑯ le piante
acquatiche
water plants

⑰ i giunchi
rushes

⑱ le felci
ferns

See also
38 Le piante da giardino e le piante da appartamento • Garden plants and houseplants **39** Il giardinaggio • Practical gardening **40** Gli attrezzi da giardinaggio • Garden tools **167-169** Le piante e gli alberi • Plants and trees

🔊

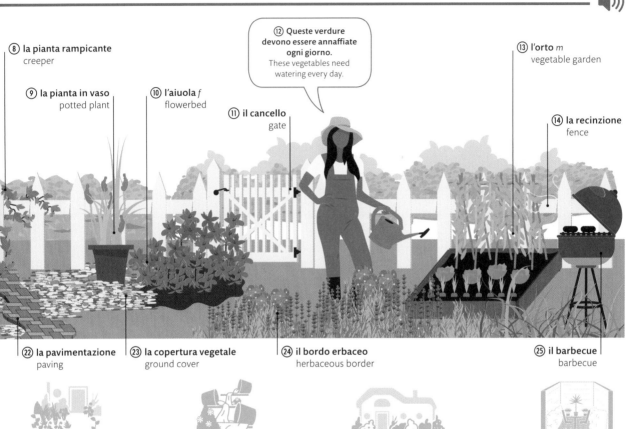

⑧ **la pianta rampicante**
creeper

⑨ **la pianta in vaso**
potted plant

⑩ **l'aiuola** *f*
flowerbed

⑪ **il cancello**
gate

⑫ **Queste verdure devono essere annaffiate ogni giorno.**
These vegetables need watering every day.

⑬ **l'orto** *m*
vegetable garden

⑭ **la recinzione**
fence

㉒ **la pavimentazione**
paving

㉓ **la copertura vegetale**
ground cover

㉔ **il bordo erbaceo**
herbaceous border

㉕ **il barbecue**
barbecue

㉚ **il giardino di erbe aromatiche**
herb garden

㉛ **il giardino d'acqua**
water garden

㉜ **il giardino all'inglese**
cottage garden

㉝ **il cortile**
courtyard

🔊

⑦ **le palme**
palms

⑧ **le conifere**
conifers

⑨ **l'arte topiaria** *f*
topiary

⑩ **la pianta rampicante**
climber

⑪ **le piante ornamentali**
ornamental plants

⑫ **le piante ombreggianti**
shade plants

⑲ **le piante alpine**
alpine plants

⑳ **le piante grasse**
succulents

㉑ **i cactus**
cacti

㉒ **gli arbusti**
shrubs

㉓ **gli arbusti da fiore**
flowering shrub

㉔ **le piante erbacee**
grasses

42.1 GLI EDIFICI E LE ALTRE CARATTERISTICHE
BUILDINGS AND OTHER FEATURES

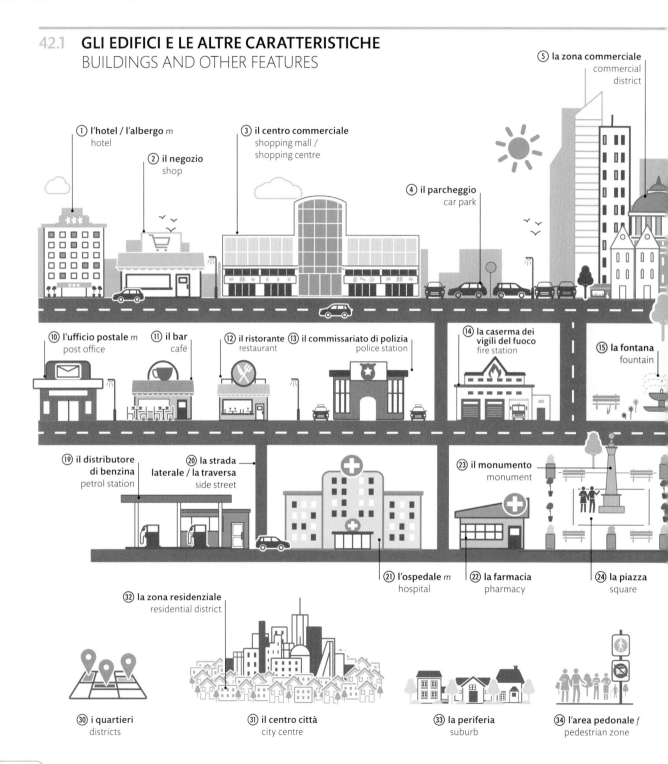

⑤ la zona commerciale
commercial district

① l'hotel / l'albergo m
hotel

② il negozio
shop

③ il centro commerciale
shopping mall / shopping centre

④ il parcheggio
car park

⑩ l'ufficio postale m
post office

⑪ il bar
café

⑫ il ristorante
restaurant

⑬ il commissariato di polizia
police station

⑭ la caserma dei vigili del fuoco
fire station

⑮ la fontana
fountain

⑲ il distributore di benzina
petrol station

⑳ la strada laterale / la traversa
side street

㉓ il monumento
monument

㉑ l'ospedale m
hospital

㉒ la farmacia
pharmacy

㉔ la piazza
square

㉜ la zona residenziale
residential district

㉚ i quartieri
districts

㉛ il centro città
city centre

㉝ la periferia
suburb

㉞ l'area pedonale f
pedestrian zone

See also
25 Un luogo in cui vivere • A place to live **43** In città (continua) • In town continued **44** Gli edifici e l'architettura • Buildings and architecture **46** Lo shopping • Shopping **47** Il centro commerciale The shopping mall **102** I treni • Trains **104** In aeroporto • At the airport **106** Il porto • The port

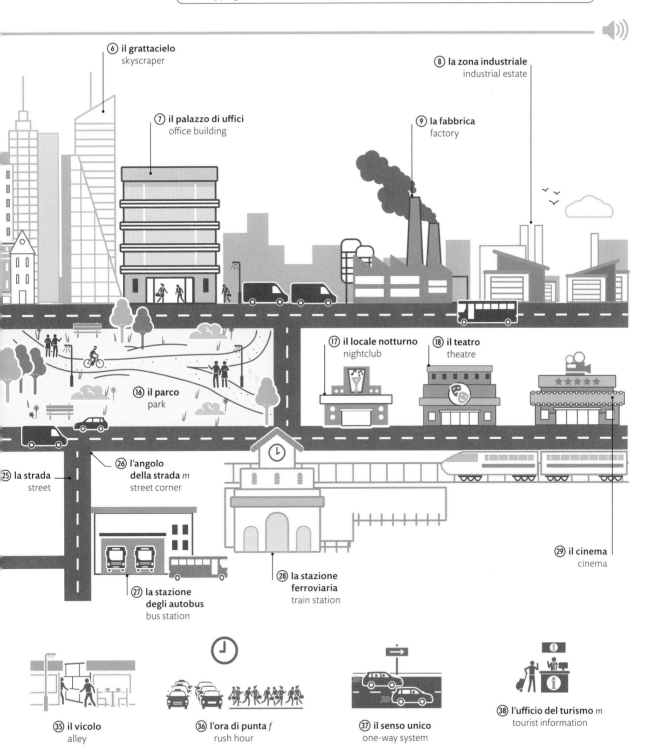

⑥ **il grattacielo**
skyscraper

⑧ **la zona industriale**
industrial estate

⑦ **il palazzo di uffici**
office building

⑨ **la fabbrica**
factory

⑯ **il parco**
park

⑰ **il locale notturno**
nightclub

⑱ **il teatro**
theatre

㉕ **la strada**
street

㉖ **l'angolo della strada** *m*
street corner

㉙ **il cinema**
cinema

㉗ **la stazione degli autobus**
bus station

㉘ **la stazione ferroviaria**
train station

㉟ **il vicolo**
alley

㊱ **l'ora di punta** *f*
rush hour

㊲ **il senso unico**
one-way system

㊳ **l'ufficio del turismo** *m*
tourist information

95

43.1 GLI EDIFICI E LE ALTRE CARATTERISTICHE · BUILDINGS AND OTHER FEATURES

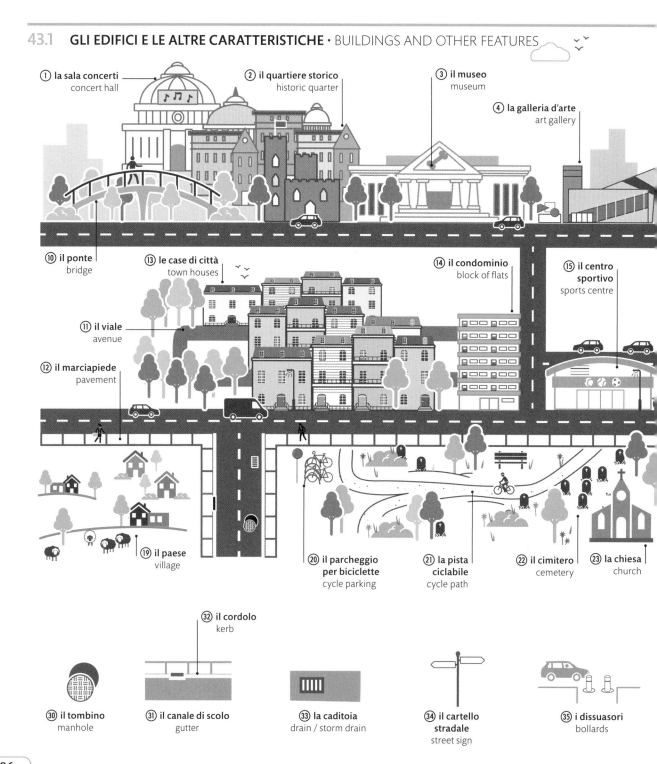

① la sala concerti
concert hall

② il quartiere storico
historic quarter

③ il museo
museum

④ la galleria d'arte
art gallery

⑩ il ponte
bridge

⑬ le case di città
town houses

⑭ il condominio
block of flats

⑮ il centro sportivo
sports centre

⑪ il viale
avenue

⑫ il marciapiede
pavement

⑲ il paese
village

⑳ il parcheggio per biciclette
cycle parking

㉑ la pista ciclabile
cycle path

㉒ il cimitero
cemetery

㉓ la chiesa
church

㉜ il cordolo
kerb

㉚ il tombino
manhole

㉛ il canale di scolo
gutter

㉝ la caditoia
drain / storm drain

㉞ il cartello stradale
street sign

㉟ i dissuasori
bollards

See also
25 Un luogo in cui vivere • A place to live **44** Gli edifici e l'architettura • Buildings and architecture **46** Lo shopping • Shopping **47** Il centro commerciale • The shopping mall **102** I treni • Trains **104** In aeroporto • At the airport **106** Il porto • The port

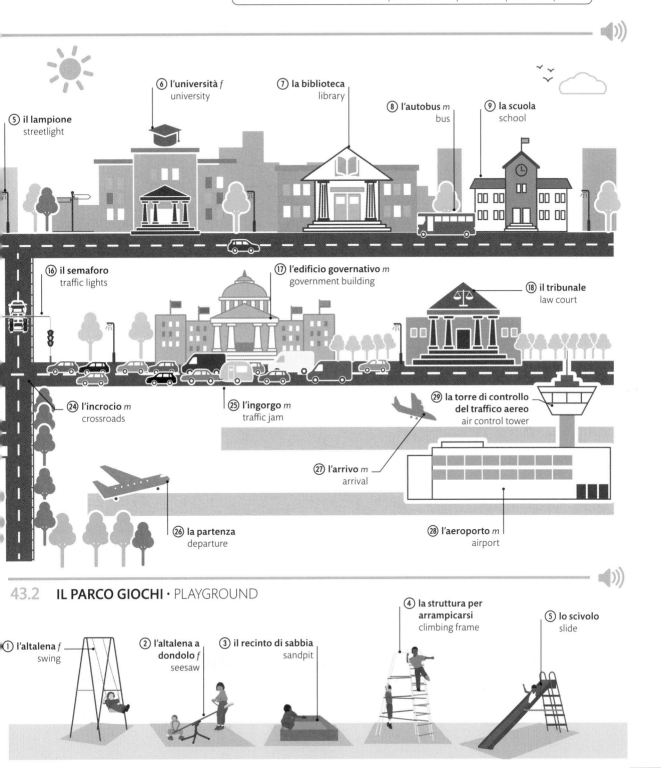

⑤ il lampione
streetlight

⑥ l'università *f*
university

⑦ la biblioteca
library

⑧ l'autobus *m*
bus

⑨ la scuola
school

⑯ il semaforo
traffic lights

⑰ l'edificio governativo *m*
government building

⑱ il tribunale
law court

㉔ l'incrocio *m*
crossroads

㉕ l'ingorgo *m*
traffic jam

㉙ la torre di controllo del traffico aereo
air control tower

㉗ l'arrivo *m*
arrival

㉖ la partenza
departure

㉘ l'aeroporto *m*
airport

43.2 IL PARCO GIOCHI · PLAYGROUND

④ la struttura per arrampicarsi
climbing frame

⑤ lo scivolo
slide

① l'altalena *f*
swing

② l'altalena a dondolo *f*
seesaw

③ il recinto di sabbia
sandpit

44 Gli edifici e l'architettura
Buildings and architecture

44.1 I TIPI DI EDIFICI · TYPES OF BUILDINGS

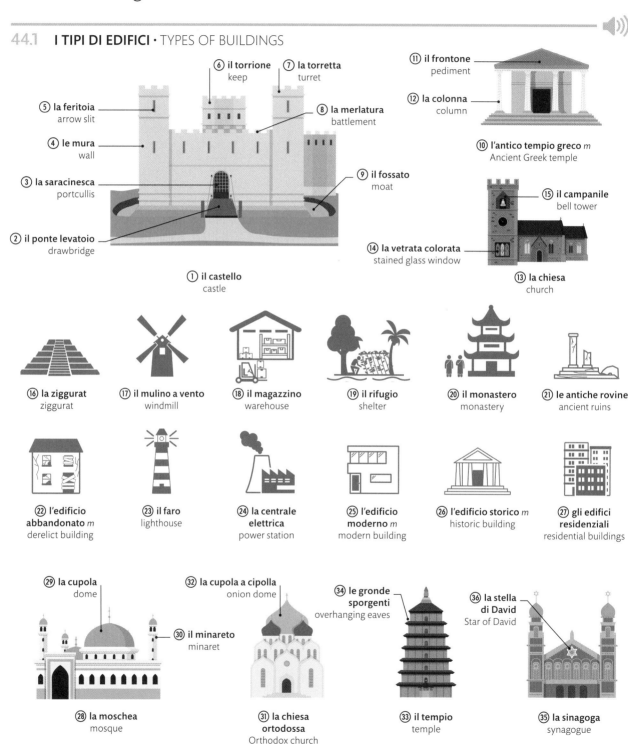

⑥ **il torrione** keep

⑦ **la torretta** turret

⑪ **il frontone** pediment

⑫ **la colonna** column

⑤ **la feritoia** arrow slit

⑧ **la merlatura** battlement

⑩ **l'antico tempio greco** *m* Ancient Greek temple

④ **le mura** wall

③ **la saracinesca** portcullis

⑨ **il fossato** moat

⑮ **il campanile** bell tower

② **il ponte levatoio** drawbridge

⑭ **la vetrata colorata** stained glass window

① **il castello** castle

⑬ **la chiesa** church

⑯ **la ziggurat** ziggurat

⑰ **il mulino a vento** windmill

⑱ **il magazzino** warehouse

⑲ **il rifugio** shelter

⑳ **il monastero** monastery

㉑ **le antiche rovine** ancient ruins

㉒ **l'edificio abbandonato** *m* derelict building

㉓ **il faro** lighthouse

㉔ **la centrale elettrica** power station

㉕ **l'edificio moderno** *m* modern building

㉖ **l'edificio storico** *m* historic building

㉗ **gli edifici residenziali** residential buildings

㉙ **la cupola** dome

㉜ **la cupola a cipolla** onion dome

㉞ **le gronde sporgenti** overhanging eaves

㊱ **la stella di David** Star of David

㉚ **il minareto** minaret

㉘ **la moschea** mosque

㉛ **la chiesa ortodossa** Orthodox church

㉝ **il tempio** temple

㉟ **la sinagoga** synagogue

See also
25 Un luogo in cui vivere · A place to live **32** La casa · House and
home **42-43** In città · In town **132** Fare un giro turistico · Sightseeing

44.2 I MONUMENTI E GLI EDIFICI FAMOSI · FAMOUS BUILDINGS AND MONUMENTS

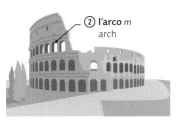

② l'arco *m*
arch

① **il Colosseo**
the Colosseum

③ **le piramidi di Giza**
the pyramids of Giza

⑤ **il muro della qibla**
qibla prayer wall

⑥ **la torre**
tower

④ **la Grande Moschea di Djenné**
the Great Mosque of Djenné

⑦ **la Casa Bianca**
the White House

⑧ **il Taj Mahal**
the Taj Mahal

⑨ **la Città Proibita**
the Forbidden City

⑩ **la cattedrale
di San Basilio**
St. Basil's cathedral

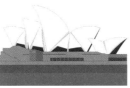

⑪ **il Teatro
dell'Opera di Sydney**
Sydney Opera House

⑰ **la piattaforma
di osservazione**
viewing
platform

⑫ **il castello di Himeji**
Himeji Castle

⑬ **il Big Ben**
Big Ben

⑭ **l'orologio** *m*
clock

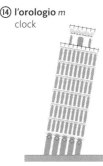

⑮ **la torre
pendente di Pisa**
the Leaning Tower of Pisa

⑯ **la Torre Eiffel**
the Eiffel Tower

⑱ **l'Empire
State Building** *m*
the Empire State Building

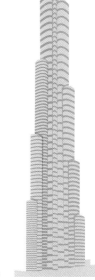

⑲ **il Burj
Khalifa**
Burj Khalifa

La banca e l'ufficio postale
The bank and post office

45.1 LA BANCA · BANK

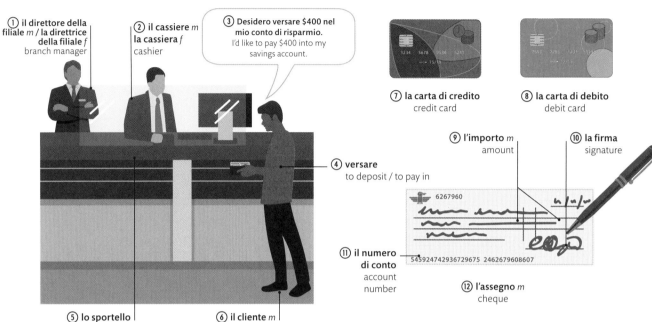

① il direttore della filiale m / la direttrice della filiale f
branch manager

② il cassiere m la cassiera f
cashier

③ Desidero versare $400 nel mio conto di risparmio.
I'd like to pay $400 into my savings account.

④ versare
to deposit / to pay in

⑤ lo sportello
counter

⑥ il cliente m la cliente f
customer

⑦ la carta di credito
credit card

⑧ la carta di debito
debit card

⑨ l'importo m
amount

⑩ la firma
signature

⑪ il numero di conto
account number

⑫ l'assegno m
cheque

⑬ il conto di risparmio
savings account

⑭ i risparmi
savings

⑮ il conto corrente
current account

⑯ l'addebito diretto m
direct debit

⑰ l'estratto conto m
bank statement

⑱ in attivo
in the black / in credit

⑲ in passivo / in rosso
in the red / in debt

⑳ lo scoperto
overdraft

㉑ i servizi bancari online
online banking

㉒ il tasso d'interesse
interest rate

㉓ il mutuo
bank loan

㉔ l'ipoteca f
mortgage

㉕ prelevare denaro
to withdraw money

㉖ trasferire denaro
to transfer money

See also
94 Il denaro e la finanza • Money and finance
131 Il viaggio e l'alloggio • Travel and accommodation

45.2 IL DENARO · MONEY

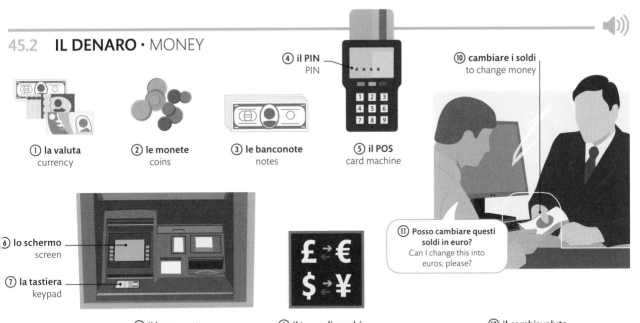

④ **il PIN**
PIN

⑩ **cambiare i soldi**
to change money

① **la valuta**
currency

② **le monete**
coins

③ **le banconote**
notes

⑤ **il POS**
card machine

⑥ **lo schermo**
screen

⑦ **la tastiera**
keypad

⑪ **Posso cambiare questi soldi in euro?**
Can I change this into euros, please?

⑧ **il bancomat**
cash machine / ATM

⑨ **il tasso di cambio**
exchange rate

⑫ **il cambiavalute**
bureau de change

45.3 L'UFFICIO POSTALE · POST OFFICE

④ **il timbro postale**
postmark

⑥ **il francobollo**
stamp

⑤ **il codice postale**
postcode

9959 North Albany St.
Mesa, AZ
85203

⑦ **la busta**
envelope

① **l'impiegato delle poste** *m*
l'impiegata delle poste *f*
postal worker

② **la bilancia**
scales

③ **la lettera**
letter

⑧ **l'indirizzo** *m*
address

⑨ **il postino** *m* / **la postina** *f*
postman / postwoman

⑩ **il pacco**
package / parcel

⑪ **il corriere**
courier

⑫ **la consegna**
delivery

⑬ **fragile**
fragile

⑭ **maneggiare con cura**
handle with care

⑮ **alto**
this way up

⑯ **non piegare**
do not bend

⑰ **la posta aerea**
airmail

⑱ **la raccomandata**
registered post

⑲ **la cassetta delle lettere**
postbox

⑳ **la buca delle lettere**
letterbox

46 Lo shopping
Shopping

NELLA VIA PRINCIPALE · ON THE HIGH STREET

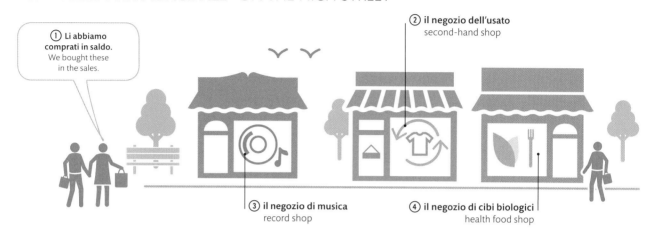

① **Li abbiamo comprati in saldo.**
We bought these in the sales.

② **il negozio dell'usato**
second-hand shop

③ **il negozio di musica**
record shop

④ **il negozio di cibi biologici**
health food shop

⑤ **il negozio di articoli da regalo**
gift shop

⑥ **la boutique**
boutique

⑦ **la gioielleria**
jeweller's

⑧ **il negozio d'arte**
art shop

⑨ **il negozio di antiquariato**
antiques shop

⑩ **il negozio di giocattoli**
toy shop

⑪ **l'ottico** *m*
optician

⑫ **la ferramenta**
hardware store

⑬ **il negozio specializzato in chiavi**
key cutting shop

⑭ **il negozio di elettronica**
electronics store

⑮ **il negozio di animali**
pet shop

⑯ **l'agenzia di viaggi** *f*
travel agent

⑰ **il mercato**
street market

⑱ **la pescheria**
fishmonger

⑲ **il macellaio**
butcher

⑳ **il panificio**
bakery

㉑ **il fruttivendolo**
greengrocer

㉒ **la gastronomia**
delicatessen

㉓ **la pasticceria**
cake shop

㉔ **il bar**
café / coffee shop

㉕ **il negozio di alcolici**
off licence

㉖ **l'edicola** *f* **il chiosco**
newsstand / kiosk

㉗ **la libreria**
bookshop

㉘ **il negozio di scarpe**
shoe shop

See also
42-43 In città • In town **47** Il centro commerciale
The shopping mall **48** Il supermercato • The supermarket

46.2 I VERBI DELLO SHOPPING · SHOPPING VERBS

㉙ **il vivaio**
garden centre

㉚ **il fiorista** *m*
la fiorista *f*
florist

① **scegliere**
to choose

② **vendere**
to sell

③ **comprare**
to buy

④ **volere**
to want

㉛ **il sarto** *m*
la sarta *f*
tailor

㉜ **la cabina per
fototessere**
photo booth

⑤ **andare bene**
to fit

⑥ **pagare**
to pay

⑦ **provare**
to try on

⑧ **contrattare**
to haggle

㉝ **la lavanderia
self-service**
launderette

㉞ **la lavanderia
a secco**
dry cleaner's

⑨ **reclamare**
to complain

⑩ **sostituire**
to exchange

⑪ **rimborsare**
to refund

⑫ **restituire**
to return

㉟ **le spese folli**
shopping spree

㊱ **guardare
le vetrine**
window shopping

㊲ **Ho dimenticato di aggiungere
il latte alla lista della spesa.**
I forgot to put milk on
my shopping list.

㊳ **la lista della spesa**
shopping list

46.3 ORDINARE ONLINE · ORDERING ONLINE

① **aggiungere
al carrello**
to add to the cart

② **aggiungere alla
lista dei desideri**
to add to wishlist

③ **procedere
al pagamento**
to proceed to checkout

④ **ordinare**
to order

⑤ **tracciare l'ordine** *m*
to track your order

Il centro commerciale
The shopping mall

47.1 IL CENTRO COMMERCIALE · SHOPPING CENTRE

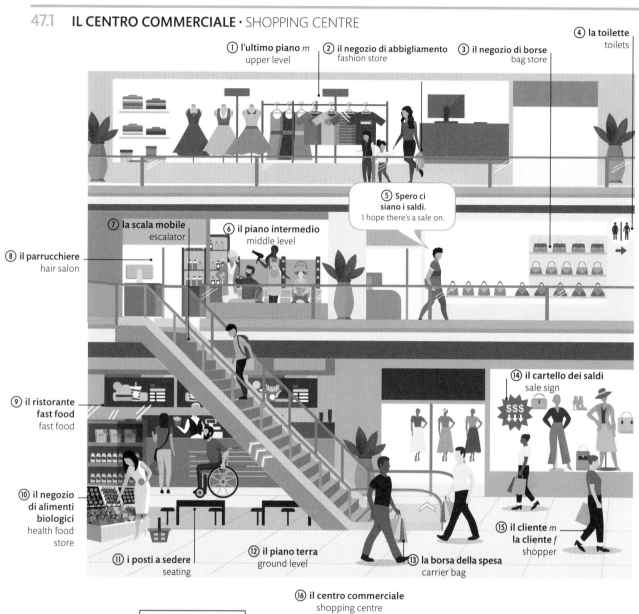

① l'ultimo piano *m*
upper level

② il negozio di abbigliamento
fashion store

③ il negozio di borse
bag store

④ la toilette
toilets

⑤ Spero ci siano i saldi.
I hope there's a sale on.

⑦ la scala mobile
escalator

⑥ il piano intermedio
middle level

⑧ il parrucchiere
hair salon

⑨ il ristorante fast food
fast food

⑩ il negozio di alimenti biologici
health food store

⑪ i posti a sedere
seating

⑫ il piano terra
ground level

⑬ la borsa della spesa
carrier bag

⑭ il cartello dei saldi
sale sign

⑮ il cliente *m*
la cliente *f*
shopper

⑯ il centro commerciale
shopping centre

⑰ il piano terra
ground floor

⑱ il primo piano
first floor

⑲ il parcheggio interrato
basement parking

⑳ il grande magazzino
department store

㉑ l'ascensore *m*
lift

㉒ di lusso
upmarket

㉓ la garanzia
guarantee

See also
13-15 Gli indumenti • Clothes **16** Gli accessori • Accessories **17** Le scarpe • Shoes
18 La bellezza • Beauty **42-43** In città • In town **46** Lo shopping • Shopping

㉔ i camerini
changing rooms

㉕ l'abbigliamento da donna *m*
womenswear

㉖ l'abbigliamento da uomo *m*
menswear

㉗ i fasciatoi
baby changing facilities

㉘ il reparto bambini
children's department

㉙ le firme
designer labels

㉚ i saldi
sale

㉛ la lingerie
lingerie

㉜ l'arredamento *m*
home furnishings

㉝ il cartellino del prezzo
price tag

㉞ l'illuminazione *m*
lighting

㉟ gli elettrodomestici
electrical appliances

㊱ la carta fedeltà
loyalty card

㊲ il fai da te
DIY (do it yourself)

㊳ la bellezza
beauty

㊴ il servizio clienti
customer service

㊵ la profumeria
perfumery

㊶ l'area ristorazione *f*
food court

47.2   IL CHIOSCO DEI FIORI · FLOWER STALL

① **il chiosco**
stall / kiosk

② **il fiorista** *m*
la fiorista *f*
florist

③ **la ghirlanda**
garland

④ **il mazzo**
bunch

⑤ **il gladiolo**
gladiolus

⑥ **la pianta in vaso**
pot plant

⑦ **il fogliame**
foliage

⑧ **la gerbera**
gerbera

⑨ **la peonia**
peony

⑩ **la gipsofila**
gypsophila

⑪ **il bouquet**
bouquet

⑫ **l'acacia** *f*
acacia

⑬ **l'orchidea** *f*
orchid

⑭ **la violacciocca**
stocks

⑮ **la fresia**
freesia

48 Il supermercato
The supermarket

IL SUPERMERCATO · SUPERMARKET

① **aperto**
open

② **chiuso**
closed

③ **il cliente** *m*
la cliente *f*
customer

④ **lo scontrino**
receipt

⑤ **l'offerta speciale** *f*
special offer

⑥ **l'affare** *m*
bargain

⑦ **la grande varietà**
wide range

⑧ **la fila**
queue

⑨ **il POS**
card machine

⑩ **lo shopping online**
online shopping

⑪ **il fattorino**
delivery man

⑫ **la consegna a domicilio**
home delivery

LA CASSA · CHECKOUT

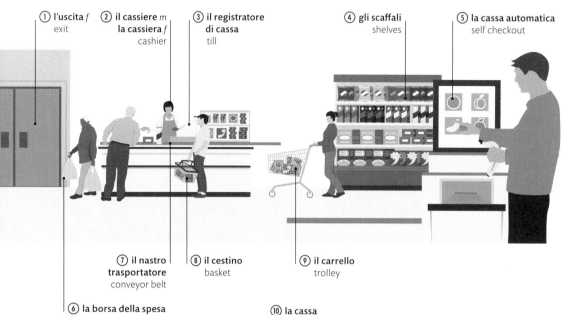

① **l'uscita** *f*
exit

② **il cassiere** *m*
la cassiera *f*
cashier

③ **il registratore di cassa**
till

④ **gli scaffali**
shelves

⑤ **la cassa automatica**
self checkout

⑦ **il nastro trasportatore**
conveyor belt

⑧ **il cestino**
basket

⑨ **il carrello**
trolley

⑥ **la borsa della spesa**
carrier bag

⑩ **la cassa**
checkout

⑪ **il codice a barre**
barcode

⑫ **il lettore di codice a barre**
scanner

⑬ **il buono sconto**
discount voucher

See also
46 Lo shopping • Shopping **53** La carne • Meat **54** Il pesce e i frutti di mare • Fish and seafood **55-56** La Verdura Vegetables **57** La frutta • Fruit **58** La frutta e la frutta a guscio • Fruit and nuts **59** Le erbe e le spezie • Herbs and spices **60** Nella dispensa • In the pantry **61** I prodotti caseari • Dairy produce **62-63** La panetteria • The bakery

48.3 LE CORSIE / I REPARTI · AISLES / SECTIONS

① **la panetteria**
bakery

② **i latticini**
dairy

③ **i cereali per la colazione**
breakfast cereals

④ **il cibo in scatola**
tinned food

⑤ **i dolciumi**
confectionery

⑥ **la verdura**
vegetables

⑦ **la frutta**
fruit

⑧ **la carne e il pollame**
meat and poultry

⑨ **il pesce**
fish

⑩ **la gastronomia**
deli

⑪ **i surgelati**
frozen food

⑫ **i cibi pronti**
convenience food

⑬ **le bevande**
drinks

⑭ **i prodotti per la casa**
household products

⑮ **gli articoli da toeletta**
toiletries

⑯ **i prodotti per bambini**
baby products

⑰ **l'elettronica** *f*
electrical goods

⑱ **il cibo per animali**
pet food

48.4 L'EDICOLA / IL CHIOSCO · NEWSSTAND / KIOSK

① **il quotidiano**
newspaper

② **la rivista**
magazine

③ **il fumetto**
comic

④ **la cartolina**
postcard

⑤ **la cartina turistica**
tourist map

⑥ **i francobolli**
stamps

⑦ **la tessera per i trasporti**
travel card

⑧ **la carta SIM**
sim card

⑨ **la barretta**
snack bar

⑩ **le patatine**
crisps

⑪ **l'acqua** *f*
water

49.1 LA FARMACIA · PHARMACY

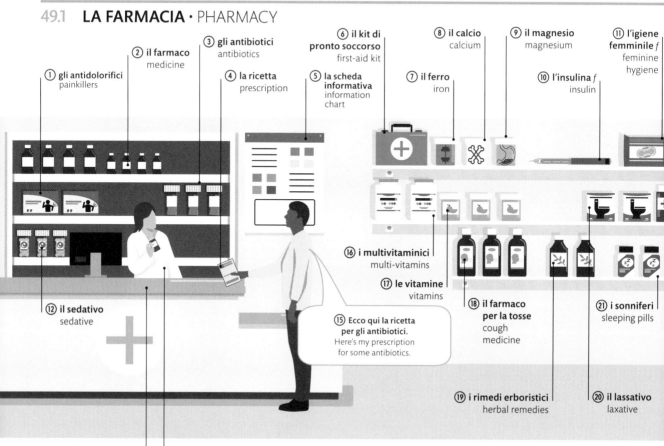

① gli antidolorifici
painkillers

② il farmaco
medicine

③ gli antibiotici
antibiotics

④ la ricetta
prescription

⑤ la scheda informativa
information chart

⑥ il kit di pronto soccorso
first-aid kit

⑦ il ferro
iron

⑧ il calcio
calcium

⑨ il magnesio
magnesium

⑩ l'insulina f
insulin

⑪ l'igiene femminile f
feminine hygiene

⑫ il sedativo
sedative

⑬ il dispensario
dispensary

⑭ il farmacista m
la farmacista f
pharmacist

⑮ Ecco qui la ricetta per gli antibiotici.
Here's my prescription for some antibiotics.

⑯ i multivitaminici
multi-vitamins

⑰ le vitamine
vitamins

⑱ il farmaco per la tosse
cough medicine

⑲ i rimedi erboristici
herbal remedies

⑳ il lassativo
laxative

㉑ i sonniferi
sleeping pills

㉒ gli effetti collaterali
side effects

㉓ il medicinale
medication

㉖ il dosaggio
dosage

㉔ le capsule
capsules

㉗ l'antinfiammatorio m
anti-inflammatory

㉕ le pastiglie / le compresse
pills / tablets

㉘ i farmaci da banco
over-the-counter drugs

㉙ la pastiglia per la gola
throat lozenge

㉛ la data di scadenza
expiry date

10/02/2028

㉚ le pillole per il mal di viaggio
travel-sickness pills

See also
19 Le malattie e le lesioni • Illness and injury **20** Andare dal medico • Visiting the doctor **21** L'ospedale • The hospital **46** Il centro commerciale • Shopping

㉝ **le ali**
wings

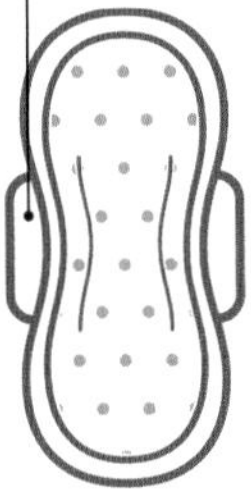

㉜ **l'assorbente** *m*
sanitary towel

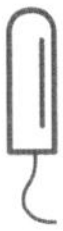

㉞ **l'assorbente interno** *m*
tampon

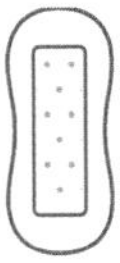

㉟ **il salvaslip**
panty liner

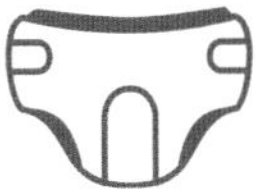

㊱ **i pannoloni per l'incontinenza**
incontinence pads

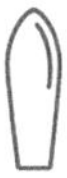

㊲ **la supposta**
suppository

㊳ **il deodorante**
deodorant

㊴ **i prodotti per la pelle**
skin care

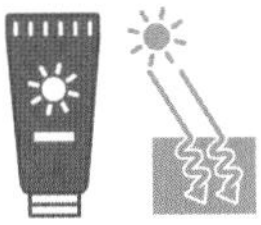

㊵ **la crema solare**
sun cream

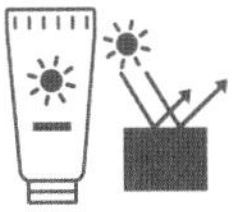

㊶ **la crema solare ad alta protezione**
sunblock

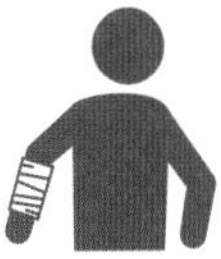

㊷ **la fasciatura**
bandage

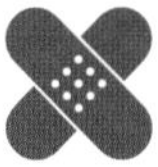

㊸ **il cerotto**
plaster

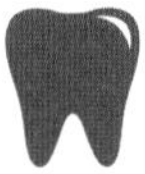

㊹ **i prodotti per l'igiene orale**
dental care

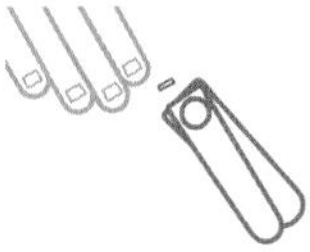

㊺ **il tagliaunghie**
nail clippers

㊻ **le salviette umidificate**
wet wipes

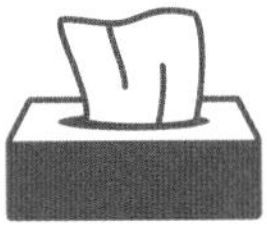

㊼ **il fazzoletto**
tissue

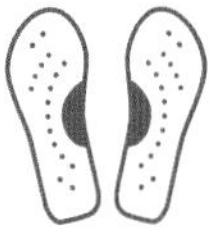

㊽ **le solette**
insoles

㊾ **gli occhiali da lettura**
reading glasses

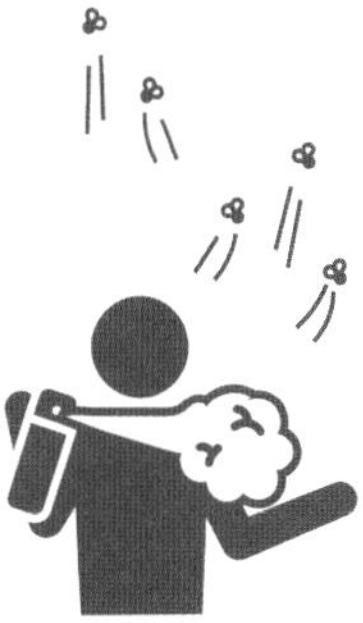

㊿ **il repellente per gli insetti**
insect repellent

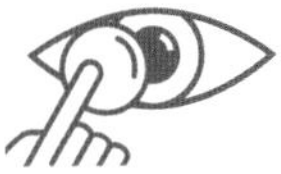

(51) **le lenti a contatto**
contact lens

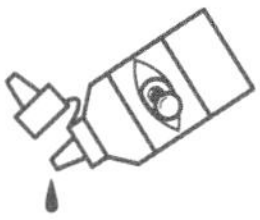

(52) **la soluzione per lenti a contatto**
lens solution

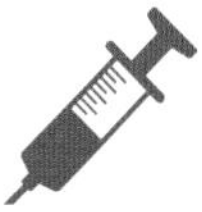

(53) **la siringa**
syringe

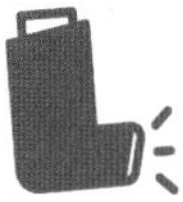

(54) **l'inalatore** *m*
inhaler

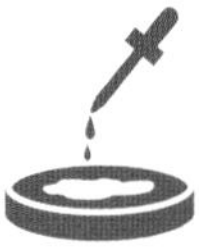

(55) **le gocce**
drops

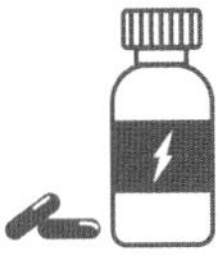

(56) **l'integratore** *m*
supplement

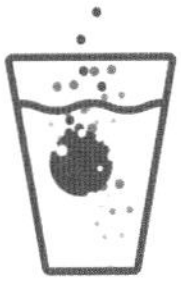

(57) **solubile**
soluble

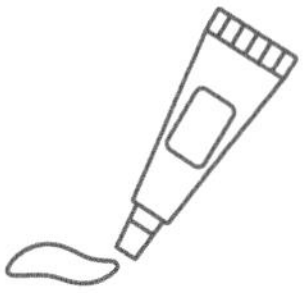

(58) **la pomata**
ointment

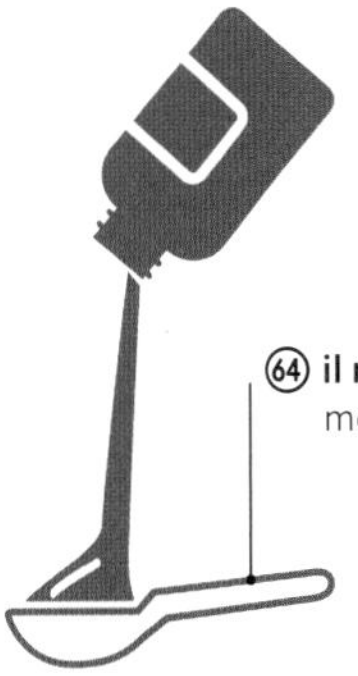

(64) **il misurino**
measuring spoon

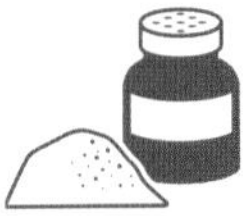

(59) **la polvere**
powder

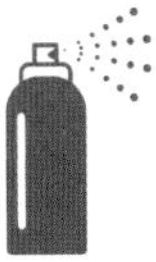

(60) **lo spray**
spray

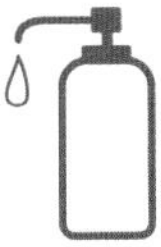

(61) **il gel**
gel

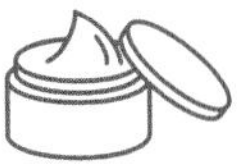

(62) **la crema**
cream

(63) **lo sciroppo**
syrup

50 I servizi di pronto intervento
Emergency services

50.1 IL PRONTO SOCCORSO · ACCIDENT AND EMERGENCY

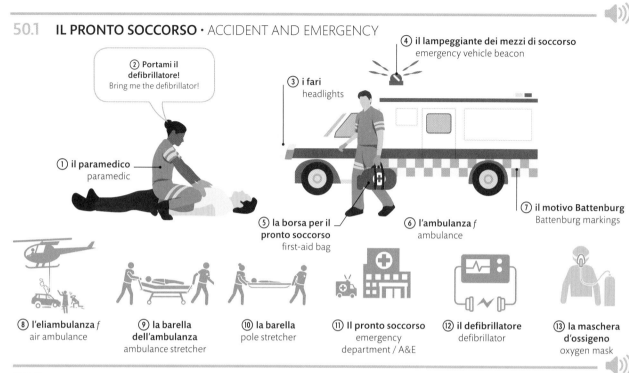

② **Portami il defibrillatore!**
Bring me the defibrillator!

④ **il lampeggiante dei mezzi di soccorso**
emergency vehicle beacon

③ **i fari**
headlights

① **il paramedico**
paramedic

⑤ **la borsa per il pronto soccorso**
first-aid bag

⑥ **l'ambulanza** f
ambulance

⑦ **il motivo Battenburg**
Battenburg markings

⑧ **l'eliambulanza** f
air ambulance

⑨ **la barella dell'ambulanza**
ambulance stretcher

⑩ **la barella**
pole stretcher

⑪ **Il pronto soccorso**
emergency department / A&E

⑫ **il defibrillatore**
defibrillator

⑬ **la maschera d'ossigeno**
oxygen mask

50.2 I VIGILI DEL FUOCO · FIRE BRIGADE

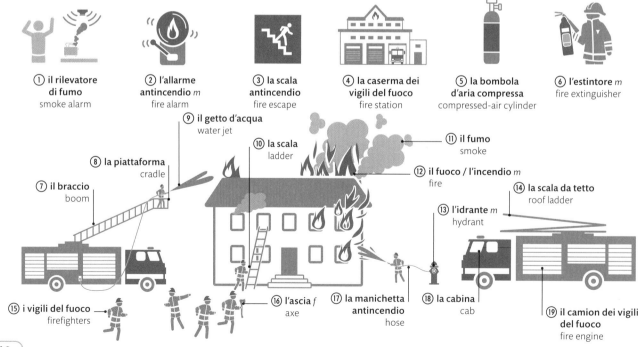

① **il rilevatore di fumo**
smoke alarm

② **l'allarme antincendio** m
fire alarm

③ **la scala antincendio**
fire escape

④ **la caserma dei vigili del fuoco**
fire station

⑤ **la bombola d'aria compressa**
compressed-air cylinder

⑥ **l'estintore** m
fire extinguisher

⑨ **il getto d'acqua**
water jet

⑩ **la scala**
ladder

⑪ **il fumo**
smoke

⑧ **la piattaforma**
cradle

⑫ **il fuoco / l'incendio** m
fire

⑦ **il braccio**
boom

⑭ **la scala da tetto**
roof ladder

⑬ **l'idrante** m
hydrant

⑮ **i vigili del fuoco**
firefighters

⑯ **l'ascia** f
axe

⑰ **la manichetta antincendio**
hose

⑱ **la cabina**
cab

⑲ **il camion dei vigili del fuoco**
fire engine

See also
19 Le malattie e le lesioni • Illness and injury
21 L'ospedale • The hospital **85** La legge • Law

50.3 **LA POLIZIA** · POLICE

① **il rilevatore di velocità**
radar speed gun

② **l'etilometro** *m*
breathalyzer

③ **la ricetrasmittente**
walkie-talkie

④ **il cane della polizia**
police dog

⑭ **il cappello da poliziotto**
police hat

⑮ **la divisa**
uniform

⑯ **il distintivo**
badge

⑰ **il cinturone**
duty belt

⑤ **la denuncia**
complaint

⑥ **il commissariato di polizia**
police station

⑦ **la cella**
police cell

⑧ **la sala interrogatori**
interrogation room

⑱ **il manganello**
truncheon

⑨ **l'investigatore** *m*
l'investigatrice *f*
detective

⑩ **l'ispettore** *m*
l'ispettrice *f*
inspector

⑪ **l'impronta digitale** *f*
fingerprint

⑫ **l'accusa** *f*
charge

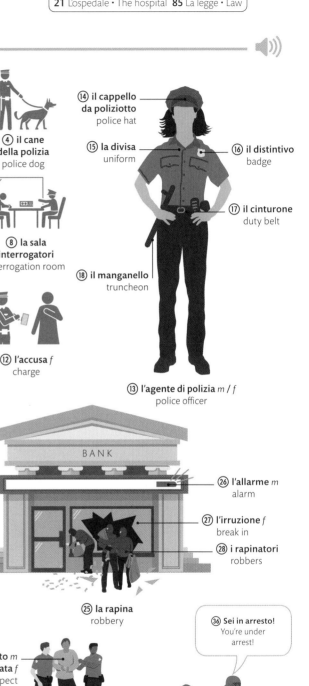

⑬ **l'agente di polizia** *m* / *f*
police officer

BANK

㉓ **le luci**
lights

㉑ **il casco**
helmet

㉒ **il megafono**
megaphone

㉖ **l'allarme** *m*
alarm

㉗ **l'irruzione** *f*
break in

㉘ **i rapinatori**
robbers

⑳ **l'agente di polizia motociclista** *m* / *f*
motorcycle police officer

⑲ **la moto della polizia**
police bike

㉔ **l'auto della polizia** *f*
police car

㉕ **la rapina**
robbery

㊱ **Sei in arresto!**
You're under arrest!

㉛ **la prova**
evidence

㉜ **la radio**
radio

㉞ **il sospettato** *m*
la sospettata *f*
suspect

㉚ **l'indagine** *f*
investigation

㉙ **la scena del crimine**
crime scene

㉝ **l'arresto** *m*
arrest

㉟ **le manette**
handcuffs

51.1 L'ENERGIA NUCLEARE E I COMBUSTIBILI FOSSILI
NUCLEAR ENERGY AND FOSSIL FUELS

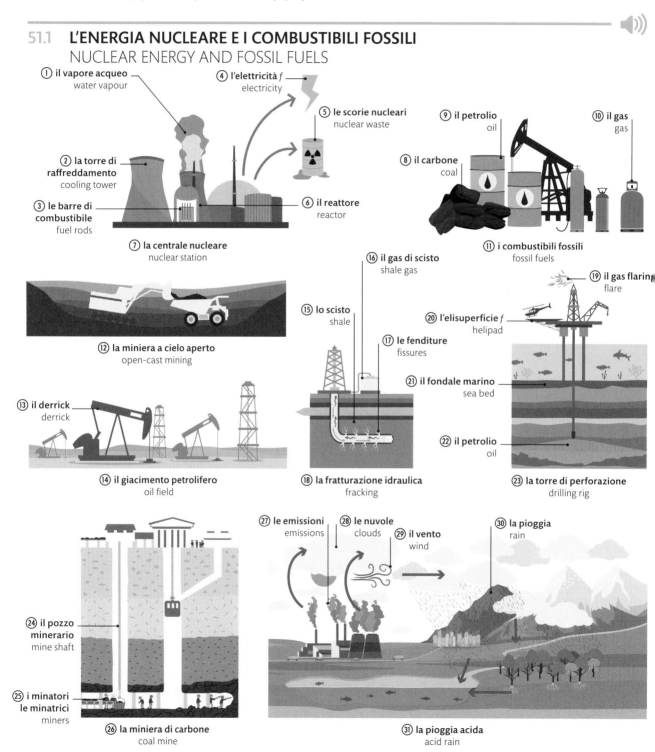

① il vapore acqueo
water vapour

④ l'elettricità f
electricity

⑤ le scorie nucleari
nuclear waste

⑨ il petrolio
oil

⑩ il gas
gas

② la torre di raffreddamento
cooling tower

⑧ il carbone
coal

③ le barre di combustibile
fuel rods

⑥ il reattore
reactor

⑦ la centrale nucleare
nuclear station

⑪ i combustibili fossili
fossil fuels

⑯ il gas di scisto
shale gas

⑲ il gas flaring
flare

⑮ lo scisto
shale

⑳ l'elisuperficie f
helipad

⑰ le fenditure
fissures

⑫ la miniera a cielo aperto
open-cast mining

㉑ il fondale marino
sea bed

⑬ il derrick
derrick

㉒ il petrolio
oil

⑭ il giacimento petrolifero
oil field

⑱ la fratturazione idraulica
fracking

㉓ la torre di perforazione
drilling rig

㉗ le emissioni
emissions

㉘ le nuvole
clouds

㉙ il vento
wind

㉚ la pioggia
rain

㉔ il pozzo minerario
mine shaft

㉕ i minatori
le minatrici
miners

㉖ la miniera di carbone
coal mine

㉛ la pioggia acida
acid rain

See also
33 Gli impianti elettrico e idraulico · Electrics and plumbing **42-43** In città · In town
145 Il pianeta Terra · Planet Earth **155** Il clima e l'ambiente · Climate and the environment

51.2 L'ENERGIA RINNOVABILE · RENEWABLE ENERGY

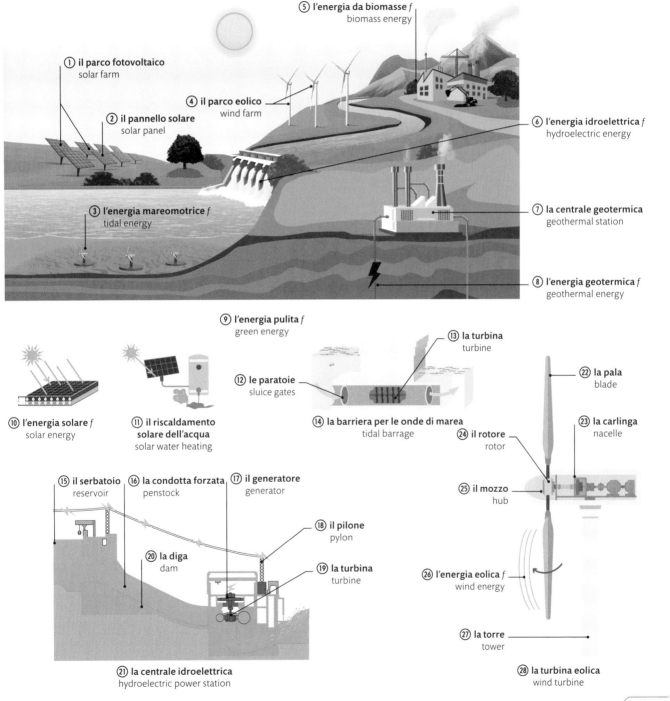

⑤ **l'energia da biomasse** *f*
biomass energy

① **il parco fotovoltaico**
solar farm

④ **il parco eolico**
wind farm

② **il pannello solare**
solar panel

⑥ **l'energia idroelettrica** *f*
hydroelectric energy

③ **l'energia mareomotrice** *f*
tidal energy

⑦ **la centrale geotermica**
geothermal station

⑧ **l'energia geotermica** *f*
geothermal energy

⑨ **l'energia pulita** *f*
green energy

⑬ **la turbina**
turbine

⑫ **le paratoie**
sluice gates

㉒ **la pala**
blade

⑩ **l'energia solare** *f*
solar energy

⑪ **il riscaldamento solare dell'acqua**
solar water heating

⑭ **la barriera per le onde di marea**
tidal barrage

㉓ **la carlinga**
nacelle

㉔ **il rotore**
rotor

⑮ **il serbatoio**
reservoir

⑯ **la condotta forzata**
penstock

⑰ **il generatore**
generator

㉕ **il mozzo**
hub

⑱ **il pilone**
pylon

⑳ **la diga**
dam

⑲ **la turbina**
turbine

㉖ **l'energia eolica** *f*
wind energy

㉗ **la torre**
tower

㉑ **la centrale idroelettrica**
hydroelectric power station

㉘ **la turbina eolica**
wind turbine

52.1 LE BEVANDE · DRINKS

① **il caffè**
coffee

② **il tè**
tea

③ **la cioccolata calda**
hot chocolate

④ **la tisana**
herbal tea

⑤ **il tè freddo**
iced tea

⑥ **la limonata**
lemonade

⑦ **il succo**
juice

⑧ **l'acqua minerale** f
mineral water

⑨ **l'acqua del rubinetto** f
tap water

⑩ **il frullato**
smoothie

⑪ **l'aranciata** f
orangeade

⑫ **la coca cola**
cola

⑬ **il frappè**
milkshake

⑭ **la bevanda energetica**
sports drink / energy drink

⑮ **il vino rosso**
red wine

⑯ **il vino bianco**
white wine

⑰ **il vino rosé**
rosé wine

⑱ **la birra**
beer

52.2 I CONTENITORI · CONTAINERS

① **la bottiglia**
bottle

② **il bicchiere**
glass

③ **il cartone**
carton

④ **il barattolo**
jar

⑤ **il sacchetto**
bag

⑥ **il pacchetto**
packet

⑦ **la scatola**
box

⑧ **la lattina**
tin

⑨ **il thermos**
flask

⑩ **la ciotola**
bowl

⑪ **il contenitore ermetico**
airtight container

⑫ **il barattolo in vetro**
Mason jar

See also
27 La cucina e le stoviglie • Kitchen and tableware **28** Gli utensili da cucina • Kitchenware **29** Cucinare • Cooking **52-72** Gli alimenti • Food

52.3 GLI AGGETTIVI · ADJECTIVES

① **dolce**
sweet

② **saporito** m / **saporita** f
savoury

③ **acido**
sour

④ **salato** m / **salata** f
salty

⑤ **amaro** m / **amara** f
bitter

⑥ **piccante**
spicy / hot

⑦ **fresco** m / **fresca** f
fresh

⑧ **andato a male** m
andata a male f
off

⑨ **forte**
strong

⑩ **con ghiaccio / freddo** m
con ghiaccio / fredda f
iced / chilled

⑪ **frizzante**
carbonated / sparkling

⑫ **naturale / non frizzante**
non-carbonated / still

⑬ **gustoso** m
gustasa f
rich

⑭ **succoso** m
succosa f
juicy

⑮ **croccante**
crunchy

⑯ **delizioso** m
deliziosa f
delicious

⑰ **disgustoso** m
disgustosa f
disgusting

⑱ **saporito** m
saporita f
tasty

④ **Alla salute!**
Cheers!

52.4 I VERBI PER MANGIARE E BERE
DRINKING AND EATING VERBS

① **mangiare**
to eat

② **masticare**
to chew

③ **assaggiare**
to taste

⑤ **cenare**
to dine

⑥ **piluccare**
to nibble

⑦ **addentare**
to bite

⑧ **inghiottire**
to swallow

⑨ **sorseggiare**
to sip

⑩ **bere**
to drink

⑪ **deglutire**
to gulp

53 La carne
Meta

53.1 IL MACELLAIO · THE BUTCHER

① biologico *m*
biologica *f*
organic

② allevato a terra *m*
allevata a terra *f*
free-range

③ la carne bianca
white meat

④ la carne rossa
red meat

⑤ la carne magra
lean meat

⑥ la carne macinata
mince

⑦ il salame
salami

⑧ il chorizo
chorizo

⑨ il prosciutto
ham

⑩ il fegato
liver

⑪ la cotoletta
chop

⑫ il gancio
da macellaio
meat hook

⑬ lo scamone
rump steak

⑭ il macellaio *m*
la macellaia *f*
butcher

⑮ il coniglio
rabbit

⑯ le salsicce
sausages

⑰ la selvaggina
game

⑱ la pancetta
streaky bacon

⑲ la lonza
back bacon

⑳ il controfiletto
sirloin steak

See also
29 Cucinare • Cooking **52** Bere e mangiare • Drinking and eating **54** Il pesce e i frutti di mare • Fish and seafood **69** Al ristorante • At the restaurant **72** Il pranzo e la cena • Lunch and dinner **165** Gli animali da fattoria • Farm animals

53.2   I TIPI DI CARNE · TYPES OF MEAT

① l'agnello *m*
lamb

② il maiale
pork

③ il manzo
beef

④ il vitello
veal

⑤ il cervo
venison

⑥ la capra
goat

⑦ il coniglio
rabbit

⑧ il cinghiale
wild boar

⑨ la carne cotta
cooked meat

⑩ la carne cruda
raw meat

⑪ i salumi
cured meat

⑫ la carne affumicata
smoked meat

53.3   IL POLLAME · POULTRY

④ l'anatra *f*
duck

⑦ Questo pollo è allevato a terra?
Is this chicken free-range?

⑧ Sì, è di provenienza locale.
Yes, it's locally sourced.

① il tacchino
turkey

② l'oca *f*
goose

③ il fagiano
pheasant

⑤ il pollo
chicken

⑥ la quaglia
quail

53.4   I TAGLI DI CARNE · CUTS OF MEAT

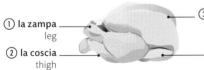

① la zampa
leg

② la coscia
thigh

③ il petto
breast

④ l'ala *f*
wing

⑤ la costoletta
rib

⑥ il filetto
fillet

⑦ i tagli
cuts

⑧ il pezzo di carne
joint

⑨ la fetta
slice

⑩ il cuore
heart

⑪ la lingua
tongue

⑫ il rene
kidney

⑬ le frattaglie
offal

54.1 IL PESCE · FISH

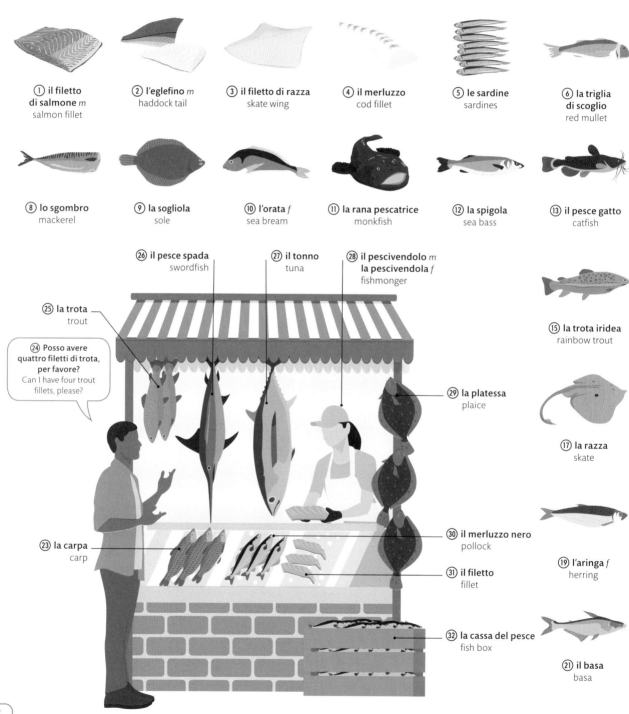

① il filetto di salmone m
salmon fillet

② l'eglefino m
haddock tail

③ il filetto di razza
skate wing

④ il merluzzo
cod fillet

⑤ le sardine
sardines

⑥ la triglia di scoglio
red mullet

⑧ lo sgombro
mackerel

⑨ la sogliola
sole

⑩ l'orata f
sea bream

⑪ la rana pescatrice
monkfish

⑫ la spigola
sea bass

⑬ il pesce gatto
catfish

㉖ il pesce spada
swordfish

㉗ il tonno
tuna

㉘ il pescivendolo m
la pescivendola f
fishmonger

㉕ la trota
trout

㉔ Posso avere quattro filetti di trota, per favore?
Can I have four trout fillets, please?

⑮ la trota iridea
rainbow trout

㉙ la platessa
plaice

⑰ la razza
skate

㉓ la carpa
carp

㉚ il merluzzo nero
pollock

㉛ il filetto
fillet

⑲ l'aringa f
herring

㉜ la cassa del pesce
fish box

㉑ il basa
basa

See also
29 Cucinare • Cooking **52** Bere e mangiare • Drinking and eating
55-56 La verdura • Vegetables **69** Al ristorante • At the restaurant
72 Il pranzo e la cena • Lunch and dinner **166** La vita negli oceani • Ocean life

54.2 I FRUTTI DI MARE · SEAFOOD

⑦ **il merlano**
whiting

⑭ **l'halibut** *m*
halibut

⑯ **il rombo**
turbot

⑱ **l'anguilla** *f*
eel

⑳ **il pesce persico**
perch

㉒ **il lucioperca**
pike perch

① **la vongola**
clam

② **il polpo**
octopus

③ **l'aragosta** *f*
lobster

④ **la capasanta**
scallop

⑤ **il gambero d'acqua dolce**
crayfish

⑥ **il gambero non sgusciato**
unpeeled prawn

⑦ **il gambero sgusciato**
peeled prawn

⑧ **il calamaro**
squid

⑬ **il cardio**
cockle

⑭ **il cannolicchio**
razor-shell

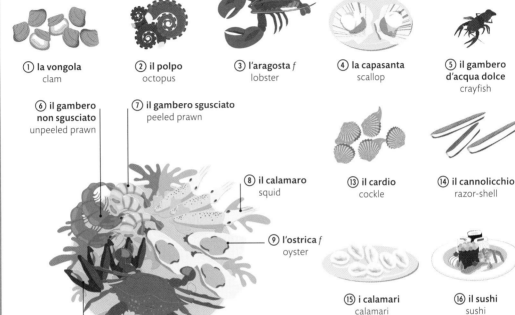

⑨ **l'ostrica** *f*
oyster

⑮ **i calamari**
calamari

⑯ **il sushi**
sushi

⑩ **la cozza**
mussel

⑪ **il piatto di frutti di mare**
seafood platter

⑫ **il granchio**
crab

54.3 LA PREPARAZIONE · PREPARATION

① **la squama**
scale

③ **la coda**
tail

② **fresco** *m* / **fresca** *f*
fresh

④ **surgelato** *m*
surgelata *f*
frozen

⑤ **affumicato** *m*
affumicata *f*
smoked

⑥ **salato** *m* / **salata** *f*
salted

⑦ **squamato** *m*
squamata *f*
descaled

⑧ **pulito** *m* / **pulita** *f*
cleaned

⑨ **spinato** *m*
spinata *f*
boned

⑩ **il filetto**
loin

119

55 La verdura
Vegetables

55.1 LA VERDURA · VEGETABLES

① le fave
broad beans

② i fagiolini
runner beans

③ i fagiolini
green beans /
French beans

④ i fagioli secchi
dried beans

⑤ il sedano
celery

⑧ il pisello
pod

⑨ il bacello
pea

⑦ i piselli
garden peas

⑩ la taccola
mangetout

⑪ l'okra *f*
okra

⑫ il bambù
bamboo

⑬ i germogli di soia
bean sprouts

⑲ i chicchi
kernel

⑮ la cicoria
chicory

⑯ il finocchio
fennel

⑰ i cuori di palma
palm hearts

**⑱ le mini pannocchie
di mais**
baby sweetcorn

⑳ il mais
corn / sweetcorn

㉓ l'indivia *f*
endive

㉔ il dente di leone
dandelion

㉕ la bietola
Swiss chard

㉖ il cavolo riccio
kale

㉗ l'acetosella *f*
sorrel

㉘ gli spinaci
spinach

㉛ il cavolo cinese
pak-choi

㉜ il cavolo rapa
kohlrabi

㊲ la cima
floret

㊳ la foglia
leaf

**㉝ i cavolini
di Bruxelles**
Brussels sprouts

**㉞ le verdure
primaverili**
spring greens

㊱ il gambo
stalk

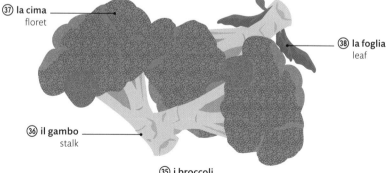

㉟ i broccoli
broccoli

See also
29 Cucinare · Cooking **52** Bere e mangiare · Drinking and eating **56** Le verdura (continua) · Vegetables continued **57** La frutta · Fruit **58** La frutta e la frutta a guscio · Fruit and nuts **59** Le erbe e le spezie Herbs and spices **69** Al ristorante · At the restaurant **72** Il pranzo e la cena · Lunch and dinner

⑥ **il cavolo**
collards

⑭ **la verza**
savoy cabbage

㉑ **il cavolo**
cabbage

㉒ **il cavolo rosso**
red cabbage

㉙ **il cavolo nero**
cavolo nero

㉚ **le foglie di barbabietola**
beet leaves

⑩ **i pesticidi**
pesticides

㊴ **le verdure biologiche**
organic vegetables

55.2 LA VERDURA DA INSALATA · SALAD VEGETABLES

① **il crescione**
cress

② **la rucola**
rocket

③ **l'insalata iceberg** f
iceberg lettuce

④ **la lattuga romana**
romaine lettuce

⑤ **la lattuga Little Gem**
little gem

⑥ **il cipollotto**
spring onion

⑦ **i pomodori ciliegini**
cherry tomatoes

⑧ **il cetriolo**
cucumber

⑨ **l'indivia riccia** f
frisée

⑩ **il crescione d'acqua**
watercress

⑪ **il radicchio**
radicchio

⑫ **la lattuga**
lettuce

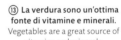

⑬ **La verdura sono un'ottima fonte di vitamine e minerali.**
Vegetables are a great source of vitamins and minerals.

⑭ **l'insalata** f
salad

56.1 DAL FRUTTIVENDOLO · AT THE GREENGROCERS

① **la rapa**
turnip

② **il ravanello**
radish

③ **la pastinaca**
parsnip

④ **il sedano rapa**
celeriac

⑤ **la manioca**
cassava

⑥ **la patata**
potato

⑦ **la castagna d'acqua**
water chestnut

⑧ **l'igname** *m*
yam

⑨ **la barbabietola**
beetroot

⑩ **la rapa svedese**
swede

⑪ **il topinambur**
Jerusalem
artichoke

⑫ **il taro**
taro root

⑬ **il rafano**
horseradish

⑭ **il frutto
dell'albero del pane**
breadfruit

⑮ **lo scalogno**
shallot

⑯ **il peperoncino**
chilli

⑰ **il pomodoro San
Marzano**
plum tomato

⑱ **la punta di
asparago**
asparagus tip

⑲ **il cuore di
carciofo**
artichoke heart

⑳ **il fungo pleurotus**
oyster mushroom

㉑ **il finferlo**
chanterelle

㉒ **il fungo shiitake**
shiitake
mushroom

㉓ **il tartufo**
truffle

㉔ **il fungo enoki**
enoki
mushroom

㉕ **lo zucchino**
marrow

㉖ **la zucca violina**
butternut
squash

㉗ **la zucca acorn**
button acorn squash

㉘ **la zucca**
pumpkin

㉙ **la zucca invernale**
buttercup squash

㉚ **la zucca bianca**
patty pan

㉛ **fresco** *m* / **fresca** *f*
fresh

㉜ **surgelato** *m*
surgelata *f*
frozen

㉝ **in scatola**
tinned

㉞ **crudo** *m* / **cruda** *f*
raw

㉟ **cotto** *m* / **cotta** *f*
cooked

㊱ **piccante**
hot / spicy

See also
29 Cucinare · Cooking **52** Bere e mangiare · Drinking and eating
57 La frutta · Fruit **58** La frutta e la frutta a guscio · Fruit and nuts
69 Al ristorante · At the restaurant **72** Il pranzo e la cena · Lunch and dinner

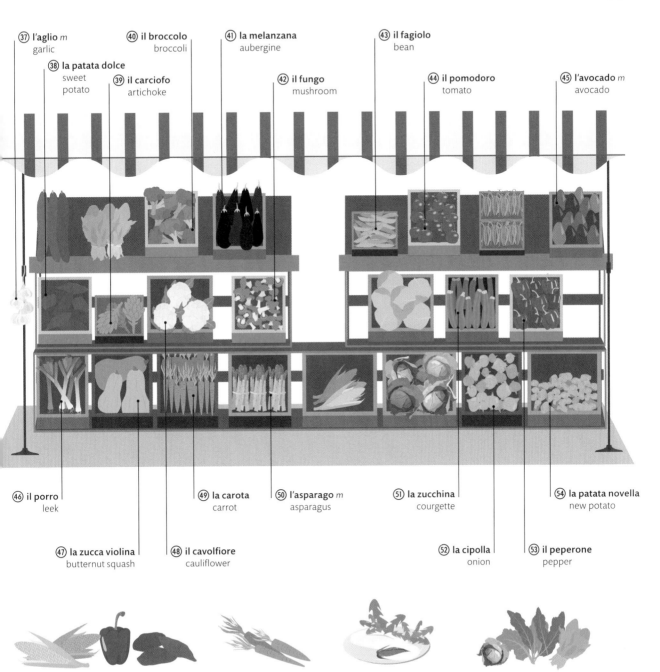

㊲ **l'aglio** m
garlic

㊳ **la patata dolce**
sweet potato

㊴ **il carciofo**
artichoke

㊵ **il broccolo**
broccoli

㊶ **la melanzana**
aubergine

㊷ **il fungo**
mushroom

㊸ **il fagiolo**
bean

㊹ **il pomodoro**
tomato

㊺ **l'avocado** m
avocado

㊻ **il porro**
leek

㊼ **la zucca violina**
butternut squash

㊽ **il cavolfiore**
cauliflower

㊾ **la carota**
carrot

㊿ **l'asparago** m
asparagus

51 **la zucchina**
courgette

52 **la cipolla**
onion

53 **il peperone**
pepper

54 **la patata novella**
new potato

55 **dolce**
sweet

56 **croccante**
crunchy

57 **amaro** m / **amara** f
bitter

58 **a foglia**
leafy

57 La frutta
Fruit

57.1 GLI AGRUMI · CITRUS FRUIT

① l'arancia f
orange

② le arance rosse
blood orange

③ il mapo
ugli fruit

④ il pomelo
pomelo

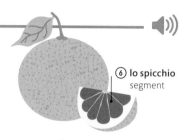
⑥ lo spicchio
segment

⑤ il pompelmo
grapefruit

⑦ la clementina
clementine

⑧ il mandarino
satsuma
satsuma

⑨ il mandarino
cinese
kumquat

⑩ il lime
lime

⑪ il limone
lemon

⑫ la scorza
zest

57.2 DESCRIVERE LA FRUTTA · DESCRIBING FRUIT

⑤ Queste pere sono mature e pronte da raccogliere.
These pears are ripe and ready to pick.

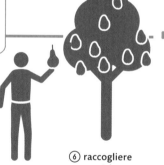
⑥ raccogliere
to pick

① il guscio della noce di cocco
coconut shell

② duro m
dura f
hard

③ morbido m
morbida f
soft

④ senza semi
seedless

⑦ la primavera
spring

⑧ l'estate f
summer

⑪ dolce
sweet

⑫ aspro m
aspra f
sour

⑬ maturo m / matura f
ripe

⑭ marcio m
marcia f
rotten

⑨ l'autunno m
autumn

⑩ la frutta stagionale
seasonal fruit

⑮ croccante
crisp

⑯ il torsolo
core

⑰ le fibre
fibre

⑱ la polpa
pulp

See also
29 Cucinare · Cooking **52** Bere e mangiare · Drinking and eating **55-56** La verdura · Vegetables
58 La frutta e la frutta a guscio · Fruit and nuts **65-66** Al bar · At the café **69** Al ristorante
At the restaurant **71** La colazione · Breakfast **72** Il pranzo e la cena · Lunch and dinner

57.3 LE BACCHE E LA FRUTTA CON IL NOCCIOLO · BERRIES AND STONE FRUIT

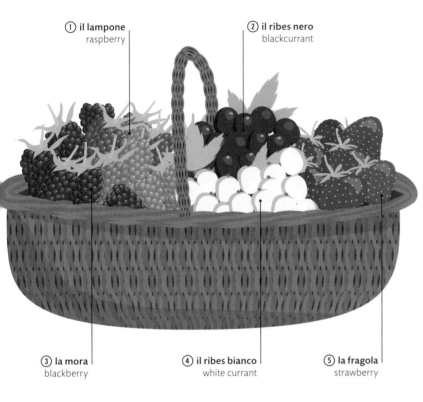

① **il lampone**
raspberry

② **il ribes nero**
blackcurrant

③ **la mora**
blackberry

④ **il ribes bianco**
white currant

⑤ **la fragola**
strawberry

⑥ **il cesto di frutta** *f*
basket of fruit

⑦ **il mirtillo rosso**
cranberry

⑧ **il mirtillo**
blueberry

⑨ **il loganberry**
loganberry

⑩ **l'alchechengi** *f*
cape gooseberry

⑪ **la bacca di goji**
goji berry

⑫ **l'uva spina** *f*
gooseberry

⑬ **il ribes rosso**
redcurrant

⑭ **il mirtillo**
bilberry

⑮ **la bacca
di sambuco**
elderberry

⑯ **l'uva** *f*
grapes

⑰ **la mora di gelso**
mulberry

⑱ **la pesca**
peach

⑲ **la pesca nettarina**
nectarine

⑳ **l'albicocca** *f*
apricot

㉑ **il mango**
mango

㉒ **la prugna**
plum

㉓ **la ciliegia**
cherry

㉔ **il dattero**
date

㉕ **il litchi**
lychee

58.1 I MELONI · MELONS

① l'anguria f
watermelon

② il cantalupo
cantaloupe

③ il melone verde
honeydew melon

④ il melone
d'inverno
Canary melon

⑤ il melone
charentais
charentais

⑥ il melone galia
galia

58.2 GLI ALTRI FRUTTI · OTHER FRUIT

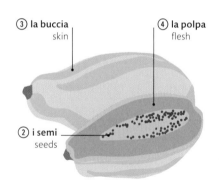

③ la buccia
skin

④ la polpa
flesh

② i semi
seeds

① la papaia
papaya

⑤ la mela cotogna
quince

⑥ il frutto
della passione
passion fruit

⑦ la guava
guava

⑧ la carambola
starfruit

⑨ il caco
persimmon

⑩ la feijoa
feijoa

⑪ l'ananas m
pineapple

⑫ il fico d'India
prickly pear

⑬ il tamarillo
tamarillo

⑭ il giaca
jackfruit

⑮ il mangostano
mangosteen

⑯ il melograno
pomegranate

⑰ la banana
banana

⑱ il kiwi
kiwi fruit

⑲ la mela
apple

⑳ le mele selvatiche
crab apples

㉑ la pera
pear

㉒ il rabarbaro
rhubarb

See also
29 Cucinare · Cooking **52** Bere e mangiare · Drinking and eating **55-56** La verdura
Vegetables **57** La frutta · Fruit **65-66** Al bar · At the café **69** Al ristorante · At the
restaurant **71** La colazione · Breakfast **72** Il pranzo e la cena · Lunch and dinner

58.3 LA FRUTTA A GUSCIO E LA FRUTTA SECCA · NUTS AND DRIED FRUIT

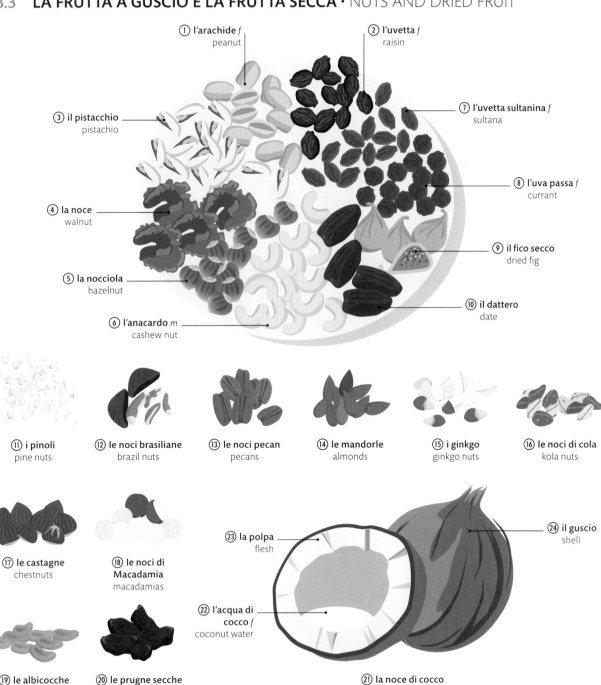

① l'arachide *f*
peanut

② l'uvetta *f*
raisin

③ il pistacchio
pistachio

⑦ l'uvetta sultanina *f*
sultana

④ la noce
walnut

⑧ l'uva passa *f*
currant

⑤ la nocciola
hazelnut

⑨ il fico secco
dried fig

⑥ l'anacardo *m*
cashew nut

⑩ il dattero
date

⑪ i pinoli
pine nuts

⑫ le noci brasiliane
brazil nuts

⑬ le noci pecan
pecans

⑭ le mandorle
almonds

⑮ i ginkgo
ginkgo nuts

⑯ le noci di cola
kola nuts

⑰ le castagne
chestnuts

⑱ le noci di
Macadamia
macadamias

㉓ la polpa
flesh

㉔ il guscio
shell

㉒ l'acqua di
cocco *f*
coconut water

⑲ le albicocche
secche
dried apricots

⑳ le prugne secche
prunes

㉑ la noce di cocco
coconut

59 Le erbe e le spezie
Herbs and spices

59.1 LE SPEZIE · SPICES

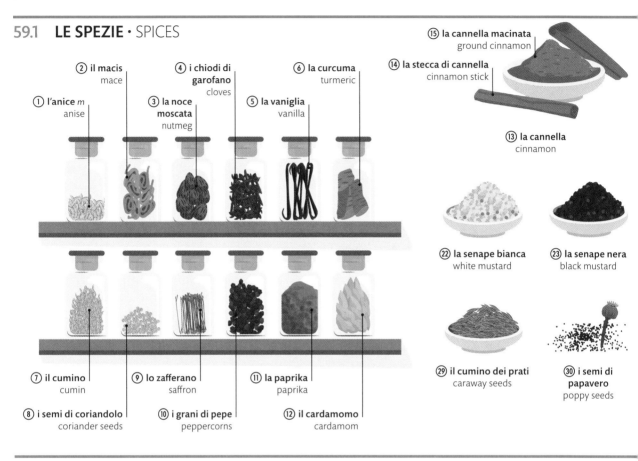

⑮ **la cannella macinata**
ground cinnamon

⑭ **la stecca di cannella**
cinnamon stick

② **il macis**
mace

④ **i chiodi di garofano**
cloves

⑥ **la curcuma**
turmeric

① **l'anice** *m*
anise

③ **la noce moscata**
nutmeg

⑤ **la vaniglia**
vanilla

⑬ **la cannella**
cinnamon

⑦ **il cumino**
cumin

⑨ **lo zafferano**
saffron

⑪ **la paprika**
paprika

⑧ **i semi di coriandolo**
coriander seeds

⑩ **i grani di pepe**
peppercorns

⑫ **il cardamomo**
cardamom

㉒ **la senape bianca**
white mustard

㉓ **la senape nera**
black mustard

㉙ **il cumino dei prati**
caraway seeds

㉚ **i semi di papavero**
poppy seeds

59.2 LE ERBE · HERBS

① **il finocchio**
fennel

② **la foglia d'alloro**
bay leaf

③ **il prezzemolo**
parsley

④ **l'erba cipollina** *f*
chives

⑤ **la menta**
mint

⑥ **il coriandolo**
coriander

⑬ **il timo**
thyme

⑭ **la salvia**
sage

⑮ **il dragoncello**
tarragon

⑯ **la maggiorana**
marjoram

⑰ **il basilico**
basil

⑱ **l'origano** *m*
oregano

See also
29 Cucinare · Cooking **52** Bere e mangiare · Drinking and eating **53** La carne Meat **55-56** La verdura · Vegetables **60** Nella dispensa · In the pantry

⑯ **l'anice stellato** *m*
star anise

⑰ **lo scotano**
sumac

⑱ **le cinque spezie**
five spice

⑲ **il ras el hanout**
ras el hanout

⑳ **il pimento**
allspice

㉑ **il curry**
curry powder

㉔ **lo zenzero**
ginger

㉕ **il peperoncino di Cayenna**
cayenne pepper

㉖ **il jalapeño**
jalapeños

㉗ **il peperoncino Thai**
bird's eye chillies

㉘ **il peperoncino in polvere**
ground chilli

㉝ **i peperoncini freschi**
fresh chillies

㉞ **il peperoncino a scaglie**
chilli flakes

㉛ **i semi di finocchio**
fennel seeds

㉜ **i semi di Nigella**
nigella seeds

⑦ **l'issopo** *m*
hyssop

⑧ **l'aneto** *m*
dill

⑨ **il rosmarino**
rosemary

⑩ **il cerfoglio**
chervil

⑪ **il levistico**
lovage

⑫ **l'acetosella**
sorrel

⑲ **la citronella**
lemongrass

⑳ **la melissa**
lemon balm

㉑ **la borragine**
borage

㉒ **le foglie di fieno greco**
fenugreek leaves

㉓ **il mazzetto aromatico** *f*
bouquet garni

60 Nella dispensa
In the pantry

60.1 GLI OLI IN BOTTIGLIA · BOTTLED OILS

① l'olio *m*
oil

② l'olio di palma *m*
palm oil

③ l'olio di girasole *m*
sunflower oil

④ l'olio di colza *m*
canola /
rapeseed oil

⑤ l'olio di mais *m*
corn oil

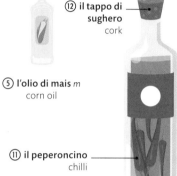

⑫ il tappo di sughero
cork

⑪ il peperoncino
chilli

⑥ l'olio di soia *m*
soybean oil

⑦ l'olio di arachide *m*
groundnut oil

⑧ l'olio di nocciola *m*
hazelnut oil

⑨ l'olio di cocco *m*
coconut oil

⑩ l'olio aromatizzato
flavoured oil

⑬ l'olio di sesamo *m*
sesame seed oil

⑭ l'olio di mandorle *m*
almond oil

⑮ l'olio di noci *m*
walnut oil

⑯ l'olio di vinaccioli *m*
grapeseed oil

⑰ l'olio di oliva *m*
olive oil

⑱ extra vergine
extra virgin

60.2 LE CREME SPALMABILI DOLCI · SWEET SPREADS

⑦ il favo
honeycomb

⑧ lo spargimie
honey dippe

④ il vasetto
jar

① la crema
al limone
lemon curd

② la confettura di
lamponi
raspberry jam

③ la confettura di
fragole
strawberry jam

⑤ il miele
cristallizzato
set honey

⑥ il miele
honey

⑭ la frutta
conservata
preserved fruit

⑨ la marmellata
di arance
marmalade

⑩ lo sciroppo
d'acero
maple syrup

⑪ il burro
di arachidi
peanut butter

⑫ la crema spalmabile
al cioccolato
chocolate spread

⑬ il barattolo
preserving jar

See also
27 La cucina e le stoviglie · Kitchen and tableware **29** Cucinare · Cooking
52 Bere e mangiare · Drinking and eating **53** La carne · Meat **55-56** La verdura
Vegetables **65-66** Al bar · At the café **69** Al ristorante · At the restaurant

60.3 **LE SALSE E I CONDIMENTI** · SAUCES AND CONDIMENTS

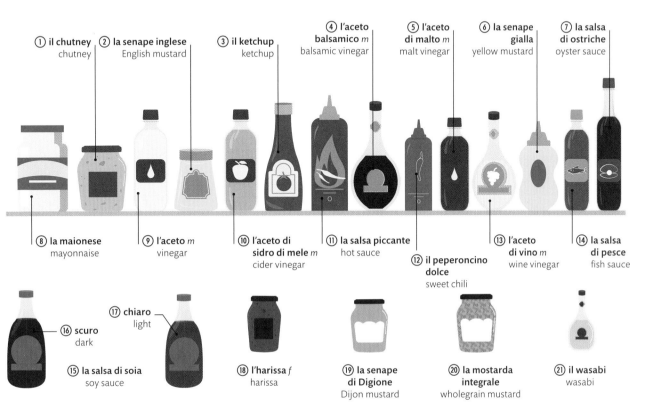

① **il chutney**
chutney

② **la senape inglese**
English mustard

③ **il ketchup**
ketchup

④ **l'aceto balsamico** *m*
balsamic vinegar

⑤ **l'aceto di malto** *m*
malt vinegar

⑥ **la senape gialla**
yellow mustard

⑦ **la salsa di ostriche**
oyster sauce

⑧ **la maionese**
mayonnaise

⑨ **l'aceto** *m*
vinegar

⑩ **l'aceto di sidro di mele** *m*
cider vinegar

⑪ **la salsa piccante**
hot sauce

⑫ **il peperoncino dolce**
sweet chili

⑬ **l'aceto di vino** *m*
wine vinegar

⑭ **la salsa di pesce**
fish sauce

⑯ **scuro**
dark

⑰ **chiaro**
light

⑮ **la salsa di soia**
soy sauce

⑱ **l'harissa** *f*
harissa

⑲ **la senape di Digione**
Dijon mustard

⑳ **la mostarda integrale**
wholegrain mustard

㉑ **il wasabi**
wasabi

60.4 **I SOTTACETI** · PICKLES

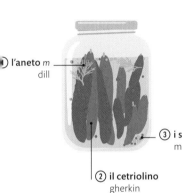

① **l'aneto** *m*
dill

② **il cetriolino**
gherkin

③ **i semi di senape**
mustard seeds

④ **i crauti**
sauerkraut

⑤ **il kimchi**
kimchi

⑥ **il lime sott'aceto**
lime pickle

⑦ **le cipolline sott'aceto**
pickled onions

⑧ **le barbabietole sott'aceto**
beetroot

⑨ **il sottaceto per sandwich**
sandwich pickle

⑩ **la giardiniera**
piccalilli

⑪ **i cetriolini sott'aceto**
cornichons

131

61.1 IL FORMAGGIO · CHEESE

① il formaggio a pasta dura
hard cheese

② il formaggio a pasta semidura
semi-hard cheese

③ il formaggio a pasta semimolle
semi-soft cheese

④ il formaggio a pasta molle
soft cheese

⑤ il pecorino
sheep's milk cheese

⑥ il formaggio di capra
goat's cheese

⑦ il formaggio erborinato
blue cheese

⑧ la crosta
rind

⑨ il formaggio grattugiato
grated cheese

⑩ il formaggio fresco
fresh cheese

⑪ i fiocchi di latte
cottage cheese

⑫ il formaggio spalmabile
cream cheese

61.2 LE UOVA · EGGS

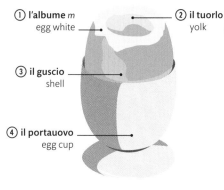

① l'albume m
egg white

② il tuorlo
yolk

③ il guscio
shell

④ il portauovo
egg cup

⑤ l'uovo sodo m
boiled egg

⑥ l'uovo al tegamino m
fried egg

⑦ le uova strapazzate
scrambled eggs

⑧ l'uovo in camicia m
poached egg

⑨ l'omelette f
omelette

⑩ l'uovo d'oca m
goose egg

⑪ l'uovo d'anatra m
duck egg

⑫ l'uovo di gallina m
hen's egg

⑬ l'uovo di quaglia m
quail egg

61.3 IL LATTE · MILK

① pastorizzato
pasteurized

② non pastorizzato
unpasteurized

③ senza lattosio
lactose free

④ omogeneizzato
homogenized

⑤ senza grassi
fat free

⑥ il latte in polvere
powdered milk

See also
29 Cucinare • Cooking **52** Bere e mangiare • Drinking and eating **65-66** Al bar • At the café **69** Al ristorante • At the restaurant **71** La colazione • Breakfast

61.4 I DERIVATI DEL LATTE · MILK PRODUCTS

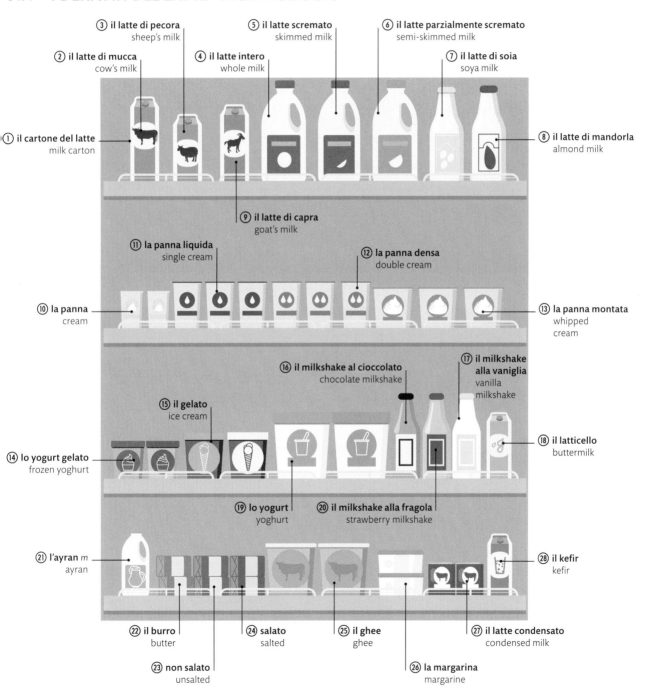

③ **il latte di pecora**
sheep's milk

⑤ **il latte scremato**
skimmed milk

⑥ **il latte parzialmente scremato**
semi-skimmed milk

② **il latte di mucca**
cow's milk

④ **il latte intero**
whole milk

⑦ **il latte di soia**
soya milk

① **il cartone del latte**
milk carton

⑧ **il latte di mandorla**
almond milk

⑨ **il latte di capra**
goat's milk

⑪ **la panna liquida**
single cream

⑫ **la panna densa**
double cream

⑩ **la panna**
cream

⑬ **la panna montata**
whipped cream

⑯ **il milkshake al cioccolato**
chocolate milkshake

⑰ **il milkshake alla vaniglia**
vanilla milkshake

⑮ **il gelato**
ice cream

⑱ **il latticello**
buttermilk

⑭ **lo yogurt gelato**
frozen yoghurt

⑲ **lo yogurt**
yoghurt

⑳ **il milkshake alla fragola**
strawberry milkshake

㉑ **l'ayran** *m*
ayran

㉘ **il kefir**
kefir

㉒ **il burro**
butter

㉔ **salato**
salted

㉕ **il ghee**
ghee

㉗ **il latte condensato**
condensed milk

㉓ **non salato**
unsalted

㉖ **la margarina**
margarine

133

62.1 I TIPI DI PANE E DI FARINA · BREADS AND FLOURS

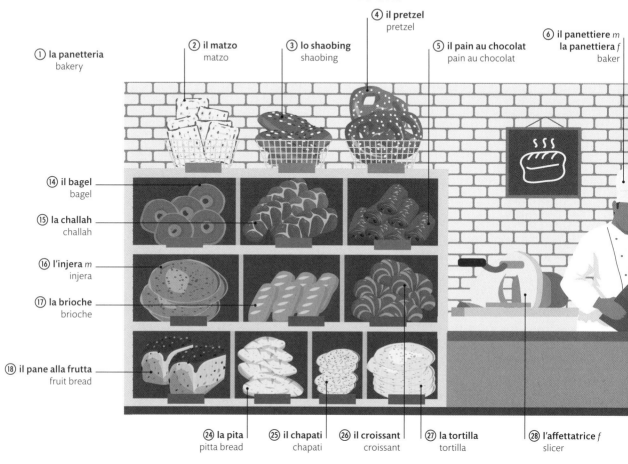

① la panetteria
bakery

② il matzo
matzo

③ lo shaobing
shaobing

④ il pretzel
pretzel

⑤ il pain au chocolat
pain au chocolat

⑥ il panettiere *m*
la panettiera *f*
baker

⑭ il bagel
bagel

⑮ la challah
challah

⑯ l'injera *m*
injera

⑰ la brioche
brioche

⑱ il pane alla frutta
fruit bread

㉔ la pita
pitta bread

㉕ il chapati
chapati

㉖ il croissant
croissant

㉗ la tortilla
tortilla

㉘ l'affettatrice *f*
slicer

㊹ le bolle di CO_2
CO_2 bubbles

㉝ la farina di grano duro
strong flour

㉞ la farina
plain flour

㉟ la farina autolievitante
self-raising flour

㊱ la farina marrone
brown flour

㊲ la farina integrale
wholemeal flour

㊳ la farina bianca
white flour

㊴ la farina senza
glutine
gluten-free flour

㊵ la farina di
grano saraceno
buckwheat flour

㊶ il lievito
disidratato
dried yeast

㊷ il lievito fresco
fresh yeast

㊸ il lievito madre
sourdough starter

See also
29 Cucinare • Cooking **52** Bere e mangiare • Drinking and eating **63** La panetteria (continua) • The bakery continued **65-66** Al bar • At the café **69** Al ristorante • At the restaurant **71** La colazione • Breakfast

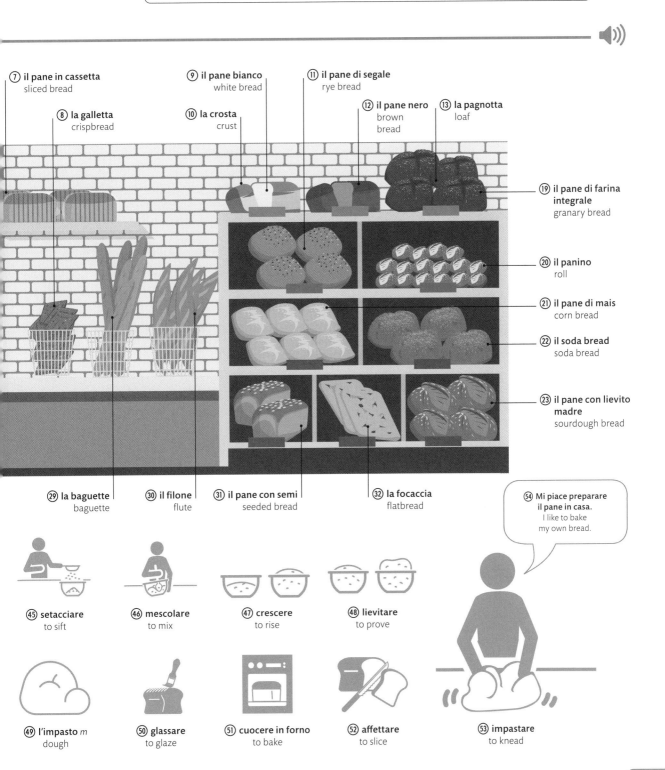

⑦ **il pane in cassetta**
sliced bread

⑧ **la galletta**
crispbread

⑨ **il pane bianco**
white bread

⑩ **la crosta**
crust

⑪ **il pane di segale**
rye bread

⑫ **il pane nero**
brown bread

⑬ **la pagnotta**
loaf

⑲ **il pane di farina integrale**
granary bread

⑳ **il panino**
roll

㉑ **il pane di mais**
corn bread

㉒ **il soda bread**
soda bread

㉓ **il pane con lievito madre**
sourdough bread

㉙ **la baguette**
baguette

㉚ **il filone**
flute

㉛ **il pane con semi**
seeded bread

㉜ **la focaccia**
flatbread

㊺ **setacciare**
to sift

㊻ **mescolare**
to mix

㊼ **crescere**
to rise

㊽ **lievitare**
to prove

㊾ **l'impasto** *m*
dough

㊿ **glassare**
to glaze

(51) **cuocere in forno**
to bake

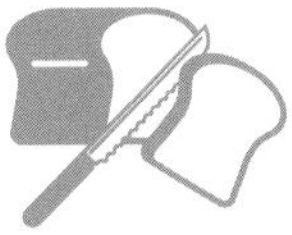

(52) **affettare**
to slice

(54) **Mi piace preparare il pane in casa.**
I like to bake my own bread.

(53) **impastare**
to knead

63 La panetteria (continua)
The bakery continued

63.1 LE TORTE E I DESSERT · CAKES AND DESSERTS

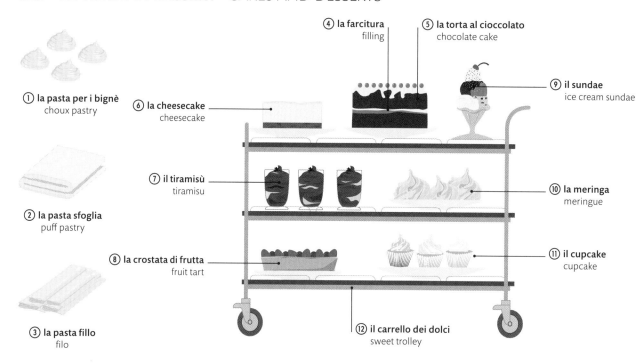

① **la pasta per i bignè**
choux pastry

② **la pasta sfoglia**
puff pastry

③ **la pasta fillo**
filo

④ **la farcitura**
filling

⑤ **la torta al cioccolato**
chocolate cake

⑥ **la cheesecake**
cheesecake

⑦ **il tiramisù**
tiramisu

⑧ **la crostata di frutta**
fruit tart

⑨ **il sundae**
ice cream sundae

⑩ **la meringa**
meringue

⑪ **il cupcake**
cupcake

⑫ **il carrello dei dolci**
sweet trolley

⑬ **la crema pasticcera**
crème pâtissière

⑭ **il mochi**
mochi

⑮ **la ciambella**
doughnut

⑯ **la ciambella alla marmellata**
jam doughnut

⑰ **la ciambella al cioccolato**
chocolate doughnut

⑱ **il muffin**
muffin

⑲ **il baklava**
baklava

⑳ **la pavlova**
pavlova

㉑ **la torta a strati**
layer cake

㉒ **il pan di Spagna**
sponge cake

㉓ **la torta alla frutta**
fruitcake

㉔ **la torta**
gateau

㉖ **la custard**
custard

㉕ **la fetta di custard**
custard slice

㉗ **l'éclair** m
éclair

㉘ **il panino glassato**
iced bun

㉙ **la pasta dolce**
pastry

㉚ **il budino di riso**
rice pudding

See also
29 Cucinare • Cooking **52** Bere e mangiare • Drinking and eating
67 I dolciumi • Sweets **71** La colazione • Breakfast

63.2 I DOLCETTI E I BISCOTTI · COOKIES AND BISCUITS

① **il biscotto con gocce di cioccolato**
chocolate chip cookie

② **il biscotto fiorentino**
Florentine

③ **il frollino**
shortbread

④ **il macaron**
macaron

⑤ **l'omino di pan di zenzero** m
gingerbread man

⑥ **i biscotti della fortuna**
fortune cookies

63.3 LE TORTE PER LE RICORRENZE · CELEBRATION CAKES

① **Vuoi un pezzo di torta?**
Would you like a piece of cake?

② **Sì, sembra davvero deliziosa.**
Yes, it looks absolutely delicious.

⑥ **il centrotorta**
cake topper

③ **lo strato superiore**
top tier

⑦ **il marzapane**
marzipan

④ **la decorazione**
decoration

⑤ **la glassa**
icing

⑧ **il nastro**
ribbon

⑨ **la torta nuziale**
wedding cake

⑩ **glassare**
to glaze

⑪ **cuocere in forno**
to bake

⑫ **decorare**
to decorate

⑮ **spegnere**
to blow out

⑭ **le candeline**
birthday candles

⑬ **la torta di compleanno**
birthday cake

137

64 La gastronomia
The delicatessen

64.1 LA GASTRONOMIA · DELICATESSEN

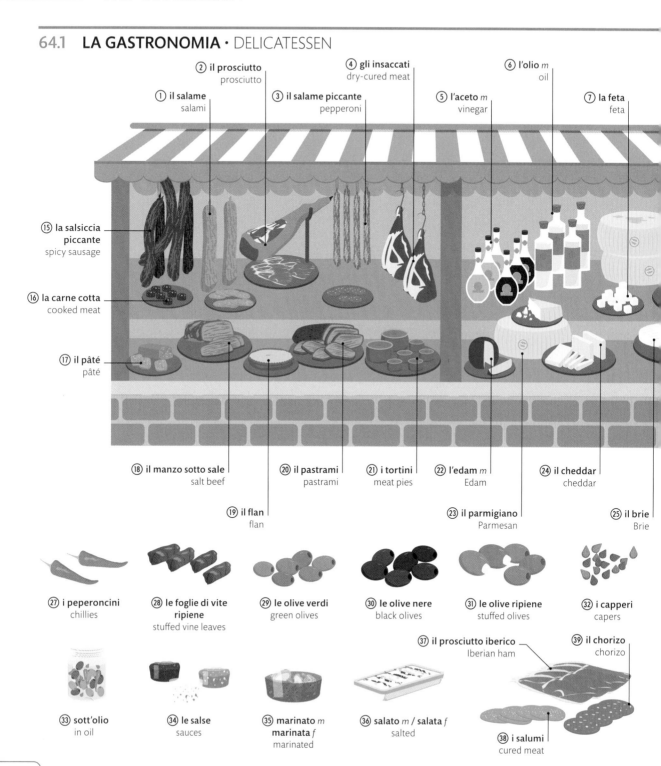

② il prosciutto
prosciutto

④ gli insaccati
dry-cured meat

⑥ l'olio *m*
oil

① il salame
salami

③ il salame piccante
pepperoni

⑤ l'aceto *m*
vinegar

⑦ la feta
feta

⑮ la salsiccia
piccante
spicy sausage

⑯ la carne cotta
cooked meat

⑰ il pâté
pâté

⑱ il manzo sotto sale
salt beef

⑳ il pastrami
pastrami

㉑ i tortini
meat pies

㉒ l'edam *m*
Edam

㉔ il cheddar
cheddar

⑲ il flan
flan

㉓ il parmigiano
Parmesan

㉕ il brie
Brie

㉗ i peperoncini
chillies

㉘ le foglie di vite
ripiene
stuffed vine leaves

㉙ le olive verdi
green olives

㉚ le olive nere
black olives

㉛ le olive ripiene
stuffed olives

㉜ i capperi
capers

㉝ sott'olio
in oil

㉞ le salse
sauces

㉟ marinato *m*
marinata *f*
marinated

㊱ salato *m* / salata *f*
salted

㊲ il prosciutto iberico
Iberian ham

㊳ i salumi
cured meat

㊴ il chorizo
chorizo

See also
29 Cucinare · Cooking **52** Bere e mangiare · Drinking and eating **53** La carne · Meat **60** Nella dispensa · In the pantry **61** I prodotti caseari · Dairy produce **65-66** Al bar · At the café **69** Al ristorante · At the restaurant **71** La colazione · Breakfast **72** Il pranzo e la cena · Lunch and dinner

⑧ **la crosta**
rind

⑨ **Provate questi diversi tipi di formaggio!**
Try these different types of cheese!

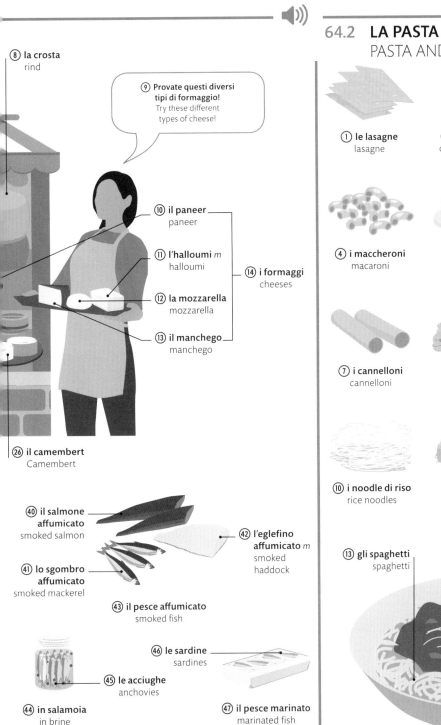

⑩ **il paneer**
paneer

⑪ **l'halloumi** *m*
halloumi

⑫ **la mozzarella**
mozzarella

⑬ **il manchego**
manchego

⑭ **i formaggi**
cheeses

㉖ **il camembert**
Camembert

㊵ **il salmone affumicato**
smoked salmon

㊶ **lo sgombro affumicato**
smoked mackerel

㊷ **l'eglefino affumicato** *m*
smoked haddock

㊸ **il pesce affumicato**
smoked fish

㊻ **le sardine**
sardines

㊺ **le acciughe**
anchovies

㊹ **in salamoia**
in brine

㊼ **il pesce marinato**
marinated fish

64.2 **LA PASTA E I NOODLE**
PASTA AND NOODLES

① **le lasagne**
lasagne

② **le conchiglie**
conchiglie / shells

③ **i fusilli**
fusilli

④ **i maccheroni**
macaroni

⑤ **gli gnocchi**
gnocchi

⑥ **le penne**
penne

⑦ **i cannelloni**
cannelloni

⑧ **i tortellini**
tortellini

⑨ **i noodle**
noodles

⑩ **i noodle di riso**
rice noodles

⑪ **il ramen**
ramen

⑫ **gli udon**
udon

⑬ **gli spaghetti**
spaghetti

⑭ **il ragù alla bolognese**
Bolognese sauce

65 Al bar
At the café

65.1 IL BAR · CAFÉ

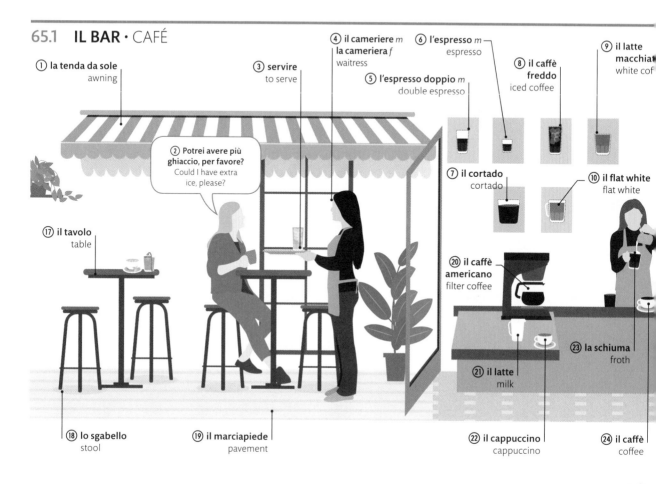

① la tenda da sole
awning

② Potrei avere più ghiaccio, per favore?
Could I have extra ice, please?

③ servire
to serve

④ il cameriere m
la cameriera f
waitress

⑤ l'espresso doppio m
double espresso

⑥ l'espresso m
espresso

⑦ il cortado
cortado

⑧ il caffè freddo
iced coffee

⑨ il latte macchia
white cof

⑩ il flat white
flat white

⑰ il tavolo
table

⑳ il caffè americano
filter coffee

㉑ il latte
milk

㉓ la schiuma
froth

㉔ il caffè
coffee

⑱ lo sgabello
stool

⑲ il marciapiede
pavement

㉒ il cappuccino
cappuccino

65.2 I SUCCHI E I MILKSHAKE · JUICES AND MILKSHAKES

① il frullatore
blender

② l'acqua di cocco f
coconut water

③ la spremuta di arancia
orange juice with pulp

④ il succo d'arancia
smooth orange juice

⑤ il succo di mela
apple juice

⑥ il succo d'ananas
pineapple juice

⑦ il succo di pomodoro
tomato juice

⑧ il succo di mango
mango juice

⑨ il succo di mirtillo rosso
cranberry juice

⑩ il frullato di fragole
strawberry smoothie

⑪ il milkshake al cioccolato
chocolate milkshake

⑫ il milkshake alla fragola
strawberry milkshake

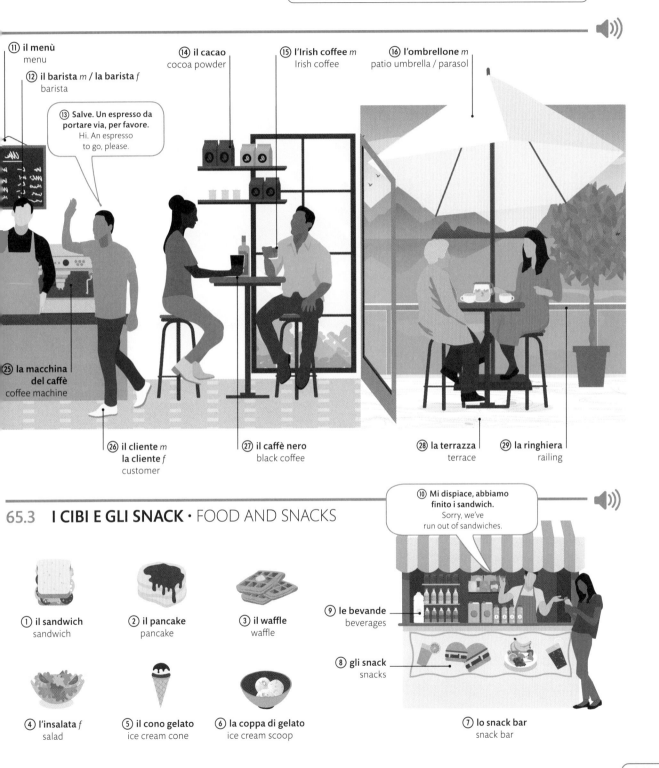

See also
27 La cucina e le stoviglie • Kitchen and tableware **52** Bere e mangiare
Drinking and eating **66** Al bar (continua) • At the café continued
70 Il fast food • Fast food **72** Il pranzo e la cena • Lunch and dinner

⑪ **il menù**
menu

⑫ **il barista** *m* **/ la barista** *f*
barista

⑬ **Salve. Un espresso da portare via, per favore.**
Hi. An espresso to go, please.

⑭ **il cacao**
cocoa powder

⑮ **l'Irish coffee** *m*
Irish coffee

⑯ **l'ombrellone** *m*
patio umbrella / parasol

㉕ **la macchina del caffè**
coffee machine

㉖ **il cliente** *m*
la cliente *f*
customer

㉗ **il caffè nero**
black coffee

㉘ **la terrazza**
terrace

㉙ **la ringhiera**
railing

65.3   I CIBI E GLI SNACK · FOOD AND SNACKS

⑩ **Mi dispiace, abbiamo finito i sandwich.**
Sorry, we've run out of sandwiches.

① **il sandwich**
sandwich

② **il pancake**
pancake

③ **il waffle**
waffle

④ **l'insalata** *f*
salad

⑤ **il cono gelato**
ice cream cone

⑥ **la coppa di gelato**
ice cream scoop

⑨ **le bevande**
beverages

⑧ **gli snack**
snacks

⑦ **lo snack bar**
snack bar

66 Al bar (continua)
At the café continued

See also
27 La cucina e le stoviglie • Kitchen and tableware
52 Bere e mangiare • Drinking and eating
72 Il pranzo e la cena • Lunch and dinner

66.1 IL TÈ · TEA

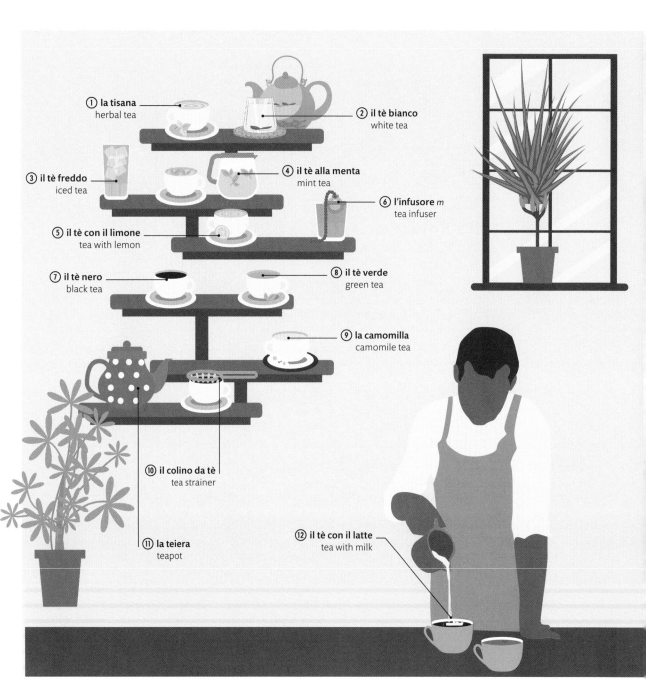

① **la tisana**
herbal tea

② **il tè bianco**
white tea

③ **il tè freddo**
iced tea

④ **il tè alla menta**
mint tea

⑥ **l'infusore** *m*
tea infuser

⑤ **il tè con il limone**
tea with lemon

⑦ **il tè nero**
black tea

⑧ **il tè verde**
green tea

⑨ **la camomilla**
camomile tea

⑩ **il colino da tè**
tea strainer

⑪ **la teiera**
teapot

⑫ **il tè con il latte**
tea with milk

67 I dolciumi
Sweets

See also
48 Il supermercato • The supermarket
62-63 La panetteria • The bakery

67.1 IL NEGOZIO DI DOLCIUMI · SWEET SHOP

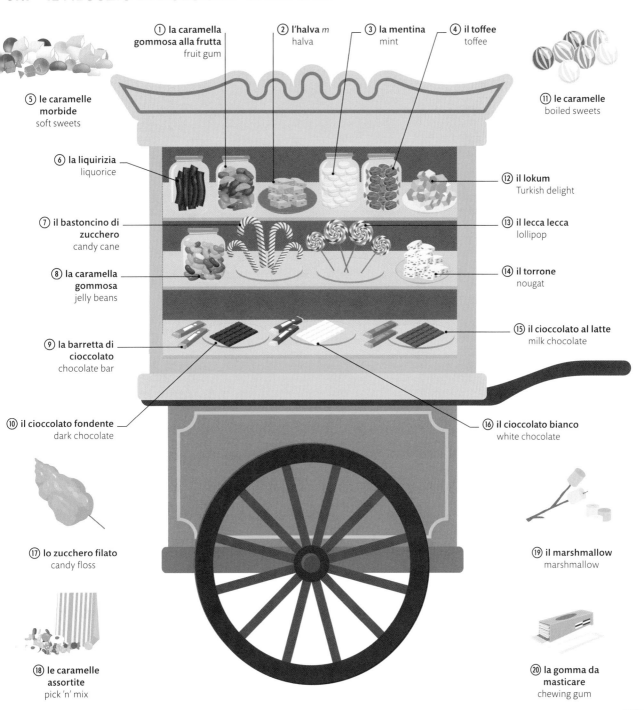

① **la caramella gommosa alla frutta**
fruit gum

② **l'halva** *m*
halva

③ **la mentina**
mint

④ **il toffee**
toffee

⑤ **le caramelle morbide**
soft sweets

⑪ **le caramelle**
boiled sweets

⑥ **la liquirizia**
liquorice

⑫ **il lokum**
Turkish delight

⑦ **il bastoncino di zucchero**
candy cane

⑬ **il lecca lecca**
lollipop

⑧ **la caramella gommosa**
jelly beans

⑭ **il torrone**
nougat

⑨ **la barretta di cioccolato**
chocolate bar

⑮ **il cioccolato al latte**
milk chocolate

⑩ **il cioccolato fondente**
dark chocolate

⑯ **il cioccolato bianco**
white chocolate

⑰ **lo zucchero filato**
candy floss

⑲ **il marshmallow**
marshmallow

⑱ **le caramelle assortite**
pick 'n' mix

⑳ **la gomma da masticare**
chewing gum

68.1 IL BAR · BAR

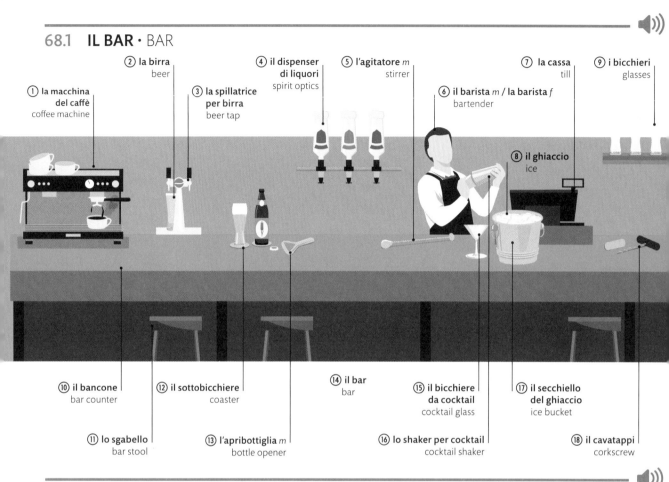

① la macchina del caffè
coffee machine

② la birra
beer

③ la spillatrice per birra
beer tap

④ il dispenser di liquori
spirit optics

⑤ l'agitatore *m*
stirrer

⑥ il barista *m* / la barista *f*
bartender

⑦ la cassa
till

⑧ il ghiaccio
ice

⑨ i bicchieri
glasses

⑩ il bancone
bar counter

⑪ lo sgabello
bar stool

⑫ il sottobicchiere
coaster

⑬ l'apribottiglia *m*
bottle opener

⑭ il bar
bar

⑮ il bicchiere da cocktail
cocktail glass

⑯ lo shaker per cocktail
cocktail shaker

⑰ il secchiello del ghiaccio
ice bucket

⑱ il cavatappi
corkscrew

68.2 LA BIRRA E IL VINO · BEER AND WINE

① la birra lager
lager

② la Pilsner
Pilsner

③ la birra di frumento
wheat beer

④ l'India Pale Ale (IPA) *f*
Indian pale ale (IPA)

⑤ la birra ale
ale

⑥ la birra stout
stout

⑦ la birra analcolica
alcohol-free beer

⑧ il vino rosso
red wine

⑨ il vino bianco
white wine

⑩ il rosé
rosé

⑪ lo spumante
sparkling wine

⑫ lo champagne
Champagne

See also
52 Bere e mangiare · Drinking and eating **69** Al ristorante
At the restaurant **72** Il pranzo e la cena · Lunch and dinner

68.3 **I DRINK** · DRINKS

① **l'acqua minerale** *f*
mineral water

② **il sidro**
cider

③ **il rum**
rum

④ **il rum e cola**
rum and cola

⑤ **la vodka**
vodka

⑥ **la vodka con succo d'arancia**
vodka and orange

⑦ **il gin tonic**
gin and tonic

⑧ **il Martini**
Martini

⑨ **il cocktail**
cocktail

⑩ **il cocktail analcolico**
mocktail

⑪ **lo sherry**
sherry

⑫ **il porto**
port

⑬ **il whisky**
whisky

⑭ **lo scotch con acqua**
Scotch and water

⑮ **il brandy**
brandy

⑯ **il liquore**
liqueur

⑰ **con ghiaccio**
with ice

⑱ **senza ghiaccio**
without ice

⑳ **doppio** *m* / **doppia** *f*
double

⑲ **singolo** *m*
singola *f*
single

㉑ **lo shottino**
shot

㉒ **la quantità**
measure

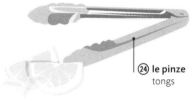

㉔ **le pinze**
tongs

㉓ **il ghiaccio e il limone**
ice and lemon

68.4 **GLI SNACK** · BAR SNACKS

① **le patatine**
crisps

② **le noci**
nuts

③ **le mandorle**
almonds

④ **gli anacardi**
cashew nuts

⑤ **le arachidi**
peanuts

⑥ **le olive**
olives

69.1 IL RISTORANTE · RESTAURANT

② la carta dei vini
wine list

③ il barista m / la barista f
bartender

④ i clienti
customers

① Quali sono le specialità del giorno?
What are today's specials?

⑫ il direttore di sala m
la direttrice di sala f
restaurant manager

⑭ Possiamo avere un tavolo per due?
May we have a table for two, please?

⑪ la cameriera
waitress

⑬ il coperto
table setting

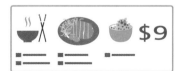

⑱ il menù fisso
set menu

⑲ il brunch
brunch

⑳ il menù del pranzo
lunch menu

㉑ il menù alla carta
à la carte menu

㉒ le specialità
specials

㉓ il menù per bambini
child's meal

㉔ il buffet
buffet

㉕ il pasto di tre portate
three-course meal

㉖ la zuppa
soup

㉗ l'antipasto m
starter

㉘ il primo piatto
main course

㉙ il contorno
side / side order

㉚ il tagliere di formaggi
cheese platter

㉛ il dessert
dessert / pudding

㉜ la bevanda
beverage

㉝ il caffè
coffee

㉞ il digestivo
digestif

See also
27 La cucina e le stoviglie • Kitchen and tableware **52** Bere e mangiare • Drinking and eating **53** La carne • Meat **54** Il pesce e i frutti di mare • Fish and seafood **55-56** La verdura • Vegetables **72** Il pranzo e la cena • Lunch and dinner

⑤ **il prezzo**
price

⑥ **il vassoio**
tray

⑦ **Buon appetito!**
Enjoy your meal!

⑧ **la cucina**
kitchen

⑨ **lo chef** m / **la chef** f
chef

⑩ **l'aiuto cuoco** m / f
commis chef

⑮ **il menù della cena**
evening menu

⑯ **il cameriere**
waiter

⑰ **il carrello dei dolci**
sweet trolley

㉟ **il sommelier** m
la sommelier f
sommelier

㊱ **mangiare fuori**
to eat out

㊲ **prenotare**
to make a reservation

㊳ **cancellare**
to cancel

㊴ **ordinare**
to order

㊵ **il conto**
bill

㊶ **pagare separatamente**
to pay separately

㊷ **dividere il conto**
to split the bill

㊸ **il prezzo del servizio**
service charge

㊹ **servizio incluso**
service included

㊺ **servizio non incluso**
service not included

㊻ **la mancia**
tip

㊼ **lo scontrino**
receipt

㊽ **il bistrot**
bistro

70.1 IN UN FAST FOOD
IN A FAST-FOOD RESTAURANT

⑤ È da mangiare qui?
Is this to eat in?

① il listino prezzi
price list

② la cannuccia
straw

④ le patatine fritte
chips

③ la bibita
soft drink

⑥ l'hamburger *m*
hamburger

⑦ il tovagliolo di carta
paper napkin

⑧ il vassoio
tray

⑨ il fast food
burger bar

⑩ mangiare sul posto
to eat in

⑪ il cibo da asporto
take-away

⑫ la consegna a domicilio
home delivery

⑬ la bancarella
street stall

⑭ il menù
menu

⑮ il milkshake
milkshake

⑯ la bibita in lattina
canned drink

⑰ la bibita gassata
fizzy drink

㉗ Il tuo ordine sta arrivando.
Your order is on its way.

⑱ l'offerta del giorno *f*
meal deal

⑲ la tazza riutilizzabile
reusable cup

⑳ la salsa
sauce

㉑ il food truck
food van

㉒ il waffle
waffle

㉓ il gelato
ice cream

㉔ il muffin
muffin

㉕ la ciambella
doughnut

㉖ il fattorino di cibo a domicilio
food delivery driver

See also
52 Bere e mangiare · Drinking and eating **60** Nella dispensa · In the pantry **65-66** Al bar · At the café **67** I dolciumi · Sweets

(29) il cheeseburger
cheeseburger

(30) l'hamburger di pollo *m*
chicken burger

(28) l'hamburger vegetariano *m*
veggie burger

(32) le crocchette di pollo
chicken nuggets

(33) il pollo fritto
fried chicken

(31) l'hamburger *m*
burger

(34) gli hash brown
hash browns

(35) il fish and chips
fish and chips

(38) la senape
mustard

(37) il ketchup
ketchup

(36) l'hot dog *m*
hot dog

(39) il kebab
kebab

(40) le costolette
ribs

(41) i noodle
noodles

(42) i ravioli
dumplings

(45) il ripieno
filling

(43) l'empanada *f*
empanada

(44) il wrap
wrap

(46) la crêpe
crêpe

(53) il forno da pizza
pizza oven

(54) la pizza
pizza

(55) il condimento
topping

(47) il taco
taco

(48) il falafel
falafel

(49) i nachos
nachos

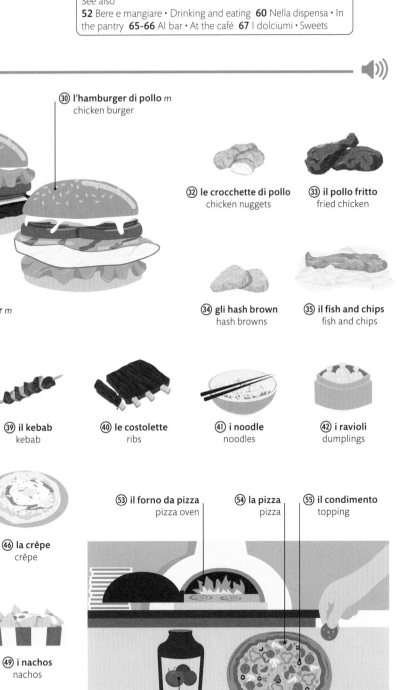

(50) il sandwich
sandwich

(51) il club sandwich
club sandwich

(52) la tartina
open sandwich

(56) la salsa di pomodoro
tomato sauce

(57) la pizzeria
pizzeria

149

71.1   **LA COLAZIONE A BUFFET** · BREAKFAST BUFFET

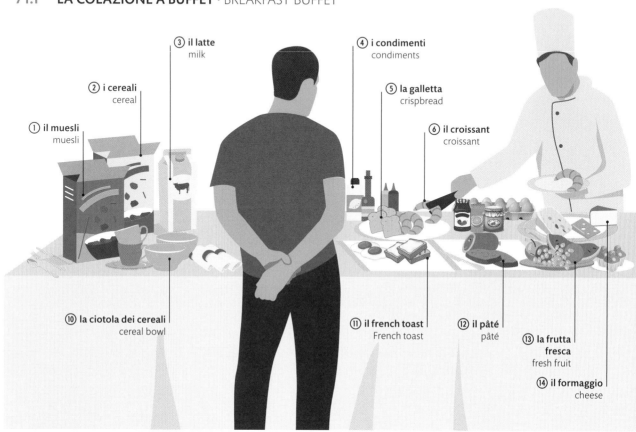

③ **il latte**
milk

④ **i condimenti**
condiments

② **i cereali**
cereal

⑤ **la galletta**
crispbread

① **il muesli**
muesli

⑥ **il croissant**
croissant

⑩ **la ciotola dei cereali**
cereal bowl

⑪ **il french toast**
French toast

⑫ **il pâté**
pâté

⑬ **la frutta fresca**
fresh fruit

⑭ **il formaggio**
cheese

⑰ **il prosciutto**
ham

⑱ **il toast**
toasted sandwich

⑲ **l'omelette** *f*
omelette

⑳ **l'avocado toast** *m*
avocado toast

㉑ **il bagel**
bagel

㉒ **il rotolo alla cannella**
cinnamon rolls

㉕ **la confettura**
jam

㉖ **la marmellata di arance**
marmalade

㉗ **il miele**
honey

㉘ **il tè**
tea

㉙ **il caffè**
coffee

㉚ **il succo di frutta**
fruit juice

See also
29 Cucinare · Cooking **52** Bere e mangiare · Drinking and eating **53** La carne · Meat
57 La frutta · Fruit **58** La frutta e la frutta a guscio · Fruit and nuts **61** I prodotti caseari
Dairy produce **64** La gastronomia · The delicatessen **65-66** Al bar · At the café

71.2 LA COLAZIONE ALL'INGLESE · COOKED BREAKFAST

① **la salsiccia**
sausage

② **le polpette di salsiccia**
sausage patties

③ **la pancetta**
bacon

④ **le aringhe affumicate**
kippers

⑤ **il salmone affumicato**
smoked salmon

⑥ **lo sgombro affumicato**
smoked mackerel

⑦ **il sanguinaccio**
black pudding / blood sausage

⑧ **i reni**
kidneys

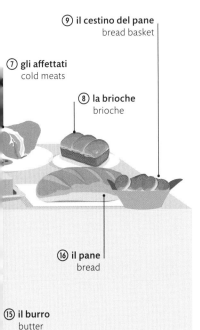

⑨ **il cestino del pane**
bread basket

⑦ **gli affettati**
cold meats

⑧ **la brioche**
brioche

⑯ **il pane**
bread

⑮ **il burro**
butter

⑫ **l'albume** *m*
egg white

⑨ **le uova strapazzate**
scrambled eggs

⑩ **l'uovo in camicia** *m*
poached egg

⑪ **l'uovo sodo** *m*
boiled egg

⑬ **il tuorlo** *m*
yolk

⑭ **l'uovo al tegamino** *m*
fried egg

⑮ **il pane tostato**
toast

⑯ **i funghi fritti**
fried mushrooms

⑰ **gli hash brown**
hash browns

㉓ **i waffle**
waffles

㉔ **la panna**
cream

⑱ **il pomodoro grigliato**
grilled tomato

⑲ **il pomodoro in scatola**
tinned tomato

⑳ **i fagioli stufati**
baked beans

㉑ **il breakfast roll**
breakfast roll

㉛ **la frutta secca**
dried fruit

㉜ **lo yogurt alla frutta**
fruit yoghurt

㉒ **il burrito**
breakfast burrito

㉓ **le frittelle di patate**
potato cakes

㉔ **i pancake**
pancakes

㉕ **il porridge**
porridge

72.1 I CIBI E I PIATTI · MEALS AND DISHES

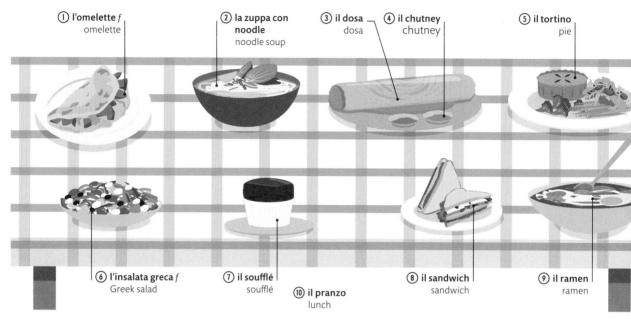

① l'omelette *f*
omelette

② la zuppa con noodle
noodle soup

③ il dosa
dosa

④ il chutney
chutney

⑤ il tortino
pie

⑥ l'insalata greca *f*
Greek salad

⑦ il soufflé
soufflé

⑩ il pranzo
lunch

⑧ il sandwich
sandwich

⑨ il ramen
ramen

⑬ il tovagliolo
napkin

⑯ la salsa di soia da intingere
soy sauce dip

⑱ le crudités
crudités

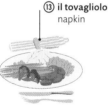

⑪ la zuppa
soup

⑫ le verdure cotte
cooked vegetables

⑭ saltato in padella *m*
saltata in padella *f*
stir-fry

⑮ l'involtino estate *m*
summer roll

⑰ l'hummus *m*
hummus

⑲ la pita
pitta bread

⑳ il riso
rice

㉑ il risotto
risotto

㉒ la paella
paella

㉓ la pasta
pasta

㉔ le polpette di carne
meatballs

㉕ i noodle
noodles

㉖ i contorni
side dishes

㉗ l'involtino primavera *m*
spring roll

㉘ l'insalata tritata *f*
chopped salad

㉙ il condimento
dressing

㉚ i sottaceti
pickles

㉛ i condimenti
condiments

See also
27 La cucina e le stoviglie · Kitchen and tableware **29** Cucinare · Cooking
52 Bere e mangiare · Drinking and eating **53** La carne · Meat **55-56** La verdura
Vegetables **65-66** Al bar · At the café **69** Al ristorante · At the restaurant

㉜ **l'insalata mista** *f*
mixed salad

㉝ **il kebab**
kebab

㉞ **il brodo**
broth

㉟ **i ravioli**
dumplings

㊱ **l'hot pot cinese** *m*
Chinese hotpot

㊲ **il pollo arrosto**
roast chicken

㊳ **il curry**
curry

㊴ **le lasagne**
lasagna

㊵ **gli spaghetti**
spaghetti

㊶ **lo stufato**
stew

㊷ **la cena**
dinner

72.2 LA PREPARAZIONE DEL CIBO · FOOD PREPARATION

① **farcito** *m*
farcita *f*
stuffed

② **grigliato** *m*
grigliata *f*
grilled

③ **marinato** *m*
marinata *f*
marinated

④ **in salsa**
in sauce

⑤ **in camicia**
poached

⑥ **bollito** *m*
bollita *f*
boiled

⑦ **cotto al forno** *m*
cotta al forno *f*
baked

⑧ **saltato in padella** *m*
saltata in padella *f*
stir-fried

⑨ **al tegame**
fried

⑩ **fritto** *m* / **fritta** *f*
deep-fried

⑪ **affumicato** *m*
affumicata *f*
smoked

⑫ **al vapore**
steamed

⑬ **schiacciato** *m*
schiacciata *f*
mashed

⑭ **condito** *m*
condita *f*
dressed

⑮ **stagionato** *m*
stagionata *f*
cured

⑯ **sott'aceto**
pickled

⑰ **il kosher**
kosher

⑱ **l'halal** *m*
halal

73 A scuola
At school

73.1 LA SCUOLA E LO STUDIO · SCHOOL AND STUDY

① la scuola
school

② l'aula *f*
classroom

③ la classe
class

④ l'insegnante *m / f*
teacher

⑤ la lavagna
whiteboard

⑥ l'alunno *m*
l'alunna *f*
pupil

⑦ il banco
desk

⑧ gli studenti *m*
le studentesse *f*
school students

⑨ lo zaino
school bag

⑩ la letteratura
literature

⑪ la matematica
maths

⑫ la geografia
geography

⑬ la storia
history

⑭ le scienze
science

⑮ la chimica
chemistry

⑯ la fisica
physics

⑰ la biologia
biology

⑱ l'inglese *m*
English

⑲ le lingue
languages

⑳ il disegno tecnico
e la tecnologia
design and technology

㉑ l'informatica *f*
information
technology

㉒ l'arte *f*
art

㉓ la musica
music

㉔ il teatro
drama

㉕ l'educazione
fisica *f*
physical education

㉖ il preside *m*
la preside *f*
head teacher /
principal

㉗ i compiti per casa
homework

㉘ la lezione
lesson

㉙ il compito in
classe
exam

㉚ il tema
essay

㉛ il voto
grade

㉜ l'enciclopedia *f*
encyclopedia

㉝ il dizionario
dictionary

㉞ l'atlante *m*
atlas

㉟ la verifica
test

See also
74 La matematica · Mathematics **75** La fisica · Physics **76** La chimica · Chemistry
77 La biologia · Biology **79** La storia · History **80** All'università · At college
83 I computer e la tecnologia · Computers and technology

73.2 I VERBI DELLA SCUOLA · SCHOOL VERBS

① **leggere**
to read

② **scrivere**
to write

③ **domandare**
to question

④ **fare una verifica**
to take an exam

⑤ **imparare**
to learn

⑥ **disegnare**
to draw

⑦ **rispondere**
to answer

⑧ **computare**
to spell

⑨ **ripassare**
to revise

⑩ **recuperare il compito**
to resit

⑪ **prendere appunti**
to take notes

⑫ **discutere**
to discuss

⑬ **andare male**
to fail

⑭ **andare bene**
to pass

⑮ **La verifica è andata bene.**
I've passed my test.

73.3 I MATERIALI · EQUIPMENT

① **la matita**
pencil

② **il temperino**
pencil sharpener

③ **la penna**
pen

④ **il pennino**
nib

⑤ **la gomma da cancellare**
rubber

⑥ **le matite colorate**
coloured pencils

⑦ **l'astuccio** *m*
pencil case

⑧ **il righello**
ruler

⑨ **la squadra**
set square

⑩ **il goniometro**
protractor

⑪ **la calcolatrice**
calculator

⑫ **il compasso**
compass

⑬ **il libro di testo**
textbook

⑭ **il quaderno**
notebook / exercise book

⑮ **il videoproiettore**
digital projector

⑯ **l'evidenziatore** *m*
highlighter

⑰ **la graffetta**
paper clip

⑱ **la cucitrice**
stapler

La matematica
Mathematics

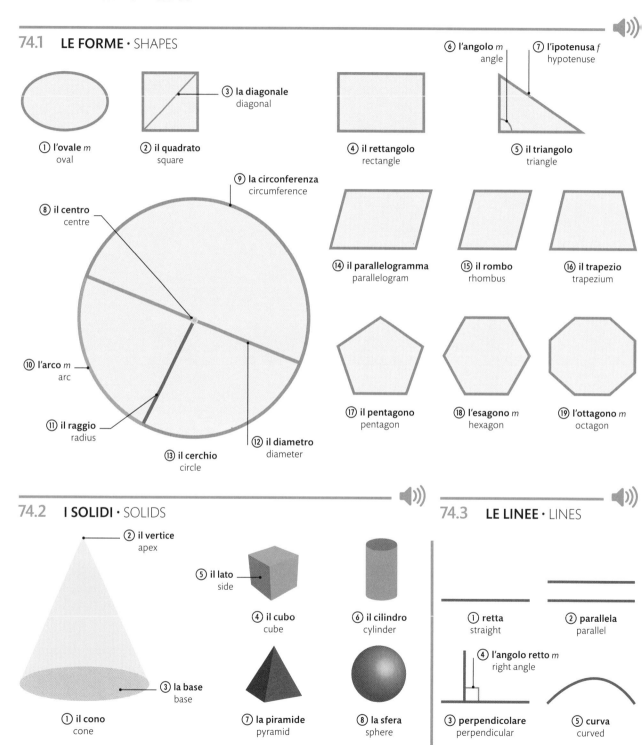

LE FORME · SHAPES

⑥ l'angolo *m*
angle

⑦ l'ipotenusa *f*
hypotenuse

③ la diagonale
diagonal

① l'ovale *m*
oval

② il quadrato
square

④ il rettangolo
rectangle

⑤ il triangolo
triangle

⑨ la circonferenza
circumference

⑧ il centro
centre

⑭ il parallelogramma
parallelogram

⑮ il rombo
rhombus

⑯ il trapezio
trapezium

⑩ l'arco *m*
arc

⑪ il raggio
radius

⑬ il cerchio
circle

⑫ il diametro
diameter

⑰ il pentagono
pentagon

⑱ l'esagono *m*
hexagon

⑲ l'ottagono *m*
octagon

74.2 **I SOLIDI** · SOLIDS

② il vertice
apex

⑤ il lato
side

④ il cubo
cube

⑥ il cilindro
cylinder

③ la base
base

① il cono
cone

⑦ la piramide
pyramid

⑧ la sfera
sphere

74.3 **LE LINEE** · LINES

① retta
straight

② parallela
parallel

④ l'angolo retto *m*
right angle

③ perpendicolare
perpendicular

⑤ curva
curved

See also
73 A scuola · At school **94** Il denaro e la finanza · Money and finance
173 I numeri · Numbers **174** I pesi e le misure · Weights and measures

74.4 LE MISURE · MEASUREMENTS

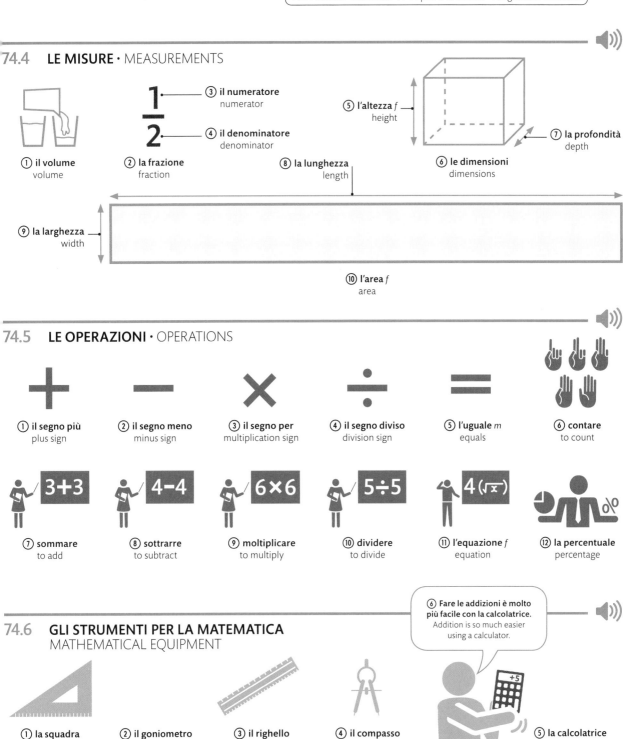

③ **il numeratore**
numerator

④ **il denominatore**
denominator

① **il volume**
volume

② **la frazione**
fraction

⑤ **l'altezza** *f*
height

⑦ **la profondità**
depth

⑥ **le dimensioni**
dimensions

⑧ **la lunghezza**
length

⑨ **la larghezza**
width

⑩ **l'area** *f*
area

74.5 LE OPERAZIONI · OPERATIONS

① **il segno più**
plus sign

② **il segno meno**
minus sign

③ **il segno per**
multiplication sign

④ **il segno diviso**
division sign

⑤ **l'uguale** *m*
equals

⑥ **contare**
to count

3+3

4-4

6×6

5÷5

4$(\sqrt{x})$

⑦ **sommare**
to add

⑧ **sottrarre**
to subtract

⑨ **moltiplicare**
to multiply

⑩ **dividere**
to divide

⑪ **l'equazione** *f*
equation

⑫ **la percentuale**
percentage

74.6 GLI STRUMENTI PER LA MATEMATICA
MATHEMATICAL EQUIPMENT

⑥ **Fare le addizioni è molto più facile con la calcolatrice.**
Addition is so much easier using a calculator.

① **la squadra**
set square

② **il goniometro**
protractor

③ **il righello**
ruler

④ **il compasso**
compass

⑤ **la calcolatrice**
calculator

75 La fisica
Physics

75.1 LA FISICA · PHYSICS

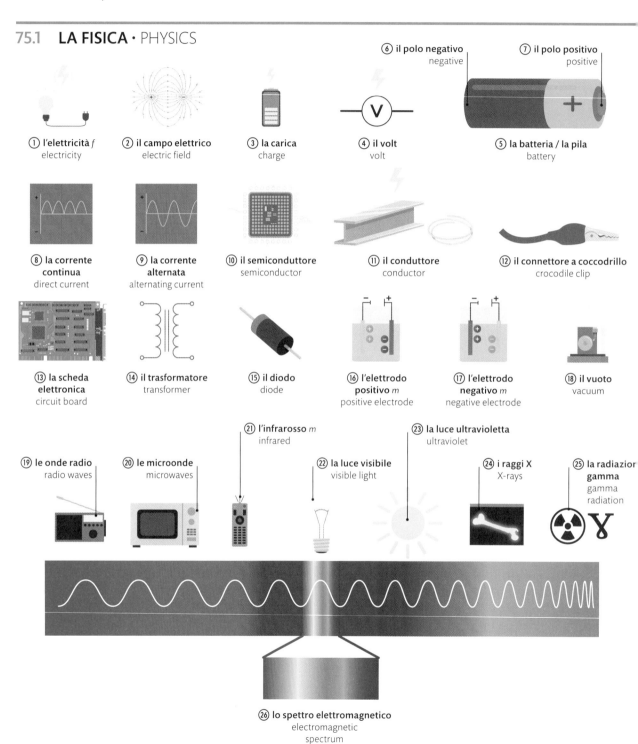

⑥ il polo negativo
negative

⑦ il polo positivo
positive

① l'elettricità *f*
electricity

② il campo elettrico
electric field

③ la carica
charge

④ il volt
volt

⑤ la batteria / la pila
battery

⑧ la corrente continua
direct current

⑨ la corrente alternata
alternating current

⑩ il semiconduttore
semiconductor

⑪ il conduttore
conductor

⑫ il connettore a coccodrillo
crocodile clip

⑬ la scheda elettronica
circuit board

⑭ il trasformatore
transformer

⑮ il diodo
diode

⑯ l'elettrodo positivo *m*
positive electrode

⑰ l'elettrodo negativo *m*
negative electrode

⑱ il vuoto
vacuum

㉑ l'infrarosso *m*
infrared

㉓ la luce ultravioletta
ultraviolet

⑲ le onde radio
radio waves

⑳ le microonde
microwaves

㉒ la luce visibile
visible light

㉔ i raggi X
X-rays

㉕ la radiazior gamma
gamma radiation

㉖ lo spettro elettromagnetico
electromagnetic spectrum

See also
73 A scuola · At school **74** La matematica · Mathematics **76** La chimica · Chemistry
77 La biologia · Biology **78** La tavola periodica · The periodic table

㉗ **il polo nord**
north pole

㉘ **il campo magnetico**
magnetic field

㉙ **il polo sud**
south pole

㉚ **il magnete**
magnet

㉛ **la forza centrifuga**
centrifugal force

㉜ **la forza centripeta**
centripetal force

㉝ **la fissione**
fission

㉞ **la fusione**
fusion

㉟ **la radioattività**
radioactivity

㊱ **la particella**
particle

㊲ **l'acceleratore di particelle** *m*
particle accelerator

75.2 **L'OTTICA** · OPTICS

① **la lente**
lens

② **la lente convessa**
convex lens

③ **la lente concava**
concave lens

⑥ **la lunghezza d'onda**
wavelength

④ **il laser**
laser

⑤ **l'onda** *f*
wave

⑦ **la riflessione**
reflection

⑧ **la refrazione**
refraction

⑨ **la diffrazione**
diffraction

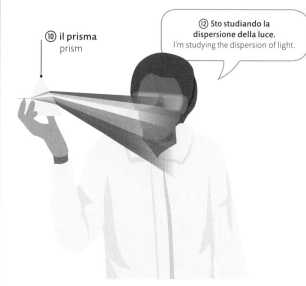

⑩ **il prisma**
prism

⑫ **Sto studiando la dispersione della luce.**
I'm studying the dispersion of light.

⑪ **la dispersione**
dispersion

76 La chimica
Chemistry

76.1 IN LABORATORIO · IN THE LABORATORY

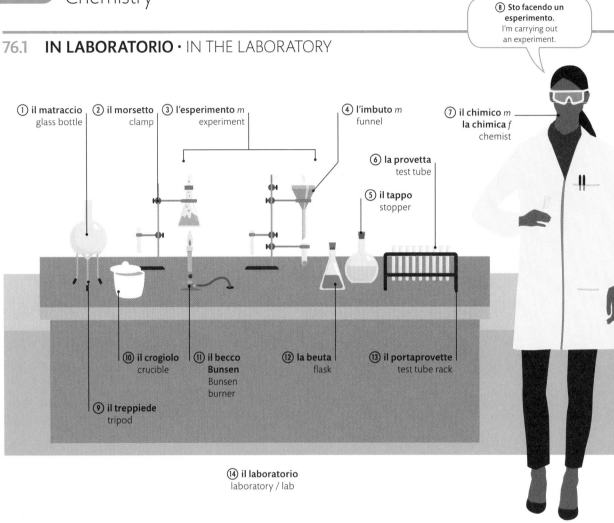

⑧ **Sto facendo un esperimento.**
I'm carrying out an experiment.

① **il matraccio** glass bottle

② **il morsetto** clamp

③ **l'esperimento** *m* experiment

④ **l'imbuto** *m* funnel

⑦ **il chimico** *m* **la chimica** *f* chemist

⑥ **la provetta** test tube

⑤ **il tappo** stopper

⑩ **il crogiolo** crucible

⑪ **il becco Bunsen** Bunsen burner

⑫ **la beuta** flask

⑬ **il portaprovette** test tube rack

⑨ **il treppiede** tripod

⑭ **il laboratorio** laboratory / lab

⑮ **la bilancia** scales

⑯ **il timer** timer

⑰ **il termometro** thermometer

⑱ **le pinze** tongs

⑲ **la spatola** spatula

⑳ **il pestello** pestle

㉑ **il mortaio** mortar

㉒ **la carta da filtro** filter paper

㉓ **il contagocce** dropper

㉔ **la pipetta** pipette

㉕ **il becher** beaker

㉖ **la bacchetta di vetro** glass rod

㉗ **gli occhiali protettivi** safety goggles

See also
73 A scuola • At school **74** La matematica • Mathematics **75** La fisica
Physics **77** La biologia • Biology **78** La tavola periodica • The periodic table

2 molecole di idrogeno
2 hydrogen molecules

1 molecola di ossigeno
1 oxygen molecule

2 molecole di acqua
2 water molecules

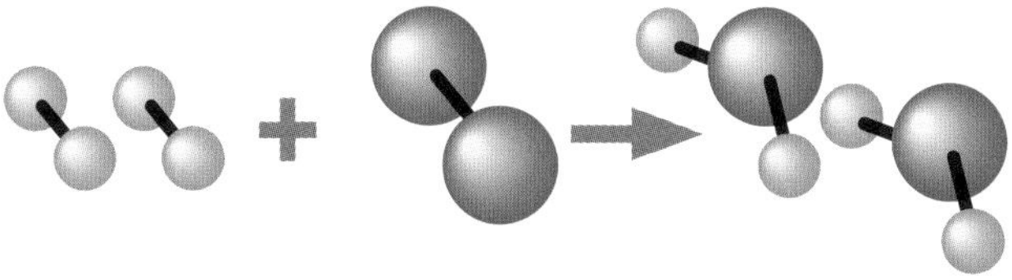

$$2H_2 + O_2 \rightarrow 2H_2O$$

(29) **il simbolo chimico**
chemical symbol

(30) **il pedice**
subscript

(28) **l'equazione chimica** *f*
chemical equation

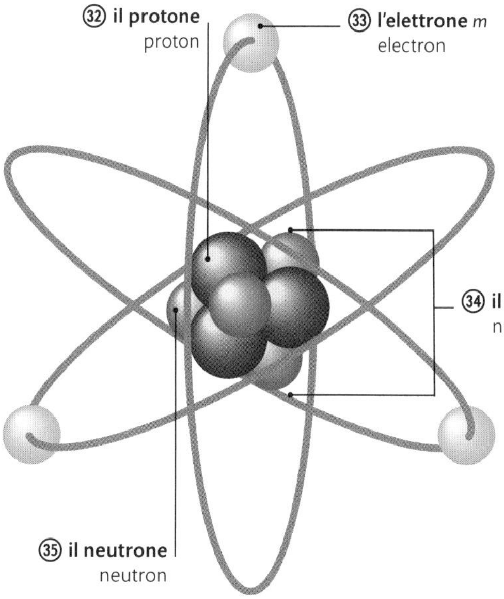

(32) **il protone**
proton

(33) **l'elettrone** *m*
electron

(34) **il nucleo**
nucleus

(35) **il neutrone**
neutron

(31) **l'atomo** *m*
atom

$$H_2O$$

(36) **la formula chimica**
chemical formula

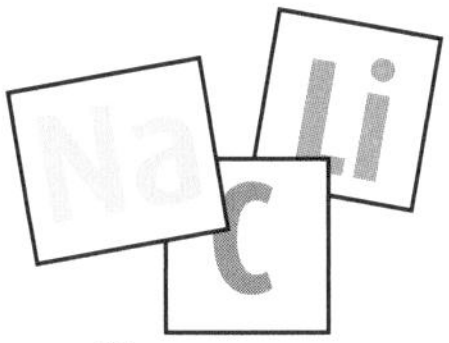

(37) **gli elementi**
elements

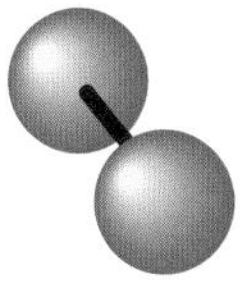

(38) **la molecola**
molecule

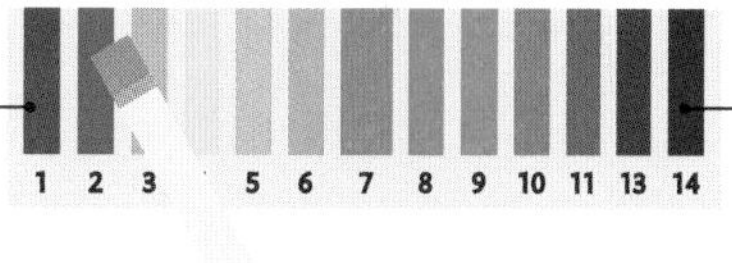

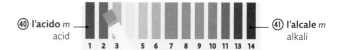

(40) **l'acido** *m*
acid

(41) **l'alcale** *m*
alkali

(39) **il valore di pH**
pH level

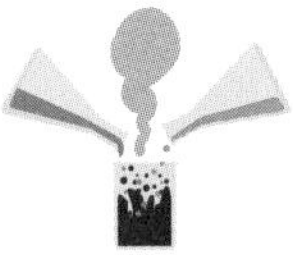

(42) **la reazione**
reaction

$$Q < K$$

(43) **la direzione di una reazione**
reaction direction

$$Q \rightleftharpoons K$$

(44) **la direzione inversa**
reversible direction

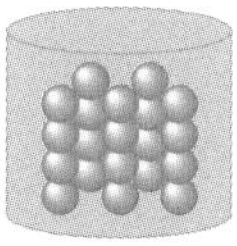

(45) **il solido**
solid

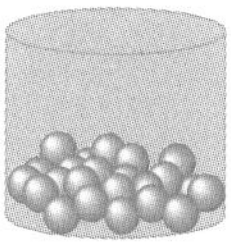

(46) **il liquido**
liquid

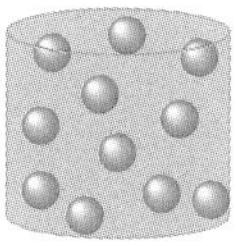

(47) **il gas**
gas

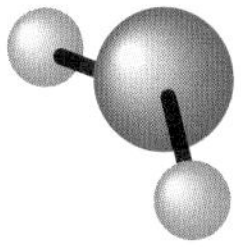

(48) **il composto**
compound

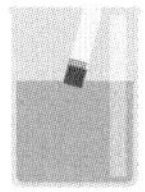

(49) **la base**
base

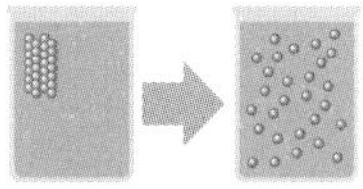

(50) **la diffusione**
diffusion

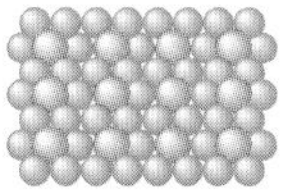

(51) **la lega**
alloy

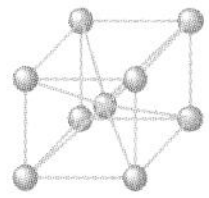

(52) **il cristallo**
crystal

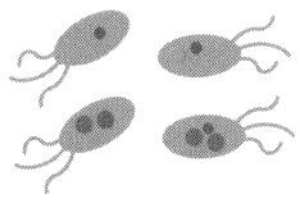

(53) **la biochimica**
biochemistry

77 La biologia
Biology

77.1 LA BIOLOGIA · BIOLOGY

① il biologo *m*
la biologa *f*
biologist

② la microbiologia
microbiology

③ il microbiologo *m*
la microbiologa *f*
microbiologist

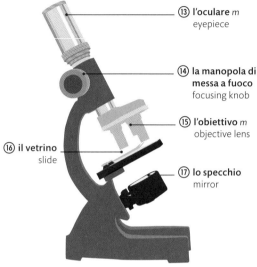

⑬ l'oculare *m*
eyepiece

⑭ la manopola di
messa a fuoco
focusing knob

⑮ l'obiettivo *m*
objective lens

⑯ il vetrino
slide

⑰ lo specchio
mirror

⑱ il microscopio
microscope

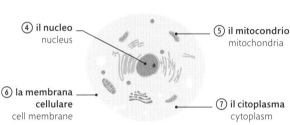

④ il nucleo
nucleus

⑤ il mitocondrio
mitochondria

⑥ la membrana
cellulare
cell membrane

⑦ il citoplasma
cytoplasm

⑧ la cellula animale
animal cell

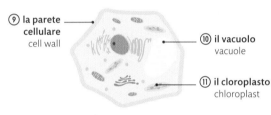

⑨ la parete
cellulare
cell wall

⑩ il vacuolo
vacuole

⑪ il cloroplasto
chloroplast

⑫ la cellula vegetale
plant cell

⑲ il globulo rosso
red blood cell

⑳ il globulo bianco
white blood cell

㉒ il gene
gene

㉑ il cromosoma
chromosome

㉓ il DNA
DNA

㉔ il virus
virus

㉕ il batterio
bacteria

㉖ la capsula Petri
petri dish

㉗ le pinzette
tweezers

㉘ il bisturi
scalpel

㉙ la siringa
syringe

㉚ la zoologia
zoology

㉛ lo zoologo *m*
la zoologa *f*
zoologist

㉜ il plancton
plankton

㉝ invertebrato *m*
invertebrata *f*
invertebrate

㉞ vertebrato *m*
vertebrata *f*
vertebrate

㉟ la specie
species

See also
157 La storia naturale · Natural history **158-159** I mammiferi · Mammals **160-161** Gli uccelli Birds **162** Gli insetti · Insects and bugs **163** Gli anfibi e i rettili · Amphibians and reptiles **166** La vita negli oceani · Ocean life **167-169** Le piante e gli alberi · Plants and trees **170** I funghi · Fungi

36 **l'ecosistema** *m*
ecosystem

37 **l'esoscheletro** *m*
exoskeleton

38 **l'endoscheletro** *m*
endoskeleton

39 **la riproduzione**
reproduction

40 **l'ibernazione** *f*
hibernation

41 **la botanica**
botany

42 **il botanico** *m*
la botanica *f*
botanist

43 **la pianta**
plant

44 **i funghi**
fungi

45 **la fotosintesi**
photosynthesis

46 **il paleontologo** *m*
la paleontologa *f*
paleontologist

47 **il fossile**
fossil

48 **l'evoluzione** *f*
evolution

77.2 LA METAMORFOSI · METAMORPHOSIS

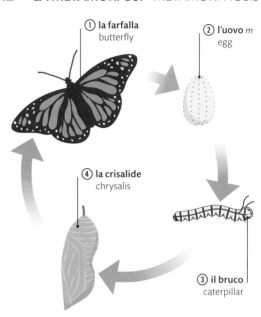

1 **la farfalla**
butterfly

2 **l'uovo** *m*
egg

3 **il bruco**
caterpillar

4 **la crisalide**
chrysalis

5 **il ciclo di vita di una farfalla**
life cycle of a butterfly

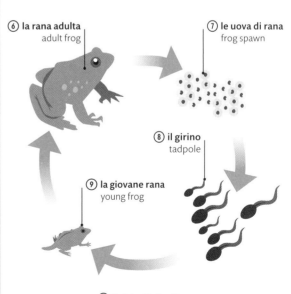

6 **la rana adulta**
adult frog

7 **le uova di rana**
frog spawn

8 **il girino**
tadpole

9 **la giovane rana**
young frog

10 **il ciclo di vita di una rana**
life cycle of a frog

78.1 LA TAVOLA PERIODICA · THE PERIODIC TABLE

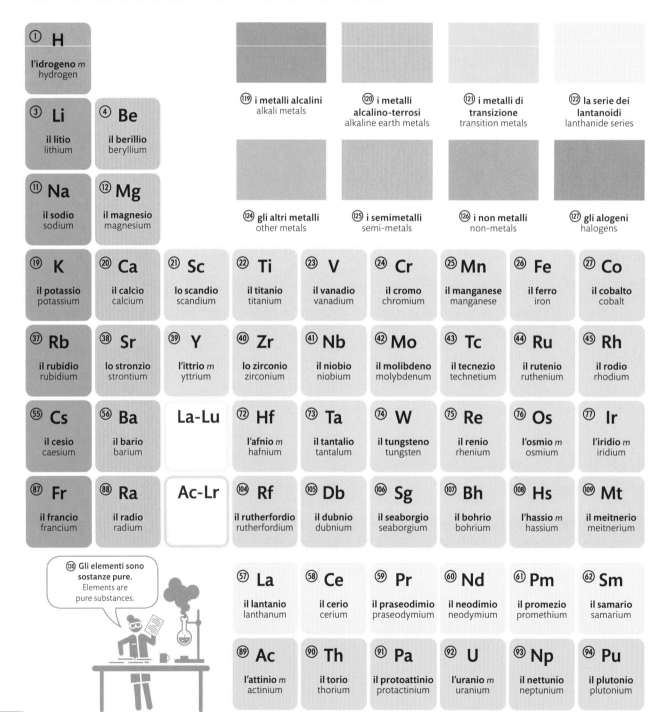

① **H**
l'idrogeno *m*
hydrogen

⑲ **i metalli alcalini**
alkali metals

⑳ **i metalli alcalino-terrosi**
alkaline earth metals

㉑ **i metalli di transizione**
transition metals

㉒ **la serie dei lantanoidi**
lanthanide series

㉔ **gli altri metalli**
other metals

㉕ **i semimetalli**
semi-metals

㉖ **i non metalli**
non-metals

㉗ **gli alogeni**
halogens

③ **Li**
il litio
lithium

④ **Be**
il berillio
beryllium

⑪ **Na**
il sodio
sodium

⑫ **Mg**
il magnesio
magnesium

⑲ **K**
il potassio
potassium

⑳ **Ca**
il calcio
calcium

㉑ **Sc**
lo scandio
scandium

㉒ **Ti**
il titanio
titanium

㉓ **V**
il vanadio
vanadium

㉔ **Cr**
il cromo
chromium

㉕ **Mn**
il manganese
manganese

㉖ **Fe**
il ferro
iron

㉗ **Co**
il cobalto
cobalt

㊲ **Rb**
il rubidio
rubidium

㊳ **Sr**
lo stronzio
strontium

㊴ **Y**
l'ittrio *m*
yttrium

㊵ **Zr**
lo zirconio
zirconium

㊶ **Nb**
il niobio
niobium

㊷ **Mo**
il molibdeno
molybdenum

㊸ **Tc**
il tecnezio
technetium

㊹ **Ru**
il rutenio
ruthenium

㊺ **Rh**
il rodio
rhodium

㊺ **Cs**
il cesio
caesium

㊻ **Ba**
il bario
barium

La-Lu

㊼ **Hf**
l'afnio *m*
hafnium

㊽ **Ta**
il tantalio
tantalum

㊾ **W**
il tungsteno
tungsten

㊿ **Re**
il renio
rhenium

⑦⑥ **Os**
l'osmio *m*
osmium

⑦⑦ **Ir**
l'iridio *m*
iridium

㊻ **Fr**
il francio
francium

㊼ **Ra**
il radio
radium

Ac-Lr

⑩④ **Rf**
il rutherfordio
rutherfordium

⑩⑤ **Db**
il dubnio
dubnium

⑩⑥ **Sg**
il seaborgio
seaborgium

⑩⑦ **Bh**
il bohrio
bohrium

⑩⑧ **Hs**
l'hassio *m*
hassium

⑩⑨ **Mt**
il meitnerio
meitnerium

⑬⓪ **Gli elementi sono sostanze pure.**
Elements are pure substances.

㊼ **La**
il lantanio
lanthanum

㊽ **Ce**
il cerio
cerium

㊾ **Pr**
il praseodimio
praseodymium

㊿ **Nd**
il neodimio
neodymium

⑥① **Pm**
il promezio
promethium

⑥② **Sm**
il samario
samarium

㊾ **Ac**
l'attinio *m*
actinium

⑨⓪ **Th**
il torio
thorium

⑨① **Pa**
il protoattinio
protactinium

⑨② **U**
l'uranio *m*
uranium

⑨③ **Np**
il nettunio
neptunium

⑨④ **Pu**
il plutonio
plutonium

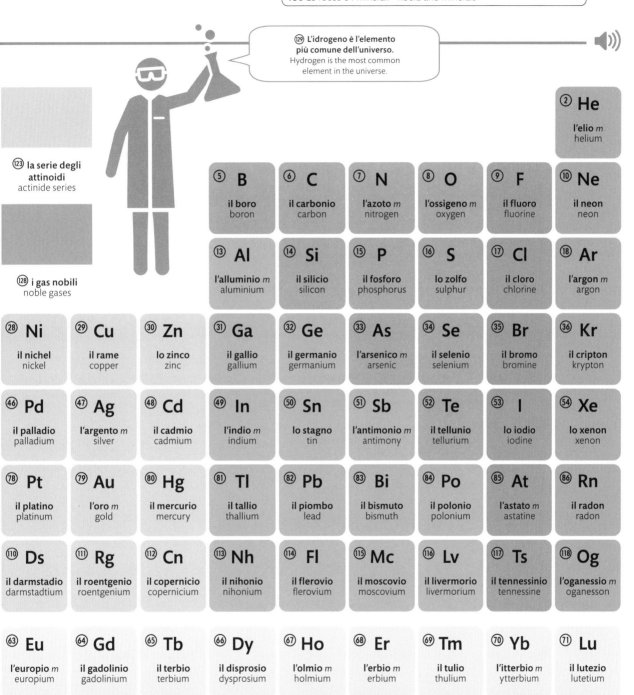

See also
73 A scuola • At school **75** La fisica • Physics **76** La chimica • Chemistry
156 Le rocce e i minerali • Rocks and minerals

㉙ **L'idrogeno è l'elemento più comune dell'universo.**
Hydrogen is the most common element in the universe.

② **He**
l'elio *m.*
helium

㉓ la serie degli attinoidi
actinide series

㉘ i gas nobili
noble gases

⑤ **B**
il boro
boron

⑥ **C**
il carbonio
carbon

⑦ **N**
l'azoto *m*
nitrogen

⑧ **O**
l'ossigeno *m*
oxygen

⑨ **F**
il fluoro
fluorine

⑩ **Ne**
il neon
neon

⑬ **Al**
l'alluminio *m*
aluminium

⑭ **Si**
il silicio
silicon

⑮ **P**
il fosforo
phosphorus

⑯ **S**
lo zolfo
sulphur

⑰ **Cl**
il cloro
chlorine

⑱ **Ar**
l'argon *m*
argon

㉘ **Ni**
il nichel
nickel

㉙ **Cu**
il rame
copper

㉚ **Zn**
lo zinco
zinc

㉛ **Ga**
il gallio
gallium

㉜ **Ge**
il germanio
germanium

㉝ **As**
l'arsenico *m*
arsenic

㉞ **Se**
il selenio
selenium

㉟ **Br**
il bromo
bromine

㊱ **Kr**
il cripton
krypton

㊺ **Pd**
il palladio
palladium

㊼ **Ag**
l'argento *m*
silver

㊽ **Cd**
il cadmio
cadmium

㊾ **In**
l'indio *m*
indium

㊿ **Sn**
lo stagno
tin

⑤ **Sb**
l'antimonio *m*
antimony

⑤ **Te**
il tellunio
tellurium

⑤ **I**
lo iodio
iodine

⑤ **Xe**
lo xenon
xenon

⑱ **Pt**
il platino
platinum

⑲ **Au**
l'oro *m*
gold

⑳ **Hg**
il mercurio
mercury

㉑ **Tl**
il tallio
thallium

㉒ **Pb**
il piombo
lead

㉓ **Bi**
il bismuto
bismuth

㉔ **Po**
il polonio
polonium

㉕ **At**
l'astato *m*
astatine

㉖ **Rn**
il radon
radon

⑩ **Ds**
il darmstadio
darmstadtium

⑪ **Rg**
il roentgenio
roentgenium

⑫ **Cn**
il copernicio
copernicium

⑬ **Nh**
il nihonio
nihonium

⑭ **Fl**
il flerovio
flerovium

⑮ **Mc**
il moscovio
moscovium

⑯ **Lv**
il livermorio
livermorium

⑰ **Ts**
il tennessinio
tennessine

⑱ **Og**
l'oganessio *m*
oganesson

㊻ **Eu**
l'europio *m*
europium

㊽ **Gd**
il gadolinio
gadolinium

㊽ **Tb**
il terbio
terbium

㊻ **Dy**
il disprosio
dysprosium

㊾ **Ho**
l'olmio *m*
holmium

㊽ **Er**
l'erbio *m*
erbium

㊾ **Tm**
il tulio
thulium

⑦ **Yb**
l'itterbio *m*
ytterbium

⑦ **Lu**
il lutezio
lutetium

㊾ **Am**
l'americio *m*
americium

㊾ **Cm**
il curio
curium

㊾ **Bk**
il berkelio
berkelium

㊾ **Cf**
il californio
californium

㊾ **Es**
l'einsteinio *m*
einsteinium

⑩ **Fm**
il fermio
fermium

⑩ **Md**
il mendelevio
mendelevium

⑩ **No**
il nobelio
nobelium

⑩ **Lr**
il laurenzio
lawrencium

79.1 LA GUERRA E LE ARMI · WAR AND WEAPONS

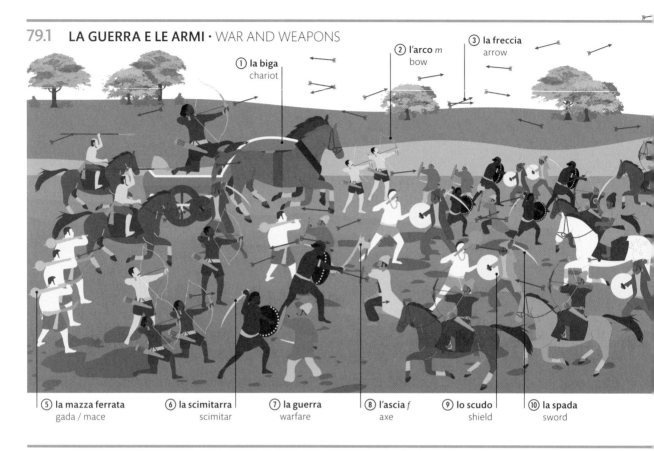

① la biga
chariot

② l'arco *m*
bow

③ la freccia
arrow

⑤ la mazza ferrata
gada / mace

⑥ la scimitarra
scimitar

⑦ la guerra
warfare

⑧ l'ascia *f*
axe

⑨ lo scudo
shield

⑩ la spada
sword

79.2 LE PERSONE NELLA STORIA · PEOPLE THROUGH TIME

② gli utensili
di selce
flint tools

① l'età della pietra *f*
the Stone Age

③ l'età del bronzo *f*
the Bronze Age

④ l'età dell'oro *f*
the Iron Age

⑤ il contadino *m*
la contadina *f*
farmer

⑥ il mercante
merchant

⑦ l'artigiano *m* / l'artigiana *f*
artisan

⑫ l'imperatore *m*
emperor

⑬ l'imperatrice *f*
empress

⑭ il re
king

⑮ la regina
queen

⑯ il principe /
la principessa
prince / princess

⑰ i nobili
nobles

⑫ l'epoca d'oro islamica f
the Islamic Golden Age

⑭ l'illuminismo *m*
the Enlightenment

⑮ la rivoluzione
industriale
the Industrial
Revolution

⑬ il filosofo
philosopher

See also
44 Gli edifici e l'architettura • Buildings and architecture **73** A scuola • At school
80 All'università • At college **88** L'esercito • Military

④ **la lancia**
spear

⑪ **il cavallo da battaglia**
warhorse

⑫ **l'elefante da battaglia** *m*
war elephant

⑬ **la battaglia**
battle

⑭ **il cannone**
cannon

⑮ **la catapulta**
catapult

⑯ **l'ariete** *m*
battering ram

⑰ **il cavaliere**
knight

⑱ **l'armatura** *f*
armour

⑲ **il guerriero**
warrior

⑧ **il fabbro**
blacksmith

⑨ **i popolani**
peasants

⑩ **il regno**
kingdom

⑪ **l'impero** *m*
empire

⑱ **il lord / la lady**
lord / lady

⑲ **il menestrello**
minstrel

⑳ **il giullare**
jester

㉑ **lo scrivano**
scribe

㉖ **la rivoluzione tecnologica** *f*
the Technological Revolution

㉗ **l'era dell'informazione** *f*
the Information Age

79.3 **LO STUDIO DEL PASSATO**
STUDYING THE PAST

① **lo storico** *m*
la storica *f*
historian

② **l'archivio** *m*
archive

③ **le fonti**
sources

④ **la pergamena**
scroll

⑤ **il documento**
document

⑥ **l'archeologia** *f*
archaeology

⑦ **l'archeologo** *m*
l'archeologa *f*
archaeologist

⑧ **lo scavo**
dig / excavation

⑩ **la torbiera**
peat bog

⑨ **i resti**
remains

⑪ **le scoperte**
finds

⑫ **la tomba**
tomb

⑬ **il sito storico**
historical site

80.1 L'UNIVERSITÀ · UNIVERSITY

③ il professore *m*
la professoressa *f*
lecturer

① il campus universitario
campus

② l'auditorium *m*
lecture theatre

④ il campo sportivo
sports field

⑤ la mensa
refectory

⑥ il dormitorio
halls of residence

⑦ la borsa di studio
scholarship

⑧ le ammissioni
admissions

⑨ lo studente della laurea
triennale *m* / la studentessa
della laurea triennale *f*
undergraduate

⑩ il diploma di laurea
diploma

⑪ la tesi
dissertation

⑫ la laurea
degree

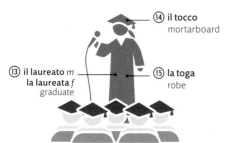

⑭ il tocco
mortarboard

⑮ la toga
robe

⑬ il laureato *m*
la laureata *f*
graduate

⑰ lo studente della
laurea magistrale *m*
la studentessa della
laurea magistrale *f*
postgraduate

⑱ la tesi
thesis

⑲ la laurea magistrale
master's degree

⑳ il dottorato
doctorate

⑯ la cerimonia di laurea
graduation ceremony

80.2 I DIPARTIMENTI E LE FACOLTÀ · DEPARTMENTS AND SCHOOLS

① gli
studi umanistici
humanities

② le scienze politiche
politics

③ la letteratura
literature

④ le lingue
languages

⑤ l'economia *f*
economics

⑥ la filosofia
philosophy

⑦ la storia
history

⑧ le scienze sociali
social sciences

⑨ la sociologia
sociology

⑩ la legge
law

⑪ la medicina
medicine

⑫ l'infermieristica *f*
nursing

See also
73 A scuola · At school **74** La matematica · Mathematics **75** La fisica · Physics
76 La chimica · Chemistry **77** La biologia · Biology **79** La storia · History
85 La legge · Law **138** I libri e la lettura · Books and reading

80.3 LA BIBLIOTECA · LIBRARY

① **la sala di lettura**
reading room

② **la lista dei libri da leggere**
reading list

③ **prendere in prestito**
to borrow

④ **rinnovare**
to renew

⑤ **restituire**
to return

⑥ **prenotare**
to reserve

⑦ **il reparto**
aisle

⑧ **lo scaffale**
bookshelf

⑨ **il bibliotecario** *m*
la bibliotecaria *f*
librarian

⑩ **la tessera della biblioteca**
library card

⑪ **la rivista**
periodical / journal

⑫ **il libro**
book

⑬ **la biblioteca**
library

⑭ **lo sportello prestiti**
loans desk

⑭ **Ho ricevuto una borsa di studio per condurre una ricerca scientifica.**
I received a grant to do scientific research.

⑬ **le scienze**
sciences

⑮ **la chimica**
chemistry

⑯ **la fisica**
physics

⑰ **la biologia**
biology

⑱ **l'ingegneria** *f*
engineering

⑲ **la zoologia**
zoology

⑳ **la scuola di musica**
music school

㉑ **la scuola di danza**
dance school

㉒ **l'istituto d'arte** *m*
art college / school

81.1 IL LAVORO D'UFFICIO · OFFICE WORK

① l'azienda *f*
company

② la filiale
branch

③ l'impiego *m*
employment

④ guadagnare
to earn

⑤ il lavoro fisso
permanent

⑥ il lavoro
temporaneo
temporary

⑩ il lavoro di otto
ore regolari
nine-to-five job

⑪ lavorare
part-time
to work part-time

⑫ fare i turni
to work shifts

⑬ le ferie annuali
annual leave

⑭ avere un giorno
libero
to have a day off

⑮ andare in
maternità
to go on maternity
leave

⑲ prendersi un
giorno di malattia
to call in sick

⑳ presentare le
dimissioni
to hand in your notice

㉑ essere licenziato *m*
essere licenziata *f*
to get fired

㉒ essere licenziato *m*
essere licenziata *f*
to be laid off

㉓ essere
disoccupato *m* /
essere disoccupata *f*
to be unemployed

㉔ il sussidio di
disoccupazione
unemployment benefit

㉞ l'uomo d'affari *m*
businessman

㊴ il manager *m*
la manager *f*
manager

㉙ la sede principale
headquarters

㉚ l'addetto alla
reception *m* / l'addetta
alla reception *f*
receptionist

㉝ l'AD (amministratore
delegato) *m*
CEO (chief executive
officer)

㊳ il tirocinante *m*
la tirocinante *f*
apprentice

㊵ l'assistente
personale *m* / *f*
PA (personal assistant)

㊶ il responsabile *m*
la responsabile *f*
leader

㉛ la sala d'attesa
waiting area

㉟ l'accordo commerciale *m*
business deal

㊱ la donna d'affari
businesswoman

㊷ i clienti
clients

㉘ la reception dell'ufficio
office reception

㉜ l'ufficio dell'amministratore delegato *m*
CEO's office

㊲ la riunione
meeting

See also
82 In ufficio • In the office **89-90** I lavori • Jobs **91** I settori e i reparti • Industries and departments **92** Fare domanda per un lavoro • Applying for a job **93** Le competenze sul luogo di lavoro • Workplace skills **95** Riunirsi e presentare • Meeting and presenting

⑦ **l'orario flessibile** *m*
flexitime

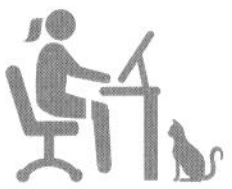
⑧ **lavorare da casa**
to work from home

⑨ **lavorare a tempo pieno**
to work full-time

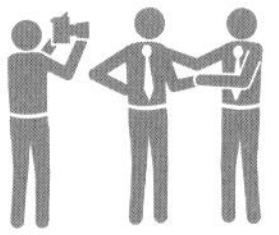
⑯ **essere promosso** *m*
essere promossa *f*
to be promoted

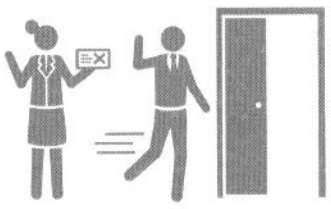
⑰ **dimettersi**
to resign

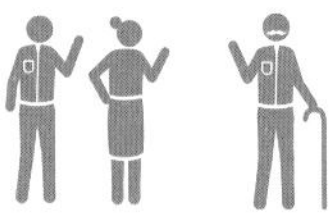
⑱ **andare in pensione**
to retire

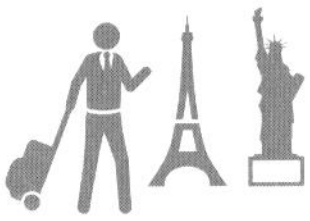
㉕ **il viaggio di lavoro**
business trip

㉖ **l'appuntamento** *m*
appointment

㉗ **il pranzo di lavoro**
business lunch

81.2 LA PAGA • PAY

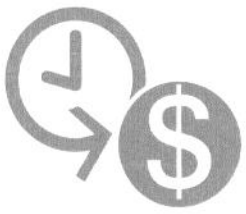
① **la tariffa oraria**
hourly rate

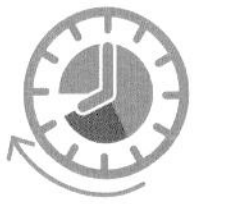
② **gli straordinari**
overtime

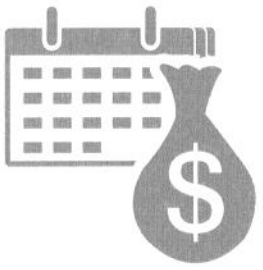
③ **il salario**
salary

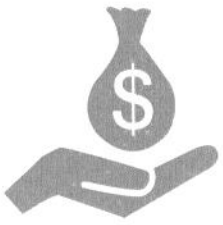
④ **lo stipendio**
wages

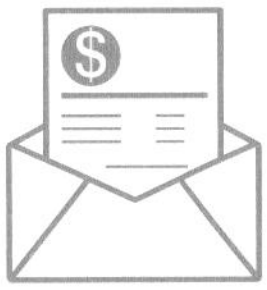
⑤ **la busta paga**
pay slip

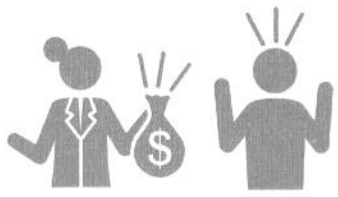
⑥ **l'incentivo** *m*
bonus

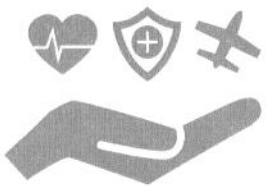
⑦ **i benefit**
benefits

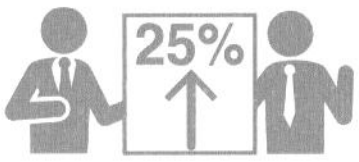

⑧ **l'aumento** *m*
raise

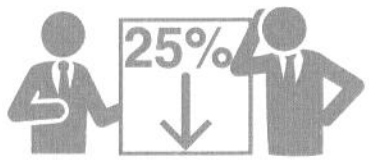

⑨ **la riduzione dello stipendio**
pay cut

㊹ **il responsabile del colloquio** *m*
la responsabile del colloquio *f*
interviewer

㊺ **il candidato** *m*
la candidata *f*
applicant

㊽ **il lavoratore** *m*
la lavoratrice *f*
worker

㊾ **il collega** *m* / **la collega** *f*
co-worker / colleague

㊿ **il dipendente** *m*
la dipendente *f*
employee

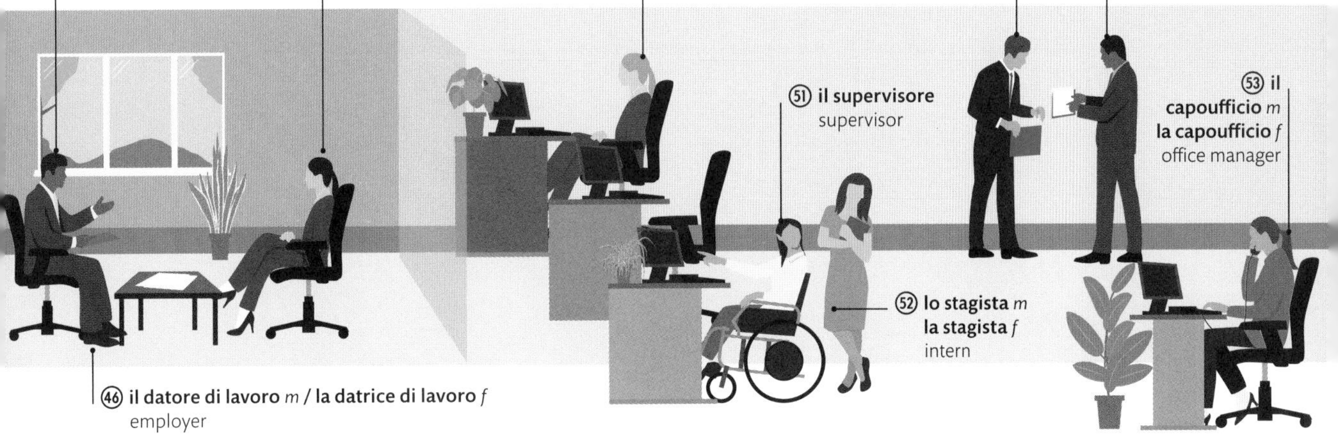

(51) **il supervisore**
supervisor

(53) **il capoufficio** *m*
la capoufficio *f*
office manager

(52) **lo stagista** *m*
la stagista *f*
intern

㊻ **il datore di lavoro** *m* / **la datrice di lavoro** *f*
employer

㊸ **il colloquio**
interview

㊼ **lo staff**
staff

82 In ufficio
In the office

82.1 L'UFFICIO · OFFICE

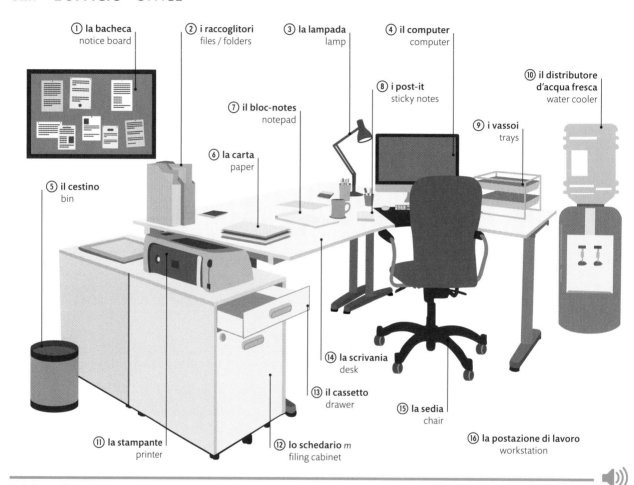

① la bacheca
notice board

② i raccoglitori
files / folders

③ la lampada
lamp

④ il computer
computer

⑩ il distributore
d'acqua fresca
water cooler

⑧ i post-it
sticky notes

⑦ il bloc-notes
notepad

⑨ i vassoi
trays

⑥ la carta
paper

⑤ il cestino
bin

⑭ la scrivania
desk

⑬ il cassetto
drawer

⑮ la sedia
chair

⑪ la stampante
printer

⑫ lo schedario *m*
filing cabinet

⑯ la postazione di lavoro
workstation

82.2 L'ATTREZZATURA PER LE SALE RIUNIONI · MEETING-ROOM EQUIPMENT

① la presentazione
presentation

② la proposta
proposal

③ la relazione
report

⑥ la lavag
fogli m
flip char

④ il proiettore
digital
projector

⑤ la riunione
meeting

⑦ il cavall
easel

See also
81 Al lavoro • At work **83** I computer e la tecnologia • Computers and technology **91** I settori e i reparti
Industries and departments **92** Fare domanda per un lavoro • Applying for a job **93** Le competenze sul
luogo di lavoro • Workplace skills **95** Riunirsi e presentare • Meeting and presenting

82.3 L'ATTREZZATURA DELL'UFFICIO · OFFICE EQUIPMENT

① **la fotocopiatrice**
photocopier

② **lo scanner**
scanner

③ **il telefono**
telephone / phone

④ **il computer portatile**
laptop

⑤ **il proiettore**
projector

⑥ **le cuffie**
headset

⑦ **il tritadocumenti**
shredder

⑧ **il cellulare**
mobile phone

⑨ **il poggiapiedi**
footrest

⑩ **la sedia con appoggio per ginocchia**
kneeling chair

⑪ **il pannello mobile**
movable panel

⑫ **la cancelleria**
stationery

⑬ **la lettera**
letter

⑭ **la busta**
envelope

⑮ **il calendario**
calendar

⑯ **l'agenda** f
diary

⑰ **il fermablocco**
clipboard

⑱ **la pinzatrice**
hole punch

⑲ **gli elastici**
rubber bands

⑳ **la pinza fermacarte**
binder clip

㉑ **le forbici**
scissors

㉒ **il temperino**
pencil sharpener

㉓ **la cucitrice**
stapler

㉔ **le graffette**
staples

㉕ **il bianchetto**
correction fluid

㉖ **il verbale**
minutes

㉗ **il raccoglitore ad anelli**
ring binder

㉘ **l'evidenziatore** m
highlighter

㉙ **la colla**
glue

㉚ **lo scotch**
tape

㉛ **la puntina da disegno**
drawing pin

㉜ **la matita**
pencil

㉝ **la penna**
pen

㉞ **le graffette**
paper clips

㉟ **la gomma da cancellare**
rubber

㊱ **il righello**
ruler

83.1 GLI APPARECCHI E LA TECNOLOGIA · GADGETS AND TECHNOLOGY

② **la webcam**
webcam

① **lo schermo**
screen

③ **il router**
router

④ **il Wi-Fi**
Wi-Fi

⑤ **il lettore di
e-book**
e-reader

⑥ **il tablet**
tablet

⑦ **il cavo**
wire

⑬ **il computer
portatile**
laptop

⑭ **la fotocamera**
camera

⑮ **lo smartwatch**
smartwatch

⑧ **il mouse**
mouse

⑨ **la scrivania del
computer**
computer desk

⑩ **la tastiera**
keyboard

⑪ **il tappetino per il
mouse**
mouse mat

⑯ **il caricabatterie
solare**
solar charger

⑰ **lo smartpho...**
smartphone

⑫ **il computer fisso**
desktop computer

⑱ **il tasto home**
home button

⑲ **il cavo di
ricarica**
charging cable

⑳ **gli altoparlanti**
speakers

㉑ **la videocamera**
camcorder

㉒ **wireless**
wireless

㉓ **la cuffia
bluetooth**
Bluetooth headset

㉔ **la batteria**
battery

㉕ **la chiavetta USB**
USB drive

㉖ **il registratore
vocale**
voice recorder

㉗ **la password**
password

㉘ **la scheda di
memoria**
memory card

㉙ **il disco fisso**
hard drive

㉚ **la presa elettrica**
plug

㉛ **il cavo di
alimentazione**
power lead

㉜ **il circuito**
circuit

㉝ **il telecomando**
remote control

㉞ **l'intelligenza
artificiale** f
artificial intelligence

See also
73 A scuola · At school **80** All'università · At college **81** Al lavoro · At work **82** In ufficio
In the office **95** Riunirsi e presentare · Meeting and presenting **140** I giochi · Games

83.2 **LA COMUNICAZIONE ONLINE** · ONLINE COMMUNICATION

① **accendere**
to turn on

② **spegnere**
to turn off

③ **accedere**
to log in

④ **uscire**
to log out

⑤ **scaricare**
to download

⑥ **caricare**
to upload

⑦ **fare il back up**
to back up

⑧ **cliccare**
to click

⑨ **collegare**
to plug in

⑩ **eliminare**
to delete

⑪ **stampare**
to print

⑫ **il contatto**
contact

⑬ **l'e-mail** *f*
email

⑭ **rispondere**
to reply

⑮ **rispondere a tutti**
to reply to all

⑯ **inviare**
to send

⑰ **inoltrare**
to forward

⑱ **la bozza**
draft

⑲ **la posta in arrivo**
inbox

⑳ **la posta in uscita**
outbox

㉑ **l'oggetto** *m*
subject

㉒ **lo spam**
junk mail / spam

㉓ **il cestino**
trash

㉔ **l'allegato** *m*
attachment

㉕ **la chat**
chat

㉖ **la videochiamata**
video chat

㉗ **la firma**
signature

㉘ **l'hashtag** *m*
hashtag

㉙ **la chiocciola**
at sign /
at symbol

㉚ **Liz, devi accendere il microfono.**
You need to turn on your microphone, Liz.

㉛ **la videoconferenza**
video conference

84 I media
Media

84.1 LO STUDIO TELEVISIVO · TELEVISION STUDIO

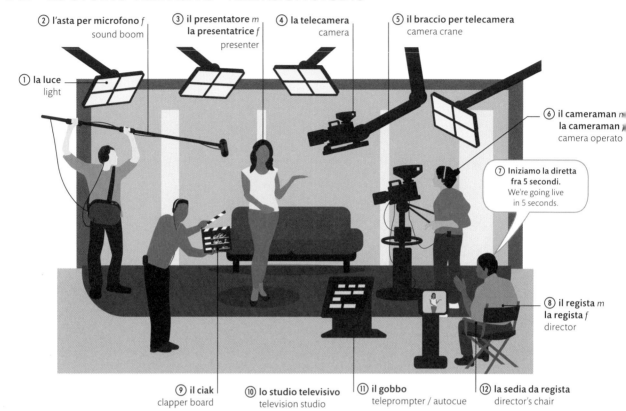

② l'asta per microfono *f*
sound boom

③ il presentatore *m*
la presentatrice *f*
presenter

④ la telecamera
camera

⑤ il braccio per telecamera
camera crane

① la luce
light

⑥ il cameraman *m*
la cameraman *f*
camera operato...

⑦ Iniziamo la diretta fra 5 secondi.
We're going live in 5 seconds.

⑧ il regista *m*
la regista *f*
director

⑨ il ciak
clapper board

⑩ lo studio televisivo
television studio

⑪ il gobbo
teleprompter / autocue

⑫ la sedia da regista
director's chair

84.2 LA RADIO · RADIO

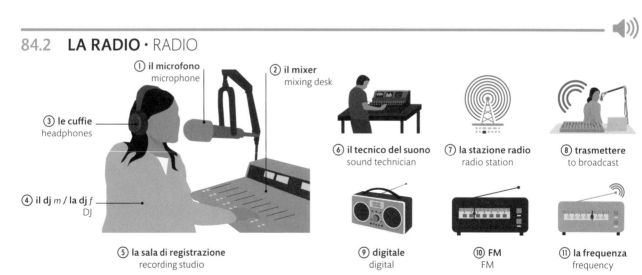

① il microfono
microphone

② il mixer
mixing desk

③ le cuffie
headphones

⑥ il tecnico del suono
sound technician

⑦ la stazione radio
radio station

⑧ trasmettere
to broadcast

④ il dj *m* / la dj *f*
DJ

⑤ la sala di registrazione
recording studio

⑨ digitale
digital

⑩ FM
FM

⑪ la frequenza
frequency

See also
83 I computer e la tecnologia · Computers and technology **128-129** La musica · Music
136 L'home entertainment · Home entertainment **137** La televisione · Television

84.3 I SOCIAL MEDIA E I MEDIA ONLINE
SOCIAL AND ONLINE MEDIA

⑨ **Il mio blog ha oltre 500 follower.**
My blog has over 500 followers.

① **seguire**
to follow

② **mettere mi piace**
to like

③ **diventare virale**
to go viral

④ **essere di tendenza**
to trend

⑤ **l'avatar** *m*
avatar

⑥ **il vlog**
vlog

⑦ **il vlogger** *m*
la vlogger *f*
vlogger

⑧ **il blog**
blog

⑩ **il blogger** *m*
la blogger *f*
blogger

⑪ **condividere**
to share

⑫ **bloccare**
to block

⑬ **postare**
to post

⑭ **inviare un messaggio diretto**
to DM someone

⑮ **l'influencer** *m / f*
influencer

⑯ **il follower**
follower

⑰ **il podcast**
podcast

⑱ **l'emoji** *f*
emoji

⑲ **l'hashtag** *m*
hashtag

⑳ **il thread**
thread

㉑ **la sezione notizie**
newsfeed

㉒ **l'aggiornamento dello stato** *m*
status update

㉔ **la piattaforma**
platform

㉕ **il cookie**
cookie

㉖ **la finestra pop-up**
pop-up

㉓ **il sistema di gestione dei contenuti**
CMS (content management system)

㉗ **il sito web di notizie**
news website

㉘ **il sito web di una rivista**
magazine website

㉙ **il sito web della community**
community website

㉚ **il trolling**
trolling

85.1 IL SISTEMA LEGALE · THE LEGAL SYSTEM

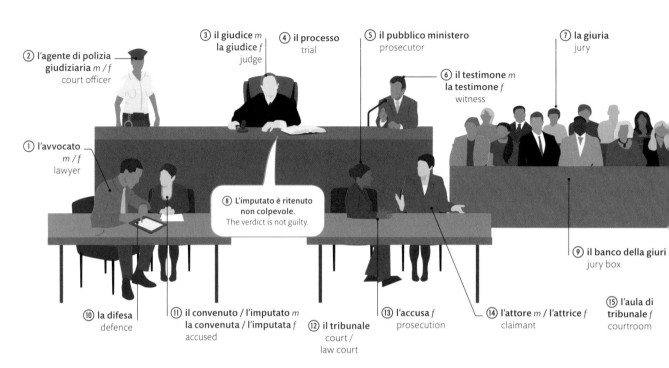

③ il giudice *m*
la giudice *f*
judge

④ il processo
trial

⑤ il pubblico ministero
prosecutor

⑦ la giuria
jury

② l'agente di polizia
giudiziaria *m / f*
court officer

⑥ il testimone *m*
la testimone *f*
witness

① l'avvocato
m / f
lawyer

⑧ L'imputato è ritenuto
non colpevole.
The verdict is not guilty.

⑨ il banco della giuri
jury box

⑩ la difesa
defence

⑪ il convenuto / l'imputato *m*
la convenuta / l'imputata *f*
accused

⑫ il tribunale
court /
law court

⑬ l'accusa *f*
prosecution

⑭ l'attore *m* / l'attrice *f*
claimant

⑮ l'aula di
tribunale *f*
courtroom

⑯ lo stenografo *m*
la stenografa *f*
stenographer

⑰ l'ufficiale giudiziario *m*
l'ufficiale giudiziaria *f*
court official

⑱ l'ufficio
dell'avvocato *m*
lawyer's office

⑲ la citazione
summons

⑳ il cliente *m*
la cliente *f*
client

㉑ il mandato
warrant

㉒ l'ordinanza *f*
writ

㉓ l'accusa *f*
charge

㉔ la consulenza
legale
legal advice

㉕ la deposizione
statement

㉛ il presidente della giuria *m*
la presidentessa della giuria *f*
foreperson

㉜ il voto
vote

㉖ l'udienza *f*
court date

㉗ il processo
court case

㉘ la sentenza
verdict

㉙ condannare
to sentence

㉚ la delibera della giuria
jury deliberation

33 l'identikit *m*
photofit

34 la prova
evidence

35 il sospettato *m*
la sospettata *f*
suspect

36 i precedenti penali
criminal record

37 il criminale *m*
la criminale *f*
criminal

38 l'imputato *m*
l'imputata *f*
accused

39 perorare / dichiararsi
to plead

40 innocente *m / f*
innocent

41 colpevole *m / f*
guilty

43 i carcerati *m*
le carcerate *f*
prisoners

42 ricorrere in appello
to appeal

44 le guardie carcerarie
prison guards

45 il carcere
prison

46 la cella
cell

47 la cauzione
bail

48 la libertà condizionale
parole

49 la multa
fine

50 essere assolto *m*
essere assolta *f*
to be acquitted

85.2 I CRIMINI · CRIME

1 la rapina
robbery / burglary

2 lo scippo
mugging

3 il furto d'auto
car theft

4 la violenza dei tifosi
hooliganism

5 il vandalismo
vandalism

6 il contrabbando
smuggling

7 la frode
fraud

8 l'hackeraggio *m*
hacking

9 il borseggio
pickpocketing

10 la corruzione
bribery

11 l'eccesso di velocità *m*
speeding

12 lo spaccio di droga
drug dealing

13 i graffiti
graffiti

14 il taccheggio
shoplifting

179

86 L'agricoltura
Farming

86.1 NELLA FATTORIA · ON THE FARM

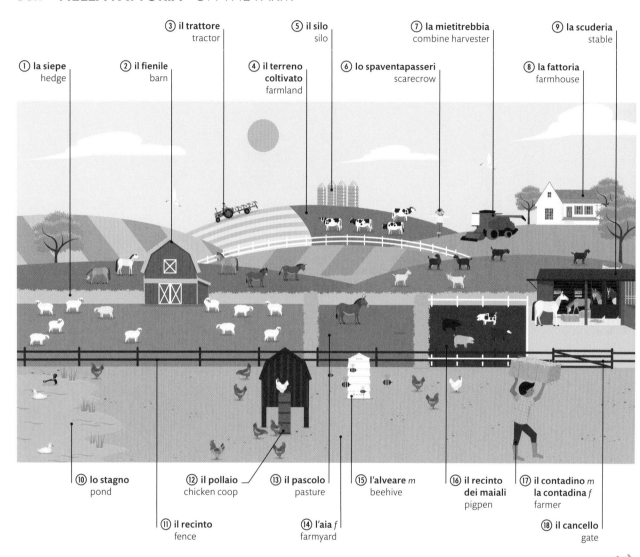

③ **il trattore**
tractor

⑤ **il silo**
silo

⑦ **la mietitrebbia**
combine harvester

⑨ **la scuderia**
stable

① **la siepe**
hedge

② **il fienile**
barn

④ **il terreno coltivato**
farmland

⑥ **lo spaventapasseri**
scarecrow

⑧ **la fattoria**
farmhouse

⑩ **lo stagno**
pond

⑫ **il pollaio**
chicken coop

⑬ **il pascolo**
pasture

⑮ **l'alveare** *m*
beehive

⑯ **il recinto dei maiali**
pigpen

⑰ **il contadino** *m*
la contadina *f*
farmer

⑪ **il recinto**
fence

⑭ **l'aia** *f*
farmyard

⑱ **il cancello**
gate

86.2 I VERBI DELL'AGRICOLTURA · FARMING VERBS

① **arare**
to plough

② **seminare**
to sow

③ **mungere**
to milk

④ **nutrire**
to feed

⑤ **piantare**
to plant

⑥ **raccogliere**
to harvest

See also
53 La carne · Meat **55-56** La verdura · Vegetables **57** La frutta · Fruit **58** La frutta e la frutta a guscio
Fruit and nuts **61** I prodotti caseari · Dairy produce **165** Gli animali da fattoria · Farm animals

86.3 I TERMINI DELL'AGRICOLTURA · FARMING TERMS

① l'azienda agricola f
arable farm

② l'azienda casearia f
dairy farm

③ l'azienda di ovinicoltura f
sheep farm

④ l'azienda avicola f
poultry farm

⑤ l'azienda suinicola f
pig farm

⑥ l'allevamento ittico m
fish farm

⑦ la mandria
herd

⑧ l'azienda ortofrutticola f
fruit farm

⑨ il vigneto
vineyard

⑩ l'orto m
vegetable garden / vegetable plot

⑪ l'erbicida m
herbicide

⑫ il pesticida
pesticide

86.4 LE COLTURE · CROPS

① il grano
wheat

② il mais
maize

③ l'orzo m
barley

④ i semi di colza
rapeseed

⑤ i girasoli
sunflowers

⑥ il fieno
hay

⑦ l'erba medica f
alfalfa

⑧ il tabacco
tobacco

⑨ il riso
rice

⑩ il tè
tea

⑪ il caffè
coffee

⑫ la canna da zucchero
sugar cane

⑬ il lino
flax

⑭ il cotone
cotton

⑮ le patate
potatoes

⑯ gli ignami m
yams

⑰ il miglio
millet

⑱ le banane platano
plantains

87 Le costruzioni
Construction

87.1 IL CANTIERE · BUILDING SITE

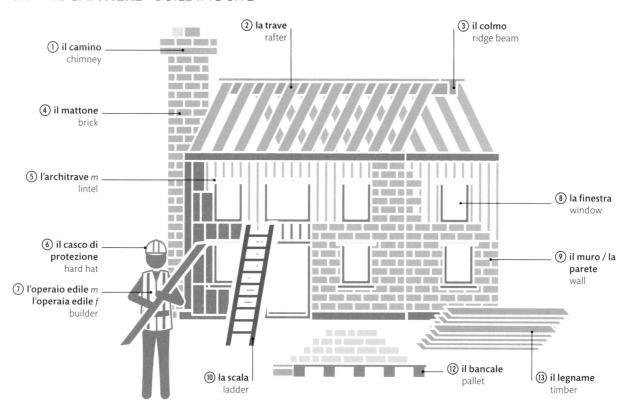

① il camino
chimney

② la trave
rafter

③ il colmo
ridge beam

④ il mattone
brick

⑤ l'architrave *m*
lintel

⑧ la finestra
window

⑥ il casco di protezione
hard hat

⑨ il muro / la parete
wall

⑦ l'operaio edile *m*
l'operaia edile *f*
builder

⑩ la scala
ladder

⑫ il bancale
pallet

⑬ il legname
timber

⑪ il cantiere
building site

⑭ la bacheca degli avvisi di sicurezza
safety notice board

⑮ il paraorecchie
ear protectors / ear muffs

⑯ il gilet ad alta visibilità
high-visibility vest

⑰ i guanti protettivi
safety gloves

⑱ gli occhiali protettivi
safety glasses

⑲ la cintura degli attrezzi
tool belt

⑳ la trave metallica
girder

㉑ la tubatura
pipe

㉒ la malta
cement / mortar

㉓ il blocco di calcestruzzo
breeze block

㉔ le tegole
roof tiles

㉕ costruire
to build

See also
25 Un luogo in cui vivere · A place to live **32** La casa · House and home **33** Gli impianti elettrico e idraulico · Electrics and plumbing **35** I lavori di miglioria della casa · Home improvements **36** Gli attrezzi · Tools **37** La decorazione · Decorating

87.2 I MACCHINARI · MACHINERY

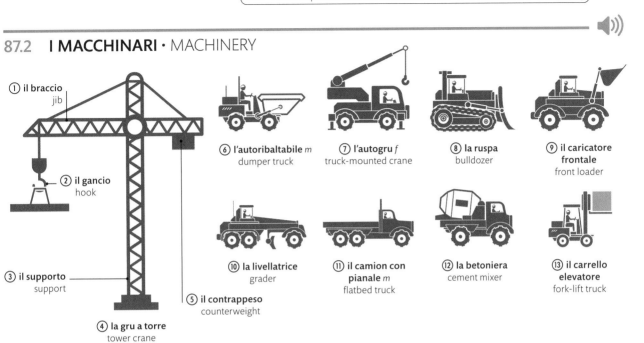

1. **il braccio** jib
2. **il gancio** hook
3. **il supporto** support
4. **la gru a torre** tower crane
5. **il contrappeso** counterweight

6. **l'autoribaltabile** *m* dumper truck
7. **l'autogru** *f* truck-mounted crane
8. **la ruspa** bulldozer
9. **il caricatore frontale** front loader

10. **la livellatrice** grader
11. **il camion con pianale** *m* flatbed truck
12. **la betoniera** cement mixer
13. **il carrello elevatore** fork-lift truck

87.3 GLI ATTREZZI E I CANTIERI STRADALI
TOOLS AND ROADWORKS

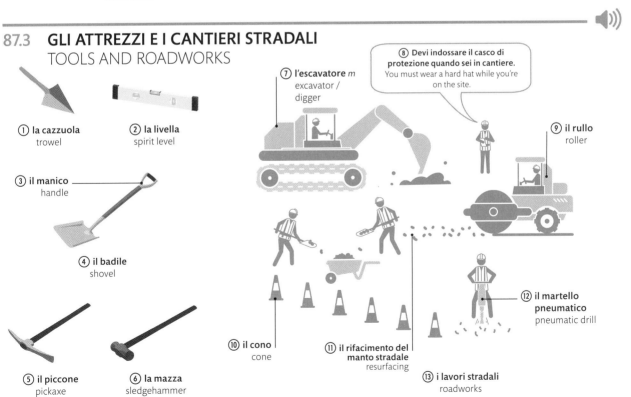

1. **la cazzuola** trowel
2. **la livella** spirit level
3. **il manico** handle
4. **il badile** shovel
5. **il piccone** pickaxe
6. **la mazza** sledgehammer

7. **l'escavatore** *m* excavator / digger
8. **Devi indossare il casco di protezione quando sei in cantiere.** You must wear a hard hat while you're on the site.
9. **il rullo** roller
10. **il cono** cone
11. **il rifacimento del manto stradale** resurfacing
12. **il martello pneumatico** pneumatic drill
13. **i lavori stradali** roadworks

88 L'esercito
Military

88.1 LE FORZE ARMATE
ARMED FORCES

⑤ la radiotrasmittente
radio

⑥ l'auricolare *m*
ear phone

① l'esercito *m*
army

⑦ la tuta mimetica
camouflage

② il marinaio
marine

③ la marina militare
navy

④ il soldato *m*
la soldatessa *f*
soldier

⑧ i marinai
sailors

⑨ il generale
general

⑩ l'ammiraglio *m*
admiral

⑫ l'aviatore *m*
airman

⑬ la divisa
uniform

⑮ la medaglia
medal

⑪ l'aeronautica militare *f*
airforce

⑭ il veterano di
guerra
veteran

88.2 I VEICOLI MILITARI
MILITARY VEHICLES

① il cannone
gun

③ il carro armato
tank

② il veicolo corazzato
armoured vehicle

④ il camion militare
military truck

⑤ il veicolo anfibio
amphibious vehicle

⑥ l'ambulanza
militare *f*
military ambulance

⑦ il veicolo da
ricognizione
reconnaissance vehicle

88.3 LE NAVI DELLA MARINA MILITARE
NAVY VESSELS

② l'isola *f*
island

① la portaerei
aircraft carrier

③ il cacciatorpediniere
destroyer

④ l'incrociatore *m*
cruiser

⑤ la fregata
frigate

⑥ il sottomarino
submarine

See also
79 La storia · History **148** Le cartine e le direzioni
Maps and directions **149-151** I Paesi · Countries

88.4 IL VELIVOLO DA COMBATTIMENTO · COMBAT AIRCRAFT

① **l'aereo da trasporto militare** *m*
military transport aircraft

② **il bombardiere**
bomber

③ **l'elicottero d'attacco** *m*
attack helicopter

④ **il caccia**
fighter

⑤ **l'aereo da ricognizione** *m*
reconnaissance aircraft

⑥ **l'elicottero da trasporto** *m*
transport helicopter

88.5 LA GUERRA E LE ARMI · WAR AND WEAPONS

① **la battaglia**
battle

② **il fronte**
front

③ **gli spari**
gunfire

④ **il ferito**
casualty

⑤ **l'ospedale da campo** *m*
field hospital

⑥ **la mensa militare**
mess

⑦ **le armi**
guns

⑧ **il mitra**
machine gun

⑨ **la pistola**
pistol

⑩ **il fucile a canna liscia**
shotgun

⑪ **il fucile**
rifle

⑬ **la granata**
grenade

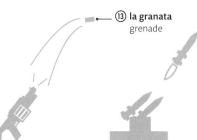

⑫ **il lanciagranate**
grenade launcher

⑭ **il missile terra-aria**
surface-to-air missile

⑮ **il missile balistico**
ballistic missile

⑯ **il missile spalleggiabile**
shoulder-launched missile

⑰ **il missile da crociera**
cruise missile

⑱ **il drone armato**
armed drone

89 I lavori
Jobs

89.1 LE OCCUPAZIONI · OCCUPATIONS

⑩ Questo tubo ha una perdita.
This pipe has sprung a leak.

① l'attore *m*
l'attrice *f*
actor

② il sociologo *m*
la sociologa *f*
sociologist

③ il barbiere
barber

④ l'editore *m*
l'editrice *f*
editor

⑤ il barista *m*
la barista *f*
bartender

⑥ il pescatore *m*
la pescatrice *f*
fisherman

⑦ il fisioterapista *m*
la fisioterapista *f*
physical therapist /
physiotherapist

⑧ l'ottico *m* / l'ottica *f*
optician

⑨ l'idraulico *m* / l'idraulica *f*
plumber

⑪ il falegname *m*
la falegname *f*
carpenter

⑫ il capitano
della nave *m* / *f*
ship's captain

⑬ il docente *m*
la docente *f*
lecturer

⑭ il comico *m*
la comica *f*
comedian

⑮ il ballerino *m*
la ballerina *f*
dancer

⑯ il clown *m* / la clown
clown

⑰ l'addetto alle
pulizie *m* / l'addetta
alle pulizie *f*
cleaner

⑱ il dottore *m*
la dottoressa *f*
doctor

⑲ l'istruttore di guida *m*
l'istruttrice di guida *f*
driving instructor

⑳ l'imbianchino *m*
l'imbianchina *f*
painter

㉑ l'elettricista *m* / *f*
electrician

㉒ il designer *m*
la designer *f*
designer

㉓ il barista *m*
la barista *f*
barista

㉔ il vigile del fuoco *m*
la vigilessa del fuoco *f*
firefighter

㉕ lo sviluppatore di app *m*
la sviluppatrice di app *f*
app developer

㉖ la spia
spy

㉗ il fiorista *m*
la fiorista *f*
florist

㉘ la manutenzione
delle aree verdi *m* / *f*
ground maintenance

㉙ il giardiniere *m*
la giardiniera *f*
gardener

㉚ il fruttivendolo *m*
la fruttivendola *f*
greengrocer

㉛ il minatore *m*
la minatrice *f*
miner

㉜ il responsabile IT *m*
la responsabile IT *f*
IT manager

㉝ il gioielliere *m*
la gioielliera *f*
jeweller

㉞ il dentista *m*
la dentista *f*
dentist

See also
81 Al lavoro • At work **82** In ufficio • In the office **90** I lavori (continua) • Jobs continued **91** I settori e i reparti • Industries and departments **92** Fare domanda per un lavoro • Applying for a job **93** Le competenze sul luogo di lavoro • Workplace skills **95** Riunirsi e presentare • Meeting and presenting

㉟ **il domestico** *m*
la domestica *f*
maid / housekeeper

㊱ **il parrucchiere** *m*
la parrucchiera *f*
hairdresser / stylist

㊲ **il meccanico** *m*
la meccanica *f*
mechanic

㊳ **l'interprete** *m / f*
interpreter

㊴ **il curatore del museo** *m* **/ la curatrice del museo** *f*
museum curator

㊵ **l'investigatore privato** *m*
l'investigatrice privata *f*
private investigator

㊶ **il capo cantiere** *m*
la capo cantiere *f*
site manager

㊷ **l'odontoiatra** *m / f*
orthodontist

㊸ **il conduttore** *m*
la conduttrice *f*
newsreader

㊹ **il farmacista** *m*
la farmacista *f*
pharmacist

㊺ **il macellaio** *m*
la macellaia *f*
butcher

㊻ **il fotografo** *m*
la fotografa *f*
photographer

㊼ **il poliziotto** *m*
la poliziotta *f*
police officer

㊽ **l'infermiere** *m*
l'infermiera *f*
nurse

㊾ **il marinaio** *m*
la marinaia *f*
sailor

㊿ **il commesso** *m*
la commessa *f*
sales assistant

(51) **la cameriera**
waitress

(52) **il cameriere**
waiter

(53) **lo scultore** *m*
la scultrice *f*
sculptor

(54) **la guardia di sicurezza**
security guard

(55) **il sarto** *m*
la sarta *f*
tailor

(56) **il maestro di sci** *m*
la maestra di sci *f*
ski instructor

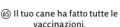

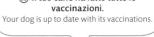

(57) **il soldato** *m*
la soldatessa *f*
soldier

(58) **il contadino** *m*
la contadina *f*
farmer

(59) **l'atleta** *m / f*
sportsperson

(60) **il pescivendolo** *m*
la pescivendola *f*
fishmonger

(61) **il cantante** *m*
la cantante *f*
singer

(62) **l'agente immobiliare** *m / f*
estate agent

(63) **il ricercatore di mercato** *m*
la ricercatrice di mercato *f*
market researcher

(65) **Il tuo cane ha fatto tutte le vaccinazioni.**
Your dog is up to date with its vaccinations.

(64) **il veterinario** *m* **/ la veterinaria** *f*
vet

90.1 LE OCCUPAZIONI · OCCUPATIONS

① la guardia di sicurezza
security guard

② il lavavetri *m*
la lavavetri *f*
window cleaner

③ l'artista *m / f*
artist

④ la guardia del corpo
bodyguard

⑤ lo psicologo *m*
la psicologa *f*
psychologist

⑥ l'uomo d'affari *m*
businessman

⑦ la donna d'affari
businesswoman

⑧ il commercialista *m*
la commercialista *f*
accountant

⑨ lo chef *m*
la chef *f*
chef

⑩ l'operaio edile *m*
l'operaia edile *f*
builder

⑪ il dj radiofonico *m*
la dj radiofonica *f*
radio DJ

⑫ l'ingegnere *m*
l'ingegnera *f*
engineer

⑬ lo stilista *m*
la stilista *f*
fashion designer

⑭ la rock star
rock star

⑮ l'istruttore di volo *m*
l'istruttrice di volo *f*
flight instructor

⑯ l'inserviente *m / f*
janitor

⑰ la guida turistica
tour guide

⑱ il postino *m*
la postina *f*
postman / postwoma

⑲ l'assistente personale *m / f*
personal assistant (PA)

⑳ il bibliotecario *m*
la bibliotecaria *f*
librarian

㉑ il fabbro *m / f*
locksmith

> **㉙ Devi fare molta esperienza in aula prima di diventare giudice.**
> You should have a lot of courtroom experience before you become a judge.

㉒ il paramedico *m*
la paramedico *f*
paramedic

㉓ l'insegnante di musica *m / f*
music teacher

㉔ l'assistente all'infanzia *m / f*
childcare provider

㉕ l'installatore di cucine *m*
l'installatrice di cucine *f*
kitchen installer / fitter

㉖ il tassista *m*
la tassista *f*
taxi driver

㉗ il custode dello zoo *m*
la custode dello zoo *f*
zookeeper

㉘ il giudice *m / **la giudice** *f*
judge

See also
81 Al lavoro · At work **82** In ufficio · In the office **91** I settori e i reparti · Industries and departments **92** Fare domanda per un lavoro · Applying for a job **93** Le competenze sul luogo di lavoro · Workplace skills **95** Riunirsi e presentare · Meeting and presenting

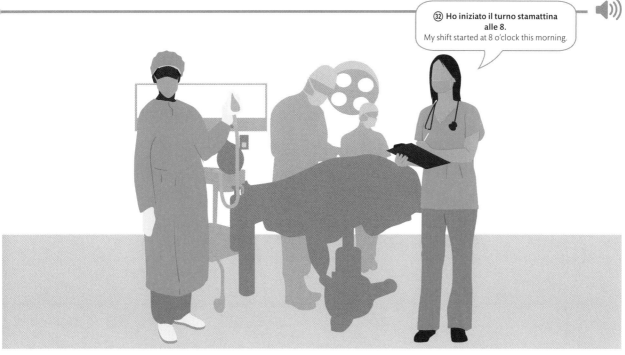

㉜ **Ho iniziato il turno stamattina alle 8.**
My shift started at 8 o'clock this morning.

㉚ **l'anestesista** *m / f*
anaesthetist

㉛ **il chirurgo** *m* / **la chirurga** *f*
surgeon

㉝ **l'autista** *m / f*
driver

㉞ **il segretario** *m*
la segretaria *f*
secretary

㉟ **l'addetto alla reception** *m*
l'addetta alla reception *f*
receptionist

㊱ **lo steward** *m*
l'hostess *f*
flight attendant

㊲ **lo scienziato** *m*
la scienziata *f*
scientist

㊳ **l'autista di autobus** *m / f*
bus driver

㊴ **il musicista** *m*
la musicista *f*
musician

㊵ **il perito** *m / f*
surveyor

㊶ **l'avvocato** *m / f*
lawyer

㊷ **l'insegnante** *m / f*
teacher

㊸ **il giornalista** *m*
la giornalista *f*
journalist

㊹ **il macchinista ferroviario** *m*
la macchinista ferroviaria *f*
train driver

㊺ **l'agente di viaggio** *m / f*
travel agent

㊻ **il camionista** *m*
la camionista *f*
lorry driver

㊼ **l'architetto** *m / f*
architect

㊽ **lo scrittore** *m*
la scrittrice *f*
writer

㊾ **l'insegnante di yoga** *m / f*
yoga teacher

㊿ **il pilota** *m*
la pilota *f*
pilot

91.1 I SETTORI · INDUSTRIES

① la pubblicità
advertising

② i servizi alla **persona**
personal services

③ l'agricoltura f
agriculture / farming

④ l'esercito m
military

⑤ il settore **immobiliare**
property

⑥ il settore **automobilistico**
automotive industry

⑩ il settore **bancario**
banking

⑪ l'industria **aerospaziale** f
aerospace

⑫ l'ingegneria del **petrolio** f
petroleum engineering

⑬ l'industria **chimica** f
chemical industry

⑭ le arti
arts

⑮ l'istruzione f
education

⑲ i videogiochi
gaming

⑳ l'energia f
energy

㉑ la ricerca
research

㉒ la moda
fashion

㉓ il riciclo
recycling

㉔ l'intrattenimento m
entertainment

㉘ le spedizioni
shipping

㉙ la vendita al **dettaglio online**
online retail

㉚ il giornalismo
journalism

㉛ il settore tessile
textiles

㉜ i media
media

㉝ il settore **hospitality**
hospitality

㊲ la consegna online
online delivery

㊳ l'acqua f
water

㊴ le arti dello **spettacolo**
performing arts

㊵ le biotecnologie
biotechnology

㊷ Le nostre azioni sono precipitate.
Our stocks have fallen dramatically.

㊶ la finanza
finance

See also
81 Al lavoro • At work **82** In ufficio • In the office **89-90** I lavori • Jobs **92** Fare domanda per un lavoro • Applying for a job **93** Le competenze sul luogo di lavoro • Workplace skills

⑧ **Questo è uno dei nostri edifici più famosi.**
This is one of our most famous buildings.

⑦ **il turismo**
tourism

⑨ **i servizi per animali domestici**
pet services

91.2 I REPARTI · DEPARTMENTS

① **il reparto contabile**
accounts / finance

② **la produzione**
production

③ **l'ufficio legale** *m*
legal

⑯ **la ristorazione**
catering / food

⑰ **l'industria farmaceutica** *f*
pharmaceuticals

⑱ **il settore edile**
construction

④ **il marketing**
marketing

⑤ **l'informatica** *f*
information technology (IT)

⑥ **i servizi per l'ufficio**
facilities / office services

㉕ **la pesca**
fishing

㉖ **l'elettronica** *f*
electronics

㉗ **la vendita al dettaglio**
retail

⑦ **le vendite**
sales

⑧ **l'amministrazione** *f*
administration

⑨ **le relazioni pubbliche**
public relations (PR)

㉞ **la sanità**
healthcare

㉟ **l'industria manifatturiera** *f*
manufacturing

㊱ **l'attività mineraria** *f*
mining

⑩ **gli acquisti**
purchasing

⑬ **Adoro queste idee per il nuovo progetto.**
I love these ideas for the new project.

⑪ **le risorse umane**
human resources (HR)

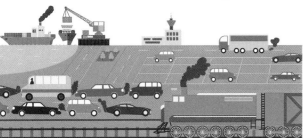

㊸ **il trasporto**
transport

⑫ **il reparto ricerca e sviluppo**
research and development (R&D)

92 Fare domanda per un lavoro
Applying for a job

92.1 LE CANDIDATURE · JOB APPLICATIONS

① **le offerte di lavoro**
job ads

② **il modulo di candidatura**
application form

③ **la lettera di accompagnamento**
cover letter

⑧ **Che tipo di lavoro sta cercando?**
What kind of work are you looking for?

⑦ **compilare un modulo**
to fill out a form

④ **il portfolio**
portfolio

⑤ **il curriculum**
CV

⑥ **il centro per l'impiego**
recruitment agency

92.2 FARE DOMANDA PER UN LAVORO
APPLYING FOR A JOB

② **i posti vacanti**
vacancies

④ **Che cosa la rende la candidata perfetta per questo lavoro?**
What makes you the perfect candidate for this job?

⑤ **Sono una gran lavoratrice e ho un forte spirito di squadra.**
I'm hardworking and I'm a team player.

① **fare domanda per un lavoro**
to apply for a job

③ **sostenere un colloquio**
to have an interview

See also
81 Al lavoro • At work **89-90** I lavori • Jobs **91** I settori e i reparti • Industries and departments **93** Le competenze sul luogo di lavoro • Workplace skills **95** Riunirsi e presentare • Meeting and presenting

92.3 IL LAVORO DI SQUADRA
TEAMWORK

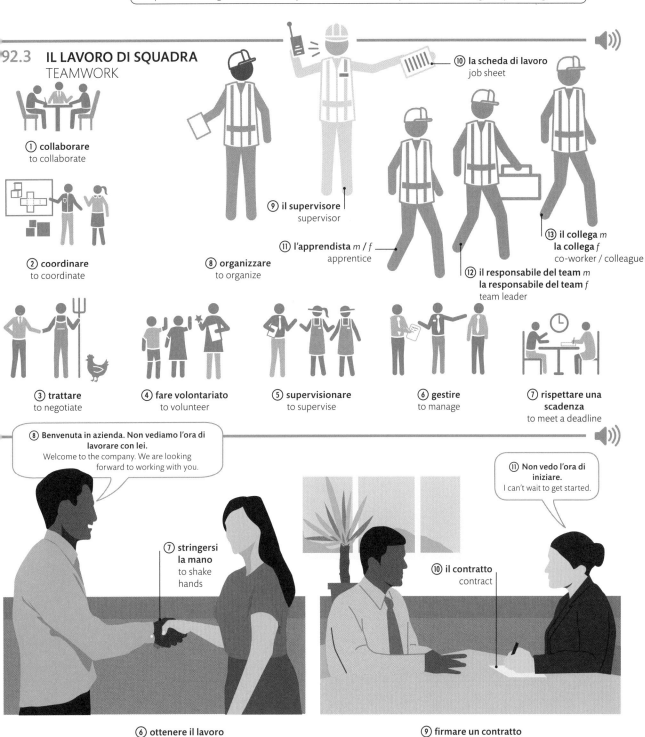

① **collaborare**
to collaborate

② **coordinare**
to coordinate

③ **trattare**
to negotiate

④ **fare volontariato**
to volunteer

⑤ **supervisionare**
to supervise

⑥ **gestire**
to manage

⑦ **rispettare una scadenza**
to meet a deadline

⑧ **organizzare**
to organize

⑨ **il supervisore**
supervisor

⑩ **la scheda di lavoro**
job sheet

⑪ **l'apprendista** *m / f*
apprentice

⑫ **il responsabile del team** *m*
la responsabile del team *f*
team leader

⑬ **il collega** *m*
la collega *f*
co-worker / colleague

⑧ **Benvenuta in azienda. Non vediamo l'ora di lavorare con lei.**
Welcome to the company. We are looking forward to working with you.

⑪ **Non vedo l'ora di iniziare.**
I can't wait to get started.

⑦ **stringersi la mano**
to shake hands

⑩ **il contratto**
contract

⑥ **ottenere il lavoro**
to get the job

⑨ **firmare un contratto**
to sign a contract

193

Le competenze sul luogo di lavoro
Workplace skills

93.1 LE QUALITÀ PROFESSIONALI · PROFESSIONAL ATTRIBUTES

① **organizzato** *m*
organizzata *f*
organized

② **paziente**
patient

③ **creativo** *m*
creativa *f*
creative

④ **onesto** *m* / **onesta** *f*
honest

⑤ **pratico** *m*
pratica *f*
practical

⑥ **professionale**
professional

⑦ **capace di adattarsi**
adaptable

⑧ **ambizioso** *m*
ambiziosa *f*
ambitious

⑨ **calmo** *m* / **calma** *f*
calm

⑩ **sicuro** *m* / **sicura** *f*
confident

⑪ **puntuale**
punctual

⑫ **affidabile**
reliable

⑬ **orientato al cliente** *m*
orientata al cliente *f*
customer-focused

⑭ **indipendente**
independent

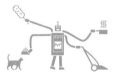

⑮ **efficiente**
efficient

⑯ **capace di lavorare in gruppo**
team player

⑰ **responsabile**
responsible

⑱ **inventivo** *m*
inventiva *f*
innovative

⑲ **motivato** *m*
motivata *f*
motivated

⑳ **determinato** *m*
determinata *f*
determined

㉑ **energico** *m*
energica *f*
energetic

㉓ Tra tutti quelli che conosco, Carlo è lo chef che lavora più duramente.
Carlo is the hardest-working chef I've ever met.

㉔ **competitivo** *m*
competitiva *f*
competitive

㉕ **assertivo** *m*
assertiva *f*
assertive

㉖ **ingegnoso** *m*
ingegnosa *f*
imaginative

㉗ **curioso** *m* / **curiosa** *f*
curious

㉒ **gran lavoratore** *m*
gran lavoratrice *f*
hard-working

㉘ **originale**
original

㉙ **preciso** *m*
precisa *f*
accurate

㉚ **buon ascoltatore** *m*
buona ascoltatrice *f*
good listener

㉛ **flessibile**
flexible

See also
10 I tratti della personalità · Personality traits **11** Le abilità e le azioni
Abilities and actions **81** Al lavoro · At work **82** In ufficio · In the office

93.2 LE COMPETENZE PROFESSIONALI · PROFESSIONAL EXPERTISE

① l'organizzazione *f*
organization

② le competenze informatiche
computer literacy

③ l'utilizzo del
computer *m*
computing

④ la risoluzione dei
problemi
problem-solving

⑤ l'analisi *f*
analytics

⑥ la capacità
decisionale
decision-making

⑦ il lavoro di
squadra
teamwork

⑧ imparare in fretta
being a
fast learner

⑨ prestare
attenzione ai dettagli
paying attention
to detail

⑩ il servizio clienti
customer service

⑪ la leadership
leadership

⑫ la ricerca
research

⑬ fluente nelle
lingue *m / f*
fluent in languages

⑭ le competenze
tecnologiche
technology literate

⑮ le capacità
oratorie
public speaking

⑯ la negoziazione
negotiating

⑰ la comunicazione
scritta
written communication

⑱ l'iniziativa *f*
initiative

⑲ il galateo
telefonico
telephone manner

⑳ lavorare bene
sotto pressione
working well
under pressure

㉑ le abilità di
calcolo
numeracy

㉒ la capacità di
guidare
ability to drive

㉓ ampiamente qualificato *m*
ampiamente qualificata *f*
well-qualified

㉔ l'autogestione *f*
self management

㉕ orientato al
servizio *m* / orientata
al servizio *f*
service focused

㉖ capace di
influenzare le persone
influencer

㉜ Devi imparare a gestire meglio il
tempo! Questa relazione è in ritardo.
You must improve your time
management! This report is late.

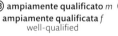

㉗ l'atteggiamento
pragmatico *m*
businesslike attitude

㉘ le capacità
relazionali
interpersonal skills

㉙ la gestione dei
progetti
project management

㉚ l'amministrazione *f*
administration

㉛ la gestione del tempo
time management

94.1 IL DENARO · MONEY

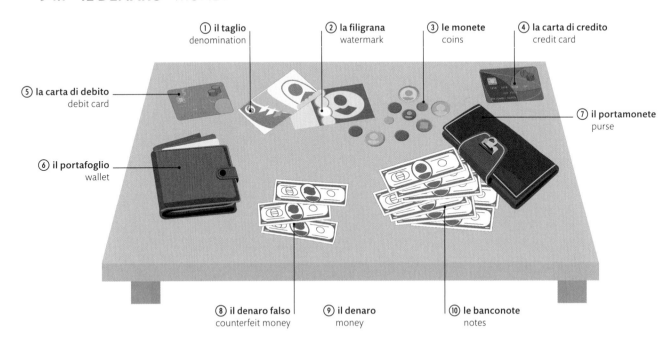

① il taglio
denomination

② la filigrana
watermark

③ le monete
coins

④ la carta di credito
credit card

⑤ la carta di debito
debit card

⑦ il portamonete
purse

⑥ il portafoglio
wallet

⑧ il denaro falso
counterfeit money

⑨ il denaro
money

⑩ le banconote
notes

⑪ il portafoglio digitale
digital wallet

⑫ la valuta digitale
digital currency

⑬ la banca
bank

⑭ i servizi bancari online
online banking

⑮ il mobile banking
mobile banking

⑯ i servizi bancari telefonici
telephone banking

⑰ la ricevuta
receipt

⑱ la valuta
currency

⑲ la fattura
invoice

⑳ Accettate i contanti qui?
Do you accept cash here?

⑳ l'assegno m
cheque

㉑ la cassa
till

㉒ pagare con carta
to pay by card

㉓ pagare in contanti
to pay with cash

See also
45 La banca e l'ufficio postale · The bank and post office
91 I settori e i reparti · Industries and departments

94.2 **LA FINANZA** · FINANCE

① **l'agente di borsa** m / f
stockbroker

② **la Borsa**
stock exchange

③ **le azioni**
shares

④ **il prezzo delle azioni**
share price

⑤ **i dividendi**
dividends

⑥ **la commissione**
commission

⑦ **il capitale netto**
equity

⑧ **l'investimento** m
investment

⑨ **il portfolio**
portfolio

⑩ **le quote azionarie**
stocks

⑪ **il tasso di cambio**
exchange rate

⑫ **il reddito**
income

⑬ **il budget**
budget

⑭ **indebitarsi**
to get into debt

⑮ **guadagnare**
to make a profit

⑯ **perdere**
to make a loss

⑰ **essere in pareggio**
to break even

⑱ **fallire**
to go out of business

㉔ **Posso consigliarle dove investire il suo denaro.**
I can advise you where to invest your money.

⑲ **lo scoperto**
overdraft

⑳ **le spese**
expenditure / outlay

㉑ **la recessione economica**
economic downturn

㉒ **il commercialista** m
la commercialista f
accountant

㉓ **il consulente finanziario** m
la consulente finanziaria f
financial advisor

95.1 RIUNIRSI · MEETING

② Maria, qual è l'ordine del giorno di oggi?
What's on the agenda today, Maria?

③ Discuteremo le presentazioni per la prossima settimana.
We're discussing the presentations for next week.

① partecipare a una riunione
to attend a meeting

④ tenere una teleconferenza
to have a conference call

⑤ redigere il verbale
to take minutes

⑥ rispondere alle domande
to take questions

⑦ essere assente
to be absent

⑧ interrompere
to interrupt

⑨ raggiungere un consenso
to reach a consensus

⑩ il voto unanime
unanimous vote

⑪ i punti di azione
action points

⑫ l'alzata di mano f
show of hands

⑬ varie ed eventuali
any other business

⑭ la sala riunioni del consiglio di amministrazione
boardroom

⑮ il consiglio di amministrazione
board of directors

⑯ raggiungere un accordo
to reach an agreement

⑰ l'assemblea generale annuale f
annual general meeting (AGM)

⑱ concludere una riunione
to wrap up the meeting

⑲ la lavagna
whiteboard

⑳ il bloc-notes
notebook

㉑ l'ordine del giorno m
agenda

See also
81 Al lavoro · At work **82** In ufficio · In the office **83** I computer
e la tecnologia · Computers and technology **84** I media · Media

95.2 **PRESENTARE** · PRESENTING

① **avviare**
to commence

② **riassumere**
to sum up

③ **esaurire il tempo a disposizione**
to run out of time

④ **la diapositiva**
slide

⑤ **il piano d'azione**
roadmap

⑥ **fare una presentazione**
to give a presentation

 ⑦ **il proiettore**
projector

 ⑧ **il timer**
timer

 ⑨ **il cavo HDMI**
HDMI cable

 ⑩ **le casse portatili**
portable speakers

⑪ **i documenti della presentazione**
handouts

 ⑫ **gli appunti**
notes

 ⑬ **la smartpen**
smartpen

 ⑭ **il microfono**
microphone

 ⑮ **le cuffie**
headphones

 ⑯ **la lavagna a fogli mobili**
flip chart

 ⑰ **condividere lo schermo**
to share your screen

 ⑱ **il telecomando per presentazioni**
presenter remote

 ⑲ **la conferenza**
conference

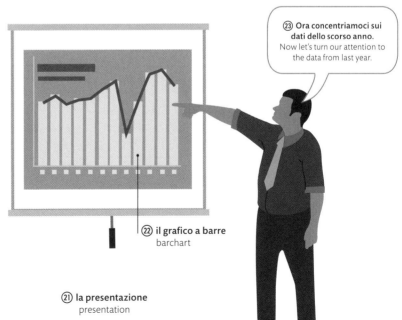

㉓ **Ora concentriamoci sui dati dello scorso anno.**
Now let's turn our attention to the data from last year.

㉒ **il grafico a barre**
barchart

 ⑳ **il relatore ospite** *m* / **la relatrice ospite** *f*
guest speaker

㉑ **la presentazione**
presentation

96 Le strade
Roads

96.1 PER LA STRADA · ON THE ROAD

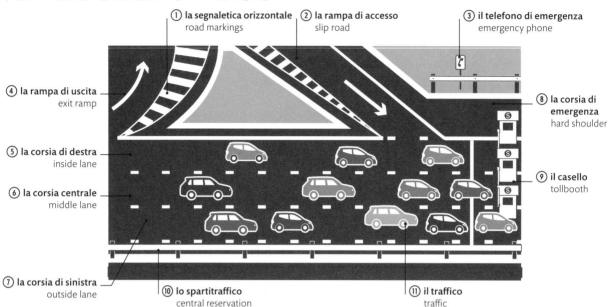

① la segnaletica orizzontale
road markings

② la rampa di accesso
slip road

③ il telefono di emergenza
emergency phone

④ la rampa di uscita
exit ramp

⑧ la corsia di emergenza
hard shoulder

⑤ la corsia di destra
inside lane

⑨ il casello
tollbooth

⑥ la corsia centrale
middle lane

⑦ la corsia di sinistra
outside lane

⑩ lo spartitraffico
central reservation

⑪ il traffico
traffic

⑫ l'autostrada f
motorway

⑭ lo spartitraffico
divider

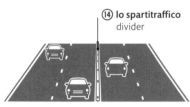

⑬ la strada a doppia carreggiata
dual carriageway

⑮ lo svincolo
junction

⑯ la rotonda
roundabout

⑰ il cavalcavia
flyover

⑱ il sottopassaggio
underpass

⑲ la barriera di sicurezza
crash barrier

⑳ la deviazione
diversion

㉑ l'autovelox m
speed camera

㉒ il semaforo
traffic light

㉓ l'ingorgo m
traffic jam

㉔ la strada a senso unico
one-way street

㉕ le strisce pedonali
pedestrian crossing

㉖ i lavori stradali
roadworks

㉗ il parcheggio per disabili
disabled parking

㉘ il posteggiatore m
la posteggiatrice f
parking attendant

㉙ il parchimetro
parking meter

See also
42-43 In città • In town **97-98** Le auto • Cars **99** Le auto e gli autobus • Cars and buses **100** I motocicli • Motorcycles **101** Il ciclismo • Cycling **123** Gli sport motoristici • Motorsports **148** Le cartine e le direzioni • Maps and directions

96.2 I CARTELLI STRADALI · ROAD SIGNS

① **il divieto di accesso**
no entry

② **il limite di velocità**
speed limit

③ **il pericolo**
hazard

④ **il divieto di svolta a destra**
no right turn

⑤ **il divieto di inversione a U**
no U-turn

⑥ **la curva a destra**
right bend

⑦ **il dare la precedenza**
give way

⑧ **il senso unico alternato**
priority traffic

⑨ **il divieto di sorpasso**
no overtaking

⑩ **l'attraversamento di bambini** m
school zone

⑪ **la strada deformata**
bumps

⑫ **l'attraversamento di animali selvatici** m
deer crossing

⑬ **la direzione obbligatoria**
direction to follow

⑭ **i lavori in corso**
roadworks ahead

⑮ **il preavviso di semaforo**
traffic light ahead

⑯ **il divieto di transito ai velocipedi**
closed to bicycles

⑰ **il divieto di transito ai pedoni**
closed to pedestrians

96.3 I VERBI DELLA GUIDA · VERBS FOR DRIVING

⑤ **il vigile urbano** m / **la vigilessa urbana** f
traffic warden

① **guidare**
to drive

② **fare retromarcia**
to reverse

③ **fermarsi**
to stop

④ **rimuovere**
to tow away

⑥ **girare a sinistra**
to turn left

⑦ **girare a destra**
to turn right

⑧ **andare dritto**
to go straight ahead / to go straight on

⑨ **prendere la prima a sinistra**
to take the first left

⑩ **prendere la seconda a destra**
to take the second right

97 Le auto
Cars

🔊

97.1 L'ESTERNO DELL'AUTO · CAR EXTERIOR

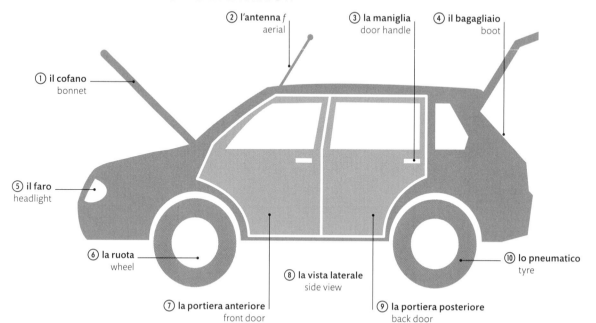

② l'antenna f
aerial

③ la maniglia
door handle

④ il bagagliaio
boot

① il cofano
bonnet

⑤ il faro
headlight

⑥ la ruota
wheel

⑧ la vista laterale
side view

⑦ la portiera anteriore
front door

⑨ la portiera posteriore
back door

⑩ lo pneumatico
tyre

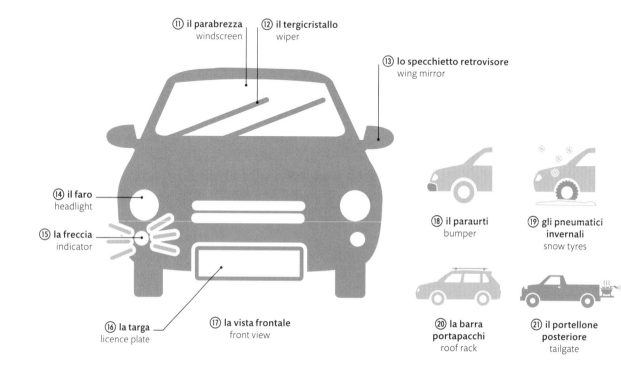

⑪ il parabrezza
windscreen

⑫ il tergicristallo
wiper

⑬ lo specchietto retrovisore
wing mirror

⑭ il faro
headlight

⑮ la freccia
indicator

⑯ la targa
licence plate

⑰ la vista frontale
front view

⑱ il paraurti
bumper

⑲ gli pneumatici
invernali
snow tyres

⑳ la barra
portapacchi
roof rack

㉑ il portellone
posteriore
tailgate

See also
42-43 In città · In town **96** Le strade · Roads **98** Le auto (continua) · Cars continued **99** Le auto e gli autobus · Cars and buses **100** I motocicli · Motorcycles **123** Gli sport motoristici · Motorsports

97.2 I TIPI DI AUTO · TYPES OF CARS

① **l'auto elettrica** *f*
electric car

② **l'auto ibrida** *f*
hybrid

③ **l'auto ibrida plug-in** *f*
plug-in hybrid

④ **la due volumi**
hatchback

⑤ **la berlina**
saloon

⑥ **la station wagon**
estate

⑦ **l'auto 4x4** *f*
four-wheel drive

⑧ **la monovolume**
people carrier

⑨ **la limousine**
limousine

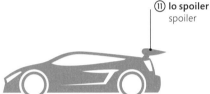

⑪ **lo spoiler**
spoiler

⑩ **l'auto sportiva** *f*
sports car

⑫ **la decappottabile**
convertible

⑬ **l'auto d'epoca** *f*
vintage

⑮ **il rollbar**
roller bar

⑭ **la dune baggy**
beach buggy

⑱ **l'alettone posteriore** *m*
rear wing

⑰ **l'alettone anteriore** *m*
front wing

⑯ **l'auto da corsa** *f*
racing car

97.3 IL DISTRIBUTORE DI BENZINA · PETROL STATION

① **la pompa di benzina**
petrol pump

② **il piazzale**
forecourt

③ **la stazione di ricarica per auto elettriche**
electric charge point

④ **il liquido per tergicristalli**
screen wash

⑤ **l'antigelo** *m*
antifreeze

⑥ **la benzina**
petrol

⑦ **senza piombo**
unleaded

⑧ **con piombo**
leaded

⑨ **il diesel**
diesel

⑩ **l'olio** *m*
oil

⑪ **l'autolavaggio** *m*
car wash

98.1 IL SOCCORSO STRADALE · BREAKDOWN ASSISTANCE

② **il meccanico** *m*
la meccanica *f*
mechanic

④ **la ruota di scorta**
spare tyre

③ **il carro attrezzi**
tow truck

⑤ **la gomma a terra**
flat tyre

① **l'officina** *f*
garage

98.2 LA MECCANICA · MECHANICS

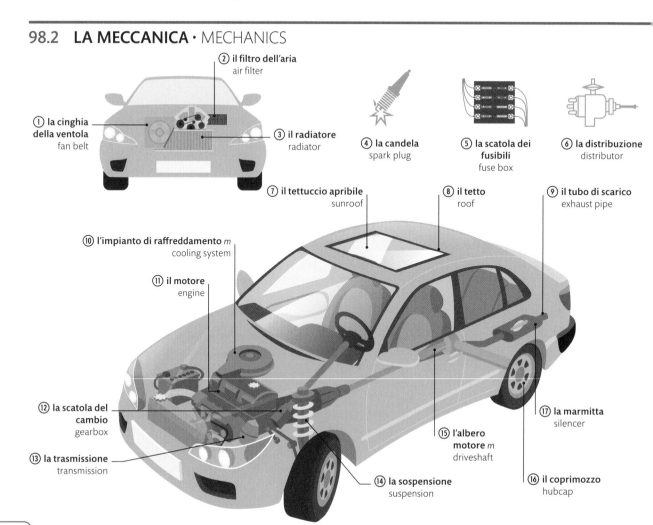

② **il filtro dell'aria**
air filter

① **la cinghia**
della ventola
fan belt

③ **il radiatore**
radiator

④ **la candela**
spark plug

⑤ **la scatola dei**
fusibili
fuse box

⑥ **la distribuzione**
distributor

⑦ **il tettuccio apribile**
sunroof

⑧ **il tetto**
roof

⑨ **il tubo di scarico**
exhaust pipe

⑩ **l'impianto di raffreddamento** *m*
cooling system

⑪ **il motore**
engine

⑫ **la scatola del**
cambio
gearbox

⑬ **la trasmissione**
transmission

⑭ **la sospensione**
suspension

⑮ **l'albero**
motore *m*
driveshaft

⑯ **il coprimozzo**
hubcap

⑰ **la marmitta**
silencer

See also
42-43 In città · In town **96** Le strade · Roads **99** Le auto e gli autobus · Cars and buses **100** I motocicli · Motorcycles **123** Gli sport motoristici · Motorsports

98.3 I VERBI DELLA GUIDA
VERBS FOR DRIVING

① **rifornire** to fill up

② **controllare l'olio** to check the oil

③ **controllare gli pneumatici** to check the tyres

④ **revisionare l'auto** to service the car

⑤ **parcheggiare** to park

⑥ **partire** to set off

⑦ **mettere la freccia** to indicate

⑧ **frenare** to brake

⑨ **rallentare** to slow down

⑩ **accelerare** to speed up

⑪ **andare a prendere qualcuno** to pick someone up

⑫ **accompagnare qualcuno** to drop someone off

⑬ **avere un incidente** to have a car accident

⑭ **rompersi** to break down

⑮ **sorpassare** to overtake

⑥ **la chiave inglese** wrench

⑦ **i bulloni delle ruote** wheel nuts

⑧ **il cric** jack

⑱ **il serbatoio del liquido per tergicristalli** screen wash reservoir

⑲ **il cofano** bonnet

⑳ **il serbatoio del liquido freni** brake fluid reservoir

㉑ **l'astina di livello** f dipstick

㉒ **il tubo di scarico** pipe

㉓ **il serbatoio del liquido di raffreddamento** coolant reservoir

㉔ **la batteria** battery

㉕ **la carrozzeria** bodywork

㉖ **la testata** cylinder head

99 Le auto e gli autobus
Cars and buses

99.1 L'INTERNO DELL'AUTO · CAR INTERIOR

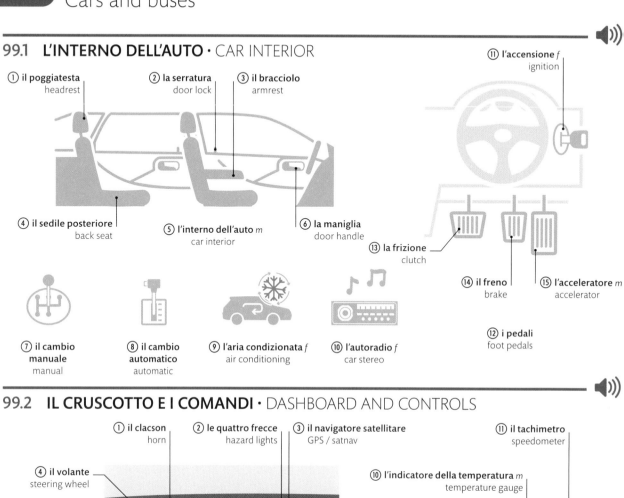

① il poggiatesta
headrest

② la serratura
door lock

③ il bracciolo
armrest

⑪ l'accensione *f*
ignition

④ il sedile posteriore
back seat

⑤ l'interno dell'auto *m*
car interior

⑥ la maniglia
door handle

⑬ la frizione
clutch

⑭ il freno
brake

⑮ l'acceleratore *m*
accelerator

⑫ i pedali
foot pedals

⑦ il cambio
manuale
manual

⑧ il cambio
automatico
automatic

⑨ l'aria condizionata *f*
air conditioning

⑩ l'autoradio *f*
car stereo

99.2 IL CRUSCOTTO E I COMANDI · DASHBOARD AND CONTROLS

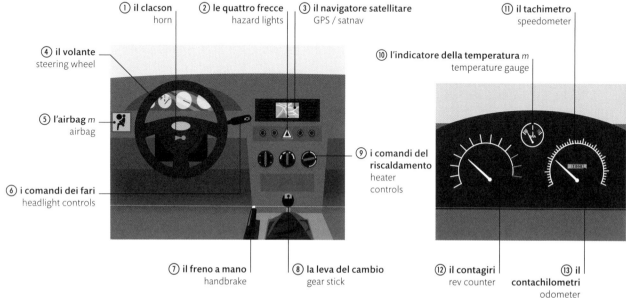

① il clacson
horn

② le quattro frecce
hazard lights

③ il navigatore satellitare
GPS / satnav

⑪ il tachimetro
speedometer

④ il volante
steering wheel

⑩ l'indicatore della temperatura *m*
temperature gauge

⑤ l'airbag *m*
airbag

⑨ i comandi del
riscaldamento
heater
controls

⑥ i comandi dei fari
headlight controls

⑦ il freno a mano
handbrake

⑧ la leva del cambio
gear stick

⑫ il contagiri
rev counter

⑬ il
contachilometri
odometer

See also
42-43 In città · In town   **96** Le strade · Roads   **97-98** Le auto · Cars
100 I motocicli · Motorcycles   **123** Gli sport motoristici · Motorsports

99.3   L'AUTOBUS · BUS

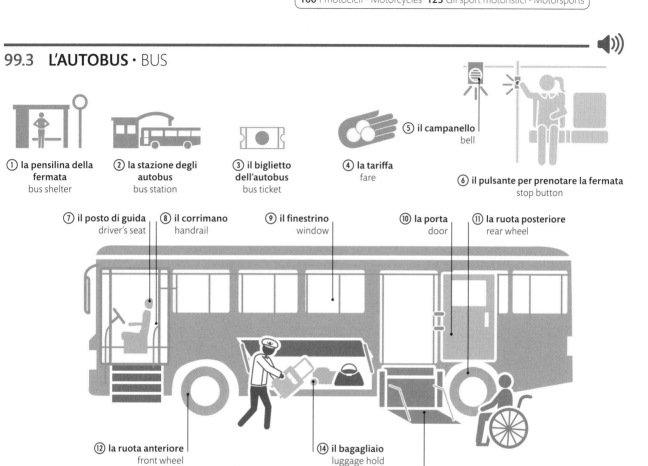

⑤ **il campanello**
bell

① **la pensilina della fermata**
bus shelter

② **la stazione degli autobus**
bus station

③ **il biglietto dell'autobus**
bus ticket

④ **la tariffa**
fare

⑥ **il pulsante per prenotare la fermata**
stop button

⑦ **il posto di guida**
driver's seat

⑧ **il corrimano**
handrail

⑨ **il finestrino**
window

⑩ **la porta**
door

⑪ **la ruota posteriore**
rear wheel

⑫ **la ruota anteriore**
front wheel

⑬ **il pullman**
coach

⑭ **il bagagliaio**
luggage hold

⑮ **l'accesso per disabili** *m*
wheelchair access

99.4   I TIPI DI AUTOBUS · TYPES OF BUSES

② **il piano superiore**
upper deck

③ **il piano inferiore**
lower deck

⑥ **fare un giro turistico** *m*
sightseeing

④ **l'autista** *m / f*
driver

① **l'autobus a due piani** *m*
double-decker bus

⑤ **l'autobus turistico** *m*
tourist bus

⑦ **il numero della linea**
route number

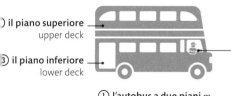

⑧ **lo scuolabus**
school bus

⑨ **il pulmino**
minibus

⑩ **l'autobus articolato** *m*
articulated bus

⑪ **la navetta**
shuttle bus

⑫ **il filobus**
trolley bus

⑬ **il tram**
tram

100.1 LA MOTO · MOTORBIKE

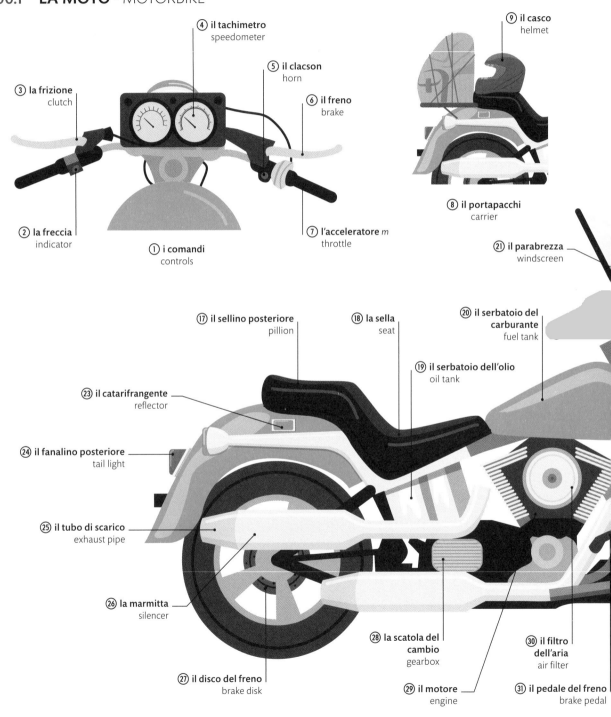

④ il tachimetro
speedometer

⑤ il clacson
horn

③ la frizione
clutch

⑥ il freno
brake

⑨ il casco
helmet

② la freccia
indicator

⑦ l'acceleratore *m*
throttle

① i comandi
controls

⑧ il portapacchi
carrier

㉑ il parabrezza
windscreen

⑰ il sellino posteriore
pillion

⑱ la sella
seat

⑳ il serbatoio del
carburante
fuel tank

⑲ il serbatoio dell'olio
oil tank

㉓ il catarifrangente
reflector

㉔ il fanalino posteriore
tail light

㉕ il tubo di scarico
exhaust pipe

㉖ la marmitta
silencer

㉘ la scatola del
cambio
gearbox

㉚ il filtro
dell'aria
air filter

㉗ il disco del freno
brake disk

㉙ il motore
engine

㉛ il pedale del freno
brake pedal

⑪ **la visiera**
visor

⑫ **la fascia catarifrangente**
reflector strap

⑬ **il guanto**
glove

⑭ **la tuta da motociclista**
leathers

⑮ **la ginocchiera**
knee pad

⑯ **lo stivale**
boot

⑩ **l'abbigliamento** *m*
clothing

⑫ **il faro**
headlight

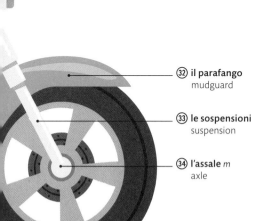

㉜ **il parafango**
mudguard

㉝ **le sospensioni**
suspension

㉞ **l'assale** *m*
axle

㉟ **lo pneumatico**
tyre

See also
42-43 In città • In town **96** Le strade • Roads **97-98** Le auto Cars **123** Gli sport motoristici • Motorsports

100.2 I TIPI DI MOTOCICLI
TYPES OF MOTORCYCLES

② **il parafango rialzato**
raised mudguard

③ **il numero di gara**
race number

④ **lo pneumatico con battistrada profondo**
deep-tread tyre

① **la moto fuoristrada**
off-road motorcycle

⑤ **la moto da corsa**
racing bike

⑥ **la moto da turismo**
tourer

⑦ **il quad**
all-terrain vehicle / quad bike

⑧ **il sidecar**
side car

⑨ **la moto elettrica**
electric motorcycle

⑩ **il monopattino elettrico**
electric scooter

⑪ **la moto a tre ruote**
three-wheeler

⑫ **lo scooter**
motor scooter

⑬ **il motociclista** *m* **la motociclista** *f*
rider

⑭ **viaggiare dietro**
to ride pillion

⑮ **salire**
to get on / mount

⑯ **scendere**
to get off / dismount

101.1 LA BICICLETTA · BICYCLE

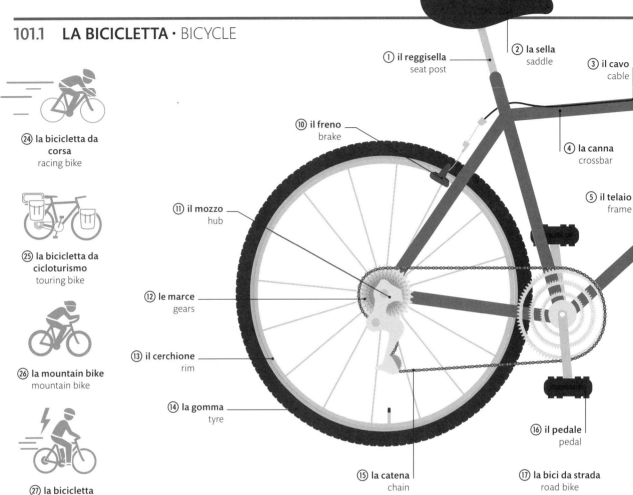

① il reggisella
seat post

② la sella
saddle

③ il cavo
cable

④ la canna
crossbar

⑤ il telaio
frame

⑩ il freno
brake

⑪ il mozzo
hub

⑫ le marce
gears

⑬ il cerchione
rim

⑭ la gomma
tyre

⑮ la catena
chain

⑯ il pedale
pedal

⑰ la bici da strada
road bike

㉔ la bicicletta da corsa
racing bike

㉕ la bicicletta da cicloturismo
touring bike

㉖ la mountain bike
mountain bike

⑳ la bicicletta elettrica
electric bike

㉘ il tandem
tandem

㉙ il cestino
basket

㉚ il seggiolino per bambini
child seat

㉛ il cavalletto
kickstand

㉜ la pastiglia dei freni
brake pad

㉝ le rotelle
stabilizers

㉞ il monociclo
unicycle

㉟ il fermapiede
toe clip

㊱ il cinturino per pedali
toe strap

㊲ la lampadina
lamp

㊳ la luce posteriore
rear light

㊴ la camera d'aria
inner tube

See also
42-43 In città · In town **96** Le strade · Roads **100** I motocicli
Motorcycles **133** Le attività all'aperto · Outdoor activities

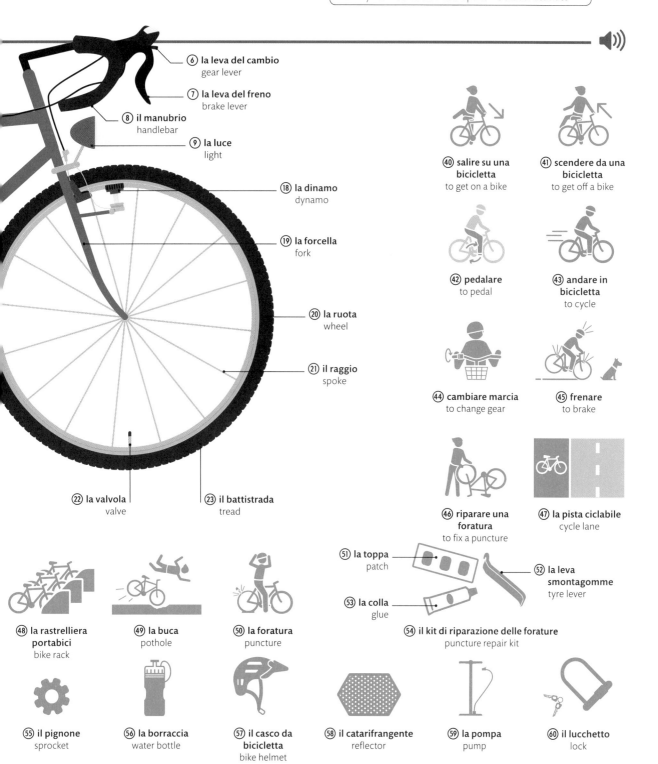

⑥ **la leva del cambio**
gear lever

⑦ **la leva del freno**
brake lever

⑧ **il manubrio**
handlebar

⑨ **la luce**
light

⑱ **la dinamo**
dynamo

⑲ **la forcella**
fork

⑳ **la ruota**
wheel

㉑ **il raggio**
spoke

㉒ **la valvola**
valve

㉓ **il battistrada**
tread

㊵ **salire su una bicicletta**
to get on a bike

㊶ **scendere da una bicicletta**
to get off a bike

㊷ **pedalare**
to pedal

㊸ **andare in bicicletta**
to cycle

㊹ **cambiare marcia**
to change gear

㊺ **frenare**
to brake

㊻ **riparare una foratura**
to fix a puncture

㊼ **la pista ciclabile**
cycle lane

㊶ **la toppa**
patch

㊸ **la colla**
glue

㊷ **la leva smontagomme**
tyre lever

㊴ **il kit di riparazione delle forature**
puncture repair kit

㊸ **la rastrelliera portabici**
bike rack

㊹ **la buca**
pothole

㊺ **la foratura**
puncture

㊻ **il pignone**
sprocket

㊼ **la borraccia**
water bottle

㊽ **il casco da bicicletta**
bike helmet

㊾ **il catarifrangente**
reflector

㊿ **la pompa**
pump

⑥⓪ **il lucchetto**
lock

211

102 I treni
Trains

102.1 LA STAZIONE FERROVIARIA · TRAIN STATION

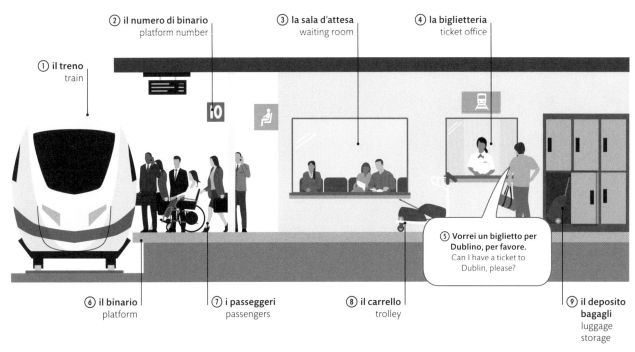

② **il numero di binario**
platform number

③ **la sala d'attesa**
waiting room

④ **la biglietteria**
ticket office

① **il treno**
train

⑤ Vorrei un biglietto per Dublino, per favore.
Can I have a ticket to Dublin, please?

⑥ **il binario**
platform

⑦ **i passeggeri**
passengers

⑧ **il carrello**
trolley

⑨ **il deposito bagagli**
luggage storage

⑩ **l'ufficio oggetti smarriti** m
lost property office

⑪ **il biglietto**
ticket

⑮ **il tabellone delle partenze**
departures board

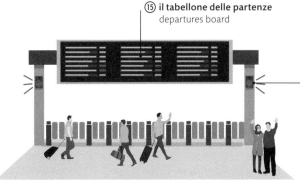

⑯ **l'altoparlante** m
public address system

⑫ **la tariffa**
fare

⑬ **il tornello**
ticket barrier

⑭ **l'atrio** m
concourse

㉒ **i pendolari**
commuters

⑰ **la rete ferroviaria**
rail network

⑱ **la cartina della metropolitana**
underground map

⑲ **l'intercity** m
intercity train

⑳ **il ritardo**
delay

㉑ **l'orario di punta** m
rush hour

㉓ **prendere un treno**
to catch a train

See also
42-43 In città · In town **131** Il viaggio
e l'alloggio · Travel and accommodation

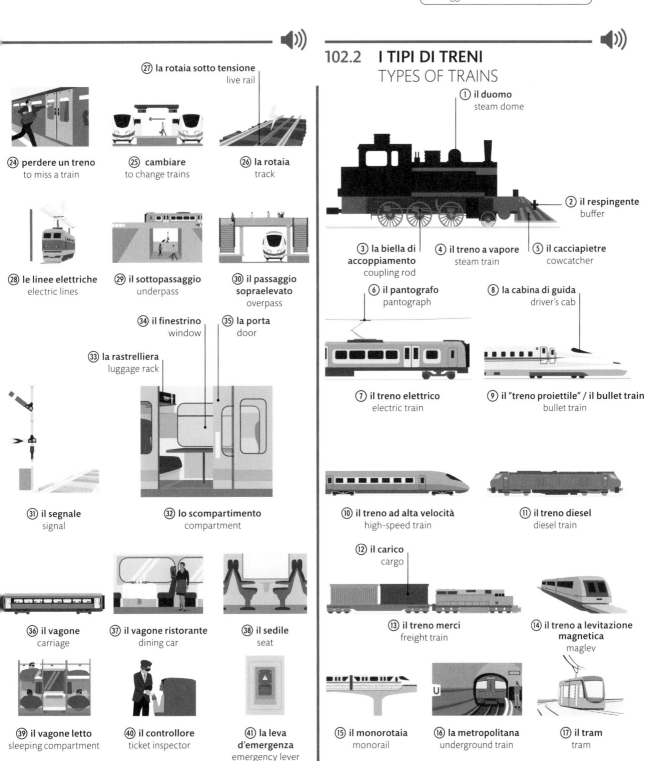

㉗ **la rotaia sotto tensione**
live rail

㉔ **perdere un treno**
to miss a train

㉕ **cambiare**
to change trains

㉖ **la rotaia**
track

㉘ **le linee elettriche**
electric lines

㉙ **il sottopassaggio**
underpass

㉚ **il passaggio sopraelevato**
overpass

㉞ **il finestrino**
window

㉟ **la porta**
door

㉝ **la rastrelliera**
luggage rack

㉛ **il segnale**
signal

㉜ **lo scompartimento**
compartment

㊱ **il vagone**
carriage

㊲ **il vagone ristorante**
dining car

㊳ **il sedile**
seat

㊴ **il vagone letto**
sleeping compartment

㊵ **il controllore**
ticket inspector

㊶ **la leva d'emergenza**
emergency lever

102.2 I TIPI DI TRENI
TYPES OF TRAINS

① **il duomo**
steam dome

② **il respingente**
buffer

③ **la biella di accoppiamento**
coupling rod

④ **il treno a vapore**
steam train

⑤ **il cacciapietre**
cowcatcher

⑥ **il pantografo**
pantograph

⑧ **la cabina di guida**
driver's cab

⑦ **il treno elettrico**
electric train

⑨ **il "treno proiettile" / il bullet train**
bullet train

⑩ **il treno ad alta velocità**
high-speed train

⑪ **il treno diesel**
diesel train

⑫ **il carico**
cargo

⑬ **il treno merci**
freight train

⑭ **il treno a levitazione magnetica**
maglev

⑮ **il monorotaia**
monorail

⑯ **la metropolitana**
underground train

⑰ **il tram**
tram

103.1 L'AEREO PASSEGGERI · AEROPLANE

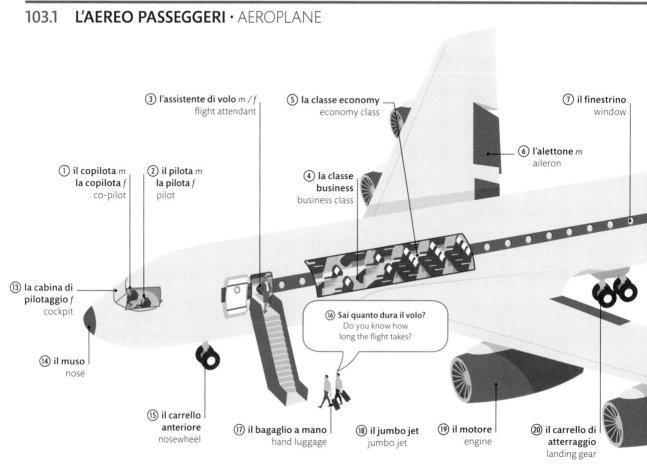

③ l'assistente di volo *m / f*
flight attendant

⑤ la classe economy
economy class

⑦ il finestrino
window

⑥ l'alettone *m*
aileron

① il copilota *m*
la copilota *f*
co-pilot

② il pilota *m*
la pilota *f*
pilot

④ la classe
business
business class

⑬ la cabina di
pilotaggio *f*
cockpit

⑯ Sai quanto dura il volo?
Do you know how
long the flight takes?

⑭ il muso
nose

⑮ il carrello
anteriore
nosewheel

⑰ il bagaglio a mano
hand luggage

⑱ il jumbo jet
jumbo jet

⑲ il motore
engine

⑳ il carrello di
atterraggio
landing gear

103.3 I TIPI DI AEROMOBILE · TYPES OF AIRCRAFT

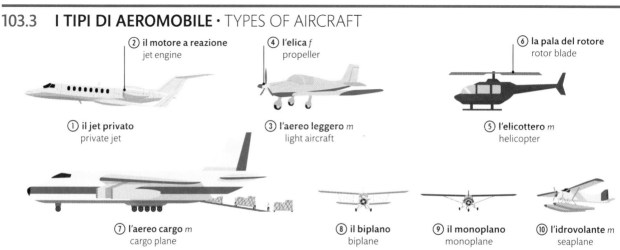

② il motore a reazione
jet engine

④ l'elica *f*
propeller

⑥ la pala del rotore
rotor blade

① il jet privato
private jet

③ l'aereo leggero *m*
light aircraft

⑤ l'elicottero *m*
helicopter

⑦ l'aereo cargo *m*
cargo plane

⑧ il biplano
biplane

⑨ il monoplano
monoplane

⑩ l'idrovolante *m*
seaplane

See also
42-43 In città · In town **104** In aeroporto · At the airport
131 Il viaggio e l'alloggio · Travel and accommodation

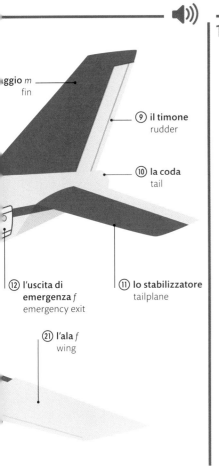

ggio *m*
fin

⑨ il timone
rudder

⑩ la coda
tail

⑫ l'uscita di
emergenza *f*
emergency exit

⑪ lo stabilizzatore
tailplane

㉑ l'ala *f*
wing

103.2   LA CABINA · CABIN

① la luce da lettura
reading light

② la ventola dell'aria
air vent

③ la cappelliera
overhead compartment

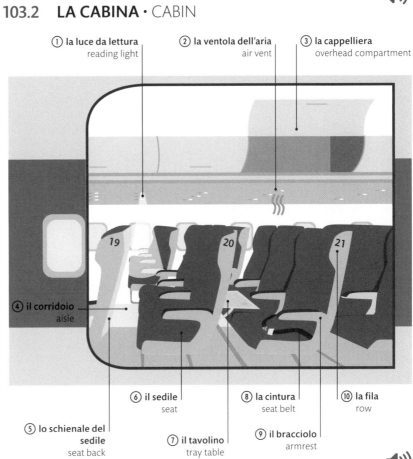

④ il corridoio
aisle

⑥ il sedile
seat

⑧ la cintura
seat belt

⑩ la fila
row

⑤ lo schienale del
sedile
seat back

⑦ il tavolino
tray table

⑨ il bracciolo
armrest

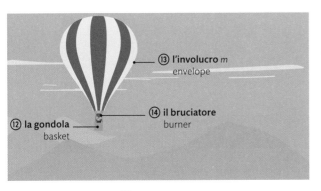

⑬ l'involucro *m*
envelope

⑭ il bruciatore
burner

⑫ la gondola
basket

⑪ la mongolfiera
hot-air balloon

⑮ il dirigibile
airship

⑯ l'ultraleggero *m*
microlight

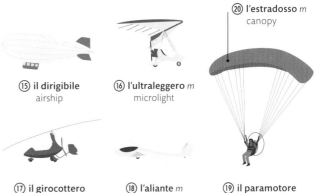

⑳ l'estradosso *m*
canopy

⑰ il girocottero
gyrocopter

⑱ l'aliante *m*
glider

⑲ il paramotore
paramotor

215

104.1 AL TERMINAL · AT THE TERMINAL

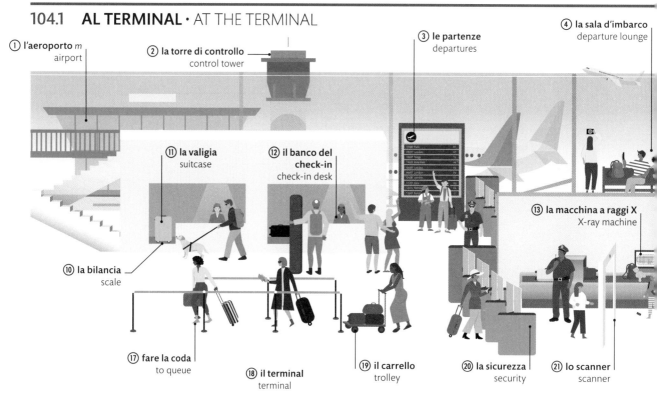

① l'aeroporto m
airport

② la torre di controllo
control tower

③ le partenze
departures

④ la sala d'imbarco
departure lounge

⑪ la valigia
suitcase

⑫ il banco del check-in
check-in desk

⑬ la macchina a raggi X
X-ray machine

⑩ la bilancia
scale

⑰ fare la coda
to queue

⑱ il terminal
terminal

⑲ il carrello
trolley

⑳ la sicurezza
security

㉑ lo scanner
scanner

㉘ il passaporto
passport

㉙ il passaporto biometrico
biometric passport

㉚ il visto
visa

㉛ il biglietto
ticket

㉜ la carta d'imbarco
boarding pass

㉝ il check-in online
online check-in

㊵ la vacanza
holiday

㊶ il volo interno
domestic flight

㊷ il volo internazionale
international flight

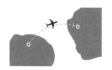

㊸ andare all'estero m
to go abroad

㊹ il volo diretto
direct flight

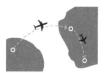

㊺ la coincidenza
connection

㊿ i bagagli in eccedenza
excess baggage

㊾ il controllo passaporti
passport control

㊾ il cambio
currency exchange

㊾ il negozio duty-free
duty-free shop

㊾ l'ufficio bagagli smarriti m
lost and found

㊾ essere in ritardo
to be delayed

See also
103 L'aeromobile • Aircraft **131** Il viaggio e l'alloggio Travel and accommodation **149-151** I Paesi • Countries

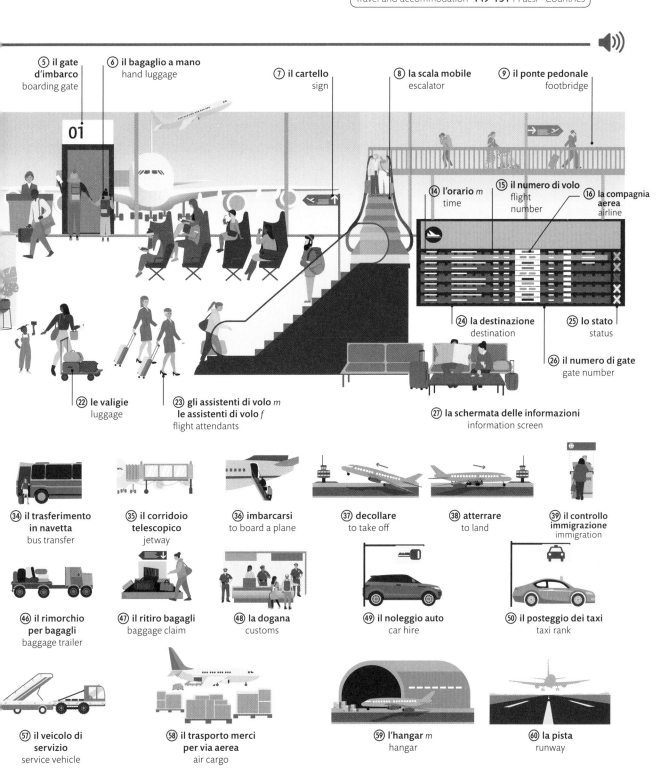

⑤ **il gate d'imbarco**
boarding gate

⑥ **il bagaglio a mano**
hand luggage

⑦ **il cartello**
sign

⑧ **la scala mobile**
escalator

⑨ **il ponte pedonale**
footbridge

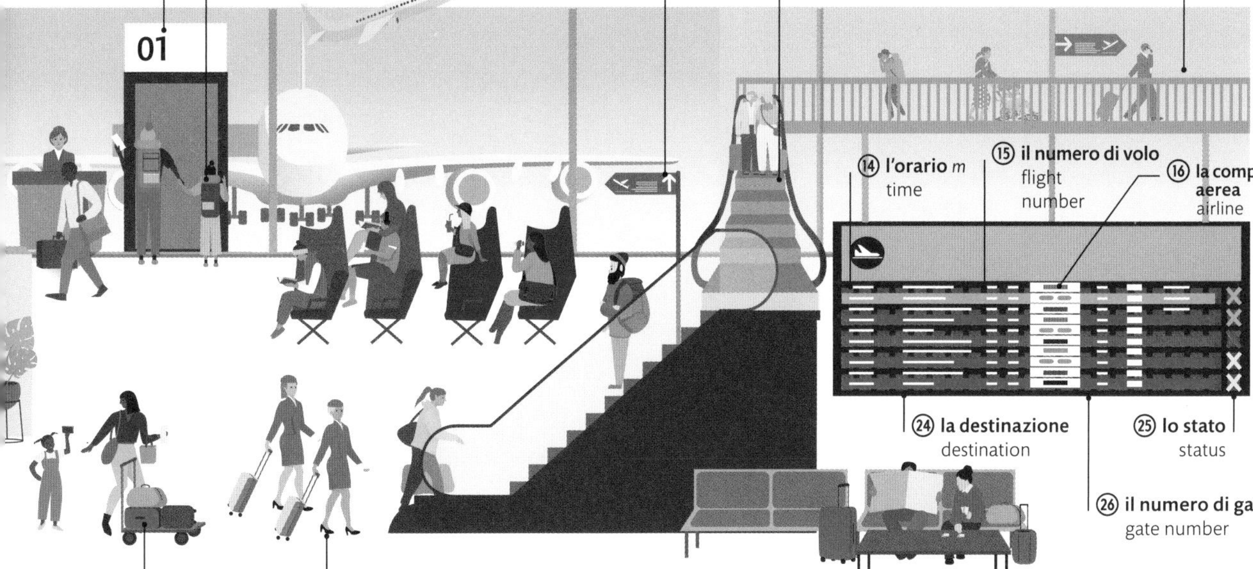

⑭ **l'orario** *m*
time

⑮ **il numero di volo**
flight number

⑯ **la compagnia aerea**
airline

㉔ **la destinazione**
destination

㉕ **lo stato**
status

㉖ **il numero di gate**
gate number

㉒ **le valigie**
luggage

㉓ **gli assistenti di volo** *m*
le assistenti di volo *f*
flight attendants

㉗ **la schermata delle informazioni**
information screen

㉞ **il trasferimento in navetta**
bus transfer

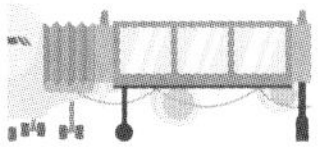

㉟ **il corridoio telescopico**
jetway

㊱ **imbarcarsi**
to board a plane

㊲ **decollare**
to take off

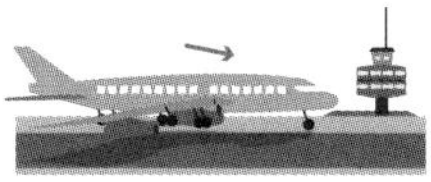

㊳ **atterrare**
to land

㊴ **il controllo immigrazione**
immigration

㊻ **il rimorchio per bagagli**
baggage trailer

㊼ **il ritiro bagagli**
baggage claim

㊽ **la dogana**
customs

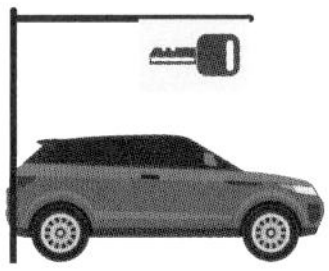

㊾ **il noleggio auto**
car hire

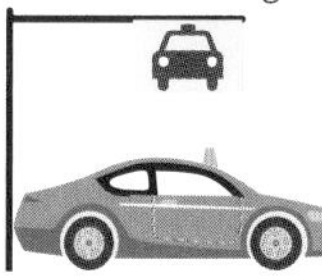

㊿ **il posteggio dei taxi**
taxi rank

(57) **il veicolo di servizio**
service vehicle

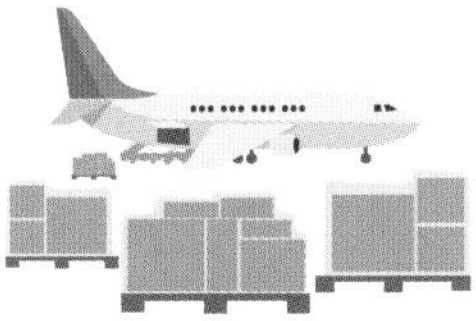

(58) **il trasporto merci per via aerea**
air cargo

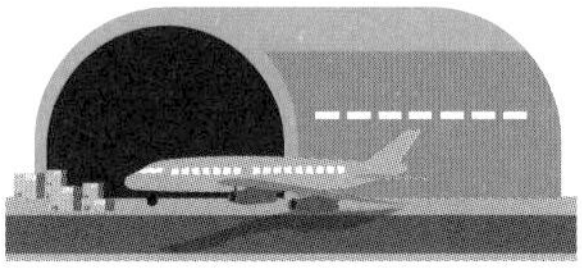

(59) **l'hangar** *m*
hangar

(60) **la pista**
runway

105.1 LA NAVE · SHIP

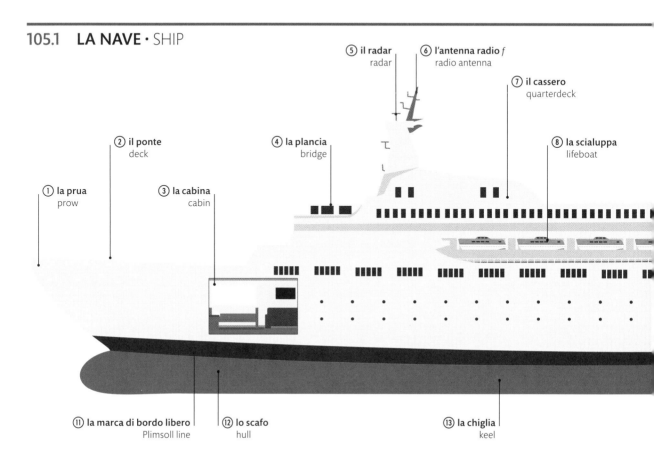

⑤ **il radar**
radar

⑥ **l'antenna radio** *f*
radio antenna

⑦ **il cassero**
quarterdeck

② **il ponte**
deck

④ **la plancia**
bridge

⑧ **la scialuppa**
lifeboat

① **la prua**
prow

③ **la cabina**
cabin

⑪ **la marca di bordo libero**
Plimsoll line

⑫ **lo scafo**
hull

⑬ **la chiglia**
keel

105.2 LE ALTRE BARCHE E NAVI · OTHER BOATS AND SHIPS

⑤ **il motore fuoribordo**
outboard motor

⑧ **l'albero** *m*
mast

① **la canoa**
canoe

② **il kayak**
kayak

③ **la barca a remi**
rowing boat

④ **il gommone**
inflatable dinghy

⑥ **il catamarano**
catamaran

⑦ **la barca a vela**
sailing boat

⑮ **il motoscafo**
speedboat

⑯ **lo yacht**
yacht

⑰ **l'aliscafo** *m*
hydrofoil

⑱ **l'hovercraft** *m*
hovercraft

⑲ **il rimorchiatore**
tugboat

⑳ **il peschereccio**
trawler

See also
106 Il porto · The port **119** La vela e gli sport acquatici · Sailing and watersports **131** Il viaggio e l'alloggio · Travel and accommodation

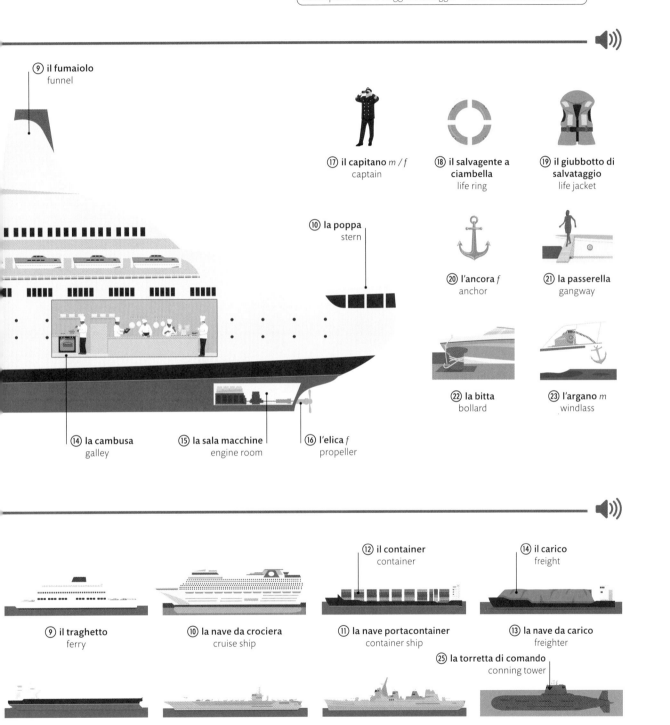

⑨ **il fumaiolo**
funnel

⑰ **il capitano** *m / f*
captain

⑱ **il salvagente a ciambella**
life ring

⑲ **il giubbotto di salvataggio**
life jacket

⑩ **la poppa**
stern

⑳ **l'ancora** *f*
anchor

㉑ **la passerella**
gangway

㉒ **la bitta**
bollard

㉓ **l'argano** *m*
windlass

⑭ **la cambusa**
galley

⑮ **la sala macchine**
engine room

⑯ **l'elica** *f*
propeller

⑨ **il traghetto**
ferry

⑩ **la nave da crociera**
cruise ship

⑫ **il container**
container

⑪ **la nave portacontainer**
container ship

⑭ **il carico**
freight

⑬ **la nave da carico**
freighter

㉑ **la petroliera**
oil tanker

㉒ **la portaerei**
aircraft carrier

㉓ **la nave da guerra**
battleship

㉕ **la torretta di comando**
conning tower

㉔ **il sottomarino**
submarine

219

106.1 AL MOLO · AT THE DOCKS

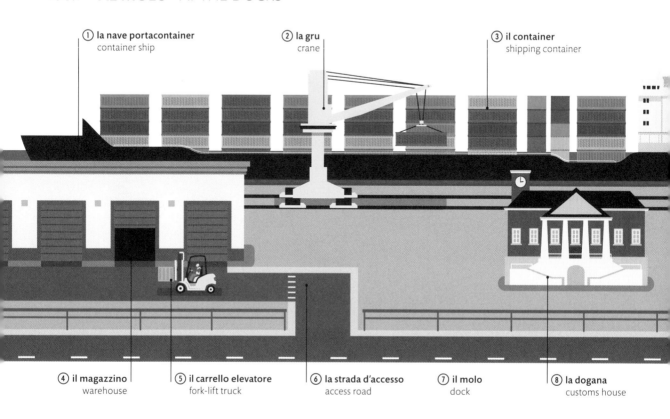

① **la nave portacontainer**
container ship

② **la gru**
crane

③ **il container**
shipping container

④ **il magazzino**
warehouse

⑤ **il carrello elevatore**
fork-lift truck

⑥ **la strada d'accesso**
access road

⑦ **il molo**
dock

⑧ **la dogana**
customs house

⑱ **il traghetto**
ferry

⑳ **i passeggeri**
passengers

⑰ **il terminal traghetti**
ferry terminal

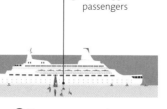

⑲ **il porto passeggeri**
passenger port

㉑ **il porto di pesca**
fishing port

㉒ **la biglietteria**
ticket office

㉗ **l'ormeggio** m
mooring

㉘ **il porto**
harbour

㉙ **la marina**
marina

㉚ **il pontile**
pier

㉛ **l'imbarcadero** m
jetty

㉜ **il cantiere navale**
shipyard

See also
96 Le strade • Roads **102** I treni • Trains
105 Le imbarcazioni • Sea vessels

106.2 I VERBI
VERBS

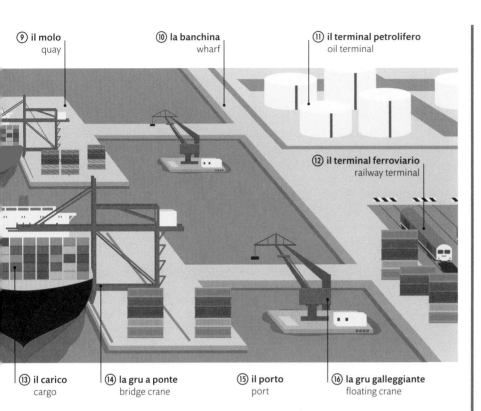

⑨ **il molo**
quay

⑩ **la banchina**
wharf

⑪ **il terminal petrolifero**
oil terminal

⑫ **il terminal ferroviario**
railway terminal

⑬ **il carico**
cargo

⑭ **la gru a ponte**
bridge crane

⑮ **il porto**
port

⑯ **la gru galleggiante**
floating crane

① **imbarcarsi**
to board

② **ormeggiare**
to moor

③ **sbarcare**
to disembark

④ **calare l'ancora**
to drop anchor

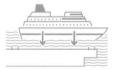

⑤ **attraccare**
to dock

⑥ **salpare**
to set sail

㉓ **il bacino di carenaggio**
dry dock

㉔ **la boa**
buoy

㉖ **la lampada**
lamp

㉕ **il faro**
lighthouse

㉞ **il cancello**
gate

㉝ **la chiusa**
lock

㉟ **la guardia costiera**
coastguard

㊱ **il capitano di porto**
harbour master

107.1 IL FOOTBALL AMERICANO · AMERICAN FOOTBALL

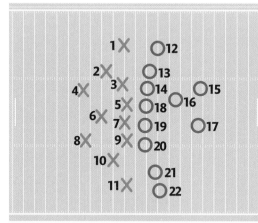

① il cornerback sinistro *m / f*
left cornerback

② il linebacker esterno *m / f*
outside linebacker

③ il defensive end sinistro *m / f*
left defensive end

④ il safety sinistro *m / f*
left safety

⑤ il defensive tackle sinistro *m / f*
left defensive tackle

⑥ il linebacker centrale *m / f*
middle linebacker

⑦ il defensive tackle destro *m / f*
right defensive tackle

⑧ il safety destro *m / f*
right safety

⑨ il defensive end destro *m / f*
right defensive end

⑩ il linebacker esterno *m / f*
outside linebacker

⑪ il cornerback destro *m / f*
right cornerback

⑫ il ricevitore *m* la ricevitrice *f*
wide receiver

⑬ l'offensive tackle destro *m / f*
right tackle

⑭ la guardia destra *m / f*
right guard

⑮ il running back / halfback *m / f*
running back / halfback

⑯ il fullback *m / f*
fullback

⑰ il quarterback *m / f*
quarterback

⑱ il centro *m / f*
centre

⑲ la guardia sinistra *m / f*
left guard

⑳ l'offensive tackle sinistro *m / f*
left tackle

㉑ ㉒ il ricevitore *m* la ricevitrice *f*
wide receiver

㉓ le posizioni del football americano
American football positions

㉔ la difesa *m / f*
defence

㉕ l'attacco *m / f*
offence

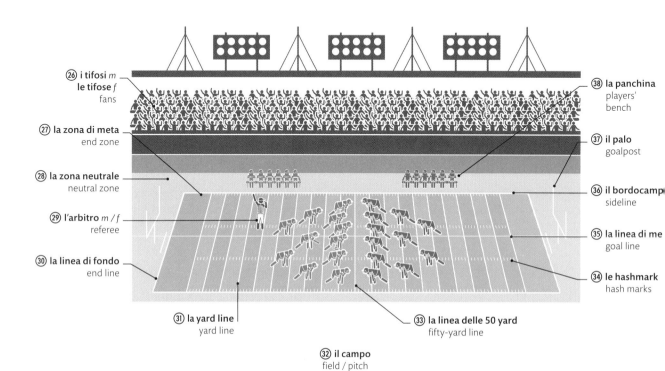

㉖ i tifosi *m* le tifose *f*
fans

㉗ la zona di meta
end zone

㉘ la zona neutrale
neutral zone

㉙ l'arbitro *m / f*
referee

㉚ la linea di fondo
end line

㉛ la yard line
yard line

㉜ il campo
field / pitch

㉝ la linea delle 50 yard
fifty-yard line

㉞ le hashmark
hash marks

㉟ la linea di me
goal line

㊱ il bordocamp
sideline

㊲ il palo
goalpost

㊳ la panchina
players' bench

See also
108 Il rugby · Rugby **109** Il calcio · Football
110 L'hockey e il lacrosse · Hockey and lacrosse

39 la mentoniera
chin strap

40 il casco
helmet

41 il paracollo
neck pad

42 la maschera facciale protettiva
face mask

43 il paraspalle
shoulder pad

44 la maglia della squadra
team jersey

46 il paragomiti
elbow pads

il polsino
wrist band

il parafianchi, il paracosce e la ginocchiera
hip, thigh, and knee pads

48 i guanti
gloves

50 i pantaloni
pants

45 il numero del giocatore *m*
il numero della giocatrice *f*
player's number

51 le scarpe da football
football boots

52 il calzino
sock

53 il giocatore di football
la giocatrice di football
football player

54 il paradenti
mouth guard

55 la protezione per il torace
chest protector

56 la squadra
team

57 placcare
to tackle

58 passare
to pass

59 prendere la palla
to catch

60 il time out
time out

61 guadagnare yard
to gain yards

62 perdere la palla
to fumble

63 lanciare
to throw

64 calciare
to kick

65 il touchdown
touchdown

66 marcare
to chase

67 il cheerleader *m*
la cheerleader *f*
cheerleader

68 la palla da football
football

70 la cucitura
lace

69 la pelle
leather

71 il tempo
time

72 la squadra di casa
home

73 la squadra ospite *m*
visitor

QTR
TOL   TOL
DOWN   TO GO   BALL ON

74 il tabellone segnapunti
scoreboard

108.1 IL RUGBY · RUGBY

① **il pilone sinistro** *m / f*
loosehead prop

② **il tallonatore** *m*
la tallonatrice *f*
hooker

③ **il pilone destro** *m / f*
tighthead prop

④ **la seconda linea** *m / f*
second row

⑤ **la seconda linea** *m / f*
second row

⑥ **la terza linea ala chiusa**
m / f
blindside flanker

⑦ **la terza linea ala aperta**
m / f
openside flanker

⑧ **la terza linea centro** *m / f*
number eight

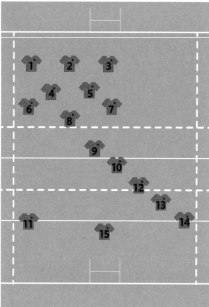

⑯ **le posizioni del rugby**
rugby positions

⑨ **il mediano di mischia**
m / f
scrum-half

⑩ **il mediano d'apertura**
m / f
fly-half

⑪ **l'ala sinistra** *m / f*
left-wing

⑫ **il primo centro** *m / f*
inside centre

⑬ **il secondo centro** *m / f*

outside centre

⑭ **l'ala destra** *m / f*
right wing

⑮ **l'estremo** *m / f*
full back

㊱ **il rugby in carrozzina**
wheelchair rugby

⑰ **il giocatore** *m*
la giocatrice *f*
player

⑱ **la palla da rugby**
rugby ball

⑲ **la maglietta da rugby**
rugby shirt

⑳ **la maglia da rugby**
rugby jersey

㉔ **i pali**
goal posts

㉓ **la protezione**
per pali
post protector

㉒ **la linea del**
pallone morto
dead ball line

㉑ **la linea di meta**
try line

㉚ **la superficie di gioco**
playing surface

㉛ **il campo da rugby**
rugby pitch

See also
107 Il football americano · American football **109** Il calcio · Football **110** L'hockey e il lacrosse · Hockey and lacrosse **112** Il basket e la pallavolo · Basketball and volleyball

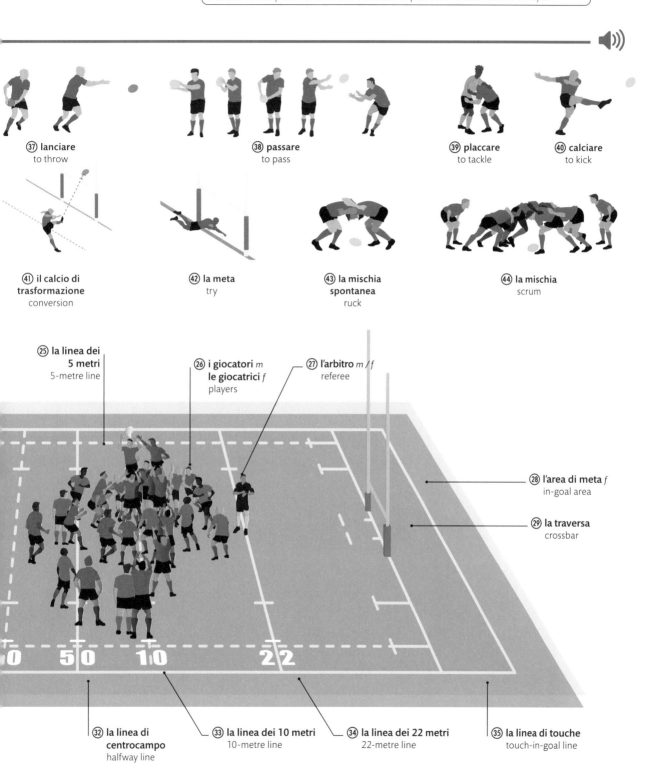

㊲ **lanciare**
to throw

㊳ **passare**
to pass

㊴ **placcare**
to tackle

㊵ **calciare**
to kick

㊶ **il calcio di trasformazione**
conversion

㊷ **la meta**
try

㊸ **la mischia spontanea**
ruck

㊹ **la mischia**
scrum

㉕ **la linea dei 5 metri**
5-metre line

㉖ **i giocatori** m **le giocatrici** f
players

㉗ **l'arbitro** m / f
referee

㉘ **l'area di meta** f
in-goal area

㉙ **la traversa**
crossbar

㉜ **la linea di centrocampo**
halfway line

㉝ **la linea dei 10 metri**
10-metre line

㉞ **la linea dei 22 metri**
22-metre line

㉟ **la linea di touche**
touch-in-goal line

225

109.1 LA PARTITA DI CALCIO · FOOTBALL GAME

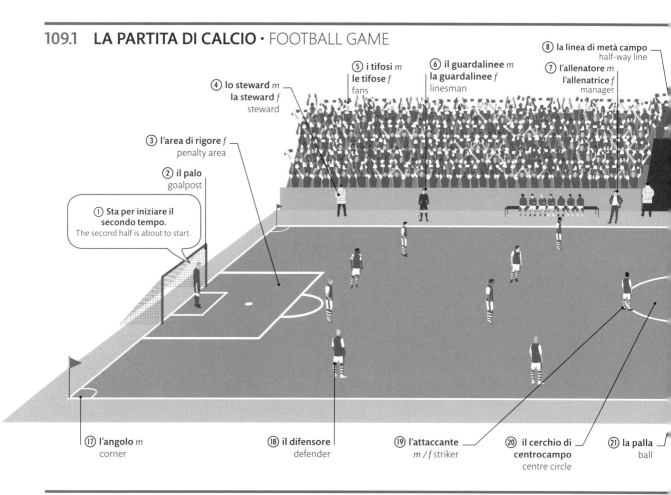

⑧ **la linea di metà campo**
half-way line

⑤ **i tifosi** *m*
le tifose *f*
fans

⑥ **il guardalinee** *m*
la guardalinee *f*
linesman

⑦ **l'allenatore** *m*
l'allenatrice *f*
manager

④ **lo steward** *m*
la steward *f*
steward

③ **l'area di rigore** *f*
penalty area

② **il palo**
goalpost

① **Sta per iniziare il secondo tempo.**
The second half is about to start.

⑰ **l'angolo** *m*
corner

⑱ **il difensore**
defender

⑲ **l'attaccante**
m / f striker

⑳ **il cerchio di centrocampo**
centre circle

㉑ **la palla**
ball

109.2 I TEMPI E LE REGOLE · TIMING AND RULES

① **il calcio d'inizio**
kickoff

② **l'intervallo** *m*
half time

③ **la fine della partita**
full time

④ **la rimessa**
throw-in

⑤ **il fischio finale**
final whistle

⑥ **il recupero**
injury time

⑨ **il calcio d'angolo**
corner kick

⑩ **il cartellino giallo**
yellow card

⑪ **il cartellino rosso**
red card

⑫ **essere espulso**
to be sent off

⑬ **pareggiare**
to draw

⑭ **perdere**
to lose

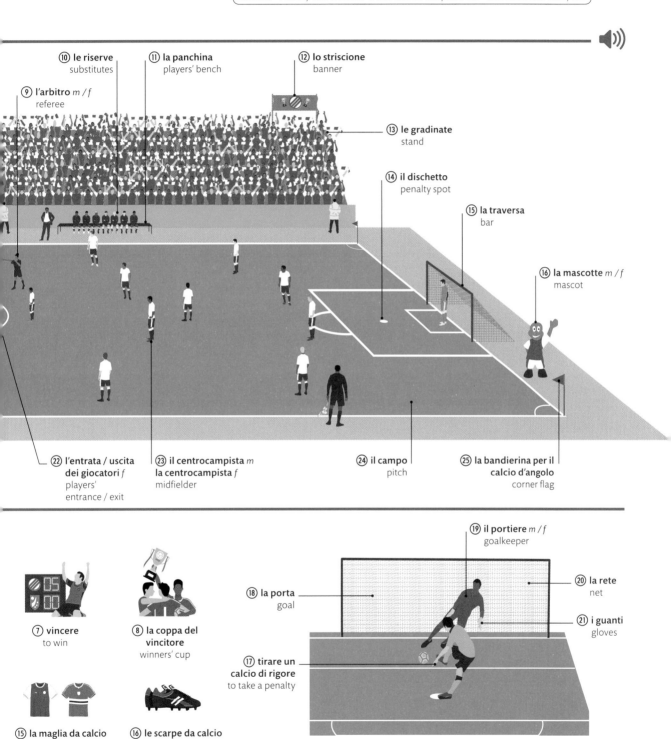

See also
107 Il football americano · American football **108** Il rugby · Rugby **110** L'hockey e il lacrosse · Hockey and lacrosse **112** Il basket e la pallavolo · Basketball and volleyball

⑩ **le riserve**
substitutes

⑪ **la panchina**
players' bench

⑫ **lo striscione**
banner

⑨ **l'arbitro** *m / f*
referee

⑬ **le gradinate**
stand

⑭ **il dischetto**
penalty spot

⑮ **la traversa**
bar

⑯ **la mascotte** *m / f*
mascot

㉒ **l'entrata / uscita dei giocatori** *f*
players' entrance / exit

㉓ **il centrocampista** *m*
la centrocampista *f*
midfielder

㉔ **il campo**
pitch

㉕ **la bandierina per il calcio d'angolo**
corner flag

⑲ **il portiere** *m / f*
goalkeeper

⑦ **vincere**
to win

⑧ **la coppa del vincitore**
winners' cup

⑱ **la porta**
goal

⑳ **la rete**
net

㉑ **i guanti**
gloves

⑰ **tirare un calcio di rigore**
to take a penalty

⑮ **la maglia da calcio**
football shirt

⑯ **le scarpe da calcio**
football boots

㉒ **il calcio di rigore**
penalty kick

110.1 L'HOCKEY SU GHIACCIO · ICE HOCKEY

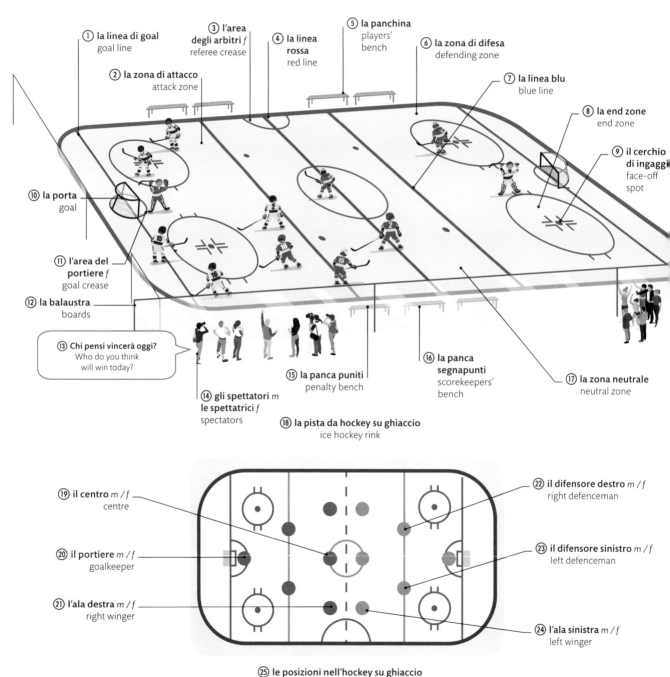

① la linea di goal
goal line

② la zona di attacco
attack zone

③ l'area degli arbitri f
referee crease

④ la linea rossa
red line

⑤ la panchina
players' bench

⑥ la zona di difesa
defending zone

⑦ la linea blu
blue line

⑧ la end zone
end zone

⑨ il cerchio di ingaggi
face-off spot

⑩ la porta
goal

⑪ l'area del portiere f
goal crease

⑫ la balaustra
boards

⑬ Chi pensi vincerà oggi?
Who do you think will win today?

⑭ gli spettatori m
le spettatrici f
spectators

⑮ la panca puniti
penalty bench

⑯ la panca segnapunti
scorekeepers' bench

⑰ la zona neutrale
neutral zone

⑱ la pista da hockey su ghiaccio
ice hockey rink

⑲ il centro m / f
centre

⑳ il portiere m / f
goalkeeper

㉑ l'ala destra m / f
right winger

㉒ il difensore destro m / f
right defenceman

㉓ il difensore sinistro m / f
left defenceman

㉔ l'ala sinistra m / f
left winger

㉕ le posizioni nell'hockey su ghiaccio
ice hockey positions

See also
107 Il football americano · American football **111** Il cricket · Cricket **112** Il basket e
la pallavolo · Basketball and volleyball **113** Il baseball · Baseball **114** Il tennis · Tennis

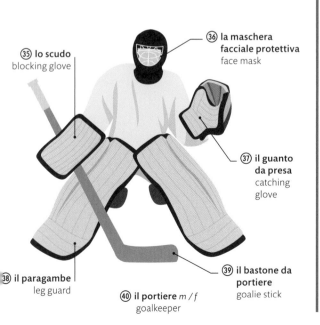

㉖ **pattinare**
to skate

㉗ **il paraspalle**
shoulder pad

㉘ **il casco**
helmet

㉙ **l'imbottitura
di protezione** *f*
protective
padding

㉚ **il guanto**
glove

㉛ **il pattino da
ghiaccio**
ice skate

㉜ **il bastone**
stick

㉝ **il disco**
puck

㉞ **il giocatore di hockey su ghiaccio** *m*
la giocatrice di hockey su ghiaccio *f*
ice hockey player

㉟ **lo scudo**
blocking glove

㊱ **la maschera
facciale protettiva**
face mask

㊲ **il guanto
da presa**
catching
glove

㊳ **il paragambe**
leg guard

㊴ **il portiere** *m / f*
goalkeeper

㊴ **il bastone da
portiere**
goalie stick

110.2 L'HOCKEY SU PRATO · FIELD HOCKEY

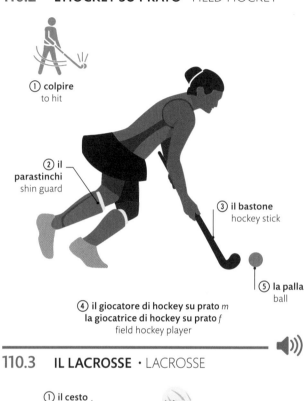

① **colpire**
to hit

② **il
parastinchi**
shin guard

③ **il bastone**
hockey stick

④ **il giocatore di hockey su prato** *m*
la giocatrice di hockey su prato *f*
field hockey player

⑤ **la palla**
ball

110.3 IL LACROSSE · LACROSSE

① **il cesto**
head pocket

② **la mazza**
crosse

③ **il parabraccia**
arm protection

④ **il manico**
handle

⑤ **il giocatore di lacrosse** *m*
la giocatrice di lacrosse *f*
lacrosse player

⑥ **passare**
to pass

⑦ **raccogliere**
to scoop

⑧ **l'ingaggio** *m*
face-off

229

111.1 IL CAMPO DA CRICKET E LE POSIZIONI
CRICKET PITCH AND POSITIONS

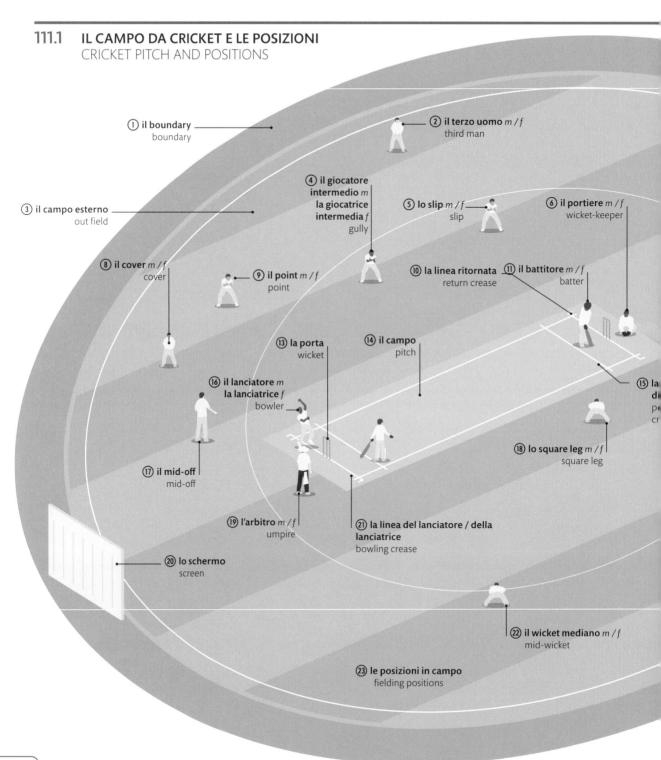

① **il boundary**
boundary

② **il terzo uomo** *m / f*
third man

③ **il campo esterno**
out field

④ **il giocatore intermedio** *m*
la giocatrice intermedia *f*
gully

⑤ **lo slip** *m / f*
slip

⑥ **il portiere** *m / f*
wicket-keeper

⑧ **il cover** *m / f*
cover

⑨ **il point** *m / f*
point

⑩ **la linea ritornata**
return crease

⑪ **il battitore** *m / f*
batter

⑬ **la porta**
wicket

⑭ **il campo**
pitch

⑮ **la
d...
p...
cr...**

⑯ **il lanciatore** *m*
la lanciatrice *f*
bowler

⑰ **il mid-off**
mid-off

⑱ **lo square leg** *m / f*
square leg

⑲ **l'arbitro** *m / f*
umpire

⑳ **lo schermo**
screen

㉑ **la linea del lanciatore / della lanciatrice**
bowling crease

㉒ **il wicket mediano** *m / f*
mid-wicket

㉓ **le posizioni in campo**
fielding positions

See also
109 Il calcio · Football **110** L'hockey e il lacrosse · Hockey and lacrosse **113** Il baseball · Baseball **115** Il golf · Golf

111.2 L'ATTREZZATURA DA CRICKET · CRICKET EQUIPMENT

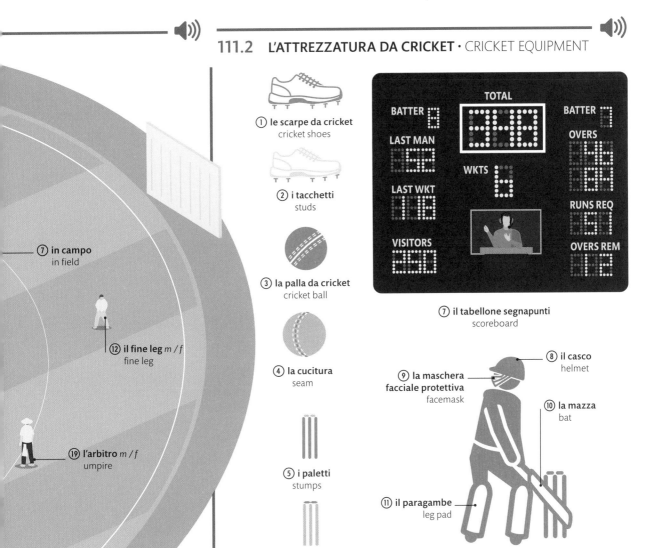

① le scarpe da cricket
cricket shoes

② i tacchetti
studs

③ la palla da cricket
cricket ball

④ la cucitura
seam

⑤ i paletti
stumps

⑥ la scanalatura del paletto
bail

⑦ il tabellone segnapunti
scoreboard

⑧ il casco
helmet

⑨ la maschera facciale protettiva
facemask

⑩ la mazza
bat

⑪ il paragambe
leg pad

⑫ il battitore *m / f*
batter / batsman

⑦ in campo
in field

⑫ il fine leg *m / f*
fine leg

⑲ l'arbitro *m / f*
umpire

111.3 I VERBI DEL CRICKET · CRICKET VERBS

① correre
to run

② lanciare
to bowl

③ battere
to bat

④ prendere la palla
to field

⑤ essere eliminato *m*
essere eliminata *f*
to strike out

⑥ eliminare colpendo il wicket
to stump

112.1 IL BASKET · BASKETBALL

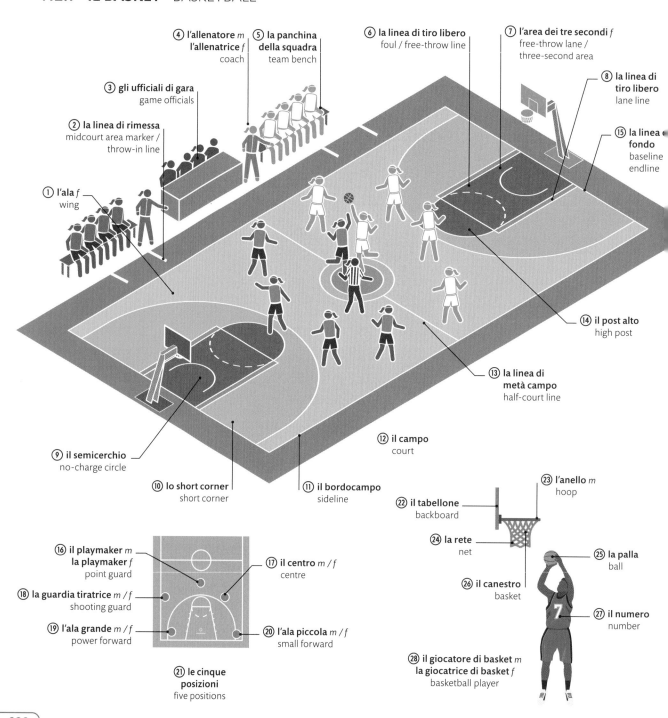

④ l'allenatore *m*
l'allenatrice *f*
coach

⑤ la panchina
della squadra
team bench

⑥ la linea di tiro libero
foul / free-throw line

⑦ l'area dei tre secondi *f*
free-throw lane /
three-second area

③ gli ufficiali di gara
game officials

⑧ la linea di
tiro libero
lane line

② la linea di rimessa
midcourt area marker /
throw-in line

⑮ la linea
fondo
baseline
endline

① l'ala *f*
wing

⑭ il post alto
high post

⑬ la linea di
metà campo
half-court line

⑨ il semicerchio
no-charge circle

⑫ il campo
court

⑩ lo short corner
short corner

⑪ il bordocampo
sideline

㉓ l'anello *m*
hoop

㉒ il tabellone
backboard

⑯ il playmaker *m*
la playmaker *f*
point guard

⑰ il centro *m / f*
centre

㉔ la rete
net

㉕ la palla
ball

⑱ la guardia tiratrice *m / f*
shooting guard

㉖ il canestro
basket

⑲ l'ala grande *m / f*
power forward

⑳ l'ala piccola *m / f*
small forward

㉗ il numero
number

㉑ le cinque
posizioni
five positions

㉘ il giocatore di basket *m*
la giocatrice di basket *f*
basketball player

See also
107 Il football americano • American football **108** Il rugby • Rugby **109** Il calcio
Football **124** In palestra • At the gym **125** Gli altri sport • Other sports

29 passare
pass

30 il fuori campo
out of bounds

31 la rimessa
throw-in

32 il rimbalzo
rebound

33 l'airball *m*
airball

34 il salto a due
jump ball

35 il fallo
foul

36 marcare
to mark

37 palleggiare
to bounce

38 schiacciare
to dunk

39 tirare
to shoot

40 bloccare
to block

112.2 **LA PALLAVOLO** · VOLLEYBALL

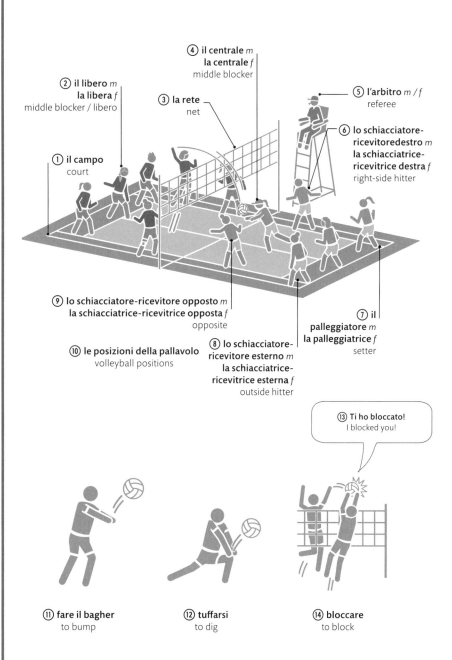

4 il centrale *m*
la centrale *f*
middle blocker

2 il libero *m*
la libera *f*
middle blocker / libero

3 la rete
net

5 l'arbitro *m / f*
referee

6 lo schiacciatore-
ricevitoredestro *m*
la schiacciatrice-
ricevitrice destra *f*
right-side hitter

1 il campo
court

9 lo schiacciatore-ricevitore opposto *m*
la schiacciatrice-ricevitrice opposta *f*
opposite

7 il
palleggiatore *m*
la palleggiatrice *f*
setter

10 le posizioni della pallavolo
volleyball positions

8 lo schiacciatore-
ricevitore esterno *m*
la schiacciatrice-
ricevitrice esterna *f*
outside hitter

13 Ti ho bloccato!
I blocked you!

11 fare il bagher
to bump

12 tuffarsi
to dig

14 bloccare
to block

233

113.1 LA PARTITA DI BASEBALL · BASEBALL GAME

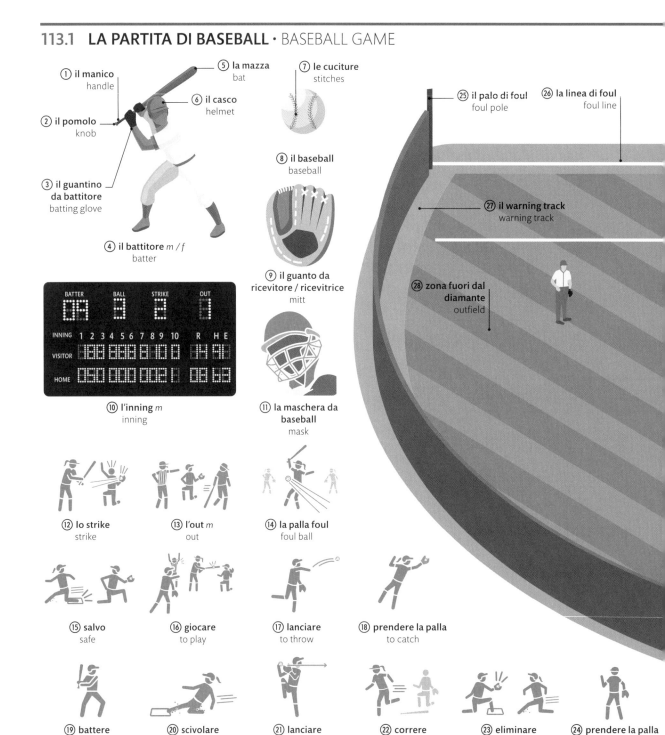

① il manico
handle

⑤ la mazza
bat

⑥ il casco
helmet

② il pomolo
knob

③ il guantino
da battitore
batting glove

④ il battitore *m / f*
batter

⑦ le cuciture
stitches

⑧ il baseball
baseball

⑨ il guanto da
ricevitore / ricevitrice
mitt

⑪ la maschera da
baseball
mask

⑩ l'inning *m*
inning

⑤ il palo di foul
foul pole

⑥ la linea di foul
foul line

⑦ il warning track
warning track

⑧ zona fuori dal
diamante
outfield

⑫ lo strike
strike

⑬ l'out *m*
out

⑭ la palla foul
foul ball

⑮ salvo
safe

⑯ giocare
to play

⑰ lanciare
to throw

⑱ prendere la palla
to catch

⑲ battere
to bat

⑳ scivolare
to slide

㉑ lanciare
to pitch

㉒ correre
to run

㉓ eliminare
to tag

㉔ prendere la palla
to field

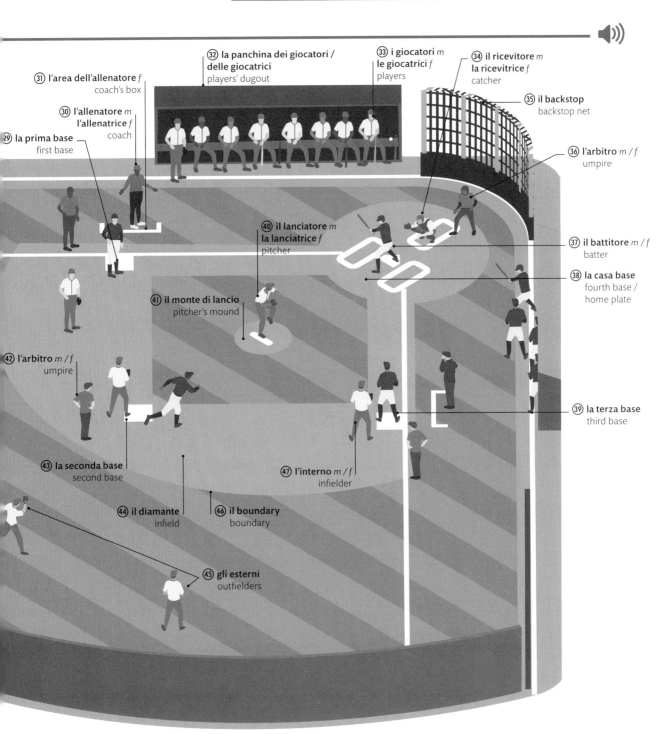

See also
107 Il football americano · American football **110** L'hockey e il lacrosse · Hockey and lacrosse **111** Il cricket · Cricket **112** Il basket e la pallavolo · Basketball and volleyball

㉛ **l'area dell'allenatore** *f*
coach's box

㉚ **l'allenatore** *m*
l'allenatrice *f*
coach

㉙ **la prima base**
first base

㉜ **la panchina dei giocatori /
delle giocatrici**
players' dugout

㉝ **i giocatori** *m*
le giocatrici *f*
players

㉞ **il ricevitore** *m*
la ricevitrice *f*
catcher

㉟ **il backstop**
backstop net

㊱ **l'arbitro** *m / f*
umpire

㊵ **il lanciatore** *m*
la lanciatrice *f*
pitcher

㊲ **il battitore** *m / f*
batter

㊳ **la casa base**
fourth base /
home plate

㊶ **il monte di lancio**
pitcher's mound

㊷ **l'interno** *m / f*
infielder

㊴ **la terza base**
third base

㊸ **l'arbitro** *m / f*
umpire

㊸ **la seconda base**
second base

㊹ **il diamante**
infield

㊻ **il boundary**
boundary

㊺ **gli esterni**
outfielders

㊽ **il campo da baseball**
baseball field

114.1 L'INCONTRO DI TENNIS · TENNIS MATCH

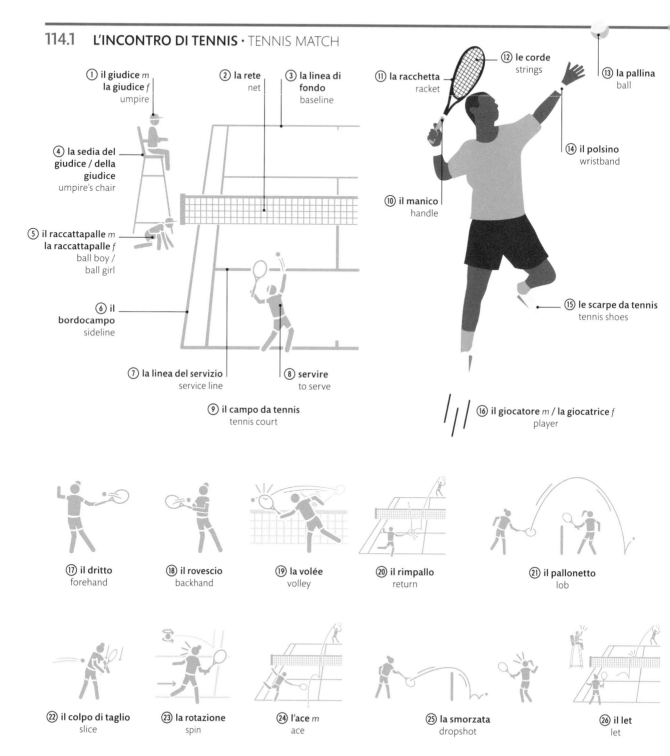

① il giudice *m*
la giudice *f*
umpire

④ la sedia del giudice / della giudice
umpire's chair

⑤ il raccattapalle *m*
la raccattapalle *f*
ball boy / ball girl

⑥ il bordocampo
sideline

② la rete
net

③ la linea di fondo
baseline

⑦ la linea del servizio
service line

⑧ servire
to serve

⑨ il campo da tennis
tennis court

⑪ la racchetta
racket

⑫ le corde
strings

⑬ la pallina
ball

⑭ il polsino
wristband

⑩ il manico
handle

⑮ le scarpe da tennis
tennis shoes

⑯ il giocatore *m* / la giocatrice *f*
player

⑰ il dritto
forehand

⑱ il rovescio
backhand

⑲ la volée
volley

⑳ il rimpallo
return

㉑ il pallonetto
lob

㉒ il colpo di taglio
slice

㉓ la rotazione
spin

㉔ l'ace *m*
ace

㉕ la smorzata
dropshot

㉖ il let
let

See also
111 Il cricket • Cricket **113** Il baseball • Baseball
115 Il golf • Golf **116** L'atletica • Athletics

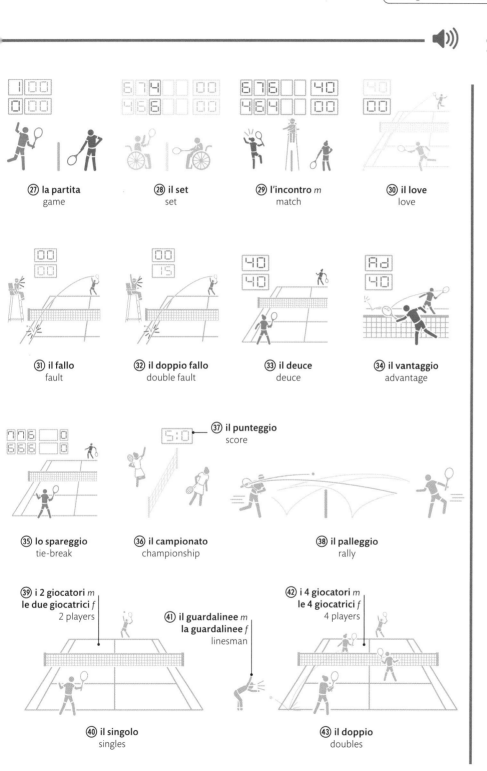

㉗ **la partita**
game

㉘ **il set**
set

㉙ **l'incontro** *m*
match

㉚ **il love**
love

㉛ **il fallo**
fault

㉜ **il doppio fallo**
double fault

㉝ **il deuce**
deuce

㉞ **il vantaggio**
advantage

㊲ **il punteggio**
score

㉟ **lo spareggio**
tie-break

㊱ **il campionato**
championship

㊳ **il palleggio**
rally

㊴ **i 2 giocatori** *m*
le due giocatrici *f*
2 players

㊶ **il guardalinee** *m*
la guardalinee *f*
linesman

㊷ **i 4 giocatori** *m*
le 4 giocatrici *f*
4 players

㊵ **il singolo**
singles

㊸ **il doppio**
doubles

114.2 I GIOCHI CON LE RACCHETTE
RACKET GAMES

① **lo squash**
squash

② **il racquetball**
racquetball

③ **il ping pong**
ping pong /
table tennis

④ **il paddle**
bat

⑤ **il badminton**
badminton

⑥ **il volano**
shuttlecock

115.1 SUL CAMPO DA GOLF · ON THE GOLF COURSE

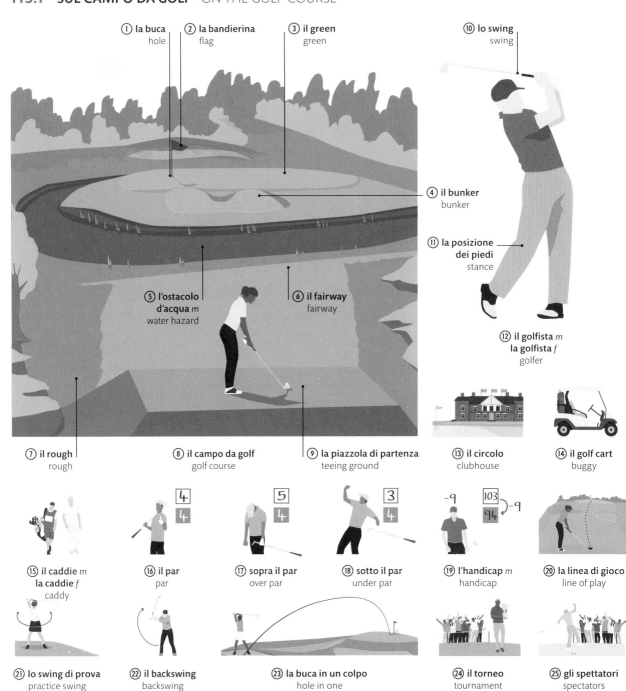

① **la buca** hole
② **la bandierina** flag
③ **il green** green
④ **il bunker** bunker
⑤ **l'ostacolo d'acqua** *m* water hazard
⑥ **il fairway** fairway
⑦ **il rough** rough
⑧ **il campo da golf** golf course
⑨ **la piazzola di partenza** teeing ground
⑩ **lo swing** swing
⑪ **la posizione dei piedi** stance
⑫ **il golfista** *m* **la golfista** *f* golfer
⑬ **il circolo** clubhouse
⑭ **il golf cart** buggy
⑮ **il caddie** *m* **la caddie** *f* caddy
⑯ **il par** par
⑰ **sopra il par** over par
⑱ **sotto il par** under par
⑲ **l'handicap** *m* handicap
⑳ **la linea di gioco** line of play
㉑ **lo swing di prova** practice swing
㉒ **il backswing** backswing
㉓ **la buca in un colpo** hole in one
㉔ **il torneo** tournament
㉕ **gli spettatori** spectators

See also
111 Il cricket · Cricket **113** Il baseball
Baseball **114** Il tennis · Tennis

115.2 **L'ATTREZZATURA DA GOLF**
GOLF EQUIPMENT

③ **il tee**
tee

① **il cappello da golf**
golf cap

② **la pallina da golf**
golf ball

⑥ **i tacchetti**
spikes

④ **il guanto**
glove

⑤ **la scarpa da golf**
golf shoe

⑧ **il sistema di trasporto**
harness

⑦ **la sacca da golf**
golf bag

⑨ **il supporto**
stand

⑩ **il carrello per sacca da golf**
golf trolley

115.3 **LE MAZZE DA GOLF** · GOLF CLUBS

① **l'impugnatura** *f*
grip

⑦ **il putter**
putter

⑧ **la suola**
sole

⑨ **il legno**
wood

⑩ **la punta**
toe

⑪ **il wedge**
wedge

③ **l'hosel** *m*
neck

② **l'asta** *f*
shaft

④ **la scanalatura**
groove

⑤ **la ghiera**
ferrule

⑫ **il ferro**
iron

⑥ **il tacco**
heel

115.4 **I VERBI DEL GOLF** · GOLF VERBS

① **iniziare una partita**
to tee off

② **tirare il drive**
to drive

③ **fare uno swing**
to swing

④ **puttare**
to putt

⑤ **tirare un chip**
to chip

⑥ **vincere**
to win

116 L'atletica
Athletics

116.1 LA PISTA DI ATLETICA · ATHLETICS TRACK

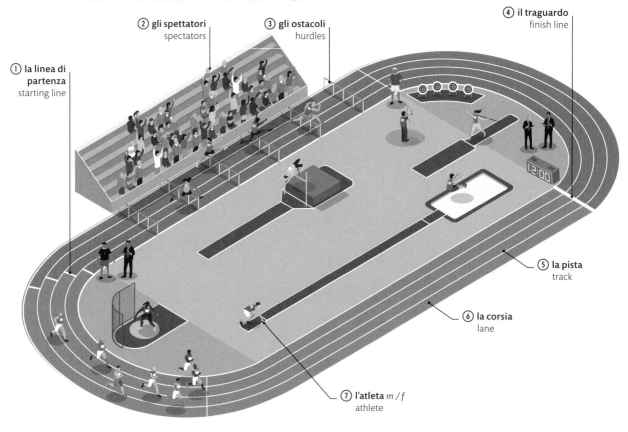

① la linea di partenza
starting line

② gli spettatori
spectators

③ gli ostacoli
hurdles

④ il traguardo
finish line

⑤ la pista
track

⑥ la corsia
lane

⑦ l'atleta *m / f*
athlete

116.2 LE GARE DI CORSA · RACING EVENTS

① la gara
race

② il blocco di partenza
starting block

③ il velocista *m*
la velocista *f*
sprinter

④ la corsa T11 (per atleti non vedenti)
T11 (visual impairment) race

⑤ la corsa in carrozzina
wheelchair race

⑥ la staffetta
relay race

⑦ il testimone
baton

⑧ la maratona
marathon

⑨ il fotofinish
photo finish

See also
117 Gli sport da combattimento · Combat sports **118** Il nuoto · Swimming **119** La vela e gli sport acquatici · Sailing and watersports **120** L'equitazione · Horse riding **122** Gli sport invernali · Winter sports **124** In palestra · At the gym **125** Gli altri sport · Other sports

116.3 L'ATLETICA LEGGERA · FIELD EVENTS

① **il lancio del disco** discus

② **il lancio del peso** shot put

③ **il lancio del martello** hammer

④ **il lancio del giavellotto** javelin

⑤ **il salto con l'asta** pole vault

⑥ **il salto in lungo** long jump

⑦ **il salto in alto** high jump

⑧ **il salto triplo** triple jump

⑨ **la sbarra** crossbar

⑩ **il laser-run** laser run

⑪ **la scherma** fencing

116.4 SUL PODIO · ON THE PODIUM

① **l'oro** *m* gold

② **l'argento** *m* silver

③ **il bronzo** bronze

④ **le medaglie** medals

⑤ **il podio** podium

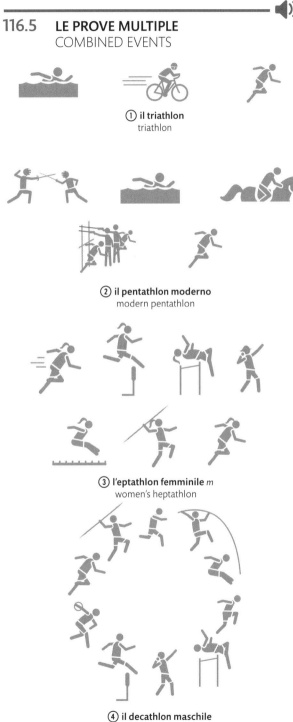

116.5 LE PROVE MULTIPLE COMBINED EVENTS

① **il triathlon** triathlon

② **il pentathlon moderno** modern pentathlon

③ **l'eptathlon femminile** *m* women's heptathlon

④ **il decathlon maschile** men's decathlon

241

117.1 LE ARTI MARZIALI · MARTIAL ARTS

① **la protezione inguinale** groin protector

⑦ **la cintura nera** black belt

⑧ **il tatami** karate mat

⑨ **l'avversario** *m* **l'avversaria** *f* opponent

④ **il casco** head guard

② **il guanto** glove

⑤ **la protezione per il torace** chest protection

③ **la cintura** belt

⑥ **il taekwondo** taekwondo

⑩ **la zona di sicurezza** safety area

⑪ **il karate** karate

⑫ **la zona di pericolo** danger area

⑮ **l'hakama** *m* hakama

⑬ **il judo** judo

⑭ **l'aikido** *m* aikido

⑯ **il kung fu** kung fu

⑰ **il jujitsu** jujitsu

⑱ **la capoeira** capoeira

㉓ **la maschera protettiva** mask

㉔ **la spada** sword

⑲ **il kickboxing** kickboxing

⑳ **il tai chi** tai chi

㉑ **il wrestling** wrestling

㉒ **il sumo** sumo wrestling

㉕ **il kendo** kendo

117.2 LE AZIONI · ACTIONS

① **cadere** to fall

② **tenere** to hold

③ **lanciare** to throw

④ **bloccare** to pin

⑤ **il calcio frontale** front kick

⑥ **il calcio volante** flying kick

See also
116 L'atletica · Athletics **124** In palestra
At the gym **125** Gli altri sport · Other sports

117.3 **LA BOXE** · BOXING

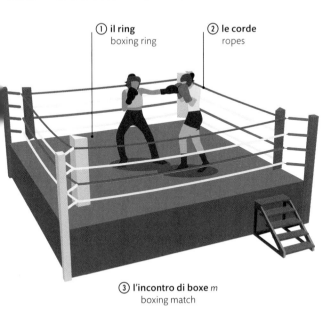

① **il ring**
boxing ring

② **le corde**
ropes

④ **il round**
round

⑤ **il K.O.**
knock out

⑥ **i guanti da boxe**
boxing gloves

⑦ **il paradenti**
mouth guard

③ **l'incontro di boxe** *m*
boxing match

⑧ **il sacco da boxe**
punchbag

117.4 **LA SCHERMA** · FENCING

① **affondare**
to lunge

② **parare**
to parry

③ **l'elsa** *f*
hilt

⑤ **la lama**
blade

④ **il fioretto**
foil

⑥ **la spada**
épée

⑦ **la sciabola**
sabre

⑦ **colpire con un pugno**
to punch

⑧ **colpire**
to strike

⑨ **bloccare**
to block

⑩ **saltare**
to jump

⑪ **spaccare**
to chop

118.1 IL NUOTO · SWIMMING

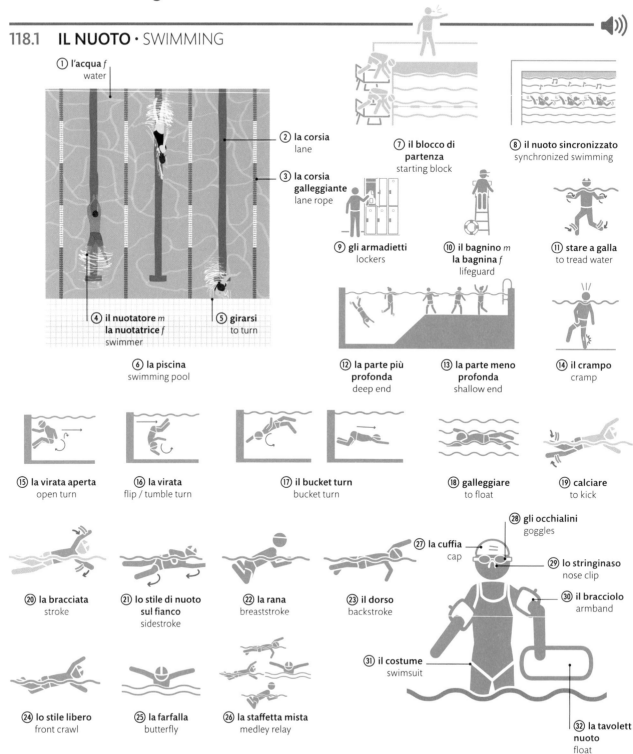

1. l'acqua *f* — water
2. la corsia — lane
3. la corsia galleggiante — lane rope
4. il nuotatore *m* / la nuotatrice *f* — swimmer
5. girarsi — to turn
6. la piscina — swimming pool
7. il blocco di partenza — starting block
8. il nuoto sincronizzato — synchronized swimming
9. gli armadietti — lockers
10. il bagnino *m* / la bagnina *f* — lifeguard
11. stare a galla — to tread water
12. la parte più profonda — deep end
13. la parte meno profonda — shallow end
14. il crampo — cramp
15. la virata aperta — open turn
16. la virata — flip / tumble turn
17. il bucket turn — bucket turn
18. galleggiare — to float
19. calciare — to kick
20. la bracciata — stroke
21. lo stile di nuoto sul fianco — sidestroke
22. la rana — breaststroke
23. il dorso — backstroke
24. lo stile libero — front crawl
25. la farfalla — butterfly
26. la staffetta mista — medley relay
27. la cuffia — cap
28. gli occhialini — goggles
29. lo stringinaso — nose clip
30. il bracciolo — armband
31. il costume — swimsuit
32. la tavoletta nuoto — float

See also
119 La vela e gli sport acquatici • Sailing and watersports
134 In spiaggia • On the beach **166** La vita negli oceani • Ocean life

118.2 **I TUFFI**
DIVING

■ **trampolino**
diving board

② **tuffarsi**
to dive

③ **la gara di tuffi**
racing dive

④ **la piattaforma**
platform

⑤ **il trampolino**
diving tower

⑥ **il tuffo da grandi altezze**
high dive

⑦ **il tuffatore** *m*
la tuffatrice *f*
diver

⑧ **la capovolta in avanti**
front-flip

⑨ **la capriola all'indietro**
back-flip

⑩ **il tuffo di testa**
head-first

⑪ **il tuffo di piedi**
feet-first

⑫ **il trampolino**
springboard

118.3 **LE IMMERSIONI** · UNDERWATER DIVING

① **il respiratore**
snorkel

② **i pesci della barriera corallina**
coral
reef fish

③ **lo snorkelling**
snorkelling

④ **la muta subacquea**
wet suit

⑤ **la cintura zavorrata**
weight belt

⑥ **la bombola**
air cylinder

⑦ **le pinne**
fins / flippers

⑧ **le immersioni subacquee**
scuba diving

⑨ **la maschera**
mask

⑩ **l'erogatore** *m*
regulator

⑪ **la videocamera subacquea**
underwater camera

⑫ **il profondimetro**
depth gauge

⑬ **la barriera corallina**
coral reef

⑭ **l'immersione ad alte profondità** *f*
deep diving

119.1 LA VELA · SAILING

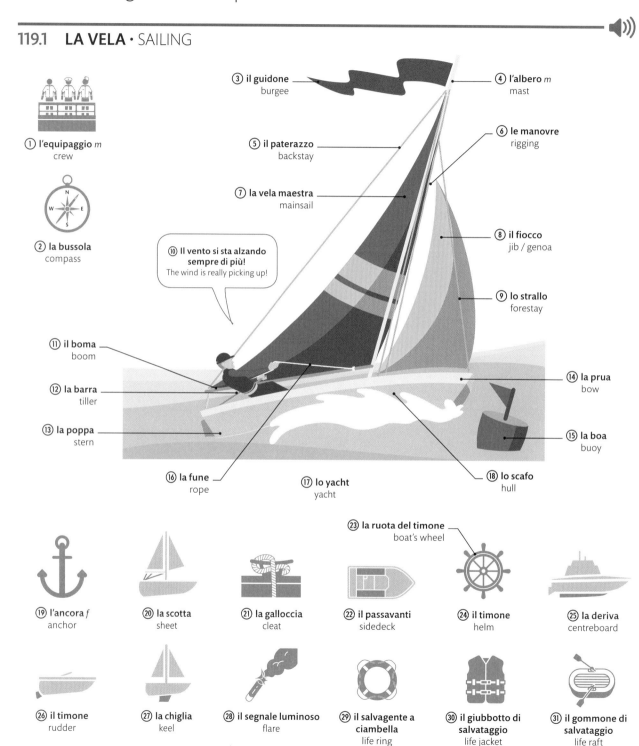

① l'equipaggio *m*
crew

② la bussola
compass

③ il guidone
burgee

④ l'albero *m*
mast

⑤ il paterazzo
backstay

⑥ le manovre
rigging

⑦ la vela maestra
mainsail

⑧ il fiocco
jib / genoa

⑨ lo strallo
forestay

⑩ Il vento si sta alzando sempre di più!
The wind is really picking up!

⑪ il boma
boom

⑫ la barra
tiller

⑬ la poppa
stern

⑭ la prua
bow

⑮ la boa
buoy

⑯ la fune
rope

⑰ lo yacht
yacht

⑱ lo scafo
hull

㉓ la ruota del timone
boat's wheel

⑲ l'ancora *f*
anchor

⑳ la scotta
sheet

㉑ la galloccia
cleat

㉒ il passavanti
sidedeck

㉔ il timone
helm

㉕ la deriva
centreboard

㉖ il timone
rudder

㉗ la chiglia
keel

㉘ il segnale luminoso
flare

㉙ il salvagente a ciambella
life ring

㉚ il giubbotto di salvataggio
life jacket

㉛ il gommone di salvataggio
life raft

See also
105 Le imbarcazioni · Sea vessels **106** Il porto · The port **118** Il nuoto
Swimming **121** La pesca · Fishing **134** In spiaggia · On the beach

119.2 GLI SPORT D'ACQUA · WATERSPORTS

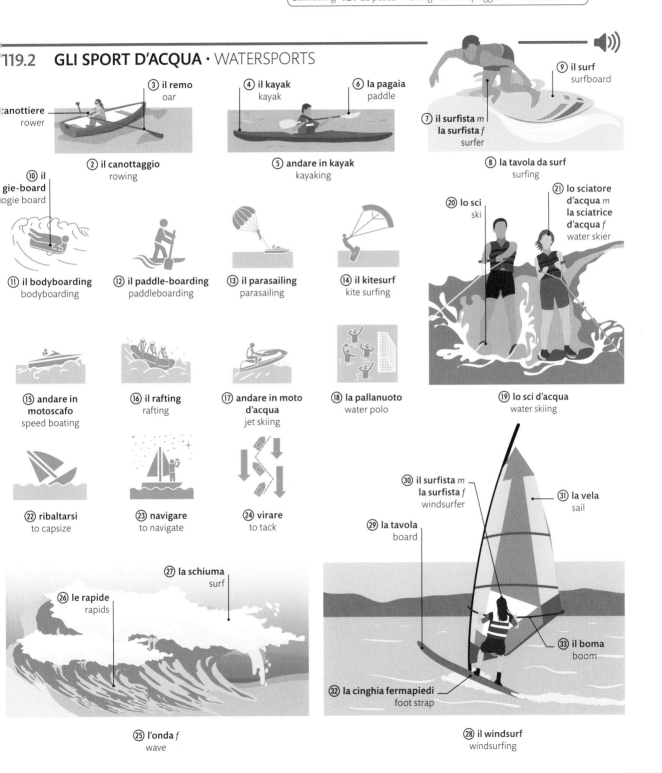

③ **il remo**
oar

④ **il kayak**
kayak

⑥ **la pagaia**
paddle

⑨ **il surf**
surfboard

canottiere
rower

⑦ **il surfista** *m*
la surfista *f*
surfer

② **il canottaggio**
rowing

⑤ **andare in kayak**
kayaking

⑧ **la tavola da surf**
surfing

⑩ **il boogie-board**
boogie board

⑳ **lo sci**
ski

㉑ **lo sciatore**
d'acqua *m*
la sciatrice
d'acqua *f*
water skier

⑪ **il bodyboarding**
bodyboarding

⑫ **il paddle-boarding**
paddleboarding

⑬ **il parasailing**
parasailing

⑭ **il kitesurf**
kite surfing

⑮ **andare in**
motoscafo
speed boating

⑯ **il rafting**
rafting

⑰ **andare in moto**
d'acqua
jet skiing

⑱ **la pallanuoto**
water polo

⑲ **lo sci d'acqua**
water skiing

㉒ **ribaltarsi**
to capsize

㉓ **navigare**
to navigate

㉔ **virare**
to tack

㉚ **il surfista** *m*
la surfista *f*
windsurfer

㉛ **la vela**
sail

㉙ **la tavola**
board

㉗ **la schiuma**
surf

㉖ **le rapide**
rapids

㉝ **il boma**
boom

㉜ **la cinghia fermapiedi**
foot strap

㉕ **l'onda** *f*
wave

㉘ **il windsurf**
windsurfing

120.1 L'EQUITAZIONE · HORSE RIDING

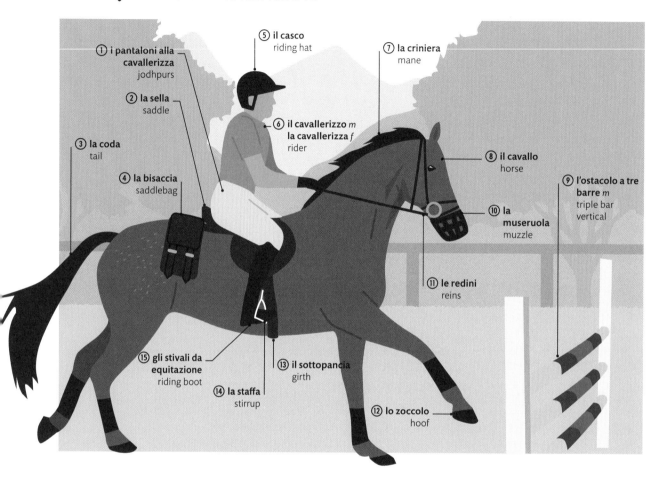

① **i pantaloni alla cavallerizza**
jodhpurs

② **la sella**
saddle

③ **la coda**
tail

④ **la bisaccia**
saddlebag

⑤ **il casco**
riding hat

⑥ **il cavallerizzo** m **la cavallerizza** f
rider

⑦ **la criniera**
mane

⑧ **il cavallo**
horse

⑨ **l'ostacolo a tre barre** m
triple bar vertical

⑩ **la museruola**
muzzle

⑪ **le redini**
reins

⑫ **lo zoccolo**
hoof

⑬ **il sottopancia**
girth

⑭ **la staffa**
stirrup

⑮ **gli stivali da equitazione**
riding boot

⑯ **il ferro di cavallo**
horseshoe

⑰ **la cavezza**
halter

⑱ **la museruola**
noseband

⑲ **il morso**
bit

⑳ **il frontalino**
browband

㉑ **le briglie**
bridle

㉒ **il pomolo**
pommel

㉓ **la sella**
seat

㉔ **il frustino**
riding crop

㉕ **il fantino**
jockey

㉖ **il cavallo da corsa**
racehorse

㉗ **gli ostacoli**
verticals

See also
116 L'atletica • Athletics **125** Gli altri sport • Other sports **133** Le attività all'aperto • Outdoor activities

㉘ **la cavalcata all'amazzone**
side-saddle

㉙ **la corsa di cavalli**
horse race

㉚ **la corsa al trotto**
harness race

㉛ **la pista senza ostacoli**
flat race

㉜ **la corsa a ostacoli**
steeplechase

㉝ **la corsa dei carri**
carriage race

㉞ **il salto a ostacoli**
showjumping

㉟ **il dressage**
dressage

㊱ **il polo**
polo

㊲ **il rodeo**
rodeo

㊳ **il trekking a cavallo**
trekking

㊴ **l'arena** *f*
arena

㊵ **l'ippodromo** *m*
racecourse

㊶ **il recinto**
paddock

㊷ **la scuderia**
stable

㊸ **lo stallone**
stallion

㊹ **la giumenta**
mare

㊺ **il puledro**
foal

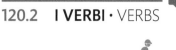

120.2   I VERBI · VERBS

① **strigliare**
to groom

② **andare al passo**
to walk

③ **andare al trotto**
to trot

④ **andare al piccolo galoppo**
to canter

⑤ **andare al galoppo**
to gallop

⑥ **saltare**
to jump

⑦ **allevare**
to breed

⑧ **pulire la stalla**
to muck out

121.1 IL PESCATORE / LA PESCATRICE · ANGLER

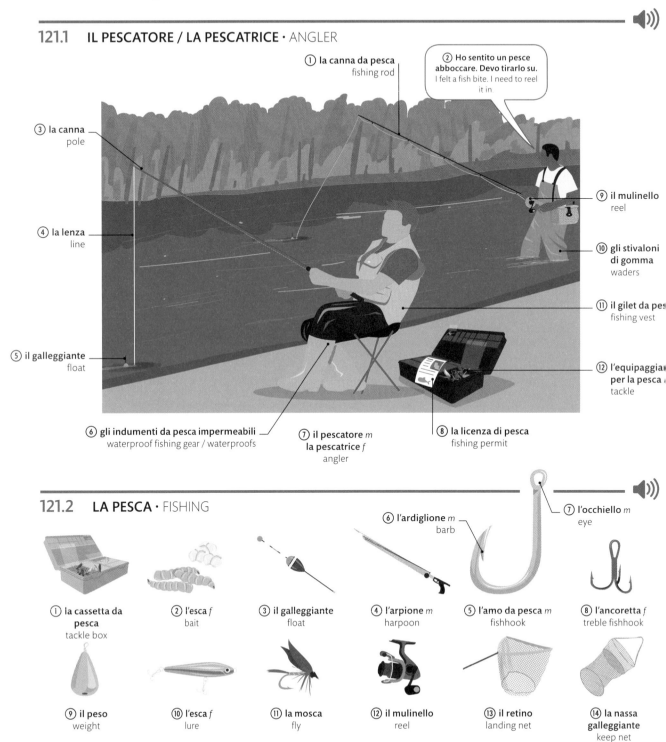

① la canna da pesca
fishing rod

② Ho sentito un pesce
abboccare. Devo tirarlo su.
I felt a fish bite. I need to reel
it in.

③ la canna
pole

④ la lenza
line

⑤ il galleggiante
float

⑥ gli indumenti da pesca impermeabili
waterproof fishing gear / waterproofs

⑦ il pescatore *m*
la pescatrice *f*
angler

⑧ la licenza di pesca
fishing permit

⑨ il mulinello
reel

⑩ gli stivaloni
di gomma
waders

⑪ il gilet da pes
fishing vest

⑫ l'equipaggia
per la pesca
tackle

121.2 LA PESCA · FISHING

⑥ l'ardiglione *m*
barb

⑦ l'occhiello *m*
eye

① la cassetta da
pesca
tackle box

② l'esca *f*
bait

③ il galleggiante
float

④ l'arpione *m*
harpoon

⑤ l'amo da pesca *m*
fishhook

⑧ l'ancoretta *f*
treble fishhook

⑨ il peso
weight

⑩ l'esca *f*
lure

⑪ la mosca
fly

⑫ il mulinello
reel

⑬ il retino
landing net

⑭ la nassa
galleggiante
keep net

See also
54 Il pesce e i frutti di mare · Fish and seafood
119 La vela e gli sport acquatici · Sailing and
watersports **166** La vita negli oceani · Ocean life

121.3   I TIPI DI PESCA · TYPES OF FISHING

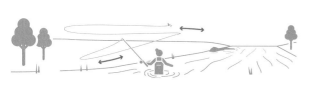

① **la pesca a mosca**
fly fishing

② **la pesca in acqua dolce**
freshwater fishing

③ **la pesca marittima**
marine fishing

④ **la pesca d'altura**
deep sea fishing

⑤ **la pesca sportiva**
sport fishing

⑥ **la pesca subacquea**
spearfishing

⑦ **la pesca su ghiaccio**
ice fishing

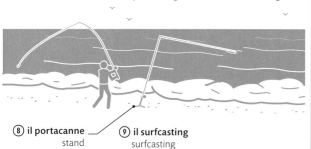

⑧ **il portacanne**
stand

⑨ **il surfcasting**
surfcasting

121.4   I VERBI DELLA PESCA · FISHING VERBS

① **mettere l'esca**
to bait

② **lanciare la lenza**
to cast

③ **abboccare**
to bite

④ **catturare**
to catch

⑤ **tirare su**
to reel in

⑥ **catturare con la rete**
to net

⑦ **liberare**
to release

121.5   I NODI · KNOTS

① **il nodo clinch**
clinch knot

② **il nodo di sangue**
blood knot

③ **il nodo Arbor**
arbor knot

④ **il nodo Snell**
snell knot

⑤ **il nodo Turle**
turle knot

⑥ **il nodo Palomar**
palomar knot

122.1 LO SCI · SKIING

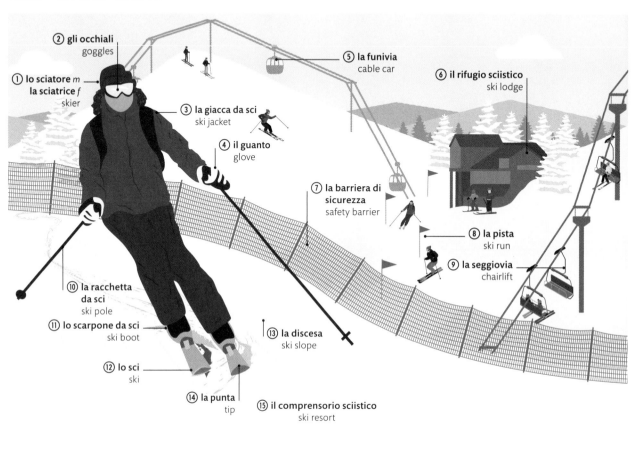

② **gli occhiali**
goggles

⑤ **la funivia**
cable car

① **lo sciatore** *m*
la sciatrice *f*
skier

⑥ **il rifugio sciistico**
ski lodge

③ **la giacca da sci**
ski jacket

④ **il guanto**
glove

⑦ **la barriera di sicurezza**
safety barrier

⑧ **la pista**
ski run

⑨ **la seggiovia**
chairlift

⑩ **la racchetta da sci**
ski pole

⑪ **lo scarpone da sci**
ski boot

⑬ **la discesa**
ski slope

⑫ **lo sci**
ski

⑭ **la punta**
tip

⑮ **il comprensorio sciistico**
ski resort

⑯ **sciare**
to ski

⑰ **lo sci da discesa**
downhill skiing

⑱ **lo slalom**
slalom

⑲ **lo slalom gigante**
giant slalom

⑳ **lo sci di fondo**
cross-country skiing

㉑ **il fuori pista**
off-piste

㉒ **il biathlon**
biathlon

㉓ **la valanga**
avalanche

㉔ **la rampa di atterraggio**
landing hill

㉕ **il cancelletto**
gate

㉖ **il salto con gli sci**
ski jump

㉗ **la rampa di salto**
jumping ramp

See also
116 L'atletica · Athletics **124** In palestra
At the gym **125** Gli altri sport · Other sports

122.2 **GLI ALTRI SPORT INVERNALI** · OTHER WINTER SPORTS

① **gli sport invernali**
winter sports

② **il pattino**
skate

③ **il pattinaggio sul ghiaccio**
ice-skating

④ **il pattinaggio di velocità**
speed skating

⑤ **il pattinaggio artistico**
figure skating

⑥ **lo snowboard**
snowboarding

⑦ **lo slittino**
luge

⑧ **lo skeleton**
skeleton

⑨ **la slitta**
sledging

⑫ **la slitta**
sleigh

⑪ **i bobbisti**
runners

⑩ **il bob**
bobsleigh

⑬ **l'arrampicata su ghiaccio** *f*
ice climbing

⑭ **il gatto delle nevi**
snowmobile

⑮ **il para hockey sul ghiaccio**
para ice hockey

⑯ **il curling in carrozzina**
wheelchair curling

⑲ **la scopa da curling**
curling brush

⑱ **il disco da curling**
curling stone

⑰ **il curling**
curling

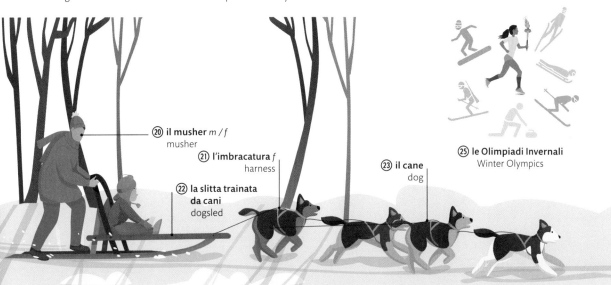

⑳ **il musher** *m / f*
musher

㉑ **l'imbracatura** *f*
harness

㉒ **la slitta trainata da cani**
dogsled

㉓ **il cane**
dog

㉕ **le Olimpiadi Invernali**
Winter Olympics

㉔ **andare sulla slitta**
dog sledding

123.1 L'AUTO DA CORSA · RACING CAR

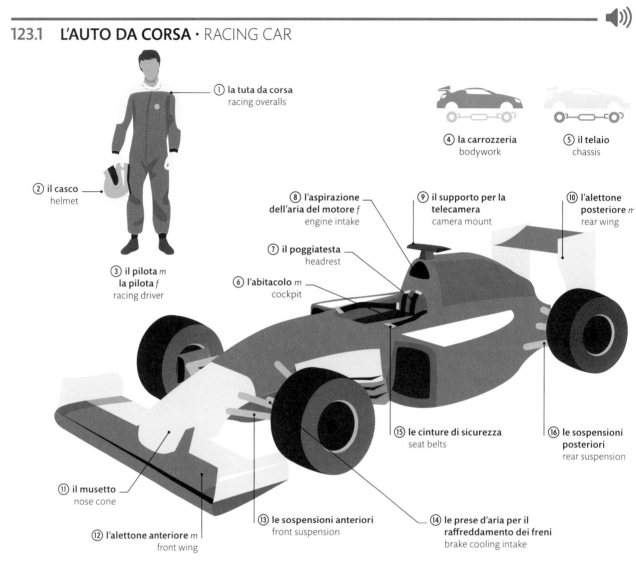

① la tuta da corsa
racing overalls

② il casco
helmet

③ il pilota *m*
la pilota *f*
racing driver

④ la carrozzeria
bodywork

⑤ il telaio
chassis

⑧ l'aspirazione
dell'aria del motore *f*
engine intake

⑦ il poggiatesta
headrest

⑥ l'abitacolo *m*
cockpit

⑨ il supporto per la
telecamera
camera mount

⑩ l'alettone
posteriore *m*
rear wing

⑪ il musetto
nose cone

⑫ l'alettone anteriore *m*
front wing

⑬ le sospensioni anteriori
front suspension

⑭ le prese d'aria per il
raffreddamento dei freni
brake cooling intake

⑮ le cinture di sicurezza
seat belts

⑯ le sospensioni
posteriori
rear suspension

123.2 I TIPI DI SPORT MOTORISTICI · TYPES OF MOTORSPORTS

① la gara automobilistica
motor racing

② il rally
rally driving

③ la gara di accelerazione
drag racing

See also
96 Le strade · Roads **97-98** Le auto · Cars **99** Le auto e gli autobus · Cars and buses **100** I motocicli · Motorcycles

123.3 **IL CIRCUITO** · RACE TRACK

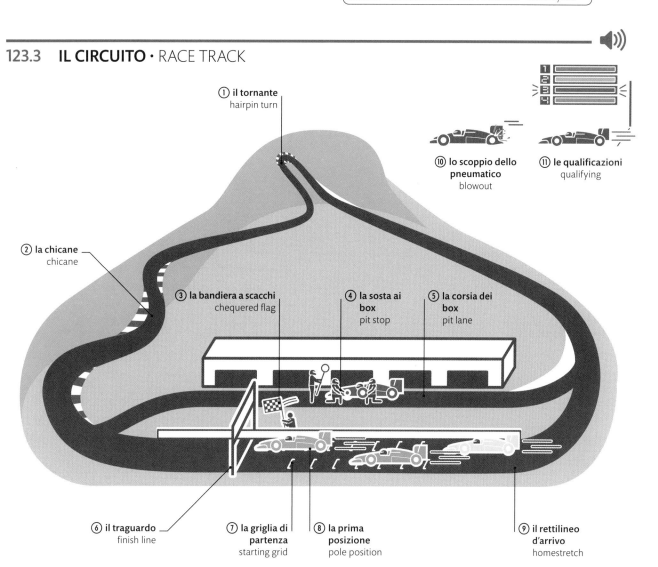

① il tornante
hairpin turn

⑩ lo scoppio dello pneumatico
blowout

⑪ le qualificazioni
qualifying

② la chicane
chicane

③ la bandiera a scacchi
chequered flag

④ la sosta ai box
pit stop

⑤ la corsia dei box
pit lane

⑥ il traguardo
finish line

⑦ la griglia di partenza
starting grid

⑧ la prima posizione
pole position

⑨ il rettilineo d'arrivo
homestretch

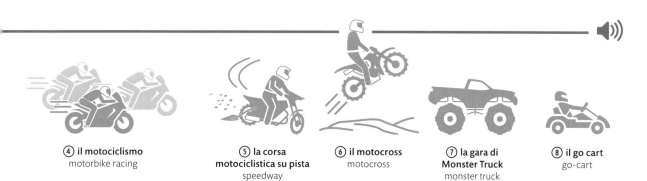

④ il motociclismo
motorbike racing

⑤ la corsa motociclistica su pista
speedway

⑥ il motocross
motocross

⑦ la gara di Monster Truck
monster truck

⑧ il go cart
go-cart

124.1 L'ALLENAMENTO · WORKING OUT

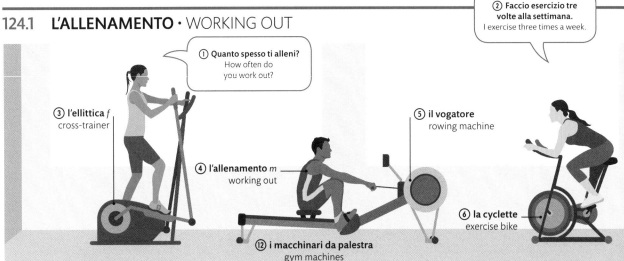

① **Quanto spesso ti alleni?**
How often do you work out?

② **Faccio esercizio tre volte alla settimana.**
I exercise three times a week.

③ **l'ellittica** *f*
cross-trainer

④ **l'allenamento** *m*
working out

⑤ **il vogatore**
rowing machine

⑥ **la cyclette**
exercise bike

⑫ **i macchinari da palestra**
gym machines

⑭ **gli armadietti**
lockers

⑬ **lo spogliatoio**
changing room

⑮ **la lezione di ginnastica**
exercise class

⑯ **il Pilates**
Pilates

⑰ **lo stretching**
stretch

⑲ **gli esercizi**
exercises

⑱ **l'allenamento a circuito** *m*
circuit training

⑳ **l'aerobica** *f*
aerobics

㉑ **il jumping jack**
star jumps

㉒ **le circonduzioni delle braccia**
arm circles

㉓ **i salti laterali**
side shuffles

㉔ **la corsa**
running

㉕ **l'affondo** *m*
lunge

㉖ **il curl dei bicipiti**
bicep curl

㉗ **lo squat**
squat

㉘ **gli addominali**
sit-up

㉙ **la fit boxe**
boxercise

㉚ **saltare la corda**
to skip

㉛ **contrarre i muscoli**
to flex

㉜ **fare corsa sul posto**
to jog on the spot

㉝ **allenarsi**
to train

㉞ **fare trazioni alla sbarra**
to pull up

㉟ **allungare**
to extend

㊱ **riscaldarsi**
to warm up

㊲ **raffreddarsi**
to cool down

See also
116 L' atletica · Athletics **117** Gli sport da combattimento · Combat sports **118** Il nuoto
Swimming **122** Gli sport invernali · Winter sports **125** Gli altri sport · Other sports

⑦ **il sollevamento pesi**
weight training

⑧ **i pesi liberi**
free weights

⑨ **il tappetino**
exercise mat

⑩ **le flessioni**
push ups / press ups

⑪ **il tapis roulant**
treadmill

③⑧ **l'iscrizione** *f*
membership

③⑨ **l'attrezzatura da
palestra** *f*
gym equipment

④⓪ **lo step**
aerobics step

④① **il manubrio**
dumbbell

④② **le manopole**
hand grips

④③ **la barra dei pesi**
barbell / weight bar

④④ **la sbarra**
bar

④⑤ **la chest press**
chest press

④⑥ **la corda da saltare**
skipping rope

④⑦ **la palla fitness**
exercise ball

④⑧ **il bastone per
torsioni**
twist bar

④⑨ **la cavigliera /
la polsiera**
ankle weights / wrist weights

⑤⓪ **la leg press**
leg press

⑤① **l'estensore per
torace** *m*
chest expander

⑤② **la ruota per
addominali** *m*
wheel roller

⑤③ **il tapis roulant**
running machine

⑤④ **la panca**
bench

⑤⑤ **il battito cardiaco**
heart rate

⑤⑥ **la sauna**
sauna

⑤⑦ **la vasca
idromassaggio**
hot tub

⑤⑧ **il personal trainer** *m*
la personal trainer *f*
personal trainer

125.1 LA GINNASTICA · GYMNASTICS

① **il tappetino**
floor mat

② **il cerchio**
hoop

③ **il nastro**
ribbon

④ **la sbarra**
horizontal bar

⑤ **la tavola da volteggio**
vault

⑪ **la pedana elastica**
springboard

⑥ **le parallele asimmetriche**
uneven bars

⑦ **la trave**
beam

⑧ **il cavallo con maniglie**
pommel horse

⑨ **gli anelli**
rings

⑩ **le parallele**
parallel bars

125.2 GLI ALTRI SPORT · OTHER SPORTS

① **il trampolino elastico**
trampoline

② **la pallamano**
handball

③ **il netball**
netball

④ **il pattinaggio a rotelle**
rollerskating

⑤ **il pattinaggio in linea**
inline skating

⑥ **lo skateboard**
skateboard

⑦ **il kickflip**
kick flip

⑧ **andare sullo skateboard**
skateboarding

⑨ **il bersaglio**
target

⑫ **l'arco** *m*
bow

⑭ **la freccia**
arrow

⑯ **la palla da bowling**
bowling ball

⑰ **il birillo**
bowling pin

⑬ **l'arciere** *m / f*
archer

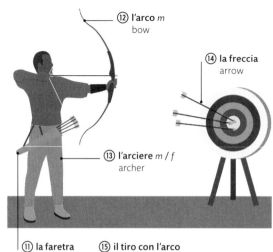

⑩ **il tiro al bersaglio**
target shooting

⑪ **la faretra**
quiver

⑮ **il tiro con l'arco**
archery

⑱ **il bowling**
bowling

See also
116 L'atletica · Athletics **117** Gli sport da combattimento · Combat sports **118** Il nuoto Swimming
120 L'equitazione · Horse riding **122** Gli sport invernali · Winter sports **124** In palestra · At the gym

125.3 I PARASPORT · PARASPORTS

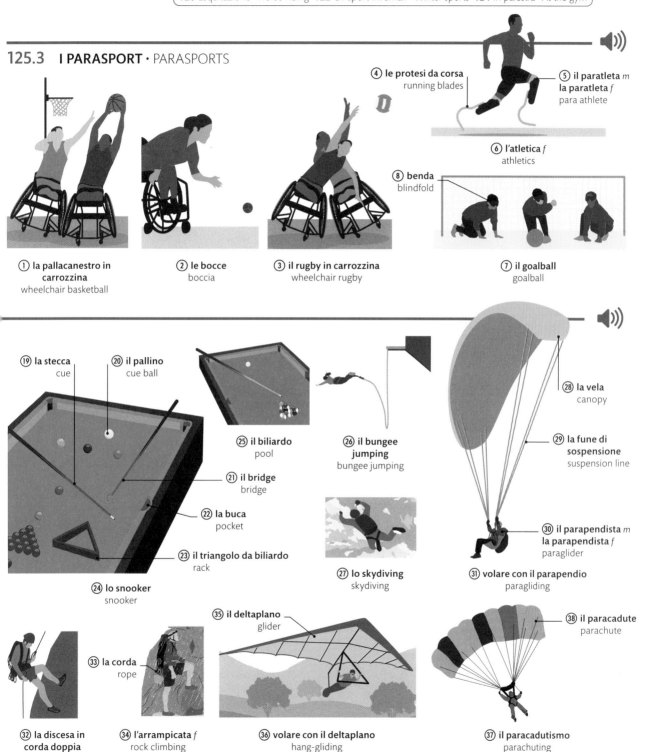

④ **le protesi da corsa**
running blades

⑤ **il paratleta** *m*
la paratleta *f*
para athlete

⑥ **l'atletica** *f*
athletics

⑧ **benda**
blindfold

① **la pallacanestro in carrozzina**
wheelchair basketball

② **le bocce**
boccia

③ **il rugby in carrozzina**
wheelchair rugby

⑦ **il goalball**
goalball

⑲ **la stecca**
cue

⑳ **il pallino**
cue ball

㉕ **il biliardo**
pool

㉖ **il bungee jumping**
bungee jumping

㉘ **la vela**
canopy

㉙ **la fune di sospensione**
suspension line

㉑ **il bridge**
bridge

㉒ **la buca**
pocket

㉓ **il triangolo da biliardo**
rack

㉔ **lo snooker**
snooker

㉗ **lo skydiving**
skydiving

㉚ **il parapendista** *m*
la parapendista *f*
paraglider

㉛ **volare con il parapendio**
paragliding

㉜ **la discesa in corda doppia**
abseiling

㉝ **la corda**
rope

㉞ **l'arrampicata** *f*
rock climbing

㉟ **il deltaplano**
glider

㊱ **volare con il deltaplano**
hang-gliding

㊳ **il paracadute**
parachute

㊲ **il paracadutismo**
parachuting

126 Sul palco
On stage

126.1 **IL TEATRO** · THEATRE

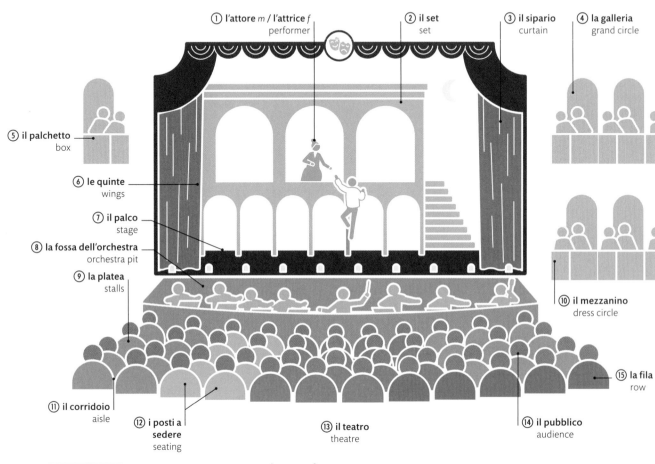

① l'attore *m* / l'attrice *f*
performer

② il set
set

③ il sipario
curtain

④ la galleria
grand circle

⑤ il palchetto
box

⑥ le quinte
wings

⑦ il palco
stage

⑧ la fossa dell'orchestra
orchestra pit

⑨ la platea
stalls

⑩ il mezzanino
dress circle

⑪ il corridoio
aisle

⑫ i posti a sedere
seating

⑬ il teatro
theatre

⑭ il pubblico
audience

⑮ la fila
row

⑯ lo spettacolo
play

⑰ i costumi
costumes

⑱ il materiale di scena
props

⑲ le scenografie
sets

⑳ lo sfondo
backdrop

㉑ il copione
script

㉒ il produttore *m*
la produttrice *f*
producer

㉓ il regista *m*
la regista *f*
director

㉔ l'attore *m*
l'attrice *f*
actor

㉕ il cast
cast

㉖ la prima
opening night

㉗ l'intervallo *m*
interval

See also
127 I film • Films **128-129** La musica • Music
139 Il fantasy e il mito • Fantasy and myth

126.2 **IL BALLETTO** · BALLET

① **il braccio**
arm

② **il ginocchio**
knee

③ **la punta**
toe box

④ **fare la pirouette**
to pirouette /
to turn

⑤ **fare il plié**
to plié /
to bend

⑥ **il ballerino**
male ballet dancer

⑦ **la ballerina**
ballerina

⑧ **il tutù**
tutu

⑨ **il body**
ballet leotard

⑩ **le scarpette**
ballet shoes

⑪ **l'esibizione** *f*
performance

⑫ **il bis**
encore

⑬ **l'applauso** *m*
applause

㉘ **il programma**
programme

㉙ **l'usciere** *m*
l'usciera *f*
usher

㉚ **la tragedia**
tragedy

㉛ **la commedia**
comedy

㉜ **il musical**
musical

㉝ **la standing ovation**
standing ovation

126.3 **L'OPERA** · OPERA

① **il basso**
bass

② **il baritono**
baritone

③ **il tenore**
tenor

④ **il teatro dell'opera**
opera house

⑤ **il contralto**
alto

⑥ **il mezzo soprano**
mezzo-soprano

⑦ **il soprano**
soprano

⑧ **la primadonna**
prima donna

⑨ **il libretto**
libretto

127.1 AL CINEMA · AT THE CINEMA

① **il film drammatico**
drama

② **il musical**
musical

③ **il film di fantascienza**
science fiction

④ **il thriller**
thriller

⑤ **la commedia**
comedy

⑥ **il film d'azione**
action movie

⑦ **l'horror** m
horror

⑧ **il cartone animato**
animation

⑨ **la commedia romantica**
romantic comedy

⑩ **il poliziesco**
crime drama

⑪ **il film western**
western

⑫ **il film storico**
historical drama

⑬ **il fantasy**
fantasy

⑭ **il film di arti marziali**
martial arts

⑮ **gli effetti speciali**
special effects

⑯ **il botteghino**
box office

⑰ **il cinema multisala**
multiplex

⑱ **i popcorn**
popcorn

⑲ **la star del cinema**
film star

⑳ **lo schermo**
screen

㉑ **il pubblico**
audience

㉒ **il cinema**
cinema

㉓ **il protagonista** m
la protagonista f
main character

㉔ **l'eroe** m / **l'eroina** f
hero

㉕ **il cattivo** m
la cattiva f
villain

See also
126 Sul palco · On stage **136** L'home entertainment
Home entertainment **137** La televisione · Television

127.2 LO STUDIO CINEMATOGRAFICO · FILM STUDIO

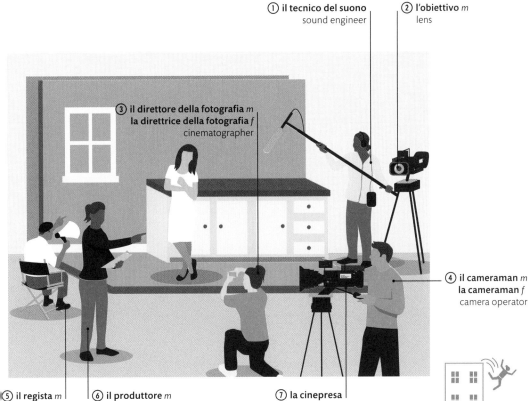

① **il tecnico del suono** sound engineer

② **l'obiettivo** *m* lens

③ **il direttore della fotografia** *m* **la direttrice della fotografia** *f* cinematographer

④ **il cameraman** *m* **la cameraman** *f* camera operator

⑤ **il regista** *m* **la regista** *f* director

⑥ **il produttore** *m* **la produttrice** *f* producer

⑦ **la cinepresa** movie camera

⑧ **il set cinematografico** film set

⑬ **l'audizione** *f* audition

⑭ **il cast** cast

⑮ **le comparse** extras

⑯ **la controfigura** stunt

⑰ **il materiale di scena** props

⑱ **la sceneggiatura** screenplay

⑲ **i costumi** costumes

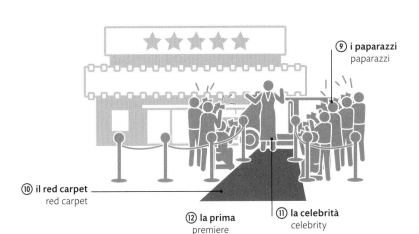

⑨ **i paparazzi** paparazzi

⑩ **il red carpet** red carpet

⑫ **la prima** premiere

⑪ **la celebrità** celebrity

⑳ **la colonna sonora** soundtrack

㉑ **lo sceneggiatore** *m* **la sceneggiatrice** *f* screenwriter

128.1 **GLI STRUMENTI DELL'ORCHESTRA** · ORCHESTRAL INSTRUMENTS

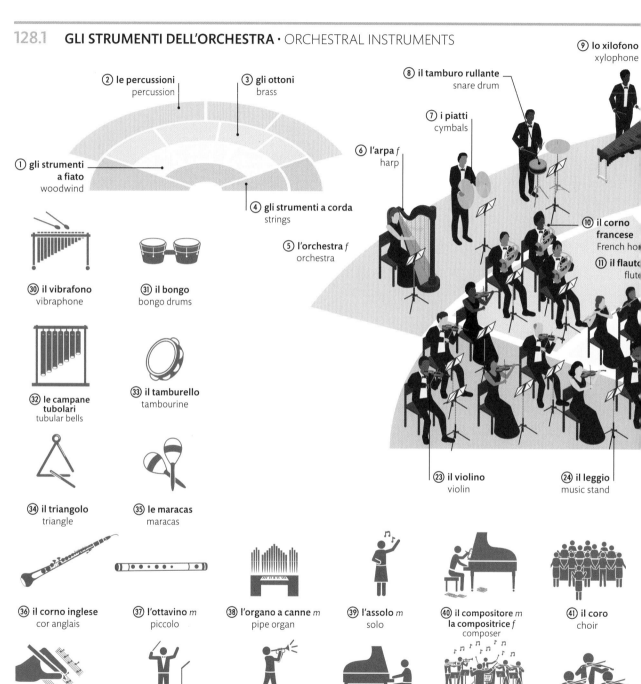

② **le percussioni** percussion

③ **gli ottoni** brass

⑧ **il tamburo rullante** snare drum

⑨ **lo xilofono** xylophone

⑦ **i piatti** cymbals

⑥ **l'arpa** *f* harp

① **gli strumenti a fiato** woodwind

④ **gli strumenti a corda** strings

⑩ **il corno francese** French horn

⑪ **il flauto** flute

⑤ **l'orchestra** *f* orchestra

㉚ **il vibrafono** vibraphone

㉛ **il bongo** bongo drums

㉜ **le campane tubolari** tubular bells

㉝ **il tamburello** tambourine

㉓ **il violino** violin

㉔ **il leggio** music stand

㉞ **il triangolo** triangle

㉟ **le maracas** maracas

㊱ **il corno inglese** cor anglais

㊲ **l'ottavino** *m* piccolo

㊳ **l'organo a canne** *m* pipe organ

㊴ **l'assolo** *m* solo

㊵ **il compositore** *m* **la compositrice** *f* composer

㊶ **il coro** choir

㊷ **comporre** to compose

㊸ **dirigere** to conduct

㊹ **suonare (la tromba)** to play (the trumpet)

㊺ **l'overture** *f* piano overture

㊻ **la sinfonia** symphony

㊼ **la sonata per violino** violin sonata

See also
126 Sul palco · On stage **127** I film · Films **129** La musica (continua)
Music continued **136** L'home entertainment · Home entertainment

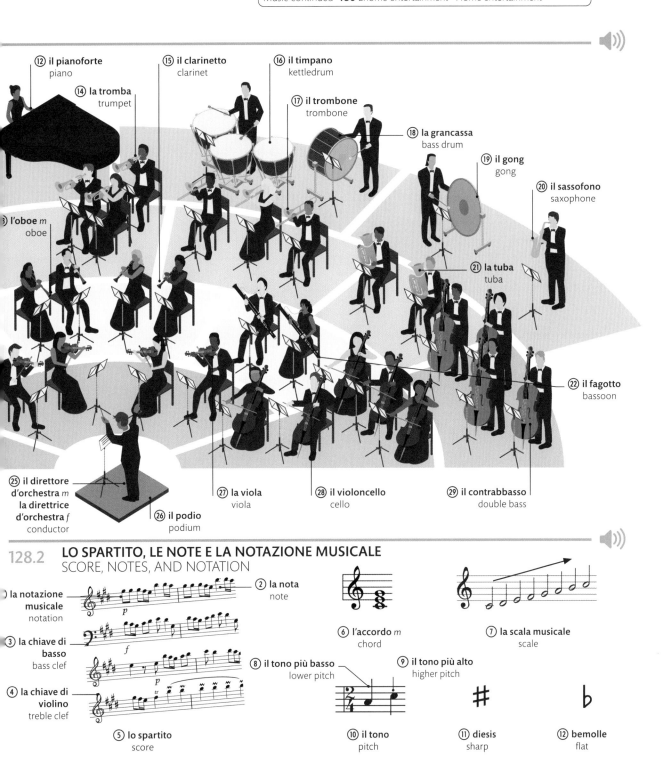

⑫ **il pianoforte**
piano

⑭ **la tromba**
trumpet

⑮ **il clarinetto**
clarinet

⑯ **il timpano**
kettledrum

⑰ **il trombone**
trombone

⑱ **la grancassa**
bass drum

⑲ **il gong**
gong

⑳ **il sassofono**
saxophone

③ **l'oboe** m
oboe

㉑ **la tuba**
tuba

㉒ **il fagotto**
bassoon

㉕ **il direttore
d'orchestra** m
**la direttrice
d'orchestra** f
conductor

㉖ **il podio**
podium

㉗ **la viola**
viola

㉘ **il violoncello**
cello

㉙ **il contrabbasso**
double bass

128.2 LO SPARTITO, LE NOTE E LA NOTAZIONE MUSICALE
SCORE, NOTES, AND NOTATION

① **la notazione
musicale**
notation

② **la nota**
note

③ **la chiave di
basso**
bass clef

④ **la chiave di
violino**
treble clef

⑤ **lo spartito**
score

⑥ **l'accordo** m
chord

⑦ **la scala musicale**
scale

⑧ **il tono più basso**
lower pitch

⑨ **il tono più alto**
higher pitch

⑩ **il tono**
pitch

⑪ **diesis**
sharp

⑫ **bemolle**
flat

129.1 LA MUSICA POP · POPULAR MUSIC

① l'attrezzatura f
rig

② il batterista m
la batterista f
drummer

③ il chitarrista acustico m
la chitarrista acustica f
acoustic guitarist

④ la voce principale f
lead singer

⑤ il chitarrista elettrico m
la chitarrista elettrica f
electric guitarist

⑥ le luci del palco
stage lights

⑦ il bassista m / la bassista f
bass guitarist

⑧ la cassa
speaker

⑨ il fan m / la fan f
fans

⑩ il concerto pop
pop concert

⑪ l'amplificatore m
amplifier

⑫ il piatto del giradischi
turntable

⑬ la console del dj
DJ console

⑭ i dischi in vinile
vinyl records

⑮ i coristi m
le coriste f
backing singers

⑯ la canzone
song

⑰ la melodia
melody

⑱ il ritmo
beat

⑲ la band
band

⑳ l'album m
album

㉑ il jazz
jazz

㉒ il blues
the blues

㉓ il punk
punk

㉔ la musica folk
folk

㉕ il pop
pop

㉖ il K-pop
K-pop

㉗ l'heavy metal m
heavy metal

㉘ l'hip hop m
hip-hop

㉙ la musica country
country

㉚ il rock
rock

㉛ il soul
soul

㉜ la musica latina
Latin

See also
126 Sul palco · On stage **127** I film · Films
136 L'home entertainment · Home entertainment

129.2 **GLI ALTRI STRUMENTI** · MORE INSTRUMENTS

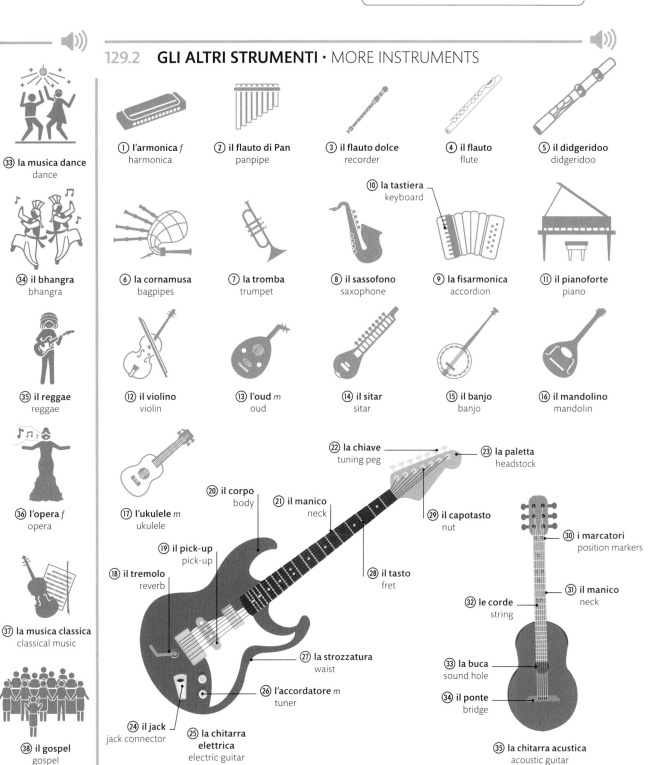

33 **la musica dance**
dance

34 **il bhangra**
bhangra

35 **il reggae**
reggae

36 **l'opera** *f*
opera

37 **la musica classica**
classical music

38 **il gospel**
gospel

1 **l'armonica** *f*
harmonica

2 **il flauto di Pan**
panpipe

3 **il flauto dolce**
recorder

4 **il flauto**
flute

5 **il didgeridoo**
didgeridoo

6 **la cornamusa**
bagpipes

7 **la tromba**
trumpet

8 **il sassofono**
saxophone

9 **la fisarmonica**
accordion

10 **la tastiera**
keyboard

11 **il pianoforte**
piano

12 **il violino**
violin

13 **l'oud** *m*
oud

14 **il sitar**
sitar

15 **il banjo**
banjo

16 **il mandolino**
mandolin

17 **l'ukulele** *m*
ukulele

18 **il tremolo**
reverb

19 **il pick-up**
pick-up

20 **il corpo**
body

21 **il manico**
neck

22 **la chiave**
tuning peg

23 **la paletta**
headstock

24 **il jack**
jack connector

25 **la chitarra elettrica**
electric guitar

26 **l'accordatore** *m*
tuner

27 **la strozzatura**
waist

28 **il tasto**
fret

29 **il capotasto**
nut

30 **i marcatori**
position markers

31 **il manico**
neck

32 **le corde**
string

33 **la buca**
sound hole

34 **il ponte**
bridge

35 **la chitarra acustica**
acoustic guitar

130.1 AL MUSEO E ALLA GALLERIA D'ARTE · AT THE MUSEUM AND ART GALLERY

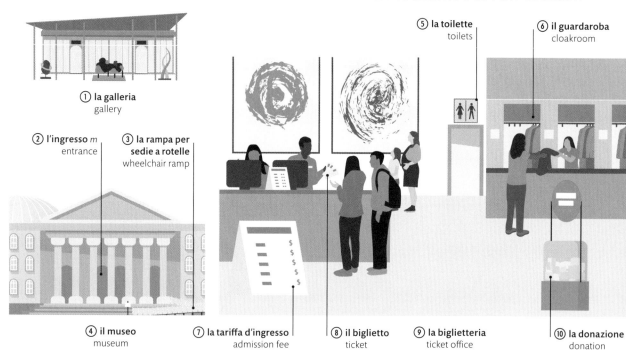

⑤ **la toilette**
toilets

⑥ **il guardaroba**
cloakroom

① **la galleria**
gallery

② **l'ingresso** *m*
entrance

③ **la rampa per sedie a rotelle**
wheelchair ramp

④ **il museo**
museum

⑦ **la tariffa d'ingresso**
admission fee

⑧ **il biglietto**
ticket

⑨ **la biglietteria**
ticket office

⑩ **la donazione**
donation

⑪ **la piantina**
floor plan

⑫ **il curatore** *m* / **la curatrice** *f*
curator

⑭ **l'opera esposta** *f*
exhibit

⑬ **la mostra**
exhibition

⑰ **l'installazione** *f*
installation

⑮ **la mostra permanente**
permanent exhibition

UNTIL MAY 14

⑯ **la mostra temporanea**
temporary exhibition

⑱ **la collezione**
collection

⑲ **il restauro**
conservation

⑳ **la guida turistica**
tour guide

㉑ **l'audioguida** *f*
audio guide

㉒ **il divieto di fotografare**
no photography

㉓ **il negozio di souvenir**
gift shop

See also
42-43 In città • In town **132** Fare un giro turistico • Sightseeing
141-142 Le arti e i mestieri • Arts and crafts

㉔ **la scultura**
sculpture

㉕ **la telecamera di sorveglianza**
surveillance camera

㉙ **Questo capolavoro è di valore inestimabile!**
This masterpiece is priceless!

㉚ **la cornice**
frame

㉖ **il cartellino**
label

㉗ **il capolavoro**
masterpiece

㉘ **l'addetto alla sicurezza** *m*
l'addetta alla sicurezza *f*
security guard

㉛ **il dipinto**
painting

㉜ **il dipinto a olio**
oil painting

㉝ **l'acquerello** *m*
watercolour

㉞ **il Classicismo**
Classicism

㉟ **l'Impressionismo** *m*
Impressionism

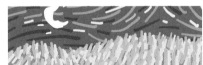

㊱ **il Post-impressionismo**
Post-Impressionism

㊶ **l'Art déco** *f*
Art Deco

㊷ **lo stile Liberty**
Art Nouveau

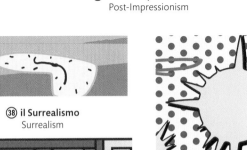

㊳ **il Surrealismo**
Surrealism

㊹ **il Bauhaus**
Bauhaus

㊵ **la Pop art**
Pop Art

㊸ **l'arte concettuale** *f*
conceptual art

㊲ **il Cubismo**
Cubism

㊴ **il Bauhaus**
Bauhaus

131.1 IL VIAGGIO · TRAVEL

① **la guida**
guidebook

② **il frasario**
phrasebook

③ **il biglietto di sola andata**
one-way ticket

④ **il biglietto di andata e ritorno**
return ticket

⑤ **prenotare una vacanza**
to book a holiday

⑥ **fare i bagagli**
to pack your bags

⑦ **andare in vacanza**
to go on a holiday

⑧ **andare in crociera**
to go on a cruise

⑨ **andare all'estero** m
to go abroad

⑩ **fare una prenotazione**
to make a reservation

⑪ **affittare un cottage**
to rent a cottage

⑫ **viaggiare con lo zaino in spalla**
to go backpacking

⑬ **fare il check-in**
to check in

⑭ **fare il check-out**
to check out

⑮ **alloggiare in albergo**
to stay in a hotel

131.2 L'ALLOGGIO · ACCOMMODATION

① **l'albergo** m
hotel

② **l'appartamento** m
apartment

③ **l'ostello** m
hostel

⑨ **la pensione**
guest house

⑩ **il bed and breakfast**
bed and breakfast

⑪ **la casa vacanze**
villa

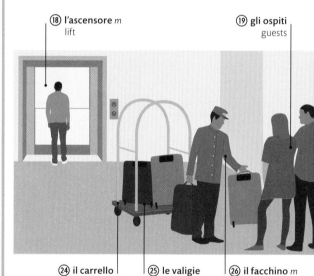

⑱ **l'ascensore** m
lift

⑲ **gli ospiti**
guests

㉔ **il carrello**
trolley

㉕ **le valigie**
luggage

㉖ **il facchino** m
la facchino f
porter

131.3 I SERVIZI · SERVICES

① **il ristorante**
restaurant

② **la palestra**
gym

③ **la piscina**
swimming pool

See also
104 In aeroporto • At the airport **132** Fare un giro turistico • Sightseeing
133 Le attività all'aperto • Outdoor activities **134** In spiaggia • On the beach

④ **lo chalet**
chalet

⑤ **la baita**
cabin

⑥ **l'ecoturismo** *m*
ecotourism

⑦ **la camera singola**
single room

⑧ **la camera doppia
con letti singoli**
twin room

⑫ **la camera doppia**
double room

⑬ **il bagno in camera**
private bathroom / en
suite bathroom

⑭ **il dormitorio**
dorm

⑮ **la camera con
vista**
room with a view

⑯ **con camere libere**
vacancies

⑰ **al completo**
no vacancies

⑳ **il receptionist** *m*
la receptionist *f*
receptionist

㉑ **la reception**
reception

㉒ **la toilette**
toilets

㉓ **l'uscita di emergenza** *f*
emergency exit

㉗ **il bancone**
counter

㉘ **la hall dell'albergo**
hotel lobby

⑤ **il vassoio della
colazione**
breakfast tray

④ **il servizio in
camera**
room service

⑥ **il servizio di
lavanderia**
laundry service

⑦ **il servizio di
pulizie**
maid service

⑧ **il minibar**
minibar

⑨ **la cassaforte**
safe

132.1 L'ATTRAZIONE TURISTICA · TOURIST ATTRACTION

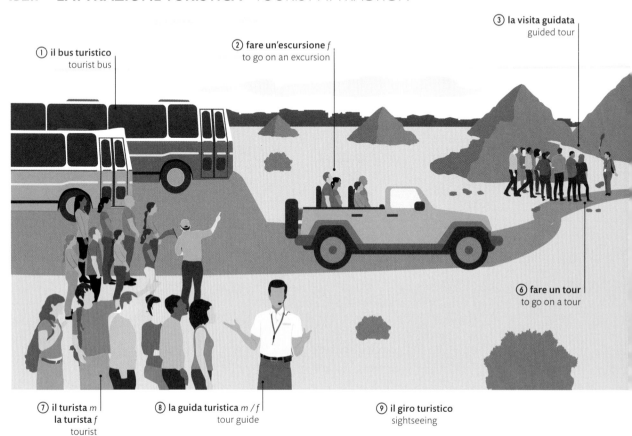

① il bus turistico
tourist bus

② fare un'escursione f
to go on an excursion

③ la visita guidata
guided tour

⑥ fare un tour
to go on a tour

⑦ il turista m
la turista f
tourist

⑧ la guida turistica m / f
tour guide

⑨ il giro turistico
sightseeing

132.2 LE ATTRAZIONI · ATTRACTIONS

① la galleria d'arte
art gallery

② il museo
museum

③ il monumento
monument

④ il palazzo
palace

⑤ l'edificio storico m
historic building

⑥ il giardino botanico
botanical gardens

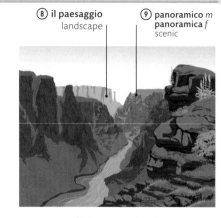

⑧ il paesaggio
landscape

⑨ panoramico m
panoramica f
scenic

⑦ il parco nazionale
national park

See also
99 Le auto e gli autobus · Cars and buses **130** I musei e le gallerie · Museums and galleries
131 Il viaggio e l'alloggio · Travel and accommodation **149-151** I Paesi · Countries

④ **il sito archeologico**
archaeological site

⑤ Dobbiamo pagare per entrare?
Do we have to pay
an admission fee?

ADMISSION

⑫ **la quota d'ingresso**
entrance fee

OPEN

⑬ **aperto** m
aperta f
open

CLOSED

⑭ **chiuso** m
chiusa f
closed

⑮ **la guida**
guidebook

⑯ **la cartolina**
postcard

⑰ **il souvenir**
souvenir

⑱ **la mappa turistica**
tourist map

⑩ **la fila**
queue

⑪ **la bancarella di souvenir**
souvenir stall

⑲ **le indicazioni**
directions

⑬ Mi può dare alcune informazioni
sulle attrazioni locali?
Can I have some information
on the local sights?

⑩ **il litorale**
waterfront

⑭ **la piantina**
floor plan

⑮ **la cartina**
map

TIMETABLE

⑰ **gli orari di apertura**
opening times

⑪ **il mercatino dell'artigianato**
craft market

⑫ **l'ufficio del turismo** m
tourist information

⑯ **gli orari**
timetable

273

133.1 LE ATTIVITÀ ALL'APERTO · OPEN-AIR ACTIVITIES

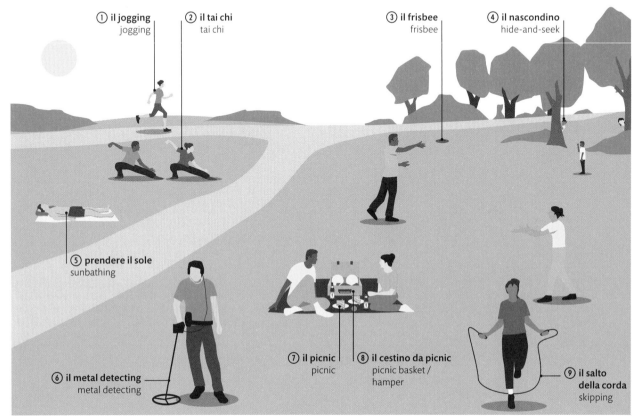

① **il jogging**
jogging

② **il tai chi**
tai chi

③ **il frisbee**
frisbee

④ **il nascondino**
hide-and-seek

⑤ **prendere il sole**
sunbathing

⑥ **il metal detecting**
metal detecting

⑦ **il picnic**
picnic

⑧ **il cestino da picnic**
picnic basket / hamper

⑨ **il salto della corda**
skipping

⑩ **il parco**
park

㉓ **la casa sull'albero**
tree house

㉔ **l'altalena** *f*
swing

㉒ **l'arrampicata sugli alberi** *f*
tree climbing

㉕ **il giardinaggio**
gardening

㉖ **il croquet**
croquet

㉗ **il bird watching**
bird-watching

㉘ **il paintball**
paintballing

㉛ **la piscina per bambini**
paddling pool

㉜ **lo skateboard**
skateboarding

㉝ **il monopattino**
scootering

㉞ **il pattinaggio in linea**
rollerblading

㉟ **andare in bicicletta**
cycling

㊱ **il parkour**
parkour

See also
11 Le abilità e le azioni • Abilities and actions **134** In spiaggia • On the beach
135 Il campeggio • Camping **148** Le cartine e le direzioni • Maps and directions

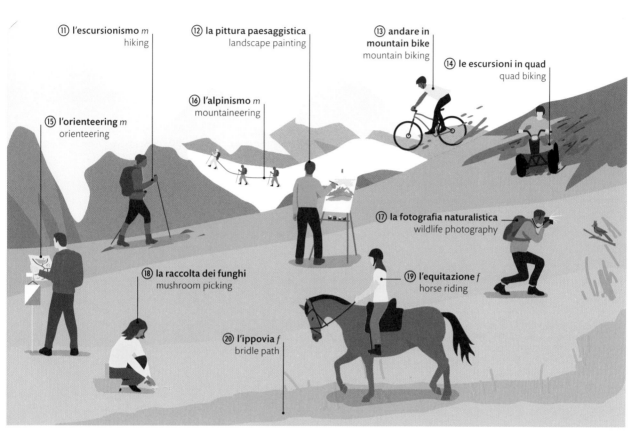

⑪ **l'escursionismo** *m*
hiking

⑫ **la pittura paesaggistica**
landscape painting

⑬ **andare in mountain bike**
mountain biking

⑭ **le escursioni in quad**
quad biking

⑯ **l'alpinismo** *m*
mountaineering

⑮ **l'orienteering** *m*
orienteering

⑰ **la fotografia naturalistica**
wildlife photography

⑱ **la raccolta dei funghi**
mushroom picking

⑲ **l'equitazione** *f*
horse riding

⑳ **l'ippovia** *f*
bridle path

㉑ **il parco nazionale**
national park

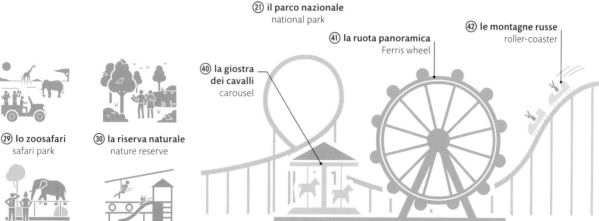

㊷ **le montagne russe**
roller-coaster

㊶ **la ruota panoramica**
Ferris wheel

㊵ **la giostra dei cavalli**
carousel

㉙ **lo zoosafari**
safari park

㉚ **la riserva naturale**
nature reserve

㊱ **lo zoo**
zoo

㊳ **l'area giochi per bambini** *f*
adventure playground

㊴ **il parco divertimenti**
theme park

134.1 **LA SPIAGGIA** · THE BEACH

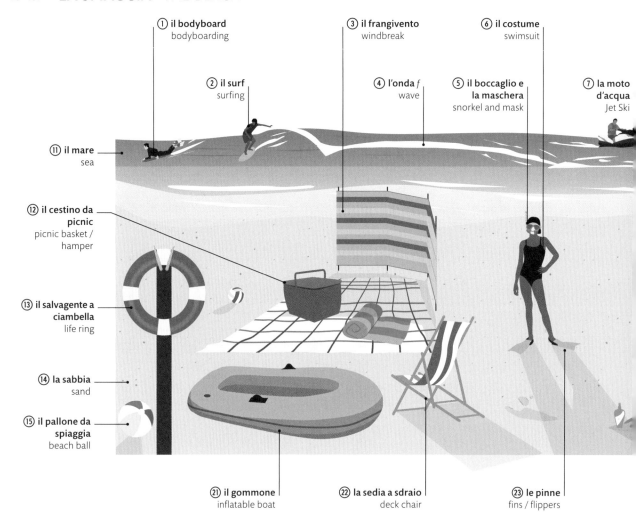

① **il bodyboard**
bodyboarding

② **il surf**
surfing

③ **il frangivento**
windbreak

④ **l'onda** *f*
wave

⑤ **il boccaglio e la maschera**
snorkel and mask

⑥ **il costume**
swimsuit

⑦ **la moto d'acqua**
Jet Ski

⑪ **il mare**
sea

⑫ **il cestino da picnic**
picnic basket / hamper

⑬ **il salvagente a ciambella**
life ring

⑭ **la sabbia**
sand

⑮ **il pallone da spiaggia**
beach ball

㉑ **il gommone**
inflatable boat

㉒ **la sedia a sdraio**
deck chair

㉓ **le pinne**
fins / flippers

㉕ **la vela**
sail

㉖ **lo yacht**
yacht

㉗ **il pontile**
boardwalk

㉘ **il lungomare**
promenade

㉙ **la cabina**
beach hut

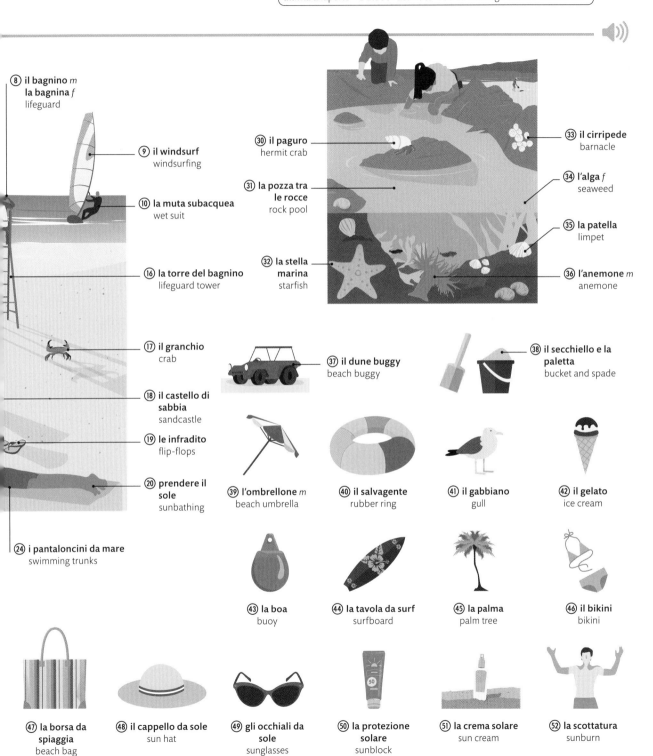

See also
105 Le imbarcazioni • Sea vessels **118** Il nuoto • Swimming **119** La vela e gli sport acquatici • Sailing and watersports **121** La pesca • Fishing **133** Le attività all'aperto • Outdoor activities **166** La vita negli oceani • Ocean life

⑧ **il bagnino** *m*
la bagnina *f*
lifeguard

⑨ **il windsurf**
windsurfing

⑩ **la muta subacquea**
wet suit

⑯ **la torre del bagnino**
lifeguard tower

⑰ **il granchio**
crab

⑱ **il castello di sabbia**
sandcastle

⑲ **le infradito**
flip-flops

⑳ **prendere il sole**
sunbathing

㉔ **i pantaloncini da mare**
swimming trunks

㉚ **il paguro**
hermit crab

㉛ **la pozza tra le rocce**
rock pool

㉜ **la stella marina**
starfish

㉝ **il cirripede**
barnacle

㉞ **l'alga** *f*
seaweed

㉟ **la patella**
limpet

㊱ **l'anemone** *m*
anemone

㊲ **il dune buggy**
beach buggy

㊳ **il secchiello e la paletta**
bucket and spade

㊴ **l'ombrellone** *m*
beach umbrella

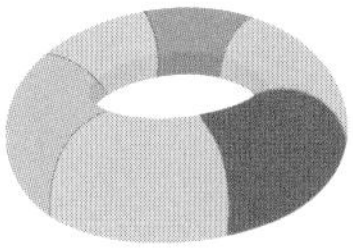

㊵ **il salvagente**
rubber ring

㊶ **il gabbiano**
gull

㊷ **il gelato**
ice cream

㊸ **la boa**
buoy

㊹ **la tavola da surf**
surfboard

㊺ **la palma**
palm tree

㊻ **il bikini**
bikini

㊼ **la borsa da spiaggia**
beach bag

㊽ **il cappello da sole**
sun hat

㊾ **gli occhiali da sole**
sunglasses

㊿ **la protezione solare**
sunblock

(51) **la crema solare**
sun cream

(52) **la scottatura**
sunburn

135.1 **LE ATTREZZATURE E LE STRUTTURE PER IL CAMPEGGIO** · CAMPING EQUIPMENT AND FACILITIES

① **fare campeggio**
to camp

② **montare la tenda**
to pitch a tent

③ **la tenda per due persone**
two-person tent

④ **l'area di campeggio** *f*
pitch

⑤ **le aree disponibili**
pitches available

⑥ **pieno**
full

⑧ **l'allaccio della luce** *m*
electric hook-up

⑨ **la roulotte**
trailer

⑩ **il camper**
camper van

⑪ **l'amaca** *f*
hammock

⑫ **il falò**
campfire

⑬ **accendere il fuoco**
to light a fire

⑮ **la carbonella**
charcoal

⑯ **il barbecue**
barbecue

⑰ **il fornello da campeggio**
single-burner camping stove

⑱ **il fornello da campeggio a due fuochi**
double-burner camping stove

⑲ **la griglia pieghevole**
folding grill

⑳ **la panca da picnic**
picnic bench

㉒ **l'area docce** *f*
shower block

㉓ **l'area bagni** *f*
toilet block

㉔ **lo smaltimento dei rifiuti**
waste disposal

㉕ **l'ufficio del responsabile dello stabilimento** *m*
l'ufficio della responsabile dello stabilimento *f*
site manager's office

㉖ **lo zaino**
backpack / rucksack

㉗ **la torcia**
torch

㉙ **la bussola**
compass

㉚ **l'abbigliamento termico** *m*
thermals

㉛ **le scarpe da trekking**
walking boots

㉜ **gli indumenti impermeabili**
waterproofs

㉝ **il coltellino svizzero**
multi-purpose knife

㉞ **il repellente per insetti**
insect repellent

㊱ **il sacco a pelo**
sleeping bag

㊲ **il materassino**
sleeping mat

㊳ **la branda**
camp bed

㊴ **il materassino autogonfiante**
self-inflating mattress

㊵ **il materasso ad aria**
air bed / air mattress

㊶ **la pompa ad aria**
air pump

See also
131 Il viaggio e l'alloggio • Travel and accommodation **133** Le attività all'aperto • Outdoor activities **146-147** La geografia • Geography

135.2   **IL CAMPEGGIO** · CAMPSITE

⑦ **il caravan**
caravan

⑭ **l'accendifuoco** *m*
firelighter

㉑ **le bottiglie d'acqua**
water bottles

㉘ **la torcia frontale**
headlamp

㉟ **la zanzariera**
mosquito net

㊷ **la pompa elettrica**
electric pump

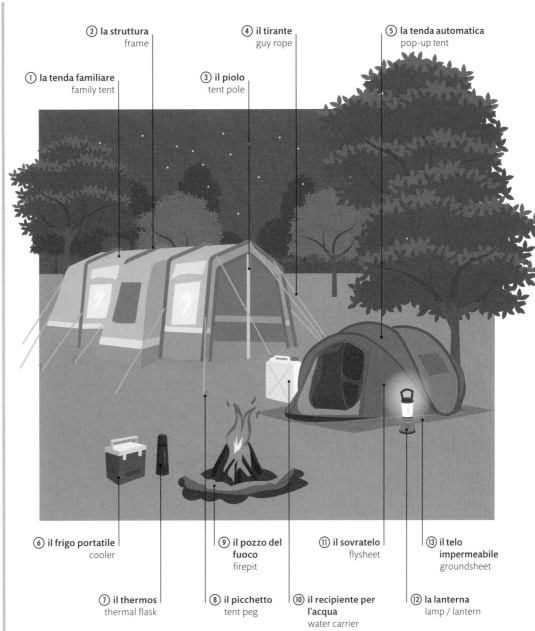

② **la struttura**
frame

④ **il tirante**
guy rope

⑤ **la tenda automatica**
pop-up tent

① **la tenda familiare**
family tent

③ **il piolo**
tent pole

⑥ **il frigo portatile**
cooler

⑨ **il pozzo del fuoco**
firepit

⑪ **il sovratelo**
flysheet

⑬ **il telo impermeabile**
groundsheet

⑦ **il thermos**
thermal flask

⑧ **il picchetto**
tent peg

⑩ **il recipiente per l'acqua**
water carrier

⑫ **la lanterna**
lamp / lantern

279

136.1 LA TELEVISIONE E I SISTEMI AUDIO · TELEVISION AND AUDIO

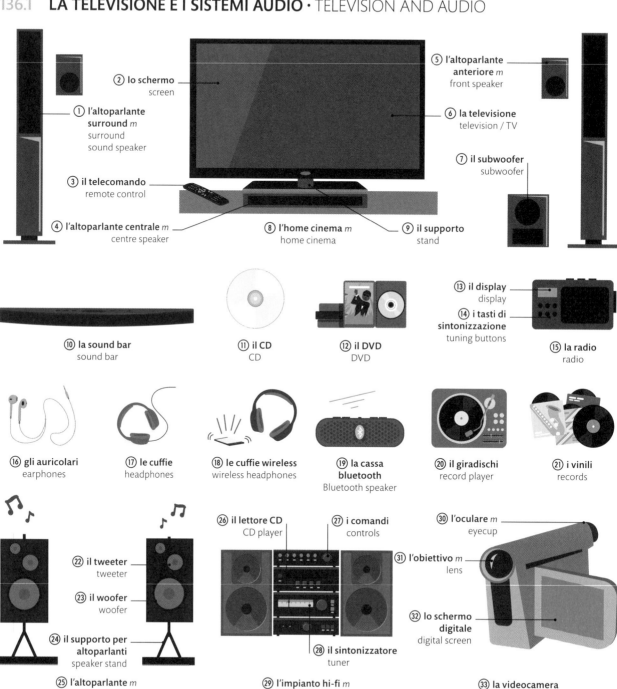

② lo schermo
screen

⑤ l'altoparlante
anteriore m
front speaker

① l'altoparlante
surround m
surround
sound speaker

⑥ la televisione
television / TV

③ il telecomando
remote control

⑦ il subwoofer
subwoofer

④ l'altoparlante centrale m
centre speaker

⑧ l'home cinema m
home cinema

⑨ il supporto
stand

⑬ il display
display

⑭ i tasti di
sintonizzazione
tuning buttons

⑩ la sound bar
sound bar

⑪ il CD
CD

⑫ il DVD
DVD

⑮ la radio
radio

⑯ gli auricolari
earphones

⑰ le cuffie
headphones

⑱ le cuffie wireless
wireless headphones

⑲ la cassa
bluetooth
Bluetooth speaker

⑳ il giradischi
record player

㉑ i vinili
records

㉒ il tweeter
tweeter

㉓ il woofer
woofer

㉔ il supporto per
altoparlanti
speaker stand

㉕ l'altoparlante m
loudspeakers

㉖ il lettore CD
CD player

㉗ i comandi
controls

㉘ il sintonizzatore
tuner

㉙ l'impianto hi-fi m
hi-fi system

㉚ l'oculare m
eyecup

㉛ l'obiettivo m
lens

㉜ lo schermo
digitale
digital screen

㉝ la videocamera
camcorder

See also
127 I film • Films **128-129** La musica • Music
137 La televisione • Television **140** I giochi • Games

34 **lo stereo**
stereo

35 **il mono**
mono

36 **sintonizzarsi**
to tune in

37 **il volume**
volume

38 **alzare il volume**
to turn up

39 **abbassare il volume**
to turn down

40 **l'antenna parabolica** *f*
satellite dish

41 **il decoder digitale**
digital box

42 **il microfono**
microphone

43 **il karaoke**
karaoke

136.2 I VIDEOGIOCHI · VIDEO GAMES

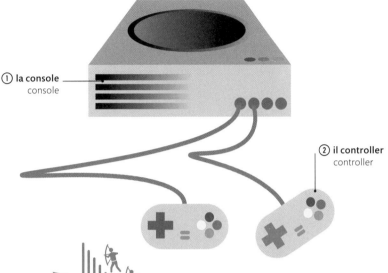

1 **la console**
console

2 **il controller**
controller

3 **il gioco di strategia**
strategy game

4 **il gioco a quiz**
trivia game

5 **il gioco a piattaforme**
platform game

6 **il gioco d'avventura**
adventure game

7 **il gioco di ruolo**
role-playing game

8 **il gioco d'azione**
action game

9 **il gioco multigiocatore**
multiplayer game

10 **il gioco di simulazione**
simulation game

11 **il gioco di sport**
sports game

12 **il puzzle**
puzzle game

13 **il gioco di logica**
logic game

281

137.1 GUARDARE LA TELEVISIONE · WATCHING TELEVISION

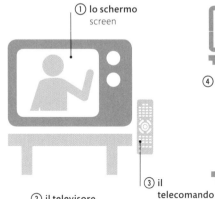

① **lo schermo**
screen

② **il televisore**
TV set

③ **il telecomando**
remote control

④ **l'alta definizione** *f*
high-definition

⑤ **la tv via cavo**
cable TV

⑥ **la tv satellitare**
satellite TV

⑦ **il video on demand**
video on demand

⑧ **il canale**
channel

⑨ **il canale pay per view**
pay-per-view channel

⑩ **l'episodio** *m*
episode

⑪ **la stagione**
series

⑫ **il programma**
programme

⑬ **i sottotitoli**
subtitles

⑭ **l'intervista** *f*
interview

⑮ **la guida tv**
TV guide / schedule

⑯ **l'anticipazione** *f*
preview

⑰ **il reporter** *m*
la reporter *f*
reporter

⑱ **il presentatore** *m*
la presentatrice *f*
presenter

⑲ **il conduttore del notiziario** *m* / **la conduttrice del notiziario** *f*
newsreader

⑳ **la pubblicità**
adverts

㉑ **le previsioni del tempo**
weather forecaster

㉒ **il pantofolaio** *m*
la pantofolaia *f*
couch potato

137.2 I VERBI DELLA TELEVISIONE · TELEVISION VERBS

① **accendere**
to turn on

② **spegnere**
to turn off

③ **alzare il volume**
to turn up the volume

④ **abbassare il volume**
to turn down the volume

⑤ **cambiare canale**
to change the channel

⑥ **trasmettere in streaming**
to stream

See also
26 Il salotto e la sala da pranzo • Living room and dining room **84** I media • Media
127 I film • Films **136** L'home entertainment • Home entertainment

137.3 I PROGRAMMI E I CANALI TELEVISIVI · TV SHOWS AND CHANNELS

① **il programma di cucina**
cooking show

② **il talk show**
chat show

③ **il programma sportivo**
sports

④ **il documentario**
documentary

⑤ **il documentario sulla natura**
nature documentary

⑥ **il dramma in costume**
period drama / costume drama

⑦ **la sitcom**
sitcom

⑧ **il quiz televisivo**
quiz show

⑨ **il programma di attualità**
current affairs

⑩ **il notiziario**
news

⑪ **il meteo**
weather

⑫ **la telenovela**
soap opera

⑬ **il gioco a premi**
game show

⑭ **la commedia**
comedy

⑮ **il cartone animato**
cartoon

⑯ **il poliziesco**
crime

⑰ **il thriller**
thriller

⑱ **la satira**
satire

⑲ **la tv per bambini**
children's TV

⑳ **il programma del mattino**
breakfast TV

㉑ **il reality**
reality TV

㉒ **la catch-up tv**
catch-up TV

㉓ **il canale di televendite**
shopping channel

㉔ **il canale musicale**
music channel

⑦ **riprodurre**
to play

⑧ **fermare**
to stop

⑨ **mettere in pausa**
to pause

⑩ **tornare indietro**
to rewind

⑪ **mandare avanti**
to fast forward

⑫ **registrare**
to record

138.1 I LIBRI · BOOKS

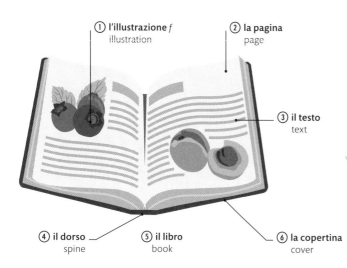

① l'illustrazione *f*
illustration

② la pagina
page

③ il testo
text

④ il dorso
spine

⑤ il libro
book

⑥ la copertina
cover

⑦ l'autore *m*
l'autrice *f*
author

⑧ il libro tascabile
paperback

⑨ il libro con
copertina rigida
hardback

⑬ la recensione
review

⑭ l'indice *m*
contents

⑮ il capitolo
chapter

138.2 LA LETTURA E I GENERI · READING AND GENRES

① la saggistica
non-fiction

② il dizionario
dictionary

③ l'enciclopedia *f*
encyclopedia

④ il libro di
giardinaggio
gardening book

⑤ la guida tv
TV guide

⑥ il manuale di
auto-aiuto
self-help

⑦ l'autobiografia *f*
autobiography

⑧ la biografia
biography

⑨ il libro di cucina
cookbook

⑩ la guida turistica
guidebook

⑪ il libro sulla
natura
nature writing

⑫ il libro di testo
textbook /
course book

⑬ la narrativa
fiction

⑭ il romanzo
novel

⑮ il libro di
fantascienza
science fiction

⑯ il libro fantasy
fantasy

⑰ il fumetto
comic

⑱ la letteratura di
viaggio
travel writing

See also
127 I film • Films **136** L'home entertainment • Home entertainment
139 Il fantasy e il mito • Fantasy and myth **175** La scrittura • Writing

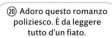
⑳ **Adoro questo romanzo poliziesco. È da leggere tutto d'un fiato.**
I love this crime novel. It's a real page-turner.

㉑ **Odio questo romanzo fantasy. La trama è assurda.**
I hate this fantasy novel. The plot is ridiculous.

⑩ **il titolo**
title

⑪ **sfogliare**
to flip through

⑫ **il lettore di e-book**
e-reader

⑯ **la bibliografia**
bibliography

⑰ **il glossario**
glossary

⑱ **l'indice** *m*
index

⑲ **la lettura**
reading

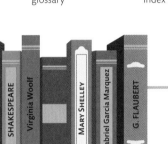
⑲ **la narrativa letteraria**
literary fiction

㉑ **il personaggio**
character

⑳ **il libro per bambini**
children's book

㉒ **il libro da colorare**
colouring book

㉓ **la favola**
fairy tale

㉔ **la storia d'amore**
romance

㉕ **il romanzo poliziesco**
crime fiction

㉖ **il libro umoristico**
humour

㉗ **l'agenda** *f*
diary

㉝ **il titolo**
headline

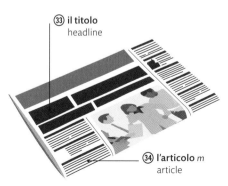

㉞ **l'articolo** *m*
article

㉘ **il bestseller**
bestseller

㉙ **l'oroscopo** *m*
horoscope

㉚ **la rivista di gossip**
gossip magazine

㉛ **l'enigmistica** *f*
puzzles

㉜ **il giornale**
newspaper

139.1 I MITI, LE STORIE E LE CREATURE FANTASTICHE · MYTHS, STORIES, AND FANTASTIC CREATURES

② C'era una volta in una terra lontana...
Once upon a time in a land far away...

⑥ fare un incantesimo
to cast a spell

⑤ la bacchetta magica
wand

④ il libro degli incantesimi
spell book

⑧ l'intruglio della strega m
witches' brew

① la favola
fairy tale

③ l'unicorno m
unicorn

⑦ il calderone
cauldron

⑨ la sfera di cristallo
crystal ball

⑩ la pozione
potion

⑪ la candela magica
candle magic

⑱ il bastone
staff

⑭ l'eroe m
l'eroina f
hero

⑬ il Minotauro
Minotaur

⑫ la mitologia greca
Greek mythology

⑮ l'elisir m
elixir

⑯ l'amuleto m
amulet

⑰ il mago m
la maga f
wizard

⑲ l'impresa f
quest

⑳ il tesoro
treasure

㉑ il tappetto volante
flying carpet

㉒ il genio
genie

㉓ la lampada
lamp

See also
127 I film • Films **137** La televisione • Television
138 I libri e la lettura • Books and reading

㉔ **il serpente marino**
sea serpent

㉕ **Hugin e Munin**
Hugin and Munin

㉖ **le Disir**
the Disir

㉗ **il mostro**
monster

㉘ **lo zombie**
zombie

㉙ **il licantropo**
werewolf

㉚ **il vampiro**
vampire

㉛ **il fantasma**
ghost

㉜ **la zucca di Halloween**
jack-o'-lantern

㉝ **il drago**
dragon

㉞ **il cavaliere**
knight

㊱ **la scopa**
broomstick

㉟ **la strega**
witch

㊲ **la fata**
fairy

㊳ **il folletto**
pixie

㊴ **il fauno**
faun

㊵ **lo gnomo**
gnome

㊶ **il leprecauno**
leprechaun

㊷ **il gremlin**
gremlin

㊸ **il goblin**
goblin

㊹ **il troll**
troll

㊺ **l'ogre** *m*
ogre

㊻ **l'orco** *m*
orc

㊼ **il gigante** *m*
la gigantessa *f*
giant

㊽ **l'elfo** *m*
elf

㊾ **il nano**
dwarf

㊿ **la sirena**
mermaid

(51) **il tritone**
merman

(52) **la fenice**
phoenix

(53) **il grifone**
griffin

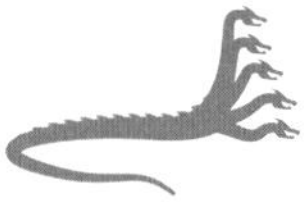

(54) **l'idra** *f*
hydra

(55) **il centauro**
centaur

(56) **la sfinge**
sphinx

(57) **Cerbero**
Cerberus

(58) **il robot cattivo**
bad robot

(59) **l'alieno** *m*
l'aliena *f*
alien

140.1 GLI SCACCHI · CHESS

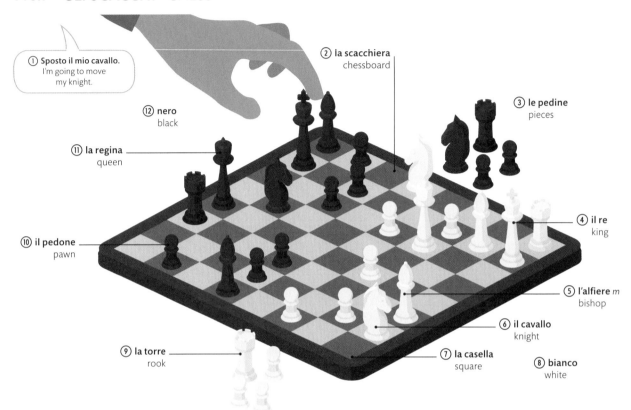

① **Sposto il mio cavallo.**
I'm going to move my knight.

② **la scacchiera**
chessboard

③ **le pedine**
pieces

⑫ **nero**
black

⑪ **la regina**
queen

④ **il re**
king

⑩ **il pedone**
pawn

⑤ **l'alfiere** *m*
bishop

⑥ **il cavallo**
knight

⑨ **la torre**
rook

⑦ **la casella**
square

⑧ **bianco**
white

140.3 I GIOCHI · GAMES

① **i giochi da tavolo**
board games

② **i punti**
points

③ **il punteggio**
score

④ **il tris**
noughts and crosses

⑤ **i dadi**
dice

⑥ **il solitario**
solitaire

⑦ **le pedine**
pieces

⑧ **il puzzle**
jigsaw puzzle

⑨ **il domino**
dominoes

⑩ **le freccette**
darts

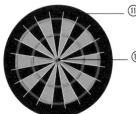

⑪ **il bersaglio**
dartboard

⑫ **il centro del bersaglio**
bullseye

See also
136 L'home entertainment · Home entertainment **138** I libri e la lettura
Books and reading **141-142** Le arti e i mestieri · Arts and crafts

140.2 **GIOCARE A CARTE** · PLAYING CARDS

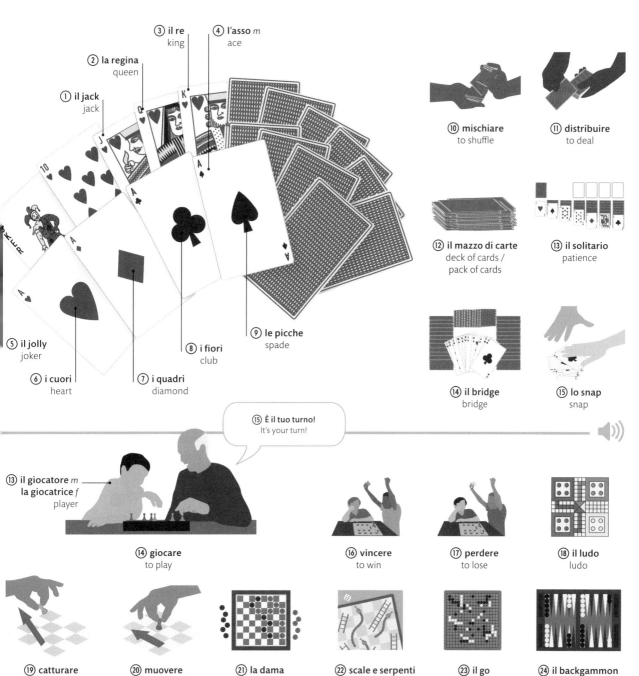

③ **il re**
king

④ **l'asso** *m*
ace

② **la regina**
queen

① **il jack**
jack

⑤ **il jolly**
joker

⑥ **i cuori**
heart

⑦ **i quadri**
diamond

⑧ **i fiori**
club

⑨ **le picche**
spade

⑩ **mischiare**
to shuffle

⑪ **distribuire**
to deal

⑫ **il mazzo di carte**
deck of cards /
pack of cards

⑬ **il solitario**
patience

⑭ **il bridge**
bridge

⑮ **lo snap**
snap

⑮ **È il tuo turno!**
It's your turn!

⑬ **il giocatore** *m*
la giocatrice *f*
player

⑭ **giocare**
to play

⑯ **vincere**
to win

⑰ **perdere**
to lose

⑱ **il ludo**
ludo

⑲ **catturare**
to take

⑳ **muovere**
to move

㉑ **la dama**
draughts

㉒ **scale e serpenti**
snakes and ladders

㉓ **il go**
go

㉔ **il backgammon**
backgammon

141.1 LA PITTURA · PAINTING

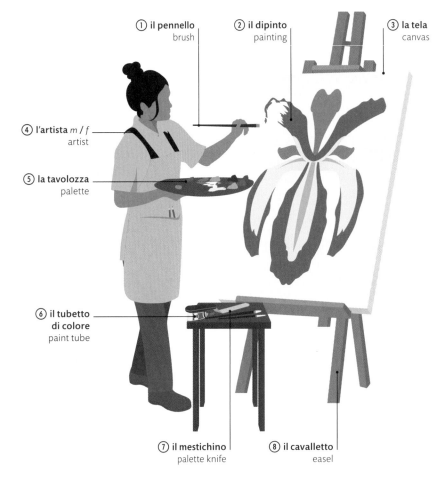

① il pennello
brush

② il dipinto
painting

③ la tela
canvas

④ l'artista m / f
artist

⑤ la tavolozza
palette

⑥ il tubetto
di colore
paint tube

⑦ il mestichino
palette knife

⑧ il cavalletto
easel

⑨ il rosso
red

⑩ lo scarlatto
scarlet

⑪ il blu
blue

⑫ il turchese
turquoise

⑬ il blu marino
navy blue

⑭ il giallo
yellow

⑮ il verde
green

⑯ l'arancione m
orange

⑰ il viola
purple

⑱ l'indaco m
indigo

⑲ il rosa
pink

⑳ il marrone
brown

㉑ il grigio
grey

㉒ il nero
black

㉓ il bianco
white

㉔ i colori a olio
oil paints

㉕ gli acquerelli
watercolour paints

㉖ i pastelli
pastels

㉗ i colori acrilici
acrylic paints

㉘ la tempera
poster paint

See also
37 La decorazione · Decorating **130** I musei e le gallerie · Museums and galleries **142** Le arti e i mestieri (continua) · Arts and crafts continued

141.2 LE ALTRE ARTI E I MESTIERI · OTHER ARTS AND CRAFTS

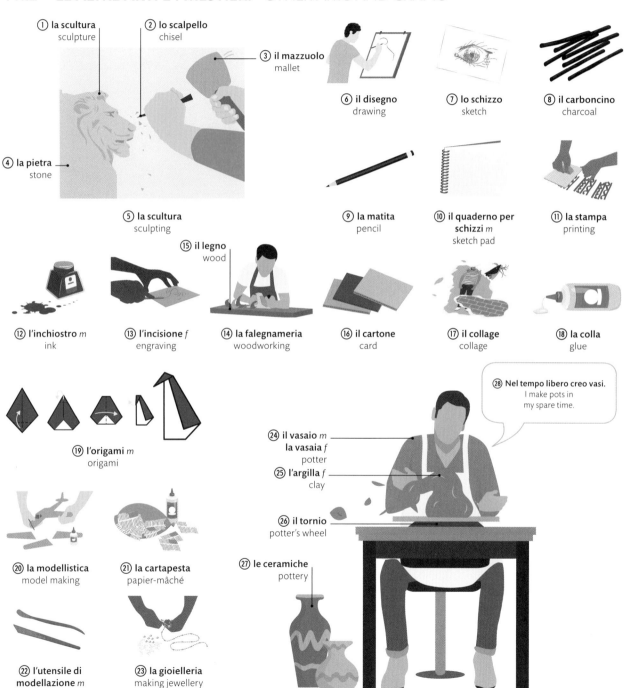

① **la scultura** sculpture

② **lo scalpello** chisel

③ **il mazzuolo** mallet

④ **la pietra** stone

⑤ **la scultura** sculpting

⑥ **il disegno** drawing

⑦ **lo schizzo** sketch

⑧ **il carboncino** charcoal

⑨ **la matita** pencil

⑩ **il quaderno per schizzi** *m* sketch pad

⑪ **la stampa** printing

⑫ **l'inchiostro** *m* ink

⑬ **l'incisione** *f* engraving

⑭ **la falegnameria** woodworking

⑮ **il legno** wood

⑯ **il cartone** card

⑰ **il collage** collage

⑱ **la colla** glue

⑲ **l'origami** *m* origami

⑳ **la modellistica** model making

㉑ **la cartapesta** papier-mâché

㉒ **l'utensile di modellazione** *m* modelling tool

㉓ **la gioielleria** making jewellery

㉔ **il vasaio** *m* **la vasaia** *f* potter

㉕ **l'argilla** *f* clay

㉖ **il tornio** potter's wheel

㉗ **le ceramiche** pottery

㉘ **Nel tempo libero creo vasi.** I make pots in my spare time.

142.1 IL CUCITO · SEWING

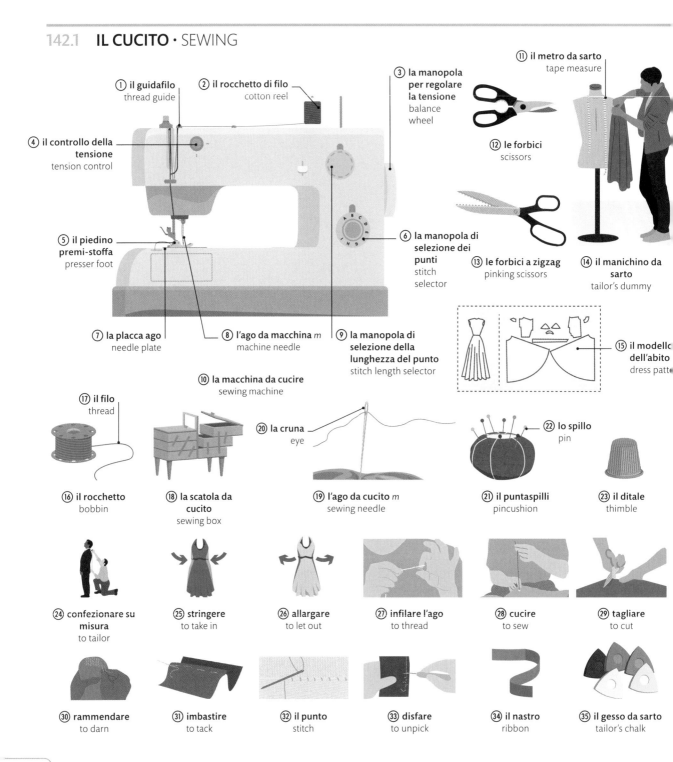

① il guidafilo
thread guide

② il rocchetto di filo
cotton reel

③ la manopola per regolare la tensione
balance wheel

④ il controllo della tensione
tension control

⑤ il piedino premi-stoffa
presser foot

⑥ la manopola di selezione dei punti
stitch selector

⑦ la placca ago
needle plate

⑧ l'ago da macchina m
machine needle

⑨ la manopola di selezione della lunghezza del punto
stitch length selector

⑩ la macchina da cucire
sewing machine

⑪ il metro da sarto
tape measure

⑫ le forbici
scissors

⑬ le forbici a zigzag
pinking scissors

⑭ il manichino da sarto
tailor's dummy

⑮ il modello dell'abito
dress pattern

⑯ il rocchetto
bobbin

⑰ il filo
thread

⑱ la scatola da cucito
sewing box

⑲ l'ago da cucito m
sewing needle

⑳ la cruna
eye

㉑ il puntaspilli
pincushion

㉒ lo spillo
pin

㉓ il ditale
thimble

㉔ confezionare su misura
to tailor

㉕ stringere
to take in

㉖ allargare
to let out

㉗ infilare l'ago
to thread

㉘ cucire
to sew

㉙ tagliare
to cut

㉚ rammendare
to darn

㉛ imbastire
to tack

㉜ il punto
stitch

㉝ disfare
to unpick

㉞ il nastro
ribbon

㉟ il gesso da sarto
tailor's chalk

See also
11 Le abilità e le azioni • Abilities and actions **13-15** Gli indumenti • Clothes
37 La decorazione • Decorating **39** Il giardinaggio • Practical gardening

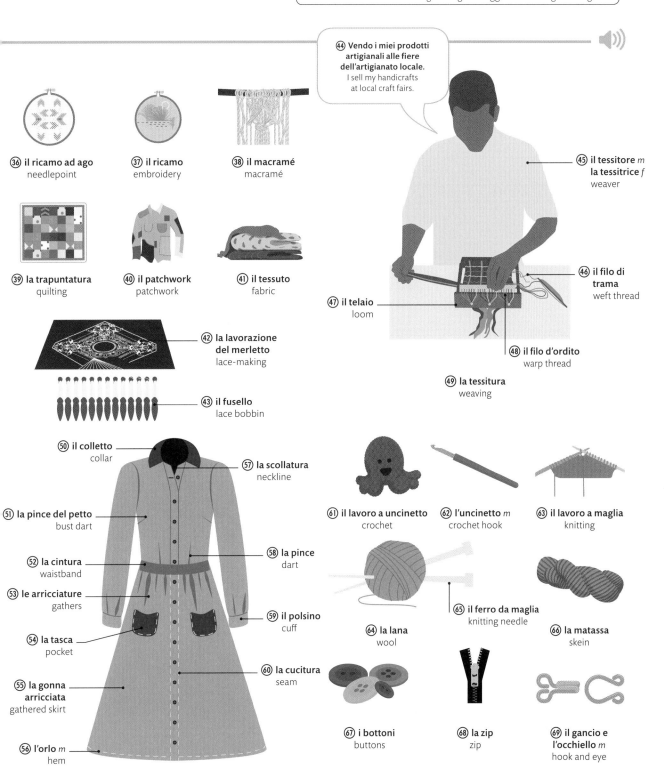

㊹ Vendo i miei prodotti artigianali alle fiere dell'artigianato locale.
I sell my handicrafts at local craft fairs.

㊱ **il ricamo ad ago**
needlepoint

㊲ **il ricamo**
embroidery

㊳ **il macramé**
macramé

㊴ **la trapuntatura**
quilting

㊵ **il patchwork**
patchwork

㊶ **il tessuto**
fabric

㊷ **la lavorazione del merletto**
lace-making

㊸ **il fusello**
lace bobbin

㊺ **il tessitore** *m*
la tessitrice *f*
weaver

㊻ **il filo di trama**
weft thread

㊼ **il telaio**
loom

㊽ **il filo d'ordito**
warp thread

㊾ **la tessitura**
weaving

㊿ **il colletto**
collar

57 **la scollatura**
neckline

51 **la pince del petto**
bust dart

52 **la cintura**
waistband

53 **le arricciature**
gathers

54 **la tasca**
pocket

55 **la gonna arricciata**
gathered skirt

56 **l'orlo** *m*
hem

58 **la pince**
dart

59 **il polsino**
cuff

60 **la cucitura**
seam

61 **il lavoro a uncinetto**
crochet

62 **l'uncinetto** *m*
crochet hook

63 **il lavoro a maglia**
knitting

64 **la lana**
wool

65 **il ferro da maglia**
knitting needle

66 **la matassa**
skein

67 **i bottoni**
buttons

68 **la zip**
zip

69 **il gancio e l'occhiello** *m*
hook and eye

293

143 Lo spazio
Space

143.1 IL SISTEMA SOLARE · THE SOLAR SYSTEM

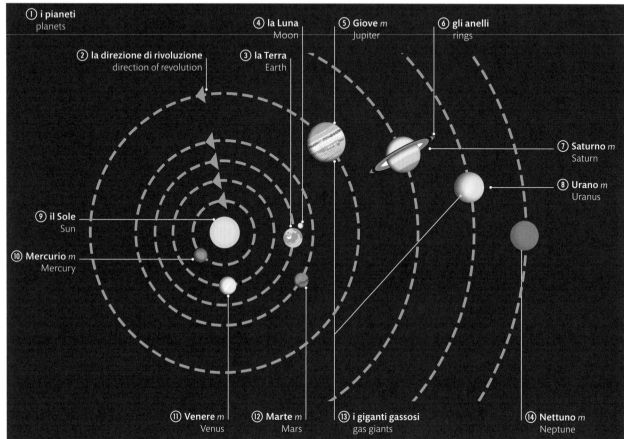

① i pianeti
planets

② la direzione di rivoluzione
direction of revolution

③ la Terra
Earth

④ la Luna
Moon

⑤ Giove *m*
Jupiter

⑥ gli anelli
rings

⑦ Saturno *m*
Saturn

⑧ Urano *m*
Uranus

⑨ il Sole
Sun

⑩ Mercurio *m*
Mercury

⑪ Venere *m*
Venus

⑫ Marte *m*
Mars

⑬ i giganti gassosi
gas giants

⑭ Nettuno *m*
Neptune

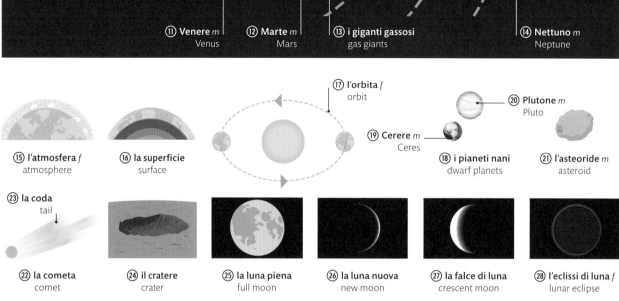

⑮ l'atmosfera *f*
atmosphere

⑯ la superficie
surface

⑰ l'orbita *f*
orbit

⑱ i pianeti nani
dwarf planets

⑲ Cerere *m*
Ceres

⑳ Plutone *m*
Pluto

㉑ l'asteoride *m*
asteroid

㉒ la cometa
comet

㉓ la coda
tail

㉔ il cratere
crater

㉕ la luna piena
full moon

㉖ la luna nuova
new moon

㉗ la falce di luna
crescent moon

㉘ l'eclissi di luna *f*
lunar eclipse

See also
74 La matematica · Mathematics **75** La fisica · Physics **83** I computer e la tecnologia · Computers and technology **144** Lo spazio (continua) · Space continued **145** Il pianeta Terra · Planet Earth **156** Le rocce e i minerali · Rocks and minerals

143.2 L'ESPLORAZIONE DELLO SPAZIO · SPACE EXPLORATION

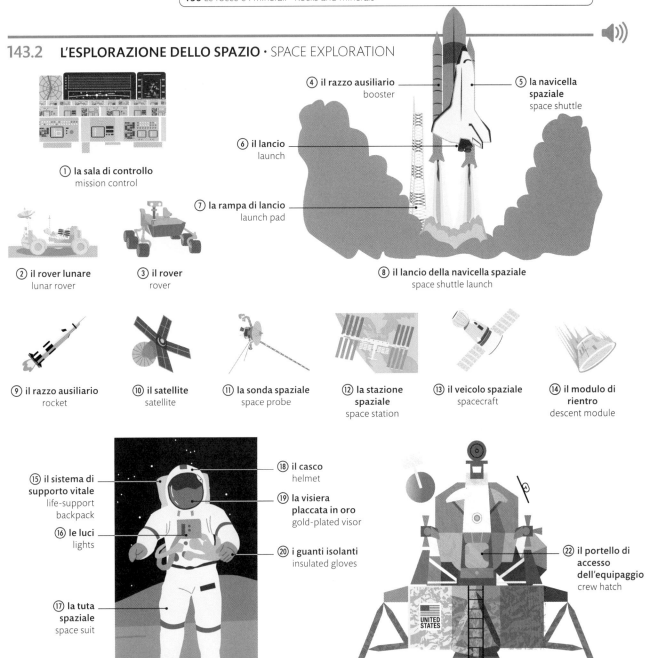

① **la sala di controllo**
mission control

② **il rover lunare**
lunar rover

③ **il rover**
rover

④ **il razzo ausiliario**
booster

⑤ **la navicella spaziale**
space shuttle

⑥ **il lancio**
launch

⑦ **la rampa di lancio**
launch pad

⑧ **il lancio della navicella spaziale**
space shuttle launch

⑨ **il razzo ausiliario**
rocket

⑩ **il satellite**
satellite

⑪ **la sonda spaziale**
space probe

⑫ **la stazione spaziale**
space station

⑬ **il veicolo spaziale**
spacecraft

⑭ **il modulo di rientro**
descent module

⑮ **il sistema di supporto vitale**
life-support backpack

⑯ **le luci**
lights

⑰ **la tuta spaziale**
space suit

⑱ **il casco**
helmet

⑲ **la visiera placcata in oro**
gold-plated visor

⑳ **i guanti isolanti**
insulated gloves

㉑ **l'astronauta** *m / f*
astronaut

㉒ **il portello di accesso dell'equipaggio**
crew hatch

㉓ **il propulsore**
thruster

㉔ **il modulo lunare**
lunar module

UNITED STATES

144.1 L'ASTRONOMIA · ASTRONOMY

① **il binocolo**
binoculars

② **il telescopio rifrattore**
refractor telescope

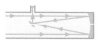

③ **il telescopio riflettore**
reflector telescope

④ **il radiotelescopio**
radio telescope

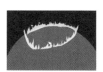

⑤ **l'osservatorio** m
observatory

⑥ **il telescopio spaziale**
space telescope

⑩ **l'oculare** m
eyepiece

⑫ **la cometa**
comet

⑪ **il cercatore**
finderscope

⑨ **Ho avvistato una cometa.**
I've just spotted a comet.

⑬ **il treppiede**
tripod

⑭ **la manopola di messa a fuoco**
focusing knob

⑮ **il telescopio**
telescope

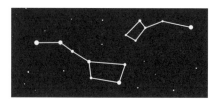

⑦ **la costellazione**
constellation

⑧ **la carta celeste**
star chart

144.2 LE STELLE E LE COSTELLAZIONI · STARS AND CONSTELLATIONS

① **la gravità**
gravity

② **l'aurora** f
aurora

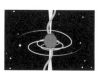

③ **la stella**
star

④ **il bagliore**
flare

⑤ **la stella binaria**
double star

⑥ **la stella di neutroni**
neutron star

⑬ **la Stella Polare**
the Pole Star / Polaris

⑭ **l'Orsa Maggiore** f
the Plough

⑮ **la Croce del Sud**
the Southern Cross

⑯ **Orione** m
Orion

⑰ **la gigante rossa**
red giant

⑱ **la nana bianca**
white dwarf

See also
74 La matematica • Mathematics **75** La fisica • Physics **83** I computer e la tecnologia • Computers and technology **145** Il pianeta Terra • Planet Earth **156** Le rocce e i minerali • Rocks and minerals

144.3 LO ZODIACO · THE ZODIAC

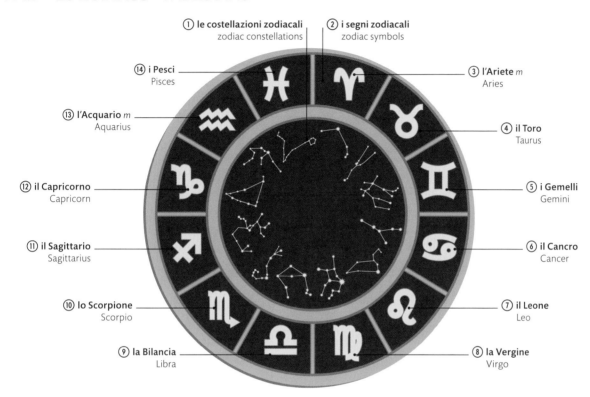

① **le costellazioni zodiacali**
zodiac constellations

② **i segni zodiacali**
zodiac symbols

⑭ **i Pesci**
Pisces

③ **l'Ariete** m
Aries

⑬ **l'Acquario** m
Aquarius

④ **il Toro**
Taurus

⑫ **il Capricorno**
Capricorn

⑤ **i Gemelli**
Gemini

⑪ **il Sagittario**
Sagittarius

⑥ **il Cancro**
Cancer

⑩ **lo Scorpione**
Scorpio

⑦ **il Leone**
Leo

⑨ **la Bilancia**
Libra

⑧ **la Vergine**
Virgo

⑦ **la supernova**
supernova

⑧ **la nebulosa**
nebula

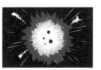

⑨ **il Big Bang**
the Big Bang

⑩ **l'ammasso stellare** m
star cluster

⑪ **la galassia ellittica**
elliptical galaxy

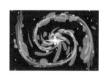

⑫ **la galassia a spirale**
spiral galaxy

⑲ **il buco nero**
black hole

la meteora
meteor

㉑ **lo sciame meteorico**
meteor shower

⑳ **la meteora**
meteor

㉒ **la Via Lattea**
the Milky Way

㉓ **l'universo** m
the universe

145.1 LA TERRA · THE EARTH

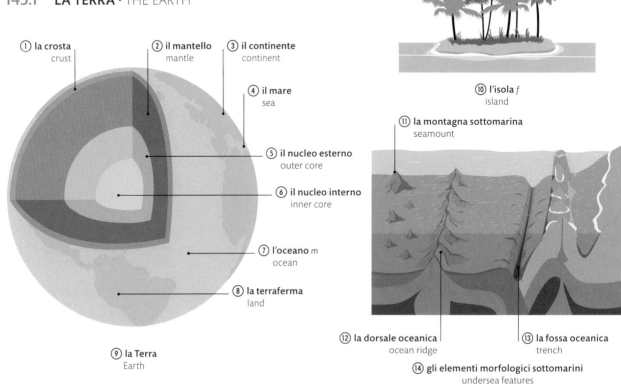

① la crosta
crust

② il mantello
mantle

③ il continente
continent

④ il mare
sea

⑤ il nucleo esterno
outer core

⑥ il nucleo interno
inner core

⑦ l'oceano *m*
ocean

⑧ la terraferma
land

⑨ la Terra
Earth

⑩ l'isola *f*
island

⑪ la montagna sottomarina
seamount

⑫ la dorsale oceanica
ocean ridge

⑬ la fossa oceanica
trench

⑭ gli elementi morfologici sottomarini
undersea features

145.2 LA TETTONICA DELLE PLACCHE · PLATE TECTONICS

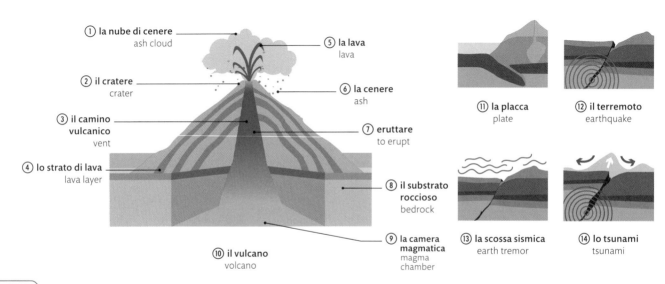

① la nube di cenere
ash cloud

② il cratere
crater

③ il camino vulcanico
vent

④ lo strato di lava
lava layer

⑤ la lava
lava

⑥ la cenere
ash

⑦ eruttare
to erupt

⑧ il substrato roccioso
bedrock

⑨ la camera magmatica
magma chamber

⑩ il vulcano
volcano

⑪ la placca
plate

⑫ il terremoto
earthquake

⑬ la scossa sismica
earth tremor

⑭ lo tsunami
tsunami

See also
143-144 Lo spazio · Space **146-147** La geografia · Geography
148 Le cartine e le direzioni · Maps and directions **149-151** I Paesi · Countries

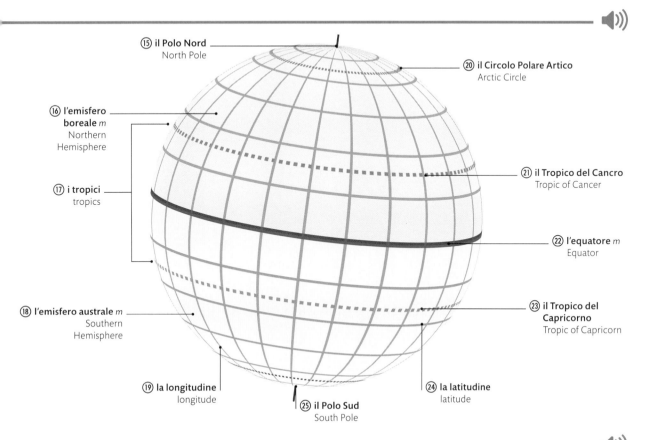

⑮ **il Polo Nord**
North Pole

⑳ **il Circolo Polare Artico**
Arctic Circle

⑯ **l'emisfero boreale** *m*
Northern Hemisphere

㉑ **il Tropico del Cancro**
Tropic of Cancer

⑰ **i tropici**
tropics

㉒ **l'equatore** *m*
Equator

⑱ **l'emisfero australe** *m*
Southern Hemisphere

㉓ **il Tropico del Capricorno**
Tropic of Capricorn

⑲ **la longitudine**
longitude

㉔ **la latitudine**
latitude

㉕ **il Polo Sud**
South Pole

145.3 LE FORMAZIONI E I FENOMENI ACQUATICI · WATER FEATURES AND PHENOMENA

① **le Cascate Vittoria**
Victoria Falls

② **la Hang Son Doong**
Hang Son Doong

③ **il Rio delle Amazzoni**
the Amazon

④ **il Mar Morto**
the Dead Sea

⑤ **il Caño Cristales**
Caño Cristales

⑥ **Pamukkale**
Pamukkale

⑦ **la barriera corallina**
the Barrier Reef

⑧ **il Gange**
the Ganges

⑨ **il Salto Ángel**
Angel Falls

⑩ **il Great Blue Hole**
the Great Blue Hole

⑪ **il lago Natron**
Lake Natron

⑫ **lo Spotted Lake**
Spotted Lake

146.1 LE CARATTERISTICHE GEOGRAFICHE E IL PAESAGGIO
GEOGRAPHICAL FEATURES AND LANDSCAPE

① **il bosco**
wood

② **la foresta pluviale**
rain forest

③ **la foresta di conifere**
coniferous forest

④ **la foresta decidua**
deciduous forest

⑤ **le rapide**
rapids

⑥ **la campagna**
countryside

⑦ **il lago**
lake

⑧ **la palude**
swamp

⑨ **la cascata**
waterfall

⑩ **il campo**
field

⑪ **la siepe**
hedge

⑫ **la valle**
valley

⑬ **il terreno coltivato**
farmland

⑭ **le zone umide**
wetlands

⑮ **il terreno erboso**
grassland

⑯ **la prateria**
prairie

⑰ **la steppa**
steppe

⑱ **la mesa**
mesa

⑲ **l'altura** f
highland

⑳ **il crinale**
ridge

㉑ **il massiccio montuoso**
mountain range

㉒ **la savana**
savannah

㉓ **la catena montuosa**
chain

㉔ **il geyser**
geyser

㉕ **la pianura**
plain

㉖ **l'oasi** f
oasis

㉗ **il deserto**
desert

㉘ **la duna**
sand dune

See also
133 Le attività all'aperto · Outdoor activites **145** Il pianeta Terra · Planet Earth **147** La geografia (continua)
Geography continued **148** Le cartine e le direzioni · Maps and directions **149-151** I Paesi · Countries

30 l'iceberg *m*
iceberg

31 la colata di fango
mudslide

32 la frana
landslide

29 il canyon
canyon

33 l'altopiano *m*
plateau

34 la regione polare
polar region

35 la tundra
tundra

36 il ghiacciaio
glacier

146.2 LE GROTTE E LA SPELEOLOGIA · CAVES AND CAVING

1 il ghiacciolo
icicle

2 la torcia frontale
headlamp

3 la colonna
column

4 il corso d'acqua
sotterraneo
subterranean
stream

5 Un casco e una torcia frontale
sono fondamentali quando si
esplorano le grotte.
A helmet and headlamp are essential
when caving.

6 la stalattite
stalactite

7 il casco
helmet

8 lo speleologo *m*
la speleologa *f*
caver

9 la stalagmite
stalagmite

147.1 LE CARATTERISTICHE COSTIERE · COASTAL FEATURES

① l'oceano *m*
ocean

② l'onda *f*
wave

③ la duna
dune

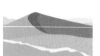

④ l'isola *f*
island

⑤ lo stretto
strait

⑥ il canale
channel

⑦ l'alta marea *f*
high tide

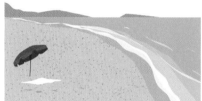

⑧ la bassa marea
low tide

⑨ il banco di scogli
reef

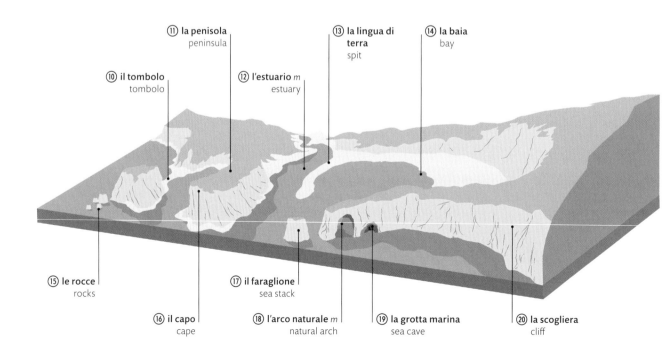

⑪ la penisola
peninsula

⑬ la lingua di terra
spit

⑭ la baia
bay

⑩ il tombolo
tombolo

⑫ l'estuario *m*
estuary

⑮ le rocce
rocks

⑰ il faraglione
sea stack

⑯ il capo
cape

⑱ l'arco naturale *m*
natural arch

⑲ la grotta marina
sea cave

⑳ la scogliera
cliff

See also
133 Le attività all'aperto • Outdoor activities **145** Il pianeta Terra • Planet Earth
148 Le cartine e le direzioni • Maps and directions **149-151** I Paesi • Countries

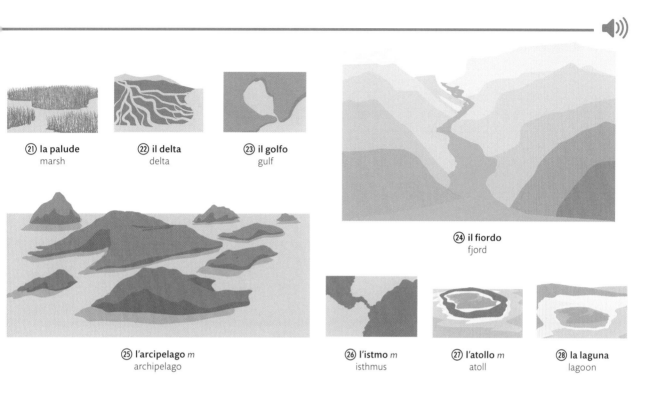

㉑ **la palude**
marsh

㉒ **il delta**
delta

㉓ **il golfo**
gulf

㉔ **il fiordo**
fjord

㉕ **l'arcipelago** *m*
archipelago

㉖ **l'istmo** *m*
isthmus

㉗ **l'atollo** *m*
atoll

㉘ **la laguna**
lagoon

147.2   LE CARATTERISTICHE FLUVIALI · RIVER FEATURES

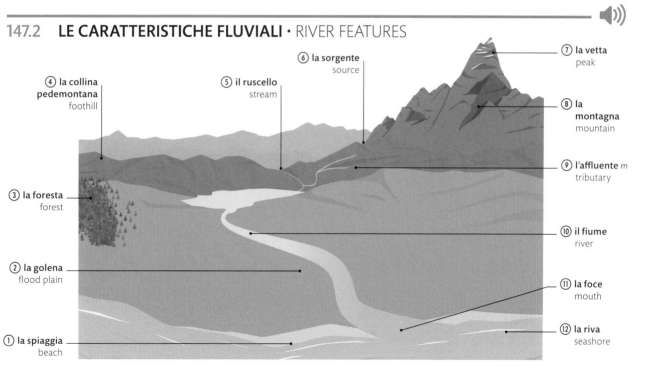

④ **la collina pedemontana**
foothill

⑤ **il ruscello**
stream

⑥ **la sorgente**
source

⑦ **la vetta**
peak

⑧ **la montagna**
mountain

③ **la foresta**
forest

⑨ **l'affluente** *m*
tributary

② **la golena**
flood plain

⑩ **il fiume**
river

⑪ **la foce**
mouth

① **la spiaggia**
beach

⑫ **la riva**
seashore

148.1 LEGGERE UNA CARTINA · READING A MAP

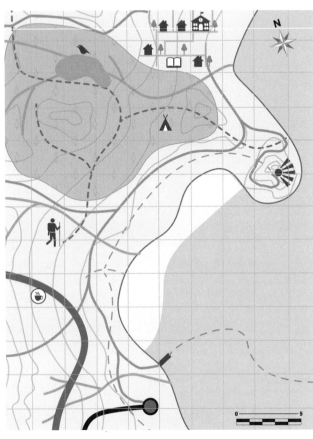

③ **il nord**
north

④ **il nordest**
northeast

⑤ **l'est** *m*
east

⑥ **il sudest**
southeast

⑦ **il sud**
south

⑩ **il nordovest**
northwest

⑨ **l'ovest** *m*
west

⑧ **il sudovest**
southwest

② **la bussola**
compass

⑪ **la strada principale**
main road

⑫ **la strada secondaria**
secondary road

⑬ **il sentiero pubblico**
public footpath

⑭ **la linea ferroviaria**
railway

⑮ **la stazione ferroviaria**
train station

⑯ **l'area campeggio** *f*
campsite

① **la cartina**
map

⑰ **l'area di sosta** *f*
service station

⑱ **le linee della griglia**
grid lines

⑲ **la riserva naturale**
nature reserve

⑳ **il punto panoramico**
viewpoint

㉑ **il percorso a piedi**
walking trail

㉒ **la città**
town

㉓ **la casa / l'edificio** *m*
house / building

㉔ **la scuola**
school

㉕ **la biblioteca**
library

㉖ **il percorso del traghetto**
ferry route

㉗ **i contorni**
contours

㉘ **il fiume**
river

㉙ **il lago**
lake

㉚ **la foresta**
forest

㉛ **la spiaggia**
beach

See also
96 Le strade · Roads **133** Le attività all'aperto · Outdoor activities **145** Il pianeta
Terra · Planet Earth **146-147** La geografia · Geography **149-151** I Paesi · Countries

㉜ **in senso orario**
clockwise

㉝ **in senso antiorario**
anticlockwise

㉞ **le coordinate**
coordinates

㉟ **l'orienteering** *m*
orienteering

㊱ **la latitudine**
latitude

㊲ **la longitudine**
longitude

0   1 km

0   1 mile

㊳ **la scala**
scale

㊴ **il cartografo** *m*
la cartografa *f*
cartographer

㊵ **la cartina online**
online map

㊶ **la cartina
escursionistica**
hiking map

㊷ **la carta stradale**
streetmap

148.2 LE PREPOSIZIONI DI LUOGO
PREPOSITIONS OF PLACE

① **accanto**
next to / beside

② **di fronte**
opposite

③ **tra**
between

④ **all'angolo** *m*
on the corner

⑤ **davanti a**
in front of

⑥ **dietro**
behind

⑦ **a sinistra**
on the left

⑧ **a destra**
on the right

148.3 I VERBI DI DIREZIONE · DIRECTION VERBS

① **girare a sinistra**
to go left /
to turn left

② **girare a destra**
to go right /
to turn right

③ **andare dritto**
to go straight
ahead / on

④ **tornare indietro**
to go back

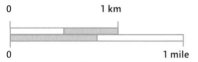

⑤ **oltrepassare**
to go past
(the restaurant)

⑥ **prendere la
prima a sinistra**
to take the first left

⑦ **prendere la
seconda a destra**
to take the
second right

⑧ **fermarsi a**
to stop at
(the hotel)

⑨ **pianificare il
percorso**
to plan your route

⑩ **perdersi**
to lose
your way

⑪ **leggere una
cartina**
to read a map

⑫ **chiedere
indicazioni**
to ask directions

305

149.1 L'AFRICA · AFRICA

① il Marocco
Morocco

② la Mauritania
Mauritania

③ Capo Verde
Cape Verde

④ il Senegal
Senegal

⑤ il Gambia
Gambia

⑥ la Guinea-Bissau
Guinea-Bissau

⑦ la Guinea
Guinea

⑧ la Sierra Leone
Sierra Leone

⑨ la Liberia
Liberia

⑩ la Costa d'Avorio
Ivory Coast

⑪ il Burkina Faso
Burkina Faso

⑫ il Mali
Mali

⑬ l'Algeria f
Algeria

⑭ la Tunisia
Tunisia

⑮ la Libia
Libya

⑯ il Niger
Niger

⑰ il Ghana
Ghana

⑱ il Togo
Togo

⑲ il Benin
Benin

⑳ la Nigeria
Nigeria

㉑ São Tomé e
Príncipe
São Tomé and Príncipe

㉒ la Guinea
Equatoriale
Equatorial Guinea

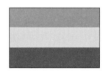
㉓ il Gabon
Gabon

㉔ il Camerun
Cameroon

㉕ il Ciad
Chad

㉖ il Ruanda
Rwanda

㉗ il Burundi
Burundi

㉘ la Tanzania
Tanzania

㉙ il Mozambico
Mozambique

㉚ il Malawi
Malawi

㉛ la Repubblica del
Congo
Republic of the Congo

㉜ la Repubblica
Democratica del Congo
Democratic Republic of
the Congo

㉝ lo Zambia
Zambia

㉞ l'Angola f
Angola

㉟ la Namibia
Namibia

㊱ il Botswana
Botswana

See also
145 Il pianeta Terra • Planet Earth **146-147** La geografia • Geography **148** Le cartine e le direzioni • Maps and directions **150-151** I Paesi (continua) • Countries continued **152-153** Le nazionalità • Nationalities

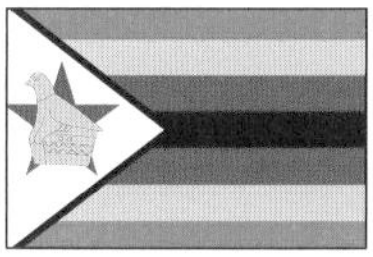

㊲ **lo Zimbabwe**
Zimbabwe

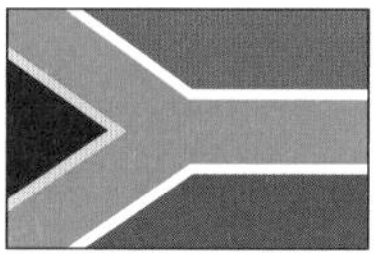

㊳ **il Sudafrica**
South Africa

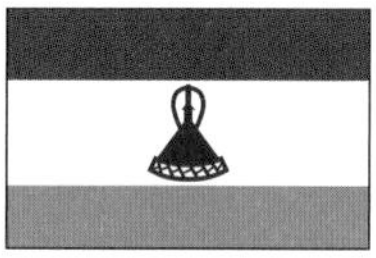

㊴ **il Lesotho**
Lesotho

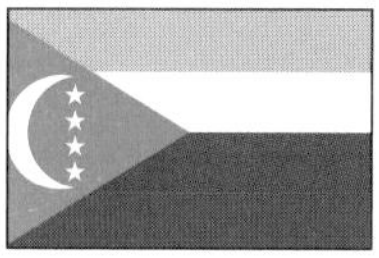

㊵ **le Comore**
Comoros

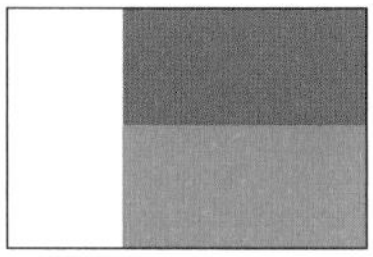

㊶ **il Madagascar**
Madagascar

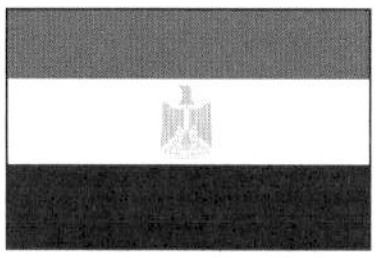

㊷ **l'Egitto** *m*
Egypt

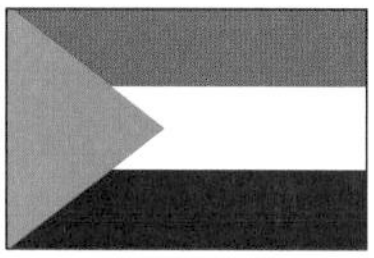

㊸ **il Sudan**
Sudan

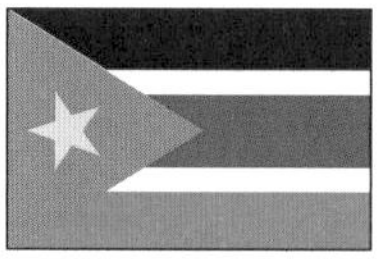

㊹ **il Sudan del Sud**
South Sudan

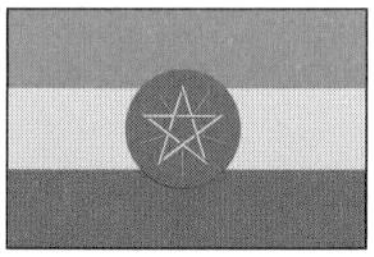

㊺ **l'Etiopia** *f*
Ethiopia

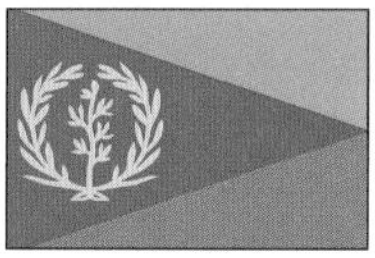

㊻ **l'Eritrea** *f*
Eritrea

㊼ **la Somalia**
Somalia

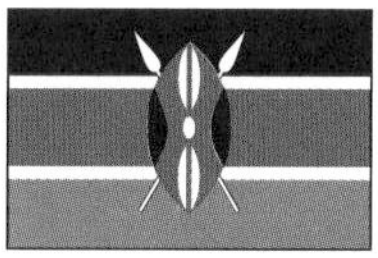

㊽ **il Kenya**
Kenya

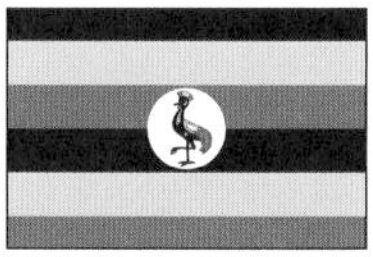

㊾ **l'Uganda** *f*
Uganda

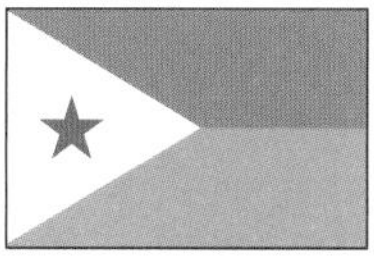

㊿ **il Gibuti**
Djibouti

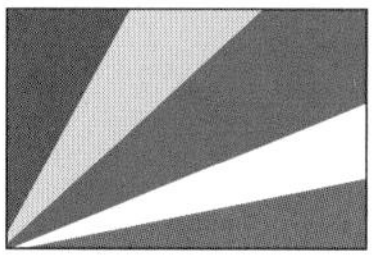

(51) **le Seychelles**
Seychelles

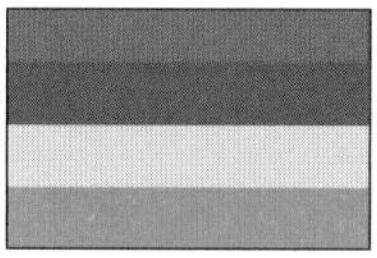

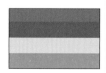

(52) **le Mauritius**
Mauritius

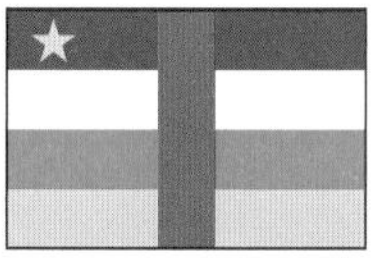

(53) **la Repubblica Centrafricana**
Central African Republic

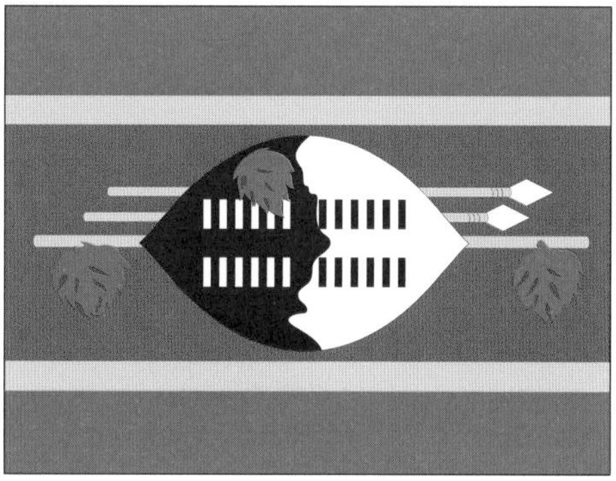

(54) **l'Eswatini** *m*
Eswatini

149.2 IL SUD AMERICA
SOUTH AMERICA

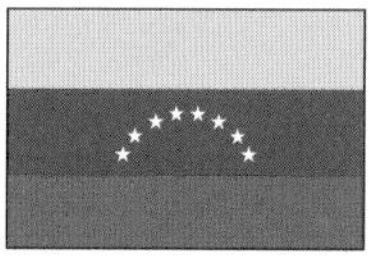

① **il Venezuela**
Venezuela

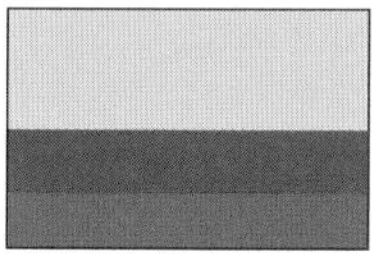

② **la Colombia**
Colombia

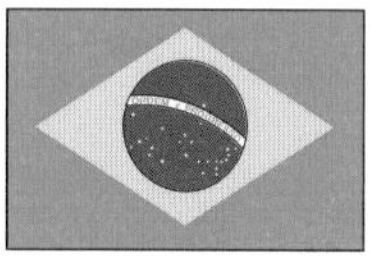

③ **il Brasile**
Brazil

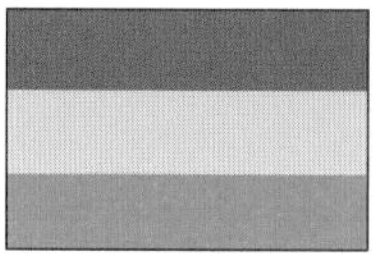

④ **la Bolivia**
Bolivia

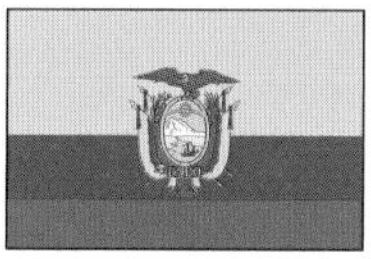

⑤ **l'Ecuador** *m*
Ecuador

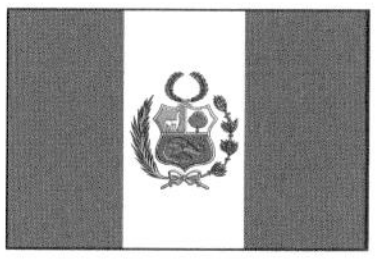

⑥ **il Perù**
Peru

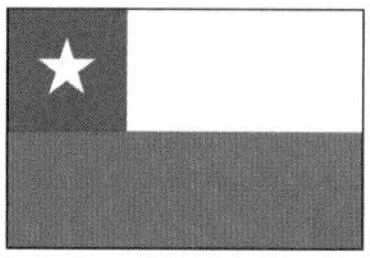

⑦ **il Cile**
Chile

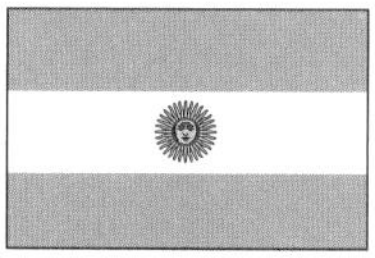

⑧ **l'Argentina** *f*
Argentina

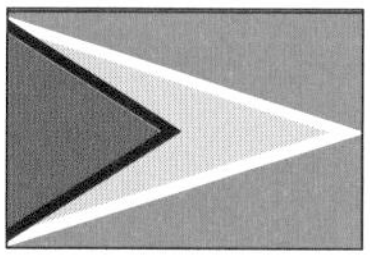

⑨ **la Guyana**
Guyana

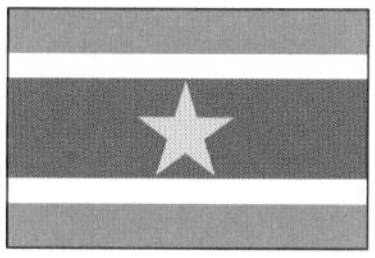

⑩ **il Suriname**
Suriname

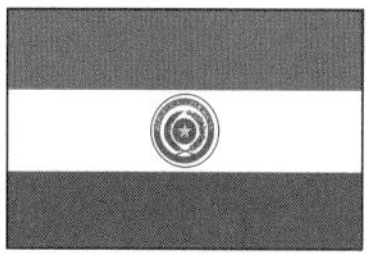

⑪ **il Paraguay**
Paraguay

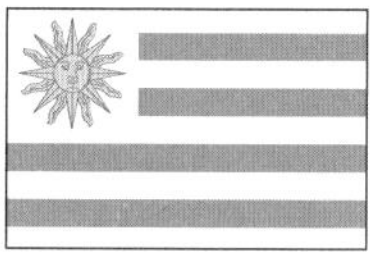

⑫ **l'Uruguay** *m*
Uruguay

150.1 IL NORD AMERICA, L'AMERICA CENTRALE E I CARAIBI
NORTH AND CENTRAL AMERICA AND THE CARIBBEAN

① **il Canada**
Canada

② **gli Stati Uniti d'America**
United States of America

③ **il Messico**
Mexico

④ **il Guatemala**
Guatemala

⑤ **il Belize**
Belize

⑥ **El Salvador**
El Salvador

⑧ **l'Honduras** *m*
Honduras

⑨ **il Nicaragua**
Nicaragua

⑩ **il Costa Rica**
Costa Rica

⑪ **Panama**
Panama

⑫ **Cuba**
Cuba

⑬ **le Bahamas**
Bahamas

⑮ **la Giamaica**
Jamaica

⑯ **Haiti**
Haiti

⑰ **la Repubblica Dominicana**
Dominican Republic

⑱ **le Barbados**
Barbados

⑲ **Trinidad e Tobago**
Trinidad and Tobago

⑳ **Saint Kitts e Nevis**
St. Kitts and Nevis

㉒ **Dominica**
Dominica
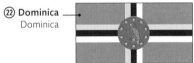
㉓ **Antigua e Barbuda**
Antigua and Barbuda

150.2 L'OCEANIA · OCEANIA

① **la Papua Nuova Guinea**
Papua New Guinea

② **l'Australia** *f*
Australia

③ **la Nuova Zelanda**
New Zealand

④ **le Isole Marshall**
Marshall Islands

⑤ **Palau**
Palau

⑥ **la Micronesia**
Micronesia

⑧ **Nauru**
Nauru

⑨ **le Kiribati**
Kiribati

⑩ **le Tuvalu**
Tuvalu

⑪ **le Samoa**
Samoa

⑫ **Tonga**
Tonga

⑬ **le Vanuatu**
Vanuatu

See also
145 Il pianeta Terra · Planet Earth **146-147** La geografia · Geography **148** Le cartine e le direzioni · Maps and directions **149-151** I Paesi (continua) · Countries continued **152-153** Le nazionalità · Nationalities

150.3 **L'ASIA** · ASIA

⑦ **Grenada**
Grenada

① **la Turchia**
Türkiye

② **la Federazione Russa**
Russian Federation

③ **la Georgia**
Georgia

④ **l'Armenia** *f*
Armenia

⑤ **l'Azerbaigian** *m*
Azerbaijan

⑭ **Saint Lucia**
St. Lucia

⑥ **l'Iraq** *m*
Iraq

⑦ **la Siria**
Syria

⑧ **il Libano**
Lebanon

⑨ **Israele**
Israel

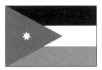
⑩ **la Giordania**
Jordan

㉑ **Saint Vincent e Grenadine**
St. Vincent and The Grenadines

⑪ **il Pakistan**
Pakistan

⑫ **l'India** *f*
India

⑬ **le Maldive**
Maldives

⑭ **lo Sri Lanka**
Sri Lanka

⑮ **la Cina**
China

⑯ **la Mongolia**
Mongolia

⑰ **la Corea del Nord**
North Korea

⑱ **la Corea del Sud**
South Korea

⑲ **il Giappone**
Japan

⑳ **il Bangladesh**
Bangladesh

⑦ **le Isole Salomone**
Solomon Islands

㉑ **il Bhutan**
Bhutan

㉒ **il Myanmar**
Myanmar (Burma)

㉓ **la Tailandia**
Thailand

㉗ **il Nepal**
Nepal

㉔ **il Laos**
Laos

㉕ **il Vietnam**
Vietnam

㉖ **la Cambogia**
Cambodia

⑭ **le Figi**
Fiji

151.1 L'ASIA (CONTINUA) · ASIA CONTINUED

① **Singapore**
Singapore

② **l'Indonesia** *f*
Indonesia

③ **il Brunei**
Brunei

④ **le Filippine**
Philippines

⑤ **Timor Est**
East Timor

⑥ **la Malesia**
Malaysia

⑦ **gli Emirati Arabi Uniti**
United Arab Emirates

⑧ **l'Oman** *m*
Oman

⑨ **il Bahrein**
Bahrain

⑩ **il Qatar**
Qatar

⑪ **il Kuwait**
Kuwait

⑫ **l'Iran** *m*
Iran

⑬ **lo Yemen**
Yemen

⑭ **l'Arabia Saudita** *f*
Saudi Arabia

⑮ **l'Uzbekistan** *m*
Uzbekistan

⑯ **il Turkmenistan**
Turkmenistan

⑰ **l'Afghanistan** *m*
Afghanistan

⑱ **il Tagikistan**
Tajikistan

⑲ **il Kirghizistan**
Kyrgyzstan

⑳ **il Kazakistan**
Kazakhstan

151.2 L'EUROPA · EUROPE

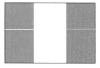

① **l'Irlanda** *f*
Ireland

② **il Regno Unito**
United Kingdom

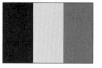

⑨ **il Belgio**
Belgium

⑩ **i Paesi Bassi**
Netherlands

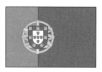

⑰ **il Portogallo**
Portugal

⑱ **la Spagna**
Spain

㉕ **il Lussemburgo**
Luxembourg

㉖ **la Germania**
Germany

㉝ **Andorra**
Andorra

㉞ **la Francia**
France

㊶ **la Danimarca**
Denmark

㊷ **la Norvegia**
Norway

See also
145 Il pianeta Terra · Planet Earth **146-147** La geografia · Geography **148** Le cartine e le direzioni · Maps and directions **152-153** Le nazionalità · Nationalities

③ **la Svezia**
Sweden

④ **la Finlandia**
Finland

⑤ **l'Estonia** f
Estonia

⑥ **la Lettonia**
Latvia

⑦ **la Lituania**
Lithuania

⑧ **la Polonia**
Poland

⑪ **la Repubblica Ceca**
Czech Republic

⑫ **l'Austria** f
Austria

⑬ **il Liechtenstein**
Liechtenstein

⑭ **l'Italia** f
Italy

⑮ **il Principato di Monaco**
Monaco

⑯ **San Marino**
San Marino

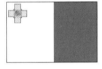
⑲ **Malta**
Malta

⑳ **la Slovenia**
Slovenia

㉑ **la Croazia**
Croatia

㉒ **l'Ungheria** f
Hungary

㉓ **la Slovacchia**
Slovakia

㉔ **l'Ucraina** f
Ukraine

㉗ **la Bielorussia**
Belarus

㉘ **la Moldavia**
Moldova

㉙ **la Romania**
Romania

㉚ **la Serbia**
Serbia

㉛ **la Bulgaria**
Bulgaria

㉜ **l'Albania** f
Albania

㉟ **la Grecia**
Greece

㊱ **l'Islanda** f
Iceland

㊲ **Cipro**
Cyprus

㊳ **il Montenegro**
Montenegro

㊴ **Città del Vaticano**
Vatican City

㊵ **la Turchia**
Türkiye

㊸ **la Bosnia-Erzegovina**
Bosnia and Herzegovina

㊹ **la Macedonia del Nord**
North Macedonia

㊺ **la Svizzera**
Switzerland

㊻ **la Federazione Russa**
Russian Federation

152 Le nazionalità
Nationalities

152.1 L'AFRICA · AFRICA

Country	Adjective	English Adjective
① **l'Africa** Africa	**africano** *m* / **africana** *f*	African
② **il Marocco** Morocco	**marocchino** *m* **marocchina** *f*	Moroccan
③ **la Mauritania** Mauritania	**mauritano** *m* / **mauritana** *f*	Mauritanian
④ **Capo Verde** Cape Verde	**capoverdiano** *m* **capoverdiana** *f*	Cape Verdean
⑤ **il Senegal** Senegal	**senegalese** *m* / *f*	Senegalese
⑥ **il Gambia** Gambia	**gambiano** *m* **gambiana** *f*	Gambian
⑦ **la Guinea-Bissau** Guinea-Bissau	**guineense** *m* / *f*	Bissau-Guinean
⑧ **la Guinea** Guinea	**guineano** *m* / **guineana** *f*	Guinean
⑨ **la Sierra Leone** Sierra Leone	**sierraleonese** *m* / *f*	Sierra Leonean
⑩ **la Liberia** Liberia	**liberiano** *m* / **liberiana** *f*	Liberian
⑪ **la Costa d'Avorio** Ivory Coast	**ivoriano** *m* / **ivoriana** *f*	Ivorian
⑫ **il Burkina Faso** Burkina Faso	**burkinabé** *m* / *f*	Burkinabe
⑬ **il Mali** Mali	**maliano** *m* / **maliana** *f*	Malian
⑭ **l'Algeria** Algeria	**algerino** *m* / **algerina** *f*	Algerian
⑮ **la Tunisia** Tunisia	**tunisino** *m* / **tunisina** *f*	Tunisian
⑯ **la Libia** Libya	**libico** *m* / **libica** *f*	Libyan
⑰ **il Niger** Niger	**nigerino** *m* / **nigerina** *f*	Nigerien
⑱ **il Ghana** Ghana	**ghanese** *m* / **ghanese** *f*	Ghanaian
⑲ **il Togo** Togo	**togolese** *m* / **togolese** *f*	Togolese
⑳ **il Benin** Benin	**beninese** *m* / **beninese** *f*	Beninese
㉑ **la Nigeria** Nigeria	**nigeriano** *m* / **nigeriana** *f*	Nigerian
㉒ **São Tomé e Príncipe** São Tomé and Príncipe	**saotomense** *m* / *f*	São Toméan
㉓ **la Guinea Equatoriale** Equatorial Guinea	**equatoguineano** *m* **equatoguineana** *f*	Equatorial Guinean
㉔ **il Camerun** Cameroon	**camerunense** *m* / *f*	Cameroonian
㉕ **il Ciad** Chad	**ciadiano** *m* / **ciadiana** *f*	Chadian
㉖ **l'Egitto** Egypt	**egiziano** *m* / **egiziana** *f*	Egyptian
㉗ **il Sudan** Sudan	**sudanese** *m* / *f*	Sudanese
㉘ **il Sudan del Sud** South Sudan	**sudsudanese** *m* / *f*	South Sudanese
㉙ **l'Eritrea** Eritrea	**eritreo** *m* / **eritrea** *f*	Eritrean
㉚ **il Gibuti** Djibouti	**gibutiano** *m* / **gibutiana** *f*	Djiboutian
㉛ **l'Etiopia** Ethiopia	**etiope** *m* / *f*	Ethiopian
㉜ **la Somalia** Somalia	**somalo** *m* / **somala** *f*	Somalian
㉝ **il Kenya** Kenya	**keniano** *m* / **keniana** *f*	Kenyan
㉞ **l'Uganda** Uganda	**ugandese** *m* / *f*	Ugandan
㉟ **la Repubblica Centrafricana** Central African Republic	**centrafricano** *m* **centrafricana** *f*	Central African
㊱ **il Gabon** Gabon	**gabonese** *m* / *f*	Gabonese
㊲ **la Repubblica del Congo** Republic of the Congo	**congolese** *m* / *f*	Congolese
㊳ **la Repubblica Democratica del Congo** Democratic Republic of the Congo	**congolese** *m* / *f*	Congolese
㊴ **il Ruanda** Rwanda	**ruandese** *m* / *f*	Rwandan
㊵ **il Burundi** Burundi	**burundese** *m* / *f*	Burundian
㊶ **la Tanzania** Tanzania	**tanzaniano** *m* **tanzaniana** *f*	Tanzanian
㊷ **il Mozambico** Mozambique	**mozambicano** *m* **mozambicana** *f*	Mozambican
㊸ **il Malawi** Malawi	**malawiano** *m* **malawiana** *f*	Malawian
㊹ **lo Zambia** Zambia	**zambiano** *m* **zambiana** *f*	Zambian
㊺ **l'Angola** Angola	**angolano** *m* **angolana** *f*	Angolan
㊻ **la Namibia** Namibia	**namibiano** *m* **namibiana** *f*	Namibian
㊼ **il Botswana** Botswana	**botswaniano** *m* **botswaniana** *f*	Botswanan
㊽ **lo Zimbabwe** Zimbabwe	**zimbabweano** *m* **zimbabweana** *f*	Zimbabwean
㊾ **il Sudafrica** South Africa	**sudafricano** *m* **sudafricana** *f*	South African
㊿ **il Lesotho** Lesotho	**lesothiano** *m* **lesothiana** *f*	Basotho
(51) **l'Eswatini** *m* Eswatini	**swazi** *m* / *f*	Swazi
(52) **le Comore** Comoros	**comoriano** *m* **comoriana** *f*	Comoran
(53) **il Madagascar** Madagascar	**malgascio** *m* **malgascia** *f*	Madagascan
(54) **le Seychelles** Seychelles	**seychellese** *m* / *f*	Seychellois
(55) **le Mauritius** Mauritius	**mauriziano** *m* **mauriziana** *f*	Mauritian

See also
145 Il pianeta Terra • Planet Earth **146-147** La geografia • Geography
148 Le cartine e le direzioni • Maps and directions **149-151** I Paesi
Countries **153** Le nazionalità (continua) • Nationalities continued

152.2 IL SUD AMERICA · SOUTH AMERICA

Country	Adjective	English Adjective	Country	Adjective	English Adjective
① Il Sud America South America	sudamericano *m* sudamericana *f*	South American	⑧ il Brasile Brazil	brasiliano *m* brasiliana *f*	Brazilian
② il Venezuela Venezuela	venezuelano *m* venezuelana *f*	Venezuelan	⑨ la Bolivia Bolivia	boliviano *m* boliviana *f*	Bolivian
③ la Colombia Colombia	colombiano *m* colombiana *f*	Colombian	⑩ il Cile Chile	cileno *m* / cilena *f*	Chilean
④ l'Ecuador *m* Ecuador	ecuadoregno *m* ecuadoregna *f*	Ecuadorian	⑪ l'Argentina Argentina	argentino *m* argentina *f*	Argentinian
⑤ il Perù Peru	peruviano *m* peruviana *f*	Peruvian	⑫ il Paraguay Paraguay	paraguaiano *m* paraguaiana *f*	Paraguayan
⑥ la Guyana Guyana	guianese *m* / *f*	Guyanese	⑬ l'Uruguay Uruguay	uruguaiano *m* uruguaiana *f*	Uruguayan
⑦ il Suriname Suriname	surinamese *m* / *f*	Surinamese			

152.3 L'AMERICA DEL NORD, L'AMERICA CENTRALE E I CARAIBI
NORTH AND CENTRAL AMERICA AND THE CARIBBEAN

Country	Adjective	English Adjective	Country	Adjective	English Adjective
① l'America del Nord, l'America centrale e i Caraibi North and Central America and the Caribbean	nordamericano, centroamericano e caraibico *m*, nordamericana centroamericana e caraibica *f*	North American, Central American, and Caribbean	⑭ la Giamaica Jamaica	giamaicano *m* giamaicana *f*	Jamaican
② il Canada Canada	canadese *m* / *f*	Canadian	⑮ Haiti Haiti	haitiano *m* haitiana *f*	Haitian
③ gli Stati Uniti d'America United States of America	statunitense *m* / *f*	American	⑯ la Repubblica Dominicana Dominican Republic	dominicano *m* dominicana *f*	Dominican
④ il Messico Mexico	messicano *m* messicana *f*	Mexican	⑰ le Barbados Barbados	barbadiano *m* barbadiana *f*	Barbadian
⑤ il Guatemala Guatemala	guatemalteco *m* guatemalteca *f*	Guatemalan	⑱ Trinidad e Tobago Trinidad and Tobago	trinidadiano o tobagoniano *m* trinidadiana o tobagoniana *f*	Trinidadian or Tobagonian
⑥ il Belize Belize	beliziano *m* / beliziana *f*	Belizean	⑲ Saint Kitts e Nevis St. Kitts and Nevis	kittitiano o nevisiano *m* kittitiana o nevisiana *f*	Kittitian or Nevisian
⑦ El Salvador El Salvador	salvadoregno *m* salvadoregna *f*	Salvadoran	⑳ Antigua e Barbuda Antigua and Barbuda	antiguo-barbudano *m* antiguo-barbudana *f*	Antiguan or Barbudan
⑧ Honduras Honduras	honduregno *m* honduregna *f*	Honduran	㉑ Dominica Dominica	dominicense *m* / *f*	Dominican
⑨ il Nicaragua Nicaragua	nicaraguense *m* / *f*	Nicaraguan	㉒ Santa Lucia St. Lucia	santaluciano *m* santaluciana *f*	St. Lucian
⑩ il Costa Rica Costa Rica	costaricano *m* costaricana *f*	Costa Rican	㉓ Saint Vincent e Grenadine St. Vincent and The Grenadines	sanvicentino *m* sanvicentina *f*	Vincentian
⑪ Panama Panama	panamense *m* / *f*	Panamanian	㉔ Grenada Grenada	grenadino *m* grenadina *f*	Grenadian
⑫ Cuba Cuba	cubano *m* / cubana *f*	Cuban			
⑬ le Bahamas Bahamas	bahamense *m* / *f*	Bahamian			

153.1 L'OCEANIA · OCEANIA

Country	Adjective	English Adjective	Country	Adjective	English Adjective
① l'Oceania Oceania	oceaniano *m* oceaniana *f*	Oceanian	⑧ Nauru Nauru	nauruano *m* / nauruana *f*	Nauruan
② la Papua Nuova Guinea Papua New Guinea	papuano *m* papuana *f*	Papua New Guinean	⑨ le Kiribati Kiribati	gilbertese *m* / *f*	Kiribati
③ l'Australia Australia	australiano *m* australiana *f*	Australian	⑩ le Tuvalu Tuvalu	tuvaluano *m* / tuvaluana *f*	Tuvaluan
④ la Nuova Zelanda New Zealand	neozelandese *m* / *f*	New Zealand	⑪ le Samoa Samoa	samoano *m* / samoana *f*	Samoan
⑤ le Isole Marshall Marshall Islands	marshallese *m* / *f*	Marshallese	⑫ Tonga Tonga	tongano *m* / tongana *f*	Tongan
⑥ Palau Palau	palauano *m* / palauana *f*	Palauan	⑬ Vanuatu Vanuatu	vanuatiano *m* vanuatiana *f*	Vanuatuan
⑦ la Micronesia Micronesia	micronesiano *m* micronesiana *f*	Micronesian	⑭ le Isole Salomone Solomon Islands	salomonese *m* / *f*	Solomon Island
			⑮ le Figi Fiji	figiano *m* / figiana *f*	Fijian

153.2 L'ASIA · ASIA

Country	Adjective	English Adjective	Country	Adjective	English Adjective
① l'Asia · Asia	asiatico *m* / asiaticia *f*	Asian	⑳ il Kazakistan Kazakhstan	kazako *m* / kazaka *f*	Kazakh
② la Turchia Türkiye	turco *m* / turca *f*	Turkish	㉑ l'Uzbekistan Uzbekistan	uzbeko *m* / uzbeka *f*	Uzbek
③ la Federazione Russa Russian Federation	russo *m* / russa *f*	Russian	㉒ il Turkmenistan Turkmenistan	turkmeno *m* turkmena *f*	Turkmen
④ la Georgia Georgia	georgiano *m* / georgiana *f*	Georgian	㉓ l'Afghanistan Afghanistan	afgano *m* / afgana *f*	Afghan
⑤ l'Armenia Armenia	armeno *m* armena *f*	Armenian	㉔ il Tagikistan Tajikistan	tagico *m* / tagica *f*	Tajikistani
⑥ l'Arzebaigian Azerbaijan	azerbaigiano *m* azerbaigiana *f*	Azerbaijani	㉕ il Kirghizistan Kyrgyzstan	kirghiso *m* / kirghisa *f*	Kyrgyz
⑦ l'Iran Iran	iraniano *m* / iraniana *f*	Iranian	㉖ il Pakistan Pakistan	pakistano *m* / pakistana *f*	Pakistani
⑧ l'Iraq Iraq	iracheno *m* / irachena *f*	Iraqi	㉗ l'India India	indiano *m* / indiana *f*	Indian
⑨ la Siria Syria	siriano *m* / siriana *f*	Syrian	㉘ le Maldive Maldives	maldiviano *m* maldiviana *f*	Maldivian
⑩ il Libano Lebanon	libanese *m* / *f*	Lebanese	㉙ lo Sri Lanka Sri Lanka	srilankese	Sri Lankan
⑪ Israele Israel	israeliano *m* istraeliana *f*	Israeli	㉚ la Cina China	cinese *m* / *f*	Chinese
⑫ la Giordania Jordan	giordano *m* / giordana *f*	Jordanian	㉛ la Mongolia Mongolia	mongolo *m* / mongola *f*	Mongolian
⑬ l'Arabia Saudita Saudi Arabia	saudita *m* / *f*	Saudi	㉜ la Corea del Nord North Korea	nordcoreano *m* nordcoreana *f*	North Korean
⑭ il Kuwait Kuwait	kuwaitiano *m* kuwaitiana *f*	Kuwaiti	㉝ la Corea del Sud South Korea	sudcoreano *m* sudcoreana *f*	South Korean
⑮ il Bahrein Bahrain	bahreinita *m* / *f*	Bahraini	㉞ il Giappone Japan	giapponese *m* / *f*	Japanese
⑯ il Qatar Qatar	qatariota *m* / *f*	Qatari	㉟ il Nepal Nepal	nepalese *m* / *f*	Nepalese
⑰ gli Emirati Arabi Uniti United Arab Emirates	emiratino *m* emiratina *f*	Emirati	㊱ il Bhutan Bhutan	butanese *m* / *f*	Bhutanese
⑱ l'Oman Oman	omanita *m* / *f*	Omani	㊲ il Bangladesh Bangladesh	bangladese *m* / *f*	Bangladeshi
⑲ lo Yemen Yemen	yemenita *m* / *f*	Yemeni	㊳ il Myanmar Myanmar (Burma)	birmano *m* / birmana *f*	Burmese
			㊴ la Tailandia Thailand	tailandese *m* / *f*	Thai

See also
145 Il pianeta Terra · Planet Earth **146-147** La geografia · Geography
148 Le cartine e le direzioni · Maps and directions **149-151** I Paesi · Countries

153.2   L'ASIA (CONTINUA) · ASIA CONTINUED

Country	Adjective	English Adjective	Country	Adjective	English Adjective
㊵ il Laos Laos	laotiano *m* / laotiana *f*	Laotian	㊹ Singapore Singapore	singaporiano *m* singaporiana *f*	Singaporean
㊶ il Vietnam Vietnam	vietnamita *m / f*	Vietnamese	㊺ l'Indonesia *f* Indonesia	indonesiano *m* indonesiana *f*	Indonesian
㊷ la Cambogia Cambodia	cambogiano *m* cambogiana *f*	Cambodian	㊻ il Brunei Brunei	bruneiano *m* bruneiana *f*	Bruneian
㊸ la Malesia Malaysia	malese *m / f*	Malaysian	㊼ le Filippine Philippines	filippino *m* / filippina *f*	Filipino
			㊽ il Timor Est East Timor	est-timorese *m / f*	Timorese

153.3   L'EUROPA · EUROPE

Country	Adjective	English Adjective	Country	Adjective	English Adjective
① l'Europa · Europe	europeo *m* / europea *f*	European	㉕ il Principato di Monaco Monaco	monegasco monegasca	Monacan
② l'Irlanda Ireland	irlandese *m / f*	Irish	㉖ San Marino San Marino	sammarinese *m / f*	Sammarinese
③ il Regno Unito United Kingdom	britannico *m* / britannica *f*	British	㉗ Malta Malta	maltese *m / f*	Maltese
④ il Portogallo Portugal	portoghese *m / f*	Portuguese	㉘ la Slovenia Slovenia	sloveno *m* / slovena *f*	Slovenian
⑤ la Spagna Spain	spagnolo *m* / spagnola *f*	Spanish	㉙ Croazia Croatia	croato *m* / croata *f*	Croatian
⑥ Andorra Andorra	andorrano *m* andorrana *f*	Andorran	㉚ l'Ungheria Hungary	ungherese *m / f*	Hungarian
⑦ la Francia France	francese *m / f*	French	㉛ la Slovacchia Slovakia	slovacco *m* slovacca *f*	Slovakian
⑧ il Belgio Belgium	belga *m / f*	Belgian	㉜ l'Ucraina Ukraine	ucraino *m* / ucraina *f*	Ukrainian
⑨ i Paesi Bassi Netherlands	olandese *m / f*	Dutch	㉝ la Bielorussia Belarus	bielorusso *m* / bielorussa *f*	Belarusian
⑩ il Lussemburgo Luxembourg	lussemburghese	Luxembourg	㉞ la Moldavia Moldova	moldavo *m* / moldava *f*	Moldovan
⑪ la Germania Germany	tedesco *m* / tedesca *f*	German	㉟ la Romania Romania	rumeno *m* / rumena *f*	Romanian
⑫ la Danimarca Denmark	danese *m / f*	Danish	㊱ la Serbia Serbia	serbo *m* / serba *f*	Serbian
⑬ la Norvegia Norway	norvegese *m / f*	Norwegian	㊲ la Bosnia -Erzegovina Bosnia and Herzegovina	bosniaco o erzegovino *m* bosniaca o erzegovina *f*	Bosnian or Herzegovinian
⑭ la Svezia Sweden	svedese *m / f*	Swedish	㊳ l'Albania Albania	albanese *m / f*	Albanian
⑮ la Finlandia Finland	finlandese *m / f*	Finnish	㊴ la Macedonia del Nord North Macedonia	macedone *m / f*	North Macedonian
⑯ l'Estonia Estonia	estone *m / f*	Estonian	㊵ la Bulgaria Bulgaria	bulgaro *m* / bulgara *f*	Bulgarian
⑰ la Lettonia Latvia	lettone *m / f*	Latvian	㊶ la Grecia Greece	greco *m* / greca *f*	Greek
⑱ la Lituania Lithuania	lituano *m* / lituana *f*	Lithuanian	㊷ il Montenegro Montenegro	montenegrino *m* montenegrina *f*	Montenegrin
⑲ la Polonia Poland	polacco *m* / polacca *f*	Polish	㊸ l'Islanda Iceland	islandese *m / f*	Icelandic
⑳ la Repubblica Ceca Czech Republic	ceco *m* / ceca *f*	Czech	㊹ Cipro Cyprus	cipriota *m / f*	Cypriot
㉑ l'Austria *f* Austria	austriaco *m* / austriaca *f*	Austrian	㊺ la Turchia Türkiye	turco *m* / turca *f*	Turkish
㉒ il Liechtenstein Liechtenstein	liechtensteinese *m / f*	Liechtensteiner	㊻ la Federazione Russa Russian Federation	russo *m* / russa *f*	Russian
㉓ la Svizzera Switzerland	svizzero *m* svizzera *f*	Swiss			
㉔ l'Italia Italy	italiano *m* / italiana *f*	Italian			

Il tempo atmosferico
Weather

① l'umidità f
humidity

② l'ondata di caldo f
heatwave

③ la siccità
drought

④ secco
dry

⑤ umido
wet

⑥ coperto
overcast

⑦ lo smog
smog

⑧ la goccia di pioggia
raindrop

⑨ il leggero piovasco
light shower

⑩ la pioggerella
drizzle

⑪ l'acquazzone m
downpour

⑫ l'alluvione f
flood

⑬ la tempesta di sabbia
sandstorm

⑭ la burrasca
gale

⑮ il temporale
storm

⑯ il tuono
thunder

⑰ il fulmine
lightning

⑱ l'arcobaleno m
rainbow

⑲ il nevischio
sleet

⑳ il fiocco di neve
snowflake

㉑ il cumulo di neve
snowdrift

㉒ la tormenta
blizzard

㉓ la tempesta di neve
snowstorm

㉔ il chicco di grandine
hailstone

㉘ Oggi piove a dirotto.
It's raining cats and dogs today.

㉕ l'uragano m
hurricane

㉖ il tornado
tornado

㉗ la pozzanghera
puddle

See also
145 Il pianeta Terra • Planet Earth **146-147** La geografia • Geography
155 Il clima e l'ambiente • Climate and the environment

154.2 **LA TEMPERATURA** · TEMPERATURE

① **gelido** m / **gelida** f
freezing

② **freddo** m / **fredda** f
cold

③ **freddo** m / **fredda** f
chilly

④ **caldo** m / **calda** f
warm

⑤ **caldissimo** m
caldissima f
hot

⑥ **soffocante**
stifling

⑦ **il punto di
congelamento**
freezing point

⑧ **il punto di
ebollizione**
boiling point

⑨ **meno 10**
minus 10

⑩ **25 gradi**
25 degrees

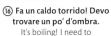

⑯ **Fa un caldo torrido! Devo
trovare un po' d'ombra.**
It's boiling! I need to
find some shade

⑪ **Celsius**
Celsius

⑫ **Fahrenheit**
Fahrenheit

⑬ **fresco** m / **fresca** f
cool

⑭ **mite**
mild

⑮ **torrido** m / **torrida** f
boiling

154.3 **GLI AGGETTIVI DEL TEMPO** · WEATHER ADJECTIVES

① **il sole → soleggiato** m
soleggiata f
sun -> sunny

② **la nuvola →
nuvoloso** m / **nuvolosa** f
cloud -> cloudy

③ **la nebbia → nebbioso**
m **nebbiosa** f
fog -> foggy

④ **la pioggia →
piovoso** m / **piovosa** f
rain -> rainy

⑤ **la neve →
nevoso** m / **nevosa** f
snow -> snowy

⑥ **il ghiaccio →
ghiacciato** m
ghiacciata f
ice -> icy

⑦ **la gelata → gelido** m
gelida f
frost -> frosty

⑧ **il vento →
ventoso** m / **ventosa** f
wind -> windy

⑨ **il temporale →
temporalesco** m
temporalesca f
storm -> stormy

⑩ **il tuono →
tempestoso** m
tempestosa f
thunder -> thundery

⑪ **la nebbiolina →
nebbioso** m
nebbiosa f
mist -> misty

⑫ **la brezza →
ventilato** m
ventilata f
breeze -> breezy

155.1 L'ATMOSFERA · ATMOSPHERE

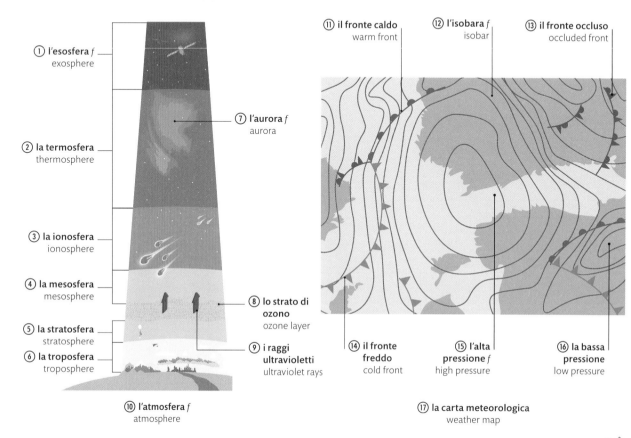

① l'esosfera *f*
exosphere

② la termosfera
thermosphere

③ la ionosfera
ionosphere

④ la mesosfera
mesosphere

⑤ la stratosfera
stratosphere

⑥ la troposfera
troposphere

⑦ l'aurora *f*
aurora

⑧ lo strato di ozono
ozone layer

⑨ i raggi ultravioletti
ultraviolet rays

⑩ l'atmosfera *f*
atmosphere

⑪ il fronte caldo
warm front

⑫ l'isobara *f*
isobar

⑬ il fronte occluso
occluded front

⑭ il fronte freddo
cold front

⑮ l'alta pressione *f*
high pressure

⑯ la bassa pressione
low pressure

⑰ la carta meteorologica
weather map

155.2 I PROBLEMI AMBIENTALI · ENVIRONMENTAL ISSUES

① la deforestazione
deforestation

② la perdita di habitat
habitat loss

⑥ il buco dell'ozono
ozone depletion

③ le specie a rischio
endangered species

⑦ la desertificazione
desertification

④ i rifiuti plastici
plastic waste

⑧ la chiazza di petrolio
oil slick

⑤ la sovrapesca
overfishing

⑨ la pioggia acida
acid rain

See also
145 Il pianeta Terra · Planet Earth **146-147** La geografia
Geography **154** Il tempo atmosferico · Weather

155.3   **IL CAMBIAMENTO CLIMATICO** · CLIMATE CHANGE

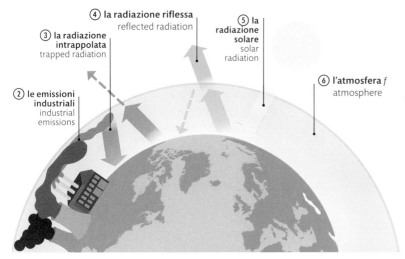

④ **la radiazione riflessa**
reflected radiation

③ **la radiazione intrappolata**
trapped radiation

⑤ **la radiazione solare**
solar radiation

② **le emissioni industriali**
industrial emissions

⑥ **l'atmosfera** *f*
atmosphere

① **l'effetto serra** *m*
greenhouse effect

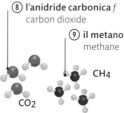

⑧ **l'anidride carbonica** *f*
carbon dioxide

⑨ **il metano**
methane

CH4

CO2

⑦ **i gas serra**
greenhouse gases

⑩ **i combustibili fossili**
fossil fuels

⑪ **le emissioni**
emissions

⑫ **l'inquinamento** *m*
pollution

⑬ **l'ecosistema** *m*
ecosystem

⑭ **emissioni zero**
zero carbon

⑮ **il restringimento dei ghiacciai**
shrinking glaciers

⑯ **lo scioglimento delle calotte polari**
melting ice caps

155.4   **I RIFIUTI E IL RICICLAGGIO** · WASTE AND RECYCLING

② **Cerco di riciclare il più possibile la plastica e la carta.**
I try to recycle plastic and paper as much as possible.

③ **i rifiuti alimentari**
food waste

④ **la carta**
paper

⑤ **la plastica**
plastic

① **differenziare i rifiuti**
to sort your rubbish

⑥ **il vetro**
glass

⑦ **il metallo**
metal

⑧ **il sacchetto compostabile**
compostable bags

⑨ **la discarica**
landfill

156.1 LE ROCCE · ROCKS

① la roccia **sedimentaria**
sedimentary

② l'**arenaria** *f*
sandstone

③ il **calcare**
limestone

④ il **gesso**
chalk

⑤ la **selce**
flint

⑥ il **conglomerato**
conglomerate

⑦ la pietra **metamorfica**
metamorphic

⑧ l'**ardesia** *f*
slate

⑨ lo **scisto**
schist

⑩ lo **gneis**
gneiss

⑪ il **marmo**
marble

⑫ la **quarzite**
quartzite

⑬ la roccia **ignea**
igneous

⑭ il **granito**
granite

⑮ l'**ossidiana** *f*
obsidian

⑯ il **basalto**
basalt

⑱ la pietra **pomice**
pumice

⑰ il **tufo vulcanico**
tuff

156.2 I MINERALI · MINERALS

① il **quarzo**
quartz

② la **mica**
mica

③ l'**agata** *f*
agate

④ l'**ematite** *f*
hematite

⑤ la **calcite**
calcite

⑥ la **malachite**
malachite

⑦ il **turchese**
turquoise

⑧ l'**onice** *f*
onyx

⑨ lo **zolfo**
sulphur

⑩ la **grafite**
graphite

⑪ il **geode**
geode

⑫ la **rosa del deserto**
sand rose

See also
76 La chimica · Chemistry **78** La tavola periodica · The periodic table
145 Il pianeta Terra · Planet Earth **146-147** La geografia · Geography

156.3 LE GEMME · GEMS

① **il diamante**
diamond

② **lo zaffiro**
sapphire

③ **lo smeraldo**
emerald

④ **il rubino**
ruby

⑤ **l'ametista** *f*
amethyst

⑥ **il topazio**
topaz

⑦ **l'acquamarina** *f*
aquamarine

⑧ **la pietra di luna**
moonstone

⑨ **l'opale** *m*
opal

⑩ **la tormalina**
tourmaline

⑪ **il granato**
garnet

⑫ **il citrino**
citrine

⑬ **la giada**
jade

⑭ **il giaietto**
jet

⑮ **il lapislazzulo**
lapis lazuli

⑯ **il diaspro**
jasper

⑰ **l'occhio di tigre** *m*
tiger's eye

⑱ **la corniola**
carnelian

156.4 I METALLI · METALS

① **l'oro** *m*
gold

② **l'argento** *m*
silver

③ **il platino**
platinum

④ **il magnesio**
magnesium

⑤ **il ferro**
iron

⑥ **il rame**
copper

⑦ **lo stagno**
tin

⑧ **l'alluminio** *m*
aluminium

⑨ **il mercurio**
mercury

⑩ **il nichel**
nickel

⑪ **lo zinco**
zinc

⑫ **il cromo**
chromium

157.1 I PERIODI GEOLOGICI · GEOLOGICAL PERIODS

⑤ il trilobite
trilobite

⑩ la cooksonia
cooksonia

② i batteri
bacteria

④ la marrella
marrella

⑦ il ciclostoma
jawless fish

⑨ lo gnatostoma
jawed fish

① il Precambriano
Precambrian

③ il Cambriano
Cambrian

⑥ il trilobite m
Ordovician

⑧ il Siluriano
Silurian

㉖ i rettili volanti
flying reptiles

㉗ il brachiosauro
brachiosaurus

㉘ lo stegosauro
stegosaurus

㉚ il tyrannosaurus rex
tyrannosaurus rex

㉕ il Giurassico
Jurassic

㉛ il triceratopo
triceratops

㉜ l'albertonecte m
albertonectes

㉝ le angiosperme
flowering plants

㉟ il gastornis
gastornis

㉙ il Cretaceo
Cretaceous

㉞ il Paleogene
Paleogene

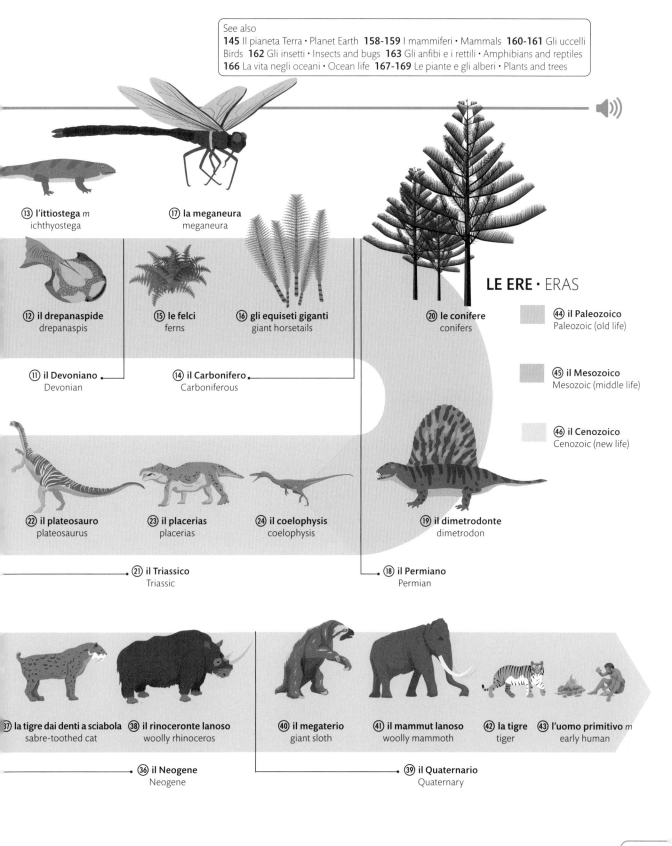

See also
145 Il pianeta Terra · Planet Earth **158-159** I mammiferi · Mammals **160-161** Gli uccelli
Birds **162** Gli insetti · Insects and bugs **163** Gli anfibi e i rettili · Amphibians and reptiles
166 La vita negli oceani · Ocean life **167-169** Le piante e gli alberi · Plants and trees

⑬ l'ittiostega *m*
ichthyostega

⑰ la meganeura
meganeura

⑫ il drepanaspide
drepanaspis

⑮ le felci
ferns

⑯ gli equiseti giganti
giant horsetails

⑳ le conifere
conifers

⑪ il Devoniano
Devonian

⑭ il Carbonifero
Carboniferous

LE ERE · ERAS

㊹ il Paleozoico
Paleozoic (old life)

㊺ il Mesozoico
Mesozoic (middle life)

㊻ il Cenozoico
Cenozoic (new life)

㉒ il plateosauro
plateosaurus

㉓ il placerias
placerias

㉔ il coelophysis
coelophysis

⑲ il dimetrodonte
dimetrodon

㉑ il Triassico
Triassic

⑱ il Permiano
Permian

㊲ la tigre dai denti a sciabola
sabre-toothed cat

㊳ il rinoceronte lanoso
woolly rhinoceros

㊵ il megaterio
giant sloth

㊶ il mammut lanoso
woolly mammoth

㊷ la tigre
tiger

㊸ l'uomo primitivo *m*
early human

㊱ il Neogene
Neogene

㊴ il Quaternario
Quaternary

158.1 LE SPECIE DI MAMMIFERI · SPECIES OF MAMMALS

② **il babbuino**
baboon

③ **l'oritteropo** *m*
aardvark

④ **il rinoceronte**
rhinoceros

① **l'impala** *m*
impala

⑧ **il ghepardo**
cheetah

⑨ **il leone**
lion

⑩ **la leonessa**
lioness

⑪ **la iena**
hyena

⑫ **la savana**
savannah

㉓ **il marsupio**
pouch

㉒ **il cucciolo di canguro**
joey

⑰ **l'ornitorinco** *m*
platypus

⑱ **l'echidna** *f*
echidna

⑲ **il diavolo della Tasmania**
Tasmanian devil

⑳ **il wombat**
wombat

㉑ **il canguro**
kangaroo

㉔ **il koala**
koala

㉕ **il coniglio**
rabbit

㉖ **il criceto**
hamster

㉘ **le vibrisse**
whiskers

㉗ **il topo**
mouse

㉙ **il ratto**
rat

㉚ **la coda**
tail

㉛ **il porcospino**
porcupine

㉜ **lo scoiattolo**
squirrel

㉝ **il riccio**
hedgehog

㉞ **lo scoiattolo volante**
flying squirrel

㉟ **il pipistrello**
bat

㊱ **la rossetta**
fruit bat

See also
157 La storia naturale • Natural history **159** I mammiferi (continua) • Mammals continued **164** Gli animali domestici • Pets **165** Gli animali da fattoria • Farm animals **166** La vita negli oceani • Ocean life

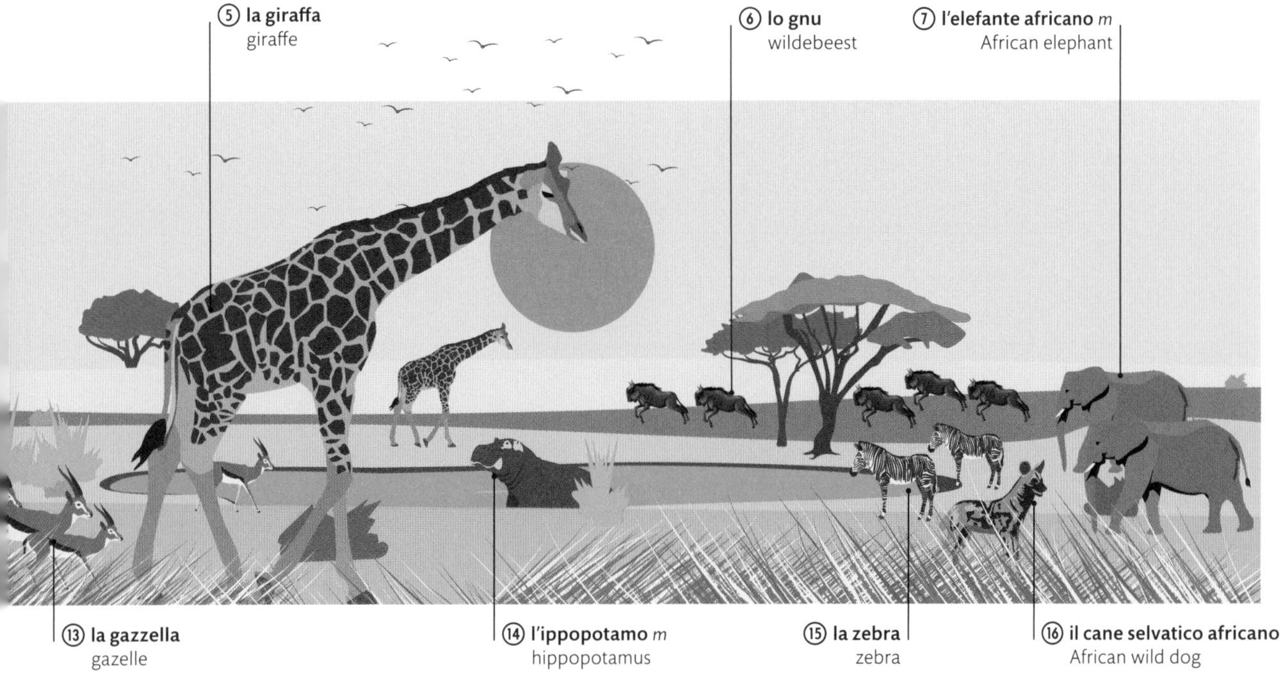
⑤ **la giraffa**
giraffe
⑥ **lo gnu**
wildebeest
⑦ **l'elefante africano** *m*
African elephant
⑬ **la gazzella**
gazelle
⑭ **l'ippopotamo** *m*
hippopotamus
⑮ **la zebra**
zebra
⑯ **il cane selvatico africano**
African wild dog

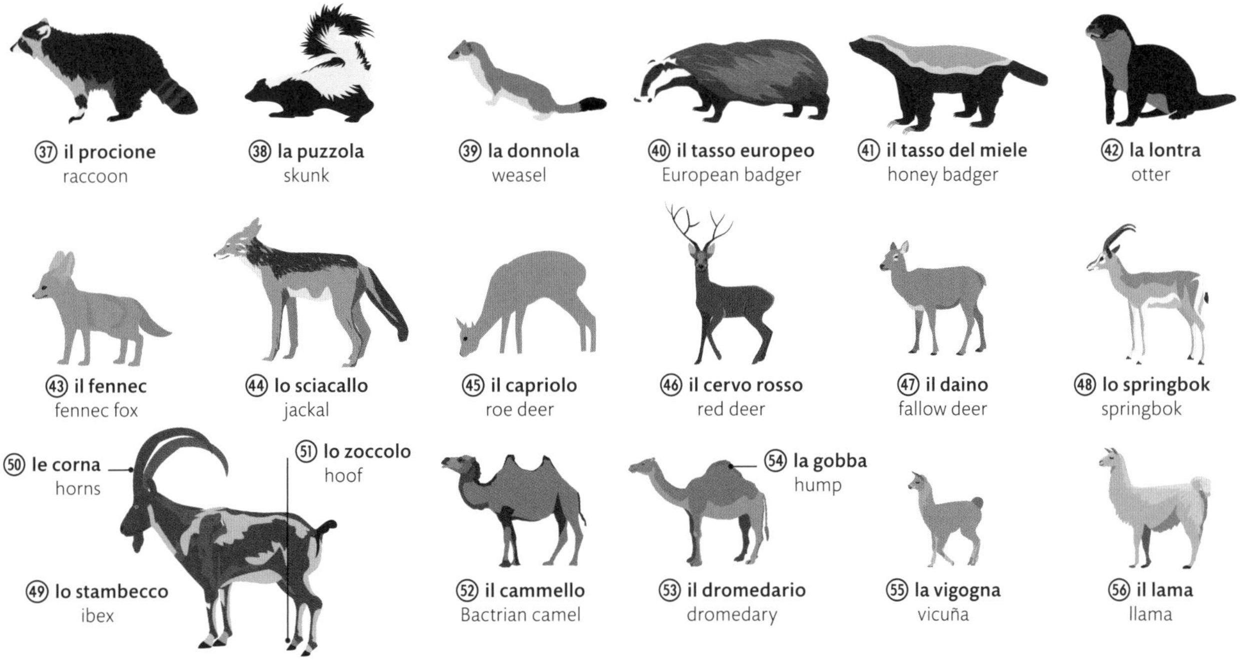
㊲ **il procione**
raccoon
㊳ **la puzzola**
skunk
㊴ **la donnola**
weasel
㊵ **il tasso europeo**
European badger
㊶ **il tasso del miele**
honey badger
㊷ **la lontra**
otter
㊸ **il fennec**
fennec fox
㊹ **lo sciacallo**
jackal
㊺ **il capriolo**
roe deer
㊻ **il cervo rosso**
red deer
㊼ **il daino**
fallow deer
㊽ **lo springbok**
springbok
㊿ **le corna**
horns
(51) **lo zoccolo**
hoof
㊾ **lo stambecco**
ibex
(52) **il cammello**
Bactrian camel
(53) **il dromedario**
dromedary
(54) **la gobba**
hump
(55) **la vigogna**
vicuña
(56) **il lama**
llama

159.1 LE SPECIE DI MAMMIFERI · SPECIES OF MAMMALS

① **la renna**
reindeer

② **il caribù**
caribou

③ **il lupo artico**
Arctic wolf

④ **la volpe artica**
Arctic fox

⑤ **il bue muschiato**
musk ox

⑪ **la volpe rossa**
red fox

⑩ **l'orso bruno** *m*
brown bear

⑧ **la foca**
seal

⑥ **l'orso polare** *m*
polar bear

⑦ **la lepre artica**
Arctic hare

⑨ **l'Artide** *f*
Arctic

⑮ **la foresta di latifoglie**
broadleaf forest

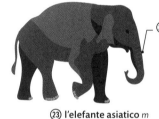

㉔ **la proboscide**
trunk

㉓ **l'elefante asiatico** *m*
Asian elephant

㉕ **il formichiere**
anteater

㉗ **il cucciolo** *m*
la cucciola *f*
cub

㉖ **la tigre**
tiger

㉘ **il leopardo**
leopard

㉟ **la coda**
tail

㉙ **il gatto selvatico**
wildcat

㉚ **la lince rossa**
bobcat

㉛ **il leopardo
delle nevi**
snow leopard

㉜ **il lemure dalla
coda ad anelli**
ring-tailed lemur

㉝ **la scimmia
cappuccina**
capuchin monkey

㉞ **la scimmia ragno**
spider monkey

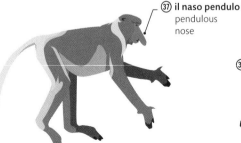

㊲ **il naso pendulo**
pendulous
nose

㊳ **il macaco**
macaque

㊴ **il mandrillo**
mandrill

㊵ **la marmosetta**
marmoset

㊶ **l'orangotango** *m*
orangutan

㊱ **la nasica**
proboscis monkey

㊷ **lo scimpanzé**
chimpanzee

㊸ **il gibbone**
gibbon

㊹ **il gorilla**
gorilla

㊺ **il panda**
panda

See also
157 La storia naturale • Natural history 164 Gli animali domestici • Pets
165 Gli animali da fattoria • Farm animals 166 La vita negli oceani • Ocean life

⑫ **la lince**
lynx
⑬ **il cinghiale**
boar
⑭ **il lupo**
wolf
⑯ **la scimmia urlatrice**
howler monkey
⑰ **il bradipo**
sloth
⑱ **la scimmia scoiattolo**
squirrel monkey
⑲ **il tapiro**
tapir
⑳ **il capibara**
capybara
㉑ **il giaguaro**
jaguar

㉒ **la foresta pluviale**
rain forest

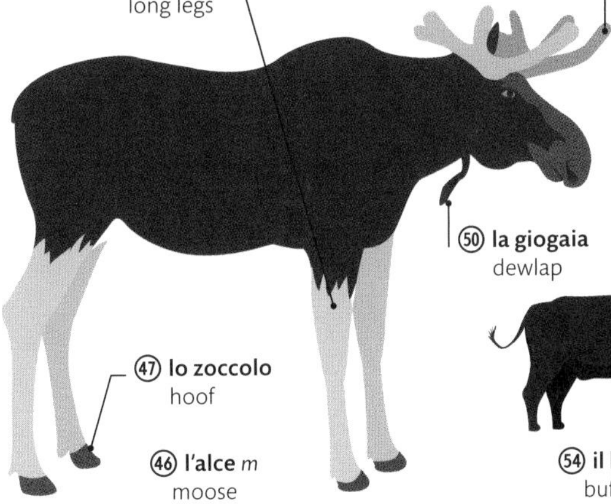
㊽ **le zampe lunghe**
long legs
㊾ **il palco**
antler
㊿ **la giogaia**
dewlap
㊼ **lo zoccolo**
hoof

㊻ **l'alce** *m*
moose

(51) **il pangolino**
pangolin

(52) **il panda rosso**
red panda

(53) **il facocero**
warthog

(54) **il bufalo**
buffalo

(55) **lo yak**
yak

(56) **l'orice** *m*
oryx

(57) **la capra delle nevi**
mountain goat

(58) **la talpa**
mole

(59) **lo scoiattolo striato**
chipmunk

(60) **la mangusta**
mongoose

(61) **l'armadillo** *m*
armadillo

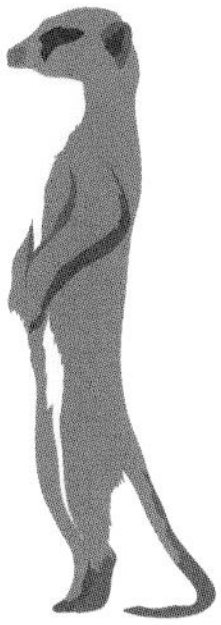
(62) **il suricato**
meerkat

(63) **cacciare**
to hunt

(64) **aggirarsi furtivamente**
to prowl

(65) **ruggire**
to roar

(66) **oscillare**
to swing

(67) **balzare**
to pounce

(68) **scavare una galleria**
to burrow

160.1 LE SPECIE DI UCCELLI · SPECIES OF BIRDS

① il picchio verde
green woodpecker

② il picchio nero
black woodpecker

③ il colibrì
hummingbird

④ il balestruccio
house martin

⑤ il gabbiano
seagull

⑧ la sterna artica
Arctic tern

⑥ il rondone
swift

⑦ la rondine riparia
sand martin

⑨ il picchio pileato
pileated woodpecker

⑩ il picchio
rosso maggiore
greater spotted
woodpecker

⑪ la coda
tail

⑫ la rondine
swallow

⑬ il canarino
canary

⑭ il parrocchetto
ondulato
budgerigar

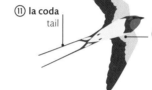

⑮ lo storno
starling

⑯ l'usignolo *m*
nightingale

⑰ il tessitore
weaverbird

⑱ l'acchiappamosche
vermiglio *m*
vermilion
flycatcher

⑲ l'albatro *m*
albatross

⑳ la fregata
frigate

㉑ l'aquila reale *f*
golden eagle

㉒ l'aquila calva *f*
bald eagle

㉓ il falco pescatore
osprey

㉔ il cormorano
cormorant

㉕ la sula
gannet

㉖ il condor
delle Ande
Andean condor

㉗ il falco pellegrino
peregrine falcon

㉘ l'avvoltoio *m*
vulture

㉙ l'aquila arpia *f*
harpy eagle

㉚ l'uria *f*
guillemot

㉛ la pulcinella
di mare
Atlantic puffin

See also
157 La storia naturale • Natural history **161** Gli uccelli (continua) Birds continued **165** Gli animali da fattoria • Farm animals

㉜ **il tucanetto smeraldino**
emerald toucan
㉝ **il tucano toco**
toco toucan
㉞ **il pettirosso europeo**
European robin
㉟ **lo scricciolo**
wren
㊱ **il passero**
sparrow
㊲ **il nido**
nest
㊳ **l'ibis scarlatto** *m*
scarlet ibis
㊴ **l'ibis sacro** *m*
sacred ibis
㊵ **il fringuello**
finch
㊶ **il piccione**
pigeon
㊷ **il merlo**
blackbird
㊸ **il corvo nero**
rook
㊹ **il corvo**
crow
㊺ **il tordo**
thrush
㊻ **il corvo imperiale**
raven
㊼ **l'uccello del paradiso** *m*
bird of paradise
㊽ **il pellicano**
pelican
㊾ **l'ostrichiere** *m*
oystercatcher
㊿ **il martin pescatore**
kingfisher
(51) **il kookaburra**
kookaburra
(52) **la cicogna**
stork
(53) **l'airone** *m*
heron
(54) **l'oca egiziana** *f*
Egyptian goose
(55) **l'oca canadese** *f*
Canada goose
(56) **l'oca delle nevi** *f*
snow goose
(57) **la gru**
crane
(58) **il fenicottero**
flamingo
(59) **lo struzzo**
ostrich
(60) **il kiwi**
kiwi
(61) **il casuario**
cassowary
(62) **l'emù** *m*
emu

161.1 LE SPECIE DI UCCELLI · SPECIES OF BIRDS

① il cacatua rosa
galah

② il pappagallo ecletto
eclectus parrot

③ il parrocchetto dal collare
rose-ringed parakeet

④ l'ara scarlatta *f*
scarlet macaw

⑤ il lorichetto
lorikeet

⑮ bubolare
to hoot

⑩ la civetta
delle navi
snowy owl

⑪ il gufo reale
eagle owl

⑫ il grande gufo grigio
great grey owl

⑬ il gufo crestato
crested owl

⑭ il barbagianni
barn owl

㉒ il cigno reale
mute swan

㉓ il cigno nero
black swan

㉔ il cigno selvatico
whooper swan

㉕ la folaga
coot

㉖ il germano reale
mallard

㉗ l'anatra mandarina *f*
mandarin duck

㉘ lo svasso
grebe

㉙ l'anatra sposa *f*
wood duck

㉚ il porciglione europeo
water rail

㉛ il chiurlo
curlew

㉜ il fagiano
pheasant

㉝ il tacchino
turkey

㉟ la ruota
feathers
displayed

㊱ il collo
neck

㉞ il pavone
peacock

See also
157 La storia naturale • Natural history
165 Gli animali da fattoria • Farm animals

⑨ Ho appena avvistato un'aquila reale!
I've just spotted a golden eagle!

⑥ **il cacatua**
cockatoo

⑦ **il pappagallo cenerino africano**
African grey parrot

⑧ **il bird watcher** *m*
la bird watcher *f*
bird-watcher

⑯ **l'allocco** *m*
tawny owl

⑰ **l'elfo dei cactus** *m*
elf owl

⑱ **il pulcino**
hatchling

⑲ **il guscio**
eggshell

⑳ **l'uccellino** *m*
fledgling

㉑ **il piumino**
soft down feathers

㊴ **l'ala** *f*
wing

㊵ **la cresta**
crest

㊶ **il becco**
bill / beak

㊳ **le piume della coda**
tail feathers

㊷ **l'artiglio** *m*
claw

㊲ **il cardinale rosso**
northern cardinal

㊸ **il pinguino imperatore**
emperor penguin

㊹ **il pinguino saltarocce**
rockhopper penguin

㊺ **il pinguino di Humboldt**
Humboldt penguin

㊻ **il pinguino Papua**
Gentoo penguin

㊼ **il pinguino minore blu**
Australian little penguin

161.2 **I VERBI**
VERBS

① **schiudersi**
to hatch

② **migrare**
to migrate

③ **sbattere**
to flap

④ **planare**
to glide

⑤ **scendere in picchiata**
to swoop

162.1 LE FARFALLE E LE FALENE · BUTTERFLIES AND MOTHS

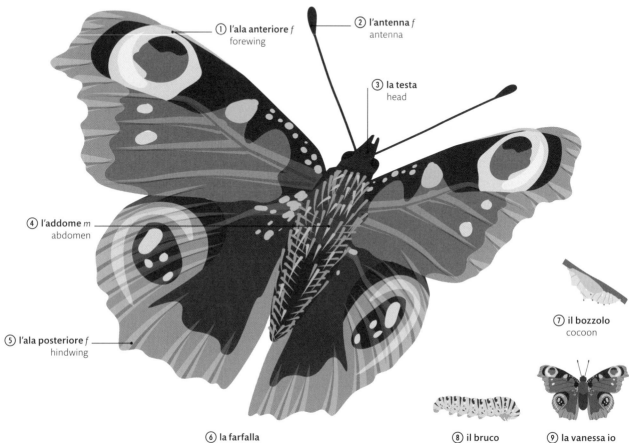

① l'ala anteriore *f*
forewing

② l'antenna *f*
antenna

③ la testa
head

④ l'addome *m*
abdomen

⑤ l'ala posteriore *f*
hindwing

⑥ la farfalla
butterfly

⑦ il bozzolo
cocoon

⑧ il bruco
caterpillar

⑨ la vanessa io
peacock butterfly

⑩ la farfalla
monarca
monarch butterfly

⑪ la vanessa del cardo
painted lady butterfly

⑫ la farfalla
papilionide
swallowtail butterfly

⑬ la farfalla dalle ali
di vetro
glasswing butterfly

⑭ la farfalla
cavolaia
cabbage white
butterfly

⑮ la farfalla
**punteggiata delle
betulle**
peppered moth

⑯ la falena di luna
luna moth

⑰ la sfinge del galio
hummingbird
hawksmoth

⑱ la falena
imperatrice
emperor moth

⑲ la farfalla cobra
atlas moth

⑳ la falena dei
vestiti
clothes moth

㉑ lo sfingide
hawk moth

See also
157 La storia naturale · Natural history **158-159** I mammiferi · Mammals
160-161 Gli uccelli · Birds **163** Gli anfibi e i rettili · Amphibians and reptiles

162.2 GLI ALTRI INSETTI E GLI INVERTEBRATI · OTHER BUGS AND INVERTEBRATES

① **il dinastino**
rhinoceros beetle

② **il cervo volante**
stag beetle

③ **il tonchio**
weevil

④ **lo scarafaggio**
cockroach

⑤ **la coccinella**
ladybird

⑥ **la mosca**
fly

⑦ **la cavalletta**
grasshopper

⑧ **la locusta**
locust

⑨ **il fillio**
leaf insect

⑩ **la mantide religiosa**
praying mantis

⑫ **il pungiglione**
sting

⑪ **lo scorpione**
scorpion

⑬ **il grillo**
cricket

⑭ **il centopiedi**
centipede

⑮ **il millepiedi**
millipede

⑯ **la libellula**
dragonfly

⑰ **la zanzara**
mosquito

⑱ **il verme**
worm

⑲ **la tarantola**
tarantula

⑳ **la vedova nera**
black widow spider

㉑ **il ragno saltatore**
jumping spider

㉒ **il ragno tessitore**
orb weaver

㉓ **la lumaca**
slug

㉔ **la chiocciola**
snail

㉕ **la termite**
termite

㉖ **la formica**
ant

㉗ **il bombo**
bumble bee

㉘ **la vespa**
wasp

㉙ **l'ape** f
honey bee

㉚ **pungere**
to sting

㉛ **volare**
to fly

㉜ **ronzare**
to buzz

㉝ **il nido di vespe**
wasp nest

㉞ **l'alveare** m
beehive

㉟ **lo sciame**
swarm

163.1 GLI ANFIBI · AMPHIBIANS

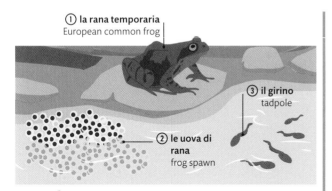

① **la rana temporaria**
European common frog

③ **il girino**
tadpole

② **le uova di rana**
frog spawn

④ **la rana volante di Wallace**
Wallace's flying frog

⑤ **la rana freccia**
poison dart frog

⑥ **la rana di Darwin**
Darwin's frog

⑦ **la raganella dagli occhi rossi**
red-eyed tree frog

⑧ **il rospo comune**
common toad

⑨ **la rana toro africana**
African bullfrog

⑩ **l'ululone dal ventre di fuoco** *m*
Oriental fire-bellied toad

⑪ **il rospo delle grandi pianure**
Great Plains toad

⑫ **la salamandra pezzata**
fire salamander

⑬ **il proteo**
olm

⑭ **l'axolotl** *m*
Mexican axolotl

⑮ **il tritone crestato**
great crested newt

⑯ **la salamandra rossa**
red salamander

163.2 I RETTILI · REPTILES

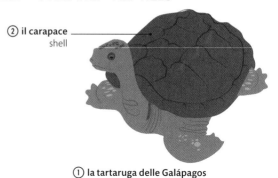

② **il carapace**
shell

① **la tartaruga delle Galápagos**
Galápagos turtle

③ **la testuggine raggiata**
radiated tortoise

④ **la mata mata**
matamata

⑤ **la tartaruga dal dorso di diamante**
diamond back terrapin

⑥ **la tartaruga dal collo di serpente**
common snake-necked turtle

⑦ **la tartaruga verde**
green sea turtle

⑧ **la tartaruga liuto**
leatherback sea turtle

⑨ **il camaleonte di Parson**
parson's chameleon

⑩ **il camaleonte del Madagascar**
panther chameleon

⑪ **il camaleonte di Jackson**
Jackson's chameleon

⑫ **il varano di Komodo**
Komodo dragon

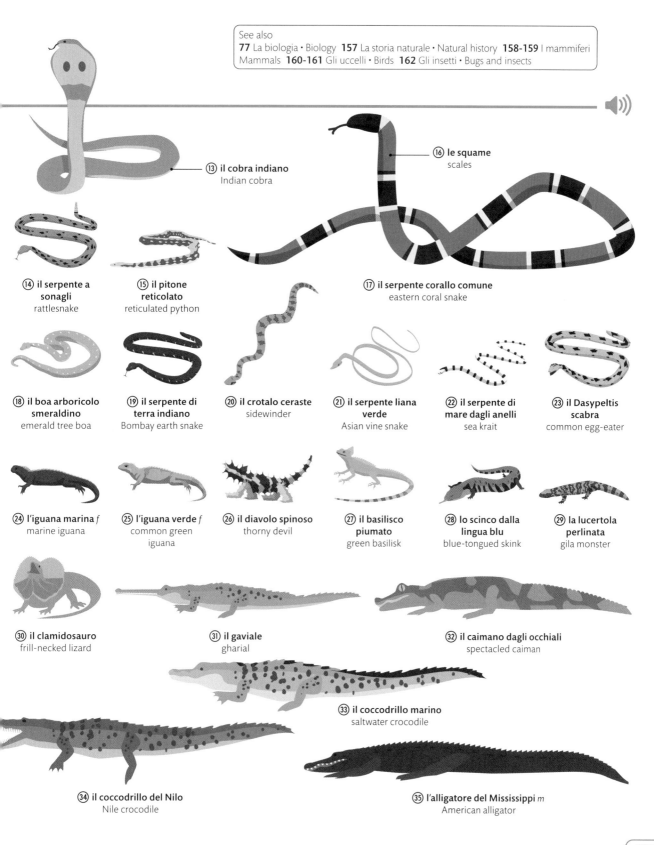

See also
77 La biologia • Biology **157** La storia naturale • Natural history **158-159** I mammiferi
Mammals **160-161** Gli uccelli • Birds **162** Gli insetti • Bugs and insects

⑬ **il cobra indiano**
Indian cobra

⑯ **le squame**
scales

⑰ **il serpente corallo comune**
eastern coral snake

⑭ **il serpente a sonagli**
rattlesnake

⑮ **il pitone reticolato**
reticulated python

⑱ **il boa arboricolo smeraldino**
emerald tree boa

⑲ **il serpente di terra indiano**
Bombay earth snake

⑳ **il crotalo ceraste**
sidewinder

㉑ **il serpente liana verde**
Asian vine snake

㉒ **il serpente di mare dagli anelli**
sea krait

㉓ **il Dasypeltis scabra**
common egg-eater

㉔ **l'iguana marina** *f*
marine iguana

㉕ **l'iguana verde** *f*
common green iguana

㉖ **il diavolo spinoso**
thorny devil

㉗ **il basilisco piumato**
green basilisk

㉘ **lo scinco dalla lingua blu**
blue-tongued skink

㉙ **la lucertola perlinata**
gila monster

㉚ **il clamidosauro**
frill-necked lizard

㉛ **il gaviale**
gharial

㉜ **il caimano dagli occhiali**
spectacled caiman

㉝ **il coccodrillo marino**
saltwater crocodile

㉞ **il coccodrillo del Nilo**
Nile crocodile

㉟ **l'alligatore del Mississippi** *m*
American alligator

164.1 LE RAZZE DI GATTI · CAT BREEDS

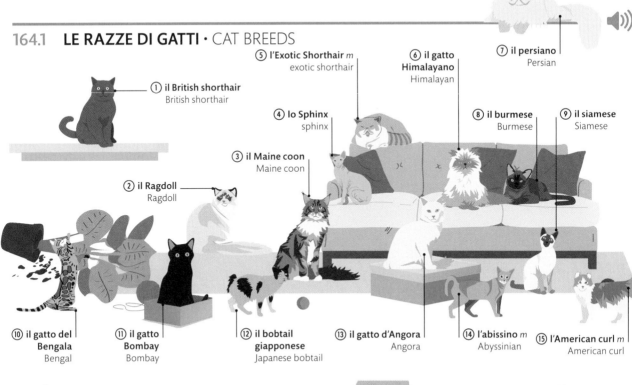

① il British shorthair
British shorthair

② il Ragdoll
Ragdoll

③ il Maine coon
Maine coon

④ lo Sphinx
sphinx

⑤ l'Exotic Shorthair *m*
exotic shorthair

⑥ il gatto Himalayano
Himalayan

⑦ il persiano
Persian

⑧ il burmese
Burmese

⑨ il siamese
Siamese

⑩ il gatto del Bengala
Bengal

⑪ il gatto Bombay
Bombay

⑫ il bobtail giapponese
Japanese bobtail

⑬ il gatto d'Angora
Angora

⑭ l'abissino *m*
Abyssinian

⑮ l'American curl *m*
American curl

⑯ miagolare
to meow

⑰ fare le fusa
to purr

⑱ nascondersi
to hide

⑲ fare la muta
to moult

⑳ il gattino *m*
la gattina *f*
kitten

164.3 GLI ALTRI ANIMALI DOMESTICI · OTHER PETS

④ squittire
to squeak

⑦ saltare
to hop

① il criceto
hamster

② il gerbillo
gerbil

③ il topo
mouse

⑤ il porcellino d'India
guinea pig

⑥ il coniglio
rabbit

⑧ il furetto
ferret

⑨ il pesce
fish

⑩ la lucertola
lizard

⑪ l'insetto stecco *m*
stick insect

⑫ la tartaruga
tortoise

⑬ il pappagallino
budgerigar / budgie

⑭ il cacatua
cockatiel

See also
158-159 I mammiferi · Mammals **160-161** Gli uccelli · Birds **162** Gli insetti
Insects and bugs **163** Gli anfibi e i rettili · Amphibians and reptiles

164.2 LE RAZZE DI CANI · DOG BREEDS

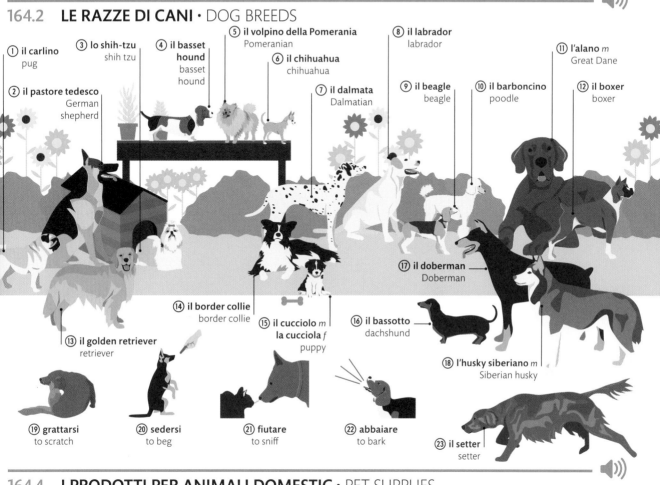

① **il carlino**
pug

② **il pastore tedesco**
German
shepherd

③ **lo shih-tzu**
shih tzu

④ **il basset
hound**
basset
hound

⑤ **il volpino della Pomerania**
Pomeranian

⑥ **il chihuahua**
chihuahua

⑦ **il dalmata**
Dalmatian

⑧ **il labrador**
labrador

⑨ **il beagle**
beagle

⑩ **il barboncino**
poodle

⑪ **l'alano** *m*
Great Dane

⑫ **il boxer**
boxer

⑰ **il doberman**
Doberman

⑬ **il golden retriever**
retriever

⑭ **il border collie**
border collie

⑮ **il cucciolo** *m*
la cucciola *f*
puppy

⑯ **il bassotto**
dachshund

⑱ **l'husky siberiano** *m*
Siberian husky

⑲ **grattarsi**
to scratch

⑳ **sedersi**
to beg

㉑ **fiutare**
to sniff

㉒ **abbaiare**
to bark

㉓ **il setter**
setter

164.4 I PRODOTTI PER ANIMALI DOMESTIC · PET SUPPLIES

① **l'acquario** *m*
fish tank /
aquarium

② **la cesta**
basket

③ **la cuccia**
kennel

④ **la gabbia**
cage

⑤ **la conigliera**
rabbit hutch

⑥ **la lettiera**
litter tray

⑦ **il guinzaglio**
leash / lead

⑧ **il terrario**
vivarium

⑨ **il becchime**
birdseed

⑩ **i premi**
treats

⑪ **i giocattoli**
toys

165.1 NELLA FATTORIA · ON THE FARM

② Do da mangiare ai polli
due volte al giorno.
I feed the chickens twice a day.

① **il pollo**
chicken

⑤ **la mucca**
cow

③ **la pecora**
sheep

④ **il pulcino**
chick

⑥ **l'agnello** *m*
lamb

⑭ **il gallo**
rooster /
cockerel

⑮ **la gallina**
hen

⑯ **il tacchino**
turkey

⑰ **il pollame**
poultry

㉑ **l'ape** *f*
bee

⑳ **l'arnia** *f*
hive

㉒ **il gregge di pecore**
flock of sheep

⑱ **il montone**
ram

⑲ **la pecora**
ewe

㉓ **la mandria di mucche**
herd of cows

㉔ **il toro**
bull

㉕ **il vitello** *m*
la vitella *f*
calf

㉖ **il bestiame**
cattle

㉗ **l'asino** *m*
donkey

See also
53 La carne · Meat **86** L'agricoltura · Farming
158-159 I mammiferi · Mammals **164** Gli animali domestici · Pets

⑦ **il cavallo**
horse

⑧ **l'oca** *f*
goose

⑨ **l'ochetta** *f*
gosling

⑩ **il maiale**
pig

⑪ **il maialino**
piglet

⑫ **l'anatra** *f*
duck

⑬ **l'anatroccolo** *m*
duckling

㉘ **lo stallone**
stallion

㉙ **la giumenta**
mare

㉚ **il puledro** *m*
la puledra *f*
foal

㉛ **la capra**
goat

㉜ **il capretto** *m*
la capretta *f*
kid

㉝ **lo struzzo**
ostrich

㉞ **il lama**
llama

㉟ **l'alpaca** *m*
alpaca

㊱ **tosare**
to shear

㊲ **trottare**
to trot

㊳ **galoppare**
to gallop

㊴ **caricare**
to charge

㊵ **cantare**
to crow

㊶ **belare**
to bleat

㊷ **sbuffare**
to snort

㊸ **grugnire**
to grunt

㊹ **ragliare**
to bray

㊺ **fare qua qua**
to quack

166.1 LE SPECIE MARINE · MARINE SPECIES

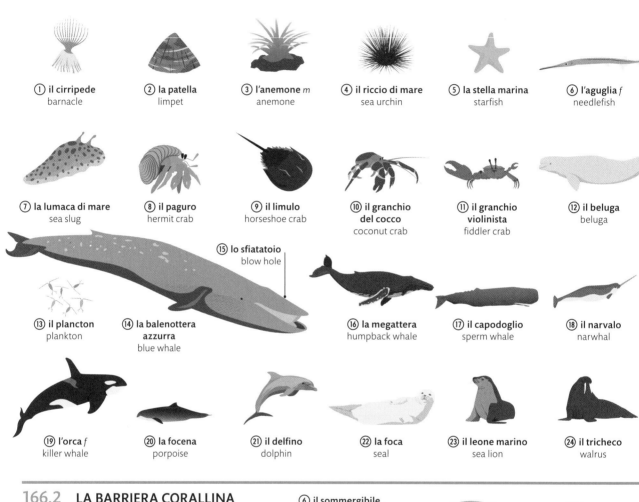

① il cirripede
barnacle

② la patella
limpet

③ l'anemone *m*
anemone

④ il riccio di mare
sea urchin

⑤ la stella marina
starfish

⑥ l'aguglia *f*
needlefish

⑦ la lumaca di mare
sea slug

⑧ il paguro
hermit crab

⑨ il limulo
horseshoe crab

⑩ il granchio
del cocco
coconut crab

⑪ il granchio
violinista
fiddler crab

⑫ il beluga
beluga

⑮ lo sfiatatoio
blow hole

⑬ il plancton
plankton

⑭ la balenottera
azzurra
blue whale

⑯ la megattera
humpback whale

⑰ il capodoglio
sperm whale

⑱ il narvalo
narwhal

⑲ l'orca *f*
killer whale

⑳ la focena
porpoise

㉑ il delfino
dolphin

㉒ la foca
seal

㉓ il leone marino
sea lion

㉔ il tricheco
walrus

166.2 LA BARRIERA CORALLINA
CORAL REEF

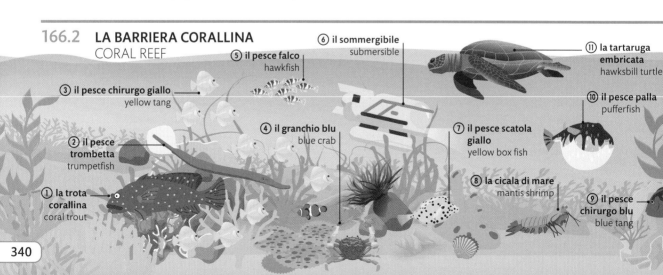

⑥ il sommergibile
submersible

⑤ il pesce falco
hawkfish

⑪ la tartaruga
embricata
hawksbill turtle

③ il pesce chirurgo giallo
yellow tang

⑩ il pesce palla
pufferfish

② il pesce
trombetta
trumpetfish

④ il granchio blu
blue crab

⑦ il pesce scatola
giallo
yellow box fish

① la trota
corallina
coral trout

⑧ la cicala di mare
mantis shrimp

⑨ il pesce
chirurgo blu
blue tang

See also
54 Il pesce e i frutti di mare • Fish and seafood **121** La pesca
Fishing **134** In spiaggia • On the beach **146-147** La geografia
Geography **157** La storia naturale • Natural history

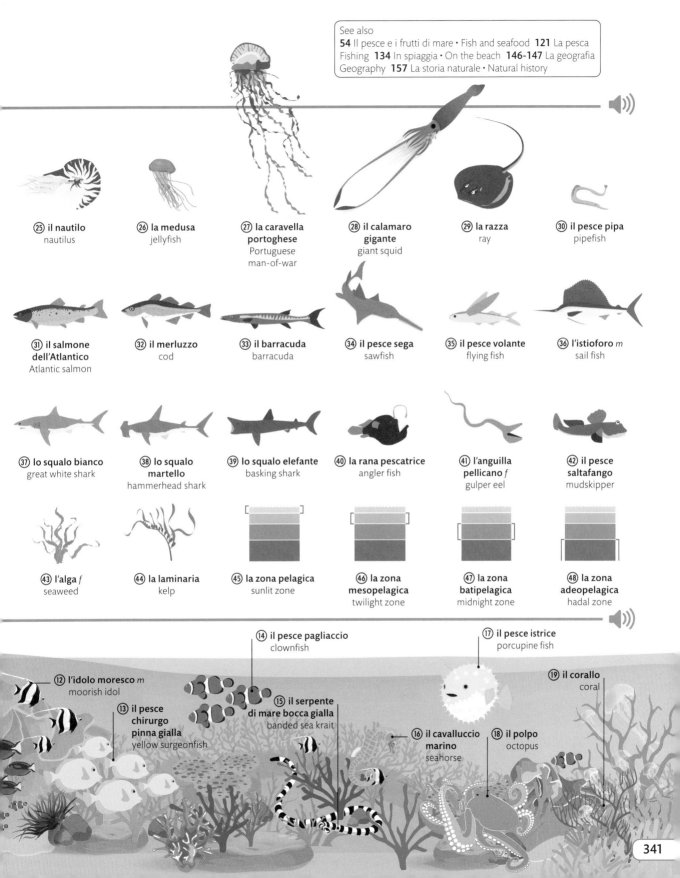

㉕ **il nautilo**
nautilus

㉖ **la medusa**
jellyfish

㉗ **la caravella portoghese**
Portuguese man-of-war

㉘ **il calamaro gigante**
giant squid

㉙ **la razza**
ray

㉚ **il pesce pipa**
pipefish

㉛ **il salmone dell'Atlantico**
Atlantic salmon

㉜ **il merluzzo**
cod

㉝ **il barracuda**
barracuda

㉞ **il pesce sega**
sawfish

㉟ **il pesce volante**
flying fish

㊱ **l'istioforo** *m*
sail fish

㊲ **lo squalo bianco**
great white shark

㊳ **lo squalo martello**
hammerhead shark

㊴ **lo squalo elefante**
basking shark

㊵ **la rana pescatrice**
angler fish

㊶ **l'anguilla pellicano** *f*
gulper eel

㊷ **il pesce saltafango**
mudskipper

㊸ **l'alga** *f*
seaweed

㊹ **la laminaria**
kelp

㊺ **la zona pelagica**
sunlit zone

㊻ **la zona mesopelagica**
twilight zone

㊼ **la zona batipelagica**
midnight zone

㊽ **la zona adeopelagica**
hadal zone

⑭ **il pesce pagliaccio**
clownfish

⑰ **il pesce istrice**
porcupine fish

⑫ **l'idolo moresco** *m*
moorish idol

⑲ **il corallo**
coral

⑬ **il pesce chirurgo pinna gialla**
yellow surgeonfish

⑮ **il serpente di mare bocca gialla**
banded sea krait

⑯ **il cavalluccio marino**
seahorse

⑱ **il polpo**
octopus

341

167.1 LE PIANTE E GLI ALBERI · PLANTS AND TREES

① l'epatica *f*
liverwort

② il muschio
moss

③ l'equiseto *m*
horsetail

④ la felce
fern

⑤ la cycas
cycad

⑥ il gingko
ginkgo

⑦ il peccio
spruce

⑧ l'abete *m*
fir

⑨ l'araucaria *f*
monkey puzzle

⑩ il tasso
yew

⑪ le conifere
conifers

⑫ il larice
larch

⑬ il cedro del **Libano**
cedar of Lebanon

⑭ il pino domestico
umbrella pine

⑮ la ninfea
water lily

⑯ la magnolia
magnolia

⑰ l'albero di **avocado** *m*
avocado tree

⑱ l'alloro *m*
laurel

⑲ la calla
arum lily

⑳ la sequoia **gigante**
giant sequoia

㉖ il bucaneve
snowdrop

㉑ l'albero di Giosuè *m*
Joshua tree

㉒ l'amarillide *f*
amaryllis

㉓ l'aspidistra *f*
cast-iron plant

㉔ la dracena
dragon tree

㉕ la campanula
English bluebell

㉗ il croco
crocus

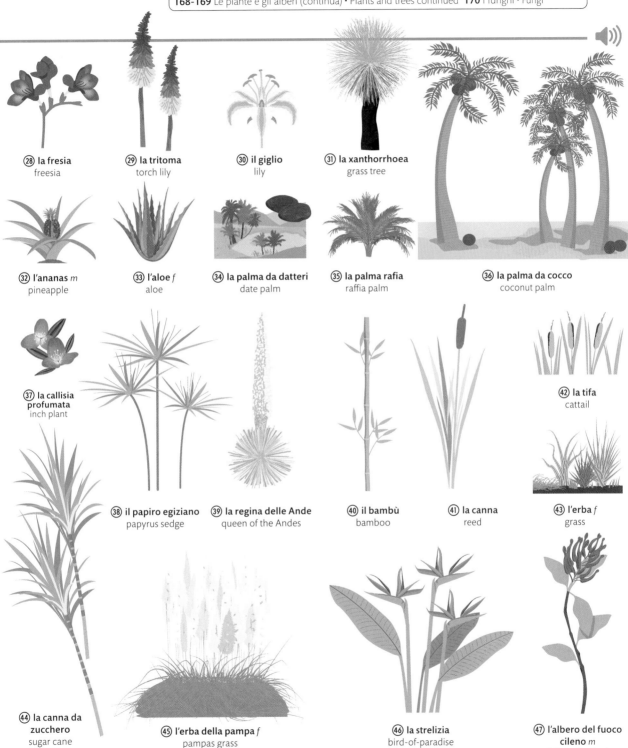

See also
38 Le piante da giardino e le piante da appartamento • Garden plants and houseplants **57** La frutta
Fruit **58** La frutta e la frutta a guscio • Fruit and nuts **157** La storia naturale • Natural history
168-169 Le piante e gli alberi (continua) • Plants and trees continued **170** I funghi • Fungi

㉘ **la fresia**
freesia

㉙ **la tritoma**
torch lily

㉚ **il giglio**
lily

㉛ **la xanthorrhoea**
grass tree

㉜ **l'ananas** *m*
pineapple

㉝ **l'aloe** *f*
aloe

㉞ **la palma da datteri**
date palm

㉟ **la palma rafia**
raffia palm

㊱ **la palma da cocco**
coconut palm

㊲ **la callisia
profumata**
inch plant

㊳ **il papiro egiziano**
papyrus sedge

㊴ **la regina delle Ande**
queen of the Andes

㊵ **il bambù**
bamboo

㊶ **la canna**
reed

㊷ **l'erba** *f*
grass

㊸ **la tifa**
cattail

㊹ **la canna da
zucchero**
sugar cane

㊺ **l'erba della pampa** *f*
pampas grass

㊻ **la strelizia**
bird-of-paradise

㊼ **l'albero del fuoco
cileno** *m*
Chilean fire bush

343

168.1 LE PIANTE E GLI ALBERI · PLANTS AND TREES

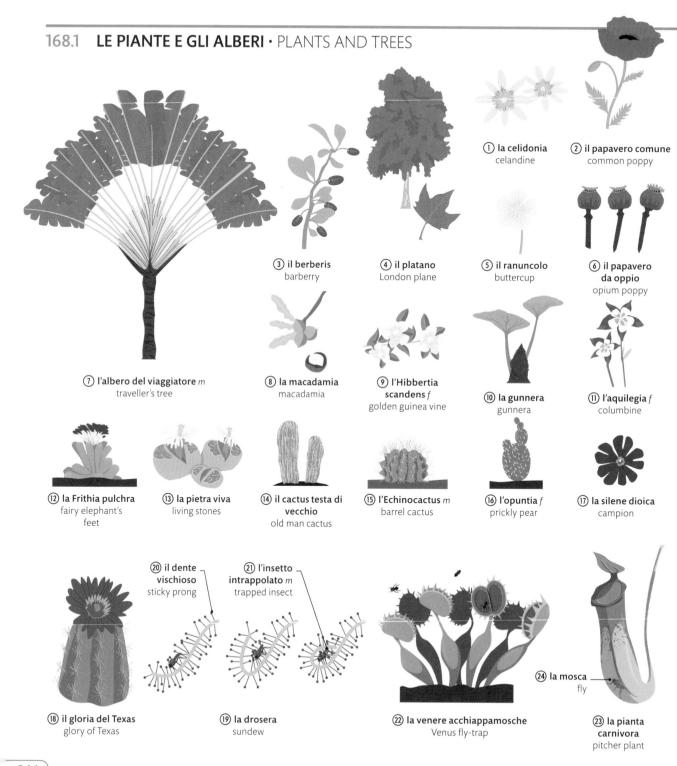

① la celidonia
celandine

② il papavero comune
common poppy

③ il berberis
barberry

④ il platano
London plane

⑤ il ranuncolo
buttercup

⑥ il papavero da oppio
opium poppy

⑦ l'albero del viaggiatore m
traveller's tree

⑧ la macadamia
macadamia

⑨ l'Hibbertia scandens f
golden guinea vine

⑩ la gunnera
gunnera

⑪ l'aquilegia f
columbine

⑫ la Frithia pulchra
fairy elephant's feet

⑬ la pietra viva
living stones

⑭ il cactus testa di vecchio
old man cactus

⑮ l'Echinocactus m
barrel cactus

⑯ l'opuntia f
prickly pear

⑰ la silene dioica
campion

⑳ il dente vischioso
sticky prong

㉑ l'insetto intrappolato m
trapped insect

㉔ la mosca
fly

⑱ il gloria del Texas
glory of Texas

⑲ la drosera
sundew

㉒ la venere acchiappamosche
Venus fly-trap

㉓ la pianta carnivora
pitcher plant

See also
38 Le piante da giardino e le piante da appartamento • Garden plants and houseplants **57** La frutta • Fruit **58** La frutta e la frutta a guscio • Fruit and nuts **157** La storia naturale • Natural history **169** Le piante e gli alberi (continua) • Plants and trees continued **170** I funghi • Fungi

㉕ **la bougainville**
bougainvillea

㉖ **l'albero di fuoco** *m*
fire tree

㉗ **il vischio**
mistletoe

㉘ **il semprevivo maggiore**
common houseleek

㉙ **la vite**
grapevine

㉚ **la Kalanchoe daigremontiana**
mother of thousands

㉛ **la peonia**
peony

㉜ **la vite americana**
Virginia creeper

㉝ **il mirto**
myrtle

㉞ **il melograno**
pomegranate

㉟ **la salcerella**
purple loosestrife

㊱ **l'henna** *f*
henna

㊲ **la Melaleuca subulata**
Tonghi bottlebrush

㊳ **la guava**
guava

㊴ **la fucsia**
fuchsia

㊵ **la mimosa**
mimosa

㊶ **l'acacia di Costantinopoli** *f*
silk tree

㊷ **il carpino**
hornbeam

㊸ **il nocciolo**
hazel

㊹ **il seme**
seed

㊺ **il noce**
walnut

㊻ **il castagno**
Spanish chestnut

㊼ **l'albero di pecan** *m*
pecan

㊽ **il faggio**
beech

㊾ **la betulla**
birch

㊿ **il pioppo**
poplar

345

169.1 LE PIANTE E GLI ALBERI · PLANTS AND TREES

② **la ghianda**
acorn

③ **l'Olneya tesota** *m*
desert ironwood
tree

④ **il ricino**
castor oil plant

⑤ **il salice**
willow

⑥ **la mangrovia**
mangrove

① **la quercia**
oak

⑦ **l'albero della gomma** *m*
rubber tree

⑧ **il fiore della passione**
passion flower

⑨ **il salice grigio**
grey willow

⑩ **l'olivello spinoso** *m*
sea buckthorn

⑱ **il fiore**
blossom

⑰ **il ramo**
branch

⑯ **le ciliegie**
cherries

⑪ **il pero**
pear

⑫ **il melo selvatico**
crab apple

⑬ **il prugno**
plum

⑭ **il fico**
fig

⑮ **il ciliegio**
cherry

⑲ **l'olivastro** *m*
oleaster

⑳ **la canapa**
hemp

㉑ **il luppolo**
hop

㉒ **la rosa canina**
dog rose

See also
38 Le piante da giardino e le piante da appartamento • Garden plants and houseplants **57** La frutta • Fruit **58** La frutta e la frutta a guscio • Fruit and nuts **157** La storia naturale • Natural history **170** I funghi • Fungi

㉓ **il cotonastro**
cotoneaster

㉔ **il sorbo**
mountain ash

㉕ **il nespolo**
medlar

㉖ **il biancospino**
hawthorn

㉗ **l'olmo** *m*
elm

㉘ **l'ortica** *f*
nettle

㊸ **la samara**
samara

㉙ **il nasturzio**
nasturtium

㉚ **la violacciocca**
wallflower

㉛ **l'ibisco cinese** *m*
Chinese hibiscus

㉜ **il cacao**
cocoa

㉝ **il tiglio**
lime / linden

㉞ **la primula**
cowslip

㉟ **il mogano cinese**
Chinese mahogany

㊱ **il baobab**
baobab tree

㊷ **la foglia estiva**
summer leaf

㊲ **l'acero** *m*
maple

㊳ **l'ippocastano** *m*
horse chestnut

㊴ **l'oleandro** *m*
oleander

㊵ **l'olivo** *m*
olive

㊶ **il sicomoro**
sycamore

㊹ **la foglia autunnale**
autumn leaf

㊺ **la campanula**
morning glory

㊻ **la belladonna**
deadly nightshade

㊼ **la cicuta**
hemlock

㊽ **il cardo**
thistle

㊾ **l'edera** *f*
ivy

㊿ **l'alchechengi** *m*
Chinese lantern

347

170.1 LE SPECIE DI FUNGHI · SPECIES OF FUNGI

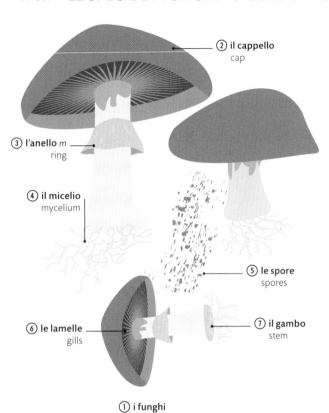

② **il cappello**
cap

③ **l'anello** *m*
ring

④ **il micelio**
mycelium

⑤ **le spore**
spores

⑥ **le lamelle**
gills

⑦ **il gambo**
stem

① **i funghi**
mushrooms

⑧ **l'Inonotus hispidus** *m*
shaggy bracket fungus

⑨ **andare a funghi**
to forage /
to pick mushrooms

⑭ **Alcuni funghi sono velenosi.
Controllo sempre prima
di raccoglierli.**
Some fungi are poisonous. I
always check before picking.

⑬ **la vescia**
common puffball

㉑ **i funghi coltivati**
cultivated mushrooms

㉒ **i funghi velenosi**
toadstools

㉓ **il cerchio delle
streghe**
fairy ring

㉔ **il Pleurotus
ostreatus**
oyster mushroom

㉕ **il boletus dal
cappello arancione**
orange-cap boletus

㉖ **il fungo
Laetiporus**
chicken of the woods

㉗ **l'Hydnum
repandum** *m*
hedgehog mushroom

㉘ **l'Hericium** *m*
bear's head tooth

㉙ **la trombetta
dei morti**
black trumpet

㉚ **il fungo
dell'inchiostro**
shaggy mane mushroom

㉛ **la grifola
frondosa**
hen of the wood

㉜ **la muffa**
mold

See also
55-56 La verdura • Vegetables   **133** Le attività all'aperto • Outdoor activities
167-169 Le piante e gli alberi • Plants and trees

⑩ **il fungo enoki**
enoki mushroom

⑪ **il fungo shiitake**
shiitake mushroom

⑫ **il cappello di cera**
waxcap

⑮ **la morchella**
morel

⑯ **la vescia gigante**
giant puffball

⑰ **il prataiolo**
field mushroom

⑱ **il tartufo**
truffle

⑲ **il porcino**
porcini

⑳ **il finferlo**
chanterelle

㉟ **l'Aleuria aurantia** *f*
orange peel fungus

㊱ **il satirione**
stinkhorn

㊲ **l'orecchio di lepre** *m*
hare's ear

㉝ **l'amanita falloide** *f*
death cap

㉞ **l'amanita virosa** *f*
death angel

㊳ **il fungo dell'olivo**
jack-o'-lantern

㊴ **lo Scleroderma citrinum**
common earthball

㊵ **il Conocybe apala**
milky conecap

㊶ **l'ovolo malefico** *m*
fly agaric

171.1 DIRE L'ORA · TELLING THE TIME

① **Che ore sono?**
What time is it?

② **Sono le tre.**
It's three o'clock.

③ **l'una** *f*
one o'clock

④ **l'una e cinque** *f*
five past one

⑤ **l'una e dieci** *f*
ten past one

⑥ **l'una e un quarto** *f*
quarter past one

⑦ **l'una e venti** *f*
twenty past one

⑧ **l'una e venticinque** *f*
twenty-five past one

⑨ **l'una e mezza** *f*
one thirty / half past one

⑩ **l'una e trentacinque**
twenty-five to two

⑪ **le due meno venti** *f*
twenty to two

⑫ **le due meno un quarto**
quarter to two

⑬ **le due meno dieci**
ten to two

⑭ **le due meno cinque**
five to two

⑮ **le due**
two o'clock

⑯ **il secondo**
second

⑰ **il minuto**
minute

⑱ **il quarto d'ora**
quarter of an hour

171.2 LE PARTI DEL GIORNO · PARTS OF THE DAY

① **l'alba** *f*
dawn

② **il sorgere del sole**
sunrise

③ **la mattina**
morning

④ **il mezzogiorno**
midday

⑤ **il pomeriggio**
afternoon

See also
172 Il calendario • The calendar **173** I numeri • Numbers
174 I pesi e le misure • Weights and measures

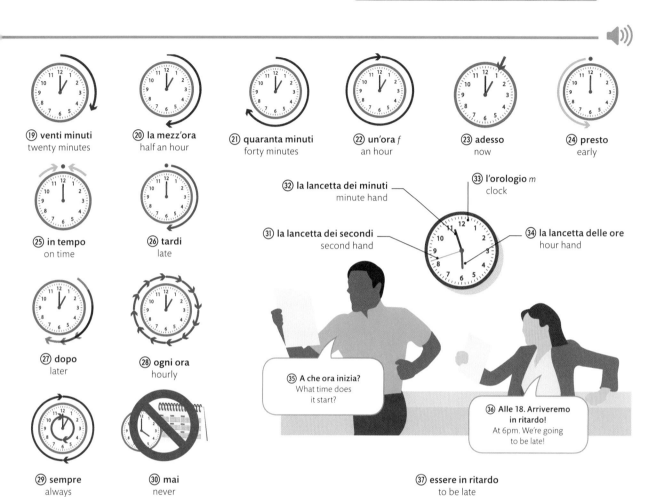

⑲ **venti minuti**
twenty minutes

⑳ **la mezz'ora**
half an hour

㉑ **quaranta minuti**
forty minutes

㉒ **un'ora** *f*
an hour

㉓ **adesso**
now

㉔ **presto**
early

㉕ **in tempo**
on time

㉖ **tardi**
late

㉗ **dopo**
later

㉘ **ogni ora**
hourly

㉙ **sempre**
always

㉚ **mai**
never

㉜ **la lancetta dei minuti**
minute hand

㉝ **l'orologio** *m*
clock

㉛ **la lancetta dei secondi**
second hand

㉞ **la lancetta delle ore**
hour hand

㉟ **A che ora inizia?**
What time does
it start?

㊱ **Alle 18. Arriveremo
in ritardo!**
At 6pm. We're going
to be late!

㊲ **essere in ritardo**
to be late

⑥ **la sera**
evening

⑦ **il tramonto**
sunset

⑧ **il crepuscolo**
dusk

⑨ **la mezzanotte**
midnight

⑩ **la notte**
night

⑪ **il giorno**
day

172.1 IL CALENDARIO E LE STAGIONI · CALENDAR AND SEASONS

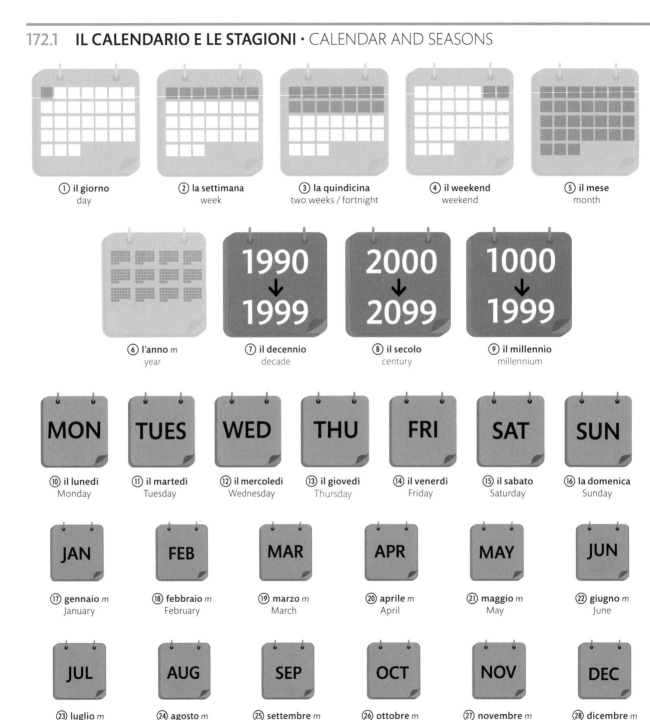

① **il giorno**
day

② **la settimana**
week

③ **la quindicina**
two weeks / fortnight

④ **il weekend**
weekend

⑤ **il mese**
month

⑥ **l'anno** *m*
year

⑦ **il decennio**
decade

⑧ **il secolo**
century

⑨ **il millennio**
millennium

⑩ **il lunedì**
Monday

⑪ **il martedì**
Tuesday

⑫ **il mercoledì**
Wednesday

⑬ **il giovedì**
Thursday

⑭ **il venerdì**
Friday

⑮ **il sabato**
Saturday

⑯ **la domenica**
Sunday

⑰ **gennaio** *m*
January

⑱ **febbraio** *m*
February

⑲ **marzo** *m*
March

⑳ **aprile** *m*
April

㉑ **maggio** *m*
May

㉒ **giugno** *m*
June

㉓ **luglio** *m*
July

㉔ **agosto** *m*
August

㉕ **settembre** *m*
September

㉖ **ottobre** *m*
October

㉗ **novembre** *m*
November

㉘ **dicembre** *m*
December

See also
171 Il tempo • Time
173 I numeri • Numbers

㉙ **millenovecento**
nineteen hundred

㉚ **millenovecentouno**
nineteen-oh-one

㉛ **millenovecentodieci**
nineteen ten

㉜ **duemila**
two thousand

㉝ **duemilauno**
two thousand and
one

㉞ **duemilatrentatré**
twenty thirty-three

㉟ **una volta alla
settimana**
once a week

㊱ **due volte alla
settimana**
twice a week

㊲ **tre volte alla
settimana**
three times a week

㊳ **ogni giorno**
every day

㊴ **ogni due giorni**
every other day

㊵ **soltanto il
weekend**
only weekends

㊶ **ogni ora**
hourly

㊷ **ogni giorno**
daily

㊸ **ogni settimana**
weekly

㊹ **ogni mese**
monthly

㊺ **la primavera**
spring

㊻ **le foglie nuove**
new leaves

㊼ **l'estate** *f*
summer

㊽ **il fogliame verde**
green foliage

㊾ **le stagioni**
seasons

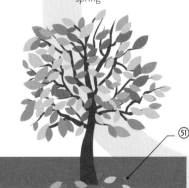

㊿ **l'autunno** *m*
autumn

㉑ **la caduta delle foglie**
leaf fall

㊾ **l'inverno** *m*
winter

㊾ **i rami spogli**
bare branches

173.1 I NUMERI CARDINALI · CARDINAL NUMBERS

1	**2**	**3**	**4**	**5**	**6**
① **uno** one	② **due** two	③ **tre** three	④ **quattro** four	⑤ **cinque** five	⑥ **sei** six

7	**8**	**9**	**10**	**11**	**12**
⑦ **sette** seven	⑧ **otto** eight	⑨ **nove** nine	⑩ **dieci** ten	⑪ **undici** eleven	⑫ **dodici** twelve

13	**14**	**15**	**16**	**17**	**18**
⑬ **tredici** thirteen	⑭ **quattordici** fourteen	⑮ **quindici** fifteen	⑯ **sedici** sixteen	⑰ **diciassette** seventeen	⑱ **diciotto** eighteen

19	**20**	**21**	**22**	**30**	**40**
⑲ **diciannove** nineteen	⑳ **venti** twenty	㉑ **ventuno** twenty-one	㉒ **ventidue** twenty-two	㉓ **trenta** thirty	㉔ **quaranta** forty

50	**60**	**70**	**80**	**90**	**100**	**0**
㉕ **cinquanta** fifty	㉖ **sessanta** sixty	㉗ **settanta** seventy	㉘ **ottanta** eighty	㉙ **novanta** ninety	㉚ **cento** one hundred	㉛ **zero** zero

173.2 I NUMERI ORDINALI · ORDINAL NUMBERS

1st	**2nd**	**3rd**	**4th**	**5th**	**6th**
① **primo** *m* / **prima** *f* first	② **secondo** *m* **seconda** *f* second	③ **terzo** *m* / **terza** *f* third	④ **quarto** *m* **quarta** *f* fourth	⑤ **quinto** *m* **quinta** *f* fifth	⑥ **sesto** *m* / **sesta** *f* sixth

7th	**8th**	**9th**	**10th**	**20th**	**21st**
⑦ **settimo** *m* **settima** *f* seventh	⑧ **ottavo** *m* **ottava** *f* eighth	⑨ **nono** *m* / **nona** *f* ninth	⑩ **decimo** *m* **decima** *f* tenth	⑪ **ventesimo** *m* **ventesima** *f* twentieth	⑫ **ventunesimo** *m* **ventunesima** *f* twenty-first

See also
74 La matematica • Mathematics **171** Il tempo • Time **172** Il calendario
The calendar **174** I pesi e le misure • Weights and measures

173.3 I GRANDI NUMERI · LARGE NUMBERS

200
① **duecento**
two hundred

250
② **duecentocinquanta**
two hundred and fifty

500
③ **cinquecento**
five hundred

750
④ **settecentocinquanta**
seven hundred and fifty

1,000
⑤ **mille**
one thousand

1,200
⑥ **milleduecento**
one thousand two
hundred

10,000
⑦ **diecimila**
ten thousand

100,000
⑧ **centomila**
one hundred thousand

1,000,000
⑨ **un milione**
one million

5,000,000
⑩ **cinque milioni**
five million

500,000,000
⑪ **cinquecento milioni / mezzo miliardo**
five hundred million / half a billion

1,000,000,000
⑫ **un miliardo**
one billion

3,846
⑬ **tremilaottocentoquarantasei**
three thousand, eight hundred and forty-six

82,043
⑭ **ottantaduemilaquarantatrè**
eighty-two thousand and forty-three

⑮ Ho perso
il conto!
I've lost count!

234,407
⑯ **duecentotrentaquattromila
quattrocentosette**
two hundred and thirty-four thousand,
four hundred and seven

3,089,342
⑰ **tre milioni ottantanovemila
trecentoquarantadue**
three million, eighty-nine thousand,
three hundred and forty-two

173.4 LE FRAZIONI, I DECIMALI E LE PERCENTUALI
FRACTIONS, DECIMALS, AND PERCENTAGES

⅛
① **un ottavo**
an eighth

¼
② **un quarto**
a quarter

⅓
③ **un terzo**
a third

½
④ **la metà**
a half

⅗
⑤ **i tre quinti**
three-fifths

⅞
⑥ **i sette ottavi**
seven-eighths

0.5
⑦ **zero virgola cinque**
nought point five

1.7
⑧ **uno virgola sette**
one point seven

3.97
⑨ **tre virgola
novantasette**
three point nine seven

1%
⑩ **uno percento**
one percent

99%
⑪ **novantanove
percento**
ninety-nine percent

100%
⑫ **cento percento**
one hundred percent

174.1 IL PESO · WEIGHT

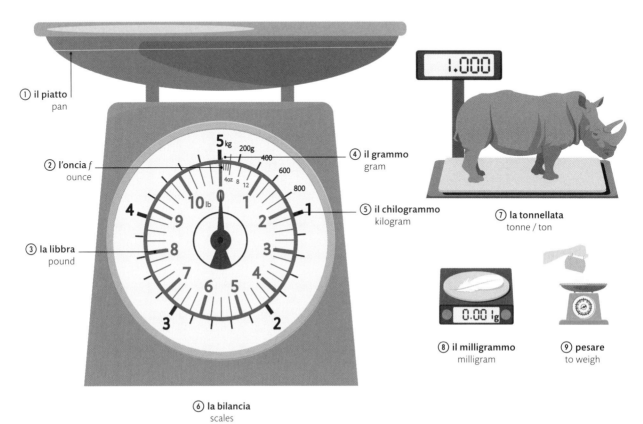

① il piatto
pan

② l'oncia *f*
ounce

③ la libbra
pound

④ il grammo
gram

⑤ il chilogrammo
kilogram

⑥ la bilancia
scales

⑦ la tonnellata
tonne / ton

⑧ il milligrammo
milligram

⑨ pesare
to weigh

174.2 LA DISTANZA, L'AREA E LA LUNGHEZZA · DISTANCE, AREA, AND LENGTH

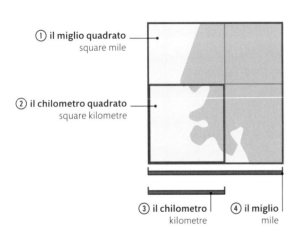

① il miglio quadrato
square mile

② il chilometro quadrato
square kilometre

③ il chilometro
kilometre

④ il miglio
mile

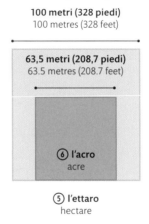

100 metri (328 piedi)
100 metres (328 feet)

63,5 metri (208,7 piedi)
63.5 metres (208.7 feet)

⑥ l'acro
acre

⑤ l'ettaro
hectare

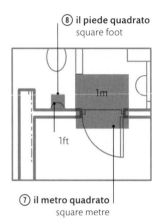

⑧ il piede quadrato
square foot

1m

1ft

⑦ il metro quadrato
square metre

See also
29 Cucinare · Cooking **35** I lavori di miglioria della casa · Home improvements **74** La matematica · Mathematics **173** I numeri · Numbers

174.3 LE MISURE / IL VOLUME DEI LIQUIDI · LIQUID MEASUREMENTS / VOLUME

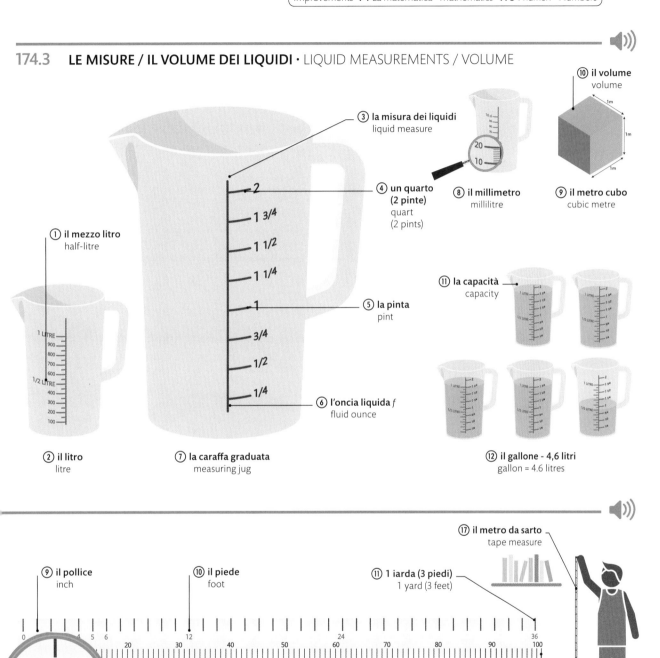

③ **la misura dei liquidi**
liquid measure

⑩ **il volume**
volume

④ **un quarto (2 pinte)**
quart (2 pints)

⑧ **il millimetro**
millilitre

⑨ **il metro cubo**
cubic metre

① **il mezzo litro**
half-litre

⑤ **la pinta**
pint

⑪ **la capacità**
capacity

⑥ **l'oncia liquida** *f*
fluid ounce

② **il litro**
litre

⑦ **la caraffa graduata**
measuring jug

⑫ **il gallone - 4,6 litri**
gallon = 4.6 litres

⑰ **il metro da sarto**
tape measure

⑨ **il pollice**
inch

⑩ **il piede**
foot

⑪ **1 iarda (3 piedi)**
1 yard (3 feet)

⑫ **il millimetro**
millimetre

⑭ **il righello**
ruler

⑮ **il metro**
metre

⑬ **il centimetro**
centimetre

⑯ **misurare**
to measure

357

175.1 LA SCRITTURA E IL MATERIALE PER SCRIVERE · WRITING AND WRITING EQUIPMENT

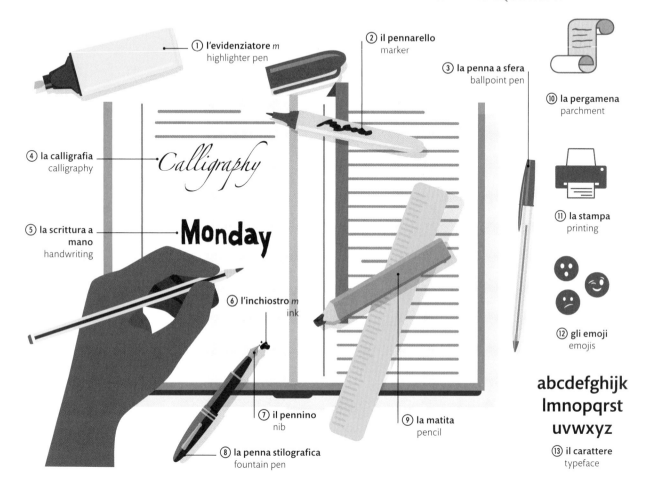

① **l'evidenziatore** *m*
highlighter pen

② **il pennarello**
marker

③ **la penna a sfera**
ballpoint pen

④ **la calligrafia**
calligraphy

⑤ **la scrittura a mano**
handwriting

⑥ **l'inchiostro** *m*
ink

⑦ **il pennino**
nib

⑧ **la penna stilografica**
fountain pen

⑨ **la matita**
pencil

⑩ **la pergamena**
parchment

⑪ **la stampa**
printing

⑫ **gli emoji**
emojis

⑬ **il carattere**
typeface

⑭ **le lettere**
letters

⑮ **le lettere maiuscole**
uppercase / capital letters

⑯ **le lettere minuscole**
lowercase

⑰ **il grassetto**
bold

⑱ **il corsivo**
italic

⑲ **le cifre**
numerals

⑳ **la legatura**
ligature

㉑ **il punto**
full stop

㉒ **il trattino**
hyphen

㉓ **la lineetta**
dash

㉔ **il trattino basso**
underscore

㉕ **la virgola**
comma

See also
73 A scuola · At school
138 I libri e la lettura · Books and reading

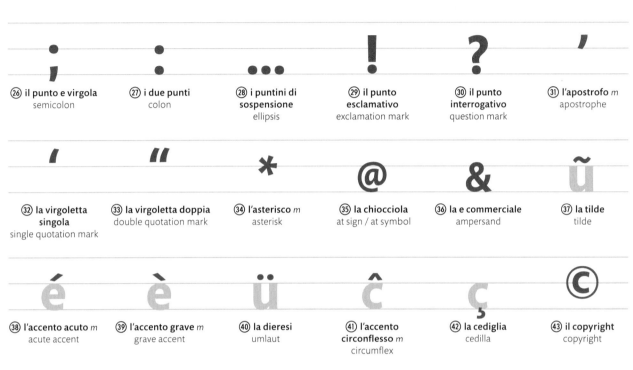

26 il punto e virgola
semicolon

27 i due punti
colon

28 i puntini di sospensione
ellipsis

29 il punto esclamativo
exclamation mark

30 il punto interrogativo
question mark

31 l'apostrofo *m*
apostrophe

32 la virgoletta singola
single quotation mark

33 la virgoletta doppia
double quotation mark

34 l'asterisco *m*
asterisk

35 la chiocciola
at sign / at symbol

36 la e commerciale
ampersand

37 la tilde
tilde

38 l'accento acuto *m*
acute accent

39 l'accento grave *m*
grave accent

40 la dieresi
umlaut

41 l'accento circonflesso *m*
circumflex

42 la cediglia
cedilla

43 il copyright
copyright

44 il marchio registrato
registered trademark

45 le parentesi
brackets

46 l'hashtag *m*
hashtag

47 l'alfabeto latino *m*
Latin alphabet

48 l'alfabeto greco *m*
Greek alphabet

49 l'alfabeto cirillico *m*
Cyrillic alphabet

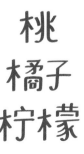

50 il Braille
Braille

51 i caratteri arabi
Arabic script

52 i caratteri giapponesi
Japanese characters

53 i caratteri cinesi
Chinese characters

54 l'alfabeto devanagari *m*
Devanagari script

55 i geroglifici dell'Antico Egitto
Ancient Egyptian hieroglyphs

176.1 **I MATERIALI** · MATERIALS

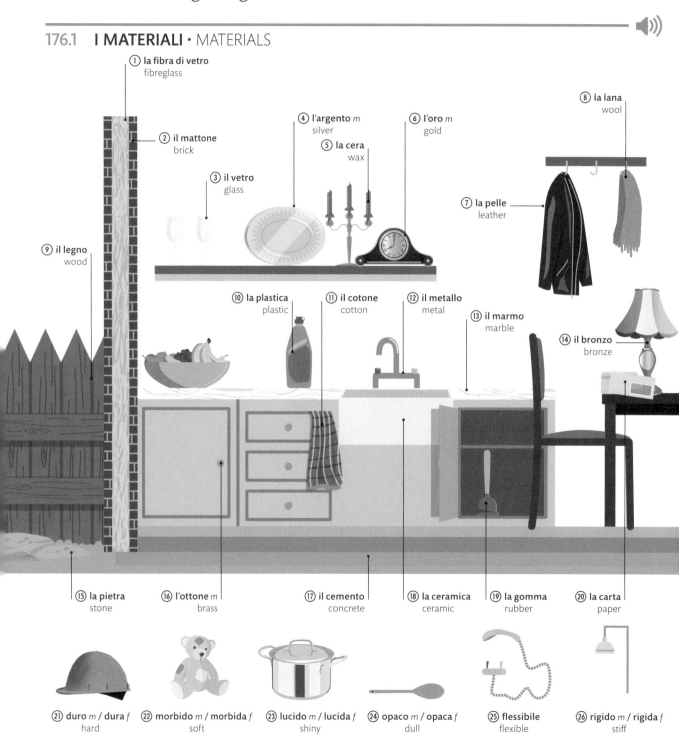

1. **la fibra di vetro** fibreglass
2. **il mattone** brick
3. **il vetro** glass
4. **l'argento** *m* silver
5. **la cera** wax
6. **l'oro** *m* gold
7. **la pelle** leather
8. **la lana** wool
9. **il legno** wood
10. **la plastica** plastic
11. **il cotone** cotton
12. **il metallo** metal
13. **il marmo** marble
14. **il bronzo** bronze
15. **la pietra** stone
16. **l'ottone** *m* brass
17. **il cemento** concrete
18. **la ceramica** ceramic
19. **la gomma** rubber
20. **la carta** paper
21. **duro** *m* / **dura** *f* hard
22. **morbido** *m* / **morbida** *f* soft
23. **lucido** *m* / **lucida** *f* shiny
24. **opaco** *m* / **opaca** *f* dull
25. **flessibile** flexible
26. **rigido** *m* / **rigida** *f* stiff

See also
32 La casa · House and home **35** I lavori di miglioria della casa · Home improvements
37 La decorazione · Decorating **87** Le costruzioni · Construction **177** Descrivere le cose (continua) · Describing things continued

176.2 **GLI AGGETTIVI** · ADJECTIVES

① **grande**
big / large

② **piccolo** *m* **piccola** *f*
small / little

③ **largo** *m* / **larga** *f*
wide

④ **stretto** *m* / **stretta** *f*
narrow

⑤ **profondo** *m* **profonda** *f*
deep

⑥ **poco profondo** *m* **poco profonda** *f*
shallow

⑦ **alto** *m* / **alta** *f*
high

⑧ **basso** *m* / **bassa** *f*
low

⑨ **pesante**
heavy

⑩ **leggero** *m* / **leggera** *f*
light

⑪ **pulito** *m* / **pulita** *f*
clean

⑫ **sporco** *m* / **sporca** *f*
dirty

⑬ **caldo** *m* / **calda** *f*
hot

⑭ **freddo** *m* / **fredda** *f*
cold

⑮ **lungo** *m* / **lunga** *f*
long

⑯ **corto** *m* / **corta** *f*
short

⑰ **allentato** *m* **allentata** *f*
loose

⑱ **stretto** *m* / **stretta** *f*
tight

⑲ **sottile**
thin

⑳ **spesso** *m* / **spessa** *f*
thick

㉑ **vicino** *m* / **vicina** *f*
near

㉒ **lontano** *m* / **lontana** *f*
far

㉓ **lento** *m* / **lenta** *f*
slow

㉔ **veloce**
fast

㉕ **nuovo** *m* / **nuova** *f*
new

㉖ **vecchio** *m* **vecchia** *f*
old

㉗ **vuoto** *m* / **vuota** *f*
empty

㉘ **pieno** *m* / **piena** *f*
full

㉙ **rumoroso** *m* **rumorosa** *f*
noisy

㉚ **silenzioso** *m* **silenziosa** *f*
quiet

㉛ **giusto** *m* / **giusta** *f*
correct

㉜ **sbagliato** *m* **sbagliata** *f*
incorrect

㉝ **luminoso** *m* **luminosa** *f*
light

㉞ **scuro** *m* / **scura** *f*
dark

177.1 LE OPINIONI · OPINIONS

② **La vista da qui è davvero mozzafiato.**
The view here is
absolutely breathtaking.

③ **entusiasmante**
exciting

① **mozzafiato**
breathtaking

④ **stupendo** *m*
stupenda *f*
beautiful

⑤ **elettrizzante**
thrilling

⑥ **divertente**
fun

⑦ **romantico** *m*
romantica *f*
romantic

⑧ **sbalorditivo** *m*
sbalorditiva *f*
stunning

⑨ **favoloso** *m*
favolosa *f*
great

⑩ **incredibile**
incredible

⑪ **importante**
important

⑫ **adorabile**
cute

⑬ **rispettoso** *m*
rispettosa *f*
respectful

⑭ **speciale**
special

⑮ **aggraziato** *m*
aggraziata *f*
graceful

⑯ **notevole**
remarkable

⑰ **eccezionale**
outstanding

⑱ **esilarante**
hilarious

⑲ **spassoso** *m*
spassosa *f*
funny

⑳ **straordinario** *m*
straordinaria *f*
extraordinary

㉑ **meraviglioso** *m*
meravigliosa *f*
wonderful

㉒ **innocuo** *m*
innocua *f*
harmless

㉓ **all'antica**
old-fashioned

See also
06 I sentimenti e gli stati d'animo • Feelings and moods **10** I tratti della personalità • Personality traits
11 Le abilità e le azioni • Abilities and actions **93** Le competenze sul luogo di lavoro • Workplace skills

㉔ **bravo** *m* / **brava** *f*
good

㉕ **incapace**
bad

㉖ **fantastico** *m*
fantastica *f*
fantastic

㉗ **terribile**
terrible

㉘ **gradevole**
pleasant

㉙ **sgradevole**
unpleasant

㉚ **brillante**
brilliant

㉛ **tremendo** *m*
tremenda *f*
dreadful

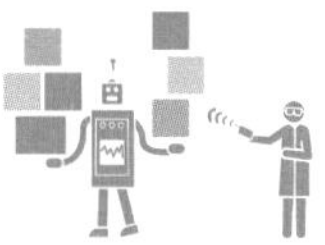
㉜ **utile**
useful

㉝ **inutile**
useless

㉞ **delizioso** *m*
deliziosa *f*
delicious

㉟ **disgustoso** *m*
disgustosa *f*
disgusting

㊱ **bello** *m* / **bella** *f*
pretty

㊲ **brutto** *m* / **brutta** *f*
ugly

㊳ **interessante**
interesting

㊴ **noioso** *m* / **noiosa** *f*
boring

㊵ **rilassante**
relaxing

㊶ **estenuante**
exhausting

㊷ **eccellente**
superb

㊸ **pessimo** *m*
pessima *f*
awful

㊹ **gentile**
nice

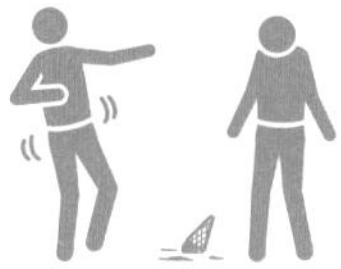
㊺ **sgarbato** *m*
sgarbata *f*
nasty

㊻ **formidabile**
amazing

㊼ **mediocre**
mediocre

㊽ **spaventoso** *m*
spaventosa *f*
frightening

㊾ **terrificante**
terrifying

㊿ **strano** *m* / **strana** *f*
strange / odd

(51) **scioccante**
shocking

(52) **fastidioso** *m*
fastidiosa *f*
annoying

(53) **orribile**
horrible

(54) **disastroso** *m*
disastrosa *f*
disastrous

(55) **poco chiaro** *m*
poco chiara *f*
confusing

(56) **stancante**
tiring

(57) **irritante**
irritating

(58) **disastroso** *m*
disastrosa *f*
dire

(59) **deludente**
disappointing

178.1 I VERBI DELLA VITA QUOTIDIANA · VERBS FOR DAILY LIFE

① calmarsi
to calm down

② rilassarsi
to chill out

③ cercare
to look for

④ crescere
to grow up

⑤ telefonare a
to call up

⑥ indossare
to put on

⑦ vestirsi elegante
to dress up

⑧ vantarsi
to show off

⑨ ammucchiare
to pile up

⑩ restituire
to give back

⑪ appisolarsi
to doze off

⑫ dormire fino a tardi
to sleep in

⑬ alzarsi
to get up

⑭ salire
to go up

⑮ scendere
to go down

⑯ raggiungere
to catch up

⑰ svagarsi
to mess around

⑱ appendere
to hang up

⑲ far entrare
to let in

⑳ strappare
to rip out

㉑ rimanere senza
to run out (of)

㉒ far scattare
to set off

㉓ inciampare
to trip over

㉔ dosare
to measure out

㉕ montare
to put together

㉖ ristrutturare
to do up

㉗ mettere via
to put away

㉙ Vi ho aspettati alzato tutta la notte!
I've been waiting up all night!

㉘ aspettare alzato *m* / aspettare alzata *f*
to wait up

㉚ compilare
to fill out

㉛ effettuare l'accesso
to log in

㉜ uscire
to log out

See also
09 Le attività quotidiane • Daily routines **11** Le abilità e le azioni
Abilities and actions **179-180** Le espressioni utili • Useful expressions

㉝ **svegliarsi**
to wake up

㉞ **pesare**
to weigh out

㉟ **accendere**
to turn on

㊱ **spegnere**
to turn off

㊲ **alzare**
to turn up

㊳ **abbassare**
to turn down

㊴ **rompersi**
to break down

㊵ **fare il pieno**
to fill up

㊶ **fare il check-in**
to check in

㊷ **fare il check-out**
to check out

㊸ **mangiare fuori**
to eat out

㊹ **servire**
to wait on

㊺ **salire**
to get on

㊻ **scendere**
to get off

㊼ **diluviare**
to pour down

㊽ **andare via / partire**
to go away

㊾ **indicare**
to point out

㊿ **accudire**
to look after

(51) **osservare**
to look at

(52) **regalare**
to give away

(53) **distribuire**
to give out

(54) **rinunciare**
to give up

(55) **lasciarsi**
to break up

(56) **annullare**
to call off

(57) **fare pace**
to make up

(58) **vedersi**
to meet up

(60) **Ciao! Sono davvero felice che siate potuti venire!**
Hi! So glad you could join us!

(59) **incontrarsi**
to get together

(61) **distribuire**
to hand out

(62) **fare le pulizie**
to clean up

(63) **raccogliere**
to pick up

(64) **buttare via**
to throw away

(65) **scappare**
to run away

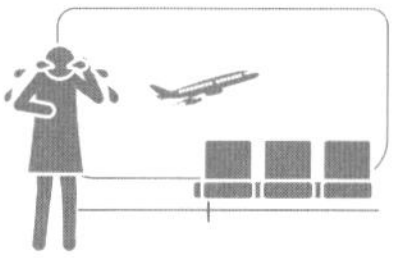

(66) **decollare**
to take off

179 Le espressioni utili
Useful expressions

179.1 I SALUTI · GREETINGS

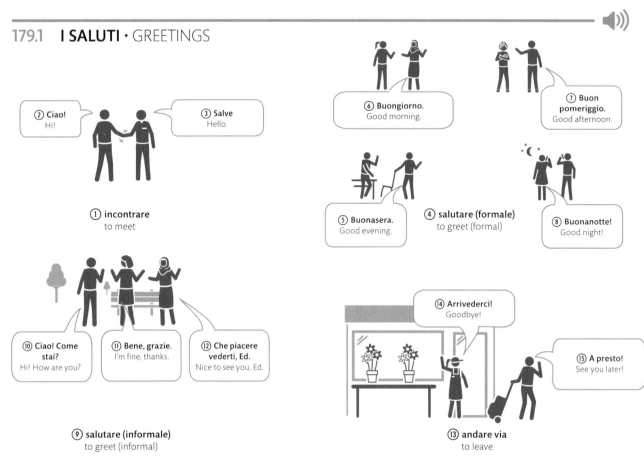

179.2 CONOSCERE QUALCUNO · GETTING TO KNOW SOMEONE

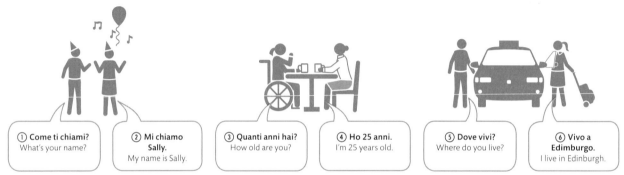

See also
09 Le attività quotidiane · Daily routines **07** Gli eventi della vita
Life events **46** Lo shopping · Shopping **180** Espressioni utili
(continua) · Useful expressions continued

179.3 **LO SHOPPING** · SHOPPING

① **Quanto costa?**
How much
is this?

② **Costa
15 dollari.**
It's 15 dollars

③ **Posso pagare
qui?**
Can I pay here?

④ **Potrebbe prendermi la tazza
rossa, per favore?**
Could you get the
red cup for me, please?

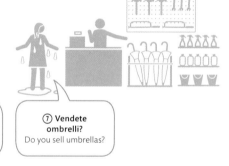

⑤ **Posso
aiutarla?**
Can I help you?

⑥ **Sto solo dando
un'occhiata, grazie.**
I'm just browsing,
thanks.

⑦ **Vendete
ombrelli?**
Do you sell umbrellas?

⑧ **Avete una taglia
più piccola di
questo modello?**
Do you have this
in a smaller size?

⑨ **Controllo subito.**
Let me check for you.

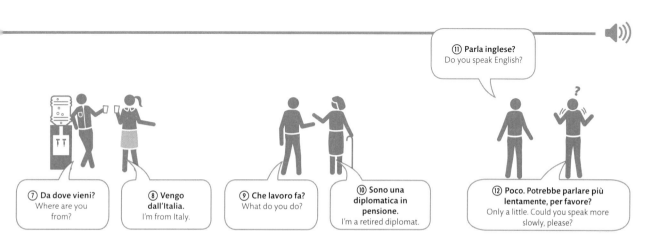

⑪ **Parla inglese?**
Do you speak English?

⑦ **Da dove vieni?**
Where are you
from?

⑧ **Vengo
dall'Italia.**
I'm from Italy.

⑨ **Che lavoro fa?**
What do you do?

⑩ **Sono una
diplomatica in
pensione.**
I'm a retired diplomat.

⑫ **Poco. Potrebbe parlare più
lentamente, per favore?**
Only a little. Could you speak more
slowly, please?

180.1 LE DIREZIONI · DIRECTIONS

① **Mi può aiutare, per favore?**
Can you help me, please?

② **Sì, certo.**
Yes, of course.

③ **Dove si trova la stazione ferroviaria?**
Where is the train station?

④ **Dista 15 minuti a piedi. Giri a sinistra al supermercato.**
It's a 15-minute walk. Turn left at the supermarket.

⑤ **Quanto dista l'hotel?**
How far is it to the hotel?

⑥ **Ci siamo persi!**
We've lost our way!

⑦ **Dovremmo chiedere aiuto.**
We should ask for help.

⑧ **Può mostrarci come si arriva al lago?**
Can you show us the way to the lake?

⑨ **Come si arriva alla spiaggia?**
How do we get to the beach?

⑩ **Sempre dritti!**
It's straight ahead!

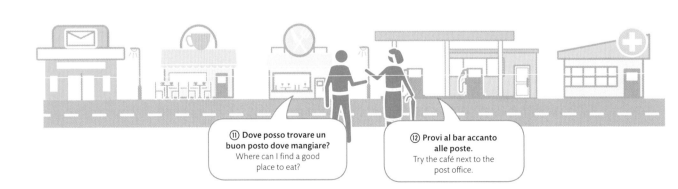

⑪ **Dove posso trovare un buon posto dove mangiare?**
Where can I find a good place to eat?

⑫ **Provi al bar accanto alle poste.**
Try the café next to the post office.

See also
42-43 In città • In town **148** Le cartine
e le direzioni • Maps and directions

180.2 **LE PREPOSIZIONI** · PREPOSITIONS

① **dentro**
in

② **fuori**
out

③ **all'interno**
inside

④ **all'esterno**
outside

⑤ **tra**
between

⑥ **sotto**
under

⑦ **sopra**
on

⑧ **accanto a**
next to / beside

⑨ **davanti a**
in front of

⑩ **dietro a**
behind

⑪ **Dov'è la gattina?**
Where is
the cat?

⑫ **Sopra lo
scaffale!**
She's on the shelf!

369

English word list

The numbers after each word or phrase refer to the units in which they can be found.

KEY

adj – adjective
adv – adverb
n – noun
num – number
phr – phrase
prep – preposition
v – verb

A

à la carte menu *n* 69
A&E *n* 21, 50
aardvark *n* 158
abdomen *n* 01, 162
abdominals *n* 03
abilities *n* 11
ability to drive *n* 93
abseiling *n* 125
Abyssinian *n* 164
acacia *n* 47
accelerator *n* 99
access road *n* 106
accessories *n* 16
accident *n* 19
accident and
   emergency *n* 50
accommodation *n* 131
accordion *n* 129
account number *n* 45
accountant *n* 90, 94
accounts *n* 91
accurate *adj* 93
accused *n* 85
ace *n* 114, 140
ache *v* 20
Achilles tendon *n* 03
acid *n* 76
acid rain *n* 51, 155
acorn *n* 169
acoustic guitar *n* 129
acoustic guitarist *n* 129
acquaintance *n* 07

acquitted *adj* 85
acre *n* 174
acrylic paint *n* 141
act *v* 11
actinide series *n* 78
actinium *n* 78
action game *n* 136
action movie *n* 127
action points *n* 95
actions *n* 11
actor *n* 89, 126
acupressure *n* 24
acupuncture *n* 24
acute accent *n* 175
Adam's apple *n* 04
adaptable *adj* 93
add *v* 11, 29, 74
add to cart *v* 46
add to wishlist *v* 46
additives *n* 23
address *n* 45
adhesive tape *n* 20
administration *n* 91, 93
admiral *n* 88
admission fee *n* 130
admissions *n* 80
admit *v* 21
adrenal gland *n* 04
adult frog *n* 77
adult teeth *n* 03
adults *n* 05
advantage *n* 114
adventure game *n* 136
adventure
   playground *n* 133
adventurous *adj* 10
advertising *n* 91
adverts *n* 137
aerate *v* 39
aerial *n* 25, 97
aerobics *n* 124
aerobics step *n* 124
aerospace *n* 91
Afghan *adj* 153
Afghanistan *n* 151, 153
Africa *n* 149, 152
African *adj* 152
African bullfrog *n* 163
African daisy *n* 38
African elephant *n* 158
African grey
   parrot *n* 161
African wild dog *n* 158
Afro *n* 12
afternoon *n* 09, 171
aftershave *n* 18, 31
agate *n* 156
agbada *n* 15
agenda *n* 95
agriculture *n* 91
aikido *n* 117

aileron *n* 103
air ambulance *n* 50
air bed *n* 135
air cargo *n* 104
air conditioning *n* 33, 99
air control tower *n* 43
air cylinder *n* 118
air filter *n* 98, 100
air mattress *n* 135
air pump *n* 135
air vent *n* 103
airbag *n* 99
airball *n* 112
aircraft carrier *n* 88, 105
aircraft *n* 103
airforce *n* 88
airline *n* 104
airmail *n* 45
airman *n* 88
airport *n* 43, 104
airship *n* 103
airtight container *n* 52
aisle, aisles *n* 48, 80,
   103, 126
alarm *n* 50
alarm clock *n* 30
alarm goes off *phr* 09
Albania *n* 151, 153
Albanian *adj* 153
albatross *n* 160
albertonectes *n* 157
album *n* 129
alcohol-free beer *n* 68
ale *n* 68
alfalfa *n* 86
Algeria *n* 149, 152
Algerian *adj* 152
Alice band *n* 16
alien *n* 139
alkali *n* 76
alkali metals *n* 78
alkaline earth metals *n* 78
all-terrain vehicle *n* 100
Allen keys *n* 36
allergic *adj* 23
allergy *n* 19
alley *n* 42
alloy *n* 76
allspice *n* 59
almond milk *n* 61
almond oil *n* 60
almonds *n* 58, 68
aloe *n* 167
alpaca *n* 165
alpine plants *n* 41
alternating current *n* 33, 75
alto *n* 126
aluminium *n* 78, 156
always *adj* 171
amaryllis *n* 167
amazed *adj* 06

amazing *adj* 177
Amazon *n* 145
ambitious *adj* 10, 93
ambulance *n* 21, 50
ambulance stretcher *n* 50
American *adj* 152
American alligator *n* 163
American curl *n* 164
American
   football field *n* 107
American football *n* 107
American football positions
   n 107
americium *n* 78
amethyst *n* 156
amount *n* 45
amp *n* 33
ampersand *n* 175
amphibians *n* 163
amphibious vehicle *n* 88
amplifier *n* 129
amulet *n* 139
amused *adj* 06
anaesthetist *n* 90
analytics *n* 93
anchor *n* 105, 119
anchovies *n* 64
Ancient Egyptian
   hieroglyphs *n* 175
Ancient Greek temple *n* 44
ancient ruins *n* 44
Andean condor *n* 160
Andorra *n* 151, 153
Andorran *adj* 153
anemone *n* 134, 166
Angel Falls *n* 145
angle *n* 74
angler *n* 121
angler fish *n* 166
Angola *n* 149, 152
Angolan *adj* 152
Angora *n* 164
angry *adj* 06
animal cell *n* 77
animation *n* 127
anise *n* 59
ankle *n* 01-02
ankle boots *n* 17
ankle strap heels *n* 17
ankle weights *n* 124
anklet *n* 16
anniversary *n* 07
annoyed *adj* 06
annoying *adj* 177
annual *n* 41
annual general
   meeting (AGM) *n* 95
annual leave *n* 81
anorak *n* 15
answer *v* 73
ant *n* 162
anteater *n* 159
antenna *n* 162
anther *n* 38

anti-inflammatory *n* 49
antibiotics *n* 49
anticlockwise *adv* 148
antifreeze *n* 97
Antigua and
   Barbuda *n* 150, 152
Antiguan *adj* 152
antimony *n* 78
antiques shop *n* 46
antiseptic *n* 20
antiseptic wipes *n* 20
antler *n* 159
anxious *adj* 06
any other business
   phr 95
apartment *n* 131
apex *n* 74
apostrophe *n* 175
app developer *n* 89
appeal *n* 85
appearance *n* 12
appendicitis *n* 19
appendix *n* 04
applause *n* 126
apple *n* 58
apple corer *n* 28
apple juice *n* 65
applicant *n* 81
application form *n* 92
apply for a job *v* 92
applying for a job *n* 92
appointment *n* 20, 81
appreciative *adj* 06
apprentice *n* 81, 92
approachable *adj* 10
apricot *n* 57
April *n* 172
apron *n* 13, 29
aquamarine *n* 156
aquarium *n* 164
Aquarius *n* 144
Arabic script *n* 175
arable farm *n* 86
arbor knot *n* 121
arc *n* 74, 112
arch *n* 02, 41, 44
arch window *n* 32
archaeological
   site *n* 132
archaeology *n* 79
archaeologist *n* 79
archer *n* 125
archery *n* 125
archipelago *n* 147
architect *n* 90
architecture *n* 44
archive *n* 79
Arctic *n* 159
Arctic Circle *n* 145
Arctic fox *n* 159
Arctic hare *n* 159
Arctic tern *n* 160
Arctic wolf *n* 159
area *n* 74, 174

arena *n* 120
Argentina *n* 149, 152
Argentinian *adj* 152
argon *n* 78
Aries *n* 144
arm, arms *n* 01, 126
arm circles *n* 124
arm protection *n* 110
armadillo *n* 159
armband *n* 118
armchair *n* 26
armed drone *n* 88
armed forces *n* 88
Armenia *n* 150, 153
Armenian *adj* 153
armour *n* 79
armoured
   vehicle *n* 88
armpit *n* 01
armrest *n* 99, 103
army *n* 88
aromatherapy *n* 24
arrest *n* 50
arrival *n* 43
arrive *v* 09
arrive early *v* 09
arrive home *v* 09
arrive late *v* 09
arrive on time *v* 09
arrogant *adj* 10
arrow *n* 79, 125
arrow slit *n* 44
arsenic *n* 78
art, arts *n* 73, 91, 141-142
art college *n* 80
Art Deco *n* 130
art gallery *n* 43, 130, 132
Art Nouveau *n* 130
art school *n* 80
art shop *n* 46
art therapy *n* 24
artery *n* 04
artichoke *n* 56
artichoke heart *n* 56
article *n* 138
articulated bus *n* 99
artificial intelligence *n* 83
artisan *n* 79
artist *n* 90, 141
arum lily *n* 167
ash *n* 145
ash cloud *n* 145
Asia *n* 150, 153
Asian *adj* 153
Asian elephant *n* 159
Asian vine snake *n* 163
ask directions *v* 148
asparagus *n* 56
asparagus tip *n* 56
assertive *adj* 10, 93
astatine *n* 78
asterisk *n* 175
asteroid *n* 143
asthma *n* 19

astigmatism *n* 22
astronaut *n* 143
astronomy *n* 144
at sign *n* 83, 175
at symbol *n* 83, 175
athlete *n* 116
athletics *n* 116, 125
athletics track *n* 116
Atlantic puffin *n* 160
Atlantic salmon *n* 166
atlas moth *n* 162
atlas *n* 73
ATM *n* 45
atmosphere *n* 143, 155
atoll *n* 147
atom *n* 76
attachment *n* 83
attack helicopter *n* 88
attack zone *n* 110
attend a meeting *v* 95
attic *n* 25
attractions *n* 132
aubergine *n* 56
auburn hair *n* 12
audience *n* 126, 127
audio *n* 136
audio guide *n* 130
audition *n* 127
August *n* 172
aunt *n* 05
aurora *n* 144, 155
Australia *n* 150, 153
Australian *adj* 153
Australian
   little penguin *n* 161
Austria *n* 151, 153
Austrian *adj* 153
author *n* 138
autobiography *n* 138
autocue *n* 84
automatic *n* 99
automotive industry
   n 91
autumn *n* 57, 172
autumn leaf *n* 169
avalanche *n* 122
avatar *n* 84
avenue *n* 43
avocado *n* 56
avocado toast *n* 71
avocado tree *n* 167
awful *adj* 177
awning *n* 65
axe *n* 36, 50, 79
axle *n* 100
ayran *n* 61
ayurveda *n* 24
azalea *n* 38
Azerbaijan *n* 150, 153
Azerbaijani *adj* 153

B

babies' clothes *n* 13
baboon *n* 158
baby *n* 05
baby bath *n* 08
baby changing
   facilities *n* 47
baby formula *n* 08
baby monitor *n* 08, 30
baby products *n* 48
baby sweetcorn *n* 55
babygro *n* 13
back *adj* 03
back *n* 26
back bacon *n* 53
back brush *n* 31
back door *n* 97
back seat *n* 99
back up *v* 83
back-flip *n* 118
backache *n* 19
backboard *n* 112
backdrop *n* 126
backgammon *n* 140
backhand *n* 114
backing singers *n* 129
backpack *n* 16, 135
backpack sprayer *n* 40
backstay *n* 119
backstop net *n* 113
backstroke *n* 118
backswing *n* 115
bacon *n* 53, 71
bacteria *n* 77, 157
Bactrian camel *n* 158
bad *adj* 52, 177
bad robot *n* 139
badge *n* 50
badge *n* 16
badminton *n* 114
bag, bags *n* 16, 52
bag store *n* 47
bagel *n* 62, 71
baggage claim *n* 104
baggage trailer *n* 104
bagpipes *n* 129
baguette *n* 62
baggy *adj* 13, 176
Bahamas *n* 150, 162
Bahamian *adj* 152
Bahrain *n* 151, 153
Bahraini *adj* 153
bail *n* 85, 111
Baisakhi *n* 07
bait *n* 121
bait *v* 121
bake *v* 29, 62-63
baked *adj* 72

baked beans *n* 71
baker *n* 62
bakery *n* 46, 48, 62-63
baking *n* 29
baking tray *n* 29
baklava *n* 63
balance wheel *n* 142
balanced diet *n* 23
balcony *n* 25
bald *adj* 12
bald eagle *n* 160
ball *n* 02, 08, 109-110,
   112, 114
ball boy *n* 114
ball girl *n* 114
ballerina *n* 126
ballet *n* 126
ballet flats *n* 17
ballet leotard *n* 126
ballet shoes *n* 126
ballistic missile *n* 88
balloon *n* 08
ballpoint pen *n* 175
balsamic vinegar *n* 60
bamboo *n* 41, 55, 167
banana *n* 58
band *n* 129
bandage *n* 20, 49
banded sea krait *n* 166
Bangladesh *n* 150, 153
Bangladeshi *adj* 153
bangle *n* 16
banister *n* 25-26
banjo *n* 129
bank *n* 45, 94
bank loan *n* 45
bank statement *n* 45
banking *n* 91
banner *n* 109
baobab tree *n* 169
baptism *n* 07
bar, bars *n* 30, 68, 109, 124
bar chart *n* 95
bar counter *n* 68
bar mitzvah *n* 07
bar snacks *n* 68
bar stool *n* 68
bar tender *n* 69
barb *n* 121
Barbadian *adj* 152
Barbados *n* 150, 152
barbecue *n* 41
barbecue *n* 135
barbell *n* 124
barber *n* 89
barberry *n* 168
Barbudan *adj* 152
barcode *n* 48
bare branches *n* 172
bargain *n* 48
barista *n* 65, 89
baritone *n* 126
barium *n* 78
bark *v* 164

barley *n* 86
barn *n* 86
barn owl *n* 161
barnacle *n* 134, 166
barracuda *n* 166
barrel cactus *n* 168
Barrier Reef *n* 145
bartender *n* 68, 89
basa *n* 54
basalt *n* 156
base *n* 74, 76
baseball *n* 113
baseball cap *n* 16
baseball cleats *n* 17
baseball game *n* 113
baseline *n* 114
basement *n* 25, 47
basil *n* 59
basin *n* 22, 33
basket *n* 48, 101, 103,
   112, 164
basket of fruit *n* 57
basketball *n* 112
basketball player *n* 112
basking shark *n* 166
Basotho *adj* 152
basque *n* 14
bass *n* 126
bass clef *n* 128
bass drum *n* 128
bass guitarist *n* 129
basset hound *n* 164
bassoon *n* 128
bat *n* 111, 113-114, 158
bat *v* 111, 113
bat mitzvah *n* 07
bath towel *n* 31
bath toys *n* 31
bath tub *n* 31
bathmat *n* 31
bathroom *n* 31
bathroom extractor
   fan *n* 31
bathroom scales *n* 31
baton *n* 116
batsman *n* 111
Battenburg markings *n* 50
batter *n* 111, 113
battering ram *n* 79
battery *n* 75, 83, 98
battery pack *n* 35
batting glove *n* 113
battle *n* 79, 88
battlement *n* 44
battleship *n* 105
Bauhaus *n* 130
bay *n* 147
bay leaf *n* 59
bay tree *n* 38
bay window *n* 25
bayonet base *n* 33
be absent *v* 95
be born *v* 07
be delayed *v* 104

brake disk *n* 100
brake fluid reservoir *n* 98
brake lever *n* 101
brake pad *n* 101
brake pedal *n* 100
brake *v* 98, 101
branch *n* 81, 169
branch manager *n* 45
brandy *n* 68
brass *adj* 176
brass *n* 128, 176
brave *adj* 10
bray *v* 165
Brazil *n* 149, 152
brazil nuts *n* 58
Brazilian *adj* 152
bread, breads *n* 62, 71
bread basket *n* 71
bread knife *n* 28
breadfruit *n* 56
break down *v* 98, 178
break even *v* 94
break in *n* 50
break up *v* 178
breakdown assistance *n* 98
breakfast *n* 26, 71
breakfast buffet *n* 71
breakfast burrito *n* 71
breakfast cereals *n* 48
breakfast roll *n* 71
breakfast tray *n* 131
breakfast TV *n* 137
breast *n* 01, 53
breastbone *n* 03
breaststroke *n* 118
Breathalyzer *n* 50
breathe *v* 02
breathtaking *adj* 177
breed *v* 120
breeze *n* 154
breeze block *n* 87
breezy *adj* 154
bribery *n* 85
brick *adj* 176
brick, bricks *n* 35, 87, 176
bride *n* 07
bridesmaid's dress *n* 15
bridge crane *n* 106
bridge *n* 02, 43, 105, 125, 129, 140
bridge pose *n* 24
bridle *n* 120
bridle path *n* 133
Brie *n* 64
briefcase *n* 16
brilliant *adj* 177
bring *v* 11
brioche *n* 62, 71
British *adj* 153
British shorthair *n* 164
broad beans *n* 55
broadcast *v* 84
broadleaf forest *n* 159
broccoli *n* 55-56

brogues *n* 17
broken bone *n* 19
bromine *n* 78
bronze *adj* 176
bronze *n* 116, 176
Bronze age *n* 79
brooch *n* 16
broom *n* 34, 40
broomstick *n* 139
broth *n* 72
brother *n* 05
brother-in-law *n* 05
browband *n* 120
brown *adj* 01
brown *n* 01, 141
brown bear *n* 159
brown bread *n* 62
brown flour *n* 62
brown hair *n* 12
bruise *n* 19
brunch *n* 69
Brunei *n* 151, 153
Bruneian *adj* 153
brush *n* 34, 141
brush *v* 22
brush your hair *v* 09
brush your teeth *v* 09
Brussels sprouts *n* 55
bubble bath *n* 18, 31
bucket *n* 34, 37, 40
bucket and spade *n* 134
bucket turn *n* 118
buckle *n* 16
buckled shoes *n* 17
buckwheat flour *n* 62
budgerigar *n* 160, 164
budget *n* 94
budgie *n* 160, 164
buffalo *n* 159
buffer *n* 102
buffet *n* 69
buggy *n* 08, 115
bugs *n* 162
build *v* 11, 87
builder *n* 87
building, buildings *n* 42-44, 148
building blocks / bricks *n* 08
building site *n* 87
built-in wardrobe *n* 30
bulb *n* 41
Bulgaria *n* 151, 153
Bulgarian *adj* 153
bull *n* 165
bull-nose pliers *n* 36
bulldozer *n* 87
bullet train *n* 102
bullseye *n* 140
bumble bee *n* 162
bump *v* 112
bumper *n* 97

bumps *n* 96
bun *n* 12
bunch *n* 47
bungalow *n* 32
bungee jumping *n* 125
bunker *n* 115
Bunsen burner *n* 76
buoy *n* 106, 119, 134
bureau de change *n* 45
burgee *n* 119
burger *n* 70
burger bar *n* 70
burglar alarm *n* 25
burglary *n* 85
Burj Khalifa *n* 44
Burkina Faso *n* 149, 152
Burkinabe *adj* 152
Burma (Myanmar) *n* 150, 153
Burmese *adj* 153
Burmese *n* 164
burn *n* 19, 29
burner *n* 27, 103
burrow *v* 159
Burundi *n* 149, 152
Burundian *adj* 152
bus, buses *n* 43, 99
bus driver *n* 90
bus shelter *n* 99
bus station *n* 42, 99
bus stop *n* 25
bus ticket *n* 99
bus transfer *n* 104
business class *n* 103
business deal *n* 81
business lunch *n* 81
business man *n* 81
business trip *n* 81
businesslike attitude *n* 93
businessman *n* 90
businesswoman *n* 81, 90
bust dart *n* 142
butcher *n* 46, 53, 89
butter *n* 61, 71
butter dish *n* 28
butter knife *n* 27
buttercup *n* 38, 168
buttercup squash *n* 56
butterfly, butterflies *n* 77, 118, 162
buttermilk *n* 61
butternut squash *n* 56
buttock *n* 03
button, buttons *n* 15, 142
button acorn squash *n* 56
button hole *n* 15
buy *v* 32, 46
buy groceries *v* 09, 34
buying a house *n* 32
buzz *v* 162

C

cab *n* 50
cabbage *n* 55
cabbage white butterfly *n* 162
cabin *n* 32, 103, 105, 131
cabinet *n* 27
cable *n* 101
cable car *n* 122
cable TV *n* 137
cacti *n* 41
caddy *n* 115
caddy bin *n* 155
cadmium *n* 78
caesium *n* 78
café *n* 42, 46, 65-66
cafetière *n* 28
cage *n* 164
cake, cakes *n* 63
cake shop *n* 46
cake tin *n* 28-29
cake topper *n* 63
calamari *n* 54
calcite *n* 156
calcium *n* 23, 49, 78
calculator *n* 73-74
calendar *n* 82, 172
calf *n* 01, 03, 165
californium *n* 78
call a friend *v* 09
call a plumber *v* 33
call in sick *v* 81
call off *v* 178
call up *v* 178
call your family *v* 09
calligraphy *n* 175
calm *adj* 06, 10, 93
calm down *v* 178
calorie-controlled diet *n* 23
calories *n* 23
Cambodia *n* 150, 153
Cambodian *adj* 153
Cambrian *adj* 157
Cambrian *n* 157
camel pose *n* 24
camellia *n* 38
Camembert *n* 64
camera *n* 83-84
camera crane *n* 84
camera mount *n* 123
camera operator *n* 84, 127
Cameroon *n* 149, 152
Cameroonian *adj* 152
camisole *n* 14
camomile tea *n* 66
camouflage *n* 88
camp *v* 135

camp bed *n* 135
camper van *n* 135
campfire *n* 135
camping *n* 135
camping equipment *n* 135
camping facilities *n* 135
campion *n* 168
campsite *n* 135, 148
campus *n* 80
Canada *n* 150, 152
Canada goose *n* 160
Canadian *adj* 152
canary *n* 160
Canary melon *n* 58
cancel *v* 69
Cancer *n* 144
candle *n* 26, 30
candle magic *n* 139
candlestick *n* 26
candy cane *n* 67
candy floss *n* 67
canes *n* 40
canines *n* 03
canned drink *n* 70
cannelloni *n* 64
cannon *n* 79
Caño Cristales *n* 145
canoe *n* 105
canola oil *n* 60
canopy *n* 103, 125
cantaloupe *n* 58
canter *v* 120
canvas *n* 141
canyon *n* 146
cap *n* 118, 170
cap sleeve *n* 15
capacity *n* 174
cape *n* 147
cape gooseberry *n* 57
Cape Verde *n* 149, 152
Cape Verdean *adj* 152
capers *n* 64
capital letters *n* 175
capoeira *n* 117
cappuccino *n* 65
Capricorn *n* 144
capsize *v* 119
capsules *n* 49
captain *n* 105
capuchin monkey *n* 159
capybara *n* 159
cars *n* 97-99
car exterior *n* 97
car hire *n* 104
car interior *n* 99
car park *n* 42
car stereo *n* 99
car theft *n* 85
car wash *n* 97
caravan *n* 135
caravan *n* 32
caraway seeds *n* 59
carbohydrates *n* 23
carbon *n* 78

circumflex n 175
cistern n 33
citrine n 156
citrus fruit n 57
city centre n 42
claimant n 85
clam n 54
clamp n 35, 76
clap v 02
clapper board n 84
clarinet n 128
class n 73
classical adj 129
Classicism n 130
classroom n 73
clavicle n 03
claw n 161
clay n 39, 141
clean adj 176
clean the bathroom v 34
clean the car v 09
clean the oven v 34
clean the windows v 34
clean up v 34, 178
cleaned adj 54
cleaner n 89
cleaning n 34
cleanser n 18
clear the table v 09, 34
cleat n 119
cleaver n 28
clementine n 57
click n 83
client, clients n 81, 85
cliff n 147
climate n 155
climate change n 155
climb v 11
climber n 41
climbing frame n 43
clinch knot n 121
clinic n 20
clipboard n 82
cloak n 15
cloakroom n 130
cloche n 16
clock n 44, 171
clock radio n 30
clockwise adv 148
clogs n 17
closed adj 48, 132
closed to bicycles adj 96
closed to
   pedestrians adj 96
cloth n 34
clothes n 13-15
clothes moth n 162
clothes peg n 34
clothesline n 34
clothing n 100
cloud, clouds n 51, 154
cloudy adj 154
cloves n 59
clown n 89

clownfish n 166
club n 140
club sandwich n 70
clubhouse n 115
clumsy adj 10
clutch n 99-100
CMS
   (content management
   system) n 84
co-pilot n 103
co-worker n 81
CO2 bubbles n 62
coach n 99, 112-113
coach's box n 113
coal n 51
coal mine n 51
coastal features n 147
coaster n 27, 68
coastguard n 106
coat hanger n 30
coats n 15
cobalt n 78
cobra pose n 24
coccyx n 03
cockatiel n 164
cockatoo n 161
cockerel n 165
cockle n 54
cockpit n 103, 123
cockroach n 162
cocktail n 68
cocktail glass n 68
cocktail shaker n 68
cocoa n 169
cocoa powder n 65
coconut n 58
coconut crab n 166
coconut oil n 60
coconut palm n 167
coconut shell n 57
coconut water n 58, 65
cocoon n 162
cod n 166
cod fillet n 54
coelophysis n 157
coffee n 52, 65, 69, 71, 86
coffee cup n 27
coffee machine n 65, 68
coffee press n 28
coffee shop n 46
coffee table n 26
coins n 45, 94
cola n 52
colander n 28
cold adj 154, 176
cold n 19
cold frame v 39
cold front n 155
cold meats n 71
cold water n 31
collaborate v 92
collage n 141
collar n 15, 142
collarbone n 03

collards n 55
colleague n 07, 81, 92
collect v 11
collection n 130
college departments n 80
college schools n 80
Colombia n 149, 152
Colombian adj 152
colon n 175
Colosseum n 44
coloured pencils n 73
colouring book n 138
columbine n 168
column n 44, 146
comb n 12
combat aircraft n 88
combat sports n 117
combination adj 18
combine harvester n 86
combined events n 116
comedian n 89
comedy n 126-127, 137
comet n 143-144
comic n 48, 138
comma n 175
commence v 95
commercial district n 42
commis chef n 69
commission n 94
common earthball n 170
common egg-eater n 163
common green
   iguana n 163
common houseleek n 168
common poppy n 168
common puffball n 170
common snake-necked
   turtle n 163
common toad n 163
community website n 84
commuters n 102
Comoran adj 152
Comoros n 149, 152
company n 81
compartment n 102
compass n 73-74, 119,
   135, 148
competitive adj 93
complain v 46
complaint n 50
compose v 128
composer n 128
compost n 40
compost bin n 40
compost heap n 41
compostable bags n 155
composter n 40
compound n 76
compressed-air
   cylinder n 50
computer,
   computers n 82-83
computer desk n 83
computer literacy n 93

computing n 93
concave lens n 75
concealer n 18
conceptual art n 130
concert hall n 43
conchiglie n 64
concourse n 102
concrete adj 176
concrete n 35, 176
concussion n 19
condensed milk n 61
condiments n 60, 71-72
conduct v 128
conductor n 75, 128
cone n 74, 87
confectionery n 48
conference n 95
confident adj 06, 10, 93
confused adj 06
confusing adj 177
conglomerate n 156
Congolese adj 152
coniferous forest n 146
conifers n 41, 157, 167
connection n 104
conning tower n 105
conservation n 130
considerate adj 10
console n 136
constellation,
   constellations n 144
construction n 87, 91
construction waste n 33
contact n 83
contact lens,
   contact lenses n 22, 49
contact lens solution n 22
container n 105
container port n 106
container ship n 105-106
containers n 52
contents n 138
continent n 145
contours n 148
contract n 92
control tower n 104
controller n 136
controls n 100, 136
convenience food n 23, 48
conversion n 108
convert the attic v 35
convert the loft v 35
convertible n 97
convex lens n 75
conveyor belt n 48
cook dinner v 09
cookbook n 138
cooked adj 56
cooked breakfast n 71
cooked meat n 53, 64
cooked vegetables n 72
cookie n 63, 84
cooking n 29
cooking show n 137

cooksonia n 157
cool adj 154
cool down v 124
coolant reservoir n 98
cooler n 135
cooling rack n 29
cooling system n 98
cooling tower n 51
coordinate v 92
coordinates n 148
coot n 161
copernicium n 78
copper n 78, 156
copy v 11
copyright n 175
cor anglais n 128
coral n 166
coral reef n 118, 166
coral reef fish n 118
coral trout n 166
cordless drill n 35
core n 57
coriander n 59
coriander seeds n 59
cork n 60
corkscrew n 28, 68
cormorant n 160
corn n 55, 86
corn bread n 62
corn oil n 60
cornea n 22
corner n 109
corner flag n 109
corner kick n 109
cornerback n 107
cornichons n 60
cornrows n 12
corpse pose n 24
correct adj 176
correction fluid n 82
cortado n 65
Costa Rica n 150, 152
Costa Rican adj 152
costume, costumes n 13,
   126-127
costume drama n 137
cot n 30
cotoneaster n 169
cottage n 32
cottage cheese n 61
cottage garden n 41
cotton adj 176
cotton n 13, 86, 176
cotton balls n 18
cotton reel n 142
cotton wool n 20
couch n 26
couch potato n 137
cough n 19
cough v 20
cough medicine n 49
counsellor n 24
count v 11, 74
counter n 45, 131

E

F

fare n 99, 102
farm n 86, 165
farm animals n 165
farmer n 79, 86, 89
farmers' market n 23
farmhouse n 86
farming n 86, 91
farming terms n 86
farmland n 86, 146
farmyard n 86
fashion n 91
fashion accessories n 16
fashion designer n 90
fashion store n 47
fast adj 176
fast food n 47, 70
fast forward v 137
fast-food restaurant n 70
fasten v 14
fastening n 16
fat free adj 61
father n 05
father-in-law n 05
fault n 114
faun n 139
feather duster n 34
feather n 161
feathers displayed n 161
February n 172
fedora n 16
feed v 86
feed the cat v 09
feed the dog v 09
feed the pets v 34
feel better v 20
feelings n 06
feet n 02
feet-first adj 118
feijoa n 58
female n 04
feminine hygiene n 49
femur n 03
fence n 41, 86
fencing n 116-117
feng shui n 24
fennec fox n 158
fennel n 55, 59
fennel seeds n 59
fenugreek leaves n 59
fermium n 78
fern, ferns n 41, 156, 167
ferret n 164
ferris wheel n 133
ferrule n 115
ferry n 105-106
ferry route n 148
ferry terminal n 106
fertilize v 39
fertilizer n 39
festivals n 07
feta n 64
fetus n 08
fever n 19
fez n 16

fiancé n 07
fiancée n 07
fibre n 23, 57
fibreglass adj 176
fibreglass n 176
fibula n 03
fiction n 138
fiddler crab n 166
field n 107, 113, 146
field v 111, 113
field events n 116
field hockey n 110
field hockey player n 110
field hospital n 88
field mushroom n 170
fielding positions n 111
fifteen num 173
fifth num 173
fifty num 173
fifty-yard line n 107
fig n 169
fighter n 88
figure skating n 122
Fiji n 150, 153
Fijian adj 153
filament n 38
file, files n 36, 82
filing cabinet n 82
Filipino adj 153
fill v 37
fill out v 178
fill out a form v 92
fill up v 98, 178
filler n 37
fillet n 53
fillet n 54
filling n 22, 63, 70
film set n 127
film star n 127
film studio n 127
films n 127
filo n 63
filter coffee n 65
filter paper n 76
fin n 103
final whistle n 109
finance n 91, 94
financial advisor n 94
finch n 160
finderscope n 144
finds n 79
fine n 85
fine leg n 111
fingernail n 02
fingerprint n 50
finish line n 116, 123
finish work v 09
Finland n 151, 153
Finnish adj 153
fins n 118, 134
fir n 167
fire n 50
fire alarm n 50
fire brigade n 50

fire engine n 50
fire escape n 50
fire extinguisher n 50
fire salamander n 163
fire station n 42, 50
fire tree n 168
firefighter,
    firefighters n 50, 89
firefighter's uniform n 13
firelighter n 135
firepit n 135
fireplace n 26
first num 173
first aid bag n 50
first base n 113
first floor n 25, 47
first-aid kit n 20, 49
fish n 48, 54, 164
fish and chips n 70
fish box n 54
fish farm n 86
fish sauce n 60
fish slice n 28
fish tank n 164
fisherman n 89
fishhook n 121
fishing n 91, 121
fishing permit n 121
fishing port n 106
fishing rod n 121
fishing vest n 121
fishmonger n 18, 54, 89
fission n 75
fissures n 51
fist n 02
fit v 14, 46
fit a carpet v 35
fitted adj 13
five num 173
five hundred num 173
five past one n 171
five positions n 112
five spice n 59
five to two n 171
fix v 11
fix a fence v 35
fix a puncture v 101
fizzy drink n 70
fjord n 147
flag n 115
flagstone n 35
flamenco dress n 15
flamingo n 160
flan n 64
flan tin n 29
flap v 161
flare n 51, 119, 144
flask n 52
flask n 76
flat adj 128
flat n 25
flat cap n 16
flat-head screwdriver n 36
flat race n 120

flat tyre n 98
flat white n 65
flat wood bit n 36
flatbed truck n 87
flatbread n 62
flats n 17
flavoured oil n 60
flax n 86
fledgling n 161
flerovium n 78
flesh n 58
flex v 124
flexible adj 93, 176
flexitime n 81
flight attendant,
    flight attendants n 90,
    103-104
flight instructor n 90
flight number n 104
flint n 156
flint tools n 79
flip n 118
flip chart n 82, 95
flip through v 138
flip-flops n 17, 134
flipper, flippers n 15,
    118, 134
float n 118, 121
float v 118
floating crane n 106
flock of sheep n 165
flood n 154
flood plain n 147
floor n 25-26, 30
floor length adj 15
floor mat n 125
floor plan n 130, 132
floorboards n 26
Florentine n 63
floret n 55
florist n 46-47, 89
floss n 22
flours n 62
flower anatomy n 38
flower stall n 47
flowerbed n 41
flowering plants n 157
flowering shrub n 41
flu n 19
fluent in languages adj 93
fluid ounce n 174
fluorine n 78
flute n 128-129
fly n 121, 162, 168
fly v 11, 162
fly agaric n 170
fly fishing n 121
fly-half n 108
flying carpet n 139
flying fish n 166
flying kick n 117
flying reptiles n 157
flying squirrel n 158
flyover n 96

flysheet n 135
FM adj 84
foal n 120, 165
focusing knob n 77, 144
foetus n 08
fog n 154
foggy adj 154
foil n 117
fold v 14
fold clothes v 34
folders n 82
folding grill n 135
foliage n 47
folk blouse n 15
folk music n 129
follow v 84
follower n 84
food n 65, 91
food allergies n 23
food bowl n 26
food compost bin n 33
food court n 47
food poisoning n 19
food preparation n 72
food processor n 27
food van n 70
food waste n 155
foot n 01, 174
foot board n 30
foot boot n 19
foot pedals n 99
foot stool n 26
foot strap n 119
football n 109
football boots n 17,
    107, 109
football game n 109
football player n 107
football rules n 109
football
    shirt n 15, 109
football timing n 109
footbridge n 104
foothill n 147
footrest n 82
forage mushrooms v 170
Forbidden City n 44
forearm n 01
forecourt n 97
forehand n 114
forehead n 01
foreperson n 85
forest n 147-148
forestay n 119
forewing n 162
forget v 11
fork n 27, 40, 101
fork-lift
    truck n 87, 106
formal garden n 41
formal wear n 15
fortnight n 172
fortune cookies n 63
forty num 173

kendo *n* 117
kennel *n* 164
Kenya *n* 149, 152
Kenyan *adj* 152
kerb *n* 43
kernel *n* 55
ketchup *n* 60, 70
kettledrum *n* 128
key, keys *n* 25, 32
key cutting shop *n* 46
keyboard *n* 83, 129
keyhole *n* 25-26
keypad *n* 45
kick *n* 108, 118
kick *v* 11, 107
kick flip *n* 125
kickboxing *n* 117
kickoff *n* 109
kickstand *n* 101
kid *n* 165
kidney,
    kidneys *n* 04, 53, 71
kids' clothes *n* 13
kids' shoes *n* 17
killer whale *n* 166
kilogram *n* 174
kilometre *n* 174
kilt *n* 15
kimchi *n* 60
kimono *n* 15
kind *adj* 10
king *n* 79, 140
kingdom *n* 79
kingfisher *n* 160
kiosk *n* 46-48
kippers *n* 71
Kiribati *adj* 153
Kiribati *n* 150, 153
kitchen *n* 27, 69
kitchen appliances *n* 27
kitchen equipment *n* 28
kitchen fitter *n* 90
kitchen installer *n* 90
kitchen knife *n* 28
kitchen scissors *n* 28
kitchenware *n* 28
kite *n* 08
kite surfing *n* 119
kitten *n* 164
kitten heels *n* 17
Kittitian *adj* 152
kiwi *n* 160
kiwi /
    kiwi fruit *n* 58
knead *v* 62
knee *n* 01, 126
knee joint *n* 03
knee pad *n* 107, 100
knee-high boots *n*
kneecap *n* 03
kneeler *n* 40
kneeling chair *n* 82
knickers *n* 14
knife *n* 27

knife sharpener *n* 28
knife stand *n* 28
knight *n* 79, 139-140
knitting *n* 142
knitting needle *n* 142
knob *n* 25-26, 113
knock down
    a wall *v* 35
knock out *n* 117
knots *n* 121
knuckle *n* 02
koala *n* 158
kohlrabi *n* 55
kola nuts *n* 58
Komodo dragon *n* 163
kookaburra *n* 160
kosher *adj* 72
krypton *n* 78
kumquat *n* 57
kung fu *n* 117
Kuwait *n* 151, 153
Kuwaiti *adj* 153
Kwanzaa *n* 07
Kyrgyz *adj* 153
Kyrgyzstan *n* 151, 153

L

lab *n* 76
lab coat *n* 13
label, labels *n* 40, 130
laboratory *n* 76
labrador *n* 164
lace *n* 17, 107
lace bobbin *n* 142
lace-making *n* 142
lace-up boots *n* 17
lacrosse *n* 110
lacrosse player *n* 110
lactose free *adj* 61
lactose intolerant *adj* 23
ladder *n* 36, 50, 87
ladle *n* 27
lady *n* 79
ladybird *n* 162
lager *n* 68
lagoon *n* 147
laid-back *adj* 10
lake *n* 146, 148
Lake Natron *n* 145
lamb *n* 53, 165
lamp *n* 26, 82, 101, 106,
    135, 139
lampshade *n* 26
land *n* 145

land *v* 104
landfill *n* 155
landing gear *n* 103
landing hill *n* 122
landing net *n* 121
landlord *n* 32
landscape *n* 132
landscape *v* 39
landscape painting *n* 133
landslide *n* 146
lane *n* 116, 118
lane line *n* 112
lane rope *n* 118
languages *n* 73, 80
lantern *n* 135
lanthanum *n* 78
lanthanide series *n* 78
Laos *n* 150, 153
Laotian *adj* 153
lapel *n* 15
lapis lazuli *n* 156
laptop *n* 82-83
larch *n* 167
large *adj* 176
large intestine *n* 04
larynx *n* 04
lasagna *n* 64, 72
laser *n* 75
laser run *n* 116
late *adj* 171
later *adj* 171
later *adv* 171
Latin *n* 129
Latin alphabet *n* 175
latissimus dorsi *n* 03
latitude *n* 145, 148
Latvia *n* 151, 153
Latvian *adj* 153
laugh *v* 02
launch *n* 143
launch pad *n* 143
Launderette *n* 46
laundry *n* 34
laundry
    basket *n* 31, 34
laundry detergent *n* 34
laundry service *n* 131
laurel *n* 167
lava *n* 145
lava layer *n* 145
lavender *n* 38
law *n* 80, 85
law court *n* 43, 85
lawn *n* 41
lawn rake *n* 40
lawnmower *n* 40
lawrencium *n* 78
lawyer *n* 85, 90
lawyer's office *n* 85
laxative *n* 49
lay bricks *v* 35
lay turf *v* 39
layer cake *n* 63
lazy *adj* 10

leaching *n* 39
lead *n* 78
lead *n* 164
lead singer *n* 129
leaded *n* 97
leader *n* 81
leadership *n* 93
leaf *n* 55
leaf blower *n* 40
leaf fall *n* 172
leafy *adj* 56
lean meat *n* 53
Leaning Tower
    of Pisa *n* 44
learn *v* 73
lease *n* 32
leash *n* 164
leather *adj* 176
leather *n* 13, 107, 176
leatherback
    sea turtle *n* 163
leathers *n* 100
leave *v* 179
leave the house *v* 09
leave work *v* 09
Lebanese *adj* 153
Lebanon *n* 150, 153
lecture theatre *n* 80
lecturer *n* 80, 89
LED (light emitting diode)
    bulb *n* 33
lederhosen *n* 15
leek *n* 56
left defenceman *n* 110
left defensive end *n* 107
left defensive tackle *n* 107
left guard *n* 107
left safety *n* 107
left tackle *n* 107
left winger *n* 110
left-wing *n* 108
leg *n* 01, 26, 53
leg guard *n* 110
leg pad *n* 111
leg press *n* 124
legal *n* 91
legal advice *n* 85
legal system *n* 85
leggings *n* 14
lemon *n* 57
lemon balm *n* 59
lemon curd *n* 60
lemon squeezer *n* 28
lemonade *n* 52
lemongrass *n* 59
length *n* 74, 174
lens *n* 22, 75, 127, 136
lens case *n* 22
lens cleaning cloth *n* 22
lens solution *n* 49
Leo *n* 144
leopard *n* 159
leotard *n* 15
leprechaun *n* 139

Lesotho *n* 149, 152
lesson *n* 73
let *n* 114
let in *v* 178
let out *v* 142
letter *n* 45, 82
letterbox *n* 25, 45
letters *n* 175
lettuce *n* 55
Liberia *n* 149, 152
Liberian *adj* 152
libero *n* 112
Libra *n* 144
librarian *n* 80, 90
library *n* 43, 80, 148
library card *n* 80
libretto *n* 126
Libya *n* 149, 152
Libyan *adj* 152
licence plate *n* 97
lick *v* 02, 11
lid *n* 28
lie down *v* 20
Liechtenstein *n* 151, 153
Liechtensteiner *adj* 153
life cycle *n* 77
life events *n* 07
life jacket *n* 105, 119
life raft *n* 119
life ring *n* 105, 119, 134
life-support
    backpack *n* 143
lifeboat *n* 105
lifeguard *n* 118, 134
lifeguard tower *n* 134
lift *n* 25, 47, 131
lift *v* 11
ligament *n* 03
ligature *n* 175
light *adj* 60, 176
light, lights *n* 32, 50, 84,
    101, 143
light a fire *v* 135
light aircraft *n* 103
light bulbs *n* 33
light shower *n* 154
light switch *n* 33
lighthouse *n* 44, 106
lighting *n* 47
lightning *n* 154
like *v* 84
lilac *n* 38
lily *n* 38, 167
lily of the valley *n* 38
lime *n* 57, 169
lime pickle *n* 60
limestone *n* 156
limousine *n* 97
limpet *n* 134, 166
linden *n* 169
line, lines *n* 74, 121
line of play *n* 115
linen chest *n* 30
linesman *n* 109, 114

medium height *adj* 12
medlar *n* 169
medley relay *n* 118
meerkat *n* 159
meet *v* 179
meet a deadline *v* 92
meet up *v* 178
meeting *n* 81, 82, 95
meeting-room
  equipment *n* 82
meganeura *n* 157
megaphone *n* 50
meitnerium *n* 78
melody *n* 129
melons *n* 58
melt butter *v* 29
melting ice caps *n* 155
membership *n* 124
memory card *n* 83
mendelevium *n* 78
men's decathlon *n* 116
menswear *n* 47
menu *n* 65, 70
meow *v* 164
merchant *n* 79
Mercury *n* 143
mercury *n* 78, 156
meringue *n* 63
mermaid *n* 139
merman *n* 139
mesa *n* 146
mesosphere *n* 155
Mesozoic
  (middle life) *adj* 157
Mesozoic
  (middle life) *n* 157
mess *n* 88
mess around *v* 178
metacarpals *n* 03
metal *adj* 176
metal, metals *n* 35, 155,
  156, 176
metal bit *n* 36
metal detecting *n* 133
metamorphic *adj* 156
metamorphosis *n* 77
metatarsals *n* 03
meteor *n* 144
meteor shower *n* 144
methane *n* 155
meticulous *adj* 10
metre *n* 174
metre line *n* 108
Mexican *adj* 152
Mexican axolotl *n* 163
Mexico *n* 150, 152
mezzo-soprano *n* 126
mica *n* 156
microbiologist *n* 77
microbiology *n* 77
microlight *n* 103
Micronesia *n* 150, 153
Micronesian *adj* 153
microphone *n* 84, 95, 136

microscope *n* 77
microwave *v* 29
microwave oven *n* 27
microwaves *n* 75
mid-off *n* 111
mid-wicket *n* 111
midcourt area
  marker *n* 112
midday *n* 171
middle blocker *n* 112
middle finger *n* 02
middle lane *n* 96
middle level *n* 47
middle linebacker *n* 107
middle-aged *adj* 12
midfielder *n* 109
midnight *n* 171
midnight zone *n* 166
midwife *n* 08
migraine *n* 19
migrate *v* 161
mild *adj* 154
mile *n* 174
military *n* 88, 91
military ambulance *n* 88
military transport
  aircraft *n* 88
military truck *n* 88
military uniform *n* 13
military vehicles *n* 88
milk *n* 61, 65, 71
milk *v* 86
milk carton *n* 61
milk chocolate *n* 67
milk products *n* 61
milk teeth *n* 22
milkshake *n* 52, 65, 70
milky conecap *n* 170
Milky Way *n* 144
millennium *n* 172
millet *n* 86
milligram *n* 174
millilitre *n* 174
millimetre *n* 174
millipede *n* 162
mimosa *n* 168
minaret *n* 44
mince *v* 29
mindfulness *n* 24
mine shaft *n* 51
miner, miners *n* 51, 89
mineral water *n* 52, 68
minerals *n* 23, 156
minibar *n* 131
minibus *n* 99
mining *n* 91
Minotaur *n* 139
minstrel *n* 79
mint *n* 59, 67
mint tea *n* 66
minus sign *n* 74
minute *n* 82, 171
minute hand *n* 171
mirror *n* 18, 30, 77

miserable *adj* 06
miss a train *v* 102
mission control *n* 143
mist *n* 154
mistletoe *n* 168
misty *adj* 154
mitochondria *n* 77
mitt *n* 113
mittens *n* 13
mix *v* 29, 62
mixed salad *n* 72
mixing bowl *n* 28
mixing desk *n* 84
moat *n* 44
mobile *n* 30
mobile banking *n* 94
mobile phone *n* 82
moccasins *n* 17
mochi *n* 63
mocktail *n* 68
model making *n* 141
modelling tool *n* 141
modern building *n* 44
modern pentathlon *n* 116
moisturizer *n* 18
molars *n* 03
mold *n* 170
Moldova *n* 151, 153
Moldovan *adj* 153
mole *n* 12, 159
molecule *n* 76
molybdenum *n* 78
Monacan *adj* 153
Monaco *n* 151, 153
monarch butterfly *n* 162
monastery *n* 44
Monday *n* 172
money *n* 45, 94
Mongolia *n* 150, 153
Mongolian *adj* 153
mongoose *n* 159
monkey puzzle *n* 167
monkey wrench *n* 36
monkfish *n* 54
mono *adj* 136
monocle *n* 22
monoplane *n* 103
monorail *n* 102
monster *n* 139
monster truck *n* 123
Montenegrin *adj* 153
Montenegro *n* 151, 153
month *n* 172
monthly *adj* 172
monthly *adv* 172
monument *n* 42, 44, 132
moods *n* 06
Moon *n* 143
moonstone *n* 156
moor *v* 106
mooring *n* 106
moorish idol *n* 166
moose *n* 159
mop *n* 34

mop the floor *v* 34
morel *n* 170
morning *n* 09, 171
morning glory *n* 169
Moroccan *adj* 152
Morocco *n* 149, 152
mortar *n* 28, 35, 76, 87
mortar and pestle *n* 28
mortarboard *n* 80
mortgage *n* 32, 45
moscovium *n* 78
Moses basket *n* 08, 30
mosque *n* 44
mosquito *n* 162
mosquito net *n* 135
moss *n* 167
mother *n* 05
mother-in-law *n* 05
mother of thousands *n*
  168
moths *n* 162
motivated *adj* 93
motor racing *n* 123
motor scooter *n* 100
motorbike *n* 100
motorbike
  racing *n* 123
motocross *n* 123
motorcycle officer *n* 50
motorsports *n* 123
motorway *n* 96
moulding *n* 26
moult *v* 164
mount *v* 100
mountain *n* 147
mountain ash *n* 169
mountain bike *n* 101
mountain biking *n* 133
mountain goat *n* 159
mountain pose *n* 24
mountain range *n* 146
mountaineering *n* 133
mouse *n* 83, 158, 164
mouse mat *n* 83
moustache *n* 12
mouth *n* 01, 147
mouth guard *n* 107, 117
mouthwash *n* 31
movable panel *n* 82
move *v* 11, 140
move in *v* 32
move out *v* 32
movie camera *n* 127
mow the lawn *v* 09, 39
Mozambican *adj* 152
Mozambique *n* 149, 152
mozzarella *n* 64
muck out *v* 120
mudguard *n* 100
mudskipper *n* 166
mudslide *n* 146
muesli *n* 71
muffin *n* 63, 70
muffin tray *n* 29

mug *n* 27
mugging *n* 85
mulberry *n* 57
mulch *v* 39
mules *n* 17
multi-purpose knife *n* 135
multi-vitamins *n* 49
multiplayer game *n* 136
multiplex *n* 127
multiplication sign *n* 74
multiply *v* 74
mum *n* 05
mumps *n* 19
muscles *n* 03
museum *n* 43, 130, 132
museum curator *n* 89
musher *n* 122
mushroom picking *n* 133
mushroom, mushrooms *n*
  56, 170
music *n* 73, 128, 129
music channel *n* 137
music school *n* 80
music stand *n* 128
music teacher *n* 90
music therapy *n* 24
musical *n* 126, 127
musician *n* 90
musk ox *n* 159
mussel *n* 54
mustard *n* 70
mustard allergy *n* 23
mustard seeds *n* 60
mute swan *n* 161
muzzle *n* 120
Myanmar
  (Burma) *n* 150, 153
mycelium *n* 170
myrtle *n* 168
myths *n* 139

N

nacelle *n* 51
nachos *n* 70
nail *n* 36
nail clippers *n* 18, 49
nail file *n* 18
nail polish *n* 18
nail polish remover
  n 18
nail scissors *n* 18
nail varnish *n* 18
Namibia *n* 149, 152
Namibian *adj* 152
napkin *n* 27, 72

napkin ring *n* 27
nappy *n* 08
nappy rash
  cream *n* 08
narrow *adj* 176
narwhal *n* 166
nasal spray *n* 20
nasturtium *n* 169
nasty *adj* 177
national park *n* 132, 133
nationalities *n* 152, 153
natural arch *n* 147
natural history *n* 157
nature documentary
  n 137
nature reserve *n* 133, 148
nature therapy *n* 24
nature writing *n* 138
naturopathy *n* 24
Nauru *n* 150, 153
Nauruan *adj* 153
nausea *n* 19
nautilus *n* 166
navel *n* 01
navigate *v* 119
navy *n* 88
navy blue *n* 141
navy vessels *n* 88
near *adj* 176
nebula *n* 144
neck *n* 01, 115, 129, 161
neck brace *n* 19
neck pad *n* 107
necklace *n* 16
neckline *n* 142
nectarine *n* 57
needle *n* 20
needlefish *n* 166
needle-nose pliers
  n 36
needle plate *n* 142
needlepoint *n* 142
negative *adj* 75
negative electrode
  n 75
negotiate *v* 92
negotiating *n* 93
neighbour *n* 07
neodymium *n* 78
Neogene *adj* 157
Neogene *n* 157
neon *n* 78
Nepal *n* 150, 153
Nepalese *adj* 153
nephew *n* 05
Neptune *n* 143
neptunium *n* 78
nerve *n* 03, 22
nervous *adj* 04, 06, 10
nest *n* 160
net *n* 109, 112, 114
net *v* 121
net curtain *n* 26
netball *n* 125

Netherlands *n* 151, 153
nettle *n* 169
neurology *n* 21
neutral *n* 33
neutral zone *n* 107, 110
neutron *n* 76
neutron star *n* 144
never *adv* 171, 172
Nevisian *adj* 152
new *adj* 176
new leaves *n* 172
new moon *n* 143
new potato *n* 56
New Year *n* 07
New Zealand
  adj 153
New Zealand
  n 150, 153
newborn baby *n* 08
news *n* 137
news website *n* 84
newsboy cap *n* 16
newsfeed *n* 84
newspaper *n* 48, 138
newsreader *n* 89, 137
newsstand *n* 46, 48
next to *prep* 148, 180
nib *n* 73, 175
nibble *v* 52
Nicaragua *n* 150, 152
Nicaraguan *adj* 152
nice *adj* 177
nickel *n* 78, 156
niece *n* 05
nigella seeds *n* 59
Niger *n* 149, 152
Nigeria *n* 149, 152
Nigerian *adj* 152
Nigerien *adj* 152
night *n* 171
night light *n* 30
nightclub *n* 42
nightgown *n* 14
nightie *n* 14
nightingale *n* 160
nightmare *n* 30
nightwear *n* 14
nihonium *n* 78
Nile crocodile *n* 163
nine *num* 173
nine-to-five job *n* 81
nineteen *num* 173
ninety *num* 173
ninth *num* 173
niobium *n* 78
nipple *n* 01, 08
nitrogen *n* 78
no entry *n* 96
no overtaking *phr* 96
no photography
  phr 130
no right turn *phr* 96
no U-turn *phr* 96
no vacancies *phr* 131

no-charge
  semi-circle *n* 112
nobelium *n* 78
noble gases *n* 78
nobles *n* 79
nod *v* 02
noisy *adj* 176
non-blood relative *n* 05
non-carbonated *adj* 52
non-fiction *n* 138
non-metals *n* 78
noodle soup *n* 72
noodles *n* 64, 70, 72
normal *adj* 18
normal hair *n* 12
north *n* 148
North America
  n 150, 152
North American
  adj 152
North Korea *n* 150, 153
North Korean *adj* 153
North
  Macedonia *n* 151, 153
North Macedonian
  adj 153
North Pole *n* 75, 145
northeast *n* 148
northern cardinal *n* 161
Northern
  Hemisphere *n* 145
northwest *n* 148
Norway *n* 151, 153
Norwegian *adj* 153
nose *n* 01, 103
nose clip *n* 118
nose cone *n* 123
noseband *n* 120
nosebleed *n* 19
nosewheel *n* 103
nostrils *n* 01
notation *n* 128
notebook *n* 73, 95
notepad *n* 82
notes *n* 45, 94
notes *n* 95, 128
notice board *n* 82
nougat *n* 67
nought point five
  num 173
noughts and
  crosses *n* 140
novel *n* 138
November *n* 172
now *adv* 171
nozzle *n* 40
nuclear energy *n* 51
nuclear power
  station *n* 51
nuclear waste *n* 51
nucleus *n* 76, 77
number *n* 112
number eight *n* 108
numbers *n* 173

numeracy *n* 93
numerals *n* 175
numerator *n* 74
nurse *n* 20, 21, 89
nursery *n* 30
nursing *n* 80
nut allergy *n* 23
nut, nuts *n* 36, 58, 68, 129
nutmeg *n* 59
nutrition *n* 23

O

oak *n* 169
oar *n* 119
oasis *n* 146
objective lens *n* 77
obliques *n* 03
oboe *n* 128
observatory *n* 144
obsidian *n* 156
obstetrician *n* 08
occluded front *n* 155
ocean *n* 145, 147
ocean life *n* 166
ocean ridge *n* 145
Oceania *n* 150, 153
Oceanian *adj* 153
octagon *n* 74
October *n* 172
octopus *n* 54, 166
odd *adj* 177
odometer *n* 99
oesophagus *n* 04
off *adj* 52
off licence *n* 46
off the shoulder *adj* 15
off-piste *n* 122
off-road motorcycle *n* 100
offal *n* 53
offence *n* 107
office *n* 82
office building *n* 42
office equipment *n* 82
office manager *n* 81
office reception *n* 81
office services *n* 91
office work *n* 81
often *adv* 172
oganesson *n* 78
ogre *n* 139
oil *n* 51, 60, 64, 97
oil field *n* 51
oil painting *n* 130
oil paints *n* 141

oil slick *n* 155
oil tank *n* 100
oil tanker *n* 105
oil terminal *n* 106
oil-filled radiator *n* 33
oily *adj* 18
ointment *n* 20, 49
okra *n* 55
old *adj* 12, 176
old man cactus *n* 168
old-fashioned *adj* 177
oleander *n* 169
oleaster *n* 169
olive *n* 68, 169
olive oil *n* 60
olm *n* 163
Oman *n* 151, 153
Omani *adj* 153
omelette *n* 61, 71, 72
on *prep* 180
on stage *adj* 126
on the corner *phr* 148
on the left *phr* 148
on the right *phr* 148
on time *adj* 131
once a week *adv* 172
oncology *n* 21
one *num* 173
one billion *num* 173
one hundred *num* 173
one million *num* 173
one o'clock *n* 171
one thirty *n* 171
one thousand *num* 173
one-way street *n* 96
one-way system *n* 42
one-way ticket *n* 131
onesie *n* 13
onion *n* 56
onion dome *n* 44
online banking *n* 45, 94
online check-in *n* 104
online
  communication *n* 83
online delivery *n* 91
online map *n* 148
online media *n* 84
online retail *n* 91
online shopping *n* 48
only child *n* 05
only weekends *adv* 172
onyx *n* 156
opal *n* 156
open *adj* 48, 132
open sandwich *n* 70
open turn *n* 118
open-air activities *n* 133
open-air hobbies *n* 133
open-cast
  mining *n* 51
open-plan *n* 32
opening night *n* 126
opening times *n* 132
openside flanker *n* 108

P

Ragdoll n 164
rail network n 102
railing n 65
railway n 148
railway
   terminal n 106
rain n 51, 154
rain forest n 146, 159
rainbow n 154
rainbow trout n 54
raincoat n 15
raindrop n 154
rainy adj 154
raise n 81
raise v 11
raised mudguard n 100
raisin n 58
rake n 40
rake (leaves) v 39
rake (soil) v 39
rally n 114
rally driving n 123
ram n 165
ramekin n 28
ramen n 64, 72
rapeseed n 86
rapeseed oil n 60
rapids n 119, 146
ras el hanout n 59
rash n 19
raspberry n 57
raspberry jam n 60
rat n 158
rattle n 08
rattlesnake n 163
raven n 160
raw adj 56
raw meat n 53
ray n 166
razor blade n 31
razor-shell n 54
reach a consensus v 95
reach an agreement v 95
reaction n 76
reaction direction n 76
reactor n 51
read v 73
read a map v 148
read a newspaper v 09
reading n 138
reading a map n 148
reading glasses n 22, 49
reading light n 103
reading list n 80
reading room n 80
reality TV n 137
reamer n 36
rear light n 101
rear suspension n 123
rear wheel n 99
rear wing n 97, 123
reasonable adj 10
rebound n 112
receipt n 48, 69, 94

receptacle n 38
reception n 131
receptionist n 81, 90, 131
reconnaissance
   aircraft n 88
reconnaissance
   vehicle n 88
record player n 136
record shop n 46
record v 137
recorder n 129
recording studio n 84
records n 136
recover v 20
recovery room n 21
recruitment
   agency n 92
rectangle n 74
recycling n 91, 155
recycling bin n 33, 34
red n 141
red blood cell n 77
red cabbage n 55
red card n 109
red carpet n 127
red deer n 158
red fox n 159
red giant n 144
red hair n 12
red line n 110
red meat n 53
red mullet n 54
red panda n 159
red salamander n 163
red wine n 52, 68
red-eyed tree frog n 163
redcurrant n 57
reed n 167
reef n 147
reel n 121
reel in v 121
refectory n 80
referee n 107-109, 112
referee crease n 110
reflected radiation n 155
reflection n 75
reflector n 100, 101
reflector strap n 100
reflector telescope n 144
reflexology n 24
refraction n 75
refractor telescope n 144
refrigerator n 27
refund v 46
reggae n 129
registered mail n 45
registered trademark n 175
regulator n 118
reiki n 24
reindeer n 159
reins n 120
relationships n 05, 07
relaxation n 24
relaxed adj 06

relaxing adj 177
relay race n 116
release v 121
reliable adj 10, 93
remains n 79
remarkable adj 177
remember v 11
remote n 137
remote
   control n 26, 83, 136
removal van n 32
renew v 80
renewable energy n 51
rent v 32
rent a cottage v 131
rent out v 32
renting a house n 32
repair v 11, 33
reply v 83
reply to all v 83
report n 82
reporter n 137
reproduction n 77
reproductive n 04
reproductive organs n 04
reptiles n 163
Republic of the
   Congo n 149, 152
research n 91, 93
research and
   development (R&D) n 91
reserve v 80
reservoir n 51
residential area n 32
residential buildings n 44
residential district n 42
resign v 81
resit v 73
respectful adj 177
respiratory n 04
responsible adj 93
rest v 20
restaurant n 42, 69, 131
restaurant manager n 69
restricted area n 112
resurfacing n 87
resuscitate v 20
retail n 91
reticulated python n 163
retina n 22
retinal camera n 22
retire v 07, 81
retriever n 164
return n 114
return v 46, 80
return crease n 111
return ticket n 131
reusable cup n 70
rev counter n 99
reverb n 129
reverse v 96
reversible direction n 76
review n 138
revise v 73

rewind v 137
rewire the house v 35
rhenium n 78
rhinoceros n 158
rhinoceros beetle n 162
rhodium n 78
rhododendron n 38
rhombus n 74
rhubarb n 58
rib n 03, 53
rib cage n 03
ribs n 70
ribbon n 63, 125, 142
rice n 72, 86
rice bowl n 27
rice noodles n 64
rice pudding n 63
rich adj 52
ride v 11
ride pillion v 100
rider n 100, 120
ridge n 146
ridge beam n 87
riding boot n 17, 120
riding crop n 120
riding hat n 120
rifle n 88
rig n 129
rigging n 119
right angle n 74
right bend n 96
right cornerback n 107
right
   defenceman n 110
right defensive end n 107
right defensive tackle n
   107
right guard n 107
right safety n 107
right side n 112
right tackle n 107
right wing n 108
right winger n 110
rim n 101
rind n 61, 64
ring n 16, 170
ring binder n 82
ring finger n 02
ring ties n 40
ring-tailed lemur n 159
rings n 125, 143
rinse v 22
rip out v 178
ripe adj 57
rise v 62
risotto n 72
river n 147, 148
river features n 147, 148
road n 96
road bike n 101
road markings n 96
road signs n 96
roadmap n 95
roadworks n 87, 96

roadworks
   ahead n 96
roar v 159
roast n 29, 72
robbers n 50
robbery n 50, 85
robe n 80
rock n 129
rock climbing n 125
rock garden n 41
rock pool n 134
rock star n 90
rocket n 143
rocket n 55
rockhopper penguin n 161
rocks n 147, 156
rocking chair n 26
rocking horse n 08
rodeo n 120
roe deer n 158
roentgenium n 78
role-playing game n 136
roll n 62
roll v 29
roller n 37, 87
roller bar n 97
roller blind n 26
roller coaster n 133
roller extension pole n 37
rollerblading n 133
rollerskating n 125
rolling pin n 29
romaine lettuce n 55
romance n 138
Romania n 151, 153
Romanian adj 153
romantic adj 10, 177
romantic comedy n 127
romper suit n 13
roof n 25, 98
roof garden n 41
roof ladder n 50
roof rack n 97
roof tiles n 87
rook n 140, 160
room service n 131
room with a view n 131
rooster n 165
root n 03
rope n 117, 119, 125
rose n 38
rosé n 68, 52
rose of Sharon n 38
rose-ringed parakeet n 161
rosemary n 38, 59
rotor n 51
rotor blade n 103
rotten adj 57
rough n 115
round n 117
round neck n 14
roundabout n 96
route number n 99
router n 35, 83

smartpen *n* 95
smartphone *n* 83
smartwatch *n* 83
smell *v* 11
smile *v* 02
smog *n* 154
smoke *n* 50
smoke alarm *n* 50
smoked *adj* 54, 72
smoked fish *n* 64
smoked haddock *n* 64
smoked mackerel *n* 64, 71
smoked meat *n* 53
smoked salmon *n* 64, 71
smooth orange juice *n* 65
smoothie *n* 52
smuggling *n* 85
snack bar *n* 48, 65
snacks *n* 65
snail *n* 162
snake plant *n* 38
snakes and
   ladders *n* 140
snap *n* 140
snare drum *n* 128
sneeze *v* 02, 20
snell knot *n* 121
Snellen chart *n* 22
sniff *v* 164
snooker *n* 125
snore *v* 02, 30
snorkel *n* 118
snorkel and mask *n* 15,
   134
snorkelling *n* 118
snort *v* 165
snow *n* 154
snow goose *n* 160
snow leopard *n* 159
snow tyres *n* 97
snowboarding *n* 122
snowdrift *n* 154
snowdrop *n* 167
snowflake *n* 154
snowmobile *n* 122
snowstorm *n* 154
snowsuit *n* 13
snowy *adj* 154
snowy owl *n* 161
soap *n* 31
soap dish *n* 31
soap opera *n* 137
social media *n* 84
social sciences *n* 80
sociologist *n* 89
sociology *n* 80
sock, socks *n* 14, 107
socket *n* 33
socket wrench *n* 36
soda bread *n* 62
sodium *n* 78
sofa *n* 26
sofa bed *n* 26
soft *adj* 57, 176

soft cheese *n* 61
soft down feathers
   n 161
soft drink *n* 70
soft sweets *n* 67
soft toy *n* 08
softwood *n* 35
soil *n* 39
soil tiller *n* 40
soil types *n* 39
solar charger *n* 83
solar energy *n* 51
solar farm *n* 51
solar panel *n* 51
solar radiation *n* 155
solar system *n* 143
solar water heating *n* 51
solder *n* 35-36
solder *v* 35
soldering iron *n* 35-36
soldier *n* 88-89
sole *n* 02, 17, 54, 115
solid, solids *n* 74, 76
solo *n* 128
Solomon Island
   adj 153
Solomon Islands
   n 150, 153
soluble *adj* 49
solvent *n* 37
Somalia *n* 149, 152
Somalian *adj* 152
sombrero *n* 16
sometimes *adj* 172
sommelier *n* 69
son *n* 05
son-in-law *n* 05
song *n* 129
soprano *n* 126
sore throat *n* 19
sorrel *n* 55, 59
sort your
   rubbish *v* 155
sorting unit *n* 33
soufflé *n* 72
soufflé dish *n* 28
soul *n* 129
sound bar *n* 136
sound boom *n* 84
sound engineer *n* 127
sound hole *n* 129
sound technician *n* 84
soundtrack *n* 127
soup *n* 69, 72
soup bowl *n* 27
soup spoon *n* 27
sour *adj* 52, 57
source *n* 147
sources *n* 79
sourdough bread *n* 62
sourdough starter *n* 62
south *n* 148
South Africa *n* 149, 152
South African *adj* 152

South America *n* 149, 152
South American *adj* 152
South Korea *n* 150, 153
South Korean *adj* 153
South Pole *n* 75, 145
South Sudan *n* 149, 152
South Sudanese *adj* 152
southeast *n* 148
Southern Cross
   n 144
Southern
   Hemisphere *n* 145
southwest *n* 148
souvenir *n* 132
souvenir stall *n* 132
sow *v* 39, 86
soy sauce *n* 60
soy sauce dip *n* 72
soya allergy *n* 23
soya milk *n* 61
soybean oil *n* 60
space *n* 143-144
space exploration *n* 143
space probe *n* 143
space shuttle *n* 143
space shuttle launch
   n 143
space station *n* 143
space suit *n* 143
space telescope *n* 144
spacecraft *n* 143
spade *n* 40, 140
spaghetti *n* 64, 72
Spain *n* 151, 153
Spanish *adj* 153
Spanish chestnut *n* 168
spanner *n* 36
spare tyre *n* 98
spark plug *n* 98
sparkling *adj* 52
sparkling wine *n* 68
sparrow *n* 160
spatula *n* 28, 76
speak *v* 11
speaker, speakers *n* 83, 129
speaker stand *n* 136
spear *n* 79
spearfishing *n* 121
special *adj* 177
special effects *n* 127
special offer *n* 48
specials *n* 69
species *n* 77
species of birds *n* 160-161
species of fungi *n* 170
species of
   mammals *n* 158-159
spectacled caiman *n* 163
spectators *n* 110, 115-116
speed boating *n* 119
speed camera *n* 96
speed limit *n* 96
speed skating *n* 122

speed up *v* 98
speedboat *n* 105
speeding *n* 85
speedometer *n* 99-100
speedway *n* 123
spell *v* 11, 73
spell book *n* 139
sperm whale *n* 166
sphere *n* 74
sphinx *n* 139, 164
spices *n* 59
spicy *adj* 52, 56
spicy sausage *n* 64
spider monkey *n* 159
spider plant *n* 38
spikes *n* 115
spin *n* 114
spinach *n* 55
spinal cord *n* 04
spine *n* 03, 138
spinning top *n* 08
spiral galaxy *n* 144
spirit dispenser *n* 68
spirit level *n* 35-36, 87
spit *n* 147
splashback *n* 27
spleen *n* 04
splinter *n* 19
split the bill *v* 69
spoiler *n* 97
spoke *n* 101
sponge *n* 31, 34, 37
sponge cake *n* 63
spontaneous *adj* 10
spores *n* 170
sport fishing *n* 121
sports bra *n* 15
sports car *n* 97
sports centre *n* 43
sports drink *n* 52
sports field *n* 80
sports game *n* 136
sports jacket *n* 15
sports
   programme *n* 137
sports shoes *n* 17
sportsperson *n* 89
sportswear *n* 15
spotted *adj* 13
Spotted Lake *n* 145
sprain *n* 19
spray *n* 49
spray *v* 39
spray nozzle *n* 40
sprayer *n* 40
spring *n* 57, 172
spring a leak *v* 33
spring greens *n* 55
spring onion *n* 55
spring roll *n* 72
springboard *n* 118, 125
springbok *n* 158
sprinkle *v* 29
sprinkler *n* 40

sprinter *n* 116
sprocket *n* 101
spruce *n* 167
spy *n* 89
square *n* 42, 74, 140
square foot *n* 174
square
   kilometre *n* 174
square leg *n* 111
square metre *n* 174
square mile *n* 174
squash *n* 114
squat *n* 124
squeak *v* 164
squeegee *n* 34
squid *n* 54
squirrel *n* 158
squirrel monkey *n* 159
Sri Lanka *n* 150, 153
Sri Lankan *adj* 153
St. Basil's cathedral
   n 44
St. Kitts and
   Nevis *n* 150, 152
St. Lucia *n* 150, 152
St. Lucian *adj* 152
St. Vincent and The
   Grenadines *n* 150, 152
stabilizers *n* 101
stable *n* 86, 120
staff *n* 81, 139
stag beetle *n* 162
stage *n* 126
stage lights *n* 129
stained glass window
   n 44
stair gate *n* 08
staircase *n* 25
stairs *n* 25
stake *v* 39
stalactite *n* 146
stalagmite *n* 146
stalk *n* 55
stall *n* 47
stallion *n* 120, 165
stalls *n* 126
stamen *n* 38
stamp, stamps *n* 45, 48
stance *n* 115
stand *n* 40, 109, 115,
   121, 136
stand up *v* 11
standing ovation
   n 126
stapler *n* 73, 82
staples *n* 82
star, stars *n* 144
star anise *n* 59
star chart *n* 144
star cluster *n* 144
star jumps *n* 124
Star of David *n* 44
starfish *n* 134, 166
starfruit *n* 58

starling n 160
start school v 07
starter n 69
starting block
    n 116, 118
starting grid n 123
starting line n 116
statement n 85
stationery n 82
status n 104
status update n 84
stay in a hotel v 131
steam v 29
steam dome n 102
steam train n 102
steamed adj 72
steeplechase n 120
steering wheel n 99
stegosaurus n 157
stem n 38, 170
stemware n 27
stencil n 37
stenographer n 85
stepbrother n 05
stepladder n 37
stepmother n 05
stepmum n 05
steppe n 146
steps n 25
stepsister n 05
stereo adj 136
stern n 105, 119
sternum n 03
stethoscope n 20
stew n 72
steward n 109
stick n 110
stick insect n 164
sticky notes n 82
sticky prong n 168
stiff adj 176
stifling adj 154
stigma n 38
stilettos n 17
still adj 52
stilt house n 32
sting n 19, 162
sting v 162
stinkhorn n 170
stir v 29
stir-fry n 29, 72
stir-fried adj 72
stirrer n 68
stirrup n 120
stitch n 142
stitches n 21, 113
stitch length selector n 142
stitch selector n 142
stock exchange n 94
stockbroker n 94
stockings n 14
stocks n 47, 94
stomach n 04
stomach ache n 19

stone adj 176
stone n 16, 141, 176
Stone age n 79
stone fruit n 57
stool n 65
stop v 96, 137
stop at (the hotel) v 148
stop button n 99
stop light ahead n 96
stopper n 76
storage n 32
stories n 139
stork n 160
storm n 154
storm drain n 43
stormy adj 154
stout n 68
straight adj 74
straight hair n 12
strainer n 28
strait n 147
strange adj 177
strapless adj 15
strategy game n 136
stratosphere n 155
straw n 70
strawberry n 57
strawberry jam n 60
strawberry
    milkshake n 61, 65
strawberry smoothie n 65
streaky bacon n 53
stream n 137, 147
street n 42
street corner n 42
street market n 46
street sign n 43
street stall n 70
streetlight n 25, 43
streetmap n 148
stress n 19
stressed adj 06
stretch n 124
stretcher n 21
strike n 113
strike v 117
strike out v 111
striker n 109
string n 129
string of pearls n 16
strings n 114, 128
strip v 37
striped n 13
stripes n 14
stroke n 118
strong adj 52
strong flour n 62
strontium n 78
stubble n 12
studs n 16, 111
study n 26
study n 73
studying the past n 79
stuffed adj 72

stuffed olives n 64
stuffed vine leaves n 64
stump v 111
stumps n 111
stunning adj 177
stunt n 127
style n 38
style your hair v 12
stylist n 89
subject n 83
submarine n 88, 105
submersible n 166
subscript n 76
subsoil n 39
substitutes n 109
subterranean stream n 146
subtitles n 137
subtract v 11, 74
suburb n 42
subwoofer n 136
succulents n 38, 41
suck v 02
suction hose n 34
Sudan n 149, 152
Sudanese adj 152
sugar n 23
sugar cane n 86, 167
sugar-snap peas n 55
suit n 15
suit (someone) v 14
suitcase n 16, 104
sulphite allergy n 23
sulphur n 78, 156
sultana n 58
sum up v 95
sumac n 59
summer n 57, 172
summer leaf n 169
summer roll n 72
summons n 85
sumo wrestling n 117
Sun n 143
sun n 154
sun bed n 18
sun cream n 134
sun hat n 14, 16, 134
sunbathing n 133-134
sunblock n 49, 134
sunburn n 19, 134
Sunday n 172
sundew n 168
sunflower,
    sunflowers n 38, 86
sunflower oil n 60
sunglasses n 22, 134
sunlit zone n 166
sunny adj 154
sunrise n 171
sunroof n 98
sunset n 171
superb adj 177
superfoods n 23
supermarket n 48
supernova n 144

supervise v 92
supervisor n 81, 92
supplement n 23, 49
support n 87
support cane n 39
supportive adj 10
suppository n 49
surf n 119
surface n 39, 143
surface cleaner n 34
surface-to-air missile n 88
surfboard n 119, 134
surfcasting n 121
surfer n 119
surfing n 119, 134
surgeon n 21, 90
surgery n 21
surgical mask n 21
Suriname n 149, 152
Surinamese adj 152
surprised adj 06
Surrealism n 130
surround sound
    speaker n 136
surveillance camera n 130
surveyor n 90
sushi n 54
sushi set n 27
suspect n 50, 85
suspenders n 14
suspension n 98, 100
suspension line n 125
swallow n 160
swallow v 52
swallowtail butterfly n 162
swamp n 146
swarm n 162
Swazi adj 152
sweat v 02
sweatpants n 15
sweater n 14
sweatshirt n 14
swede n 56
Sweden n 151, 153
Swedish adj 153
sweep the floor v 34
sweet adj 52, 56-57
sweet chilli n 60
sweet potato n 56
sweet shop n 67
sweet spreads n 60
sweet trolley n 63, 69
sweetcorn n 55
sweets n 67
swift n 160
swimmer n 118
swimming n 118
swimming pool n 118, 131
swimming trunks
    n 15, 134
swimsuit n 15, 118, 134
swing n 43, 115, 133
swing v 115, 159
Swiss adj 153

Swiss chard n 55
Swiss cheese plant n 38
Switzerland n 151, 153
swoop v 161
sword n 79, 117
swordfish n 54
sycamore n 169
Sydney Opera House n 44
sympathetic adj 06
symphony n 128
symptoms n 19
synagogue n 44
synchronized
    swimming n 118
synthetic n 13
Syria n 150, 153
Syrian adj 153
syringe n 20, 49, 77
syrup n 49

T

T-shirt n 14
T-strap heels n 17
T11 (visual impairment)
    race n 116
tabard n 13
tabi boots n 17
table n 26, 65
table setting n 69
table tennis n 114
tablecloth n 26
tablespoon n 27
tablet n 83
tablets n 20, 49
tableware n 27
tack v 119, 142
tackle n 108, 121
tackle v 107
tackle box n 121
taco n 70
tadpole n 77, 163
taekwondo n 117
tag v 113
tagine n 28
tai chi n 117, 133
tail n 54, 103, 120,
    143, 158-160
tail feathers n 161
tail light n 100
tailbone sacrum n 03
tailgate n 97
tailor n 46, 89
tailor v 142
tailor's chalk n 142

upper level *n* **47**
uppercase *n* **175**
upset *adj* **06**
upstairs *adv, n* **25**
uranium *n* **78**
Uranus *n* **143**
urinary *n* **04**
urology *n* **21**
Uruguay *n* **149, 152**
Uruguayan *adj* **152**
USB drive *n* **83**
useful *adj* **177**
useful
   expressions *n* **179-180**
useless *adj* **177**
usher *n* **126**
uterus *n* **04, 08**
utility knife *n* **36-37**
UV tubes *n* **18**
Uzbek *adj* **153**
Uzbekistan *n* **151, 153**

V

V-neck *n* **14**
vacancies *n* **92, 131**
vaccination *n* **08, 20**
vacuole *n* **77**
vacuum *n* **75**
vacuum cleaner *n* **34**
vacuum the carpet *v* **34**
vagina *n* **04**
Vaisakhi *n* **07**
valance *n* **30**
valley *n* **146**
valve *n* **101**
vampire *n* **139**
vanadium *n* **78**
vandalism *n* **85**
vanilla milkshake *n* **61**
Vanuatu *n* **150, 153**
Vanuatuan *adj* **153**
varnish *n* **37**
vase *n* **26**
Vatican City *n* **151**
vault *n* **125**
veal *n* **53**
vegan *adj* **23**
vegan *n* **23**
vegetable garden *n* **41, 86**
vegetable plot *n* **86**
vegetables *n* **48, 55-56**
vegetarian *adj* **23**
vegetarian *n* **23**
veggie burger *n* **70**

veil *n* **15**
vein *n* **04**
Venetian blinds *n* **26**
Venezuela *n* **149, 152**
Venezuelan *adj* **152**
venison *n* **53**
vent *n* **145**
Venus *n* **143**
Venus fly-trap *n* **168**
verdict *n* **85**
vermilion
   flycatcher *n* **160**
vertebrate *n* **77**
verticals *n* **120**
vest *n* **14**
vet *n* **89**
veteran *n* **88**
vial *n* **36**
vibraphone *n* **128**
Victoria Falls *n* **145**
vicuña *n* **158**
video chat *n* **83**
video conference *n* **83**
video games *n* **136**
video on demand *n* **137**
Vietnam *n* **150, 153**
Vietnamese *adj* **153**
view a house *v* **32**
viewing platform *n* **44**
viewpoint *n* **148**
villa *n* **32, 131**
village *n* **43**
villain *n* **127**
Vincentian *adj* **152**
vinegar *n* **60, 64**
vineyard *n* **86**
vintage *adj* **13**
vintage *n* **97**
vinyl records *n* **129**
viola *n* **128**
violet *n* **38**
violin *n* **128-29**
violin sonata *n* **128**
Virginia creeper *n* **168**
Virgo *n* **144**
virus *n* **19, 77**
visa *n* **104**
visible light *n* **75**
vision *n* **22**
visitor *n* **107**
visor *n* **100**
vitamins *n* **23, 49**
vivarium *n* **164**
vlog *n* **84**
vlogger *n* **84**
vocal cords *n* **04**
vodka *n* **68**
vodka and orange *n* **68**
voice recorder *n* **83**
volcano *n* **145**
volley *n* **114**
volleyball *n* **112**
volleyball positions *n* **112**
volt *n* **75**

voltage *n* **33**
volume *n* **74, 136, 174**
volunteer *v* **92**
vomit *v* **20**
vote *n* **85**
vulture *n* **160**

W

waders *n* **121**
waffle, waffles *n* **65, 70-71**
wages *n* **81**
waist *n* **01, 129**
waistband *n* **15, 142**
waistcoat *n* **15**
wait on *v* **178**
wait up *v* **178**
waiter *n* **69, 89**
waiting room *n* **20, 102**
waitress *n* **65, 69, 89**
wake up *v* **09, 178**
walk *v* **120**
walk the dog *v* **09**
walkie-talkie *n* **50**
walking boots *n* **135**
walking trail *n* **148**
wall *n* **25, 44, 87**
wall light *n* **26**
Wallace's flying frog *n* **163**
wallet *n* **94**
wallflower *n* **169**
wallpaper *n* **37**
wallpaper *v* **37**
wallpaper border *n* **37**
wallpaper brush *n* **37**
wallpaper paste *n* **37**
wallpaper roll *n* **37**
wallpaper stripper *n* **37**
walnut *n* **58, 168**
walnut oil *n* **60**
walrus *n* **166**
wand *n* **139**
want *v* **46**
war *n* **79, 88**
war elephant *n* **79**
ward *n* **21**
wardrobe *n* **30**
warehouse *n* **44, 106**
warfare *n* **79**
warhorse *n* **79**
warm *adj* **154**
warm front *n* **155**
warning track *n* **113**
warp thread *n* **142**
warrant *n* **85**

warrior *n* **79**
warrior pose *n* **24**
warthog *n* **159**
wasabi *n* **60**
wash the car *v* **34**
wash up *v* **09**
wash your face *v* **09**
wash your hair *v* **09, 12**
washer *n* **36**
washing line *n* **34**
washing machine *n* **34**
washing-up
   liquid *n* **34**
wasp *n* **162**
wasp nest *n* **162**
waste *n* **33**
waste disposal *n* **135**
waste pipe *n* **33**
watch *n* **16**
watch TV *v* **09**
watching television
   n **137**
water *n* **48, 91, 118**
water *v* **39**
water bottle,
   water bottles *n* **101, 135**
water carrier *n* **135**
water chestnut *n* **56**
water cooler *n* **82**
water features *n* **145**
water garden *n* **41**
water hazard *n* **115**
water jet *n* **50**
water lilies *n* **167**
water phenomena
   n **145**
water plants *n* **41**
water polo *n* **119**
water rail *n* **161**
water shoes *n* **17**
water skier *n* **119**
water skiing *n* **119**
water sports *n* **119**
water the plants *v* **09, 34**
water vapour *n* **51**
watercolour *n* **130**
watercolour
   paints *n* **141**
watercress *n* **55**
waterfall *n* **146**
waterfront *n* **132**
watering *n* **40**
watering can *n* **40**
watermark *n* **94**
watermelon *n* **58**
waterproof
   fishing gear *n* **121**
waterproofs *n* **121, 135**
wave *n* **75, 119, 134, 147**
wave *v* **02**
wavelength *n* **75**
wavy hair *n* **12**
wax *adj* **176**
wax *n* **18, 176**

waxcap *n* **170**
weapons *n* **79, 88**
wear *v* **14**
weasel *n* **158**
weather *n* **137, 154**
weather forecaster *n* **137**
weather map *n* **155**
weaver *n* **142**
weaverbird *n* **160**
weaving *n* **142**
webcam *n* **83**
wedding *n* **07**
wedding cake *n* **63**
wedding dress *n* **15**
wedge *n* **115**
wedge sandals *n* **17**
Wednesday *n* **172**
weedkiller *n* **39**
weeds *n* **41**
week *n* **172**
weekends *n* **172**
weekly *adj* **172**
weekly *adv* **172**
weevil *n* **162**
weft thread *n* **142**
weigh *v* **174**
weigh out *v* **178**
weight, weights *n* **121, 174**
weight bar *n* **124**
weight belt *n* **118**
weight training *n* **124**
well-qualified *adj* **93**
wellies *n* **40**
wellington boots *n* **17**
werewolf *n* **139**
west *n* **148**
western *n* **127**
wet *adj* **154**
wet suit *n* **118, 134**
wet wipe,
   wet wipes *n* **08, 49**
wetlands *n* **146**
wharf *n* **106**
wheat allergy *n* **23**
wheat beer *n* **68**
wheel *n* **97, 101**
wheel nuts *n* **98**
wheel pose *n* **24**
wheel roller *n* **124**
wheelbarrow *n* **40**
wheelchair *n* **21**
wheelchair access *n* **99**
wheelchair
   basketball *n* **125**
wheelchair curling *n* **122**
wheelchair race *n* **116**
wheelchair ramp *n* **130**
wheelchair
   rugby *n* **108, 125**
wheelie bin *n* **25**
whiplash *n* **19**
whipped cream *n* **61**
whisk *n* **28**
whisk *v* **29**

whiskers *n* 158
whisky *n* 68
whisper *v* 11
white *adj* 140-141
white *n* 140-141
white blood cell *n* 77
white bread *n* 62
white chocolate *n* 67
white coffee *n* 65
white currant *n* 57
white dwarf *n* 144
white flour *n* 62
White House *n* 44
white meat *n* 53
white mustard *n* 59
white spirit *n* 37
white tea *n* 66
white vinegar *n* 34
white wine *n* 52, 68
whiteboard *n* 73, 95
whitening *n* 22
whiting *n* 54
whole milk *n* 61
wholegrain
   mustard *n* 60
wholemeal flour *n* 62
whooper swan *n* 161
Wi-Fi *n* 83
wicket *n* 111
wicket-keeper *n* 111
wide *adj* 176
wide range *n* 48
wide receiver *n* 107
widow *n* 05
width *n* 74
wife *n* 05
wig *n* 12
wigwam *n* 32
wildcat *n* 159
wildebeest *n* 158
wildlife photography
   n 133
willow *n* 169
win *v* 11, 109, 115, 140
win a prize *v* 07
wind *n* 51, 154
wind energy *n* 51
wind farm *n* 51
wind turbine *n* 51
windbreak *n* 134
windlass *n* 105
windmill *n* 44
window cleaner *n* 90
window shopping *n* 46
windscreen *n* 97, 100
windsurfer *n* 119
windsurfing *n* 119, 134
windy *adj* 154
wine *n* 68
wine list *n* 69
wine vinegar *n* 60
wineglass *n* 27
wing *n* 53, 103, 112, 161
wing mirror *n* 97

wings *n* 49, 126
wink *v* 02
winners' cup *n* 109
winter *n* 172
Winter Olympics *n* 122
winter sports *n* 122
wipe the surfaces *v* 34
wiper *n* 97
wire *n* 35, 83
wire cutters *n* 36
wire strippers *n* 36
wire wool *n* 36
wireless *adj* 83
wireless
   headphones *n* 136
wires *n* 33
wiring *n* 33
wisteria *n* 38
witch *n* 139
witches' brew *n* 139
with ice *adj* 68
withdraw money *v* 45
without ice *adj* 68
witness *n* 85
wizard *n* 139
wok *n* 28
wolf *n* 159
woman *n* 05
womb *n* 04, 08
wombat *n* 158
women's
   heptathlon *n* 116
womenswear *n* 47
wonderful *adj* 177
wood *adj* 176
wood *n* 35, 115, 141, 146,
   176
woods *n* 176
wood duck *n* 161
wood glue *n* 35
wood preserver *n* 37
wooden spoon *n* 28
woodwind *n* 128
woodworking *n* 141
woofer *n* 136
wool *adj* 176
wool *n* 142, 176
woollen *n* 13
woolly mammoth
   n 157
woolly rhinoceros
   n 157
work *n* 81
work *v* 11
work bench *n* 35
work boots *n* 17
work from home *v* 81
work full-time *v* 81
work part-time *v* 81
work shifts *v* 81
workclothes *n* 13
worker *n* 81
working out *n* 124
working well

under pressure *n* 93
workplace skills *n* 93
workstation *n* 82
worktop *n* 27
worm *n* 162
worried *adj* 06
wound *n* 19
wrap *n* 70
wrap up the meeting
   v 95
wren *n* 160
wrestling *n* 117
wrinkles *n* 12
wrist *n* 01-02
wrist band *n* 107
wrist weights *n* 124
wristband *n* 114
writ *n* 85
write *v* 73
writer *n* 90
writing *n* 175
writing equipment
   n 175
written
   communication
   n 93

XY

X-ray, X-rays *n* 19, 21, 75
X-ray machine *n* 104
xenon *n* 78
xylophone *n* 128
yacht *n* 105, 119, 134
yak *n* 159
yam *n* 56, 86
yard *n* 174
yard line *n* 107
yarmulke *n* 16
yawn *v* 02
year *n* 172
yellow *n* 141
yellow box fish *n* 166
yellow card *n* 109
yellow mustard *n* 60
yellow surgeonfish *n* 166
yellow tang *n* 166
Yemen *n* 151, 153
Yemeni *adj* 153
yew *n* 167
yo-yo *n* 08
yoga *n* 24
yoga class *n* 24
yoga pants *n* 24
yoga teacher *n* 90
yoghurt *n* 61
yolk *n* 61, 71
young *adj* 12
young frog *n* 77
ytterbium *n* 78

yttrium *n* 78
yucca *n* 38
yurt *n* 32

Z

Zambia *n* 149, 152
Zambian *adj* 152
zebra *n* 158
zero carbon *adj* 155
zest *n* 57
ziggurat *n* 44
Zimbabwe *n* 149, 152
Zimbabwean *adj* 152
zinc *n* 78, 156
zip *n* 17, 142
zirconium *n* 78
zodiac *n* 144
zodiac
   constellations *n* 144
zodiac symbols *n* 144
zombie *n* 139
zoo *n* 133
zookeeper *n* 90
zoologist *n* 77
zoology *n* 77, 80

Italian word list

The numbers after each word or phrase refer to the units in which they can be found.

boxer **14**, **164**
bozza **83**
bozzolo **162**
bracciale **21**
bracciale rigido **16**
bracciale / braccialetto **16**
bracciata **118**
braccio **01**, **50**, **87**, **126**
braccio per telecamera **84**
bracciolo **99**, **103**, **118**
brachiosauro **157**
bradipo **159**
Braille **175**
branda **135**
brandy **68**
Brasile **149**, **152**
brasiliano / brasiliana **152**
bravo / brava **177**
breakfast roll **71**
brezza **154**
bricolage **35**
bridge **125**, **140**
brie **64**
briglie **120**
brillante **177**
brioche **62**, **71**
brividi **19**
broccolo **55**, **56**
brodo **72**
bromo **78**
bronzo **116**, **176**
bruciare **29**
bruciatore **103**
bruciatura **19**
bruco **77**, **162**
brugole **36**
brunch **69**
Brunei **151**, **153**
bruneiano / bruneiana **153**
brutto / brutta **177**
bubolare **161**
buca **101**, **115**, **125**, **129**
buca delle lettere **25**, **45**
buca in un colpo **115**
bucaneve **167**
bucato e pulizie **34**
buccia **58**
bucket turn **118**
buco della serratura **25**
buco dell'ozono **155**
buco nero **144**
budget **94**
budino di riso **63**
bue muschiato **159**
bufalo **159**
buffet **69**
bulbo **41**
bulbo oculare **22**

Bulgaria **151**, **153**
bulgaro / bulgara **153**
bullone **36**
bulloni delle ruote **98**
bungalow **32**
bungee jumping **125**
bunker **115**
buon appetito **69**
buon ascoltatore / buona
   ascoltatrice **93**
buon pomeriggio **179**
buonanotte **179**
buonasera **179**
buongiorno **179**
buono sconto **48**
Burj Khalifa **44**
Burkina Faso **149**, **152**
burkinabé **152**
burmese **164**
burrasca **154**
burriera **28**
burrito **71**
burro **61**, **71**
burrocacao **18**
burro di arachidi **60**
burundese **152**
Burundi **149**, **152**
bus turistico **132**
bussola **119**, **135**, **148**
busta **45**, **82**
busta paga **81**
butanese **153**
buttare via **178**

C

cabina **50**, **103**, **105**, **134**
cabina di guida **102**
cabina di pilotaggio **103**
cabina per fototessere **46**
cablaggio **33**
cacao **65**, **169**
cacatua **161**, **164**
cacatua rosa **161**
caccia **88**
cacciapietre **102**
cacciare **159**
cacciatorpediniere **88**
cacciavite a stella **36**
cacciavite a testa piatta **36**
caco **58**
cactus **41**

cactus testa di vecchio **168**
caddie **115**
cadere **11**, **117**
caditoia **43**
cadmio **78**
caduco / caduca **41**
caduta delle foglie **172**
caffè **52**, **65**, **69**, **71**, **86**
caffè americano **65**
caffè freddo **65**
caffè nero **65**
caffettiera **27**
caffettiera a stantuffo **28**
caimano dagli occhiali **163**
calamari **54**
calamaro **54**
calamaro gigante **166**
calare l'ancora **106**
calcare **156**
calciare **11**, **107**, **108**, **118**
calcio **23**, **49**, **78**, **109**
calcio d'angolo **109**
calcio di rigore **109**
calcio di trasformazione
   108
calcio d'inizio **109**
calcio frontale **117**
calcio volante **117**
calcite **156**
calcolatrice **73**, **74**
calderone **139**
caldissimo / caldissima **154**
caldo / calda **154**, **176**
calendario **82**, **172**
calendula **38**
calici **27**
californio **78**
calla **167**
calligrafia **175**
callisia profumata **167**
calmarsi **178**
calmo / calma **06**, **10**, **93**
calorie **23**
calvo / calva **12**
calze **14**
calzini **14**
calzino **107**
camaleonte del
   Madagascar **163**
camaleonte di Jackson **163**
camaleonte di Parson **163**
cambiamento climatico
   155
cambiare **102**
cambiare canale **137**
cambiare i soldi **45**
cambiare le lenzuola **34**
cambiare marcia **101**
cambiare una
   lampadina **35**

cambiarsi **14**
cambiavalute **45**
cambio **104**
cambio automatico **99**
cambio manuale **99**
Cambogia **150**, **153**
cambogiano /
   cambogiana **153**
Cambriano **157**
cambusa **105**
camelia **38**
camembert **64**
camera con vista **131**
camera da letto **30**
camera d'aria **101**
camera doppia **131**
camera doppia con letti
   singoli **131**
camera magmatica **145**
camera singola **131**
cameraman **84**, **127**
cameriere / cameriera **65**,
   69, **89**
camerini **47**
Camerun **149**, **152**
camerunense **152**
camice da laboratorio **13**
camicetta **14**
camicetta folkloristica **15**
camicia **15**
camicia a maniche corte
   14
camicia da notte **14**
camicia della divisa
   scolastica **13**
caminetto **26**
camino **25**, **32**, **87**
camino vulcanico **145**
camion con pianale **87**
camion dei traslochi **32**
camion dei vigili del fuoco
   50
camion militare **88**
camionista **90**
cammello **158**
camomilla **66**
campagna **146**
campane tubolari **128**
campanello **25**, **99**
campanile **44**
campanula **167**, **169**
campeggio **135**
camper **135**
campionato **114**
campo **107**, **109**, **111**, **112**,
   146
campo da baseball **113**
campo da cricket **111**
campo da golf **115**
campo da rugby **108**

campo da tennis **114**
campo elettrico **75**
campo esterno **111**
campo magnetico **75**
campo sportivo **80**
campus universitario **80**
Canada **150**, **152**
canadese **152**
canale **137**, **147**
canale di scolo **43**
canale di televendite **137**
canale musicale **137**
canale pay per view **137**
canali televisivi **137**
canapa **169**
canarino **160**
cancellare **69**
cancelleria **82**
cancelletto **122**
cancelletto di sicurezza **08**
cancello **32**, **41**, **86**, **106**
Cancro **144**
candeggina **34**
candela **26**, **98**
candela magica **139**
candeline **63**
candidato / candidata **81**
candidature **92**
cane **122**
cane a testa in giù **24**
cane della polizia **50**
cane selvatico africano
   158
canestro **112**
canguro **158**
canini **03**
canna **101**, **121**, **167**
canna da giardino **40**
canna da pesca **121**
canna da zucchero **86**, **167**
cannella **59**
cannella macinata **59**
cannelloni **64**
cannolicchio **54**
cannone **79**, **88**
cannuccia **70**
Caño Cristales **145**
canoa **105**
canotta **14**
canottaggio **119**
canottiera **14**
canottiere **119**
canovaccio **28**
cantalupo **58**
cantante **89**
cantare **11**, **165**
cantiere **87**
cantiere navale **106**
cantieri stradali **87**
cantina **25**

colonna sonora **128**
colonna vertebrale **03**
colori a olio **141**
colori acrilici **141**
Colosseo **44**
colpevole **06, 85**
colpire **11, 110, 117**
colpire con un pugno **117**
colpo di frusta **19**
colpo di taglio **114**
coltellino svizzero **135**
coltello **27**
coltello da burro **27**
coltello da cucina **28**
coltello da pane **28**
coltivare **39**
colture **86**
comandi **99, 100, 136**
comandi dei fari **99**
comandi del riscaldamento **99**
combustibili fossili **51, 155**
cometa **143, 144**
comico / comica **89**
comignolo **25**
commedia **126, 127, 137**
commedia romantica **127**
commercialista **90, 94**
commesso / commessa **89**
commissariato di polizia **42, 50**
commissione **94**
commozione cerebrale **19**
comodino **30**
Comore **149, 152**
comoriano / comoriana **152**
compagnia aerea **104**
comparse **127**
compasso **73, 74**
compensato **35**
competenze informatiche **93**
competenze professionali **93**
competenze sul luogo di lavoro **93**
competenze tecnologiche **93**
competitivo / competitiva **93**
compilare **178**
compilare un modulo **92**
compitare **11**
compiti per casa **73**
compito in classe **73**
compleanno **07**
completo **15**
comporre **128**
compositore / compositrice **128**

compost **40**
compostiera **40, 41**
composto **76**
comprare **46**
comprensivo / comprensiva **06**
comprensorio sciistico **122**
compresse **20, 49**
compressioni toraciche **20**
computare **73**
computer **82, 83**
computer fisso **83**
computer portatile **82, 83**
comunicazione online **83**
comunicazione scritta **93**
con camere libere **131**
con ghiaccio **52, 68**
con le spalle scoperte **15**
con motivo cachemire **13**
con motivo scozzese **13**
con piombo **97**
concerto pop **129**
conchiglie **64**
concimare **39**
concime **39**
concludere una riunione **95**
condannare **85**
condimenti **60, 71, 72**
condimento **70, 72**
condito / condita **72**
condividere **84**
condividere lo schermo **95**
condominio **25, 43**
condor delle Ande **160**
condotta forzata **51**
conduttore **75**
conduttore del notiziario / conduttrice del notiziario **137**
conduttore / conduttrice **89**
conferenza **95**
confettura **71**
confettura di fragole **60**
confettura di lamponi **60**
confezionare su misura **142**
confuso / confusa **06**
congelare **29**
conglomerato **156**
congolese **152**
conifere **41, 157, 167**
conigliera **164**
coniglio **53, 158, 164**
connettore a coccodrillo **75**
cono **74, 87**
cono gelato **65**
Conocybe apala **170**

conoscente **07**
conoscere qualcuno **179**
consegna **45**
consegna a domicilio **48, 70**
consegna online **91**
consiglio di amministrazione **95**
console **136**
console del dj **129**
costellazioni **144**
consulente finanziario / consulente finanziaria **94**
consulenza legale **85**
contachilometri **99**
contadino / contadina **79, 86, 89**
contagiri **99**
contagocce **76**
container **105, 106**
contaminuti **28**
contare **11, 74**
contatore elettrico **33**
contatto **83**
contenitore dei giocattoli **08**
contenitore ermetico **52**
contenitore per il compost **33**
contenitori **52**
contento / contenta **06**
continente **145**
conto corrente **45**
conto di risparmio **45**
contorni **72, 148**
conto **69**
contrabbando **85**
contrabbasso **128**
contralto **126**
contrappeso **87**
contrarre i muscoli **124**
contrattare **46**
contratto **46**
contratto d'affitto **32**
controfigura **127**
controfiletto **53**
controllare gli pneumatici **98**
controllare le e-mail **09**
controllare l'olio **98**
controller **136**
controllo della tensione **142**
controllo immigrazione **104**
controllo passaporti **104**
controllore **102**
convenuto / convenuta **85**
convertire il loft **35**
cookie **84**

cooksonia **157**
coordinare **92**
coordinate **148**
coperchio **28**
copernicio **78**
coperta **26, 30**
coperta elettrica **30**
copertina **138**
coperto **69, 154**
copertura vegetale **41**
copiare **11**
copilota **103**
copione **126**
coppa del vincitore **109**
coppa di gelato **65**
coppia **07**
coppia di fidanzati **07**
coppia sposata **07**
coppola **16**
copricapi **16**
copriletto **30**
coprimozzo **98**
coprire con zolle erbose **39**
copyright **175**
coraggioso / coraggiosa **10**
corallo **166**
corda **125**
corda da saltare **124**
corda per saltare **08**
corde **114, 117, 129**
corde vocali **04**
cordolo **43**
cordone ombelicale **08**
Corea del Nord **150, 153**
Corea del Sud **150, 153**
coriandolo **59**
coristi / coriste **129**
cormorano **160**
corna **158**
cornamusa **129**
cornea **22**
cornerback destro **107**
cornerback sinistro **107**
cornice **26, 130**
corniola **156**
corno francese **128**
corno inglese **128**
coro **128**
corpo **02, 129**
corpo sano **24**
corpo umano **01**
corrente alternata **33, 75**
corrente continua **33, 75**
corrente elettrica **33**
correre **11, 111, 113**
correttore **18**
corridoio **103, 126**
corridoio telescopico **104**
corriere **45**

corrimano **25, 99**
corruzione **85**
corsa **124**
corsa a ostacoli **120**
corsa al trotto **120**
corsa dei carri **120**
corsa di cavalli **120**
corsa in carrozzina **116**
corsa motociclistica su pista **123**
corsa T11 (per atleti non vedenti) **116**
corsetto **14**
corsia **116, 118**
corsia centrale **96**
corsia dei box **123**
corsia di destra **96**
corsia di emergenza **96**
corsia di sinistra **96**
corsia galleggiante **118**
corsie **48**
corsivo **175**
corso d'acqua sotterraneo **146**
cortado **65**
cortile **25, 41**
corto / corta **13, 176**
corvo **160**
corvo imperiale **160**
corvo nero **160**
coscia **01, 53**
cose **176, 177**
cospargere **29**
Costa d'Avorio **149, 152**
Costa Rica **150, 152**
costaricano / costaricana **152**
costellazione **144**
costellazioni zodiacali **144**
costola **03**
costoletta **53**
costolette **70**
costruire **11, 87**
costruzioni **87**
costume **13, 118, 134**
costume da bagno **15**
costumi **127**
cotoletta **53**
cotonastro **169**
cotone **13, 86, 176**
cottage **32**
cottage con il tetto di paglia **32**
cotto / cotta **56**
cotto al forno / cotta al forno **72**
cover **111**
cozza **54**
crampo **19, 118**
cranio **03**

G

H

I

S

427

XY

Z

W

Acknowledgments

The publisher would like to thank:

Dr. Steven Snape for his assistance with hieroglyphs. Elizabeth Blakemore for editorial assistance; Mark Lloyd, Charlotte Johnson, and Anna Scully for design assistance; Simon Mumford for national flags; Sunita Gahir and Ali Jayne Scrivens for additional illustration; Adam Brackenbury for art colour correction; Claire Ashby and Romaine Werblow for images; William Collins for fonts; Lori Hand, Kayla Dugger, and Jane Perlmutter for Americanization; Justine Willis for proofreading; Elizabeth Blakemore for indexing; Helen Peters for the wordlists; Christine Stroyan for audio recording management and ID Audio for audio recording and production.

DK India

Senior Art Editors Vikas Sachdeva, Ira Sharma; **Art Editor** Anukriti Arora; **Assistant Art Editors** Ankita Das, Adhithi Priya; **Editors** Hina Jain, Saumya Agarwal; **DTP Designer** Manish Upreti

DK WHAT WILL YOU LEARN NEXT?

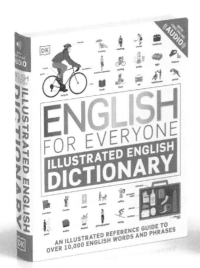

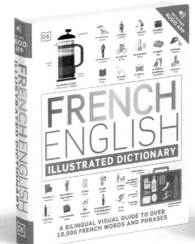

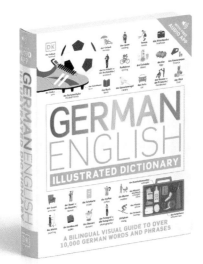

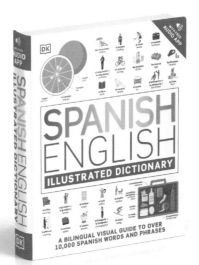